Introduction to Econometrics

Third Edition

G.S. Maddala

Formerly of Ohio State University

JOHN WILEY & SONS, LTD

Chichester • New York • Weinheim • Brisbane • Toronto • Singapore

Other Wiley Editorial Offices

John Wiley & Sons, Inc., 605 Third Avenue,
New York, NY 10158-0012, USA

Wiley-VCH Verlag GmbH, Pappelallee 3,
D-69469 Weinheim, Germany

John Wiley & Sons Australia Ltd, 33 Park Road, Milton,
Queensland 4064, Australia

John Wiley & Sons (Asia) Pte Ltd, 2 Clementi Loop #02-01,
Jin Xing Distripark, Singapore 129809

John Wiley & Sons (Canada) Ltd, 22 Worcester Road,
Rexdale, Ontario M9W 1L1, Canada

British Library Cataloguing in Publication Data

A catalogue record for this book is available from the British Library

ISBN 0-471-49728-2

Typeset in 10/12pt Times by Laser Words, Madras, India.
Printed and bound in Great Britain by Biddles Ltd, Guildford and King's Lynn.
This book is printed on acid-free paper responsibly manufactured from sustainable forestry in which at least
two trees are planted for each one used for paper production.

Contents

Foreword

I would like to thank Professor Kajal Lahiri for his help with the publication of this edition. After my husband G. S. Maddala passed away, Jo Ducey (his assistant) gave me the manuscript he had worked on until the last day of his life. Looking at the notes on his desk, I remembered how worried he was about being able to complete the revisions before he died. Because I could not allow my husband's final effort to go to waste, I immediately sought the help of Kajal Lahiri, my husband's former student and long-time friend. He graciously organized the manuscript, incorporated my husband's revisions, and edited the text to provide a smooth transition between the old and new material. Lahiri also addressed other questions that my husband's passing left unanswered. For instance, readers will notice that the last three chapters do not include exercises. From my husband's personal notes and computer files, Lahiri determined that my husband intentionally omitted exercises from the chapter on panel data. As for Chapters 16 (Large-Sample Theory) and 17 (Small-Sample Inference: Resampling Methods), my husband did not have those ready at the time of his death. We elected not to add new exercises, in order to preserve my husband's influence on the entire book. Without Lahiri's immense help and advice, this book would not have been published. I am very grateful for his hard work and dedication to this text.

I would also like to thank Ms. Samantha Whittaker and Mr. Steve Hardman for their invaluable help and encouragement in preparing this manuscript for publication.

This volume is dedicated to all of G. S. Maddala's students, who meant so much to him.

Kay Maddala
October 2000

Preface to the Second Edition

There have been many important developments in econometrics during the last two decades, but introductory books in the field still deal mostly with what econometrics was in the 1960s. The present book is meant to familiarize students (and researchers) with some of these developments, explaining them with very simple models without cluttering up the exposition with too much algebraic detail. Where proofs involve complicated expressions they are omitted and appropriate references are given. Ten of the more difficult sections have been marked with an asterisk indicating that they are optional. Beginning students can skip them and proceed. The book also contains several examples illustrating the techniques at each stage, and where illustrations are not given, some data sets have been provided so that students can compute the required results themselves.

Since the book covers quite a few topics, only a few examples have been given to illustrate *each* point. Giving too many illustrations for a single point might be boring for some students and would have made the book much too bulky. The instructor's manual contains more illustrative examples and questions and answers. The exercises given at the end of each chapter are somewhat challenging. However, the instructor's manual contains answers or guidelines. The instructor's manual also gives a "guided tour" of the material in each chapter as well as some detailed explanations for some points that are touched briefly in the book.

Some of the questions at the end of the chapters have been taken from the examinations at several U.S. and U.K. universities, and from P. C. B. Phillips and M. R. Wickens, *Exercises in Econometrics* (Cambridge, MA: Ballinger Publishing Co., 1978), Vol. I. (Many of the questions in that book are from examinations in the U.K. universities.) Since questions tend to get repeated with minor changes, I have not bothered to quote the exact source for each question.

There are many distinguishing features of the book, some of which are:

1. A discussion of aims and methodology of econometrics in Chapter 1.
2. A critique of conventional significance levels in Chapter 2.
3. A discussion of direct versus reverse regression and inverse prediction in Chapter 3.
4. A thorough discussion of several practically useful results in multiple regression (Chapter 4), some of which are not to be found even in specialized books on regression.
5. Discussion of several new tests for heteroskedasticity, choice of linear versus log-linear models, and use of deflators (in Chapter 5).
6. A thorough discussion of the use and limitations of the Durbin–Watson test, showing that it is almost useless in practice, and a discussion of Sargan's test, ARCH test, LM test, etc. (Chapter 6).
7. A critical discussion of the use and limitations of condition numbers, variance inflation factors (VIF's), ridge regression, and principal component regression in the analysis of multicollinearity (Chapter 7). Many of these techniques are often used uncritically, because computer programs are readily available.
8. The use of dummy variables to obtain predictions and standard errors of predictions, the relationship between discriminant analysis and the linear probability model, the logit, probit, and tobit models (Chapter 8).
9. Inference in underidentified simultaneous equation models, criteria for normalization, and tests for exogeneity and causality (Chapter 9).
10. The discussion of partial adjustment models, error correction models, rational expectations models, and tests for rationality (Chapter 10).
11. Reverse regression, proxy variables (Chapter 11).
12. Different types of residuals and their use in diagnostic checking, model selection, choice of F-ratios in the selection of regressors, Hausman's specification error test, tests of nonnested hypotheses (Chapter 12).

These are not new topics for advanced texts but these topics (most of which are never dealt with in introductory texts) are important in econometric practice. The book explains them all with simple models so that students (and researchers) who have not had exposure to advanced texts and advanced courses in econometrics can still learn them and use them.

I have avoided any special discussion of computer programs. Nowadays, there are several computer packages available that one can choose from. Also, they change so rapidly that the lists have to be expanded and updated very often. The instructor's manual will provide some guidance on this. I feel that it is more important to know the answers to the questions of what to compute, why to compute, how to interpret the results, what is wrong with the model, and how we can improve the model. Learning how to compute is rather easy. In the 1960s this last question received more attention because computer technology had not progressed enough and not many efficient computer programs were readily available. With the advances in computer technology and the large number of computer programs readily available, everyone can easily learn "how to compute." That is why I have tried to minimize the discussion of computer programs or the presentation of computer output. Moreover, there is no single program that will do all the things discussed in the book. But by simple adaptation many of the computer programs available will do the job.

   Instructors using the book might find it difficult to cover all the material. However, it is always better to have some topics in the book that instructors can choose from depending on their interests and needs. Chapters 1 through 9 cover the basic material. The last three chapters, on models of expectations, errors in variables, and model selection, are topics that instructors can pick and choose from. A one-semester course would cover Chapters 1 to 6 (or 7). A two-semester course would cover Chapters 1 to 9 and parts of Chapters 10–12. In either case Chapter 2 need not be covered but can be used as a reference.

Second Edition

1. *Addition of matrix algebra.* Many who have used the first edition found the omission of matrix algebra a handicap. Since the purpose of the book was to convey the basic ideas without using the "crutches" of matrix notation, I have decided to retain the original format and add matrix algebra in the appendices to Chapters 2, 4, 5, 7, 9, and 12. The appendix to Chapter 2 gives all the necessary background in matrix algebra and there are some exercises at the end of the appendix.
2. *Exercises on statistical inference.* Chapter 2 presents a review of statistical inference. Those who used the book found the review too short, but expanding it would have made the book unnecessarily long. However, students are expected to have had a beginning statistics course. To make the review more useful, a list of questions has been added to Chapter 2. Students will get a sufficient review by attempting to solve these questions.
3. *Addition of chapters on time series, unit roots, and cointegration.* One major drawback of the first edition has been the complete omission of time-series analysis. This has been corrected by adding Chapter 13. In addition, the important recent developments of unit roots and cointegration have been covered in Chapter 14. There is currently no book that covers these topics at an introductory level.

   Some instructors might want to cover Chapters 6, 10, 13, and 14 together because they are all on time-series topics. There is no need to cover the topics in the order in which they appear in the book.

   At some places I have a reference to my earlier book: *Econometrics* (New York: McGraw-Hill, 1977) for details. I saw no point in reproducing some proofs or derivations where they were not absolutely necessary for understanding the points being made. At several others, there is a footnote saying that the result or proof can be found in many books in econometrics, and I give a reference to my earlier book with page numbers. However, the same result can be often found in other standard references, such as:

J. Johnston, *Econometric Methods*, 3rd ed. (New York: McGraw-Hill, 1984).
J. Kmenta, *Elements of Econometrics*, 2nd ed. (New York: Macmillan, 1986).
H. Theil, *Principles of Econometrics* (New York: Wiley, 1971).
G. G. Judge, C. R. Hill, W. E. Griffiths, H. Lütkepohl, and T. C. Lee, *Theory and Practice of Economics*, 2nd ed. (New York: Wiley, 1985).

E. Malinvaud, *Statistical Methods of Econometrics*, 3rd ed. (Amsterdam: North-Holland, 1976).

Since I did not find it practicable to give detailed page numbers for every book, I have just referred to my earlier book.

I would like to thank Jack Repcheck for first encouraging me to write this book and Ken MacLeod and John Travis for bringing the first edition to completion. I would also like to thank Caroline Carney for initiating this second edition and Jill Lectka and David Boelio for their encouragement in bringing it to completion.

I would like to thank Richard Butler, Melanie Courchene, Jinook Jeong, Fred Joutz, Sang-Heung Kang, In-Moo Kim, Jongmin Lee, Wanki Moon, Marc Nerlove, Mark Rush, W. Douglas Shaw, Robert Trost, Ken White, Jisoo Yoo, and many others for their comments and suggestions.

I would like to thank Kajal Lahiri, Scott Shonkwiler, and Robert P. Trost for their help on the first edition.

I would like to thank In-Moo Kim for his invaluable help in preparing this second edition. Without his assistance, this edition would have taken much longer to complete. I would also like to thank Ann Crisafulli for typing several versions of the additions and corrections cheerfully and efficiently. Finally, I would like to thank all those who used the book and also passed on helpful comments.

G. S. Maddala

Preface to the Third Edition

This edition contains a reorganization of the chapters in the second edition, corrections in the errors, and the addition of several new chapters covering new material. The additions include new chapters on panel data, large-sample theory (maximum likelihood and GMM), and resampling methods (Monte Carlo and bootstrap) for small-sample inference. In each case, the discussion is at an elementary and easily understandable level. The chapters are also organized into three parts. Parts I and II are appropriate for undergraduate courses. Part III can be added for (two-semester) beginning graduate and MBA courses (with selective deletions if necessary). With the expanded and comprehensive coverage this book should also be of use to graduate students and empirical researchers alike. To make space for the new material and for the convenience of students, the data sets in the second edition (as well as new data sets) have been put on to a Website.

In addition to the people I thanked in my preface to the second edition, I would like to thank the following. First of all I would like to thank Min Qi at Kent State University for her detailed comments on the second edition, suggestions for the topics to be added to this third edition, and constant encouragement in the preparation of this edition. Without her help this edition would not have been completed. I would also like to thank Hongyi Li at the Chinese University of Hong Kong for his help with the data sets, and Yong Hoon Koo for several corrections to the second edition. Yasushi Toda is thanked for supplying one of the large data sets. Mark N. Harris and Lachlan R. Macquarie from Monash University provided several useful suggestions, and references for this revision, for which I am very thankful. Others who provided some helpful comments include Badi Baltagi, Kajal Lahiri, In-Moo Kim, Tom Means, Mary McGarvey, Robert Trost, Yong Yin and several others (too many to list) who used the earlier editions of this book. Finally I would like to thank Jo Ducey and Shaowen Wu for typing the additions to the second edition.

G. S. Maddala

Obituary[1]

On June 4, 1999 G. S. Maddala (popularly and affectionately known as GS) passed away in Columbus, OH at the age of 66. A leading figure in the econometrics profession for more than three decades, he held the University Eminent Scholar Professorship in the Department of Economics at Ohio State University at the time of his death. GS is survived by his wife Kameswari, "Kay," and several members of his immediate family: his daughter, Tara, of Houston; his son, Vivek, of San Francisco; and two sisters who live in India.

GS's previous university affiliations include Stanford University (1963–1967), University of Rochester (1967–1975), and University of Florida (1975–1993). At Florida, he was a Graduate Research Professor and the Director of the Center for Econometrics and Decision Sciences. He held visiting appointments at Cornell, Yale, CORE, Monash, Columbia, the California Institute of Technology (as the Fairchild Distinguished Scholar), and many other institutions. At the time of his death, GS was an Advisory Editor of *Econometric Theory*, an Associate Editor of the *Journal of Statistical Planning and Inference*, and a long-time Fellow and active participant of the Econometric Society. He was an Associate Editor of *Econometrica* during 1970–1979 and an Associate Editor of the *Journal of Applied Econometrics* from 1993 to 1996.

GS had a passion for writing and research and the gift of a brilliant expositor — the ability to cut through the technical superstructure to reveal essential detail only, yet in the process of simplification never to lose the nerve center of the methods he sought to explain. This skill was apparent in all his writing and was the central element in his textbook expositions. His 1977 econometrics text redefined the boundaries of econometrics that could be integrated into graduate econometrics teaching and became a new standard for subsequent econometrics textbooks. His 1983 Econometric Society monograph, "Limited Dependent and Qualitative Variables in Econometrics," was an immediate best seller and was declared a citation classic in *Current Contents* (Vol. 30, July 26, 1993). It has fueled

---

[1]This obituary first appeared in the journal *Econometric Theory*, published by Cambridge University Press.

much of the innovative applied research in this area during the last 15 years, and it has served as a bible to empirical researchers in applied microeconomics.

Born in India to a family of very modest means, GS came to the Department of Economics at the University of Chicago as a Fulbright Scholar with a B.A. in Mathematics from Andhra University and an M.A. in Statistics from Bombay University. Since completing his doctorate at Chicago in 1963, GS has been a prolific writer, producing over 110 articles and 12 books covering almost every emerging area of econometrics throughout his career.

According to the Social Science Citation Index, GS has been one of the top five most cited econometricians during each of the years 1988–1994. This is undeniable testimony to his influence on contemporary econometric thought. He has worked on an enormous range of topics in econometrics, coming close to covering the entire field. In econometric methodology, he has contributed to distributed lags, generalized least squares, panel data, simultaneous equations, errors in variables, income distribution, switching regressions, disequilibrium models, qualitative and limited dependent variable models, self-selection models, outliers and bootstrap methods, unit roots and cointegration methods, and Bayesian econometrics, among other topics. In empirical economics, GS has written papers in such diverse areas as consumption, production and cost functions, money demand, regulation, pseudo-data, returns to college education, housing market discrimination, survey data on expectations, and risk premia in futures markets. How remarkable it is that he has made significant contributions to such varied areas of econometrics. Yet, in his often self-deprecating way, GS used to say that he never made any hard decisions to do anything in life, he just tumbled onto them—that his whole attitude in these matters was influenced by the Indian philosophy that "nothing matters."

Even though his most influential contributions have been in methodology, he loved to write econometrics in plain English and had an extraordinary talent to penetrate to the essence of problems, conveying basic ideas lucidly in simple words. This exceptional expository capability made him revered by applied and theoretical econometricians alike. GS's style was often to take a critical but constructive look at evolving econometric techniques, in particular those that have little practical application. In doing so, he never hesitated to go against the tide of the profession. He was one of the few econometricians who constantly asked whether the questions being answered are worth asking, always maintaining a clear perspective on a wide range of issues in econometrics and their relationship to economic problems. In oral presentations at seminars and conferences, he was well known for making points with a characteristic sense of wit and humor, not to mention his self-deprecating, oft-stated remark that "it was all in the paper," representing a humorous counterculture to present-day demonstrative live-data-show presentations. Those close to him were constantly aware of GS's pervasive sense of humor. Without his presence, conferences will never be the same.

GS has been a mentor and a source of inspiration to more than 50 doctoral students whom he has supervised over the years. They have benefited from the durability of his insights and the power of his analytical mind. Until the last day of his life, GS kept doing what he liked to do the most—talking to graduate students, worrying about them, and writing papers and books with them. After hearing the news of his death, one of GS's current Ph.D. students sent the following e-mail message to all his Ohio State University professors and fellow graduate students, "I started to work with GS almost a year ago. Even though it is a short amount of time, I realized a clear fact that anyone who was close to GS must have realized: GS's quality as a person was even greater than his qualities as an econometrician. As an econometrician, he wrote many books and papers that anyone can read. However, his quality as a person was only enjoyed by a few who were close to him. I feel truly blessed that God gave me the opportunity to be close to him during this year." There could be no more fitting epitaph for a teacher to whom his students meant so much, and none that GS himself would have prized more highly than that. With his death, the economics profession has lost one of its most prolific, energetic, influential, and articulate members, a man who was loved by so many of us.

Kajal Lahiri
State University of New York, Albany

Peter C. B. Phillips
Yale University

June 1999

Part I Introduction and the Linear Regression Model

This part consists of four chapters.

Chapter 1 discusses the changes in the methodology that have taken place since the 1950s and 1960s and gives an outline of the book.

Chapter 2 reviews some basic results in statistics. Most students will have covered this introductory material in courses in statistics. This chapter also provides an introduction to matrix algebra.

Chapter 3 covers the simple regression model and Chapter 4 the multiple regression model in detail. This forms the basics of linear regression under the assumption of independent and identically distributed normal errors. These assumptions are relaxed in Part II.

1 What is Econometrics?

What is in this Chapter?

This chapter explains the scope and methodology of econometrics. Econometrics deals with the application of statistical tools to economic data. The first task an econometrician faces is that of formulating an economic relationship, which is necessarily a simplified model of the real-world process. Estimation and testing of these models with observed data, and the use of the estimated models for prediction and policy analysis are the other two major goals of econometrics.

This chapter also contains a schematic depiction of the various methodological steps involved in an econometric analysis.

1.1 What is Econometrics?

Literally speaking, the word "econometrics" means "measurement in economics." This is too broad a definition to be of any use because most of economics is concerned with measurement. We measure our gross national product, employment, money supply, exports, imports, price indexes, and so on. What we mean by *econometrics* is:

> The application of statistical and mathematical methods to the analysis of economic data, with a purpose of giving empirical content to economic theories and verifying them or refuting them.

In this respect econometrics is distinguished from mathematical economics, which consists of the application of mathematics only, and the theories derived need not necessarily have an empirical content.

The application of statistical tools to economic data has a very long history. Stigler[1] notes that the first "empirical" demand schedule was published in 1699 by Charles Davenant and that the first modern statistical demand studies were made by Rodulfo Enini, an Italian statistician, in 1907. The main impetus to the development of econometrics, however, came with the establishment of the Econometric Society in 1930 and the publication of the journal *Econometrica* in January 1933.

Before any statistical analysis with economic data can be done, one needs a clear mathematical formulation of the relevant economic theory. To take a very simple example, saying that the demand curve is downward sloping is not enough. We have to write the statement in mathematical form. This can be done in several ways. For instance, defining q as the quantity demanded and p as price, we can write

$$q = \alpha + \beta p \quad \beta < 0$$

or

$$q = A p^{\beta} \quad \beta < 0$$

As we will see later in the book, one of the major problems we face is the fact that economic theory is rarely informative about functional forms. We have to use statistical methods to choose the functional form, as well.

1.2 Economic and Econometric Models

The first task an econometrician faces is that of formulating an econometric model. What is a model?

A *model* is a simplified representation of a real-world process. For instance, saying that the quantity demanded of oranges depends on the price of oranges is a simplified representation because there are a host of other variables that one can think of that determine the demand for oranges. For instance, income of consumers, an increase in diet consciousness ("drinking coffee causes cancer, so you better switch to orange juice," etc.), an increase or decrease in the price of apples, and so on. However, there is no end to this stream of other variables. In a remote sense even the price of gasoline can affect the demand for oranges.

Many scientists have argued in favor of simplicity because simple models are easier to understand, communicate, and test empirically with data. This is the position of Karl Popper[2] and Milton Friedman.[3] The choice of a simple model to explain complex real-world phenomena leads to two criticisms:

1. The model is oversimplified.
2. The assumptions are unrealistic.

---

[1]G. J. Stigler, "The Early History of Empirical Studies of Consumer Behavior," *The Journal of Political Economy*, 1954 [reprinted in G. J. Stigler, *Essays in the History of Economics* (Chicago: University of Chicago Press, 1965)].

[2]K. F. Popper, *The Logic of Scientific Discovery* (London: Hutchinson, 1959), p. 142.

[3]M. Friedman, "The Methodology of Positive Economics," in *Essays in Positive Economics* (Chicago: University of Chicago Press, 1953), p. 14.

For instance, in our example of the demand for oranges, to say that it depends on only the price of oranges is an oversimplification and also an unrealistic assumption. To the criticism of oversimplification, one can argue that it is better to start with a simplified model and progressively construct more complicated models. This is the idea expressed by Koopmans.[4] On the other hand, there are some who argue in favor of starting with a very general model and simplifying it progressively based on the data available.[5] The famous statistician L. J. (Jimmy) Savage used to say that "a model should be as big as an elephant." Whatever the relative merits of this alternative approach area, we will start with simple models and progressively build more complicated models.

The other criticism we have mentioned is that of "unrealistic assumptions." To this criticism Friedman argued that the assumptions of a theory are never descriptively realistic. He says:[6]

> The relevant question to ask about the "assumptions" of a theory is not whether they are descriptively "realistic" for they never are, but whether they are sufficiently good approximations for the purpose at hand. And this question can be answered by only seeing whether the theory works, which means whether it yields sufficiently accurate predictions.

Returning to our example of demand for oranges, to say that it depends only on the price of oranges is a descriptively unrealistic assumption. However, the inclusion of other variables, such as income and price of apples in the model, does not render the model more descriptively realistic. Even this model can be considered to be based on unrealistic assumptions because it leaves out many other variables (like health consciousness, etc.). But the issue is which model is more useful for predicting the demand for oranges. This issue can be decided only from the data we have and the data we can get.

In practice, we include in our model all the variables that we think are relevant for our purpose and dump the rest of the variables in a basket called "disturbance." This brings us to the distinction between an economic model and an econometric model.

An *economic model* is a set of assumptions that approximately describes the behavior of an economy (or a sector of an economy). An *econometric model* consists of the following:

1. A set of behavioral equations derived from the economic model. These equations involve some observed variables and some "disturbances" (which are a catchall for all the variables considered as irrelevant for the purpose of this model as well as all unforeseen events).
2. A statement of whether there are errors of observation in the observed variables.
3. A specification of the probability distribution of the "disturbances" (and errors of measurement).

With these specifications we can proceed to test the empirical validity of the economic model and use it to make forecasts or use it in policy analysis.

Taking the simplest example of a demand model, the econometric model usually consists of:

---

[4]T. C. Koopmans, *Three Essays on the State of Economics Science* (New York: McGraw-Hill, 1957), pp. 142–143.

[5]This is the approach suggested by J. D. Sargan and notably David F. Hendry.

[6]Friedman, "Methodology," pp. 14–15.

1. The behavioral equation

$$q = \alpha + \beta p + u$$

   where q is the quantity demanded and p the price. Here p and q are the observed variables and u is a disturbance term.
2. A specification of the probability distribution of u which says that $E(u|p) = 0$ and that the values of u for the different observations are independently and normally distributed with mean zero and variance σ^2.

With these specifications one proceeds to test empirically the law of demand or the hypothesis that $\beta < 0$. One can also use the estimated demand function for prediction and policy purposes.

1.3 The Aims and Methodology of Econometrics

The aims of econometrics are:

1. Formulation of econometric models, that is, formulation of economic models in an empirically testable form. Usually, there are several ways of formulating the econometric model from an economic model because we have to choose the functional form, the specification of the stochastic structure of the variables, and so on. This part constitutes the *specification aspect* of the econometric work.
2. Estimation and testing of these models with observed data. This part constitutes the *inference aspect* of the econometric work.
3. Use of these models for prediction and policy purposes.

During the 1950s and 1960s the inference aspect received a lot of attention and the specification aspect very little. The major preoccupation of econometricians had been the statistical estimation of correctly specified econometric models. During the late 1940s the Cowles Foundation provided a major breakthrough in this respect, but the statistical analysis presented formidable computational problems. Thus the 1950s and 1960s were spent mostly in devising alternative estimation methods and alternative computer algorithms. Not much attention was paid to errors in the specification or to errors in observations.[7] With the advent of high-speed computers, all this has, however, changed. The estimation problems are no longer formidable and econometricians have turned attention to other aspects of econometric analysis.

We can schematically depict the various steps involved in an econometric analysis, as was done before the emphasis on specification analysis. This is shown in Figure 1.1. Since the entries in the boxes are self-explanatory, we will not elaborate on them. The only box that needs an explanation is box 4, "prior information." This refers to any information that we might have on the unknown parameters in the model. This information can come from economic theory or from previous empirical studies.

---

[7]There was some work on specification errors in the early 1960s by Theil and Griliches, but this referred to omitted-variable bias (see Chapter 4). Griliches' lecture notes (unpublished) at the University of Chicago were titled "Specification Errors in Econometrics."

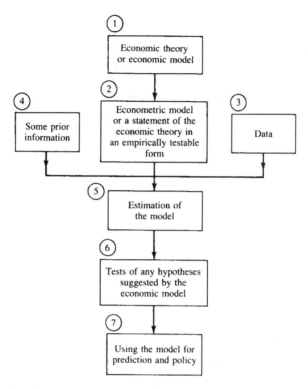

Figure 1.1 Schematic description of the steps involved in an econometric analysis of economic models

There has, however, been considerable dissatisfaction with the scheme shown in Figure 1.1. Although one can find instances of dissatisfaction earlier, it was primarily during the 1970s that arguments were levied against the one-way traffic shown in Figure 1.1. We will discuss three of these arguments.

1. In Figure 1.1 there is no feedback from the econometric testing of economic theories to the formulation of economic theories (i.e., from box 6 to box 1). It has been argued that econometricians are not just handmaidens of economic theorists. It is not true that they just take the theories they are given and test them, learning nothing from the tests. So we need an arrow from box 6 to box 1.
2. The same is true regarding the data collection agencies. It is not true that they just gather whatever data they can and the econometricians use whatever data are given them. (The word *data* comes from the Latin word *datum*, which means *given*.) There ought to be feedback from boxes 2 and 5 to box 3.
3. Regarding box 6 itself, it has been argued that the hypothesis testing refers only to the hypotheses suggested by the original economic model. This depends on the assumption that the specification adopted in box 2 is correct. However, what we should be doing is testing the adequacy of the original specification as well. Thus we need an extra

box of specification testing and diagnostic checking. There will also be feedback from this box to box 2, that is, the specification tests will result in a new specification for the econometric models. These problems, which have been one of the most important major developments in econometrics in the 1970s, are treated in Chapter 12.

The new developments that have been suggested are shown figuratively in Figure 1.2. Some of the original boxes have been deleted or condensed. The schematic description in Figure 1.2 is illustrative only and should not be interpreted literally. The important things to note are the feedback:

1. From econometric results to economic theory.
2. From specification testing and diagnostic checking to revised specification of the economic model.
3. From the econometric model to data.

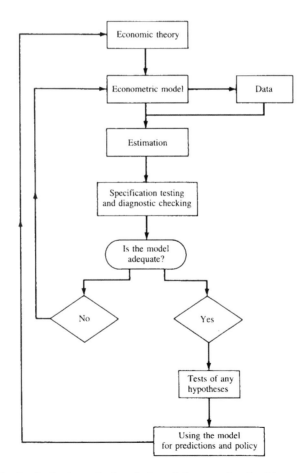

Figure 1.2   Revised schematic description of the steps involved in an econometric
analysis of economic models

In the foregoing scheme we have talked of only one theory, but often there are many competing theories, and one of the main purposes of econometrics is to help in the choice among competing theories. This is the problem of model selection, which is discussed in Chapter 12.

1.4   What Constitutes a Test of an Economic Theory?

Earlier, we stated that one of the aims of econometrics was that of testing economic theories. An important question that arises is: What constitutes a test? As evidence of a successful test of economic theory, it is customary to report that the signs of the estimated coefficients in an econometric model are correct. This approach may be termed the approach of *confirming* economic theories. The problem with this approach is that, as Mark Blaug points out:[8]

> In many areas of economics, different econometric studies reach conflicting conclusions and, given the available data, there are frequently no effective methods for deciding which conclusion is correct. In consequence, contradictory hypotheses continue to co-exist sometimes for decades or more.

A more valid test of an economic theory is if it can give predictions that are better than those of alternative theories suggested earlier. Thus one needs to compare a given model with earlier models. This approach of evaluating alternative theories has received greater attention in recent years. The problems associated with model comparison and model selection are dealt with in Chapter 12.

Summary and an Outline of the Book

The preceding discussion suggests some changes that have taken place during the last decade in the development of econometric methods. The earlier emphasis (during the 1950s and 1960s) was on efficient estimation of a given model. The emphasis has now shifted to specification testing, diagnostic checking, model comparison, and an adequate formulation of the expectational variables given the pervasive role of expectations in almost all economic theories.

A large part of the book, however, will be devoted to developments that took place in the 1950s and 1960s because these developments form the basis for recent work. However, Chapters 12–15 are devoted to recent advances in the areas of specification testing and model selection in time series and panel data models. Chapters 16 and 17 will deal with some current developments in the area of inference in large as well as small samples. In addition, the other chapters also describe recent developments. For instance, rational expectations models are discussed in Chapter 10, recent developments on tests for serial correlation are reviewed in Chapter 6, and vector autoregressions, unit roots, and cointegration are discussed in Chapter 14.

---

[8]M. Blaug, *The Methodology of Economics* (Cambridge: Cambridge University Press, 1980), p. 261.

The book is divided into three parts.

Part I: Introduction and the Linear Regression Model consists of four chapters. Chapter 2 is a review of basic results in statistics. It also has an introduction to matrix algebra. Further results in matrix algebra on characteristic roots and vectors are in the appendix to Chapter 7. Chapter 3 is on the simple regression model and Chapter 4 is on the multiple regression model. These chapters cover the basics of regression based on the assumption that the errors are IN$(0, \sigma^2)$.

Part II: Violation of the Assumptions of the Basic Model has seven chapters. Chapter 5 is on heteroskedasticity and Chapter 6 is on autocorrelation. Chapter 7 is on multicollinearity. Chapter 8 is on dummy variables and truncated variables. Chapter 9 is on simultaneous equations. Chapter 10 is on nonlinear models, expectations and nonnormality. Chapter 11 is on errors in variables.

These chapters relax the several assumptions made regarding the basic regression model discussed in Part I.

Part III: Special Topics consists of six chapters. Chapter 12 is on diagnostic checking, specification testing and model selection. Chapters 13 and 14 are on time series, unit roots and cointegration. Chapters 15, 16, and 17 are new chapters in this book. Chapter 15 is on panel data. Chapter 16 is on large-sample theory. Chapter 17 is on small-sample inference and bootstrap methods.

2 Statistical Background and Matrix Algebra

What is in this Chapter?

This chapter reviews the basics of statistical inference that students would have learnt in a course in statistics. The concepts discussed are: probability, conditional probability and Bayes' theorem, random variables and probability distributions, the normal and related distributions (χ^2, t, F), classical and Bayesian inference, properties of estimators (small sample and asymptotic), sampling distributions, interval estimation and tests of hypotheses.

The distinction between statistical significance and economic significance is emphasized. Also, reasons are given why one should not use the 5% or 1% significance levels all the time.

Finally, a method of combining several independent tests is outlined. This is a problem that occurs frequently in practice.

The chapter next gives an introduction to matrix algebra (in the appendix). The topics discussed are addition and multiplication of matrices, finding the inverse of a matrix, definition of the rank, Cramer's rule for solving systems of equations, positive and negative definite matrices, idempotent matrices, the multivariate normal distribution, idempotent matrices and their relationship to χ^2-distributions.

The mastery of all these concepts in matrix algebra is important to understand portions of the book where matrix notation is used (this is avoided in the beginning chapters, Chapters 1–11). The appendices of the respective chapters, however, discuss the topics in matrix notation.

The appendix to Chapter 7 discusses more topics in matrix algebra, such as characteristic roots and vectors.

2.1   Introduction

In this chapter we review some basic results in probability and statistics that are used in the book. Most of the results are generally covered in a course in introductory statistics that students take before entering a course in econometrics. Hence the discussion is concise, and proofs are omitted. However, exercises at the end of the chapter will provide some practice in the use of concepts and results presented here. Students should attempt to work on these questions as well, as part of this review. This chapter serves two purposes:

1. As a review of some material covered in previous courses in statistics.
2. As a reference for some results when needed.

In this chapter we omit discussion of methods of estimation: method of moments, method of least squares, and the method of maximum likelihood as they are discussed in Chapter 3 when we cover simple regression.

The other thing this chapter provides is an introduction to matrix algebra. This is included in an appendix because the main body of the text does not involve matrix notation and explains the basic concepts with simple models. Chapters 4, 5, 7, 9, and 12 also contain appendices that contain proofs of some results stated without proof in the respective chapters. These proofs need the matrix notation. Thus students wishing to learn the proofs and the matrix notation would start with this appendix and then go through the appendices to the other chapters. The appendix to this chapter also contains exercises on matrix algebra that students are advised to work on.

2.2   Probability

The term *probability* is used to give a quantitative measure to the uncertainty associated with our statements. The earliest notions of probability were first applied to gambling. Backgammon was known thousands of years ago. Although most of the gamblers presumably calculated some probabilities, it is Gerolamo Cardano (1501–1576), an Italian physician, mathematician, and astrologer, who is credited with the first systematic computation of probabilities. He defined probability as

$$\text{probability} = \frac{\text{number of favorable outcomes}}{\text{total number of possible outcomes}}$$

This is called the *classical view* of probability. Suppose that we roll a balanced die. What is the probability of getting a 6? The number of favorable outcomes is one since there is only one 6. The total number of possible outcomes is six (1, 2, 3, 4, 5, 6). Hence the probability is $\frac{1}{6}$.

Another definition of probability is that of the relative frequency of the occurrence of an event in a large number of repetitions. In the case of the die, we calculate the probability of a 6 by rolling the die a large number of times and then observing the proportion of times we get a 6. This observed proportion will give us the probability of a 6. You would think that nobody would have the patience to compute probabilities this way. However, there is a well-known example of Kerrick, who while interned in Denmark during World War II, performed several such experiments. For instance, he tossed a coin 10,000 times! Initially, the relative frequency of heads fluctuated widely, but it finally settled close to 0.5, with a value of 0.507 on the final toss. The experiments are described in J. E. Kerrick, *An Experimental Introduction to the Theory of Probability* (Copenhagen: Jorgensen, 1946).

The *frequency view* of probability, first given by the French mathematician Poisson in 1837, says that if n is the number of trials and $n(E)$ the number of occurrences of the event E, then the probability of E, denoted by $P(E)$ is

$$P(E) = \lim_{n \to \infty} \frac{n(E)}{n}$$

According to the classical view, probability is a *theoretical number* defined as the ratio of the number of favorable cases to the total number of possible cases. According to the frequency view, it is a limit of the *observed* relative frequency as the number of repetitions becomes very large.

A third view is the *subjective view* of probability, which is based on personal beliefs. Suppose you say that the probability that the New York Giants will win is $\frac{3}{4}$. Consider a bet where you are given \$1 if the Giants win and you pay \$3 if they lose. Your probability indicated that this is a "fair" bet. If you are not willing to take this bet, your subjective probability that the Giants will win is $< \frac{3}{4}$. If you are too anxious to take this bet, your subjective probability that the Giants will win is $> \frac{3}{4}$. Because of the "betting" basis for subjective probability, it is also called "personal pignic probability." The work "pignic" comes from the Latin word *pignus* (a bet).

Addition Rules of Probability

Fortunately, however, whatever view of probability we adopt, the rules for the calculation of probability are the same. Before we discuss these, we have to define some terms. Events $A_1, A_2, A_3, \ldots$ are said to be *mutually exclusive* if when one occurs, the others do not. They are said to be *exhaustive* if they exhaust all the possibilities. In the case of a die, the events $A_1, A_2, \ldots, A_6$ that the die shows 1, 2, 3, 4, 5, and 6 are mutually exclusive as well as exhaustive.

We write $P(A + B)$ as the probability that A or B of the events A and B occur. This is called the *union* of the two events. We write $P(AB)$ as the probability of the joint occurrence of A and B. This is called the *intersection* of the events A and B.

For example, if we define A and B as:

$$A : \quad \text{The die shows 1, 3, or 5}$$

$$B : \quad \text{The die shows 3}$$

then

$$A + B : \quad \text{The die shows 1, 3, or 5}$$

$$AB : \quad \text{The die shows 3}$$

The *addition rule* of probability states that

$$P(A + B) = P(A) + P(B) - P(AB)$$

(We can show this by drawing a diagram known as the *Venn diagram*. This is left as an exercise.) If A and B are mutually exclusive, they cannot occur jointly, so $P(AB) = 0$. Thus for mutually exclusive events we have

$$P(A + B) = P(A) + P(B)$$

If, in addition, A and B are exhaustive, $P(A) + P(B) = 1$.

We denote by $\overline{A}$ the *complement* of A. $\overline{A}$ *represents the nonoccurrence of A.* Since either A occurs or does not (i.e., $\overline{A}$ occurs), A and $\overline{A}$ are mutually exclusive and exhaustive. Hence $P(A) + P(\overline{A}) = 1$ or $P(\overline{A}) = 1 - P(A)$. We can also write $P(A) = P(AB) + P(A\overline{B})$ because A can occur jointly with B or without B.

Conditional Probability and the Multiplication Rule

Sometimes we restrict our attention to a subset of all possible events. For instance, suppose that when we throw a die, the cases 1, 2, and 3 do not count. Thus the restricted set of events is that the die shows 4, 5, or 6. There are three possible outcomes. Consider the event A that the die shows a 6. The probability of A is now $\frac{1}{3}$ since the total number of outcomes is 3, not 6. Conditional probability is defined as follows: The probability of an event A, given that another event B has occurred, is denoted by $P(A|B)$ and is defined by

$$P(A|B) = \frac{P(AB)}{P(B)}$$

In the case above, $P(AB) = \frac{1}{6}$, $P(B) = \frac{3}{6}$, and hence $P(A|B) = \frac{1}{3}$. We shall now define *independent events*. A and B are said to be independent if the probability of the occurrence of one does not depend on whether or not the other has occurred. Thus if A and B are independent, the conditional and unconditional probabilities are the same, that is, $P(A|B) = P(A)$ and $P(B|A) = P(B)$. Since $P(A|B) = P(AB)/P(B)$ and $P(A|B) = P(A)$, we get the *multiplication rule*, which says that

$$P(AB) = P(A) \times P(B) \quad \text{if } A \text{ and } B \text{ are independent}$$

As an example, suppose that we throw a die two times:

$$A = \text{event that the first throw shows a 6}$$

$$B = \text{event that the second throw shows a 6}$$

Clearly, A and B are independent events. Hence Prob(we get a double 6) $= P(AB) = P(A) \cdot P(B) = \frac{1}{36}$.

Bayes' Theorem

Bayes' theorem is based on conditional probability. We have

$$P(A|B) = \frac{P(AB)}{P(B)} \quad \text{and} \quad P(B|A) = \frac{P(AB)}{P(A)}$$

Write the second equation as

$$P(AB) = P(B|A) \cdot P(A)$$

Then we get

$$P(A|B) = \frac{P(B|A) \cdot P(A)}{P(B)}$$

This is known as Bayes' theorem. It appeared in a text published in 1763 by Reverend Thomas Bayes, a part-time mathematician.

Let H_1 and H_2 denote two hypotheses and D denote the observed data. Let us substitute H_1 and H_2 in turn for A and substitute D for B. Then we get

$$P(H_1|D) = \frac{P(D|H_1) \cdot P(H_1)}{P(D)} \quad \text{and} \quad P(H_2|D) = \frac{P(D|H_2) \cdot P(H_2)}{P(D)}$$

Hence we get

$$\frac{P(H_1|D)}{P(H_2|D)} = \frac{P(D|H_1)}{P(D|H_2)} \cdot \frac{P(H_1)}{P(H_2)}$$

The left-hand side of this equation is called *posterior odds*. The first term on the right-hand side is called the *likelihood ratio*, and the second term is called the *prior odds*. We shall make use of this in Chapter 12 for the problem of choice between two models. For the present let us consider the following example.

We have two urns: the first has 1 red ball and 4 white balls, and the second has 2 red balls and 2 white balls. An urn is chosen at random and a ball drawn. The ball is white. What is the probability that it came from the first urn? Let us define:

$$H_1: \quad \text{The first urn was chosen}$$

$$H_2: \quad \text{The second urn was chosen}$$

$$D: \quad \text{Data, that is, the ball is white}$$

We have $P(H_1) = P(H_2) = \frac{1}{2}$. Also, $P(D|H_1) = \frac{4}{5}$ and $P(D|H_2) = \frac{1}{2}$. Hence $P(H_1|D)/P(H_2|D) = \frac{8}{5}$ or $P(H_1|D) = \frac{8}{13}$ and $P(H_2|D) = \frac{5}{13}$. The required probability is $\frac{8}{13}$.

Summation and Product Operations

In the examples we considered, we often had only two events. If we have n events, we have to use the summation operator $\sum$ and the product operator $\prod$. Since we shall be using these in other contexts as well, we shall discuss them here.

The summation operator $\sum$ is defined as follows:

$$\sum_{i=1}^{n} X_i = X_1 + X_2 + \cdots X_n$$

Some important properties of this operator are:

1. $\sum_{i=1}^{n} c = nc$, where c is a constant.
2. $\sum_{i=1}^{n} (x_i + y_i) = \sum_{i=1}^{n} x_i + \sum_{i=1}^{n} y_i$.
3. $\sum_{i=1}^{n} (c + bx_i) = nc + b \sum_{i=1}^{n} x_i$.

Where there is no confusion we will just write $\sum_i X_i$ or $\sum X_i$ to denote $\sum_{i=1}^{n} X_i$, that is, summation over all the X's.

Sometimes we use the double-summation operator, which is defined as follows:

$$\sum_{i=1}^{n} \sum_{j=1}^{m} X_{ij} = X_{11} + X_{12} + \cdots + X_{1m}$$

$$+ X_{21} + X_{22} + \cdots + X_{2m}$$

$$\cdots \cdots$$

$$+ X_{n1} + X_{n2} + \cdots + X_{nm}$$

Again, where there is no confusion that i runs from 1 to n and j runs from 1 to m, we will just write $\sum_i \sum_j X_{ij}$. Yet another notation is $\sum_i \sum_{j, i \neq j} X_{ij}$, which denotes summation over all values of i and j except those for which $i = j$. For instance, suppose that i goes from 1 to 3 and j goes from 1 to 2. Then

$$\sum_i \sum_j X_{ij} = X_{11} + X_{12} + X_{21} + X_{22} + X_{31} + X_{32}$$

But

$$\sum_{\substack{i \\ i \neq j}} \sum_j X_{ij} = X_{12} + X_{21} + X_{31} + X_{32}$$

That is, we have to omit all the terms for which $i = j$. As yet another example, consider

$$(X_1 + X_2 + X_3)^2 = X_1^2 + X_2^2 + X_3^2 + 2X_1X_2 + 2X_2X_3 + 2X_1X_3$$

We can write this as

$$\left(\sum_i X_i \right)^2 = \sum_i \sum_j X_i X_j$$

$$= \sum_i X_i^2 + \sum_{\substack{i \\ i \neq j}} \sum_j X_i X_j$$

The product operator $\prod$ is defined as

$$\prod_{i=1}^{n} X_i = X_1 X_2 \cdots X_n$$

Again, where there is no confusion as to the limits of i, we will just write $\prod_i X_i$ or $\prod X_i$. As with the $\sum$ operator, we can also use the double-product operator, $\prod \prod$. For instance, if we have variables X_1, X_2, X_3 and Y_1, Y_2, then $\prod_i \prod_j X_i Y_j = X_1 X_2 X_3 Y_1 Y_2$.

2.3   Random Variables and Probability Distributions

A variable X is said to be a *random variable* (rv) if for every real number a there exists a probability $P(X \leq a)$ that X takes on a value less than or equal to a. We shall denote random variables by capital letters X, Y, Z, and so on. We shall use lowercase letters, x, y, z, and so on, to denote particular values of the random variables. Thus $P(X = x)$ is the probability that the random variable X takes the value x. $P(x_1 \leq X \leq x_2)$ is the probability that the random variable X takes values between x_1 and x_2, both inclusive.

If the random variable X can assume only a particular finite (or countably infinite) set of values, it is said to be a *discrete* random variable. A random variable is said to be *continuous* if it can assume any value in a certain range. An example of a discrete random variable is the number of customers arriving at a store during a certain period (say, the first hour of business). An example of a continuous random variable is the income of a family in the United States. In actual practice, use of continuous random variables is popular because the mathematical theory is simpler. For instance, when we say that income is a continuing random variable, we do not mean that it is continuous (in fact, strictly speaking, it is discrete) but that it is a convenient approximation to treat it that way.

A formula giving the probabilities for different values of the random variable X is called a *probability distribution* in the case of discrete random variables, and *probability density function* (denoted by p.d.f.) for continuous random variables. This is usually denoted by $f(x)$.

In general, for a continuous random variable, the occurrence of any *exact* value of X may be regarded as having a zero probability. Hence probabilities are discussed in terms of some ranges. These probabilities are obtained by integrating $f(x)$ over the desired range. For instance, if we want Prob($a \leq X \leq b$), this is given by

$$\text{Prob}(a \leq X \leq b) = \int_a^b f(x)\, dx$$

The probability that the random variable X takes on values at or below a number c is often written as $F(c) = \text{Prob}(X \leq c)$. The function $F(x)$ represents, for different values of x, the cumulated probabilities and hence is called the *cumulative distribution function* (denoted by c.d.f.). Thus

$$F(c) = \text{Prob}(X \leq c) = \int_{-\infty}^{c} f(x)\,dx$$

Joint, Marginal, and Conditional Distributions

We are often interested in not just one random variable but in the relationship between several random variables. Suppose that we have two random variables, X and Y. Now we have to consider:

1. The joint p.d.f.: $f(x, y)$.
2. The marginal p.d.f.'s: $f(x)$ and $f(y)$.
3. The conditional p.d.f.'s:
    (a) $f(x|y)$, which is the distribution of X given $Y = y$.
    (b) $f(y|x)$, which is the distribution of Y given $X = x$.

The joint density can be written as the product of the marginal and conditional densities. Thus

$$f(x, y) = f(x)f(y|x)$$
$$= f(y)f(x|y)$$

If $f(x, y) = f(x)f(y)$ for all x and y, then x and y are said to be *independent*. Note that if they are independent,

$$f(x|y) = f(x) \quad \text{and} \quad f(y|x) = f(y)$$

that is, the conditional distributions are the same as the marginals. This makes intuitive sense because for X, whether or not Y is fixed at a certain level, is irrelevant. Similarly, for Y it should be irrelevant at what level we fix X.

Illustrative Example

Consider, for instance, the discrete distribution of X and Y defined by the following probabilities:

x / y	3	4	5	$f(y) \neq$	$f(y\|x=3) \neq$	$f(y\|x=4) \neq$	$f(y\|x=5)$
2	0.2	0	0.2	0.4	0.5	0	0.5
4	0	0.2	0	0.2	0	1.0	0
6	0.2	0	0.2	0.4	0.5	0	0.5
$f(x)$	0.4	0.2	0.4				

Since the conditional distributions of y depend on the values of x, X and Y cannot be independent. On the other hand, if the distribution of X and Y is defined as

x y	3	4	5	$f(y) =$	$f(y|x=3) =$	$f(y|x=4) =$	$f(y|x=5)$
2	0.2	0.2	0.1	0.5	0.5	0.5	0.5
4	0.12	0.12	0.06	0.3	0.3	0.3	0.3
6	0.08	0.08	0.04	0.2	0.2	0.3	0.2
$f(x)$	0.4	0.4	0.2				

we see that the conditional distributions of y for the different values of x and the marginal distribution of y are the same and hence X and Y are independent.

2.4 The Normal Probability Distribution and Related Distributions

If we are given the probability distribution of a random variable X, we can determine the probability that X lies in an interval (a, b). There are some probability distributions for which the probabilities have been tabulated and which are considered suitable descriptions for a wide variety of phenomena. These are the normal distribution and the χ^2, t, and F distributions. We discuss these and also the lognormal and bivariate normal distributions. There are other distributions as well, such as the gamma and beta distributions, for which extensive tables are available. In fact, the χ^2-distribution is a particular case of the gamma distribution, and the t and F distributions are particular cases of the beta distribution. We do not need all these relationships here.

There is also a question of whether the normal distribution is an appropriate one to use to describe economic variables. However, even if the variables are not normally distributed, one can consider transformations of the variables so that the transformed variables are normally distributed.

The Normal Distribution

The normal distribution is a bell-shaped distribution which is used most extensively in statistical applications in a wide variety of fields. Its probability density function is given by

$$f(x) = \frac{1}{\sigma\sqrt{2\pi}} \exp\left[-\frac{1}{2\sigma^2}(x - \mu)^2\right] \quad -\infty < x < +\infty$$

Its mean is μ and its variance is σ^2. When x has the normal distribution with mean μ and variance σ^2, we write this compactly as $x \sim N(\mu, \sigma^2)$.

An important property of the normal distribution is that *any* linear function of normally distributed variables is also normally distributed. This is true whether the variables are independent or correlated. If

$$x_1 \sim N(\mu_1, \sigma_1^2) \quad \text{and} \quad x_2 \sim N(\mu_2, \sigma_2^2)$$

and the correlation between x_1 and x_2 is ρ, then

$$a_1 x_1 + a_2 x_2 \sim N(a_1\mu_1 + a_2\mu_2, a_1^2\sigma_1^2 + a_2^2\sigma_2^2 + 2\rho a_1 a_2 \sigma_1 \sigma_2)$$

In particular,

$$x_1 + x_2 \sim N(\mu_1 + \mu_2, \sigma_1^2 + \sigma_2^2 + 2\rho\sigma_1\sigma_2)$$

and

$$x_1 - x_2 \sim N(\mu_1 - \mu_2, \sigma_1^2 + \sigma_2^2 - 2\rho\sigma_1\sigma_2)$$

Related Distributions

In addition to the normal distribution, there are other probability distributions that we will be using frequently. These are the χ^2, t, and F distributions tabulated in the appendix. These distributions are derived from the normal distribution and are defined as described below.

χ^2-Distribution

If $x_1, x_2, \ldots, x_n$ are independent normal variables with mean zero and variance 1, that is, $x_i \sim \text{IN}(0, 1), i = 1, 2, \ldots, n$, then

$$Z = \sum_i x_i^2$$

is said to have the χ^2-distribution with degrees of freedom (d.f.) n, and we will write this as $Z \sim \chi_n^2$. The subscript n denotes the d.f. The χ_n^2-distribution is the distribution of the sum of squares of n independent standard normal variables.

If $x_i \sim \text{IN}(0, \sigma^2)$, then Z should be defined as

$$Z = \sum_i \frac{x_i^2}{\sigma^2}$$

The χ^2-distribution also has an "additive property," although it is different from the property of the normal distribution and is much more restrictive. The property is:

If $Z_1 \sim \chi_n^2$ and $Z_2 \sim \chi_m^2$ and Z_1 and Z_2 are *independent*,

then $Z_1 + Z_2 \sim \chi_{n+m}^2$.

Note that we need independence and we can consider simple additions only, not any general linear combinations. Even this limited property is useful in practical applications. There are many distributions for which even this limited property does not hold.

t-Distribution

If $x \sim N(0, 1)$ and $y \sim \chi_n^2$ and x and y are independent, $Z = x/\sqrt{y/n}$ has a *t*-distribution with d.f. n. We write this as $Z \sim t_n$. The subscript n again denotes the d.f. Thus the *t*-distribution is the distribution of a standard normal variable divided by the square root of an independent averaged χ^2 variable (χ^2 variable divided by its degrees of freedom). The *t*-distribution is a symmetric probability distribution like the normal distribution but is flatter than the normal and has longer tails. As the d.f. n approaches infinity, the *t*-distribution approaches the normal distribution.

F-Distribution

If $y_1 \sim \chi_{n1}^2$ and $y_2 \sim \chi_{n2}^2$ and y_1 and y_2 are independent, $Z = (y_1/n_1)/(y_2/n_2)$ has the *F*-distribution with d.f. n_1 and n_2. We write this as

$$Z \sim F_{n1,n2}$$

The first subscript, n_1, refers to the d.f. of the numerator, and the second subscript, n_2, refers to the d.f. of the denominator. The *F*-distribution is thus the distribution of the ratio of two independent averaged χ^2 variables.

2.5 Classical Statistical Inference

Statistical inference is the area that describes the procedures by which we use the observed data to *draw conclusions* about the population from which the data came or about the process by which the data were generated. Our assumption is that there is an unknown process that generates the data we have and that this process can be described by a probability distribution, which, in turn, can be characterized by some unknown parameters. For instance, for a normal distribution the unknown parameters are μ and σ^2.

Broadly speaking, statistical inference can be classified under two headings: classical inference and Bayesian inference. Classical statistical inference is based on two premises:

1. The sample data constitute the only relevant information.
2. The construction and assessment of the different procedures for inference are based on long-run behavior under essentially similar circumstances.

In Bayesian inference we combine sample information with prior information. Suppose that we draw a random sample $y_1, y_2, \ldots, y_n$ of size n from a normal population with mean μ and variance σ^2 (assumed known), and we want to make inferences about μ.

In classical inference we take the sample mean $\bar{y}$ as our estimate of μ. Its variance is σ^2/n. The inverse of this variance is known as the *sample precision*. Thus the sample precision is n/σ^2.

In Bayesian inference we have prior information on μ. This is expressed in terms of a probability distribution known as the *prior distribution*. Suppose that the prior distribution is normal with mean μ_0 and variance σ_0^2, that is, precision $1/\sigma_0^2$. We now combine this with the sample information to obtain what is known as the *posterior distribution* of μ. This distribution can be shown to be normal. Its mean is a weighted average of the sample mean $\bar{y}$ and the prior mean μ_0, weighted by the sample precision and prior precision, respectively. Thus

$$\mu(\text{Bayesian}) = \frac{w_1 \bar{y} + w_2 \mu_0}{w_1 + w_2}$$

where
$$w_1 = n/\sigma^2 = \text{sample precision}$$

$$w_2 = 1/\sigma_0^2 = \text{prior precision}$$

Also, the precision (or inverse of the variance) of the posterior distribution of μ is $w_1 + w_2$, that is, the sum of sample precision and prior precision.

For instance, if the sample mean is 20 with variance 4 and the prior mean is 10 with variance 2, we have

$$\text{posterior mean} = \frac{\frac{1}{4}(20) + \frac{1}{2}(10)}{\frac{1}{4} + \frac{1}{2}}$$

$$= \frac{10}{\frac{3}{4}} = 13.33$$

$$\text{posterior variance} = (\tfrac{1}{4} + \tfrac{1}{2})^{-1} = \tfrac{4}{3} = 1.33$$

The posterior mean will lie between the sample mean and the prior mean. The posterior variance will be less than both the sample and prior variances.

We do not discuss Bayesian inference in this book, because this would take us into a lot more detail than we intend to cover.[1] However, the basic notion of combining the sample mean and prior mean in inverse proportion to their variances will be a useful one to remember.

Returning to classical inference, it is customary to discuss classical statistical inference under three headings:

1. Point estimation.
2. Interval estimation.
3. Testing of hypotheses.

Point Estimation

Suppose that the probability distribution involves a parameter θ and we have a sample of size n, namely $y_1, y_2, \ldots, y_n$, from this probability distribution. In *point estimation* we construct a function $g(y_1, y_2, \ldots, y_n)$ of these observations and say that g is our estimate (guess) of θ. The common terminology is to call the function $g(y_1, y_2, \ldots, y_n)$ an *estimator* and its value in a *particular* sample an *estimate*. Thus an estimator is a random variable and an estimate is a particular value of this random variable. For instance, if θ is the

---

[1] For more discussion of Bayesian econometrics, refer to A. Zellner, *Introduction to Bayesian Analysis in Econometrics* (New York: Wiley, 1971), and E. E. Leamer, *Specification Searches: Ad Hoc Inference with Non-experimental Data* (New York: Wiley, 1978).

population mean and $g(y_1, y_2, \ldots, y_n) = (1/n) \sum y_i = \overline{y}$ is the sample mean, $\overline{y}$ is an estimator of θ. If $\overline{y} = 4$ in a particular sample, 4 is an estimate of θ.

In *interval estimation* we construct two functions, $g_1(y_1, y_2, \ldots, y_n)$ and $g_2(y_1, y_2, \ldots, y_n)$, of the sample observations and say that θ lies between g_1 and g_2 with a certain probability. In *hypothesis testing* we suggest a hypothesis about θ (say, $\theta = 4.0$) and examine the degree of evidence in the sample in favor of the hypothesis, on the basis of which we either accept or reject the hypothesis.

In practice what we need to know is how to construct the point estimator g, the interval estimator (g_1, g_2), and the procedures for testing hypotheses. In the classical statistical inference all these are based on *sampling distributions*. Sampling distributions are probability distributions of functions of sample observations. For instance, the sample mean $\overline{y}$ is a function of the sample observations and its probability distribution is called the sampling distribution of $\overline{y}$. In classical statistical inference the properties of estimators are discussed in terms of the properties of their sampling distributions.

2.6 Properties of Estimators

There are some desirable properties of estimators that are often mentioned in the book. These are:

1. Unbiasedness.
2. Efficiency.
3. Consistency.

The first two are small-sample properties. The third is a large-sample property.

Unbiasedness

An estimator g is said to be *unbiased* for θ if $E(g) = \theta$, that is, the mean of the sampling distribution of g is equal to θ. What this says is that if we calculate g for each sample and repeat this process infinitely many times, the average of all these estimates will be equal to θ. If $E(g) \neq \theta$, then g is said to be biased and we refer to $E(g) - \theta$ as the *bias*.

Unbiasedness is a desirable property but not at all costs. Suppose that we have two estimators g_1 and g_2, and g_1 can assume values far away from θ and yet have its mean equal to θ, whereas g_2 always ranges close to θ but has its mean slightly away from θ. Then we might prefer g_2 to g_1 because it has smaller variance even though it is biased. If the variance of the estimator is large, we can have some unlucky samples where our estimate is far from the true value. Thus the second property we want our estimators to have is a small variance. One criterion that is often suggested is the mean-squared error (MSE), which is defined by

$$\text{MSE} = (\text{bias})^2 + \text{variance}$$

The MSE criterion gives equal weights to these components. Instead, we can consider a weighted average $W(\text{bias})^2 + (1 - W)$ variance. Strictly speaking, instead of doing something ad hoc like this, we should specify a loss function that gives the loss in using $g(y_1, \ldots, y_n)$ as an estimator of θ and choose g to minimize expected loss.

Efficiency

The property of efficiency is concerned with the variance of estimators. Obviously, it is a relative concept and we have to confine ourselves to a particular class. If g is an unbiased estimator and it has the minimum variance in the class of unbiased estimators, g is said to be an *efficient* estimator. We say that g is an MVUE (a minimum-variance unbiased estimator).

If we confine ourselves to linear estimators, that is, $g = c_1 y_1 + c_2 y_2 + \cdots + c_n y_n$, where the c's are constants which we choose so that g is unbiased and has minimum variance, g is called a BLUE (a best linear unbiased estimator).

Consistency

Often it is not possible to find estimators that have desirable small-sample properties such as unbiasedness and efficiency. In such cases it is customary to look at desirable properties in large samples. These are called *asymptotic* properties. Three such properties often mentioned are consistency, asymptotic unbiasedness, and asymptotic efficiency.

Suppose that $\hat{\theta}_n$ is the estimator of θ based on a sample of size n. Then the sequence of estimators $\hat{\theta}_n$ is called a *consistent* sequence if for any arbitrarily small positive numbers ε and δ there is a sample size n_0 such that

$$\text{Prob}[|\hat{\theta}_n - \theta| < \varepsilon] > 1 - \delta \quad \text{for all } n > n_0$$

That is, by increasing the sample size n the estimator $\hat{\theta}_n$ can be made to lie arbitrarily close to the true value of θ with probability arbitrarily close to 1. This statement is also written as

$$\lim_{n \to \infty} P(|\hat{\theta}_n - \theta| < \varepsilon) = 1$$

and more briefly we write it as

$$\hat{\theta}_n^p \to \theta \quad \text{or} \quad \text{plim } \hat{\theta}_n = \theta$$

(plim is "probability limit"). $\hat{\theta}_n$ is said to *converge in probability* to θ. In practice we drop the subscript n on $\hat{\theta}_n$ and also drop the words "sequence of estimators" and merely say that $\hat{\theta}$ is a consistent estimator for θ.

A sufficient condition for $\hat{\theta}$ to be consistent is that the bias and variance should both tend to zero as the sample size increases. This condition is often useful to check in practice, but it should be noted that the condition is not necessary. An estimator can be consistent even if the bias does not tend to zero.

There are also some relations in probability limits that are useful in proving consistency. These are

1. $\mathrm{plim}(c_1 y_1 + c_2 y_2) = c_1 \mathrm{~plim~} y_1 + c_2 \mathrm{~plim~} y_2$, where c_1 and c_2 are constants.
2. $\mathrm{plim}(y_1 y_2) = (\mathrm{plim~} y_1)(\mathrm{plim~} y_2)$.
3. $\mathrm{plim}(y_1/y_2) = (\mathrm{plim~} y_1)/(\mathrm{plim~} y_2)$ provided that $\mathrm{plim~} y_2 \neq 0$.
4. If $\mathrm{plim~} y = c$ and $g(y)$ is a continuous function of y, then $\mathrm{plim~} g(y) = g(c)$.

Other Asymptotic Properties

In addition to consistency, there are two other concepts, *asymptotic unbiasedness* and *asymptotic efficiency*, that are often used in discussions in econometrics. To explain these concepts we first have to define the concept of *limiting distribution*, which is as follows: If we consider a sequence of random variables y_1, y_2, y_3, $\ldots$ with corresponding distribution functions $F_1, F_2, F_3, \ldots$, this sequence is said to converge in distribution to a random variable y with distribution function F if $F_n(x)$ converges to $F(x)$ as $n \to \infty$ for all continuity points of F.

It is important to note that the moments of F are not necessarily the moments of F_n. In fact, in econometrics, it is often the case that F_n does not have moments but F does.

Example

Suppose that x is a random variable with mean $\mu \neq 0$ and variance σ^2 and $P(x = 0) = c > 0$. Suppose that we have a random sample of size n: $x_1, x_2, \ldots, x_n$. Let $\bar{x}_n$ be the sample mean. The subscript n denotes the sample size. Define the random variable $y_n = 1/\bar{x}_n$. Then $E(y_n)$ does not exist because there is a positive probability that $x_1 = x_2 = \cdots = x_n = 0$. Thus $y_n = \infty$ if $\bar{x}_n = 0$. However, in this case it can be shown that $\sqrt{n}(1/\bar{x}_n - 1/\mu)$ has a limiting distribution that is normal with mean 0 and variance σ^2/μ^4. Thus even if the distribution of y_n does not have a mean and variance, its limiting distribution has a mean $1/\mu$ and variance $\sigma^2/n\mu^4$.

When we consider asymptotic distributions, we consider $\sqrt{n}$ times the estimator because otherwise the variance is of order $1/n$, which $\to 0$ as $n \to \infty$. Thus when we compare two estimators T_1 and T_2, the variances of the asymptotic distributions both $\to 0$ as $n \to \infty$. Hence in discussions of efficiency, we compare the variances of the distributions of $\sqrt{n}T_1$ and $\sqrt{n}T_2$. We shall now define asymptotic unbiasedness and asymptotic efficiency formally.

Asymptotic Unbiasedness

The estimator $\hat{\theta}_n$, based on a sample of size n, is an asymptotically unbiased estimator of θ if the mean of the limiting distribution of $\sqrt{n}(\hat{\theta}_n - \theta)$ is zero. We denote this by writing

$$\mathrm{AE}(\hat{\theta}_n) = \theta \qquad (\mathrm{AE} = \text{asymptotic expectations})$$

Sometimes, an alternative definition is used: $\hat{\theta}_n$ is an asymptotically unbiased estimator of θ if $\lim_{n \to \infty} E(\hat{\theta}_n) = \theta$. The problem with this definition is that $E(\hat{\theta}_n)$ may not exist, as in the case of the example we cited earlier.

Asymptotic Variance

Again we have two definitions: one the variance of the limiting distribution, the other the limit of variances. The problem with the latter definition is that $\text{var}(\hat{\theta}_n)$ may not exist. The two definitions are:

1. $\text{AE}[\sqrt{n}(\hat{\theta}_n - \theta)]^2$ if we consider the variance of the limiting distribution.
2. $\lim_{n \to \infty} E[\sqrt{n}(\hat{\theta}_n - \theta)]^2$ if we consider the limit of variances.

Some Examples

Consistency and asymptotic unbiasedness are different, and the two concepts of unbiasedness are also different; that is, $\text{plim}(\hat{\theta}_n)$, $\text{AE}(\hat{\theta}_n)$, and $\lim E(\hat{\theta}_n)$ are not all the same. Suppose that we have a sample of size n from a normal distribution $N(\theta, 1)$. Consider $\hat{\theta}_n = \bar{x}$ as an estimator of θ. Then

$$\text{plim}(\hat{\theta}_n) = \text{AE}(\hat{\theta}_n) = \lim E(\hat{\theta}_n) = \theta$$

But suppose that we define

$$\hat{\theta}_n = \frac{1}{2}x_1 + \frac{1}{2n} \sum_2^n x_i$$

Then

$$E(\hat{\theta}_n) = \frac{1}{2}\theta + \frac{n-1}{2n}\theta \quad \text{and} \quad \lim_{n \to \infty} E(\hat{\theta}_n) = \theta$$

But $\text{plim}(\hat{\theta}_n) = \frac{1}{2}x_1 + \frac{1}{2}\theta \neq \theta$. Thus $\text{plim}(\hat{\theta}_n) \neq \lim E(\theta_n)$. Thus we have an asymptotically unbiased estimator of θ that is not consistent. As another example, consider $1/\bar{x}_n$ as an estimator of $1/\theta$. We have $\text{plim}(1/\bar{x}_n) = 1/\theta$, so that the estimator is consistent. Also, $\text{AE}(1/\bar{x}_n) = 1/\theta$. But $\lim E(1/\bar{x}_n)$ does not exist. Thus the estimator is asymptotically unbiased or not depending on what definition we use.

Very often in the econometric literature, the asymptotic variances are obtained by replacing AE by plim and evaluating plims. (The implicit assumption is that they are equal.) Thus the asymptotic variance of $\hat{\theta}_n$ is evaluated as

$$\text{AE}[\sqrt{n}(\hat{\theta}_n - \theta)]^2 = \text{plim}[\sqrt{n}(\hat{\theta}_n - \theta)]^2$$

2.7 Sampling Distributions for Samples from a Normal Population

The most commonly used sampling distributions are those for samples from normal populations. We state the results here (without proof). Suppose that we have a sample of n independent observations, namely, $y_1, y_2, \ldots, y_n$, from a normal population with mean

μ and variance σ^2. Consider the following:

$$\bar{y} = \frac{1}{n} \sum y_i \qquad \text{sample mean}$$

(2.1)

$$S^2 = \frac{1}{n-1} \sum (y_i - \bar{y})^2 \qquad \text{sample variance}$$

Then

1. The sampling distribution of the sample mean $\bar{y}$ is also normal with mean μ and variance σ^2/n.
2. $(n-1)S^2/\sigma^2$ has a χ^2-distribution with d.f. $(n-1)$. Further, the distributions of $\bar{y}$ and S^2 are independent.
3. Since

$$\frac{\sqrt{n}(\bar{y} - \mu)}{\sigma} \sim N(0, 1) \quad \text{and} \quad \frac{(n-1)S^2}{\sigma^2} \sim \chi^2_{n-1}$$

and these distributions are independent, we have (by the definition of the t-distribution as the distribution of a standard normal variable divided by the square root of an independent averaged χ^2 variable) that $\sqrt{n}(\bar{y} - \mu)/S$ has a t-distribution with d.f. $(n-1)$.

4. Also, $E(\bar{y}) = \mu$ and $E(S^2) = \sigma^2$ and thus $\bar{y}$ and S^2 are unbiased estimators for μ and σ^2, respectively.

These sampling distributions will also be used to get interval estimates and for testing hypotheses about μ and σ^2.

2.8 Interval Estimation

In interval estimation we construct two functions $g_1(y_1, y_2, \ldots, y_n)$ and $g_2(y_1, y_2, \ldots, y_n)$ of the sample observations such that

$$\text{Prob}(g_1 < \theta < g_2) = \alpha, \text{ a given probability} \qquad (2.2)$$

α is called the *confidence coefficient* and the interval (g_1, g_2) is called the *confidence interval*. Since θ is a parameter (or a constant that is unknown), the probability statement (2.2) is a statement about g_1 and g_2 and not about θ. What it implies is that if we use the formulas $g_1(y_1, y_2, \ldots, y_n)$ and $g_2(y_1, y_2, \ldots, y_n)$ repeatedly with different samples and in each case construct the confidence intervals using these formulas, then in 100α percent of all the cases (samples) the interval given will include the true value.

As an illustration of how to use the sampling distributions to construct confidence intervals, consider a sample $y_1, y_2, \ldots, y_n$ of n independent observations from a normal population with mean μ and variance σ^2. Then

$$\frac{(n-1)S^2}{\sigma^2} \sim \chi^2_{n-1} \quad \text{and} \quad \frac{\sqrt{n}(\bar{y} - \mu)}{S} \sim t_{n-1}$$

where $\bar{y}$ and S^2 are the sample mean and sample variance defined in equations (2.1).

If the sample size n is 20, so that the d.f. $= n - 1 = 19$, we can refer to the χ^2-tables with 19 degrees of freedom and say that

$$\text{Prob}\left(\frac{19S^2}{\sigma^2} > 32.852\right) = 0.025 \tag{2.3}$$

or

$$\text{Prob}\left(10.117 < \frac{19S^2}{\sigma^2} < 30.144\right) = 0.90 \tag{2.4}$$

Also, referring to the t-tables with 19 degrees of freedom, we find that

$$\text{Prob}\left[-2.093 < \frac{\sqrt{n}(\bar{y} - \mu)}{S} < 2.093\right] = 0.95 \tag{2.5}$$

From equation (2.4) we get

$$\text{Prob}\left(\frac{19S^2}{30.144} < \sigma^2 < \frac{19S^2}{10.117}\right) = 0.90$$

and if $S^2 = 9.0$ we get the 90% confidence interval for σ^2 as (5.7, 16.9). From equation (2.5) we get

$$\text{Prob}\left(\bar{y} - \frac{2.093S}{\sqrt{n}} < \mu < \bar{y} + \frac{2.093S}{\sqrt{n}}\right) = 0.95$$

If $\bar{y} = 5$ and $S = 3.0$ we get the 95% confidence interval for μ as (3.6, 6.4).

These intervals are called *two-sided* intervals. One can also construct *one-sided* intervals. For instance, equation (2.3) implies that

$$\text{Prob}\left(\sigma^2 < \frac{19S^2}{32.852}\right) = 0.025$$

or

$$\text{Prob}\left(\sigma^2 > \frac{19S^2}{32.852}\right) = 0.975$$

If $S^2 = 9$, we get the 97.5% (right-sided) confidence interval for σ^2 as (5.205, ∞). We can construct a similar one-sided confidence interval for μ.

2.9   Testing of Hypotheses

We list here some essential points regarding hypothesis testing.

1. A statistical hypothesis is a statement about the values of some parameters in the hypothetical population from which the sample is drawn.

2. A hypothesis which says that a parameter has a specified value is called a *point hypothesis*. A hypothesis which says that a parameter lies in a specified interval is called an *interval hypothesis*. For instance, if μ is the population mean, then $H: \mu = 4$ is a point hypothesis; $H: 4 \leq \mu \leq 7$ is an interval hypothesis.

3. A hypothesis test is a procedure that answers the question of whether the observed difference between the *sample value* and the *population value* hypothesized is real or due to chance variation. For instance, if the hypothesis says that the population mean $\mu = 6$ and the sample mean $\bar{y} = 8$, then we want to know whether this difference is real or due to chance variation.

4. The hypothesis we are testing is called the *null hypothesis* and is often denoted by H_0.[2] The alternative hypothesis is denoted by H_1. The probability of rejecting H_0 when, in fact, it is true, is called the *significance level*. To test whether the observed difference between the data and what is expected under the null hypothesis H_0 is real or due to chance variation, we use a *test statistic*. A desirable criterion for the test statistic is that its sampling distribution be tractable, preferably with tabulated probabilities. Tables are already available for the normal, χ^2, t, and F distributions, and hence the test statistics chosen are often those that have these distributions.

5. The *observed significance level* or *P-value* is the probability of getting a value of the test statistic that is as extreme or more extreme than the observed value of the test statistic. This probability is computed on the basis that the null hypothesis is correct. For instance, consider a sample of n independent observations from a normal population with mean μ and variance σ^2. We want to test

$$H_0 : \mu = 7 \quad \text{against} \quad H_1 : \mu \neq 7$$

The test statistic we use is

$$t = \frac{\sqrt{n}(\bar{y} - \mu)}{S}$$

which has a t-distribution with $(n - 1)$ degrees of freedom. Suppose that $n = 25, \bar{y} = 10, S = 5$. Then under the assumption that H_0 is true, the observed value of t is $t_0 = 3$. Since high positive values of t are evidence against the null hypothesis H_0, the P-value is [since d.f. $(n - 1) = 24$]

$$P = \text{Prob}(t_{24} > 3)$$

This is the observed significance level.

6. It is common practice to say simply that the result of the test is (statistically) significant or not significant and not report the actual *P*-values. The meaning of the two terms is as follows:

Statistically significant. Sampling variation is an unlikely explanation of the discrepancy between the null hypothesis and sample values.
Statistically insignificant. Sampling variation is a likely explanation of the discrepancy between the null hypothesis and the sample value.

Also, the terms *significant* and *highly significant* are customarily used to denote "significant at the 0.05 level" and "significant at the 0.01 level", respectively. However,

---

[2]This terminology is unfortunate because "null" means "zero, void, insignificant, amounts to nothing, etc." A hypothesis $\mu = 0$ can be called a null hypothesis, but a hypothesis $\mu = 100$ should not be called a "null" hypothesis. However, this is the standard terminology that was introduced in the 1930s by the statisticians Jerzy Neyman and E. S. Pearson.

consider two cases where the *P*-values are 0.055 and 0.045, respectively. Then in the former case one would say that the results are "not significant" and in the latter case one would say that the results are "significant," although the sample evidence is marginally different in both cases. Similarly, two tests with *P*-values of 0.80 and 0.055 will both be considered "not significant," although there is a tremendous difference in the compatibility of the sample evidence with the null hypothesis in the two cases. That is why many computer programs print out *P*-values.[3]

7. *Statistical significance* and *practical significance* are not the same thing. A result that is highly significant statistically may be of no practical significance at all. For instance, suppose that we consider a shipment of cans of cashews with expected mean weight of 450 g. If the actual sample mean of weights is 449.5 g, the difference may be practically insignificant but could be highly statistically significant if we have a large enough sample or a small enough sampling variance (note that the test statistic has $\sqrt{n}$ in the numerator and S in the denominator). On the other hand, in the case of precision instruments, a part is expected to be of length 10 cm and a sample had a mean length of 9.9 cm. If n is small and S is large, the difference could not be statistically significant but could be practically very significant. The shipment could simply be useless.

8. It is customary to reject the null hypothesis H_0 when the test statistic is statistically significant at a chosen significance level and not to reject H_0 when the test statistic is not statistically significant at the chosen significance level. There is, however, some controversy on this issue which we discuss later in item 9. In reality, H_0 may be either true or false. Corresponding to the two cases of reality and the two conclusions drawn, we have the following four possibilities:

	Reality	
Result of the Test	H_0 is True	H_0 is False
Significant (reject H_0)	Type I error or α error	Correct conclusion
Not significant (do not reject H_0)	Correct conclusion	Type II error or β error

There are two possible errors that we can make:

1. Rejecting H_0 when it is true. This is called the type I error or α error.
2. Not rejecting H_0 when it is not true. This is called the type II error or β error.

Thus

$$\alpha = \text{Prob(rejecting } H_0 | H_0 \text{ is true)}$$

$$\beta = \text{Prob(not rejecting } H_0 | H_0 \text{ is not true)}$$

---

[3] A question of historical interest is: "How did the numbers 0.05 and 0.01 creep into all these textbooks?" The answer is that they were suggested by the famous statistician Sir R. A. Fisher (1890–1962), the "father" of modern statistics, and his prescription has been followed ever since.

α is just the significance level, defined earlier. $(1 - \beta)$ is called the *power* of the test. The power of the test cannot be computed unless the alternative hypothesis H_1 is specified; that is, H_0 is not true means that H_1 is true.

For example, consider the problem of testing the hypothesis

$$H_0 : \mu = 10 \quad \text{against} \quad H_1 : \mu = 15$$

for a normal population with mean μ and variance σ^2. The test statistic we use is $t = \sqrt{n}(\bar{x} - \mu)/S$. From the sample data we get the values of $n, \bar{x}$, and S. To calculate α we use $\mu = 10$, and to calculate β we use $\mu = 15$. The two errors are

$$\alpha = \text{Prob}(t > t^* | \mu = 10)$$
$$\beta = \text{Prob}(t < t^* | \mu = 15)$$

where t^* is the cutoff point of t that we use to reject or not reject H_0. The distributions of t under H_0 and H_1 are shown in Figure 2.1. In our example α is the *right-hand* tail area from the distribution of t under H_0 and β is the *left-hand* tail area from the distribution of t under H_1. If the alternative hypothesis H_1 says that $\mu < 0$, then the distribution of t under H_1 would be to the left of the distribution of t under H_0. In this case α would be the left-hand tail area of the distribution of t under H_0 and β would be the right-hand tail area of the distribution of t under H_1.

The usual procedure that is suggested (which is called the Neyman–Pearson approach) is to fix α at a certain level and minimize β, that is, choose the test statistic that has the most power. In practice, the tests we use, such as the χ^2, t, and F tests, have been shown to be the most powerful tests.

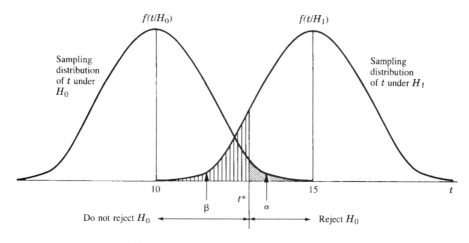

Figure 2.1   Type I and type II errors in testing a hypothesis

9. There are some statisticians who disagree with the ideas of the Neyman–Pearson theory. For instance, Kalbfleisch and Sprott[4] argue that it is a gross simplification to regard a test of significance as a decision rule for accepting or rejecting a hypothesis. They argue that such decisions are made on more than just experimental evidence. Thus the purpose of a significance test is just to quantify the strength of evidence in the data against a hypothesis expressed in a (0, 1) scale, not to suggest an accept–reject rule (see item 7). There are some statisticians who think that the significance level used should depend on the sample size.

The problem with a preassigned significance level is that if the sample size is large enough, we can reject every null hypothesis. This is often the experience of those who use large cross-sectional data sets with thousands of observations. Almost every coefficient is significant at the 5% level. Lindley[5] argues that for large samples one should use lower significance levels and for smaller samples higher significance levels. Leamer[6] derives significance levels in the case of regression models for different sample sizes that show how significance levels should be much higher than 5% for small sample sizes and much lower than 5% for large sample sizes.

Very often the purpose of a test is to simplify an estimation procedure. This is the "pretesting" problem, where the test is a prelude to further estimation. In the case of such pretests it has been found that the significance levels to be used should be much higher than the conventional 5% (sometimes 25 to 50% and even 99%). The important thing to note is that tests of significance have several purposes and one should not use a uniform 5% significance level.[7]

2.10   Relationship Between Confidence Interval Procedures and Tests of Hypotheses

There is a close relationship between confidence intervals and tests of hypotheses. Suppose that we want to test a hypothesis at the 5% significance level. Then we can construct a 95% confidence interval for the parameter under consideration and see whether the hypothesized value is in the interval. If it is, we do not reject the hypothesis. If it is not, we reject the hypothesis. This relationship holds good for tests of parameter values. There are other tests, such as goodness of fit tests, tests of independence in contingency tables, and so on, for which there is no confidence interval counterpart.

As an example, consider a sample of 20 independent observations from a normal distribution with mean μ and variance σ^2. Suppose that the sample mean is $\overline{y} = 5$ and sample variance $S^2 = 9$. We saw from equation (2.5) that the 95% confidence interval

---

[4]J. G. Kalbfleisch and D. A. Sprott, "On Tests of Significance," in W. L. Harper and C. A. Hooker (eds.), *Foundations of Probability Theory, Statistical Inference, and Statistical Theory of Science*, Vol. 2 (Boston: D. Reidel, 1976), pp. 259–272.

[5]D. V. Lindley, "A Statistical Paradox," *Biometrika*, 1957, pp. 187–192.

[6]Leamer, *Specification Searches*.

[7]A good discussion of this problem is in the series of papers "For What Use Are Tests of Hypotheses and Tests of Significance" in *Communications in Statistics, A. Theory and Methods*, Vol. 5, No. 8, 1976.

was (3.6, 6.4). Suppose that we consider the problem of testing the hypothesis

$$H_0 : \mu = 7 \quad \text{against} \quad H_1 : \mu \neq 7$$

If we use a 5% level of significance we should reject H_0 if

$$\left| \frac{\sqrt{n}(\bar{y} - 7)}{S} \right| > 2.093$$

since 2.093 is the point from the t-tables for 19 degrees of freedom such that $\text{Prob}(-2.093 < t < 2.093) = 0.95$ or $\text{Prob}(|t| > 2.093) = 0.05$. In our example $\sqrt{n}(\bar{y} - 7)/S = -3$ and hence we reject H_0. Actually, we would be rejecting H_0 at the 5% significance level whenever H_0 specifies μ to be a value outside the interval (3.6, 6.4).

For a one-tailed test we have to consider the corresponding one-sided confidence interval. If $H_0 : \mu = 7$ and $H_1 : \mu < 7$, then we reject H_0 for low values of $t = \sqrt{n}(\bar{y} - 7)/S$. From the t-tables with 19 degrees of freedom, we find that $\text{Prob}(t < -1.73) = 0.05$. Hence we reject H_0 if the observed $t < -1.73$. In our example it is -3 and hence we reject H_0. The corresponding 95% one-sided confidence interval is given by

$$\text{Prob}\left[-1.73 < \frac{\sqrt{n}(\bar{y} - \mu)}{S} \right] = 0.95$$

which gives (on substituting $n = 20$, $\bar{y} = 5$, $S = 3$) the confidence interval $(-\infty, 6.15)$.

2.11   Combining Independent Tests

Very often in practical applications there are several independent tests of the same hypothesis — rejecting or not rejecting the null at different significance levels. For instance, to the question of whether unions have any effect on wages, there may be studies from several industries, some showing an effect and others not. The problem is to combine the evidence from all these independent tests.

There have been several tests suggested in the literature, but it has been found that the test suggested by R. A. Fisher[8] dominates the others. This test, also known as the P_λ test, is as follows.

Let P_i be the P-value (observed significance level) of test i. Then $\lambda = -2\sum_i \log_e P_i$ has a χ^2-distribution with d.f. $2n$, where n is the number of tests. This result follows from the fact that if a random variable y has a uniform distribution in the range $[0, 1]$, then $-2\log_e y$ has a χ^2-distribution with d.f. 2. (You can prove this by making transformation of variables.)

The Fisher test is very useful in several econometric applications. It will be discussed in Chapter 14 when considering panel data unit root tests.

Summary

1. If two random variables are uncorrelated, this does not necessarily imply that they are independent. A simple example is given in Section 2.3.

---

[8]R. A. Fisher, *Statistical Methods for Research Workers*, 4th ed. (Edinburgh: Oliver and Boyd).

2. The normal distribution and the related distributions: χ^2, t, and F form the basis of all statistical inference in the book. Although many economic data do not necessarily satisfy the assumption of normality, we can make some transformations that would produce approximate normality. For instance, we consider log wages rather than wages.

3. The advantage of the normal distribution is that any linear function of normally distributed variables is normally distributed. For the χ^2-distribution a weaker property holds. The sum of independent χ^2 variables has a χ^2-distribution. These properties are very useful in deriving probability distributions of sample statistics. The χ^2, t, and F distributions are explained in Section 2.4.

4. A function of the sample observations is called a statistic (e.g., sample mean, sample variance). The probability distribution of a statistic is called the sampling distribution of the statistic.

5. Classical statistical inference is based entirely on sampling distributions. By contrast, Bayesian inference makes use of sample information and prior information. We do not discuss Bayesian inference in this book, but the basic idea is explained in Section 2.5. Based on the prior distribution (which incorporates prior information) and the sample observations, we obtain what is known as the posterior distribution and all our inferences are based on this posterior distribution.

6. Classical statistical inference is usually discussed under three headings: point estimation, interval estimation, and testing of hypotheses. Three desirable properties of point estimators — unbiasedness, efficiency, and consistency — are discussed in Section 2.6.

7. There are three commonly used methods of deriving point estimators:

   (a) The method of moments.
   (b) The method of least squares.
   (c) The method of maximum likelihood.

These are discussed in Chapter 3.

8. Section 2.8 presents an introduction to interval estimation and Section 2.9 gives an introduction to hypothesis testing. The interrelationship between the two is explained in Section 2.10.

9. The main elements of hypothesis testing are discussed in detail in Section 2.9. Most important, arguments are presented as to why it is not desirable to use the usual 5% significance level in all problems.

10. A method due to R. A. Fisher of combining several independent tests is discussed in Section 2.11.

Exercises

1. The COMPACT computer company has four applicants, all equally qualified, of whom two are male and two female. The company has to choose two candidates, and it does not discriminate on the basis of sex. If it chooses the two candidates at random, what is the probability that the two candidates chosen will be the same sex? A student answered this question as follows: There are three possible outcomes: two

female, two male, one female and one male. The number of favorable outcomes is two. Hence the probability is $\frac{2}{3}$. Is this correct?

2. Your friend John says: "Let's toss coins. Each time I'll toss first and then you. If either coin comes up heads, I win. If neither, you win." You say, "There are three possibilities. You may get heads first and the game ends there. Or you may get tails and I get heads, or we may both get tails. In two of the three possible cases, you win." "Right," says your friend, "I have two chances to your one. So I'll put up $2 against $1." Is this a fair bet?

3. A major investment company wanted to know what proportions of investors bought stocks, bonds, both stocks and bonds, and neither stocks nor bonds. The company entrusted this task to its statistician, who, in turn, asked her assistant to conduct a telephone survey of 200 potential investors chosen at random. The assistant, however, was a moonlighter with some preconceptions of his own, and he cooked up the following results without actually doing a survey. For a sample of 200, he reported the following results:

Invested in stocks: 100

Invested in bonds: 75

Invested in both stocks and bonds: 45

Invested in neither: 90

The statistician saw these results and fired his moonlighting assistant. Why?

4. *(The birthday problem)* (In this famous problem it is easier to calculate the probability of a complementary event than the probability of the given event.) Suppose your friend, a teacher, says that she will pick 30 students at random from her school and offer you an even bet that there will be *at least* two students who have the same birthday. Should you accept this bet?

5. *(Getting the answer without being sure you have asked the question)* This is the *randomized response technique* due to Stanley L. Warner's paper in *Journal of the American Statistical Association*, Vol. 60, 1965, pp. 63–69. You want to know the proportion of college students who have used drugs. A direct question will not give frank answers. Instead, you give the students a box containing 4 blue, 3 red, and 4 white balls. Each student is asked to draw a ball (you do not see the ball) and abide by the following instructions, based on the color of the ball drawn:

Blue: Answer the question "Have you used drugs?"

Red: Answer "yes."

White: Answer "no."

If 40% of the students answered "yes," what is the percentage of students who have used drugs?

6. A petroleum company intends to drill for oil in four different wells. Use the subscripts 1, 2, 3, 4 to denote the different wells. Each well is given an equally likely chance of being successful. Consider the following events:

Event A: There are exactly two successful wells.

Event B: There are at least three successful wells.

Event C: Well number 3 is successful.

Event D: There are fewer than three successful wells.

Compute the following probabilities:

(a) $P(A)$	**(b)** $P(B)$	**(c)** $P(C)$	**(d)** $P(D)$
(e) $P(AB)$	**(f)** $P(A+B)$	**(g)** $P(BC)$	**(h)** $P(B+C)$
(i) $P(BD)$	**(j)** $P(A|B)$	**(k)** $P(B|C)$	**(l)** $P(C|D)$
(m) $P(D|C)$			

7. On the TV show "Let's Make a Deal," one of the three boxes (A, B, C) on the stage contains keys to a Lincoln Continental. The other two boxes are empty. A contestant chooses box B. Boxes A and C remain on the table. Monty Hall, the energetic host of the show, suggests that the contestant surrender her box for $500. The contestant refuses. Monty Hall then opens one of the remaining boxes, box A, which turns out to be empty. Monty now offers $1000 to the contestant to surrender her box. She again refuses but asks whether she can trade her box B for box C on the table. Monty exclaims, "That's weird." But is it really weird, or does the contestant know how to calculate probabilities? *Hint:* Suppose that there are n boxes. The probability that the key is in any of the $(n-1)$ boxes on the stage $= (n-1)/n$. Monty opens p boxes, which turn out to be empty. The probability that the key is in any of the $(n-p-1)$ boxes is $(n-1)/n(n-p-1)$. Without switching, the probability that the contestant wins remains at $1/n$. Hence it is better to switch. In this case $n=3$, $p=1$. The probability of winning without a switch is $\frac{1}{3}$. The probability of winning by switching is $\frac{2}{3}$.

8. You are given 10 white and 10 black balls and two boxes. You are told that your instructor will draw a ball from one of the two boxes. If it is white, you pass the exam. If it is black, you fail. How should you arrange the balls in the boxes to maximize your chance of passing?

9. Suppose that the joint probability distribution of X and Y is given by the following table:

x \ y	2	4	6
1	0.2	0	0.2
2	0	0.2	0
3	0.2	0	0.2

(a) Are X and Y independent? Explain.

(b) Find the marginal distributions of X and Y.

(c) Find the conditional distribution of Y given $X = 1$ and hence $E(Y|X=1)$ and $\text{var}(Y|X=1)$.

(d) Repeat part (c) for $X=2$ and $X=3$ and hence verify the result that $V(Y) = EV(Y|X) + VE(Y|X)$, that is the variance of a random variable is equal to the expectation of its conditional variance plus the variance of its conditional expectation.

10. The density function of a continuous random variable X is given by

$$f(x) = \begin{cases} kx(2-x) & \text{for } 0 \le x \le 2 \\ 0 & \text{otherwise} \end{cases}$$

(a) Find k.
(b) Find $E(X)$ and $V(X)$.

11. Answer Exercise 10 when

$$f(x) = \begin{cases} kx & \text{for } 0 \le x \le 1 \\ k(2-x) & \text{for } 1 \le x \le 2 \\ 0 & \text{otherwise} \end{cases}$$

12. Suppose that X and Y are continuous random variables with the joint probability density function

$$f(x, y) = \begin{cases} k(x+y) & \text{for } 0 \le x \le 1, 0 \le y \le 2 \\ 0 & \text{otherwise} \end{cases}$$

(a) Find k, $E(X)$, $E(Y)$, $V(X)$, $V(Y)$, and $\text{cov}(X, Y)$. Are X and Y independent?
(b) Find the marginal densities of X and Y.
(c) Find the conditional density of X given $Y = \frac{1}{2}$ and hence $E(X|Y = \frac{1}{2})$ and $V(Y|X = \frac{1}{2})$.

13. Answer Exercise 12 if $f(x, y)$ is defined as follows:

$$f(x, y) = \begin{cases} k(1-x)(2-y) & \text{for } 0 \le x \le 1, 0 \le y \le 2 \\ 0 & \text{otherwise} \end{cases}$$

14. Let dependent random variables X, Y, and Z be defined by the joint distribution

$$P(X = 1, Y = 2, Z = 3) = 0.25$$
$$P(X = 2, Y = 1, Z = 3) = 0.35$$
$$P(X = 2, Y = 3, Z = 1) = 0.40$$

In this case, $P(X < Y) = 0.65$, $P(X < Z) = 0.6$, and $P(Y < Z) = 0.6$, which shows that Z is the largest. However, direct observation shows that

$$P(X = \text{minimum of } X, Y, Z) = 0.25$$
$$P(Y = \text{minimum of } X, Y, Z) = 0.35$$
$$P(Z = \text{minimum of } X, Y, Z) = 0.40$$

which shows that Z is most likely to be the smallest. What can you conclude? (See C. R. Blyth, *Journal of the American Statistical Association*, Vol. 67, 1972, pp. 364–366 and 366–381.)

15. The number of hot dogs sold at a football stand has the following probability distribution:

x	Probability
800	0.05
900	0.10
1000	0.25
1100	0.35
1200	0.10
1300	0.10
1400	0.05

The hot dog vendor pays 30 cents for each hot dog and sells it for 45 cents. Thus for every hot dog sold, he makes a profit of 15 cents, and for every hot dog unsold, he loses 30 cents. What are the expected value and variance of his profit if the number of hot dogs he orders is: (a) 1100; (b) 1200; and (c) 1300? If he wants to maximize his expected profits, how many hot dogs should he order?

16. An instructor wishes to "grade on the curve." The students' scores seem to be normally distributed with mean 70 and standard deviation 8. If the instructor wishes to give 20% A's, what should be the dividing line between an A grade and a B grade?

17. Suppose that you replace every observation x by $y = 3x + 7$ and the mean μ by $\eta = 3\mu + 7$. What happens to the t-value you use?

18. *(Reading the N, χ^2, t, F tables)*
 (a) Given that $X \sim N(2, 9)$, find $P(-2 < X < 3)$.
 (b) If $X \sim t_{20}$, find x_1 and x_2 such that

$$P(X < x_1) = 0.95$$

$$P(-x_1 < X < x_1) = 0.90$$

$$P(x_1 < X < x_2) = 0.90$$

Note that in the last case, we have several sets of x_1 and x_2. Find three sets.
 (c) If $X \sim \chi^2_{10}$, find x_1 and x_2 such that $P(X < x_1) = 0.95$ and $P(X > x_1) = 0.95$. Find two values x_1 and x_2 such that $P(x_1 < X < x_2) = 0.90$.

Note again that we can have several sets of x_1 and x_2. Find three sets.
 (d) If $X \sim F_{2,20}$, find x_1 such that $P(X > x_1) = 0.05$ and $P(X > x_1) = 0.01$. Can you find x_1 if you are told that $P(X > x_1) = 0.50$?

19. Given that $y = e^x$ is normal with mean 2 and variance 4, find the mean and variance of x.

20. Let $x_1, x_2, \ldots, x_n$ be a sample of size n from a normal distribution $N(\mu, \sigma^2)$. Consider the following point estimators of μ:

$$\hat{\mu}_1 = \bar{x}, \text{ the sample mean}$$

$$\hat{\mu}_2 = x_1$$

$$\hat{\mu}_3 = \frac{x_1}{2} + \frac{1}{2(n-1)}(x_2 + x_3 + \cdots + x_n)$$

(a) Which of these are unbiased?
(b) Which of these are consistent?
(c) Find the relative efficiencies: $\hat{\mu}_1$ to $\hat{\mu}_2$, $\hat{\mu}_1$ to $\hat{\mu}_3$, and $\hat{\mu}_2$ to $\hat{\mu}_3$. What can you conclude from this?
(d) Are all unbiased estimators consistent?
(e) Is the assumption of normality needed to answer parts (a) to (d)? For what purposes is this assumption needed?

21. In Exercise 20 consider the point estimators of σ^2:

$$\hat{\sigma}_1^2 = \frac{1}{n-1} \sum_{i=1}^{n} (x_i - \bar{x})^2$$

$$\hat{\sigma}_2^2 = \frac{1}{n} \sum_{i=1}^{n} (x_i - \bar{x})^2$$

$$\hat{\sigma}_3^2 = (x_1 - \bar{x})^2$$

Which of these estimators are
(a) Unbiased?
(b) Consistent?

Is the assumption of normality needed to answer this question? For what purposes is the normality assumption needed?

22. Suppose that $\hat{\alpha}$ is an estimator of α derived from a sample of size T. We are given that $E(\hat{\alpha}) = \alpha + 2/T$ and $\text{var}(\hat{\alpha}) = 4\alpha/T + \alpha^2/T^2$.
(a) Examine whether, as an estimator of α, $\hat{\alpha}$ is (1) unbiased, (2) consistent, (3) asymptotically unbiased, and (4) asymptotically efficient.
(b) What is the asymptotic variance of $\hat{\alpha}$?

23. Explain, using the estimators for μ in Exercise 20, the difference between $\lim E$, AE, and plim. Give some examples of how they differ.

24. Examine whether the following statements are true or false. Explain your answer briefly.
(a) The null hypothesis says that the effect is zero.
(b) The alternative hypothesis says that nothing is going on besides chance variation.
(c) A hypothesis test tells you whether or not you have a useful sample.
(d) A significance level tells you how important the null hypothesis is.
(e) The P-value will tell you at what level of significance you can reject the null hypothesis.
(f) Calculation of P-values is useless for significance tests.
(g) It is always better to use a significance level of 0.01 than a level of 0.05.
(h) If the P-value is 0.45, the null hypothesis looks plausible.

25. Examine whether the following statements are true or false. If false, correct the statement.
(a) With small samples and large σ, quite large differences may not be statistically significant but may be real and of great practical significance.

(b) The conclusions from the data cannot be summarized in the P-value. Conclusions should always have a practical meaning in terms of the problem at hand.

(c) The power of a test at the null hypothesis H_0 is equal to the significance level.

(d) In practice the alternative hypothesis H_1 has no important role except in deciding what the nature of the rejection region should be (left-sided, right-sided, or two-sided).

(e) If you are sufficiently resourceful, you can always reject any null hypothesis.

26. Define *type I error*, *type II error*, and *power of a test*. What is the relationship between type I error and the confidence coefficient in a confidence interval?

27. In each of the following cases, set up the null hypothesis and the alternative: explain how you will proceed in testing the hypothesis.

(a) A biscuit manufacturer is packaging 16-oz. packages. The production manager feels that something is wrong with the packaging and that the packages contain too many biscuits.

(b) A tire manufacturer advertises that its tires last for at least 30,000 miles. A consumer group does not believe it.

(c) A manufacturer of weighing scales believes that something is going wrong in the production process and the scale does not show the correct weight.

In each of the problems above, can you identify the costs of mistaken decisions if we view the hypothesis-testing problem as a decision problem?

28. An examination of sample items from a shipment showed that 51% of the items were good and 49% were defective. The company president asked the statistician, "What is the probability that over half the items are good?" The statistician replied that the question cannot be answered from the data. Is this correct? Does the question make sense? Explain why.

29. A local merchant owns two grocery stores at opposite ends of town. He wants to determine if the variability in business is the same at both locations. Two independent random samples yield

$$n_1 = 16 \text{ days} \quad n_2 = 16 \text{ days}$$
$$s_1 = \$200 \qquad s_2 = \$300$$

(a) Is there enough evidence that the two stores have different variability in sales?

(b) The merchant reads in a trade magazine that stores similar to his have a population standard deviation in daily sales of $210 and that stores with higher variability are badly managed. Is there any evidence to suggest that either one of the two stores the merchant owns has a standard deviation of sales greater than $210?

30. A stockbroker wants to compare mean returns and risk (measured by variance) of two stocks and gets the following results:

First stock	Second stock
$n_1 = 31$	$n_2 = 31$
$\bar{x}_1 = 0.45$	$\bar{x}_2 = 0.35$
$s_1 = 0.60$	$s_2 = 0.40$

Are there any significant differences in the mean returns and risks? (Assume that daily price changes are normally distributed.)

31. If p has a uniform distribution in the range $(0, 1)$ show that $-2 \log_e p$ has a χ^2-distribution with d.f. 2. If there are k independent tests, each with a p-value, then $\lambda = - \sum_{i=1}^{b} 2 \log p_i$ has a χ^2-distribution with d.f. $2k$. This statistic can be used for an overall rejection or acceptance of the null hypothesis based on the k independent tests. [See G. S. Maddala, *Econometrics* (New York: McGraw-Hill, 1977), p. 48. The test is from C. R. Rao, *Advanced Statistical Methods in Biometric Research* (New York: Wiley, 1952), p. 44.]

32. The weekly cash inflows (x) and outflows (y) of a business firm are random variables. The following data give values of x and y for 30 weeks. Assume that x and y are normally distributed.

x	y	x	y	x	y
42	25	70	39	93	20
65	37	82	36	86	68
76	83	90	82	68	72
92	36	68	30	53	60
37	73	82	72	87	65
47	23	28	39	63	80
27	97	61	27	47	62
23	36	75	38	52	36
63	70	83	27	38	43
40	51	60	78	90	57

(a) Obtain unbiased estimates of the means and variances of x, y, and $x - y$. Also obtain 95% confidence intervals for these six variables.

(b) Test the hypothesis $\mu_x > \mu_y$ assuming that:
  (1) x and y are independent.
  (2) x and y are correlated.

Appendix to Chapter 2

Matrix Algebra

In this appendix we present an introduction to matrix notation. This will facilitate the exposition of some material in later chapters — in particular, Chapter 4.

A *matrix* is a rectangular array of elements; for example,

$$\begin{bmatrix} 2 & 1 & 7 & 4 \\ 1 & 2 & -2 & 1 \\ 4 & 1 & 2 & -3 \end{bmatrix}$$

We shall denote this by **A** and say that it is of order 3×4. The first number is the number of rows, and the second number is the number of columns. A matrix of order $1 \times n$ is called a *row vector*, and a matrix of order $m \times 1$ is called a *column vector*; for example,

$\mathbf{b} = (1, 2, 7, 3)$ is a row vector and $\mathbf{c} = \begin{bmatrix} 2 \\ 8 \\ -10 \end{bmatrix}$ is a column vector. Henceforth we shall follow the convention of writing column vectors without a prime and row vectors with a prime; for example, if $\mathbf{b} = \begin{bmatrix} 1 \\ 2 \\ 7 \\ 3 \end{bmatrix}$ is a column vector, $\mathbf{b}' = [1, 2, 7, 3]$ is a row vector.

A *transpose* of a matrix, $\mathbf{A}$, denoted by $\mathbf{A}'$, is the same matrix $\mathbf{A}$ with rows and columns interchanged. In the example above,

$$\mathbf{A}' = \begin{bmatrix} 2 & 1 & 4 \\ 1 & 2 & 1 \\ 7 & -2 & 2 \\ 4 & 1 & -3 \end{bmatrix}$$

We shall now define matrix addition, subtraction, and multiplication. *Matrix addition* (or subtraction) is done by adding (subtracting) the corresponding elements and is defined only if the matrices are of the same order. If they are not of the same order, then there are no corresponding elements. For example, if

$$\mathbf{A} = \begin{bmatrix} 1 & 2 & 7 \\ -1 & 0 & 6 \end{bmatrix} \quad \text{and} \quad \mathbf{B} = \begin{bmatrix} 3 & 4 & 2 \\ -3 & -7 & 10 \end{bmatrix}$$

then

$$\mathbf{A} + \mathbf{B} = \begin{bmatrix} 4 & 6 & 9 \\ -4 & -7 & 16 \end{bmatrix} \quad \text{and} \quad \mathbf{A} - \mathbf{B} = \begin{bmatrix} -2 & -2 & 5 \\ 2 & 7 & -4 \end{bmatrix}$$

Obviously, $\mathbf{A} + \mathbf{B}'$ is not defined because $\mathbf{A}$ is of order 2×3 and $\mathbf{B}'$ is of order 3×2. Also note that $\mathbf{A} + \mathbf{B} = \mathbf{B} + \mathbf{A}$. As we shall see later, this commutative law does not hold for matrix multiplication; that is, $\mathbf{AB}$ and $\mathbf{BA}$ need not be defined, and they need not be equal even if they are defined.

Multiplication of a Matrix by a Scalar

This is done by multiplying each element of the matrix by the scalar. For instance, if

$$\mathbf{A} = \begin{bmatrix} 2 & 3 & 1 \\ 0 & 1 & 7 \end{bmatrix} \quad \text{then} \quad 4\mathbf{A} = \begin{bmatrix} 8 & 12 & 4 \\ 0 & 4 & 28 \end{bmatrix}$$

Matrix Equality

Two matrices $\mathbf{A}$ and $\mathbf{B}$ are said to be equal if they are of the same order and they have all the corresponding elements equal. In this case, $\mathbf{A} - \mathbf{B} = \mathbf{0}$ (a matrix with all elements zero; such a matrix is known as a *null matrix*).

Scalar Product of Vectors

If $\mathbf{b}$ and $\mathbf{c}$ are two vectors of the same order, so that $\mathbf{b}' = (b_1, b_2, \ldots, b_n)$ and $\mathbf{c}' = (c_1, c_2, \ldots, c_n)$, the scalar product of the two vectors is defined as $\mathbf{b}'\mathbf{c} = b_1 c_1 + b_2 c_2 + \cdots + b_n c_n$. The multiplication is row–column wise and is achieved by multiplying the corresponding elements and adding up the result. For example, if $\mathbf{b}' = (2, -1, 2)$ and $\mathbf{c}' = (0, 3, 3)$ then $\mathbf{b}'\mathbf{c} = [(2)(0) + (-1)(3) + (2)(3)] = 0 - 3 + 6 = 3$. The scalar product is not defined if the vectors are not of the same order.

Matrix Multiplication

A matrix can be considered as a series of row vectors or a series of column vectors. Matrix multiplication is also done row–column wise. If we have two matrices $\mathbf{B}$ and $\mathbf{C}$ and we need the product $\mathbf{BC}$, we write $\mathbf{B}$ as a series of row vectors and $\mathbf{C}$ as a series of column vectors and then take scalar products of the row vectors in $\mathbf{B}$ and the column vectors in $\mathbf{C}$. Clearly, for this to be possible the number of elements in each of the rows of $\mathbf{B}$ should be equal to each of the columns of $\mathbf{C}$. If $\mathbf{B}$ is of order $m \times n$ and $\mathbf{C}$ is of order $n \times k$, $\mathbf{BC}$ is defined because the number of elements in the row vectors in $\mathbf{B}$ and the column vectors in $\mathbf{C}$ are both n. But if $\mathbf{B}$ is $n \times k$ and $\mathbf{C}$ is $m \times n$, $\mathbf{BC}$ is not defined. If $\mathbf{B}$ is an $m \times n$ matrix and $\mathbf{C}$ is an $n \times k$ matrix, we can write $\mathbf{B}$ as a set of m row vectors and $\mathbf{C}$ as a set of k column vectors; each of order n. That is,

$$\mathbf{B} = \begin{bmatrix} b_1' \\ b_2' \\ b_m' \end{bmatrix} \quad \text{and} \quad \mathbf{C} = [c_1, c_2, \ldots, c_k]$$

Then $\mathbf{BC}$ is defined as

$$\mathbf{BC} = \begin{bmatrix} b_1'c_1 & b_1'c_2 & b_1'c_k \\ b_2'c_1 & b_2'c_2 & b_2'c_k \\ \vdots & \vdots & \vdots \\ b_m'c_1 & b_m'c_2 & b_m'c_k \end{bmatrix}$$

$\mathbf{BC}$ is of order $m \times k$. It has as many rows as $\mathbf{B}$ and as many columns as $\mathbf{C}$. As an example, consider

$$\mathbf{B} = \begin{bmatrix} 2 & 1 & 3 \\ 0 & 1 & 2 \end{bmatrix} \quad \text{and} \quad \mathbf{C} = \begin{bmatrix} 7 & 5 \\ 8 & 6 \end{bmatrix}$$

$\mathbf{B}$ is of order 2×3 and $\mathbf{C}$ of order 2×2. Hence $\mathbf{BC}$ is not defined. But $\mathbf{B}'\mathbf{C}$ is defined.

$$\mathbf{B}'\mathbf{C} = \begin{bmatrix} 2 & 0 \\ 1 & 1 \\ 3 & 2 \end{bmatrix} \begin{bmatrix} 7 & 5 \\ 8 & 6 \end{bmatrix} = \begin{bmatrix} (2)(7) + (0)(8) & (2)(5) + (0)(6) \\ (1)(7) + (1)(8) & (1)(5) + (1)(6) \\ (3)(7) + (2)(8) & (3)(5) + (2)(6) \end{bmatrix} = \begin{bmatrix} 14 & 10 \\ 15 & 11 \\ 37 & 27 \end{bmatrix}$$

Note that $\mathbf{BC}$ is not defined but $\mathbf{CB}$ is defined.

$$\mathbf{CB} = \begin{bmatrix} 7 & 5 \\ 8 & 6 \end{bmatrix} \begin{bmatrix} 2 & 1 & 3 \\ 0 & 1 & 2 \end{bmatrix} = \begin{bmatrix} 14 & 12 & 31 \\ 16 & 14 & 36 \end{bmatrix}$$

Note: Given two matrices, **B** and **C**, one or both of the products **BC** and **CB** may not be defined, and even if they are both defined, they may not be of the same order, and even if they are of the same order, they may not be equal. For instance, if **B** is 2×3 and **C** is 3×2, then **BC** is defined and of order 2×2, and **CB** is also defined but is of order 3×3. Suppose that $\mathbf{B} = \begin{bmatrix} 2 & 0 \\ 1 & 1 \end{bmatrix}$ and $\mathbf{C} = \begin{bmatrix} 3 & 6 \\ 1 & 3 \end{bmatrix}$; then **BC** and **CB** are both of order 2×2, but they are not equal. We have

$$\mathbf{BC} = \begin{bmatrix} 6 & 12 \\ 4 & 9 \end{bmatrix} \quad \text{and} \quad \mathbf{CB} = \begin{bmatrix} 12 & 6 \\ 5 & 3 \end{bmatrix}$$

Because of all these complications, when we say that a matrix **B** is multiplied by a matrix **C**, we have to specify whether **B** is *premultiplied* by **C** so that we have **CB** or whether it is *postmultiplied* by **C** so that we have **BC**.

Reversal Law for Transpose of a Product

If **B** and **C** are matrices such that **BC** is defined, then $(\mathbf{BC})' = \mathbf{C}'\mathbf{B}'$. This result can easily be verified and hence we shall not prove it.

Identity Matrix

An $n \times n$ matrix with 1 in the diagonal and zeros elsewhere is called an identity matrix of order n and is denoted by $\mathbf{I}_n$. For example,

$$\mathbf{I}_3 = \begin{bmatrix} 1 & 0 & 0 \\ 0 & 1 & 0 \\ 0 & 0 & 1 \end{bmatrix}$$

The identity matrix plays the same role in matrix multiplication as the number 1 in scalar multiplication, except that the order of $\mathbf{I}_n$ must be defined properly for pre- and postmultiplication; for example, if **B** is 3×4, then $\mathbf{I}_3\mathbf{B} = \mathbf{B}$ and $\mathbf{B}\mathbf{I}_4 = \mathbf{B}$.

Inverse of a Matrix

The inverse of a square matrix, **A**, denoted by $\mathbf{A}^{-1}$, is a matrix such that $\mathbf{A}^{-1}\mathbf{A} = \mathbf{A}\mathbf{A}^{-1} = \mathbf{I}$. This is analogous to the result in ordinary scalar multiplication $yy^{-1} = y^{-1}y = 1$. To find $\mathbf{A}^{-1}$ given **A**, we need to go through a few results on determinants.

Determinants

Corresponding to each square matrix **A** there is a scalar value known as the determinant, which is denoted by $|\mathbf{A}|$. There are n^2 elements in **A**, and the determinant of **A** is an algebraic function of these n^2 elements. Formally, the definition is

$$|\mathbf{A}| = \sum (\pm) a_{1*} a_{2*} \cdots a_{n*}$$

where the second subscript is a permutation of the numbers $(1, 2, \ldots, n)$. The summation is over all the $(n!)$ permutations, and the sign of any element is positive if it is an even permutation and negative if it is an odd permutation. The permutation is odd (even) if we need an odd (even) number of interchanges in the elements to arrive at the given permutation. For example, if we have a 3×3 matrix,

$$\mathbf{A} = \begin{bmatrix} a_{11} & a_{12} & a_{13} \\ a_{21} & a_{22} & a_{23} \\ a_{31} & a_{32} & a_{33} \end{bmatrix}$$

we have to consider permutations of the numbers $(1, 2, 3)$. The permutation $(3, 2, 1)$ is odd because we need one interchange. The permutation $(3, 1, 2)$ is even because we need two interchanges. There are $(3!) = 6$ permutations in all. These are, with the appropriate signs: $+(1, 2, 3)$, $-(1, 3, 2)$, $-(2, 1, 3)$, $+(2, 3, 1)$, $-(3, 2, 1)$, $+(3, 1, 2)$. Hence we have

$$|\mathbf{A}| = a_{11}a_{22}a_{33} - a_{11}a_{23}a_{32} - a_{12}a_{21}a_{33} + a_{12}a_{23}a_{31} - a_{13}a_{22}a_{31} + a_{13}a_{21}a_{32}$$

Note that the first subscripts are always $(1, 2, 3)$. We can write this in terms of the elements of the first row as follows:

$$|\mathbf{A}| = a_{11}(a_{22}a_{33} - a_{23}a_{32}) + a_{12}(-a_{21}a_{33} + a_{23}a_{31}) + a_{13}(a_{21}a_{32} - a_{22}a_{31})$$

The terms in parentheses are called the *cofactors* of the respective elements. Thus if we denote the cofactor of a_{11} by A_{11}, of a_{12} by A_{12}, and of a_{13} by A_{13}, we have

$$|\mathbf{A}| = a_{11}A_{11} + a_{12}A_{12} + a_{13}A_{13}$$

We can equally well write $|\mathbf{A}|$ in terms of the elements and the corresponding cofactors of any other row or column. For example, if we consider the third column, we can write

$$|\mathbf{A}| = a_{13}A_{13} + a_{23}A_{23} + a_{33}A_{33}$$

The cofactor is nothing but the determinant of a submatrix obtained by deleting that row and column, with an appropriate sign. For example, if we want to get the cofactor for a_{13}, we delete the first row and third column, calculate the value of the determinant of the 2×2 matrix, and multiply it by $(-1)^{1+3} = 1$. To get the cofactor of a_{ij} in a matrix $\mathbf{A}$, we delete the ith row and jth column in $\mathbf{A}$, compute the determinant, and multiply it by $(-1)^{i+j}$. For a 2×2 matrix $\mathbf{A} = \begin{bmatrix} a_{11} & a_{12} \\ a_{21} & a_{22} \end{bmatrix}$, we have $|\mathbf{A}| = a_{11}a_{22} - a_{12}a_{21}$.

Properties of Determinants

There are several useful properties of determinants that can be derived by just considering the definition of a determinant.

1. If $\mathbf{A}^*$ is a matrix obtained by interchanging any two rows or columns of $\mathbf{A}$, then $|\mathbf{A}^*| = -|\mathbf{A}|$. This is because all odd permutations become even and even permutations

become odd — with one extra interchange. For example,

$$\begin{vmatrix} 1 & 3 & 7 \\ 2 & 0 & 1 \\ 5 & 1 & 8 \end{vmatrix} = - \begin{vmatrix} 2 & 0 & 1 \\ 1 & 3 & 7 \\ 5 & 1 & 8 \end{vmatrix}$$

2. From property 1 it follows that if two rows (or columns) of a matrix $\mathbf{A}$ are identical, then $|\mathbf{A}| = 0$ because by interchanging these rows (or columns) the value is unaltered. Thus $|\mathbf{A}| = |\mathbf{A}^*| = -|\mathbf{A}|$. Hence $|\mathbf{A}| = 0$. For example,

$$\begin{vmatrix} 1 & 3 & 7 \\ 1 & 3 & 7 \\ 5 & 1 & 8 \end{vmatrix} = 0$$

3. Expansion of a determinant by "alien" cofactors is equal to zero. By "alien" cofactors, we mean cofactors of another row or column. For example, consider a 3×3 matrix. The first row is (a_{11}, a_{12}, a_{13}) with cofactors (A_{11}, A_{12}, A_{13}). The second row is (a_{21}, a_{22}, a_{23}) with cofactors (A_{21}, A_{22}, A_{23}). Then

$$a_{11}A_{11} + a_{12}A_{12} + a_{13}A_{13} = \text{expansion by own cofactors}$$

$$a_{11}A_{21} + a_{12}A_{22} + a_{13}A_{23} = \text{expansion by alien cofactors}$$

We know that the first expansion is $|\mathbf{A}|$. The second expansion would be a correct expansion if $a_{11} = a_{21}$, $a_{12} = a_{22}$, and $a_{13} = a_{23}$, that is, if the first and second rows of $\mathbf{A}$ are identical. But we know from property 2 that in this case, $|\mathbf{A}| = 0$. Hence we have

$$a_{11}A_{21} + a_{12}A_{22} + a_{13}A_{23} = 0$$

or expansion by alien cofactors is zero.

4. The value of a determinant is unaltered by adding to any of its rows (or columns) any multiples of other rows (or columns). For example, consider adding three times the second row to the first row for a 3×3 matrix. We then have, expanding by the elements and cofactors of the first row,

$$\begin{vmatrix} a_{11} + 3a_{21} & a_{12} + 3a_{22} & a_{13} + 3a_{23} \\ a_{21} & a_{22} & a_{23} \\ a_{31} & a_{32} & a_{33} \end{vmatrix} = (a_{11} + 3a_{21})A_{11} + (a_{12} + 3a_{22})A_{12}$$

$$+ (a_{13} + 3a_{23})A_{13} = (a_{11}A_{11} + a_{12}A_{12} + a_{13}A_{13}) + 3(a_{21}A_{11} + a_{22}A_{12} + a_{23}A_{13})$$

The first term in parentheses is $|\mathbf{A}|$, and the second is zero, because it is an expansion by alien cofactors.

This property is useful for evaluating the values of determinants. For instance, consider

$$|\mathbf{A}| = \begin{vmatrix} 2 & 8 & 16 \\ 3 & 4 & 10 \\ -1 & 2 & 3 \end{vmatrix}$$

Now consider (row 1) − (row 2) − 2(row 3). The value of the determinant is unaltered. But we get

$$\begin{vmatrix} 1 & 0 & 0 \\ 3 & 4 & 10 \\ -1 & 2 & 3 \end{vmatrix}$$

Now expand by the elements of the first row. It is easy because we have two zeros. We get

$$|\mathbf{A}| = 1 \cdot \begin{vmatrix} 4 & 10 \\ 2 & 3 \end{vmatrix} = 12 - 20 = -8$$

5. From property 4 we can deduce the important property that if a row (or column) of a matrix $\mathbf{A}$ can be expressed as a linear combination of the other rows (or columns), the determinant of $\mathbf{A}$ is zero. For example, consider

$$\mathbf{A} = \begin{bmatrix} 3 & -1 & 1 \\ 4 & 2 & 8 \\ 10 & 3 & 16 \end{bmatrix}$$

Here the third column of $\mathbf{A}$ = (first column) + 2(second column). In such cases we say that the columns are *linearly dependent*. When we evaluate $|\mathbf{A}|$ we can subtract (column $1 + 2$ column 2) from column 3 and get all zeros. Then the expansion by the elements of column 3 gives us $|\mathbf{A}| = 0$. From this property we can derive the following theorem:

> *Theorem:* The determinant of a matrix $\mathbf{A}$ is nonzero if and only if there are no linear dependencies between the columns (or rows) of $\mathbf{A}$. If $|\mathbf{A}| \neq 0$, $\mathbf{A}$ is said to be *nonsingular*. If $|\mathbf{A}| = 0$, $\mathbf{A}$ is said to be *singular*.

Note that each row (or column) of a matrix is a vector. A set of vectors is said to be *linearly independent* if none can be expressed as a linear combination of the rest. For example, $(1, -1, 0)$, $(2, 3, 1)$, and $(4, 1, 1)$ are not linearly independent because the third vector = 2(the first vector) + 1(the second vector). There cannot be more than n linearly independent vectors of order n.

Determinants of the Third Order

There is a simple procedure for evaluating determinants of the third order. For higher-order determinants we have to follow the expansion by cofactors and the simplification rule 4.

Consider

$$\begin{vmatrix} 4 & 3 & 3 \\ 3 & 1 & 4 \\ 3 & 4 & 1 \end{vmatrix}$$

What we do is append the first two columns to this and take products of the diagonal elements. There are three products going down and three products going up. The products going down are positive; the products going up are negative. The value of the determinant is $76 - 82 = -6$.

$$9 + 64 + 9 = 82$$

$$\begin{vmatrix} 4 & 3 & 3 \\ 3 & 1 & 4 \\ 3 & 4 & 1 \end{vmatrix}\begin{matrix} 4 & 3 \\ 3 & 1 \\ 3 & 4 \end{matrix}$$

$$4 + 36 + 36 = 76$$

As another example, consider

$$\begin{vmatrix} 3 & -1 & 1 \\ 4 & 2 & 8 \\ 1 & 2 & 3 \end{vmatrix}$$

We have

$$2 + 48 - 12 = 38$$

$$\begin{vmatrix} 3 & -1 & 1 \\ 4 & 2 & 8 \\ 1 & 2 & 3 \end{vmatrix}\begin{matrix} 3 & -1 \\ 4 & 2 \\ 1 & 2 \end{matrix}$$

$$18 - 8 + 8 = 18$$

The value of the determinant is $18 - 38 = -20$.

Finding the Inverse of a Matrix

To get the inverse of a matrix $\mathbf{A}$, we first replace each element of $\mathbf{A}$ by its cofactor, transpose the matrix, and then divide each element by $|\mathbf{A}|$. For instance, with the 3×3 matrix $\mathbf{A}$ that we have been considering,

$$\mathbf{A}^{-1} = \frac{1}{|\mathbf{A}|}\begin{bmatrix} A_{11} & A_{12} & A_{13} \\ A_{21} & A_{22} & A_{23} \\ A_{31} & A_{32} & A_{33} \end{bmatrix}'$$

Noting that expansion by own cofactors gives $|\mathbf{A}|$ and expansion by alien cofactors gives zero, we get

$$\mathbf{A}^{-1}\mathbf{A} = \frac{1}{|\mathbf{A}|}\begin{bmatrix} A_{11} & A_{21} & A_{31} \\ A_{12} & A_{22} & A_{32} \\ A_{13} & A_{23} & A_{33} \end{bmatrix}\begin{bmatrix} a_{11} & a_{12} & a_{13} \\ a_{21} & a_{22} & a_{23} \\ a_{31} & a_{32} & a_{33} \end{bmatrix}$$

$$= \frac{1}{|\mathbf{A}|}\begin{bmatrix} |A| & 0 & 0 \\ 0 & |A| & 0 \\ 0 & 0 & |A| \end{bmatrix} = \mathbf{I}$$

We can also check that $\mathbf{A}\mathbf{A}^{-1} = \mathbf{I}$. If $|\mathbf{A}| = 0$, then $\mathbf{A}^{-1}$ does not exist. Thus for a *singular* matrix, the inverse does not exist. As an example of computing an inverse, consider the matrix

$$\mathbf{A} = \begin{bmatrix} 3 & -1 & 1 \\ 4 & 2 & 8 \\ 1 & 2 & 3 \end{bmatrix}$$

To find the inverse, first we have to find the matrix of cofactors and also $|\mathbf{A}|$. The matrix of cofactors is

$$\begin{bmatrix} -10 & -4 & 6 \\ 5 & 8 & -7 \\ -10 & -20 & 10 \end{bmatrix}$$

and $|\mathbf{A}| = -20$. Hence

$$\mathbf{A}^{-1} = \frac{1}{-20} \begin{bmatrix} -10 & 5 & -10 \\ -4 & 8 & -20 \\ 6 & -7 & 10 \end{bmatrix}$$

Reversal Law

Inverses follow a reversal law, just like transposes. If $\mathbf{B}$ and $\mathbf{C}$ both have inverses, then

$$(\mathbf{BC})^{-1} = \mathbf{C}^{-1}\mathbf{B}^{-1}$$

Orthogonal Matrices

Two vectors $\mathbf{b}_1$ and $\mathbf{b}_2$ are said to be orthogonal if $\mathbf{b}_1'\mathbf{b}_2 = 0$. They are also of unit length if $\mathbf{b}_1'\mathbf{b}_1 = \mathbf{b}_2'\mathbf{b}_2 = 1$. A matrix $\mathbf{B}$ is said to be an *orthogonal matrix* if its rows are orthogonal and of unit length. We have

$$\mathbf{B}'\mathbf{B} = \begin{bmatrix} \mathbf{b}_1' \\ \mathbf{b}_2' \\ \mathbf{b}_n' \end{bmatrix} [\mathbf{b}_1, \mathbf{b}_2, \dots, \mathbf{b}_n] = \begin{bmatrix} 1 & 0 & \cdots & 0 \\ 0 & 1 & \cdots & 0 \\ \cdots & \cdots & \cdots & \cdots \\ 0 & 0 & \cdots & 1 \end{bmatrix}$$

$$= \mathbf{I} \quad \text{the identity matrix}$$

Postmultiplying both sides by $\mathbf{B}^{-1}$, we get

$$\mathbf{B}' = \mathbf{B}^{-1}$$

Thus for an orthogonal matrix, the inverse is just the transpose. Premultiplying both sides by $\mathbf{B}$, we get $\mathbf{BB}' = \mathbf{I}$. Thus for an orthogonal matrix the rows as well as columns are orthogonal. Also, $|\mathbf{B}'\mathbf{B}| = 1$. Hence $|\mathbf{B}| = \pm 1$.

Rank of a Matrix

A matrix of order $m \times n$ can be regarded as a set of m row vectors or a set of n column vectors. The *row rank* of the matrix is the number of linearly independent row vectors. The *column rank* of the matrix is the number of linearly independent column vectors.

The row rank is $\leq m$ and the column rank is $\leq n$. There are three important results on the rank of a matrix (which we shall state without proof).

1. Row rank = column rank.
2. If $\mathbf{A}$ and $\mathbf{B}$ are two matrices such that their product $\mathbf{AB}$ is defined, rank($\mathbf{AB}$) is not greater than rank $\mathbf{A}$ or rank $\mathbf{B}$.
3. The rank of a matrix is unaltered by pre- or postmultiplication by a nonsingular matrix. This says that rank is unaltered by taking linear combinations of rows (or columns).

Solution of Linear Equations

For simplicity let us consider a system of three equations in three unknowns:

$$a_{11}x_1 + a_{12}x_2 + a_{13}x_3 = b_1$$

$$a_{21}x_1 + a_{22}x_2 + a_{23}x_3 = b_2$$

$$a_{31}x_1 + a_{32}x_2 + a_{33}x_3 = b_3$$

We can write them compactly in matrix notation as $\mathbf{Ax} = \mathbf{b}$, where

$$\mathbf{A} = \begin{bmatrix} a_{11} & a_{12} & a_{13} \\ a_{21} & a_{22} & a_{23} \\ a_{31} & a_{32} & a_{33} \end{bmatrix} \quad \mathbf{x} = \begin{bmatrix} x_1 \\ x_2 \\ x_3 \end{bmatrix} \quad \mathbf{b} = \begin{bmatrix} b_1 \\ b_2 \\ b_3 \end{bmatrix}$$

If $\mathbf{b} = \mathbf{0}$, the system of equations is said to be *homogeneous*. In this case we have $\mathbf{Ax} = 0$. This says that the vector $\mathbf{x}$ is orthogonal to the row vectors of $\mathbf{A}$. But since $\mathbf{A}$ is 3×3 and there can be at most three linearly independent vectors of order 3, a necessary and sufficient condition for the existence of a nonzero solution to the set of equations is rank $\mathbf{A} < 3$. In the general case of n equations, the condition is rank $\mathbf{A} < n$. If rank $\mathbf{A} = r < n$, there are $(n - r)$ linearly independent solutions $\mathbf{x}$ that satisfy the equations $\mathbf{Ax} = 0$.

Now consider the case of the *nonhomogeneous* equations: $\mathbf{Ax} = \mathbf{b}$. We can write these equations as follows:

$$x_1 \begin{bmatrix} a_{11} \\ a_{21} \\ a_{31} \end{bmatrix} + x_2 \begin{bmatrix} a_{12} \\ a_{22} \\ a_{32} \end{bmatrix} + x_3 \begin{bmatrix} a_{13} \\ a_{23} \\ a_{33} \end{bmatrix} = \begin{bmatrix} b_1 \\ b_2 \\ b_3 \end{bmatrix}$$

What this says is that $\mathbf{b}$ is a linear combination of the columns of $\mathbf{A}$. Hence a necessary and sufficient condition for the existence of a solution to this set is: rank$(\mathbf{A}) = $ rank$(\mathbf{A}|\mathbf{b})$.

Cramer's Rule

There is one convenient rule for solving a system of nonhomogeneous equations. This rule, known as Cramer's rule, is as follows. Consider the system of nonhomogeneous equations $\mathbf{Ax} = \mathbf{b}$ where $\mathbf{x}' = (x_1, x_2, \ldots, x_n)$. Let us denote by $\mathbf{A}_1$, the matrix $\mathbf{A}$ with the first column replaced by the vector $\mathbf{b}$. Similarly, $\mathbf{A}_2$ denotes the matrix $\mathbf{A}$ with the second column replaced by the vector **b**. We define $A_3, A_4, \ldots, A_n$ similarly. Then Cramer's rule says:

$$x_1 = |\mathbf{A}_1| \div |\mathbf{A}|, x_2 = |\mathbf{A}_2| \div |\mathbf{A}|, x_3 = |\mathbf{A}_3| \div |\mathbf{A}|$$

and so on. As an example, consider the system of equations:

$$4x_1 + 3x_2 + x_3 = 13$$

$$x_1 - x_2 + x_3 = 2$$

$$2x_1 - x_2 + 3x_3 = 9$$

Then

$$|\mathbf{A}| = \begin{vmatrix} 4 & 3 & 1 \\ 1 & -1 & 1 \\ 2 & -1 & 3 \end{vmatrix} = -10$$

$$|\mathbf{A}_1| = \begin{vmatrix} 13 & 3 & 1 \\ 2 & -1 & 1 \\ 9 & -1 & 3 \end{vmatrix} = -10$$

$$|\mathbf{A}_2| = \begin{vmatrix} 4 & 13 & 1 \\ 1 & 2 & 1 \\ 2 & 9 & 3 \end{vmatrix} = -20$$

$$|\mathbf{A}_3| = \begin{vmatrix} 4 & 3 & 13 \\ 1 & -1 & 2 \\ 2 & -1 & 9 \end{vmatrix} = -30$$

Hence, $x_1 = -10/-10 = 1$, $x_2 = -20/-10 = 2$, $x_3 = -30/-10 = 3$.

Another example we shall consider is that of the existence of a solution for which we require $\text{rank}(\mathbf{A}) = \text{rank}(\mathbf{A}|\mathbf{b})$. Consider the question: For what value of c will the following equations admit a solution? (Note that this is a case where Cramer's rule breaks down because $|\mathbf{A}| = 0$.)

$$2x_1 - x_2 + 5x_3 = 4$$

$$4x_1 \qquad + 6x_3 = 1$$

$$-2x_2 + 4x_3 = 7 + c$$

Note that what we need to show is

$$\text{rank} \begin{bmatrix} 2 & -1 & 5 \\ 4 & 0 & 6 \\ 0 & -2 & 4 \end{bmatrix} = \text{rank} \begin{bmatrix} 2 & -1 & 5 & 4 \\ 4 & 0 & 6 & 1 \\ 0 & -2 & 4 & 7+c \end{bmatrix}$$

Since rank is unaltered by taking linear combinations of rows (or columns), subtract 2(row 1) from row 2. We get

$$\begin{bmatrix} 2 & -1 & 5 & 4 \\ 0 & 2 & -4 & -7 \\ 0 & -2 & 4 & 7+c \end{bmatrix}$$

Now add row 2 to row 3. We get

$$\begin{bmatrix} 2 & -1 & 5 & 4 \\ 0 & 2 & -4 & -7 \\ 0 & 0 & 0 & c \end{bmatrix}$$

Now

$$\text{rank}(\mathbf{A}) = \text{rank} \begin{bmatrix} 2 & -1 & 5 \\ 0 & 2 & -4 \\ 0 & 0 & 0 \end{bmatrix} = 2$$

because the third row has all zeros.

$$\text{rank}(\mathbf{A}|\mathbf{b}) = \text{rank} \begin{bmatrix} 2 & -1 & 5 & 4 \\ 0 & 2 & -4 & -7 \\ 0 & 0 & 0 & c \end{bmatrix} = 2 \quad \text{only if } c = 0$$

Hence the required answer is $c = 0$.

Linear and Quadratic Forms

Suppose that we have the vectors $\mathbf{a}$, $\mathbf{x}$, and the matrix $\mathbf{A}$ defined as

$$\mathbf{a} = \begin{pmatrix} a_1 \\ a_2 \\ a_3 \end{pmatrix} \quad \mathbf{x} = \begin{pmatrix} x_1 \\ x_2 \\ x_3 \end{pmatrix} \quad \mathbf{A} = \begin{pmatrix} a_{11} & a_{12} & a_{13} \\ a_{21} & a_{22} & a_{23} \\ a_{31} & a_{32} & a_{33} \end{pmatrix}$$

Then $L = \mathbf{a}'\mathbf{x} = a_1 x_1 + a_2 x_2 + a_3 x_3$ is said to be a *linear form* in x's. $Q = \mathbf{x}'\mathbf{A}\mathbf{x} = a_{11}x_1^2 + a_{12}x_1x_2 + a_{13}x_1x_3 + a_{21}x_1x_2 + a_{22}x_2^2 + a_{23}x_2x_3 + a_{31}x_1x_3 + a_{32}x_2x_3 + a_{33}x_3^2$ is called a *quadratic form* in x's. The generalization to the case of n x's is obvious. In subsequent chapters we shall need differentiation of the linear function L and the quadratic function Q with respect to the x's.

Note that $\partial L/\partial x_1 = a_1$, $\partial L/\partial x_2 = a_2$, and $\partial L/\partial x_3 = a_3$. We shall denote the vector of partial derivatives

$$\begin{bmatrix} \dfrac{\partial L}{\partial x_1} \\[2mm] \dfrac{\partial L}{\partial x_2} \\[2mm] \dfrac{\partial L}{\partial x_3} \end{bmatrix}$$

by $\partial L/\partial \mathbf{x}$. Thus we have $\partial L/\partial \mathbf{x} = \mathbf{a}$. Also,

$$\frac{\partial Q}{\partial x_1} = (a_{11}x_1 + a_{12}x_2 + a_{13}x_3) + (a_{11}x_1 + a_{21}x_2 + a_{31}x_3)$$

with similar expressions for $\partial Q/\partial x_2$ and $\partial Q/\partial x_3$. Collecting these and writing in matrix notation, we get

$$\frac{\partial Q}{\partial \mathbf{x}} = \mathbf{A}\mathbf{x} + \mathbf{A}'\mathbf{x} = 2\mathbf{A}\mathbf{x} \quad \text{if } \mathbf{A} \text{ is symmetric}$$

Thus we get

$$\frac{\partial}{\partial \mathbf{x}}(\mathbf{a}'\mathbf{x}) = \mathbf{a} \quad \text{and} \quad \frac{\partial}{\partial \mathbf{x}}(\mathbf{x}'\mathbf{A}\mathbf{x}) = (\mathbf{A} + \mathbf{A}')\mathbf{x}$$

We shall use this result in the appendix to Chapter 4.

Covariance Matrix of a Set of Random Variables

Let $\mathbf{x}' = (x_1, x_2, \ldots, x_n)$ be a set of n independent random variables with mean zero and common variance σ^2. Earlier we defined $\mathbf{x}'\mathbf{x}$ as a scalar product. This is equal to $\sum_1^n x_i^2$. If we consider $\mathbf{x}\mathbf{x}'$, this will be an $n \times n$ matrix. The covariance matrix of the variables is (since their mean is 0)

$$\mathbf{V} = E \begin{bmatrix} x_1^2 & x_1 x_2 & \cdots & x_1 x_n \\ x_1 x_2 & x_2^2 & \cdots & x_2 x_n \\ \cdots & \cdots & \cdots & \cdots \\ x_1 x_n & x_2 x_n & \cdots & x_n^2 \end{bmatrix} = E(\mathbf{x}\mathbf{x}')$$

Since

$$E(x_i x_j) = \begin{cases} \sigma^2 & \text{if } i = j \\ 0 & \text{if } i \neq j \end{cases}$$

we have $\mathbf{V} = \mathbf{I}\sigma^2$. In the general case where $E(x_i) = \mu_i$ and $\text{cov}(x_i, x_j) = \sigma_{ij}$, we have $E(\mathbf{x}) = \boldsymbol{\mu}$, where $\boldsymbol{\mu}$ is the vector of means, and the covariance matrix is $\mathbf{V} = E(\mathbf{x} - \boldsymbol{\mu})(\mathbf{x} - \boldsymbol{\mu})' = \boldsymbol{\Sigma}$, an $n \times n$ matrix whose (i,j)th element is σ_{ij}.

Positive Definite and Negative Definite Matrices

In the case of scalars, a number y is said to be positive if $y > 0$, negative if $y < 0$, nonnegative if $y \geq 0$, and nonpositive if $y \leq 0$. In the case of matrices, the corresponding concepts are *positive definite, negative definite, positive semidefinite*, and *negative semidefinite*, respectively. Corresponding to a square matrix $\mathbf{B}$ we define the quadrative form $Q = \mathbf{x}'\mathbf{B}\mathbf{x}$, where $\mathbf{x}$ is a nonnull vector. Then:

$\mathbf{B}$ is said to be positive definite if $Q > 0$.
$\mathbf{B}$ is said to be positive semidefinite if $Q \geq 0$.
$\mathbf{B}$ is said to be negative definite if $Q < 0$.
$\mathbf{B}$ is said to be negative semidefinite if $Q \leq 0$.

All these relations should hold for any nonnull vector $\mathbf{x}$.

For a positive definite matrix $\mathbf{B}$, leading (diagonal) determinants of all orders are > 0. In particular, the diagonal elements are > 0 and $|\mathbf{B}| > 0$. For example, consider the matrix

$$\mathbf{B} = \begin{bmatrix} 3 & 1 & -3 \\ -4 & 2 & 2 \\ 6 & -4 & 7 \end{bmatrix}$$

The diagonal elements are 3, 2, and 7, all positive. The diagonal determinants of order 2 are

$$\begin{vmatrix} 3 & 1 \\ -4 & 2 \end{vmatrix} = 10, \quad \begin{vmatrix} 3 & -3 \\ 6 & 7 \end{vmatrix} = 39, \quad \text{and} \quad \begin{vmatrix} 2 & 2 \\ -4 & 7 \end{vmatrix} = 22$$

which are all positive. Also, $|\mathbf{B}| = 94 > 0$. Hence $\mathbf{B}$ is positive definite.

As yet another example, consider the quadratic form

$$Q = 4x_1^2 + 9x_2^2 + 2x_3^2 + 6x_1x_2 + 6x_1x_2 + 6x_1x_3 + 8x_2x_3$$

Is this positive for all values of x_1, x_2, and x_3? To answer this question, we write $Q = \mathbf{x}'\mathbf{B}\mathbf{x}$. The matrix $\mathbf{B}$ is given by

$$\mathbf{B} = \begin{bmatrix} 4 & 3 & 3 \\ 3 & 9 & 4 \\ 3 & 4 & 2 \end{bmatrix}$$

The diagonal terms are all positive. As for the three leading determinants of order 2, they are

$$\begin{vmatrix} 4 & 3 \\ 3 & 9 \end{vmatrix}, \quad \begin{vmatrix} 9 & 4 \\ 4 & 2 \end{vmatrix}, \quad \text{and} \quad \begin{vmatrix} 4 & 3 \\ 3 & 2 \end{vmatrix}$$

The first two are positive, but the last one is not. Also, $|\mathbf{B}| = -19$. Hence $\mathbf{B}$ is not positive definite. The answer to the question asked is "no."

For a negative definite matrix all leading determinants of odd order are < 0 and all leading determinants of even order are > 0. For semidefinite matrices we replace > 0 by ≥ 0 and < 0 by ≤ 0. For example, the matrix

$$\begin{bmatrix} 3 & 1 & -3 \\ -4 & 0 & 2 \\ 6 & -4 & 7 \end{bmatrix}$$

is positive semidefinite. Suppose that $\mathbf{A}$ is an $m \times n$ matrix. Then $\mathbf{A}'\mathbf{A}$ and $\mathbf{A}\mathbf{A}'$ are square matrices of order $n \times n$ and $m \times m$, respectively. We can show that both these matrices are positive semidefinite.

Consider $\mathbf{B} = \mathbf{A}\mathbf{A}'$. Then $\mathbf{x}'\mathbf{B}\mathbf{x} = \mathbf{x}'\mathbf{A}\mathbf{A}'\mathbf{x}$. Define $\mathbf{y} = \mathbf{A}'\mathbf{x}$. Then $\mathbf{x}'\mathbf{B}\mathbf{x} = \mathbf{y}'\mathbf{y} = \sum y_i^2$, which is ≥ 0. Hence $\mathbf{x}'\mathbf{B}\mathbf{x} \geq 0$; that is, $\mathbf{B}$ is positive semidefinite.

Finally, consider two positive semidefinite matrices $\mathbf{B}$ and $\mathbf{C}$. We shall write $\mathbf{B} \geq \mathbf{C}$ if $\mathbf{B} - \mathbf{C}$ is positive semidefinite. Consider

$$\mathbf{A} = \begin{bmatrix} 1 & 2 \\ 0 & 1 \\ 2 & 1 \end{bmatrix}$$

Then

$$\mathbf{B} = \mathbf{A}'\mathbf{A} = \begin{bmatrix} 5 & 4 \\ 4 & 6 \end{bmatrix} \quad \text{and} \quad \mathbf{C} = \mathbf{A}\mathbf{A}' = \begin{bmatrix} 5 & 2 & 4 \\ 2 & 1 & 1 \\ 4 & 1 & 5 \end{bmatrix}$$

are both positive definite.

The Multivariate Normal Distribution

Let $\mathbf{x}' = (x_1, x_2, \ldots, x_n)$ be a set of n variables which are normally distributed with mean vector $\boldsymbol{\mu}$ and covariance matrix $\mathbf{V}$. Then $\mathbf{x}$ is said to have an n-variate normal distribution $N_n(\boldsymbol{\mu}, \mathbf{V})$. Its density function is given by

$$f(x) = \frac{1}{(2\pi)^{n/2}|\mathbf{V}|^{1/2}} \exp[(\mathbf{x} - \boldsymbol{\mu})'\mathbf{V}^{-1}(\mathbf{x} - \boldsymbol{\mu})]$$

Note that with $n = 1$, we have $\mathbf{V} = \sigma^2$ and we can see the analogy with the density function for the univariate normal we considered earlier.

Consider the simpler case $\boldsymbol{\mu} = \mathbf{0}$. Also make the transformation

$$\mathbf{y} = \mathbf{V}^{-1/2}\mathbf{x}$$

Then the y's are linear functions of the x's and hence have a normal distribution. The covariance matrix of the y's is

$$E(\mathbf{y}\mathbf{y}') = E[\mathbf{V}^{-1/2}\mathbf{x}\mathbf{x}'\mathbf{V}^{-1/2}]$$
$$= \mathbf{V}^{-1/2}E(\mathbf{x}\mathbf{x}')\mathbf{V}^{-1/2}$$
$$= \mathbf{V}^{-1/2}\mathbf{V}\mathbf{V}^{-1/2} = \mathbf{I}$$

Thus the y's are independent normal with mean 0 and variance 1. Hence $\sum y_i^2$ has a χ^2-distribution with d.f. n. But

$$\sum y_i^2 = \mathbf{y}'\mathbf{y} = \mathbf{x}'\mathbf{V}^{-1/2}\mathbf{V}^{-1/2}\mathbf{x} = \mathbf{x}'\mathbf{V}^{-1}\mathbf{x}$$

Hence we have the result

> If $\mathbf{x} \sim N_n(\mathbf{0}, \mathbf{V})$, then $\mathbf{x}'\mathbf{V}^{-1}\mathbf{x} \sim \chi_n^2$

Idempotent Matrices and the χ^2-Distribution

A matrix $\mathbf{A}$ is said to be *idempotent* if $\mathbf{A}^2 = \mathbf{A}$. For example, consider $\mathbf{A} = \mathbf{X}(\mathbf{X}'\mathbf{X})^{-1}\mathbf{X}'$. Then $\mathbf{A}^2 = \mathbf{X}(\mathbf{X}'\mathbf{X})^{-1}\mathbf{X}'\mathbf{X}(\mathbf{X}'\mathbf{X})^{-1}\mathbf{X}' = \mathbf{X}(\mathbf{X}'\mathbf{X})\mathbf{X}' = \mathbf{A}$. Thus $\mathbf{A}$ is idempotent. Such matrices play an important role in econometrics. We shall state two important theorems regarding the relationship between idempotent matrices and the χ^2-distribution (proofs are omitted).[9]

Let $\mathbf{x}' = (x_1, x_2, \ldots, x_n)$ be a set of independent normal variables with mean 0 and variance 1. We know that $\mathbf{x}'\mathbf{x} = \sum x_i^2$ has a χ^2-distribution with d.f. n. But some other quadratic forms also have a χ^2-distribution, as stated in the following theorems:

> *Theorem 1:* If $\mathbf{A}$ is an $n \times n$ idempotent matrix of rank r, then $\mathbf{x}'\mathbf{A}\mathbf{x}$ has a χ^2-distribution with d.f. r.

---

[9]For proofs, see G. S. Maddala, *Econometrics* (New York: McGraw-Hill, 1977), pp. 455–456.

Theorem 2: If $\mathbf{A}_1$ and $\mathbf{A}_2$ are two idempotent matrices with ranks r_1 and r_2, respectively, and $\mathbf{A}_1\mathbf{A}_2 = \mathbf{0}$, then $\mathbf{x}'\mathbf{A}_1\mathbf{x}$ and $\mathbf{x}'\mathbf{A}_2\mathbf{x}$ have *independent* χ^2-*distributions* with d.f. r_1 and r_2, respectively.

We shall be using this result in statistical inference in the multiple regression model in Chapter 4.

Trace of a Matrix

The *trace* of a matrix $\mathbf{A}$ is the sum of its diagonal elements. We denote this by Tr($\mathbf{A}$). These are a few important results regarding traces:

$$\text{Tr}(\mathbf{A} + \mathbf{B}) = \text{Tr}(\mathbf{A}) + \text{Tr}(\mathbf{B})$$

$$\text{Tr}(\mathbf{AB}) = \text{Tr}(\mathbf{BA}) \text{ if both } \mathbf{AB} \text{ and } \mathbf{BA} \text{ are defined}$$

These results can be checked by writing down the appropriate expressions. As an example, let

$$\mathbf{A} = \begin{bmatrix} 1 & 2 \\ 0 & 1 \\ 1 & 1 \end{bmatrix} \quad \text{and} \quad \mathbf{B} = \begin{bmatrix} 2 & 0 & 1 \\ 1 & 1 & 1 \end{bmatrix}$$

Then

$$\mathbf{AB} = \begin{bmatrix} 4 & 2 & 3 \\ 1 & 1 & 1 \\ 3 & 1 & 2 \end{bmatrix} \quad \text{and} \quad \mathbf{BA} = \begin{bmatrix} 3 & 5 \\ 2 & 4 \end{bmatrix}$$

Tr($\mathbf{AB}$) = Tr($\mathbf{BA}$) = 7. Another important result we shall be using (in the case of the multiple regression model) is the following:[10]

If $\mathbf{A}$ is an idempotent matrix, then rank($\mathbf{A}$) = Tr($\mathbf{A}$)

Characteristic Roots and Vectors

This topic is discussed in the appendix to Chapter 7.

Exercises on Matrix Algebra

1. Consider $\mathbf{A} = \begin{bmatrix} 1 & 0 & 1 \\ 2 & 1 & 1 \end{bmatrix}$, $\mathbf{B} = \begin{bmatrix} 1 & 0 \\ 0 & 1 \\ 1 & 0 \end{bmatrix}$, and $\mathbf{C} = \begin{bmatrix} 2 & 1 \\ 1 & 1 \end{bmatrix}$

   (a) Compute $\mathbf{ABC}$, $\mathbf{CAB}$, $\mathbf{BCA}$, $\mathbf{CB}'\mathbf{A}'$, $\mathbf{C}'\mathbf{B}'\mathbf{A}'$.
   (b) Verify that $(\mathbf{ABC})' = \mathbf{C}'\mathbf{B}'\mathbf{A}'$.
   (c) Find the inverses of these matrices. Verify that $(\mathbf{ABC})^{-1} = \mathbf{C}^{-1}(\mathbf{AB})^{-1}$.
   (d) Verify that Tr($\mathbf{BCA}$) = Tr($\mathbf{ABC}$) = Tr($\mathbf{CAB}$).

---

[10]For a proof, see Maddala, *Econometrics*, pp. 444–445.

2. Solve the following set of equations using matrix methods:

$$x_1 + 2x_2 + 2x_3 = 1$$
$$2x_1 + 2x_2 + 3x_3 = 3$$
$$x_1 - x_2 + 3x_3 = 5$$

3. Determine those values of λ for which the following set of equations may possess a nontrivial solution:

$$3x_1 + x_2 - \lambda x_3 = 0$$
$$4x_1 - 2x_2 - 3x_3 = 0$$
$$2\lambda x_1 + 4x_2 + \lambda x_3 = 0$$

For each permissible value of λ, determine the most general solution.

4. If $\mathbf{AB} = \mathbf{AC}$, where $\mathbf{A}$ is a square matrix, when does it necessarily follow that $\mathbf{B} = \mathbf{C}$? Give an example in which this does not follow.

5. $\mathbf{A}$ and $\mathbf{B}$ are symmetric matrices. Show that $\mathbf{AB}$ is also symmetric if and only if $\mathbf{A}$ and $\mathbf{B}$ are commutative.

6. If $\mathbf{A}$ is a square matrix, the matrix obtained by replacing each element of $\mathbf{A}$ by its cofactor and then transposing the resulting matrix is known as the adjoint of $\mathbf{A}$ and is denoted by Adj($\mathbf{A}$). Note that $\mathbf{A}^{-1} = (1/|A|\text{Adj}(\mathbf{A}))$. Show that if $\mathbf{A}$ and $\mathbf{B}$ are square matrices, Adj($\mathbf{AB}$) = Adj($\mathbf{A}$) $\times$ Adj($\mathbf{B}$).

7. In Exercise 1, show that $\mathbf{A}(\mathbf{A'A})^{-1}\mathbf{A'}$ and $\mathbf{B}(\mathbf{B'B})^{-1}\mathbf{B'}$ are both idempotent. What are the ranks of these two matrices?

8. Determine whether the quadratic form $Q = x_1^2 + 2x_2^2 + x_3^2 - 2x_1x_2 + 2x_2x_3$ is positive definite or not. Answer the same for $Q = 2x_1^2 + 3x_2^2 + x_3^2 + x_4^2 + 2x_1x_2 - 2x_1x_3 + 8x_2x_3 + 4x_2x_4 + 4x_3x_4$.

9. Show that the set of equations

$$2x_1 - 2x_2 + x_3 = \lambda x_1$$
$$2x_1 - 3x_2 + 2x_3 = \lambda x_2$$
$$-x_1 + 2x_2 \qquad = \lambda x_3$$

can possess a nontrivial solution only if $\lambda = 1$ or -3. Obtain the general solution in each case.

10. Construct a set of three mutually orthogonal vectors that are linear combinations of the vectors (1, 1, 0, 1), (1, 1, 0, 0), and (1, 0, 2, 2).

3 Simple Regression

What is in this Chapter?

This chapter starts with a linear regression model with one explanatory variable, and states the assumptions of this basic model. It then discusses two methods of estimation: the method of moments and the method of least squares. The method of maximum likelihood is discussed in the appendix.

Next there is a discussion of statistical inference in this model, analysis of variance, and prediction problems. Alternative functional forms for regression equations and how they can be reduced to the linear regression model are discussed.

There are three topics: inverse prediction in the linear regression model, stochastic regressors and regression fallacy, that can be omitted at first. The inverse prediction problem, however, is very important in practice but is rarely discussed. It describes Fieller's method. The problem is to predict a value of x given a value of y.

The appendix to this chapter contains proofs of some results in least squares estimation omitted in the main part of the chapter, the maximum likelihood method of estimation and the associated large-sample tests: LR, Wald, LM. Methods of solving the likelihood equations are also outlined.

A more advanced discussion of the maximum likelihood method is given in Chapter 16.

3.1 Introduction

Regression analysis is one of the most commonly used tools in econometric work. We will, therefore, start our discussion with an outline of regression analysis. The subsequent chapters will deal with some modifications and extensions of this basic technique that need to be made when analyzing economic data.

We start with a basic question: What is regression analysis? Regression analysis is concerned with describing and evaluating the relationship between a given variable (often called the *explained* or *dependent* variable) and one or more other variables (often called the *explanatory* or *independent* variables). We will denote the explained variable by y and the explanatory variables by $x_1, x_2, \ldots, x_k$.

The dictionary definition of "regression" is "backward movement, a retreat, a return to an earlier stage of development." Paradoxical as it may sound, regression analysis as it is currently used has nothing to do with regression as dictionaries define the term.

The term *regression* was coined by Sir Francis Galton (1822–1911) from England, who was studying the relationship between the height of children and the height of parents. He observed that although tall parents had tall children and short parents had short children, there was a tendency for children's heights to converge toward the average. There is thus a "regression of children's heights toward the average." Galton, in his aristocratic way, termed this a "regression toward mediocrity."

Something similar to what Galton found has been noted in some other studies as well (studies of test scores, etc.). These examples are discussed in Section 3.12 under the heading "regression fallacy." For the present we should note that regression analysis as currently used has nothing to do with regression or backward movement.

Let us return to our notation of the explained variable to be denoted by y and explanatory variables denoted by $x_1, x_2, \ldots, x_k$. If $k = 1$, that is, there is only one of the x variables, we have what is known as *simple regression*. This is what we discuss in this chapter. If $k > 1$, that is, there are more than one x variables, we have what is known as *multiple regression*. This is discussed in Chapter 4. First we give some examples.

Example 1: Simple Regression

$$y = \text{sales}$$

$$x = \text{advertising expenditures}$$

Here we try to determine the relationship between sales and advertising expenditures.

Example 2: Multiple Regression

$$y = \text{consumption expenditures of a family}$$

$$x_1 = \text{family income}$$

$$x_2 = \text{financial assets of the family}$$

$$x_3 = \text{family size}$$

Here we try to determine the relationship between consumption expenditures on the one hand and family income, financial assets of the family, and family size on the other.

There are several objectives in studying these relationships. They can be used to:

1. Analyze the effects of policies that involve changing the individual x's. In Example 1 this involves analyzing the effect of changing advertising expenditures on sales.

Table 3.1 Classification of variables in regression analysis

y	$x_1, x_2, \ldots, x_k$
(a) Predictand	Predictors
(b) Regressand	Regressors
(c) Explained variable	Explanatory variables
(d) Dependent variable	Independent variables
(e) Effect variable	Causal variables
(f) Endogenous variable	Exogenous variables
(g) Target variable	Control variables

2. Forecast the value of y for a given set of x's.

3. Examine whether any of the x's have a significant effect on y.

In Example 2 we would want to know whether family size has a significant effect on consumption expenditures of the family. The exact meaning of the word "significant" is discussed in Section 3.5.

Given the way we have set up the problem until now, the variable y and the x variables are not on the same footing. Implicitly we have assumed that the x's are variables that influence y or are variables that we can control or change and y is the effect variable. There are several alternative terms used in the literature for y and $x_1, x_2, \ldots, x_k$. These are shown in Table 3.1.

Each of these terms is relevant for a particular view of the use of regression analysis. Terminology (a) is used if the purpose is prediction. For instance, sales is the predictand and advertising expenditures is the predictor. The terminology in (b), (c), and (d) is used by different people in their discussion of regression models. They are all equivalent terms. Terminology (e) is used in studies of causation. Terminology (f) is specific to econometrics. We use this terminology in Chapter 9. Finally, terminology (g) is used in control problems. For instance, our objective might be to achieve a certain level of sales (target variable) and we would like to determine the level of advertising expenditures (control variable) to achieve our objective.

In this and subsequent chapters we use the terminology in (c) and (d). Also, we consider here the case of one explained (dependent) variable and one explanatory (independent) variable. This, as we said earlier, is called simple regression. Further, as we said earlier, the variables y and x are not treated on the same footing. A detailed discussion of this issue is postponed to Chapter 11.

3.2 Specification of the Relationships

As mentioned in Section 3.1, we will discuss the case of one explained (dependent) variable, which we denote by y, and one explanatory (independent) variable, which we denote by x. The relationship between y and x is denoted by

$$y = f(x) \tag{3.1}$$

where $f(x)$ is a function of x.

At this point we need to distinguish between two types of relationships:

1. A *deterministic* or mathematical relationship.
2. A *statistical* relationship which does not give unique values of *y* for given values of *x* but can be described exactly in probabilistic terms.

What we are going to talk about in regression analysis here is relationships of type 2, not of type 1. As an example, suppose that the relationship between sales *y* and advertising expenditures *x* is

$$y = 2500 + 100x - x^2$$

This is a deterministic relationship. The sales for different levels of advertising expenditures can be determined exactly. These are as follows:

x	y
0	2500
20	4100
50	5000
100	2500

On the other hand, suppose that the relationship between sales *y* and advertising expenditures *x* is

$$y = 2500 + 100x - x^2 + u$$

where $u = +500$ with probability $\frac{1}{2}$
$\quad\quad = -500$ with probability $\frac{1}{2}$

Then the values of *y* for different values of *x* cannot be determined exactly but can be described probabilistically. For example, if advertising expenditures are 50, sales will be 5500 with probability $\frac{1}{2}$ and 4500 with probability $\frac{1}{2}$.

The values of *y* for different values of *x* are now as follows:

x	y
0	2000 or 3000
20	3600 or 4600
50	4500 or 5500
100	2000 or 3000

The data on *y* that we observe can be any one of the eight possible cases. For instance, we can have

x	y
0	2000
20	4600
50	5500
100	2000

If the error term u has a continuous distribution, say a normal distribution with mean 0 and variance 1, then for each value of x we have a normal distribution for y and the value of y we observe can be any observation from this distribution. For instance, if the relationship between y and x is

$$y = 2 + x + u$$

where the error term u is $N(0, 1)$, then for each value of x, y will have a normal distribution. This is shown in Figure 3.1. The line we have drawn is the deterministic relationship $y = 2 + x$. The actual values of y for each x will be some points on the vertical lines shown. The relationship between y and x in such cases is called a *stochastic* or statistical relationship.

Going back to equation (3.1), we will assume that the function $f(x)$ is linear in x, that is,

$$f(x) = \alpha + \beta x$$

and we will assume that this relationship is a stochastic relationship, that is,

$$y = \alpha + \beta x + u \tag{3.2}$$

where u, which is called an *error* or *disturbance*, has a known probability distribution (i.e., is a random variable).

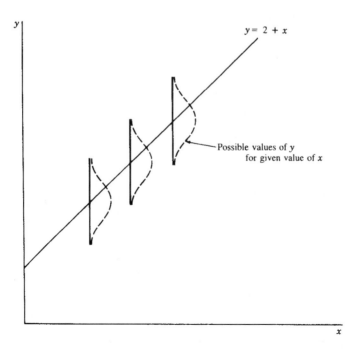

Figure 3.1   A stochastic relationship

In equation (3.2), $\alpha + \beta x$ is the deterministic component of y and u is the stochastic or random component. α and β are called *regression coefficients* or *regression parameters* that we estimate from the data on y and x.

There is no reason why the deterministic and stochastic components must be additive. But we will start our discussion with a simple model and introduce complications later. For this reason we have taken $f(x)$ to be a linear function and have assumed an additive error. Some simple alternative functional forms are discussed in Section 3.8.

Why should we add an error term u? What are the sources of the error term u in equation (3.2)? There are three main sources:

1. *Unpredictable element of randomness in human responses.* For instance, if $y =$ consumption expenditure of a household and $x =$ disposable income of the household, there is an unpredictable element of randomness in each household's consumption. The household does not behave like a machine. In one month the people in the household are on a spending spree. In another month they are tightfisted.
2. *Effect of a large number of omitted variables.* Again in our example x is not the only variable influencing y. The family size, tastes of the family, spending habits, and so on, affect the variable y. The error u is a *catchall* for the effects of all these variables, some of which may not even be quantifiable, and some of which may not even be identifiable. To a certain extent some of these variables are those that we refer to in source 1.
3. *Measurement error in y.* In our example this refers to measurement error in the household consumption. That is, we cannot measure it accurately. This argument for u is somewhat difficult to justify, particularly if we say that there is no measurement error in x (household disposable income). The case where both y and x are measured with error is discussed in Chapter 11. Since we have to go step by step and not introduce all the complications initially, we will accept this argument; that is, there is a measurement error in y but not in x.

In summary, the sources of the error term u are:

1. Unpredictable element of randomness in human response.
2. Effect of a large number of variables that have been omitted.
3. Measurement error in y.

If we have n observations on y and x, we can write equation (3.2) as

$$y_i = \alpha + \beta x_i + u_i \quad i = 1, 2, \ldots, n \tag{3.3}$$

Our objective is to get estimates of the unknown parameters α and β in equation (3.3) given the n observations on y and x. To do this we have to make some assumptions about the error terms u_i. The assumptions we make are:

1. *Zero mean.* $E(u_i) = 0$ for all i.
2. *Common variance.* $\mathrm{var}(u_i) = \sigma^2$ for all i.
3. *Independence.* u_i and u_j are independent for all $i \neq j$.

4. *Independence of x_j.* u_i and x_j are independent for all i and j. This assumption automatically follows if x_j are considered nonrandom variables. With reference to Figure 3.1, what this says is that the distribution of u does not depend on the value of x.

5. *Normality.* u_i are normally distributed for all i. In conjunction with assumptions 1, 2, and 3 this implies that u_i are independently and normally distributed with mean zero and a common variance σ^2. We write this as $u_i \sim \text{IN}(0, \sigma^2)$.

These are the assumptions with which we start. We will, however, relax some of these assumptions in later chapters.

Assumption 2 is relaxed in Chapter 5.
Assumption 3 is relaxed in Chapter 6.
Assumption 4 is relaxed in Chapter 9.

As for the normality assumption, we retain it because we will make inferences on the basis of the normal distribution and the t and F distributions. The first assumption is also retained throughout.

Since $E(u_i) = 0$ we can write equation (3.3) as

$$E(y_i) = \alpha + \beta x_i \tag{3.4}$$

This is also often termed the *population regression function*. When we substitute estimates of the parameters α and β in this, we get the *sample regression function*.

We will discuss three methods for estimating the parameters α and β:

1. The method of moments.
2. The method of least squares.
3. The method of maximum likelihood.

The first two methods are discussed in the next two sections. The last method is discussed in the appendix to this chapter. In the case of the simple regression model we are considering, all three methods give identical estimates. When it comes to generalizations, the methods give different estimates.

3.3   The Method of Moments

The assumptions we have made about the error term u imply that

$$E(u) = 0 \quad \text{and} \quad \text{cov}(x, u) = 0$$

In the method of moments, we replace these conditions by their sample counterparts.

Let $\hat{\alpha}$ and $\hat{\beta}$ be the estimators for α and β, respectively. The sample counterpart of u_i is the estimated error $\hat{u}_i$ (which is also called the *residual*), defined as

$$\hat{u}_i = y_i - \hat{\alpha} - \hat{\beta} x_i$$

The two equations to determine $\hat{\alpha}$ and $\hat{\beta}$ are obtained by replacing population assumptions by their sample counterparts:

Population Assumption	Sample Counterpart
$E(u) = 0$	$\frac{1}{n} \sum \hat{u}_i = 0$ or $\sum \hat{u}_i = 0$
$\text{cov}(x, u) = 0$	$\frac{1}{n} \sum x_i \hat{u}_i = 0$ or $\sum x_i \hat{u}_i = 0$

In these and the following equations, $\sum$ denotes $\sum_{i=1}^{n}$. Thus we get the two equations

$$\sum \hat{u}_i = 0 \quad \text{or} \quad \sum (y_i - \hat{\alpha} - \hat{\beta} x_i) = 0$$

$$\sum x_i \hat{u}_i = 0 \quad \text{or} \quad \sum x_i (y_i - \hat{\alpha} - \hat{\beta} x_i) = 0$$

These equations can be written as (noting that $\sum \hat{\alpha} = n \hat{\alpha}$)

$$\sum y_i = n \hat{\alpha} + \hat{\beta} \sum x_i$$

$$\sum x_i y_i = \hat{\alpha} \sum x_i + \hat{\beta} \sum x_i^2$$

Solving these two equations, we get $\hat{\alpha}$ and $\hat{\beta}$. These equations are also called "normal equations." In Section 3.4, we will show further simplifications of the equations as well as methods of making statistical inferences. First, we consider an illustrative example.

Illustrative Example

Consider the data on advertising expenditures (x) and sales revenue (y) for an athletic sportswear store for 5 months. The observations are as follows:

Month	Sales Revenue, y (thousands of dollars)	Advertising Expenditure, x (hundreds of dollars)
1	3	1
2	4	2
3	2	3
4	6	4
5	8	5

To get $\hat{\alpha}$ and $\hat{\beta}$, we need to compute $\sum x$, $\sum x^2$, $\sum xy$, and $\sum y$. We have

Observation	x	y	x^2	xy	$\hat{u}_i$
1	1	3	1	3	0.8
2	2	4	4	8	0.6
3	3	2	9	6	−2.6
4	4	6	16	24	0.2
5	5	8	25	40	1.0
Total	15	23	55	81	0

The normal equations are (since $n = 5$)

$$5\hat{\alpha} + 15\hat{\beta} = 23$$

$$15\hat{\alpha} + 55\hat{\beta} = 81$$

These give $\hat{\alpha} = 1.0$, $\hat{\beta} = 1.2$. Thus the sample regression equation is

$$\hat{y} = 1.0 + 1.2x$$

The sample observations and the estimated regression line are shown in Figure 3.2.

The intercept 1.0 gives the value of y when $x = 0$. This says that if advertising expenditures are zero, sales revenue will be $1000. The slope coefficient is 1.2. This says that if x is changed by an amount Δx, the change in y is $\Delta y = 1.2\Delta x$. For example, if advertising expenditures are increased by 1 unit ($100), sales revenue increases by 1.2 units ($1200) *on the average*. Clearly, there is no certainty in this prediction. The estimates 1.0 and 1.2 have some uncertainty attached. We discuss this in Section 3.5, on statistical inference in the linear regression model. For the present, what we have shown is how to obtain estimates of the parameters α and β. One other thing to note is that it is not appropriate to obtain predictions too far from the range of observations. Otherwise, the owner of the store might conclude that by raising the advertising expenditures by $100,000, she can increase sales revenue by $1,200,000.

We have also shown the estimated errors or the residuals, which are given by

$$\hat{u}_i = y_i - 1.0 - 1.2x_i$$

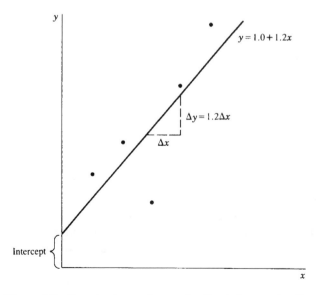

Figure 3.2 Sample observations and estimated regression line

These are the errors we would make if we tried to predict the value of y on the basis of the estimated regression equation and the values of x. Note that we are not trying to predict any future values of y. We are considering only *within-sample prediction errors*. We cannot get $\hat{u}_i$ for $x_i = 0$ or $x_i = 6$ because we do not have the corresponding values of y_i. Out-of-sample prediction is considered in Section 3.7.

Note that $\sum \hat{u}_i = 0$ by virtue of the first condition we imposed. The sum of squares of the residuals is

$$\sum \hat{u}_i^2 = (0.8)^2 + (0.6)^2 + (-2.6)^2 + (0.2)^2 + (1.0)^2 = 8.8$$

The method of least squares described in the next section is based on the principle of choosing $\hat{\alpha}$ and $\hat{\beta}$ so that $\sum \hat{u}_i^2$ is minimum. That is, the sum of squares of prediction errors is the minimum. With this method we get the same estimates of α and β as we have obtained here because we get the same normal equations.

3.4 The Method of Least Squares

The method of least squares is the automobile of modern statistical analysis; despite its limitations, occasional accidents, and incidental pollution, it and its numerous variations, extensions and related conveyances carry the bulk of statistical analysis, and are known and valued by all.

Stephen M. Stigler[1]

The method of least squares requires that we should choose $\hat{\alpha}$ and $\hat{\beta}$ as estimates of α and β, respectively, so that

$$Q = \sum_{i=1}^{n} (y_i - \hat{\alpha} - \hat{\beta} x_i)^2 \tag{3.5}$$

is a minimum. Q is also the sum of squares of the (within-sample) prediction errors when we predict y_i given x_i and the estimated regression equation. We will show in the appendix to this chapter that the least squares estimators have desirable optimal properties. As before, this property is often abbreviated as BLUE (best linear unbiased estimator). We are relegating the proof to the appendix so that readers not interested in proofs can proceed.

The intuitive idea behind the least squares procedure can be described figuratively with reference to Figure 3.2, which gives a graph of the points (x_i, y_i). We pass the regression line through the points in such a way that it is "as close as possible" to the points. The question is what is meant by "close." The procedure of minimizing Q in equation (3.5) implies that we minimize the sum of squares of vertical distances of the points from the line. Some alternative methods of measuring closeness are illustrated in Figure 3.4.

With the readily available computer programs, readers interested in just obtaining results need not even know how all the estimators are derived. However, it is advisable to know

---

[1]S. M. Stigler, "Gauss and the Invention of Least Squares," *The Annals of Statistics*, Vol. 9, No. 3, 1981, pp. 465–474.

a little bit about the derivation of the least squares estimators. Readers not interested in the algebraic detail can go to the illustrative examples.

To minimize Q in equation (3.5) with respect to $\hat{\alpha}$ and $\hat{\beta}$, we equate its first derivatives with respect to $\hat{\alpha}$ and $\hat{\beta}$ to zero. This procedure yields (in the following equations, $\sum$ denotes $\sum_{i=1}^{n}$)

$$\frac{\partial Q}{\partial \hat{\alpha}} = 0 \Rightarrow \sum 2(y_i - \hat{\alpha} - \hat{\beta} x_i)(-1) = 0$$

or

$$\sum y_i = n\hat{\alpha} + \hat{\beta} \sum x_i$$

or

$$\bar{y} = \hat{\alpha} + \hat{\beta}\bar{x} \tag{3.6}$$

and

$$\frac{\partial Q}{\partial \hat{\beta}} = 0 \Rightarrow \sum 2(y_i - \hat{\alpha} - \hat{\beta} x_i)(-x_i) = 0$$

or

$$\sum y_i x_i = \hat{\alpha} \sum x_i + \hat{\beta} \sum x_i^2 \tag{3.7}$$

Equations (3.6) and (3.7) are called the *normal equations*. Substituting the value of $\hat{\alpha}$ from (3.6) into (3.7), we get

$$\sum y_i x_i = \sum x_i(\bar{y} - \hat{\beta}\bar{x}) + \hat{\beta} \sum x_i^2 \tag{3.8}$$

$$= n\bar{x}(\bar{y} - \hat{\beta}\bar{x}) + \hat{\beta} \sum x_i^2$$

Let us define

$$S_{yy} = \sum (y_i - \bar{y})^2 = \sum y_i^2 - n\bar{y}^2$$

$$S_{xy} = \sum (x_i - \bar{x})(y_i - \bar{y}) = \sum x_i y_i - n\bar{x}\bar{y}$$

and

$$S_{xx} = \sum (x_i - \bar{x})^2 = \sum x_i^2 - n\bar{x}^2$$

Then equation (3.8) can be written as

$$\hat{\beta} S_{xx} = S_{xy} \text{ or } \hat{\beta} = \frac{S_{xy}}{S_{xx}} \tag{3.9}$$

Hence the least squares estimators for α and β are

$$\boxed{\hat{\beta} = \frac{S_{xy}}{S_{xx}} \quad \text{and} \quad \hat{\alpha} = \bar{y} - \hat{\beta}\bar{x}} \tag{3.10}$$

The estimated residuals are

$$\hat{u}_i = y_i - \hat{\alpha} - \hat{\beta} x_i$$

The two normal equations show that these residuals satisfy the equations

$$\sum \hat{u}_i = 0 \quad \text{and} \quad \sum x_i \hat{u}_i = 0$$

The residual sum of squares (to be denoted by RSS) is given by

$$\begin{aligned}
\text{RSS} &= \sum (y_i - \hat{\alpha} - \hat{\beta} x_i)^2 \\
&= \sum [y_i - \bar{y} - \hat{\beta}(x_i - \bar{x})]^2 \\
&= \sum (y_i - \bar{y})^2 + \hat{\beta}^2 \sum (x_i - \bar{x})^2 - 2\hat{\beta} \sum (y_i - \bar{y})(x_i - \bar{x}) \\
&= S_{yy} + \hat{\beta}^2 S_{xx} - 2\hat{\beta} S_{xy}
\end{aligned}$$

But $\hat{\beta} = S_{xy}/S_{xx}$. Hence we have

$$\text{RSS} = S_{yy} - \frac{S_{xy}^2}{S_{xx}} = S_{yy} - \hat{\beta} S_{xy}$$

S_{yy} is usually denoted by TSS (total sum of squares) and $\hat{\beta} S_{xy}$ is usually denoted by ESS (explained sum of squares). Thus

$$\begin{array}{ccc}
\text{TSS} = & \text{ESS} & + & \text{RSS} \\
\text{(total)} & \text{(explained)} & & \text{(residual)}
\end{array}$$

Some other authors like to use RSS to denote regression sum of squares and ESS as error sum of squares. The confusing thing here is that both the words "explained" and "error" start with the letter "e" and the words "regression" and "residual" start with the letter "r." However, we prefer to use RSS for residual sum of squares and ESS for explained sum of squares.[2] We will reserve the word *residual* to denote $\hat{u} = y - \hat{\alpha} - \hat{\beta} x$ and the word *error* to denote the disturbance u in equation (3.3). Thus *residual is the estimated error*.

The proportion of the total sum of squares explained is denoted by r_{xy}^2, where r_{xy} is called the *correlation coefficient*. Thus $r_{xy}^2 = \text{ESS}/\text{TSS}$ and $1 - r_{xy}^2 = \text{RSS}/\text{TSS}$. If r_{xy}^2 is high (close to 1), then x is a good "explanatory" variable for y. The term r_{xy}^2 is called the *coefficient of determination* and must fall between zero and 1 for any given regression. If r_{xy}^2 is close to zero, the variable x explains very little of the variation in y. If r_{xy}^2 is close to 1, the variable x explains most of the variation in y.

The coefficient of determination r_{xy}^2 is given by

$$\boxed{r_{xy}^2 = \frac{\text{ESS}}{\text{TSS}} = \frac{\text{TSS} - \text{RSS}}{\text{TSS}} = \frac{\hat{\beta} S_{xy}}{S_{yy}}}$$

---

[2]This is also the notation used in J. Johnston, *Econometric Methods*, 3rd ed. (New York: McGraw-Hill, 1984).

Summary

The estimates for the regression coefficients are

$$\hat{\beta} = \frac{S_{xy}}{S_{xx}} \quad \text{and} \quad \hat{\alpha} = \bar{y} - \hat{\beta}\bar{x}$$

The residual sum of squares is given by

$$\text{RSS} = S_{yy} - \frac{S_{xy}^2}{S_{xx}} = S_{yy} - \hat{\beta}S_{xy} = S_{yy}(1 - r_{xy}^2)$$

and the coefficient of determination is given by

$$r_{xy}^2 = \frac{S_{xy}^2}{S_{xx}S_{yy}} = \frac{\hat{\beta}S_{xy}}{S_{yy}}$$

The least squares estimators $\hat{\beta}$ and $\hat{\alpha}$ yield an estimated straight line that has a smaller RSS than any other straight line.

Reverse Regression

We have until now considered the regression of y on x. This is called the *direct regression*. Sometimes one has to consider the regression of x on y as well. This is called the *reverse regression*. The reverse regression has been advocated in the analysis of sex (or race) discrimination in salaries. For instance, if

$$y = \text{salary}$$

$$x = \text{qualifications}$$

and we are interested in determining if there is sex discrimination in salaries, we can ask:

1. Whether men and women with the same qualifications (value of x) are getting the same salaries (value of y). This question is answered by the direct regression, regression of y on x. Alternatively, we can ask:
2. Whether men and women with the same salaries (value of y) have the same qualifications (value of x). This question is answered by the reverse regression, regression of x on y.[3]

In this example both the questions make sense and hence we have to look at both these regressions. For the reverse regression the regression equation can be written as

$$x_i = \alpha' + \beta'y_i + v_i$$

---

[3]We discuss this problem further in Chapter 11.

where v_i are the errors that satisfy assumptions similar to those stated earlier in Section 3.2 for u_i. Interchanging x and y in the formulas that we derived, we get

$$\hat{\beta}' = \frac{S_{xy}}{S_{yy}} \quad \text{and} \quad \hat{\alpha}' = \bar{x} - \hat{\beta}'\bar{y}$$

Denoting the residual sum of squares in this case by RSS', we have

$$\text{RSS}' = S_{xx} - \frac{S_{xy}^2}{S_{yy}}$$

Note that

$$\hat{\beta}\hat{\beta}' = \frac{S_{xy}^2}{S_{xx}S_{yy}} = r_{xy}^2$$

Hence if r_{xy}^2 is close to 1, the two regression lines will be close to each other.

We now illustrate with an example.

Illustrative Example

Consider the data in Table 3.2. The data are for 10 workers:

$$x = \text{labor-hours of work}$$

$$y = \text{output}$$

We wish to determine the relationship between output and labor-hours of work. We have

$$\bar{x} = \frac{80}{10} = 8$$

$$\bar{y} = \frac{96}{10} = 9.6$$

Table 3.2 Labor-hours of work and output

Observation	x	y	x^2	y^2	xy
1	10	11	100	121	110
2	7	10	49	100	70
3	10	12	100	144	120
4	5	6	25	36	30
5	8	10	64	100	80
6	8	7	64	49	56
7	6	9	36	81	54
8	7	10	49	100	70
9	9	11	81	121	99
10	10	10	100	100	100
Total	80	96	668	952	789

$$S_{xx} = 668 - 10(8)^2 = 668 - 640 = 28$$

$$S_{xy} = 789 - 10(8)(9.6) = 789 - 768 = 21$$

$$S_{yy} = 952 - 10(9.6)^2 = 952 - 921.6 = 30.4$$

$$r_{xy} = \frac{21}{\sqrt{28(30.4)}} \simeq \frac{21}{29} = 0.724 \quad \text{or} \quad r_{xy}^2 = 0.52$$

$$\hat{\beta} = \frac{S_{xy}}{S_{xx}} = \frac{21}{28} = 0.75$$

$$\hat{\alpha} = \bar{y} - \hat{\beta}\bar{x} = 9.6 - 0.75(0.8) = 3.6$$

Hence the regression of y on x is

$$y = 3.6 + 0.75x$$

Since x is labor-hours of work and y is output, the slope coefficient 0.75 measures the marginal productivity of labor. As for the intercept 3.6, it means that output will be 3.6 when labor-hours of work is zero! Clearly, this does not make sense. However, this merely illustrates the point we made earlier — that we should not try to get predicted values of y too far out of the range of sample values. Here x ranges from 5 to 10.

As for the reverse regression we have

$$\hat{\beta}' = \frac{S_{xy}}{S_{yy}} = \frac{21}{30.4} \simeq 0.69$$

and

$$\hat{\alpha}' = \bar{x} - \hat{\beta}'\bar{y} = 8.0 - 9.6(0.69) = 1.37$$

Hence the regression of x on y is

$$x = 1.37 + 0.69y$$

Note that the product of the two slopes $= \hat{\beta}\hat{\beta}' = 0.75(0.69) = 0.52 = r_{xy}^2$. These two regression lines are presented in Figure 3.3. The procedure used in the two regressions is illustrated in Figure 3.4. If we consider a scatter diagram of the observations, the procedure of minimizing

$$\sum_{i=1}^{n}(y_i - \hat{\alpha} - \hat{\beta}x_i)^2$$

amounts to passing a line through the observations so as to minimize the sum of squares of the vertical distances of the points in the scatter diagram from the line. This is shown in Figure 3.4(a). The line shows the regression of y on x.

On the other hand, the procedure of minimizing

$$\sum_{i=1}^{n}(x_i - \hat{\alpha}' - \hat{\beta}'y_i)^2$$

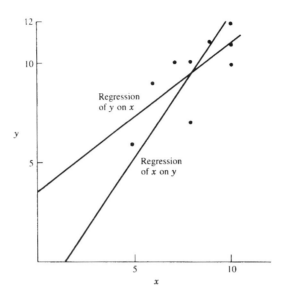

Figure 3.3   Regression lines for regression of y on x and x on y

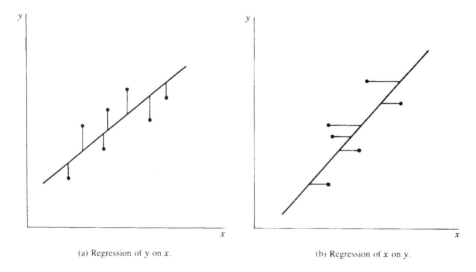

(a) Regression of y on x.   (b) Regression of x on y.

Figure 3.4   Minimization of residual sum of squares in the regression of y on x and x on y

amounts to passing a line through the observations so as to minimize the sum of squares of the horizontal distances of the points in the scatter diagram from the line. This is shown in Figure 3.4(b). The line shows the regression of x on y.

We can also think of passing a line in such a way that we minimize the sum of squares of the *perpendicular* distances of the points from the line. This is called *orthogonal regression*.

Since a discussion of orthogonal regression is beyond the scope of this book, we will confine our discussion to only the other two regressions: regression of y on x and of x on y. A question arises as to which of these is the appropriate one. Following are some general guidelines on this problem.

1. If the model is such that the direction of causation is known (e.g., if we say that advertising expenditures at time t influence sales at time t but not the other way around), we should estimate the regression using sales as the explained variable and advertising expenditures as the explanatory variable. The opposite regression does not make sense. We should estimate this equation whether our objective is to estimate sales for given advertising expenditures or to estimate advertising expenditures for given sales (i.e., always estimate a regression of an effect variable on a causal variable).
2. In problems where the direction of causation is not as clear cut, and where y and x have a joint normal distribution, both the regressions y on x and x on y make sense and one should estimate a regression of y on x to predict y given x and a regression of x on y to predict x given y.
3. In models where y and x are both measured with error, we have to estimate both the regressions of y on x and x on y to get "bounds" on β. This problem is discussed in Chapter 11.
4. The case of salary discrimination mentioned earlier is an example where the problem can be posed in two different and equally meaningful ways. In such cases both regressions make sense.
5. Sometimes, which regression makes sense depends on how the data are generated. Consider the data presented in Table 3.2. x is labor-hours of work and y is output, and the observations are for different workers. Which of the two regressions makes sense depends on the way the data were generated. If the workers are given some hours of work (x), and the output they produced (y) was observed, then a regression of y on x is the correct one to look at. In this case x is the controlled variable. On the other hand, if the workers were assigned some amount of output (y) and the hours of work (x) that they took to produce that output was observed, it is a regression of x on y that is meaningful. In this case y is the controlled variable. Here what we are considering is an experiment where one of the variables is controlled or fixed. With experimental data, which of the variables should be treated as dependent and which as independent will be clear from the way the experiment was conducted. With most economic data, however, this is not a clear-cut choice.

3.5 Statistical Inference in the Linear Regression Model

In Section 3.4 we discussed procedures for obtaining the least squares estimators. To obtain the least squares estimators of α and β we do not need to assume any particular probability distribution for the errors u_i. But to get interval estimates for the parameters and to test any hypotheses about them, we need to assume that the errors u_i have a normal distribution. As proved in the appendix to this chapter, the least squares estimators are:

1. Unbiased.
2. Have minimum variance among the class of all linear unbiased estimators.

These properties hold even if the errors u_i do not have the normal distribution provided that the other assumptions we have made are satisfied. These assumptions, we may recall, are:

1. $E(u_i) = 0$.
2. $V(u_i) = \sigma^2$ for all i.
3. u_i and u_j are independent for $i \neq j$.
4. x_j are nonstochastic.

We will now make the additional assumption that the errors u_i are normally distributed and show how we can get confidence intervals for α and β and test any hypotheses about α and β. We will relegate the proofs of the propositions to the appendix and state the results here.

First, we need the sampling distributions of $\hat{\alpha}$ and $\hat{\beta}$. We can prove that they have a normal distribution (proofs are given in the appendix). Specifically, we have the following results:

$\hat{\alpha}$ and $\hat{\beta}$ are jointly normally distributed with

$$E(\hat{\alpha}) = \alpha \qquad \text{var}(\hat{\alpha}) = \sigma^2 \left(\frac{1}{n} + \frac{\bar{x}^2}{S_{xx}} \right)$$

$$E(\hat{\beta}) = \beta \qquad \text{var}(\hat{\beta}) = \frac{\sigma^2}{S_{xx}}$$

and

$$\text{cov}(\hat{\alpha}, \hat{\beta}) = \sigma^2 \left(\frac{-\bar{x}}{S_{xx}} \right)$$

These results would be useful if the error variance σ^2 were known. Unfortunately, in practice, σ^2 is not known, and has to be estimated.

If RSS is the residual sum of squares, then

$$\hat{\sigma}^2 = \frac{\text{RSS}}{n-2} \text{ is an unbiased estimator for } \sigma^2$$

Also

$$\frac{\text{RSS}}{\sigma^2} \text{ has a } \chi^2\text{-distribution with d.f. } (n-2)$$

Further, the distribution of RSS is independent of the distributions of $\hat{\alpha}$ and $\hat{\beta}$. (Proofs of these propositions are relegated to the appendix.)

This result can be used to get confidence intervals for σ^2 or to test hypotheses about σ^2. However, we are still left with the problem of making inferences about α and β. For this purpose we use the t-distribution.

We know that if we have two variables $x_1 \sim N(0, 1)$ and $x_2 \sim \chi^2$ with d.f. k and x_1 and x_2 independent, then

$$x = \frac{x_1}{\sqrt{x_2/k}} = \frac{\text{standard normal}}{\sqrt{\text{independent averaged } \chi^2}}$$

has a t-distribution with d.f. k.

In this case $(\hat{\beta} - \beta)/\sqrt{\sigma^2/S_{xx}} \sim N(0, 1)$. (We have subtracted the mean and divided it by the standard deviation.) Also, $\text{RSS}/\sigma^2 \sim \chi^2_{n-2}$ and the two distributions are independent. Hence we compute the ratio

$$\frac{\hat{\beta} - \beta}{\sqrt{\sigma^2/S_{xx}}} \bigg/ \sqrt{\frac{\text{RSS}}{(n-2)\sigma^2}}$$

which has a t-distribution with d.f. $(n-2)$. Now σ^2 cancels out and writing $\text{RSS}/(n-2)$ as $\hat{\sigma}^2$ we get the result that $(\hat{\beta} - \beta)/\sqrt{\hat{\sigma}^2/S_{xx}}$ has a t-distribution with d.f. $(n-2)$. Note that the variance of $\hat{\beta}$ is σ^2/S_{xx}. Since σ^2 is not known, we use an unbiased estimator $\text{RSS}/(n-2)$. Thus $\hat{\sigma}^2/S_{xx}$ is the estimated variance of $\hat{\beta}$ and its square root is called the *standard error* denoted by $\text{SE}(\hat{\beta})$.

We can follow a similar procedure for $\hat{\alpha}$. We substitute $\hat{\sigma}^2$ for σ^2 in the variance of $\hat{\alpha}$ and take the square root to get the standard error $\text{SE}(\hat{\alpha})$.

Thus we have the following result:

> $(\hat{\alpha} - \alpha)/\text{SE}(\hat{\alpha})$ and $(\hat{\beta} - \beta)/\text{SE}(\hat{\beta})$ each have a t-distribution with d.f. $(n-2)$. These distributions can be used to get confidence intervals for α and β and to test hypotheses about α and β.

$\hat{\sigma}$ is usually called the *standard error of the regression*. It is denoted by SER (sometimes by SEE).

Illustrative Example

As an illustration of the calculation of standard errors, consider the data in Table 3.2. Earlier we obtained the regression equation of y on x as

$$\hat{y} = 3.6 + 0.75x$$

We will now calculate the standard errors of $\hat{\alpha}$ and $\hat{\beta}$. These are obtained by:

1. Computing the variances of $\hat{\alpha}$ and $\hat{\beta}$ in terms of σ^2.
2. Substituting $\hat{\sigma}^2 = \text{RSS}/(n-2)$ for σ^2.
3. Taking the square root of the resulting expressions.

We have

$$V(\hat{\alpha}) = \sigma^2 \left(\frac{1}{n} + \frac{\bar{x}^2}{S_{xx}} \right) = \sigma^2 \left(\frac{1}{10} + \frac{64}{28} \right) = 2.39\sigma^2$$

$$V(\hat{\beta}) = \frac{\sigma^2}{S_{xx}} = \frac{\sigma^2}{28} = 0.036\sigma^2$$

$$\hat{\sigma}^2 = \frac{1}{n-2} \left(S_{yy} - \frac{S_{xy}^2}{S_{xx}} \right) = \frac{1}{8} \left[30.4 - \frac{(21)^2}{28} \right] = 1.83$$

$$SE(\hat{\alpha}) = \sqrt{(2.39)(1.83)} = 2.09$$

$$SE(\hat{\beta}) = \sqrt{(0.036)(1.83)} = 0.256$$

The standard errors are usually presented in parentheses under the estimates of the regression coefficients.

Confidence Intervals for α, β, and σ²

Since $(\hat{\alpha} - \alpha)/SE(\hat{\alpha})$ and $(\hat{\beta} - \beta)/SE(\hat{\beta})$ have t-distributions with d.f. $(n-2)$, using the table of the t-distribution (in the appendix) with $n - 2 = 8$ degrees of freedom we get

$$\text{Prob} \left[-2.306 < \frac{\hat{\alpha} - \alpha}{SE(\hat{\alpha})} < 2.306 \right] = 0.95$$

and

$$\text{Prob} \left[-2.306 < \frac{\hat{\beta} - \beta}{SE(\hat{\beta})} < 2.306 \right] = 0.95$$

These give confidence intervals for α and β. Substituting the values of $\hat{\alpha}$, $\hat{\beta}$, $SE(\hat{\alpha})$, and $SE(\hat{\beta})$ and simplifying we get the 95% confidence limits for α and β as $(-1.22, 8.42)$ for α and $(0.16, 1.34)$ for β. Note that the 95% confidence limits for α are $\hat{\alpha} \pm 2.306 SE(\hat{\alpha})$ and for β are $\hat{\beta} \pm 2.306 SE(\hat{\beta})$. Although it is not often used, we will also illustrate the procedure of finding a confidence interval for σ^2. Since we know that RSS/σ^2 has a χ^2-distribution with d.f. $(n-2)$, we can use the tables of the χ^2-distribution for getting any required confidence interval. Suppose that we want a 95% confidence interval. Note that we will write $RSS = (n-2)\hat{\sigma}^2$.

From the tables of the χ^2-distribution with d.f. 8, we find that the probability of obtaining a value < 2.18 is 0.025 and of obtaining a value > 17.53 is 0.025. Hence

$$\text{Prob} \left(2.18 < \frac{8\hat{\sigma}^2}{\sigma^2} < 17.53 \right) = 0.95$$

or

$$\text{Prob} \left(\frac{8\hat{\sigma}^2}{17.53} < \sigma^2 < \frac{8\hat{\sigma}^2}{2.18} \right) = 0.95$$

Since $\hat{\sigma}^2 = 1.83$, substituting this value, we get the 95% confidence limits for σ^2 as (0.84, 6.72).

Note that the confidence intervals for α and β are symmetric around $\hat{\alpha}$ and $\hat{\beta}$, respectively (because the t-distribution is a symmetric distribution). This is not the case with the confidence interval for σ^2. It is not symmetric around $\hat{\sigma}^2$.

The confidence intervals we have obtained for α, β, and σ^2 are all very wide. We can produce narrower intervals by reducing the confidence coefficient. For instance, the 80% confidence limits for β are

$$\hat{\beta} \pm 1.397 \mathrm{SE}(\hat{\beta}) \quad \text{since} \quad \mathrm{Prob}(-1.397 < t < 1.397) = 0.80$$

from the t-tables with 8 degrees of freedom.

We therefore get the 80% confidence limits for β as

$$0.75 \pm 1.397(0.256) = (0.39, 1.11)$$

The confidence intervals we have constructed are two-sided intervals. Sometimes we want upper or lower limits for β, in which case we construct one-sided intervals. For instance, from the t-tables with 8 degrees of freedom we have

$$\mathrm{Prob}(t < 1.86) = 0.95$$

and

$$\mathrm{Prob}(t > -1.86) = 0.95$$

Hence for a one-sided confidence interval, the upper limit for β is

$$\hat{\beta} + 1.86 \mathrm{SE}(\hat{\beta}) = 0.75 + 1.86(0.256) = 0.75 + 0.48 = 1.23$$

The 95% confidence interval is $(-\infty, 1.23)$. Similarly, the lower limit for β is

$$\hat{\beta} - 1.86 \mathrm{SE}(\hat{\beta}) = 0.75 - 0.48 = 0.27$$

Thus the 95% confidence interval is $(0.27, +\infty)$.

We will give further examples of the use of one-sided intervals after we discuss tests of hypotheses.

Testing of Hypotheses

Turning to the problem of testing of hypotheses, suppose we want to test the hypothesis that the true value of β is 1.0. We know that

$$t_0 = \frac{\hat{\beta} - \beta}{\mathrm{SE}(\hat{\beta})}$$

has a t-distribution with $(n - 2)$ degrees of freedom. Let t_0 be the observed t-value. If the alternative hypothesis is $\beta \neq 1$ then we consider $|t_0|$ as the test statistic. Hence if the true value of β is 1.0, we have

$$t_0 = \frac{0.75 - 1.0}{0.256} = -0.98$$

Hence $|t_0| = 0.98$.

Looking at the t-tables for 8 degrees of freedom, we see that

$$\text{Prob}(t > 0.706) = 0.25$$

and

$$\text{Prob}(t > 1.397) = 0.10$$

Thus $\text{Prob}(t > 0.98)$ is roughly 0.19 (by linear interpolation) or $\text{Prob}(|t| > 0.98) \simeq 0.38$. This probability is not very low and we do not reject the hypothesis that $\beta = 1.0$. It is customary to use 0.05 as a low probability and to reject the suggested hypothesis if the probability of obtaining as extreme a t-value as the observed t_0 is less than 0.05. In this case either the suggested hypothesis is not true or it is true but an improbable event has occurred.

Note that for 8 degrees of freedom, the 5% probability points are ± 2.306 for a two-sided test and ± 1.86 for a one-sided test. Thus if *both* high and low t-values are to be considered as evidence against the suggested hypothesis, we reject it if the observed t_0 is > 2.306 or < -2.306. On the other hand, if only very high *or* very low t-values are to be considered as evidence against the suggested hypothesis, we reject it if $t_0 > 1.86$ or $t_0 < -1.86$, depending on the suggested direction of deviation.

Although it is customary to use the 5% probability level for rejection of the suggested hypothesis, there is nothing sacred about this number. The theory of significance tests with the commonly used significance levels of 0.05 and 0.01 owes its origins to the famous British statistician Sir R. A. Fisher (1890–1962). He is considered the father of modern statistical methods and the numbers 0.05 and 0.01 suggested by him have been adopted universally.

Another point to note is that the hypothesis being tested (in this case $\beta = 1$) is called the *null hypothesis*. Again the terminology is misleading and owes its origin to the fact that the initial hypotheses tested were that some parameters were zero. Thus a hypothesis $\beta = 0$ can be called a null hypothesis but not a hypothesis $\beta = 1$. In any case for the present we will stick to the standard terminology and call the hypothesis tested the null hypothesis and use the standard significance levels of 0.05 and 0.01.

Finally, it should be noted that there is a correspondence between the confidence intervals derived earlier and tests of hypotheses. For instance, the 95% confidence interval we derived earlier for β is $(0.16 < \beta < 1.34)$. Any hypothesis that says $\beta = \beta_0$, where β_0 is in this interval, will not be rejected at the 5% level for a two-sided test. For instance, the hypothesis $\beta = 1.27$ will not be rejected, but the hypothesis $\beta = 1.35$ or $\beta = 0.10$ will be. For one-sided tests we consider one-sided confidence intervals.

It is also customary to term some regression coefficients as "significant" or "not significant" depending on the t-ratios, and attach asterisks to them if they are significant. This procedure should be avoided. For instance, in our illustrative example the regression equation is sometimes presented as

$$y = \underset{(2.09)}{3.6} + \underset{(0.256)}{0.75^* x}$$

The* on the slope coefficient indicates that it is "significant" at the 5% level. However, this statement means that "it is significantly different from 'zero' " and this statement is meaningful only if the hypothesis being tested is $\beta = 0$. Such a hypothesis would not be meaningful in many cases. For instance, in our example, if y is output and x is labor-hours of work, a hypothesis $\beta = 0$ does not make any sense. Similarly, if y is a posttraining score and x is a pretraining score, a hypothesis $\beta = 0$ would imply that the pretraining score has no effect on the posttraining score and no one would be interested in testing such an extreme hypothesis.

Example of Comparing Test Scores from the GRE and GMAT Tests[4]

In the College of Business Administration at the University of Florida, two different tests are used to measure aptitude for graduate work. The economics department relies on GRE scores and the other graduate departments rely on GMAT scores. To allocate graduate assistantships and fellowships, it is important to be able to compare the scores of these two tests. A rough rule of thumb that was suggested was the following:

$$\text{GRE score} = 2(\text{GMAT score}) + 100$$

A question arose as to the adequacy of this rule.

To answer this question data were obtained on 262 current and recent University of Florida students who had taken both tests. The GRE and GMAT scores were highly correlated. The correlation coefficients were 0.71 for U.S. students and 0.80 for foreign students.

If we have GRE scores on some students and GMAT scores on others, we can convert all scores to GRE scores, in which case we use the regression of GRE score on GMAT score. Alternatively, we can convert all scores to GMAT scores, in which case we use the regression of GMAT score on GRE score. These two regressions were as follows (figures in parentheses are standard errors):

Students	Numbers	Regression	R^2
		Regression of GRE on GMAT	
All	255	$\widehat{\text{GRE}} = 333 + 1.470\text{GMAT}$ (0.087)	0.53
U.S.	211	$\widehat{\text{GRE}} = 336 + 1.458\text{GMAT}$ (0.101)	0.50
Foreign	44	$\widehat{\text{GRE}} = 284 + 1.606\text{GMAT}$ (0.183)	0.64
		Regression of GMAT on GRE	
All	255	$\widehat{\text{GMAT}} = 125 + 0.363\text{GRE}$ (0.021)	0.53
U.S.	211	$\widehat{\text{GMAT}} = 151 + 0.345\text{GRE}$ (0.024)	0.50
Foreign	44	$\widehat{\text{GMAT}} = 60 + 0.400\text{GRE}$ (0.046)	0.64

Although we can get predictions for the U.S. students and foreign students separately, and for the GRE given GMAT and GMAT given GRE, we shall present only one set of

---

[4]I would like to thank my colleague Larry Kenny for this example and the computations.

predictions and compare this with the present rule. The predictions, from the regression of GRE on GMAT (for all students), are as follows:

GMAT	GR̂E	Current Rule[a]
400	921	900
450	995	1000
500	1068	1100
550	1142	1200
600	1215	1300
650	1289	1400
700	1362	1500

[a]GRE = 2(GMAT) + 100.

Thus, except for scores at the low end (which are not particularly relevant because students with low scores are not admitted), the current rule overpredicts the GRE based on the GMAT score. Thus, the current conversion biases decisions in favor of those taking the GMAT test as compared to those taking the GRE test. Since the students entering the economics department take the GRE test, the current rule results in decisions unfavorable to the economics department.

Regression with No Constant Term

Sometimes the regression equation is estimated with the constant term excluded. This is called regression through the origin. This arises either because economic theory suggests an equation with no constant term or we end up with a regression equation with no constant term because of some transformations in the variables. (These are discussed in Section 5.4.)

In this case the normal equations and other formulas will be the same as before, except that there will be no "mean corrections." That is $S_{xx} = \sum x_i^2$, $S_{xy} = \sum x_i y_i$ and $S_{yy} = \sum y_i^2$, etc. Consider the data in Table 3.2. We have

$$S_{xx} = 668, S_{xy} = 789 \text{ and } S_{yy} = 952$$

$$\hat{\beta} = S_{xy}/S_{xx} = 789/688 = 1.181$$

$$\hat{\sigma}^2 = \frac{1}{n-1}(S_{yy} - S_{xy}^2/S_{xx}) = \frac{1}{9}\left[952 - \frac{(789)^2}{668}\right] = 2.23$$

$$\text{estimate of } V(\hat{\beta}) = \hat{\sigma}^2/S_{xx} = 2.23/668 = 0.00334$$

$$\text{SE}(\hat{\beta}) = 0.058$$

$$r^2 = S_{xy}^2/(S_{xx}S_{yy}) = 0.979$$

Thus, the regression equation is

$$y = 1.181x \quad r^2 = 0.98$$
$$\underset{(0.058)}{}$$

Compared to the regression with the constant term, the results look better! The t-ratio for $\hat{\beta}$ has increased from 3 to 20. The r^2 has increased dramatically from 0.52 to 0.98. Students often come to me with high R^2's (sometimes 0.9999) when they fit a regression without a constant term and claim that they got better fits. But this is spurious; one has to look at which equation predicts better.

Some computer regression programs allow the option of not including a constant term but do not give the correct r^2. Note that $1 - r^2 = \text{RSS}/S_{yy}$. If the RSS is calculated from a regression with no constant term, but S_{yy} is calculated with the mean correction, then we can even get a negative r^2. Even if we do not get a negative r^2, we can get a very low r^2. For instance, in the example with data from Table 3.2, we have RSS = 20.08 from the regression with no constant term and S_{yy} (with mean correction) = 30.4. Hence, $r^2 = 0.34$ when calculated (wrongly) this way.

3.6 Analysis of Variance for the Simple Regression Model

Yet another item that is often presented in connection with the simple linear regression model is the *analysis of variance*. This is the breakdown of the total sum of squares (TSS) into the explained sum of squares (ESS) and the residual sum of squares (RSS). The purpose of presenting the table is to test the significance of the explained sum of squares. In this case this amounts to testing the significance of β. Table 3.3 presents the breakdown of the total sum of squares.

Under the assumptions of the model, RSS/σ^2 has a χ^2-distribution with $(n - 2)$ degrees of freedom. ESS/σ^2, on the other hand, has a χ^2-distribution with 1 degree of freedom *only if* the true β is equal to zero. Further, these two χ^2-distributions are independent. (All these results are proved in the appendix to this chapter.)

Thus under the assumption that $\beta = 0$, we have the F-statistic (σ^2 cancels) $F = (\text{ESS}/1)/(\text{RSS}/(n - 2))$, which has an F-distribution with d.f. 1 and $(n - 2)$. This F-statistic can be used to test the hypothesis that $\beta = 0$.

For the data in Table 3.2 we are considering, the analysis of variance is presented in Table 3.4. The F-statistic is $F = 15.75/1.83 = 8.6$.

Note that the t-statistic for testing the significance of β is $\hat{\beta}/\text{SE}(\hat{\beta}) = 0.75/0.256 = 2.93$ and the F-statistic obtained from the analysis of variance Table 3.4 is the square of the t-statistic. Thus in the case of a simple linear regression model, the analysis of variance table does not give any more information. We will see in Chapter 4 that in the case of multiple regression this is not the case. What the analysis of variance table provides there

Table 3.3 Analysis of variance for the simple regression model

Source of Variation	Sum of Squares	Degrees of Freedom	Mean Square
x	$\text{ESS} = \hat{\beta}S_{xy}$	1	ESS/1
Residual	$\text{RSS} = S_{yy} - \hat{\beta}S_{xy}$	$n - 2$	$\text{RSS}/(n - 2)$
Total	$\text{TSS} = S_{yy}$	$n - 1$	

Table 3.4   Analysis of variance for the data in
Table 3.2

Source of Variation	Sum of Squares	Degrees of Freedom	Mean Square
x	15.75	1	15.75
Residual	14.65	8	1.83
Total	30.4	9	

is a test of significance for all the regression parameters together. Note that

$$\text{ESS} = \hat{\beta}S_{xy} = r^2 S_{yy}$$

and

$$\text{RSS} = S_{yy} - \hat{\beta}S_{xy} = (1 - r^2)S_{yy}$$

Hence the F-statistic can also be written as

$$F = \frac{r^2}{(1 - r^2)/(n - 2)} = \frac{(n - 2)r^2}{1 - r^2}$$

Since $F = t^2$ we get

$$r^2 = \frac{t^2}{t^2 + (n - 2)}$$

We can check in our illustrative example that $t^2 = 8.6$ and $(n - 2) = 8$. Hence

$$r^2 = \frac{8.6}{8.6 + 8} = \frac{8.6}{16.6} = 0.52$$

as we obtained earlier. The formula

$$\boxed{r^2 = \frac{t^2}{t^2 + (n - 2)}}$$

gives the relationship between the t-ratio for testing the hypothesis $\beta = 0$ and the r^2. We will derive a similar formula in Chapter 4.

3.7   Prediction with the Simple Regression Model

The estimated regression equation $\hat{y} = \hat{\alpha} + \hat{\beta}x$ is used for predicting the value of y for given values of x and the estimated equation $\hat{x} = \hat{\alpha}' + \hat{\beta}'y$ is used for predicting the values of x for given values of y. We will illustrate the procedures with reference to the prediction of y given x.

Let x_0 be the given value of x. Then we predict the corresponding value y_0 of y by

$$\hat{y}_0 = \hat{\alpha} + \hat{\beta} x_0 \qquad (3.11)$$

The true value y_0 is given by

$$y_0 = \alpha + \beta x_0 + u_0$$

where u_0 is the error term.

Hence the prediction error is

$$\hat{y}_0 - y_0 = (\hat{\alpha} - \alpha) + (\hat{\beta} - \beta)x_0 - u_0$$

Since $E(\hat{\alpha} - \alpha) = 0$, $E(\hat{\beta} - \beta) = 0$, and $E(u_0) = 0$ we have

$$E(\hat{y}_0 - y_0) = 0$$

This equation shows that the predictant given by equation (3.11) is unbiased. Note that the predictant is unbiased in the sense that $E(\hat{y}_0) = E(y_0)$ since both $\hat{y}_0$ and y_0 are random variables.

The variance of the prediction error is

$$V(\hat{y}_0 - y_0) = V(\hat{\alpha} - \alpha) + x_0^2 V(\hat{\beta} - \beta) + 2x_0 \operatorname{cov}(\hat{\alpha} - \alpha, \hat{\beta} - \beta) + V(u_0)$$

$$= \sigma^2 \left(\frac{1}{n} + \frac{\bar{x}^2}{S_{xx}} \right) + \sigma^2 \frac{x_0^2}{S_{xx}} - 2x_0 \sigma^2 \frac{\bar{x}}{S_{xx}} + \sigma^2$$

$$= \sigma^2 \left[1 + \frac{1}{n} + \frac{(x_0 - \bar{x})^2}{S_{xx}} \right]$$

Thus the variance increases the farther away the value of x_0 is from $\bar{x}$, the mean of the observations on the basis of which $\hat{\alpha}$ and $\hat{\beta}$ have been computed. This is illustrated in Figure 3.5, which shows the confidence bands for y.

If x_0 lies within the range of the sample observations on x, we can call it within-sample prediction, and if x_0 lies outside the range of the sample observations, we call the prediction out-of-sample prediction. As an illustration, consider a consumption function estimated on the basis of 12 observations. The equation is (this is just a hypothetical example)

$$y = 10.0 + 0.90x$$

where y = consumer expenditures
$\quad\quad\ \ x$ = disposable income

We are given $\hat{\sigma}^2 = 0.01$, $\bar{x} = 200$, and $S_{xx} = 4000$. Given $x_0 = 250$, our prediction of y_0 is

$$\hat{y}_0 = 10.0 + 0.9(250) = 235$$

$$\mathrm{SE}(\hat{y}_0) = \sqrt{0.01 \left(1 + \frac{1}{12} + \frac{2500}{4000} \right)} = 0.131$$

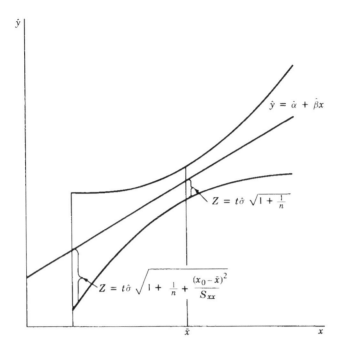

Figure 3.5 Confidence bands for prediction of y given x. [Confidence bands shown are $\hat{y} \pm Z$, where $Z = t\text{SE}(\hat{y})$ and t is the t-value used]

Since $t = 2.228$ from the t-tables with 10 degrees of freedom, the 95% confidence interval for y_0 is $235 \pm 2.228(0.131) = 235 \pm 0.29$, that is $(234.71, 235.29)$.

Prediction of Expected Values

Sometimes given x_0, it is not y_0 but $E(y_0)$ that we would be interested in predicting; that is, we are interested in the mean of y_0, not y_0 as such. We will give an illustrative example of this. Since $E(y_0) = \alpha + \beta x_0$, we would be predicting this by $\hat{E}(y_0) = \hat{\alpha} + \hat{\beta} x_0$, which is the same as $\hat{y}_0$ that we considered earlier. Thus our prediction would be the same whether it is y_0 or $E(y_0)$ that we want to predict. However, the prediction error would be different and the variance of the prediction error would be different (actually smaller). This means that the confidence intervals we generate would be different. The prediction error now is

$$\hat{E}(y_0) - E(y_0) = (\hat{\alpha} - \alpha) + (\hat{\beta} - \beta)x_0$$

Note that this is the same as the prediction error $\hat{y}_0 - y_0$ with $-u_0$ missing. Since the variance of this is σ^2, we have to subtract σ^2 from the error variance we obtained earlier. Thus

$$\text{var}[\hat{E}(y_0) - E(y_0)] = \sigma^2 \left[\frac{1}{n} + \frac{(x_0 - \bar{x})^2}{S_{xx}} \right]$$

The standard error of the prediction is given by the square root of this expression after substituting $\hat{\sigma}^2$ for σ^2. The confidence intervals are given by $\hat{E}(y_0) \pm t\text{SE}$, where t is the appropriate t-value.

Illustrative Example

Consider the sample of the athletic sportswear store considered in Section 3.3 earlier. The regression equation estimated from the data from 5 months presented there is

$$\hat{y} = 1.0 + 1.2x \quad \bar{x} = 3.0 \quad \text{RSS} = 8.8$$

Suppose that the sales manager wants us to predict what the sales revenue will be if advertising expenditures are increased to \$600. He would also like a 90% confidence interval for his prediction.

We have $x_0 = 6$. Hence

$$\hat{y}_0 = 1.0 + 1.2(6) = 8.2$$

The variance of the prediction error is

$$\sigma^2 \left[1 + \frac{1}{5} + \frac{(6-3)^2}{10} \right] = 2.1\sigma^2$$

Since

$$\hat{\sigma}^2 = \frac{\text{RSS}}{\text{d.f.}} = \frac{8.8}{3} = 2.93$$

the standard error of the prediction is

$$\sqrt{2.1(2.93)} = \sqrt{6.153} = 2.48$$

The 5% point from the t-distribution with d.f. 3 is 2.353. The 90% confidence interval for y_0 given $x_0 = 6$ is, therefore

$$8.2 \pm 2.48(2.353) = (2.36, 14.04)$$

Thus the 90% confidence interval for sales revenue if advertising expenditures are \$600 is (\$2360; \$14,040).

Consider now the case where the sales manager wants us to predict the *average* sales per month over the next two years when advertising expenditures are \$600 per month. He also wants a 90% confidence interval for the prediction.

Now we are interested in predicting $E(y_0)$, not y_0. The prediction is still given by $1.0 + 1.2(6) = 8.2$. The variance of the prediction error is now

$$\sigma^2 \left[\frac{1}{5} + \frac{(6-3)^2}{10} \right] = 1.1\sigma^2$$

Substituting $\hat{\sigma}^2 = 2.93$ as before and taking the square root, we now get the standard error as

$$\text{SE}[\hat{E}(y_0)] = 1.795$$

The 90% confidence interval now is

$$8.20 \pm 2.353(1.795) = 8.20 \pm 4.22$$

Thus the 90% confidence interval for the *average* sales is ($3980; $12,420). Note that this confidence interval is narrower than the one we obtained for $\hat{y}_0$.

3.8 Outliers

Very often it happens that the estimates of the regression parameters are influenced by a few extreme observations or outliers. This problem can be detected if we study the residuals from the estimated regression equation. Actually, a detailed analysis of residuals should accompany every estimated equation. Such analysis will enable us to see whether we are justified in making the assumptions that:

1. The error variance $V(u_i) = \sigma^2$ for all i. This problem is treated in Chapter 5.
2. The error terms are serially independent. This problem is treated in Chapter 6.
3. The regression relationship is linear. This problem is treated in Section 3.9.

What we will be concerned with here is detecting some outlying observations using analysis of residuals. A more detailed discussion of analysis of residuals is given in Chapter 12. Actually, what we are doing is a diagnostic checking of our patient (regression equation) to see whether anything is wrong.

An *outlier* is an observation that is far removed from the rest of the observations. This observation is usually generated by some unusual factors. However, when we use the least squares method this single observation can produce substantial changes in the estimated regression equation. In the case of a simple regression we can detect outliers simply by plotting the data. However, in the case of multiple regression such plotting would not be possible and we have to analyze the residuals $\hat{u}_i$.

A good example to show that a simple presentation of the regression equation with the associated standard errors and r^2 does not give us the whole picture is given by Anscombe.[5] There are four data sets presented in Table 3.5. The values of x for the first three data sets are the same. All four data sets give the same regression equation.

For all of the four data sets, we have the following statistics:

$$n = 11 \qquad \bar{x} = 9.0 \qquad \bar{y} = 7.5$$
$$S_{xx} = 110.0 \qquad S_{yy} = 41.25 \qquad S_{xy} = 55.0$$

The regression equation is

$$\hat{y} = 3.0 + \underset{(0.118)}{0.5x} \quad r^2 = 0.667$$

$$\text{regression sum of squares} = 27.50 \ (1 \text{ d.f.})$$

$$\text{residual sum of squares} = 13.75 \ (9 \text{ d.f.})$$

---

[5]F. J. Anscombe, "Graphs in Statistical Analysis," *The American Statistician*, Vol. 27, No. 1, February 1973, pp. 17–21.

Table 3.5 Four data sets that give an identical regression equation

Data Set:		1–3	1	2	3	4	4
Variable:		x	y	y	y	x	y
Observation	1	10.0	8.04	9.14	7.46	8.0	6.58
	2	8.0	6.95	8.14	6.77	8.0	5.76
	3	13.0	7.58	8.74	12.74	8.0	7.71
	4	9.0	8.81	8.77	7.11	8.0	8.0
	5	11.0	8.33	9.26	7.81	8.0	8.47
	6	14.0	9.96	8.10	8.84	8.0	7.04
	7	6.0	7.24	6.13	6.08	8.0	5.25
	8	4.0	4.26	3.10	5.39	19.0	12.50
	9	12.0	10.84	9.13	8.15	8.0	5.56
	10	7.0	4.82	7.26	6.42	8.0	7.91
	11	5.0	5.68	4.74	5.73	8.0	6.89

Although the regression equations are identical, the four data sets exhibit widely different characteristics. This is revealed when we see the plots of the four data sets. These plots are shown in Figure 3.6.

Data set 1 shown in Figure 3.6(i) shows no special problems. Figure 3.6(ii) shows that the regression line should not be linear. Figure 3.6(iii) shows how a single outlier has twisted the regression line slightly. If we omit this one observation (observation 3), we would have obtained a slightly different regression line. Figure 3.6(iv) shows how an outlier can produce an entirely different picture. If that one observation (observation 8) is omitted, we would have a vertical regression line.

We have shown graphically how outliers can produce drastic changes in the regression estimates. Next we give some real-world examples.

Some Illustrative Examples

Example 1

This example consists of the estimation of the consumption function for the United States for the period 1929–1984. Table 3.6 gives the data on per capita disposable income (Y) and per capita consumption expenditures (C) both in constant dollars for the United States. The data are not continuous. They are for 1929, 1933, and then continuous from 1939. The continuous data for 1929–1939 can be obtained from an earlier President's Economic Report (say, for 1972), but these data are in 1958 dollars and thus we have to link the two series.[6] We have not attempted this.

We will estimate a regression of C on Y. It was estimated by the SAS regression package. The results are as follows:

$$\hat{C} = \underset{(58.124)}{-24.944} + \underset{(0.018)}{0.911Y} \quad r^2 = 0.9823$$

---

[6]The data for 1929–1970 at 1958 prices have been analyzed in G. S. Maddala, *Econometrics* (New York: McGraw-Hill, 1977), pp. 84–86. These data are given as an exercise.

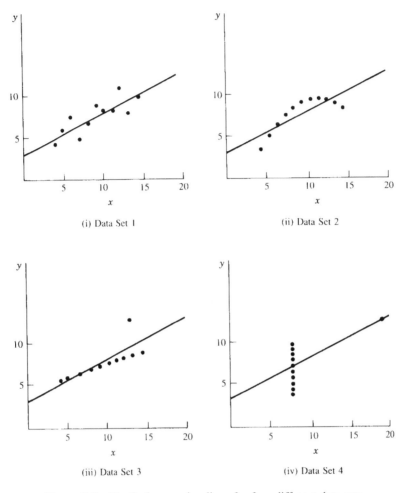

Figure 3.6 Identical regression lines for four different data sets

The t-value for β is $0.911/0.018 = 50.47$ and it can be checked that $r^2 = t^2/[t^2 + (n - 2)]$ and $n = 48$. (The figures have all been rounded to three decimals from the computer output.) The next step is to examine the residuals. These are presented in Table 3.7. One can easily notice the large negative residuals for observations 6, 7, 8, and 9. These observations are outliers. They correspond to the war years 1942–1945 with strict controls on consumer expenditures. We therefore discard these observations and reestimate the equation. The equation now is

$$\hat{C} = \underset{(22.353)}{85.725} + \underset{(0.007)}{0.885Y} \quad r^2 = 0.9975$$

Earlier the intercept was not significantly different from zero. Now it is significantly positive. Further, the estimate of the marginal propensity to consume is significantly lower

Table 3.6 Per capita personal consumption expenditures (C) and per capita disposable personal income (Y) (in 1972 dollars) for the United States, 1929–1984

Year	C	Y	Year	C	Y	Year	C	Y
1929	1765	1883	1957	2416	2660	1977	3924	4280
1933	1356	1349	1958	2400	2645	1978	4057	4441
1939	1678	1754	1959	2487	2709	1979	4121	4512
1940	1740	1847	1960	2501	2709	1980	4093	4487
1941	1826	2083	1961	2511	2742	1981	4131	4561
1942	1788	2354	1962	2583	2813	1982	4146	4555
1943	1815	2429	1963	2644	2865	1983	4303	4670
1944	1844	2483	1964	2751	3026	1984	4490	4941
1945	1936	2416	1965	2868	3171			
1946	2129	2353	1966	2979	3290			
1947	2122	2212	1967	3032	3389			
1948	2129	2290	1968	3160	3493			
1949	2140	2257	1969	3245	3564			
1950	2224	2392	1970	3277	3665			
1951	2214	2415	1971	3355	3752			
1952	2230	2441	1972	3511	3860			
1953	2277	2501	1973	3623	4080			
1954	2278	2483	1974	3566	4009			
1955	2384	2582	1975	3609	4051			
1956	2410	2653	1976	3774	4158			

Source: Economic Report of the President, 1984, p. 261.

Table 3.7 Residuals for the consumption function estimated from the data in Table 3.6 (rounded to the first decimal)

Observation	Residual	Observation	Residual	Observation	Residual
1	75.0	17	24.2	33	24.1
2	152.4	18	41.6	34	−35.9
3	105.5	19	57.4	35	−37.1
4	82.8	20	18.8	36	20.5
5	−46.1	21	18.4	37	−67.9
6	−330.9	22	16.0	38	−60.2
7	−372.2	23	44.8	39	−55.4
8	−392.4	24	58.8	40	12.1
9	−239.4	25	38.7	41	51.0
10	11.0	26	46.0	42	37.4
11	132.4	27	59.7	43	36.7
12	68.4	28	20.1	44	31.5
13	109.4	29	5.0	45	2.1
14	70.5	30	7.6	46	22.5
15	39.5	31	−29.5	47	74.8
16	31.8	32	3.7	48	15.0

(0.885 compared to 0.911).[7] The estimated residuals from this equation are presented in Table 3.8. We do not see any exceptionally large residual (except perhaps for observation 5, which is 1941), nor the long runs of positive and negative residuals as in Table 3.7.

Example 2

As a second example, consider the data presented in Table 3.9. They give teenage unemployment rates and unemployment benefits in Australia for the period 1962–1980. We will estimate some simple regressions of unemployment rates on unemployment benefits (in constant dollars) and present an analysis of the residuals.[8]

Defining

$$y_1 = \text{unemployment rate for male teenagers}$$

$$y_2 = \text{unemployment rate for female teenagers}$$

$$x = \text{unemployment benefit (constant dollars)}$$

we get the following regressions:

$$\hat{y}_1 = \underset{(1.234)}{2.478} + \underset{(0.035)}{0.212x} \quad r^2 = 0.690$$

$$\hat{y}_2 = \underset{(1.410)}{3.310} + \underset{(0.039)}{0.226x} \quad r^2 = 0.660$$

Table 3.8 Estimated residuals for the consumption function omitting the war years (1942–1945)

Observation	Residual	Observation	Residual	Observation	Residual
1	12.4	20	−24.2	35	−52.1
2	76.1	21	−24.4	36	8.3
3	39.6	22	−27.2	37	−74.5
4	19.2	23	3.2	38	−68.6
5	−103.7	24	17.2	39	−62.8
10	−39.7	25	−2.0	40	7.5
11	78.1	26	7.1	41	49.5
12	16.1	27	22.1	42	40.0
13	56.3	28	−13.4	43	41.1
14	20.8	29	−24.8	44	35.2
15	−9.6	30	−19.1	45	7.7
16	−16.6	31	−53.8	46	28.0
17	−22.7	32	−17.8	47	83.2
18	−5.8	33	4.3	48	30.3
19	12.6	34	−53.1		

[7]There is an increase in r^2 as well but the two r^2's are not comparable. To compare the two we have to calculate the r^2 between C and $\hat{C}$ from the first equation for just the 44 observations (excluding the war years). Then this recomputed r^2 will be comparable to the r^2 reported here.

[8]These are not the equations estimated by Gregory and Duncan. We are just estimating some simple regressions which may not be very meaningful.

Table 3.9 Teenage unemployment rates and unemployment benefits

Year	Teenage Unemployment Rate (%)		Unemployment Benefit for 16- and 17-Year-Olds	
	Males	Females	Nominal Dollars	Constant Dollars 1981
1962	4.5	5.9	3.50	13.3
1963	3.4	4.5	3.50	13.2
1964	2.5	4.4	3.50	12.7
1965	4.4	5.1	3.50	12.2
1966	3.1	5.5	3.50	11.9
1967	4.1	5.7	3.50	11.6
1968	4.7	6.0	3.50	11.3
1969	5.8	6.3	4.50	14.1
1970	5.7	5.1	4.50	13.4
1971	6.9	6.1	4.50	12.5
1972	8.6	9.3	7.50	20.0
1973	7.6	7.8	23.00	54.1
1974	11.9	12.3	31.00	62.7
1975	14.6	16.7	36.00	63.8
1976	13.6	15.6	36.00	55.8
1977	17.1	18.8	36.00	51.1
1978	16.4	18.8	36.00	47.4
1979	15.9	18.9	36.00	43.1
1980	15.7	17.6	36.00	39.5

Source: R. G. Gregory and R. C. Duncan, "High Teenage Unemployment: The Role of Atypical Labor Supply Behavior," *Economic Record*, Vol. 56, December 1980, pp. 316–330.

The equation suggests that an increase in unemployment benefit leads to an increase in the unemployment rate. However, the residuals from the two equations presented in Table 3.10 show very large absolute residuals for 1973, 1974, and 1977–1980.

Suppose that, as in Example 1, we delete these observations and reestimate the equations. The estimates are

$$\hat{y}_1 = \underset{(0.610)}{2.156} + \underset{(0.023)}{0.203x} \quad r^2 = 0.876$$

$$\hat{y}_2 = \underset{(0.394)}{2.799} + \underset{(0.015)}{0.225x} \quad r^2 = 0.955$$

The estimates of the coefficients of x did not change much. The r^2 values are higher but again to compare the r^2 values we have to compute the implied r^2 from the first equation using just these 13 observations. (The r^2 we compute is for y and $\hat{y}$.)

However, is the deletion of the six observations with high residuals the correct procedure in this case? The answer is "no." In Example 1 the deletion of the war years was justified because the behavior of consumers was affected by wartime controls. In

Table 3.10 Residuals from the regressions of
unemployment rates on unemployment
benefits

Year	Regression of y_1	Regression of y_2
1962	−0.80	−0.42
1963	−1.88	−1.80
1964	−2.67	−1.78
1965	−0.67	−0.97
1966	−1.90	−0.50
1967	−0.84	−0.23
1968	−0.18	0.13
1969	0.33	−0.20
1970	0.38	−1.24
1971	1.77	−0.04
1972	1.88	1.47
1973	−6.34	−7.73
1974	−3.89	−5.20
1975	−1.42	−1.04
1976	−0.72	−0.33
1977	3.78	3.93
1978	3.86	4.77
1979	4.27	5.84
1980	5.04	5.35

this example there are no such controls. However, the large residuals are due to lags in behavior. First, with an increase in unemployment benefit rate, there will be an increase in the labor force participation. There will be time lags involved in this. Next there are the time lags involved in qualifying for benefits, filing of claims, receipt of benefits, and so on. Thus there are substantial time lags between x and y_1, and x and y_2. The large negative residuals in 1973 and 1974 and the positive residuals in 1977–1980 are a consequence of this. Further, one can see a trend in these residuals from 1973 to 1980. Thus the solution to this problem is not a deletion of observations as in the previous example of the consumption function but a reformulation of the problem taking account of labor force participation rates, time lags, and so on. This analysis is much too complicated for our purpose here. The example serves to illustrate the point that not all "outliers" should be deleted.

3.9 Alternative Functional Forms for Regression Equations

We saw earlier with reference to Figure 3.6(ii) that sometimes the relationship between y and x can be nonlinear rather than linear. In this case we have to assume an appropriate functional form for the relationship. There are several functional forms that can be used which, after some transformations of the variables, can be brought into the usual linear regression framework that we have been discussing.

For instance, for the data points depicted in Figure 3.7(a), where y is increasing more slowly than x, a possible functional form is $y = \alpha + \beta \log x$. This is called a *semilog form*,

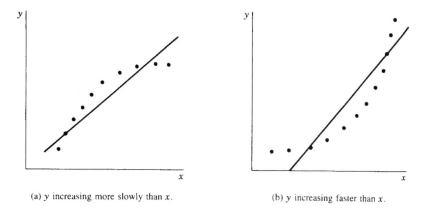

(a) y increasing more slowly than x.   (b) y increasing faster than x.

Figure 3.7   Data sets for which linear regression is inappropriate

since it involves the logarithm of only one of the two variables x and y. In this case, if we redefine a variable $X = \log x$, the equation becomes $y = \alpha + \beta X$. Thus we have a linear regression model with the explained variable y and the explanatory variable $X = \log x$.

For the data points depicted in Figure 3.7(b), where y is increasing faster than x, a possible functional form is $y = Ae^{\beta x}$. In this case we take logs of both sides and get another kind of semilog specification:

$$\log y = \log A + \beta x$$

If we define $Y = \log y$ and $\alpha = \log A$, we have

$$Y = \alpha + \beta x$$

which is in the form of a linear regression equation.

An alternative model one can use is

$$y = Ax^{\beta}$$

In this case taking logs of both sides, we get

$$\log y = \log A + \beta \log x$$

In this case β can be interpreted as an elasticity. Hence this form is popular in econometric work. This is called a *double-log specification* since it involves logarithms of both x and y. Now define $Y = \log y$, $X = \log x$, and $\alpha = \log A$. We have

$$Y = \alpha + \beta X$$

which is in the form of a linear regression equation. An illustrative example is given at the end of this section.

There is, of course, a difference between those functional forms in which we transform the variable x and those in which we transform the variable y. This becomes clear when we introduce the error term u. For instance, when we write the transformed equation with an additive error, which we do before we use the least squares method, that is, we write

$$Y = \alpha + \beta X + u$$

we are assuming that the original equation in terms of the untransformed variables is

$$y = Ax^\beta e^u$$

that is, the error term enters exponentially and in a multiplicative fashion. If we make the assumption of an additive error term in the original equation, that is,

$$y = Ax^\beta + u$$

then there is no way of transforming the variables that would enable us to use the simple methods of estimation described here. Estimation of this model requires nonlinear least squares.

Some other functional forms that are useful when the data points are as shown in Figure 3.8 are

$$Y = \alpha + \frac{\beta}{x}$$

or

$$Y = \alpha + \frac{\beta}{\sqrt{x}}$$

In the first case we define $X = 1/x$ and in the second case we define $X = 1/\sqrt{x}$. In both cases the equation is linear in the variables after the transformation. It is

$$Y = \alpha + \beta X$$

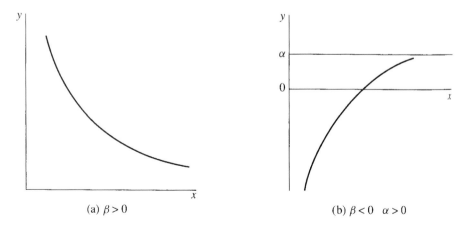

(a) $\beta > 0$ (b) $\beta < 0$ $\alpha > 0$

Figure 3.8 (a) y decreases with increasing x; (b) y increases with increasing x

If $\beta > 0$, the relationship is as shown in Figure 3.8(a). If $\beta < 0$, the relationship is as shown in Figure 3.8(b).

Some other nonlinearities can be handled by what is known as "search procedures." For instance, suppose that we have the regression equation

$$y = \alpha + \frac{\beta}{x + \gamma} + u$$

The estimates of α, β, and γ are obtained by minimizing

$$\sum \left(y_i - \alpha - \frac{\beta}{x_i + \gamma} \right)^2$$

We can reduce this problem to one of the simple least squares as follows: For each value of γ, we define the variable $Z_i = 1/(x_i + \gamma)$ and estimate α and β by minimizing

$$\sum (y_i - \alpha - \beta z_i)^2$$

We look at the residual sum of squares in each case and then choose that value of γ for which the residual sum of squares is minimum. The corresponding estimates of α and β are the least squares estimates of these parameters. Here we are "searching" over different values of γ. This search would be a convenient one only if we had some prior notion of the range of this parameter. In any case there are convenient nonlinear regression programs available nowadays. Our purpose here is to show how some problems that do not appear to fall in the framework of simple regression at first sight can be transformed into that framework by a suitable redefinition of the variables.

Illustrative Example

In Table 3.11 we present data on output, labor input, and capital input for the United States for the period 1929–1967. The variables are

$X =$ index of gross national product in constant dollars

$L_1 =$ labor input index (number of persons adjusted for hours of work

and educational level)

$L_2 =$ persons engaged

$K_1 =$ capital input index (capital stock adjusted for rates of utilization)

$K_2 =$ capital stock in constant dollars

Since output depends on both labor and capital inputs we have to estimate a regression equation of X on L and K. This is what we will illustrate in Chapter 4. For the present let us study the relationship between output and labor input, and output and capital input. We will use L_1 for labor input and K_1 for capital input.

From the data it is clear that X has risen faster than L_1 or K_1. Hence we have a situation depicted in Figure 3.7(b). This suggests a semilogarithmic form or a double-logarithmic form. The advantage with the latter is that we can interpret the coefficients as elasticities.

Table 3.11   Output, labor input, and capital input for the United
States, 1929–1967

Year	X	L_1	L_2	K_1	K_2
1929	189.8	173.3	44.151	87.8	888.9
1930	172.1	165.4	41.898	87.8	904.0
1931	159.1	158.2	36.948	84.0	900.2
1932	135.6	141.7	35.686	78.3	883.6
1933	132.0	141.6	35.533	76.6	851.4
1934	141.8	148.0	37.854	76.0	823.7
1935	153.9	154.4	39.014	77.7	805.3
1936	171.5	163.5	40.765	79.1	800.4
1937	183.0	172.0	42.484	80.0	805.5
1938	173.2	161.5	40.039	77.6	817.6
1939	188.5	168.6	41.443	81.4	809.8
1940	205.5	176.5	43.149	87.0	814.1
1941	236.0	192.4	46.576	96.2	830.3
1942	257.8	205.1	49.010	104.4	857.9
1943	277.5	210.1	49.695	110.0	851.4
1944	291.1	208.8	48.668	107.8	834.6
1945	284.5	202.1	47.136	102.1	819.3
1946	274.0	213.4	49.950	97.2	812.3
1947	279.9	223.6	52.350	105.9	851.3
1948	297.6	228.2	53.336	113.0	888.3
1949	297.7	221.3	51.469	114.9	934.6
1950	328.9	228.8	52.972	124.1	964.6
1951	351.4	239.0	55.101	134.5	1021.4
1952	360.4	241.7	55.385	139.7	1068.5
1953	378.9	245.2	56.226	147.4	1100.3
1954	375.8	237.4	54.387	148.9	1134.6
1955	406.7	245.9	55.718	158.6	1163.2
1956	416.3	251.6	56.770	167.1	1213.9
1957	422.8	251.5	56.809	171.9	1255.5
1958	418.4	245.1	55.023	173.1	1287.9
1959	445.7	254.9	56.215	182.5	1305.8
1960	457.3	259.6	56.743	189.0	1341.4
1961	466.3	258.1	56.211	194.1	1373.9
1962	495.3	264.6	57.078	202.3	1399.1
1963	515.5	268.5	57.540	205.4	1436.7
1964	544.1	275.4	58.508	215.9	1477.8
1965	579.2	285.3	60.055	225.0	1524.4
1966	615.6	297.4	62.130	236.2	1582.2
1967	631.1	305.0	63.162	247.9	1645.3

Source: L. R. Christensen and D. W. Jorgenson, "U.S. Real Product and
Real Factor Input 1929–67," *Review of Income and Wealth*, March 1970.

Moreover, even though X has been rising faster than L_1 (or K_1), it has not been rising
that fast to justify a regression of $\log X$ on L_1 (or K_1). We will therefore estimate the
equation in the double-logarithmic form:

$$\log X = \alpha + \beta \log L_1 + u$$

A regression of X on L_1 gave the following results (figures in parentheses are standard errors):

$$\hat{X} = -338.01 + 3.052L_1 \quad r^2 = 0.9573$$
$$\underset{(23.55)}{} \quad \underset{(0.106)}{}$$

When we examined the residuals,[9] they were positive for the first 12 observations, negative for the middle 17 observations, and positive again for the last 10 observations. This is what we would expect if the relationship is as shown in Figure 3.7(b) and we estimate a linear function.

The results of a regression of $\log X$ on $\log L_1$ gave the following results (figures in parentheses are standard errors):

$$\log \hat{X} = -5.480 - 2.084 \log L_1 \quad r^2 = 0.9851$$
$$\underset{(0.226)}{} \quad \underset{(0.042)}{}$$

This equation still exhibited some pattern in the residuals, although not to the same extent as the linear form.

The log-linear form is more easy to interpret. The elasticity of output with respect to the labor input is about 2. This is, of course, very high, but this is because of the omission of the capital input. In Chapter 4 we estimate the production function with the capital input included.

In this particular example, estimation in the linear form is not very meaningful. A linear production function assumes perfect substitutability between capital and labor inputs. However, it is given here as an example illustrating Figure 3.7(b).

Note that r^2 is higher in the log-linear form than in the linear form. But this comparison does not mean anything because the dependent variables in the two equations are different. (This point is discussed in greater detail in Section 5.6.)

Finally, in the case of a simple regression it is always easy to plot the points on a graph and see what functional form is the most appropriate for the problem. This is not possible in the case of multiple regression with several explanatory variables. Hence greater use is made of the information from the residuals.

*3.10 Inverse Prediction in the Least Squares Regression Model

At times a regression model of y on x is used to make a prediction of the value of x which could have given rise to a new observation y. As an illustration suppose that we have data on sales and advertising expenditures for a number of firms in an industry. There is a new firm whose sales are known but advertising expenditures are not. In this case we would want to get an estimate of the advertising expenditures of this firm.

In this example we have the estimated regression equation

$$\hat{y} = \hat{\alpha} + \hat{\beta}x$$

---

[9]To economize on space, we are not presenting the residuals here. We present residuals for some multiple regression equations in Chapter 12.

*Optional section.

and given a new value y_0 of y we have to estimate the value x_0 of x that could have given rise to y_0 and obtain a confidence interval for x_0.

To simplify the algebra we will write $x' = x - \bar{x}$ and $y' = y - \bar{y}$. Then the estimated regression equation can be written as

$$\hat{y}' = \hat{\beta} x' \tag{3.12}$$

We are given the value y_0 of y and we are asked to estimate the value x_0 of x that could have given rise to y_0. Define $y_0' = y_0 - \bar{y}$ and $x_0' = x_0 - \bar{x}$. The estimate of x_0' given from equation (3.12) is

$$\hat{x}_0' = \frac{y_0'}{\hat{\beta}} \tag{3.13}$$

The main problem is that of obtaining confidence limits for $\hat{x}_0'$ because both y_0' and $\hat{\beta}$ are normally distributed. One can use a method suggested by Fieller for this purpose.[10] This method can be used to obtain confidence intervals for ratios of estimators. These problems also arise in our discussion of simultaneous equation models and distributed lag models in later chapters. Another problem that falls in this same category is to estimate the value of x at which the value of y is zero. This is given by

$$\hat{x} = -\frac{\hat{\alpha}}{\hat{\beta}}$$

and $\hat{\alpha}$ and $\hat{\beta}$ have joint normal distribution.

Let us define $\theta = E(y_0'/\beta)$ (θ is just x_0' and is thus a constant). Then the variable $y_0' - \theta\hat{\beta}$ is normally distributed with mean zero and variance

$$\sigma^2 \left(1 + \frac{1}{n}\right) + \theta^2 \frac{\sigma^2}{S_{xx}} \tag{3.14}$$

[since $\text{var}(y_0') = \text{var}(y_0 - \bar{y}) = \sigma^2 + \sigma^2/n$ and $\text{cov}(y_0, \hat{\beta}) = 0$]. Substituting the estimate $\hat{\sigma}^2$ of σ^2 derived earlier into equation (3.14), we get the estimated variance. Thus

$$t = \frac{y_0' - \theta\hat{\beta}}{\sqrt{\hat{\sigma}^2(1 + 1/n) + \theta^2(\hat{\sigma}^2/S_{xx})}}$$

has a t-distribution with d.f. $(n - 2)$. This can be used to construct a confidence interval for θ, which is what we need. For instance, to get a 95% confidence interval for θ, we find a value t_0 of t (from the t-tables for $n - 2$ degrees of freedom) such that

$$\text{Prob}(t^2 < t_0^2) = 0.95$$

To get the limits for θ we solve the quadratic equation

$$(y_0' - \hat{\beta}\theta)^2 - t_0^2\hat{\sigma}^2 \left(1 + \frac{1}{n} + \frac{\theta^2}{S_{xx}}\right) = 0 \tag{3.15}$$

---

[10]C. E. Fieller, "A Fundamental Formula in the Statistics of Biological Assay and Some Applications," *Quarterly Journal of Pharmacy*, 1944, pp. 117–123.

The roots θ_1 and θ_2 of this equation give the confidence limits.

As an illustration, suppose that we have estimated a consumption function on the basis of 10 observations and the equation is[11]

$$y = 10.0 + 0.9x$$

and $\bar{x} = 200$, $\bar{y} = 185$, $\hat{\sigma}^2 = 5.0$, and $S_{xx} = 400$. Consider the predicted value of x for $y = 235$. This is clearly $\hat{x}_0 = 250$.

To get the confidence interval for x_0 we solve equation (3.15). Note that $y_0' = 235 - 185 = 50$ and $t_0 = 2.306$ from the t-tables for 8 degrees of freedom. Thus we have to solve the equation

$$(50 - 0.9\theta)^2 - (2.306)^2(5)\left(1 + \frac{1}{10} + \frac{\theta^2}{400}\right) = 0$$

or

$$2500 - 90\theta + 0.81\theta^2 = 29.25 + 0.066\theta^2$$

or

$$0.744\theta^2 - 90\theta + 2470.75 = 0$$

The two roots are $\theta_1 = 42.12$ and $\theta_2 = 78.85$. Thus the 95% confidence interval for x_0' is (42.12, 78.85) or for x_0 it is (242.12, 278.85). Note that the confidence interval obtained by the Fieller method need not be symmetric around the predicted point value (which in this case is $x_0 = 250$).

If the samples are large, we can use the asymptotic distributions and this will give symmetric intervals. However, for small samples we have to use the method described here.

*3.11   Stochastic Regressors

In Section 3.2 we started explaining the regression model saying that the values x_1, x_2, ..., x_n of x are given constants, that is, x is not a random variable. This view is perhaps valid in experimental work but not in econometrics. In econometrics we view x as a random variable (except in special cases where x is time or some dummy variable). In this case the observations x_1, x_2, ..., x_n are realizations of the random variable x. This is what is meant when we say that the regressor is stochastic.

Which of the results we derived earlier are valid in this case? First, regarding the unbiasedness property of the least squares estimators, that property holds provided that the random variables x and u are independent. (This is proved in the appendix to this chapter.) Second, regarding the variances of the estimators and the tests of significance that we derived, these have to be viewed as conditional on the realized values of x.

---

[11] We have changed the illustrative example slightly from the one we discussed in Section 3.7 because with $\hat{\sigma}^2 = 0.01$ and $S_{xx} = 4000$ we get a symmetric confidence interval for θ. We have changed the example to illustrate the point that we need not get a symmetric confidence interval.

To obtain any concrete results, with stochastic regressors, we need to make some assumptions about the joint distribution of y and x. It has been proved that when y and x are jointly normally distributed, the formulas we have derived for the estimates of the regression parameters, their standard errors, and the test statistics are all valid. Since the proof of this proposition is beyond the scope of this book, we will not pursue it here.[12]

Thus, with stochastic regressors the formulas we have derived are valid if y and x are jointly normally distributed. Otherwise, they have to be considered as valid conditional on the observed x's.

*3.12   The Regression Fallacy

In the introduction to this chapter we mentioned a study by Galton, who analyzed the relationship between the height of children and the height of parents. Let

$$x = \text{mid-parent height}$$

$$y = \text{mean height (at maturity) of all children whose}$$

$$\text{mid-parent height is } x$$

Galton plotted y against x and found that the points lay close to a straight line but the slope was less than 1.0. What this means is that if the mid-parent height is 1 inch above $\bar{x}$, the children's height (on the average) is less than 1 inch above $\bar{y}$. There is thus a "*regression* of children's heights toward the average."

A phenomenon like the one observed by Galton could arise in several situations where y and x have a bivariate normal distribution and thus is a mere statistical artifact. That is why it is termed a "regression fallacy." To see this, first we have to derive the conditional distributions $f(x|y)$ and $f(y|x)$ when x and y are jointly normal. We will show that both these conditional distributions are normal.

The Bivariate Normal Distribution

Suppose that X and Y are *jointly* normally distributed with means, variances, and covariance given by

$$E(X) = m_x \quad E(Y) = m_y \quad V(X) = \sigma_x^2 \quad V(Y) = \sigma_y^2$$

and

$$\text{cov}(X, Y) = \rho \sigma_x \sigma_y$$

Then the joint density of X and Y is given by

$$f(x, y) = \left(2\pi\sigma_x\sigma_y\sqrt{1-\rho^2}\right)^{-1}\exp(Q)$$

---

[12] In the case of multiple regression, proof of this proposition can be found in several papers. A clear exposition of all the propositions is given in: Allan R. Simpson, "A Tale of Two Regressions," *Journal of the American Statistical Association*, September 1974, pp. 682–689.

where

$$Q = -\frac{1}{2(1-\rho^2)} \left[\left(\frac{x-m_x}{\sigma_x} \right)^2 - 2\rho \frac{x-m_x}{\sigma_x} \frac{y-m_y}{\sigma_y} + \left(\frac{y-m_y}{\sigma_y} \right)^2 \right]$$

Now completing the square in x and simplifying, we get

$$Q = -\frac{1}{2(1-\rho^2)} \left(\frac{x-m_x}{\sigma_x} - \rho \frac{y-m_y}{\sigma_y} \right)^2 - \frac{1}{2} \left(\frac{y-m_y}{\sigma_y} \right)^2$$

Thus

$$f(x, y) = f(x|y)f(y)$$

where

$$f(y) = \frac{1}{\sqrt{2\pi}\sigma_y} \exp \left[-\frac{1}{2\sigma_y^2} (y-m_y)^2 \right]$$

and

$$f(x|y) = \frac{1}{\sqrt{2\pi}\sigma_x \sqrt{1-\rho^2}} \exp \left[-\frac{1}{2\sigma_x^2(1-\rho^2)} (x-m_{x \cdot y})^2 \right]$$

where

$$m_{x \cdot y} = m_x + \frac{\rho\sigma_x}{\sigma_y} (y-m_y)$$

Thus we see that the marginal distribution of y is normal with mean m_y and variance σ_y^2. The conditional distribution of x given y is also normal with

$$\text{mean} = m_x + \frac{\rho\sigma_x}{\sigma_y} (y-m_y)$$

and

$$\text{variance} = \sigma_x^2(1-\rho^2)$$

The conditional distribution of y given x is just obtained by interchanging x and y in the foregoing relationships.

Thus for a bivariate normal distribution, both the marginal and conditional distributions are univariate normal.[13] Note that the converse need not be true, that is, if the marginal distributions of X and Y are normal, it does not necessarily follow that the joint distribution of X and Y is bivariate normal. In fact, there are many nonnormal bivariate distributions for which the marginal distributions are both normal.[14]

---

[13]This result is more general. For the multivariate normal distribution we can show that all marginal and conditional distributions are also normal.

[14]C. J. Kowalski, "Non-normal Bivariate Distributions with Normal Marginals," *The American Statistician*, Vol. 27, No. 3, June 1973, pp. 103–106; K. V. Mardia, *Families of Bivariate Distributions* (London: Charles Griffin, 1970).

Galton's Result and the Regression Fallacy

Consider now the mean of Y for given value of X. We have seen that it is given by

$$E(Y|X = x) = m_y + \frac{\rho \sigma_y}{\sigma_x}(x - m_x)$$

The slope of this line is $\rho \sigma_y / \sigma_x$ and if $\sigma_x \simeq \sigma_y$, since $\rho < 1$ we have the result that the slope is less than 1, as observed by Galton.

By the same token, if we consider $E(X|Y = y)$ we get

$$E(X|Y = y) = m_x + \frac{\rho \sigma_x}{\sigma_y}(y - m_y)$$

Since we have assumed that $\sigma_x = \sigma_y$, the slope of this line is also less than unity (note that we are taking dx/dy as the slope in this case). Thus if Galton had considered the conditional means of parents' heights for given values of offspring's heights, he would have found a "regression" of parents' heights toward the mean. It is not clear what Galton would have labeled this regression.

Such "regression" toward average is often found when considering variables that are jointly normally distributed and that have almost the same variance. This has been a frequent finding in the case of test scores. For example, if

$$x = \text{score on the first test}$$

and

$$y = \text{score on the second test}$$

then considering the conditional means of y for given values of x shows a regression toward the mean in the second test. This does not mean that the students' abilities are converging toward the mean. This finding in the case of test scores has been named a *regression fallacy* by the psychologist Thorndike.[15]

This, then, is the story of the term "regression." The term as it is used now has no implication that the slope be less than 1.0, nor even the implication of linearity.

A Note on the Term: "Regression"

Throughout this chapter (and subsequent chapters as well) the regression of a random variable y on another variable x was understood to be the *mean* of y conditional on x. Manski[16] argues that one can also consider median or mode instead of mean. Then we have "median regression," "mode regression," and in fact "variance regression," and so on. Since a discussion of these concepts is too involved for our purpose, we shall not discuss them in detail here.

---

[15]F. L. Thorndike, "Regression Fallacies in the Matched Group Experiment," *Psychometrika*, Vol. 7, No. 2, 1942, pp. 85–102.

[16]C. F. Manski, "Regression," *Journal of Economic Literature*, Vol. 29, 1991, pp. 34–50.

Summary

1. The present chapter discusses the simple linear regression model with one explained variable and one explanatory variable. The term regression literally means "backwardation," but that is not the way it is used today, although that is the way it originated in statistics. A brief history of the term is given in Section 3.1, but it is discussed in greater detail in Section 3.12 under the title "regression fallacy."

2. Two methods — the method of moments (Section 3.3) and the method of least squares (Section 3.4) — are described for the estimation of the parameters in the linear regression model. A third method, the method of maximum likelihood (ML), is presented in the appendix. For the normal linear regression model all of them give the same results.

3. Given two variables y and x there is always the question of whether to regress y on x or to regress x on y. This question can always be answered if we know how the data were generated or if we know the direction of causality. In some cases both the regressions make sense. These issues are discussed in the latter part of Section 3.4.

4. In Sections 3.5 and 3.6 we discuss the procedures of obtaining:

(a) Standard errors of the coefficients.
(b) Confidence intervals for the parameters.
(c) Tests of hypotheses about the parameters.

The exact formulas need not be repeated here because they are summarized in the respective sections. The main results that need to be presented are:

(a) The estimates of the regression parameters with their standard errors. Sometimes the t-ratios are given instead of the standard errors. If we are interested in obtaining confidence intervals, the standard errors are more convenient. If we are interested in tests of hypotheses, presentation of the t-ratios is sometimes more convenient.
(b) The coefficient of determination of r^2.
(c) SEE or SER. This is an estimate of the standard deviation σ of the error term.

However, these statistics by themselves are not sufficient. In Section 3.8 we give an example of four different data sets that give the same regression output.

5. While considering the predictions from the linear regression model, it is important to note whether we are obtaining predictions for the particular value of y or for the mean value of y. Although the point prediction is the same for the two cases, the variance of the prediction error and the confidence intervals we generate will be different. This is illustrated with an example in Section 3.7. Sometimes we are interested in the inverse prediction: prediction of x given y. This problem is discussed in Section 3.10.

6. In regression analysis it is important to examine the residuals and see whether there are any systematic patterns in them. Such analysis would be useful in detecting outliers and judging whether the linear functional form is appropriate. The problem of detection of outliers and what to do with them is discussed in Section 3.8. In Section 3.9 we discuss different functional forms where the least squares model can be used with some transformations of the data.

7. Throughout the chapter, the explanatory variable is assumed to be fixed (or a nonrandom variable). In Section 3.10 (optional) we discuss briefly what happens if this assumption is relaxed.

8. The last three sections and the appendix, which contains some derivations of the results and a discussion of the ML estimation method and the LR test, can be omitted by beginning students.

Exercises

More difficult exercises are marked with an asterisk.

1. Comment briefly on the meaning of each of the following:
   (a) Estimated coefficient.
   (b) Standard error.
   (c) *t*-Statistic.
   (d) *R*-squared.
   (e) Sum of squared residuals.
   (f) Standard error of the regression.
   (g) Best linear unbiased estimator.

2. A store manager selling TV sets observes the following sales on 10 different days. Calculate the regression of y on x where

$$y = \text{number of TV sets sold}$$

$$x = \text{number of sales representatives}$$

y	3	6	10	5	10	12	5	10	10	8
x	1	1	1	2	2	2	3	3	3	2

Present all the items mentioned in Exercise 1.

3. The following data present experience and salary structure of University of Michigan economists in 1983–1984. The variables are

$$y = \text{salary (thousands of dollars)}$$

$$x = \text{years of experience (defined as years since receiving Ph.D.)}$$

y	x	y	x	y	x	y	x
63.0	43	44.5	22	45.0	18	51.3	12
54.3	32	43.0	21	50.7	17	50.3	12
51.0	32	46.8	20	37.5	17	62.4	10
39.0	30	42.4	20	61.0	16	39.3	10
52.0	26	56.5	19	48.1	16	43.2	9
55.0	25	55.0	19	30.0	16	40.4	7
41.2	23	53.0	19	51.5	15	37.7	6
47.7	22	55.0	18	40.6	13	27.7	3

Source: R. H. Frank, "Are Workers Paid Their Marginal Products?," *The American Economic Review*, September 1984, Table 1, p. 560.

Calculate the regression of y on x. Present all the items mentioned in Exercise 1. Give reasons why the regression does or does not make sense. Calculate the residuals to see whether there are any outliers. Would you discard these observations or look for other explanations?

4. Show that the simple regression line of y against x coincides with the simple regression line of x against y if and only if $r^2 = 1$ (where r is the sample correlation coefficient between x and y).

5. In the regression model $y_i = \alpha + \beta x_i + u_i$ if the sample mean $\bar{x}$ of x is zero, show that $\text{cov}(\hat{\alpha}, \hat{\beta}) = 0$, where $\hat{\alpha}$ and $\hat{\beta}$ are the least squares estimators of α and β.

6. The following are data on

$$y = \text{quit rate per 100 employees in manufacturing}$$

$$x = \text{unemployment rate}$$

The data are for the United States and cover the period 1960–1972.

Year	y	x	Year	y	x
1960	1.3	6.2	1967	2.3	3.6
1961	1.2	7.8	1968	2.5	3.3
1962	1.4	5.8	1969	2.7	3.3
1963	1.4	5.7	1970	2.1	5.6
1964	1.5	5.0	1971	1.8	6.8
1965	1.9	4.0	1972	2.2	5.6
1966	2.6	3.2			

(a) Calculate a regression of y on x.

$$y = \alpha + \beta x + u$$

(b) Construct a 95% confidence interval for β.
(c) Test the hypothesis $H_0 : \beta = 0$ against the alternative $\beta \neq 0$ at the 5% significance level.
(d) Construct a 90% confidence interval for $\sigma^2 = \text{var}(u)$.
(e) What is likely to be wrong with the assumptions of the classical normal linear model in this case? Discuss.

7. Let $\hat{u}_i$ be the residuals in the least squares fit of y_i against x_i $(i = 1, 2, \ldots, n)$. Derive the following results:

$$\sum_{i=1}^{n} \hat{u}_i = 0 \quad \text{and} \quad \sum_{i=1}^{n} x_i \hat{u}_i = 0$$

8. Given data on y and x explain what functional form you will use and how you will estimate the parameters if
(a) y is a proportion and lies between 0 and 1.
(b) $x > 0$ and x assumes very large values relative to y.
(c) You are interested in estimating a constant elasticity of demand function.

9. At a large state university seven undergraduate students who are majoring in economics were randomly selected from the population and surveyed. Two of the survey questions asked were: (1) What was your grade-point average (GPA) in the preceding term? (2) What was the average number of hours spent per week last term in the Orange and Brew? The Orange and Brew is a favorite and only watering hole on campus. Using the data below, estimate with ordinary least squares the equation

$$G = \alpha + \beta H$$

where G is GPA and H is hours per week in Orange and Brew. What is the expected sign for β? Do the data support your expectations?

Student	GPA, G	Hours per Week in Orange and Brew, H
1	3.6	3
2	2.2	15
3	3.1	8
4	3.5	9
5	2.7	12
6	2.6	12
7	3.9	4

10. Two variables y and x are believed to be related by the following stochastic equation:

$$y = \alpha + \beta x + u$$

where u is the usual random disturbance with zero mean and constant variance σ^2. To check this relationship one researcher takes a sample size of 8 and estimates β with OLS. A second researcher takes a different sample size of 8 and also estimates β with OLS. The data they used and the results they obtained are as follows:

Researcher 1		Researcher 2	
y	x	y	x
4.0	3	2.0	1
4.5	3	2.5	1
4.5	3	2.5	1
3.5	3	1.5	1
4.5	4	11.5	10
4.5	4	10.5	10
5.5	4	10.5	10
5.0	4	11.0	10

$$\hat{y} = \underset{(1.20)}{1.875} + \underset{(0.339)}{0.750x}$$

$$r^2 = 0.45$$

$$\hat{\sigma} = 0.48$$

$$\hat{y} = \underset{(0.27)}{1.5} + \underset{(0.038)}{0.970x}$$

$$r^2 = 0.99$$

$$\hat{\sigma} = 0.48$$

Can you explain why the standard error of $\hat{\beta}$ for the first researcher is larger than the standard error of $\hat{\beta}$ for the second researcher?

11. Since the variance of the regression coefficient $\hat{\beta}$ varies inversely with the variance of x, it is often suggested that we should drop all the observations in the middle range of x and use only the extreme observations on x in the calculation of $\hat{\beta}$. Is this a desirable procedure?

12. Suppose you are attempting to build a model that explains aggregate savings behavior as a function of the level of interest rates. Would you rather sample during a period of fluctuating interest rates or a period of stable interest rates? Explain.

13. A small grocery store notices that the price it charges for oranges varies greatly throughout the year. In the off-season the price was as high as 60 cents per orange, and during the peak season they had special sales where the price was as low as 10 cents, 20 cents, and 30 cents per orange. Below are six weeks of data on the quantity of oranges sold (y) and price (x):

Oranges Sold, y (100s)	Price per Orange, x (cents)
6	10
4	20
5	30
4	40
3	50
1	60

Assuming that the demand for oranges is given by the linear equation

$$y = \alpha + \beta x + u$$

estimate the parameters of this equation. Calculate a 90% confidence interval for the quantity of oranges sold in week seven if the price is 25 cents per orange during that week.

14. In Exercise 9 we considered the relationship between grade-point average (GPA) and weekly hours spent in the campus pub. Suppose that a freshman economics student has been spending 15 hours a week in the Orange and Brew during the first two weeks of class. Calculate a 90% confidence interval for his GPA in his first quarter of college if he continues to spend 15 hours per week in the Orange and Brew. Suppose that this freshman remains in school for four years and completes the required 12 quarters for graduation. Calculate a 90% confidence interval for his final cumulative GPA. Suppose that the minimum requirements for acceptance into most graduate schools for economics is 3.25. What are the chances that this student will be able to go to graduate school after completing his undergraduate studies?

15. A local night entertainment establishment in a small college town is trying to decide whether they should increase their weekly advertising expenditures on the campus radio station. The last six weeks of data on monthly revenue (y) and radio advertising expenditures (x) are given in the accompanying table. What would their predicted revenues be next week if they spent \$500 on radio commercials. Give a 90% confidence interval for next week's revenues. Suppose that they spend \$500 per week for the next 10 weeks. Give a 90% confidence interval for the *average* revenue over the next 10 weeks.

Week	Revenue, y (thousands of dollars)	Radio Advertising Expenditure, x (hundreds of dollars)
1	1.5	1.0
2	2.0	2.5
3	1.0	0.0
4	2.0	3.0
5	3.5	4.0
6	1.5	2.0

*16. In the model $y_i = \alpha + \beta x_i + u_i, i = 1, \ldots, N$, the following sample moments have been calculated from 10 observations:

$$\sum y_i = 8 \quad \sum x_i = 40 \quad \sum y_i^2 = 26 \quad \sum x_i^2 = 200 \quad \sum x_i y_i = 20$$

(a) Calculate the predictor of y for $x = 10$ and obtain a 95% confidence interval for it.

(b) Calculate the value of x that could have given rise to a value of $y = 1$ and explain how you would find a 95% confidence interval for it.

*17. (*Instrumental variable method*) Consider the linear regression model

$$y_i = \alpha + \beta x_i + u_i$$

One of the assumptions we have made is that x_i are uncorrelated with the errors u_i. If x_i are correlated with u_i, we have to look for a variable that is uncorrelated with u_i (but correlated with x_i). Let us call this variable z_i. z_i is called an *instrumental variable*. Note that as explained in Section 3.3, the assumptions $E(u) = 0$ and $\text{cov}(x, u) = 0$ are replaced by

$$\sum \hat{u}_i = 0 \quad \text{and} \quad \sum x_i \hat{u}_i = 0$$

However, since x and u are correlated we cannot use the second condition. But since z and u are uncorrelated, we use the condition $\text{cov}(z, u) = 0$. This leads to the normal equations

$$\sum \hat{u}_i = 0 \quad \text{and} \quad \sum z_i \hat{u}_i = 0$$

The estimates of α and β obtained using these two equations are called the instrumental variable estimates. From a sample of 100 observations, the following data are obtained:

$$\sum y_i^2 = 350$$

$$\sum x_i y_i = 150 \qquad \sum x_i^2 = 400$$

$$\sum z_i y_i = 100 \qquad \sum z_i x_i = 200 \qquad \sum z_i^2 = 400$$

$$\sum y_i = 100 \qquad \sum x_i = 100 \qquad \sum z_i = 50$$

Calculate the instrumental variables estimates of α and β.

Let the instrumental variable estimator of β be denoted by β^* and the least squares estimator of β by $\hat{\beta}$. Show that $\beta^* = S_{zy}/S_{zx}$ with S_{zy} and S_{zx} defined in a similar manner to S_{xx}, S_{xy} and S_{yy}. Show that

$$\text{var}(\beta^*) = \sigma^2 \cdot \frac{S_{zz}}{(S_{zx})^2} = \frac{\sigma^2}{S_{xx}} \left(\frac{1}{r_{xz}^2} \right)$$

Hence, $\text{var}(\beta^*) \geq \text{var}(\hat{\beta})$. To test whether x and u are correlated or not, the following test has been suggested (Hausman's test discussed in Chapter 12):

$$t = \frac{\beta^* - \hat{\beta}}{\sqrt{\hat{V}(\beta^*) - \hat{V}(\hat{\beta})}} \sim N(0, 1)$$

Apply this test to test whether $\text{cov}(x, u) = 0$ with the data provided.

*18. *(Stochastic regressors)* In the linear regression model

$$y_i = \alpha + \beta x_i + u_i$$

suppose that $x_i \sim \text{IN}(0, \lambda^2)$. What is the (asymptotic) distribution of the least squares estimator $\hat{\beta}$? Just state the result. Proof not required.

*19. Consider the regression model

$$y_i = \alpha + \beta x_i + u_i$$

$$u_i \sim \text{IN}(0, 1) \qquad i = 1, 2, \ldots, T$$

Suppose that the model refers to semiannual data, but the data available are either:
1. Annual data, that is

$$\bar{y}_1 = y_1 + y_2$$

$$\bar{y}_2 = y_3 + y_4$$

$$\bar{y}_3 = y_5 + y_6 \quad \text{etc.}$$

with $\bar{x}_1, \bar{x}_2, \bar{x}_3, \ldots$ defined analogously (assuming that T is even), or:

2. Moving average data, that is

$$y_1^* = \frac{y_1 + y_2}{2}$$

$$y_2^* = \frac{y_2 + y_3}{2}$$

$$y_3^* = \frac{y_3 + y_4}{2} \quad \text{etc.}$$

with $x_1^*, x_2^*, x_3^*, \ldots$ defined analogously.
   (a) What are the properties of the error term in the regression model with each set of data: (y_i, x_i), $(\bar{y}_i, \bar{x}_i)$, and (y_i^*, x_i^*)?
   (b) How would you estimate β in the case of annual data?
   (c) How would you estimate β in the case of moving average data?
   (d) Would you rather have the annual data or moving average data? Why?

*20. Given data on y and x explain how you will estimate the parameters in the following equations by using the ordinary least squares method. Specify the assumptions you make about the errors.
   (a) $y = \alpha x^\beta$
   (b) $y = \alpha e^{\beta x}$
   (c) $y = \alpha + \beta \log x$

   (d) $y = \dfrac{x}{\alpha x - \beta}$

   (e) $y = \dfrac{e^{\alpha + \beta x}}{1 + e^{\alpha + \beta x}}$

   (f) $y = \alpha + \beta \sqrt{x}$

   (g) $y = \alpha + e^{\beta x}$

   (h) $y = \alpha + \dfrac{\beta}{x - c}$

Appendix to Chapter 3

In the following proofs we will use the compact notation $\sum y_i$ for $\sum_{i=1}^{n} y_i$.

(1) Proof That the Least Squares Estimators are Best Linear Unbiased Estimators (BLUE)

Consider the regression model

$$y_i = \beta x_i + u_i \quad i = 1, 2, \ldots, n$$

For simplicity we have omitted the constant term. We assume that u_i are independently distributed with mean 0 and variance σ^2. Since x_i are given constants, $E(y_i) = \beta x_i$ and $\text{var}(y_i) = \sigma^2$.

The least squares estimator of β is

$$\hat{\beta} = \frac{\sum x_i y_i}{\sum x_i^2} = \sum c_i y_i$$

where $c_i = x_i / \sum x_i^2$. Thus $\hat{\beta}$ is a linear function of the sample observations y_i and hence is called a *linear estimator*. Also,

$$E(\hat{\beta}) = \sum c_i E(y_i)$$

$$= \sum \left(\frac{x_i}{\sum x_i^2} \right) (\beta x_i) = \beta \frac{\sum x_i^2}{\sum x_i^2} = \beta$$

Hence $\hat{\beta}$ is an *unbiased linear estimator*. We have to show that this is the best (i.e., has minimum variance among the class of linear unbiased estimators). Consider any linear estimator

$$\tilde{\beta} = \sum d_i y_i$$

If it is unbiased, we have

$$E(\tilde{\beta}) = \sum d_i E(y_i) = \sum d_i (x_i \beta) = \beta$$

Hence we should have $\sum d_i x_i = 1$. Since y_i are independent with a common variance σ^2, we have

$$\mathrm{var}(\tilde{\beta}) = \sum d_i^2 \sigma^2$$

We have to find d_i so that this variance is minimum subject to the condition that $\sum d_i x_i = 1$.

Hence we minimize $\sum d_i^2 - \lambda(\sum d_i x_i - 1)$, where λ is the Lagrangian multiplier. Differentiating with respect to d_i and equating to zero, we get

$$2d_i - \lambda x_i = 0 \quad \text{or} \quad d_i = \frac{\lambda}{2} x_i$$

Multiplying both sides by x_i and summing over i, we get

$$\sum d_i x_i = \frac{\lambda}{2} \sum x_i^2$$

But $\sum d_i x_i = 1$. Hence

$$\lambda = \frac{2}{\sum x_i^2}$$

Thus we get

$$d_i = \frac{\lambda}{2} x_i = \frac{x_i}{\sum x_i^2}$$

which are the least squares coefficients c_i. Thus the least squares estimator has the minimum variance in the class of linear unbiased estimators. This minimum variance is

$$\text{var}(\hat{\beta}) = \sum c_i^2 \sigma^2 = \sum \left(\frac{x_i}{\sum x_i^2}\right)^2 \sigma^2 = \frac{\sigma^2}{\sum x_i^2}$$

Note that what we have shown is that the least squares estimator has the minimum variance among the class of linear unbiased estimators. It is possible in some cases that we can find nonlinear estimators that are unbiased but have a smaller variance than the linear estimators. However, if u_i are independently and *normally* distributed, then the least squares estimator has minimum variance among all (linear and nonlinear) unbiased estimators. Proofs of these propositions are beyond our scope and hence are omitted.

(2) Derivation of the Sampling Distributions of the Least Squares Estimators

Consider the regression model

$$y_i = \alpha + \beta x_i + u_i \quad u_i \sim \text{IN}(0, \sigma^2)$$

We have seen that the least squares estimators are

$$\hat{\beta} = \frac{S_{xy}}{S_{xx}} \quad \text{and} \quad \hat{\alpha} = \bar{y} - \hat{\beta}\bar{x}$$

To derive the sampling distributions, we will use the following result:
If $y_1, y_2, \ldots, y_n$ are independent normal with variance σ^2, and if

$$L_1 = \sum c_i y_i \quad \text{and} \quad L_2 = \sum d_i y_i$$

are two linear functions of y_i, then L_1 and L_2 are jointly normally distributed

$$\text{var}(L_1) = \sigma^2 \sum c_i^2 \quad \text{var}(L_2) = \sigma^2 \sum d_i^2$$

and

$$\text{cov}(L_1, L_2) = \sigma^2 \sum c_i d_i$$

We now write $\hat{\beta}$ and $\hat{\alpha}$ as linear functions of y_i. First we write

$$S_{xy} = \sum (x_i - \bar{x})(y_i - \bar{y})$$

$$= \sum (x_i - \bar{x}) y_i - \bar{y} \sum (x_i - \bar{x})$$

$$= \sum (x_i - \bar{x}) y_i$$

The last term is zero since $\sum (x_i - \bar{x}) = 0$. Thus

$$\hat{\beta} = \frac{S_{xy}}{S_{xx}} = \sum c_i y_i$$

where $c_i = (x_i - \bar{x})/S_{xx}$. Also,

$$\hat{\alpha} = \bar{y} - \hat{\beta}\bar{x} = \frac{1}{n}\sum y_i - \bar{x}\frac{\sum(x_i - \bar{x})y_i}{S_{xx}} = \sum d_i y_i$$

where

$$d_i = \frac{1}{n} - \frac{\bar{x}(x_i - \bar{x})}{S_{xx}}$$

Thus

$$\operatorname{var}(\hat{\beta}) = \sum c_i^2 \sigma^2 = \frac{\sigma^2}{(S_{xx})^2}\sum(x_i - \bar{x})^2 = \frac{\sigma^2}{S_{xx}}$$

$$\operatorname{var}(\hat{\alpha}) = \sum d_i^2 \sigma^2$$

$$= \sigma^2 \sum\left[\frac{1}{n^2} + \left(\frac{\bar{x}}{S_{xx}}\right)^2(x_i - \bar{x})^2 - \frac{2\,\bar{x}}{n\,S_{xx}}(x_i - \bar{x})\right]$$

But

$$\sum(x_i - \bar{x}) = 0 \quad \sum(x_i - \bar{x})^2 = S_{xx} \quad \sum\frac{1}{n^2} = \frac{1}{n}$$

Hence

$$\operatorname{var}(\hat{\alpha}) = \sigma^2\left(\frac{1}{n} + \frac{\bar{x}^2}{S_{xx}}\right)$$

$$\operatorname{cov}(\hat{\alpha}, \hat{\beta}) = \sum c_i d_i \sigma^2$$

$$= \sigma^2 \sum\left(\frac{x_i - \bar{x}}{S_{xx}}\right)\left[\frac{1}{n} - \frac{\bar{x}(x_i - \bar{x})}{S_{xx}}\right]$$

$$= \sigma^2\left(-\frac{\bar{x}}{S_{xx}}\right)$$

Also, $\hat{\alpha}$ and $\hat{\beta}$ are unbiased estimators. So $E(\hat{\alpha}) = \alpha$ and $E(\hat{\beta}) = \beta$. We can show this by noting that

$$E(\hat{\beta}) = \sum c_i E(y_i) = \sum c_i(\alpha + \beta x_i) = \beta$$

(since $\sum c_i\alpha = 0$ and $\sum c_i x_i = 1$). Also,

$$E(\hat{\alpha}) = E(\bar{y}) - \hat{\beta}\bar{x} = \alpha + \beta\bar{x} - \beta\bar{x} = \alpha$$

Thus we get the following results:

1. $\hat{\alpha}$ has a normal distribution with mean α and variance

$$\sigma^2\left(\frac{1}{n} + \frac{\bar{x}^2}{S_{xx}}\right)$$

2. $\hat{\beta}$ has a normal distribution with mean β and variance σ^2/S_{xx}.
3. $\text{cov}(\hat{\alpha}, \hat{\beta}) = \sigma^2(-\bar{x}/S_{xx})$.

(3) Distribution of RSS

Note that the derivation of the t-tests in the regression model depends on the result that RSS$/\sigma^2$ has a χ^2-distribution with d.f. $(n - 2)$ and that this distribution is independent of the distribution of $\hat{\alpha}$ and $\hat{\beta}$. The exact proof of this is somewhat complicated.[17] However, some intuitive arguments can be given as follows.

The estimated residual is

$$\hat{u}_i = y_i - \hat{y}_i$$

Note that $\hat{y}_i = \hat{\alpha} + \hat{\beta}x_i$ and $\hat{y}_i$ and $\hat{u}$ are uncorrelated because

$$\sum \hat{y}_i \hat{u}_i = \hat{\alpha} \sum \hat{u}_i + \hat{\beta} \sum x_i \hat{u}_i = 0$$

by virtue of the normal equations. This proves the independence between $\hat{u}_i$ and $(\hat{\alpha}, \hat{\beta})$. Note that under the assumption of normality zero correlation implies independence.

The next thing to note is that $\sum u_i^2/\sigma^2$ has a χ^2-distribution with d.f. n and $\sum u_i^2$ can be partitioned into two components as follows:

$$\sum u_i^2 = \sum (y_i - \alpha - \beta x_i)^2 = \sum (y_i - \hat{y}_i + \hat{y}_i - \alpha - \beta x_i)^2$$

$$= \sum \hat{u}_i^2 + \sum [(\hat{\alpha} - \alpha) + (\hat{\beta} - \beta)x_i]^2$$

(the cross-product term vanishes)

$$= Q_1 + Q_2 \quad \text{(say)}$$

Q_1/σ^2 has a χ^2-distribution with d.f. $(n - 2)$ and Q_2/σ^2 has a χ^2-distribution with d.f. 2. Presentation of a detailed proof involves more algebra than is intended here.

(4) The Method of Maximum Likelihood

The method of maximum likelihood (ML) is a very general method of estimation that is applicable in a large variety of problems. In the linear regression model, however, we get the same estimators as those obtained by the method of least squares.

The model is

$$y_i = \alpha + \beta x_i + u_i \quad u_i \sim \text{IN}(0, \sigma^2)$$

This implies that y_i are independently and normally distributed with respective means $\alpha + \beta x_i$ and a common variance σ^2. The joint density of the observations, therefore, is

$$f(y_1, \ldots, y_n) = \prod_{i=1}^{n} \left(\frac{1}{2\pi\sigma^2} \right)^{1/2} \exp \left[-\frac{1}{2\sigma^2} (y_i - \alpha - \beta x_i)^2 \right]$$

---

[17]It is easier to prove it with the use of matrix algebra for the multiple regression model. This proof can be found in any textbook of econometrics. See, for instance, Maddala, *Econometrics*, pp. 456–457.

This function, when considered as a function of the parameters $(\alpha, \beta, \sigma^2)$, is called the *likelihood function* and is denoted by $L(\alpha, \beta, \sigma^2)$. The ML method of estimation suggests that we choose as our estimates the values of the parameters that maximize this likelihood function. In many cases it is convenient to maximize the logarithm of the likelihood function rather than the likelihood function itself, and we get the same results since $\log L$ and L attain the maximum at the same point.

For the linear regression model we have

$$\log L = \sum_{i=1}^{n} \left[-\frac{1}{2} \log(2\pi\sigma^2) - \frac{1}{2\sigma^2}(y_i - \alpha - \beta x_i)^2 \right]$$

$$= c - \frac{n}{2} \log \sigma^2 - \frac{Q}{2\sigma^2}$$

where $c = -(n/2)\log(2\pi)$ does not involve any parameters
$$Q = \sum(y_i - \alpha - \beta x_i)^2$$

We will maximize $\log L$ first with respect to α and β and then with respect to σ. Note that it is only the third term in $\log L$ that involves α and β and maximizing this is the same as minimizing Q (since this term has a negative sign). *Thus the ML estimators of α and β are the same as the least squares estimators $\hat{\alpha}$ and $\hat{\beta}$ we considered earlier.*

Substituting $\hat{\alpha}$ for α and $\hat{\beta}$ for β we get the likelihood function which is now a function of σ only. We now have

$$\log L(\sigma) = \text{const.} - \frac{n}{2}\log\sigma^2 - \frac{\hat{Q}}{2\sigma^2}$$

$$= \text{const.} - n\log\sigma - \frac{\hat{Q}}{2\sigma^2}$$

where $\hat{Q} = \sum(y_i - \hat{\alpha} - \hat{\beta}x_i)^2$ is nothing but the residual sum of squares RSS. Differentiating this with respect to σ and equating the derivative to zero, we get

$$-\frac{n}{\hat{\sigma}} + \frac{\hat{Q}}{\hat{\sigma}^3} = 0$$

This gives the ML estimator for σ^2 as

$$\hat{\sigma}^2 = \frac{\hat{Q}}{n} = \frac{\text{RSS}}{n}$$

Note that this is different from the unbiased estimator for σ^2 which we have been using, namely, $\text{RSS}/(n-2)$. For large n the estimates obtained by the two methods will be very close. The ML method is a large-sample estimation method.

Substituting $\hat{\sigma}^2 = \hat{Q}/n$ in $\log L(\sigma)$ we get the maximum value of the log-likelihood as

$$\max_{\alpha,\beta,\sigma} \log L = c - \frac{n}{2}\log\frac{\hat{Q}}{n} - \frac{n}{2}$$

$$= c - \frac{n}{2}\log\hat{Q} + \frac{n}{2}\log n - \frac{n}{2}$$

This expression is useful for deriving tests for α, β, σ using the ML method. Since we do not change the sample size n, we will just write

$$\max \log L = \text{const.} - \frac{n}{2} \log \hat{Q}$$

or

$$\max L = \text{const.} \, (\hat{Q})^{-n/2} = \text{const.} \, (\text{RSS})^{-n/2}$$

(5) The Likelihood Ratio Test

The likelihood ratio (LR) test is a general large-sample test based on the ML method. Let θ be the set of parameters in the model and $L(\theta)$ the likelihood function. In our example θ consists of the three parameters α, β, and σ. Hypotheses such as $\beta = 0$ or $\beta = 1, \sigma = 0$ impose restrictions on these parameters. What the LR test says is that we first obtain the maximum of $L(\theta)$ without any restrictions, and with the restrictions imposed by the hypothesis to be tested. We then consider the ratio

$$\lambda = \frac{\max L(\theta) \text{ under the restrictions}}{\max L(\theta) \text{ without the restrictions}}$$

λ will necessarily be less than 1 since the restricted maximum will be less than the unrestricted maximum. If the restrictions are not valid, λ will be significantly less than 1. If they are valid, λ will be close to 1. The LR test consists of using $-2 \log_e \lambda$ as a χ^2 with d.f. k, where k is the number of restrictions. Note that it is log to the base e (natural logarithm).

In our least squares model, suppose that we want to test the hypothesis $\beta = 0$. What we do is obtain

$$\text{URSS} = \text{unrestricted residual sum of squares}$$

and

$$\text{RRSS} = \text{restricted residual sum of squares}$$

As derived in the preceding section, we have the unrestricted maximum of the likelihood function $= C(\text{URSS})^{-n/2}$ and the restricted maximum $= C(\text{RRSS})^{-n/2}$. Thus

$$\lambda = \left(\frac{\text{RRSS}}{\text{URSS}} \right)^{-n/2}$$

Hence

$$-2 \log_e \lambda = n(\log_e \text{RRSS} - \log_e \text{URSS})$$

and we use this as a χ^2 with d.f. 1. In the case of our simple regression model, this test might sound complicated. But the point is that if we want to test the hypothesis $\beta = 0$, note that

$$\text{RRSS} = S_{yy}$$

$$\text{URSS} = S_{yy}(1 - r^2)$$

Hence $-2\log_e\lambda = -n\log_e(1-r^2) = n\log_e[1/(1-r^2)]$. This we use as χ^2 with d.f. 1. Of course, in the simple regression model we would not be using this test, but the LR test is applicable in a very wide class of situations and is used in nonlinear models where small sample tests are not available.

(6) The Wald and Lagrangian Multiplier Tests

There are two other commonly used large sample tests that are based on the ML method: the W (Wald) test and the LM (Lagrangian multiplier) test. We will derive the expressions for these test statistics in the case of the simple regression model.

Note that the t-test for the hypothesis $\beta = 0$ is based on the statistic

$$t = \frac{\hat{\beta}}{\text{SE}(\hat{\beta})}$$

and in deriving $\text{SE}(\hat{\beta})$ we use an unbiased estimator for σ^2. Instead, suppose that we use the ML estimator $\hat{\sigma}^2 = \text{RSS}/n$ that we derived earlier. Then we get the Wald test. Note that since this is a large sample test we use the standard normal distribution, or the χ^2-distribution if we consider the squared test statistic. Thus

$$W = \frac{\hat{\beta}^2}{\text{estimate of } \text{var}(\hat{\beta})}$$

which we use as χ^2 with d.f. 1. Estimate of $\text{var}(\hat{\beta}) = \hat{\sigma}^2/S_{xx}$, where

$$\hat{\sigma}^2 = \frac{S_{yy}(1-r^2)}{n}$$

Noting that $\hat{\beta} = S_{xy}/S_{xx}$ we get, on simplification,

$$W = \frac{nr^2}{1-r^2}$$

For the LM test we use the restricted residual sum of squares (i.e., residual sum of squares with $\beta = 0$). This is nothing but S_{yy} and $\hat{\sigma}^2 = S_{yy}/n$. Thus, the LM test statistic is

$$LM = nr^2$$

which again has a χ^2-distribution with d.f. 1.

In summary, we have

$$\boxed{\begin{aligned} LR &= n\log(1/(1-r^2)) \\ W &= nr^2/(1-r^2) \\ LM &= nr^2 \end{aligned}}$$

Each has a χ^2-distribution with d.f. 1. These simple formulas are useful to remember and will be used in subsequent chapters. There is an interesting relationship between these test statistics that is valid for linear regression models. This is

$$W \geq LR \geq LM$$

Note that $W/n = r^2/(1 - r^2)$. Hence, $LM/n = r^2 = (W/n)/(1 + W/n)$. Also, $LR/n = \log(1/(1 - r^2)) = \log(1 + W/n)$. For $x > 0$, there is a famous inequality

$$x \geq \log_e(1 + x) \geq x/(1 + x)$$

Substituting $x = W/n$ we get

$$\frac{W}{n} \geq \frac{LR}{n} \geq \frac{LM}{n}$$

or

$$W \geq LR \geq LM$$

What this suggests is that a hypothesis can be rejected by the W test but not rejected by the LM test. An example is provided in Section 4.12.

The LR test was suggested by Neyman and Pearson in 1928. The W test was suggested by Abraham Wald in 1943. The LM test was suggested by C. R. Rao in 1948 but the name "Lagrangian multiplier" test was given in 1959 by S. D. Silvey. The test should more appropriately be called "Rao's Score Test" but since the "LM test" terminology is more common in econometrics, we shall use it here. The inequality between the test statistics was first pointed out by Berndt and Savin in 1977.

For the LR test we need the ML estimates from both the restricted and unrestricted maximization of the likelihood function. For the W test we need only the unrestricted ML estimates. For the LM test we need only the restricted ML estimates. Since the last estimates are the easiest to obtain, the LM test is very popular in econometric work.[18]

(7) Intuition Behind the LR, W, and LM Tests

The three tests described here are all based on ML estimation. Before we discuss their interrelationships, we present a few results in the theory of ML estimation.

1. $\partial \log L/\partial \theta$ is called the *score function* and is denoted by $S(\theta)$. The ML estimator $\hat{\theta}$ of θ is obtained by solving $S(\theta) = 0$.
2. The quantity $E[(-\partial^2 \log L)/\partial \theta^2]$ is called the *information on θ in the sample* and is denoted by $I(\theta)$. Intuitively speaking, the second derivative measures the curvature of the function (in this case the likelihood function). The sharper the peak is, the more the information in the sample on θ. If the likelihood function is relatively flat at the

---

[18] There is a lot of literature on the W, LR and LM tests. For a survey, see R. F. Engle, "Wald, Likelihood Ratio, and Lagrange Multiplier Tests in Econometrics," in Z. Griliches and M. D. Intrilligator (eds.), *Handbook of Econometrics*, Vol. 2 (North Holland Publishing Co., 1984).

top, this means that many values of θ are almost equally likely; that is, there is no information on θ in the sample.

3. The expression $I(\theta)$ plays a central role in the theory of ML estimation. It has been proved that under fairly general conditions, the ML estimator $\hat{\theta}$ is consistent and asymptotically normally distributed with variance $[I(\theta)]^{-1}$. This quantity is also called the information limit to the variance or the *Cramer–Rao lower bound* for the variance of the estimator $\hat{\theta}$. It is called the lower bound because it has been shown that the variance of any other consistent estimator is not less than this; that is, the ML estimator has the least variance.

4. In practice, we estimate $I(\theta)$ by $(-\partial \log L/\partial \theta^2)$, that is, omitting the expectation part. Since the derivative of a function at a point is the slope of the tangent to that function at that point, $(-\partial^2 \log L/\partial \theta^2)$ is the slope of the score function. The question is: At what point is this slope calculated? For the W test, this slope is calculated at the point given by the ML estimate $\hat{\theta}$. For the LM test, it is calculated at the point $\theta = \theta_0$ specified by the null hypothesis.

We can now show the relationship between the LR, W, and the LM tests geometrically.[19] Consider testing the null hypothesis $H_0 : \theta = \theta_0$.

Figure 3.9 shows the graph of the score function $S(\theta) = \partial \log L/\partial \theta$. The ML estimator $\hat{\theta}$ is the value of θ for which $S(\theta) = 0$. This is shown as the point C, where $S(\theta)$ crosses the θ-axis. Since

$$\int \frac{\partial \log L}{\partial \theta} d\theta = \log L(\theta)$$

we have $\int_{-\infty}^{\hat{\theta}} S(\theta) \, d\theta = \log L(\hat{\theta})$ and $\int_{-\infty}^{\theta_0} S(\theta) \, d\theta = \log L(\theta_0)$. The LR statistic is $LR = -2[\log L(\theta_0) - \log L(\hat{\theta})] = 2[\log L(\hat{\theta}) - \log L(\theta_0)]$. Hence we get

$$\boxed{LR = 2 \times (\text{area } BAC)}$$

Now consider approximating area BAC by a triangle. Draw a tangent to $S(\theta)$ at point C (i.e., $\theta = \hat{\theta}$). As mentioned earlier, $I(\theta)$ is estimated by the slope of this tangent, that is, by AD/AC.

$$\text{var}(\hat{\theta}) = \frac{1}{I(\theta)} = \frac{AC}{AD}$$

The Wald statistic is $W = (\hat{\theta} - \theta_0)^2/\text{var}(\hat{\theta}) = AC^2/(AC/AD) = (AC \times AD)$. Hence we get

$$\left| W = 2 \times (\text{area of the triangle } ADC) \right|$$

<hr />

[19]This geometric interpretation is from A. R. Pagan, "Reflections on Australian Macro Modelling," Working Paper, Australian National University, September 1981.

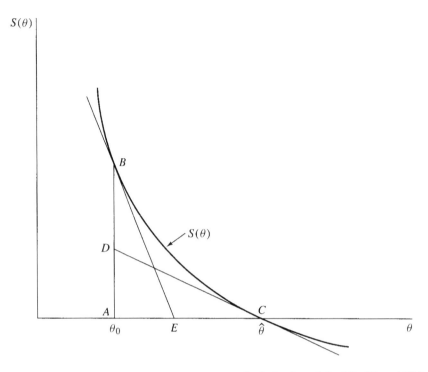

Figure 3.9 Graph of the score function and geometric derivation of the LR, W, and LM test statistics. $LR/2 = $ area BAC, $W/2 = $ area DAC, $LM/2 = $ area BAE

Now draw a tangent to $S(\theta)$ at point B (i.e., $\theta = \theta_0$). By a similar argument, we get

$$LM = 2 \times \text{(area of the triangle } BAE)$$

Thus the W and LM statistics amount to using two different triangle approximations to area BAC under the curve $S(\theta)$. They differ in computing the value of $I(\theta)$. The W statistic computes its value at $\theta = \hat{\theta}$, the ML estimate. The LM statistic computes it at $\theta = \theta_0$ and is easier to calculate because we have to estimate the model with fewer parameters (the restricted model with $\theta = \theta_0$).

(8) Methods of Solving the Likelihood Equations

Earlier (see item 4 in the appendix) we discussed the ML estimation of the parameters in the linear regression model. There we saw that the ML estimates of α and β were the same as the least squares estimates.

In many cases the computation of the ML estimates is not as straightforward and we need some iterative techniques to compute them. Here we shall explain two of the iteration methods commonly used: the Newton–Raphson method and the scoring method. For ease of exposition we shall consider the case of a single parameter θ. The generalization to several parameters involves writing down the corresponding expressions in matrix notation (using the appendix to Chapter 2).

Consider a sample of n independent observations $(y_1, y_2, \ldots, y_n)$ from a density function $f(y, \theta)$. Let $L(\theta)$ be the likelihood function. Then $\log L(\theta) = \sum_{i=1}^{n} \log f(y_i, \theta)$. A necessary condition that $\log L(\theta)$ is maximum at $\theta = \hat{\theta}$ is

$$\frac{\partial \log L}{\partial \theta} \bigg|_{\theta = \hat{\theta}} = 0$$

The equation $\partial \log L / \partial \theta = 0$ is called the likelihood equation. Sometimes it can be solved easily. But often we have to use iterative methods.

Let θ_0 be a trial value of the estimate. Then expanding $(\partial \log L / \partial \theta)$ and retaining only the first power of $\delta\theta = \theta - \theta_0$ we get

$$\frac{\partial \log L}{\partial \theta} \simeq \frac{\partial \log L}{\partial \theta_0} + \delta\theta \cdot \frac{\partial^2 \log L}{\partial \theta_0^2}$$

At the maximum $\partial \log L / \partial \theta = 0$, this gives us $\delta\theta$. Thus, the correction for the next iteration is given by

$$\theta_1 - \theta_0 = \delta\theta = \left[-\frac{\partial^2 \log L}{\partial \theta_0^2} \right]^{-1} \left[\frac{\partial \log L}{\partial \theta_0} \right]$$

We now proceed with the first and second derivatives at θ_1 and get a new estimate θ_2. We continue this iterative procedure until convergence (we should also check the value of $\log L$ at each iteration). This is the *Newton–Raphson* method. The quantity $\partial \log L / \partial \theta_0$ is sometimes called the *score* at θ_0 and is denoted by $S(\theta_0)$. Also $E[-\partial^2 \log L / \partial \theta^2]$ is called the *information on θ in the sample* and is denoted by $I(\theta)$. In the *method of scoring* we substitute $I(\theta_0)$ for $(-\partial^2 \log L / \partial \theta^2)$ in the Newton–Raphson method. The iteration method, in the method of scoring gives

$$\theta_1 = \theta_0 + S(\theta_0)/I(\theta_0)$$

The difference between the Newton–Raphson method and the method of scoring is that the former depends on *observed* second derivatives and the latter depends on *expected values* of the second derivatives.

As an illustration of the scoring method, consider the following regression model:

$$y_i = \frac{1}{x_i - \beta} + u_i$$

where u_i are IN(0, 1). We assume the variance of u_i to be unity, since we want to discuss the single-parameter case here. The log-likelihood function is

$$\log L = \text{const.} - 1/2 \sum \left(y_i - \frac{1}{x_i - \beta} \right)^2$$

$$\frac{\partial \log L}{\partial \beta} = S(\beta) = \sum \left(y_i - \frac{1}{x_i - \beta} \right) \frac{1}{(x_i - \beta)^2} = 0$$

is the likelihood equation. This is a nonlinear equation in β.

$$\frac{\partial^2 \log L}{\partial \beta^2} = \sum \left[\frac{2y_i}{(x_i - \beta)^3} - \frac{3}{(x_i - \beta)^4} \right]$$

Since

$$E(y_i) = \frac{1}{x_i - \beta}$$

we have

$$I(\beta) = E\left(\frac{-\partial^2 \log L}{\partial \beta^2} \right) = \sum \frac{1}{(x_i - \beta)^4}$$

Suppose we start with an initial value β_0. Then we calculate $S(\beta_0)$ and $I(\beta_0)$. The next value is given by

$$\beta_1 = \beta_0 + \frac{S(\beta_0)}{I(\beta_0)}$$

We next calculate $S(\beta_1)$ and $I(\beta_1)$ and proceed with this equation until convergence.

The expression $I(\beta)$ plays a central role in the theory of ML estimation. It has been proved that, under fairly general conditions, the ML estimator is consistent and asymptotically normally distributed with variance $[I(\beta)]^{-1}$. Thus, in the above problem at the final step of the iteration we get an estimate of asymptotic variance of the ML estimator as $[I(\hat{\beta})]^{-1}$.

The quantity $[I(\beta)]^{-1}$ is also known as the information limit to the variance, or alternatively as the *Cramer–Rao lower bound* for the variance of the estimator $\hat{\beta}$.

(9) Stochastic Regressors

Consider the regression model

$$y_i = \beta x_i + u_i \quad i = 1, 2, \ldots, n$$

u_i are independent with mean zero and common variance σ^2. x_i are random variables but x_i and u_j are independent for all i and j. We will show that the least squares estimator $\hat{\beta}$ is an unbiased estimator for β. We have

$$\hat{\beta} = \sum c_i y_i$$

where

$$c_i = \frac{x_i}{\sum_{j=1}^{n} x_j^2}$$

Substituting the value of y_i and simplifying, we get

$$\hat{\beta} = \beta + \sum c_i u_i$$

Since x_i and u_j are independent for all i and j, we know that c_i and u_i are independent. Thus $E(c_i u_i) = E(c_i) \cdot E(u_i) = 0$. Since $E(u_i) = 0$, we need not worry about evaluating

$E(c_i)$. Hence we get the result that

$$E(\hat{\beta}) = \beta + E\left(\sum c_i u_i\right) = \beta$$

Thus the least squares estimator is unbiased even if x_i are random variables, provided that they are independent of the error terms.

However, when we consider the variance of $\hat{\beta}$, we have to evaluate $E(c_i^2) \cdot E(u_i^2)$. The latter term is σ^2, but the former term is rather cumbersome to compute in general — hence the conclusions stated in Section 3.11.

4 Multiple Regression

What is in this Chapter?

The previous chapter considered a regression model with one explanatory variable. This chapter discusses regression models with several explanatory variables.

We start with a model with two explanatory variables, and consider statistical inference in this model. These results are then generalized to the case of k explanatory variables.

Next the concepts of multiple and partial correlations are introduced and their interrelationships are discussed.

Then there is a discussion of the prediction problems in multiple regression, analysis of variance and tests of hypotheses, and consequences of omission of relevant and inclusion of irrelevant variables.

The next topic on degrees of freedom and adjusted R^2 or $\overline{R}^2$ leads to consequences of dropping and adding explanatory variables to the equation.

Then we consider tests for stability. Here we discuss the analysis of variance test and the predictive test for stability (commonly known as the Chow test).

The final section (which is optional) discusses the LR, W, and LM tests in the multiple regression model.

This chapter is a thorough discussion of the different problems associated with multiple regression. Its mastery is essential.

The appendix to this chapter contains a discussion of the multiple regression model in matrix notation.

4.1 Introduction

In simple regression we study the relationship between an explained variable y and an explanatory variable x. In multiple regression we study the relationship between y and a number of explanatory variables $x_1, x_2, \ldots, x_k$. For instance, in demand studies we study the relationship between quantity demanded of a good and price of the good, prices of substitute goods and the consumer's income. The model we assume is

$$y_i = \alpha + \beta_1 x_{1i} + \beta_2 x_{2i} + \cdots + \beta_k x_{ki} + u_i \quad i = 1, 2, \ldots, n$$

The errors u_i are again due to measurement errors in y and errors in the specification of the relationship between y and the x's. We make the same assumptions about u_i that we made in Chapter 3. These are:

1. $E(u_i) = 0$.
2. $V(u_i) = \sigma^2$ for all i.
3. u_i and u_j are independent for all $i \neq j$.
4. u_i and x_j are independent for all i and j.
5. u_i are normally distributed for all i.
6. There are no linear dependencies in the explanatory variables, i.e., none of the explanatory variables can be expressed as an exact linear function of the others. (This assumption will be relaxed in Chapter 17.)

Also, it will be assumed that y_i is a continuous variable. (The case where it is observed as a dummy variable or as a truncated variable will be discussed in Chapter 8.)

Under the first four assumptions, we can show that the method of least squares gives estimators α, $\beta_1, \beta_2, \ldots, \beta_k$, that are unbiased and have minimum variance among the class of linear unbiased estimators. (The proofs are similar to those in Chapter 3 and are given in the appendix.)

Assumption 5 is needed for tests of significance and confidence intervals. It is not needed to prove the optimal properties of least squares estimators.

In addition to these assumptions, which are similar to those we make in the case of simple regression, we will also assume (assumption 6) that $x_1, x_2, \ldots, x_k$ are not collinear, that is, there is no deterministic linear relationship among them. For instance, suppose that we have the regression equation

$$y = \alpha + \beta_1 x_1 + \beta_2 x_2 + u$$

but x_1 and x_2 are connected by the deterministic linear relationship

$$2x_1 + x_2 = 4$$

then we can express x_2 in terms of x_1 and get $x_2 = 4 - 2x_1$ and the regression equation becomes

$$y = \alpha + \beta_1 x_1 + \beta_2 (4 - 2x_1) + u$$
$$= (\alpha + 4\beta_2) + (\beta_1 - 2\beta_2) x_1 + u$$

Thus we can estimate $(\alpha + 4\beta_2)$ and $(\beta_1 - 2\beta_2)$ but not α, β_1, β_2 separately.

A case where there is an exact linear relationship between the explanatory variables is known as exact or *perfect collinearity*. In the case of the two variables we considered, the exact relationship implies that the correlation coefficient between x_1 and x_2 is $+1$ or -1. In our analysis in this chapter we rule out perfect collinearity but not the case where the correlation between the variables is high but not perfect. When it comes to the analysis of the effect of several variables $x_1, x_2, \ldots, x_k$ on y, we have to distinguish between joint effects and partial effects. For instance, suppose that we are estimating the effect of price and income on quantity demanded; then we have to consider the joint effect of income and price and the partial effects:

1. Effect of price on quantity demanded holding income constant.
2. Effect of income on quantity demanded holding price constant.

These are the problems that we will be dealing with in this chapter. If price and income are highly correlated with each other, it is intuitively clear that it would be difficult to disentangle the separate effects of the two variables.

We start our analysis with the case of two explanatory variables and then present the formulas for the case of k explanatory variables.

4.2   A Model with Two Explanatory Variables

Consider the model

$$y_i = \alpha + \beta_1 x_{1i} + \beta_2 x_{2i} + u_i \quad i = 1, 2, \ldots, n \tag{4.1}$$

The assumptions we have made about the error term u imply that

$$E(u) = 0 \quad \text{cov}(x_1, u) = 0 \quad \text{cov}(x_2, u) = 0$$

As in the case of the simple regression model discussed in Section 3.3, we can replace these assumptions by their sample counterparts.

Let $\hat{\alpha}$, $\hat{\beta}_1$, and $\hat{\beta}_2$ be the estimators of α, β_1, and β_2, respectively. The sample counterpart of u_i is the residual

$$\hat{u}_i = y_i - \hat{\alpha} - \hat{\beta}_1 x_{1i} - \hat{\beta}_2 x_{2i}$$

The three equations to determine $\hat{\alpha}$, $\hat{\beta}_1$, and $\hat{\beta}_2$ are obtained by replacing the population assumptions by their sample counterparts:

Population Assumption	Sample Counterpart		
$E(u) = 0$	$(1/n) \sum \hat{u}_i = 0$	or	$\sum \hat{u}_i = 0$
$\text{cov}(u, x_1) = 0$	$(1/n) \sum x_{1i} \hat{u}_i = 0$	or	$\sum x_{1i} \hat{u}_i = 0$
$\text{cov}(u, x_2) = 0$	$(1/n) \sum x_{2i} \hat{u}_i = 0$	or	$\sum x_{2i} \hat{u}_i = 0$

These equations can also be obtained by the use of the least squares method and are referred to as the "normal equations."

The Least Squares Method

The least squares method says that we should choose the estimators $\hat{\alpha}$, $\hat{\beta}_1$, $\hat{\beta}_2$ of α, β_1, β_2 so as to minimize

$$Q = \sum (y_i - \hat{\alpha} - \hat{\beta}_1 x_{1i} - \hat{\beta}_2 x_{2i})^2$$

Differentiate Q with respect to $\hat{\alpha}$, $\hat{\beta}_1$, and $\hat{\beta}_2$ and equate the derivatives to zero. We get

$$\frac{\partial Q}{\partial \hat{\alpha}} = 0 \Rightarrow \sum 2(y_i - \hat{\alpha} - \hat{\beta}_1 x_{1i} - \hat{\beta}_2 x_{2i})(-1) = 0 \tag{4.2}$$

$$\frac{\partial Q}{\partial \hat{\beta}_1} = 0 \Rightarrow \sum 2(y_i - \hat{\alpha} - \hat{\beta}_1 x_{1i} - \hat{\beta}_2 x_{2i})(-x_{1i}) = 0 \tag{4.3}$$

$$\frac{\partial Q}{\partial \hat{\beta}_2} = 0 \Rightarrow \sum 2(y_i - \hat{\alpha} - \hat{\beta}_1 x_{1i} - \hat{\beta}_2 x_{2i})(-x_{2i}) = 0 \tag{4.4}$$

These three equations, as mentioned earlier, are called the "normal equations." They can be simplified as follows. Equation (4.2) can be written as

$$\sum y_i = n\hat{\alpha} + \hat{\beta}_1 \sum x_{1i} + \hat{\beta}_2 \sum x_{2i}$$

or

$$\bar{y} = \hat{\alpha} + \hat{\beta}_1 \bar{x}_1 + \hat{\beta}_2 \bar{x}_2 \tag{4.5}$$

where

$$\bar{y} = \frac{1}{n} \sum y_i \quad \bar{x}_1 = \frac{1}{n} \sum x_{1i} \quad \bar{x}_2 = \frac{1}{n} \sum x_{2i}$$

Equation (4.3) can be written as

$$\sum x_{1i} y_i = \hat{\alpha} \sum x_{1i} + \hat{\beta}_1 \sum x_{1i}^2 + \hat{\beta}_2 \sum x_{1i} x_{2i}$$

Substituting the value of $\hat{\alpha}$ from (4.5) into this equation, we get

$$\sum x_{1i} y_i = n\bar{x}_1(\bar{y} - \hat{\beta}_1 \bar{x}_1 - \hat{\beta}_2 \bar{x}_2) + \hat{\beta}_1 \sum x_{1i}^2 + \hat{\beta}_2 \sum x_{1i} x_{2i} \tag{4.6}$$

We can simplify this equation by the use of the following notation. Let us define

$$S_{11} = \sum x_{1i}^2 - n\bar{x}_1^2 \qquad S_{1y} = \sum x_{1i} y_i - n\bar{x}_1 \bar{y}$$

$$S_{12} = \sum x_{1i} x_{2i} - n\bar{x}_1 \bar{x}_2 \qquad S_{2y} = \sum x_{2i} y_i - n\bar{x}_2 \bar{y}$$

$$S_{22} = \sum x_{2i}^2 - n\bar{x}_2^2 \qquad S_{yy} = \sum y_i^2 - n\bar{y}^2$$

Equation (4.6) can be written as

$$S_{1y} = \hat{\beta}_1 S_{11} + \hat{\beta}_2 S_{12} \tag{4.7}$$

By a similar simplification, equation (4.4) can be written as

$$S_{2y} = \hat{\beta}_1 S_{12} + \hat{\beta}_2 S_{22} \tag{4.8}$$

Now we can solve these two equations to get $\hat{\beta}_1$ and $\hat{\beta}_2$. We get

$$\hat{\beta}_1 = \frac{S_{22}S_{1y} - S_{12}S_{2y}}{\Delta}$$

$$\hat{\beta}_2 = \frac{S_{11}S_{2y} - S_{12}S_{1y}}{\Delta} \tag{4.9}$$

where $\Delta = S_{11}S_{22} - S_{12}^2$. Once we obtain $\hat{\beta}_1$ and $\hat{\beta}_2$ we can get $\hat{\alpha}$ from equation (4.5). We have

$$\hat{\alpha} = \bar{y} - \hat{\beta}_1 \bar{x}_1 - \hat{\beta}_2 \bar{x}_2$$

Thus the computational procedure is as follows:

1. Obtain all the means: $\bar{y}, \bar{x}_1, \bar{x}_2$.
2. Obtain all the sums of squares and sums of products: $\sum x_{1i}^2, \sum x_{2i}^2, \sum x_{1i}x_{2i}$, and so on.
3. Obtain $S_{11}, S_{12}, S_{22}, S_{1y}, S_{2y}$, and S_{yy}.
4. Solve equations (4.7) and (4.8) to get $\hat{\beta}_1$ and $\hat{\beta}_2$.
5. Substitute these in equation (4.5) to get $\hat{\alpha}$.

In the case of simple regression we also defined the following:

$$\text{residual sum of squares} = S_{yy} - \hat{\beta}S_{xy}$$

$$\text{regression sum of squares} = \hat{\beta}S_{xy}$$

$$r_{xy}^2 = \frac{\hat{\beta}S_{xy}}{S_{yy}}$$

The analogous expressions in multiple regression are

$$\text{RSS} = S_{yy} - \hat{\beta}_1 S_{1y} - \hat{\beta}_2 S_{2y}$$

$$\text{regression sum of squares} = \hat{\beta}_1 S_{1y} + \hat{\beta}_2 S_{2y}$$

$$R_{y\cdot12}^2 = \frac{\hat{\beta}_1 S_{1y} + \hat{\beta}_2 S_{2y}}{S_{yy}}$$

$R_{y\cdot12}^2$ is called the *coefficient of multiple determination* and its positive square root is called the *multiple correlation coefficient*. The first subscript is the explained variable. The subscripts after the dot are the explanatory variables. To avoid cumbersome notation we have written 12 instead of x_1x_2. Since it is only x's that have subscripts, there is no confusion in this notation.

The procedure in the case of three explanatory variables is analogous. The normal equations give

$$\hat{\alpha} = \bar{y} - \hat{\beta}_1 \bar{x}_1 - \hat{\beta}_2 \bar{x}_2 - \hat{\beta}_3 \bar{x}_3$$

and

$$S_{1y} = \hat{\beta}_1 S_{11} + \hat{\beta}_2 S_{12} + \hat{\beta}_3 S_{13}$$

$$S_{2y} = \hat{\beta}_1 S_{12} + \hat{\beta}_2 S_{22} + \hat{\beta}_3 S_{23}$$

$$S_{3y} = \hat{\beta}_1 S_{13} + \hat{\beta}_2 S_{23} + \hat{\beta}_3 S_{33}$$

We can solve these equations by successive elimination. But this is cumbersome. There are computer programs now available that compute all these things once the basic data are fed in. Thus we will concentrate more on the interpretation of the coefficients rather than on solving the normal equations. Again,

$$\text{RSS} = S_{yy} - \hat{\beta}_1 S_{1y} - \hat{\beta}_2 S_{2y} - \hat{\beta}_3 S_{3y}$$

and

$$R^2_{y \cdot 123} = \frac{\hat{\beta}_1 S_{1y} + \hat{\beta}_2 S_{2y} + \hat{\beta}_3 S_{3y}}{S_{yy}}$$

Note that $\text{RSS} = S_{yy}(1 - R^2)$ in all cases.

One other important relationship to note, which we have also mentioned in Chapter 3, is that if we consider the residual $\hat{u}_i$ we note that

$$\hat{u}_i = y_i - \hat{\alpha} - \hat{\beta}_1 x_{1i} - \hat{\beta}_2 x_{2i}$$

Thus the normal equations (4.2)–(4.4) imply that

$$\sum \hat{u}_i = 0 \quad \sum \hat{u}_i x_{1i} = 0 \quad \sum \hat{u}_i x_{2i} = 0 \tag{4.10}$$

These equations imply that $\text{cov}(\hat{u}, x_1) = 0$ and $\text{cov}(\hat{u}, x_2) = 0$. Thus the sum of the residuals is equal to zero and the residuals are uncorrelated with both x_1 and x_2.

Illustrative Example

With many computer packages readily available for multiple regression analysis one does not need to go through the details of the calculations involved. However, it is instructive to see what computations are done by the computer programs. The following simple example illustrates the computations.

In Table 4.1 we present data on a sample of five persons randomly drawn from a large firm giving their annual salaries, years of education, and years of experience with the firm they are working for:

$$Y = \text{annual salary (thousands of dollars)}$$

$$X_1 = \text{years of education past high school}$$

$$X_2 = \text{years of experience with the firm}$$

Table 4.1 Data on salaries, years of education, and years of experience

Y	X_1	X_2	$Y - \overline{Y}$	$X_1 - \overline{X}_1$	$X_2 - \overline{X}_2$
30	4	10	0	-1	0
20	3	8	-10	-2	-2
36	6	11	6	1	1
24	4	9	-6	-1	-1
40	8	12	10	3	2

The means are $\overline{Y} = 30$, $\overline{X}_1 = 5$, $\overline{X}_2 = 10$. The sums of squares of deviations from the respective means are

$$S_{11} = 16 \qquad S_{12} = 12 \qquad S_{1y} = 62$$
$$S_{22} = 10 \qquad S_{2y} = 52$$
$$S_{yy} = 272$$

The normal equations are

$$16\hat{\beta}_1 + 12\hat{\beta}_2 = 62$$
$$12\hat{\beta}_1 + 10\hat{\beta}_2 = 52$$

Solving these equations, we get

$$\hat{\beta}_1 = -0.25 \quad \hat{\beta}_2 = 5.5$$
$$\hat{\alpha} = \overline{Y} - \hat{\beta}_1\overline{X}_1 - \hat{\beta}_2\overline{X}_2 = 30 - (-1.25) - 55 = -23.75$$
$$R^2 = \frac{\hat{\beta}_1 S_{1y} + \hat{\beta}_2 S_{2y}}{S_{yy}} = \frac{271.5}{272} = 0.998$$

Thus the regression equation is

$$\hat{Y} = -23.75 - 0.25X_1 + 5.5X_2 \quad R^2 = 0.998$$

This equation suggests that years of experience with the firm is far more important than years of education (which actually has a negative sign). The equation says that we can predict that one more year of experience, after allowing for years of education (or holding it constant), results in an annual increase in salary of $5500. That is, if we consider the persons with the same level of education, the one with one more year of experience can be expected to have a higher salary of $5500. Similarly, if we consider two people with the same experience, the one with an education of one more year can be expected to have a *lower* annual salary of $250. Of course, all these numbers are subject to some uncertainty, which we will be discussing in Section 4.3. It will then be clear that we should be dropping the variable X_1 completely.

What about the interpretation of the constant term -23.75? Clearly, that is the salary one would get with no experience and only high school education. But a negative salary is not possible. What of the case when $X_2 = 0$, that is, a person just joined the firm? Again, the equation predicts a negative salary! So what is wrong?

What we have to conclude is that the sample we have is not a truly representative sample from all the people working in the firm. The sample must have been drawn from a subgroup. We have persons with experience ranging from 8 to 12 years in the firm. So we cannot extrapolate the results too far out of this sample range. We cannot use the equation to predict what a new entrant would earn.

It would be interesting to see what the simple regressions in this example give us. We get

$$\hat{Y} = 10.625 + 3.875X_1 \quad R^2 = 0.883$$
$$\hat{Y} = -22.0 + 5.2X_2 \quad R^2 = 0.994$$

The simple regression equation predicts that an increase of one year of education results in an increase of $3875 in annual salary. However, after allowing for the effect of years of experience we find from the multiple regression equation that it does not result in any increase in salary. Thus omission of the variable "years of experience" gives us wrong conclusions about the effect of years of education on salaries.

4.3   Statistical Inference in the Multiple Regression Model

Again we will consider the results for a model with two explanatory variables first and then the general model. If we assume that the errors u_i are normally distributed, this, together with the other assumptions we have made, implies that $u_i \sim \text{IN}(0, \sigma^2)$; the following results can be derived. (Proofs are similar to those in Chapter 3 and are omitted.)

1. $\hat{\alpha}$, $\hat{\beta}_1$, and $\hat{\beta}_2$ have normal distributions with means α, β_1, β_2, respectively.
2. If we denote the correlation coefficient between x_1 and x_2 by r_{12}, then

$$\text{var}(\hat{\beta}_1) = \frac{\sigma^2}{S_{11}(1 - r_{12}^2)}$$

$$\text{var}(\hat{\beta}_2) = \frac{\sigma^2}{S_{22}(1 - r_{12}^2)}$$

$$\text{cov}(\hat{\beta}_1, \hat{\beta}_2) = \frac{-\sigma^2 r_{12}^2}{S_{12}(1 - r_{12}^2)}$$

$$\text{var}(\hat{\alpha}) = \frac{\sigma^2}{n} + \bar{x}_1^2 \, \text{var}(\hat{\beta}_1) + 2\bar{x}_1\bar{x}_2 \, \text{cov}(\hat{\beta}_1, \hat{\beta}_2) + \bar{x}_2^2 \, \text{var}(\hat{\beta}_2)$$

$$\text{cov}(\hat{\alpha}, \hat{\beta}_1) = -[\bar{x}_1 \, \text{var}(\hat{\beta}_1) + \bar{x}_2 \, \text{cov}(\hat{\beta}_1, \hat{\beta}_2)]$$

$$\text{cov}(\hat{\alpha}, \hat{\beta}_2) = -[\bar{x}_1 \, \text{cov}(\hat{\beta}_1, \hat{\beta}_2) + \bar{x}_2 \, \text{var}(\hat{\beta}_2)]$$

Comments

1. Note that the higher the value of r_{12} (other things staying the same), the higher the variances of $\hat{\beta}_1$ and $\hat{\beta}_2$. If r_{12} is very high, we cannot estimate β_1 and β_2 with much precision.
2. Note that $S_{11}(1 - r_{12}^2)$ is the residual sum of squares from a regression of x_1 on x_2. Similarly, $S_{22}(1 - r_{12}^2)$ is the residual sum of squares from a regression of x_2 on x_1. We can now see the analogy between the expressions for the variances in the case of simple regression $\text{var}(\hat{\beta}_1) = \sigma^2/\text{RSS}_1$, where RSS_1 is the residual sum of squares after regressing x_1 on the other variable, that is, after removing the effect of the other variable. This result generalizes to the case of several explanatory variables. In that case RSS_1 is the residual sum of squares from a regression of x_1 on *all* the other x's.

Analogous to the other results in the case of simple regression, we have the following results:

3. If RSS is the residual sum of squares then RSS/σ^2 has a χ^2-distribution with d.f. $(n-3)$. This result can be used to make confidence interval statements about σ^2.
4. If $\hat{\sigma}^2 = \text{RSS}/(n-3)$, then $E(\hat{\sigma}^2) = \sigma^2$ or $\hat{\sigma}^2$ is an unbiased estimator for σ^2.
5. If we substitute $\hat{\sigma}^2$ for σ^2 in the expressions in result 2, we get the estimated variances and covariances. The square roots of the estimated variances are called the standard errors (denoted SE). Then

$$\frac{\hat{\alpha} - \alpha}{\text{SE}(\hat{\alpha})} \quad \frac{\hat{\beta}_1 - \beta_1}{\text{SE}(\hat{\beta}_1)} \quad \frac{\hat{\beta}_2 - \beta_2}{\text{SE}(\hat{\beta}_2)}$$

each have a *t*-distribution with d.f. $(n-3)$.

In addition to results 3 to 5, which have counterparts in the case of simple regression, we have one extra item in the case of multiple regression, that of confidence regions and joint tests for parameters. We have the following result:

6. $F = (1/2\hat{\sigma}^2)[S_{11}(\hat{\beta}_1 - \beta_1)^2 + 2S_{12}(\hat{\beta}_1 - \beta_1)(\hat{\beta}_2 - \beta_2) + S_{22}(\hat{\beta}_2 - \beta_2)^2]$ has an F-distribution with d.f. 2 and $(n-3)$. This result can be used to construct a *confidence region* for β_1 and β_2 together and to test β_1 and β_2 together.

Later we shall state results 1 to 6 for the general case of k explanatory variables. But first we will consider an illustrative example.

Illustrative Example

A production function is specified as

$$y_i = \alpha + \beta_1 x_{1i} + \beta_2 x_{2i} + u_i \quad u_i \sim \text{IN}(0, \sigma^2)$$

where

$$y = \log \text{output}$$

$$x_1 = \log \text{labor input}$$

$$x_2 = \log \text{capital input}$$

The variables x_i are nonstochastic. The following data are obtained from a sample of size $n = 23$ (23 individual firms):

$$\bar{x}_1 = 10 \qquad \bar{x}_2 = 5 \qquad \bar{y} = 12$$
$$S_{11} = 12 \qquad S_{12} = 8 \qquad S_{22} = 12$$
$$S_{1y} = 10 \qquad S_{2y} = 8 \qquad S_{yy} = 10$$

(a) Compute $\hat{\alpha}$, $\hat{\beta}_1$, and $\hat{\beta}_2$ and their standard errors. Present the regression equation.
(b) Find the 95% confidence intervals for α, β_1, β_2, and σ^2 and test the hypotheses $\beta_1 = 1.0$ and $\beta_2 = 0$ separately at the 5% significance level.
(c) Find a 95% confidence region for $\hat{\beta}_1$ and $\hat{\beta}_2$ and show it in a figure.
(d) Test the hypothesis $\beta_1 = 1$, $\beta_2 = 0$ at the 5% significance level.

Solution

(a) The normal equations are

$$12\hat{\beta}_1 + 8\hat{\beta}_2 = 10$$
$$8\hat{\beta}_1 + 12\hat{\beta}_2 = 8$$

These give $\hat{\beta}_1 = 0.7$ and $\hat{\beta}_2 = 0.2$. Hence $\hat{\alpha} = \bar{y} - \hat{\beta}_1\bar{x}_1 - \hat{\beta}_2\bar{x}_2 = 12 - 0.7(10) - 0.2(5) = 4$.

$$R_{y\cdot12}^2 = \frac{\hat{\beta}_1 S_{1y} + \hat{\beta}_2 S_{2y}}{S_{yy}}$$

$$= \frac{0.7(10) + 0.2(8)}{10} = 0.86$$

RSS $= S_{yy}(1 - R^2) = 10(1 - 0.86) = 1.4$. Hence

$$\hat{\sigma}^2 = \frac{\text{RSS}}{n - 3} = \frac{1.4}{20} = 0.07$$

$$r_{12}^2 = \frac{S_{12}^2}{S_{11}S_{22}} = \frac{64}{144}$$

Hence we have

$$S_{11}(1 - r_{12}^2) = 12\left(\frac{80}{144}\right) = \frac{80}{12} = \frac{20}{3}$$

Hence

$$\text{var}(\hat{\beta}_1) = \frac{\sigma^2}{S_{11}(1 - r_{12}^2)} = \frac{3}{20}\sigma^2$$

$$\text{var}(\hat{\beta}_2) = \frac{3}{20}\sigma^2$$

and

$$\text{cov}(\hat{\beta}_1, \hat{\beta}_2) = \frac{-\sigma^2 r_{12}^2}{S_{12}(1 - r_{12}^2)}$$

$$= \frac{-\sigma^2(64/144)}{8(80/144)} = -\frac{\sigma^2}{10}$$

Also, since $\bar{x}_1 = 10$ and $\bar{x}_2 = 5$, we have

$$V(\hat{\alpha}) = \sigma^2 \left[\frac{1}{23} + (10)^2 \left(\frac{3}{20} \right) - \frac{2(10)(5)}{10} + \frac{(5)^2(3)}{20} \right] = 8.7935\sigma^2$$

Substituting the estimate of σ^2, which is 0.07, in these expressions and taking the square roots, we get

$$\text{SE}(\hat{\beta}_1) = \text{SE}(\hat{\beta}_2) = \sqrt{\frac{0.21}{20}} = 0.102$$

$$\text{SE}(\hat{\alpha}) = 0.78$$

Thus the regression equation is

$$\hat{y} = \underset{(0.78)}{4.0} + \underset{(0.102)}{0.7x_1} + \underset{(0.102)}{0.2x_2} \quad R^2 = 0.86$$

Figures in parentheses are standard errors.

(b) Using the t-distribution with d.f. 20, we get the 95% confidence intervals for α, β_1, and β_2 as

$$\hat{\alpha} \pm 2.086\text{SE}(\hat{\alpha}) = 4.0 \pm 1.63 = (2.37, 5.63)$$

$$\hat{\beta}_1 \pm 2.086\text{SE}(\hat{\beta}_1) = 0.7 \pm 0.21 = (0.49, 0.91)$$

$$\hat{\beta}_2 \pm 2.086\text{SE}(\hat{\beta}_2) = 0.2 \pm 0.21 = (-0.01, 0.41)$$

The hypothesis $\beta_1 = 1.0$ will be rejected at the 5% significance level since $\beta_1 = 1.0$ is outside the 95% confidence interval for β_1. The hypothesis $\beta_2 = 0$ will not be rejected because $\beta_2 = 0$ is a point in the 95% confidence interval for β_2. Using the χ^2-distribution for d.f. 20, we have

$$\text{Prob}\left(9.59 < \frac{20\hat{\sigma}^2}{\sigma^2} < 34.2 \right) = 0.95$$

or

$$\text{Prob}\left(\frac{20\hat{\sigma}^2}{34.2} < \sigma^2 < \frac{20\hat{\sigma}^2}{9.95} \right) = 0.95$$

Thus the 95% confidence interval for σ^2 is

$$\left(\frac{20(0.07)}{34.2}, \frac{20(0.07)}{9.59} \right) \quad \text{or} \quad (0.041, 0.146)$$

(c) The 5% point for the F-distribution with d.f. 2 and 20 is 3.49. Hence using result 6, we can write the 95% *confidence region* for β_1 and β_2 as

$$[S_{11}(\hat{\beta}_1 - \beta_1)^2 + 2S_{12}(\hat{\beta}_1 - \beta_1)(\hat{\beta}_2 - \beta_2) + S_{22}(\hat{\beta}_2 - \beta_2)^2] \leq 3.49(2\hat{\sigma}^2)$$

or

$$[12(0.7 - \beta_1)^2 + 16(0.7 - \beta_1)(0.2 - \beta_2) + 12(0.2 - \beta_2)^2] \leq 3.49(2)(0.07)$$

Or, dividing by 12 throughout and changing $\hat{\beta}_1 - \beta_1$ to $\beta_1 - \hat{\beta}_1$ and $\hat{\beta}_2 - \beta_2$ to $\beta_2 - \hat{\beta}_2$, we get

$$(\beta_1 - 0.7)^2 + \tfrac{4}{3}(\beta_1 - 0.7)(\beta_2 - 0.2) + (\beta_2 - 0.2)^2 \leq 0.041$$

This is an ellipse with center at (0.7, 0.2). It is plotted in Figure 4.1. There are two important things to note: first that the ellipse will be slanting to the left if $\text{cov}(\hat{\beta}_1, \hat{\beta}_2) < 0$ as in our case, and will be slanting to the right if $\text{cov}(\hat{\beta}_1, \hat{\beta}_2) > 0$. In the case of the two explanatory variables this will depend on the sign of S_{12}. The second point to note is that the limits for β_1 and β_2 that we obtain from the ellipse will be different from the 95% confidence limits we obtained earlier for β_1 and β_2 separately. The limits are $(-0.07, 0.47)$ for β_2 and $(0.43, 0.97)$ for β_1. This is because what we have here are *joint* confidence limits. If $\hat{\beta}_1$ and $\hat{\beta}_2$ are independent, the confidence coefficient for the joint interval will simply be the product of the confidence coefficients for $\hat{\beta}_1$ and $\hat{\beta}_2$ separately. Otherwise, it will be different.

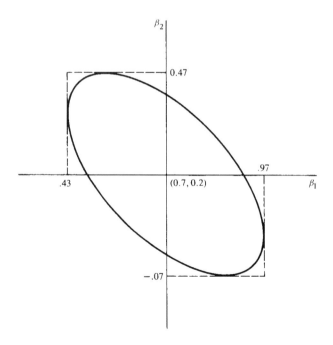

Figure 4.1 Confidence ellipse for β_1 and β_2 in multiple regression

This distinction between *separate intervals and joint intervals*, and between *separate tests and joint tests* should be kept in mind when we talk of statistical inference in the multiple regression model. We discuss this in detail in Section 4.8.

(d) To test the hypothesis $\beta_1 = 1$, $\beta_2 = 0$ at the 5% confidence level we can check whether the point is in the 95% confidence ellipse. But since we do not plot the confidence ellipse all the time, we will apply the F-test discussed in result 6 earlier. We have that

$$F = \frac{1}{2\hat{\sigma}^2}[S_{11}(\hat{\beta}_1 - \beta_1)^2 + 2S_{12}(\hat{\beta}_1 - \beta_1)(\hat{\beta}_2 - \beta_2) + S_{22}(\hat{\beta}_2 - \beta_2)^2]$$

has an F-distribution with d.f. 2 and $n - 3$.

The observed value F_0 is

$$F_0 = \frac{1}{2(0.07)}[12(0.7 - 1.0)^2 + 2(8)(0.7 - 1.0)(0.2 - 0) + 12(0.2 - 0)^2] = 4.3$$

The 5% point from the F-tables with d.f. 2 and 20 is 3.49. Since $F_0 > 3.49$ we reject the hypothesis at the 5% significance level.

Formulas for the General Case of k Explanatory Variables

We have given explicit expressions for the case of two explanatory variables so as to highlight the differences between simple and multiple regressions. The expressions for the general case can be written down neatly in matrix notation, and are given in the appendix to this chapter.

If we have the multiple regression equation with k regressors, that is,

$$y_i = \alpha + \beta_1 x_{1i} + \beta_2 x_{2i} + \cdots + \beta_k x_{ki} + u_i$$

then we have to make the following changes in the earlier results. In result 2, in the expressions for $V(\hat{\beta}_1)$, $V(\hat{\beta}_2)$, and so on, the denominator now will be the residual sum of squares from a regression of that variable on *all* the other x's. Thus

$$\text{var}(\hat{\beta}_i) = \frac{\sigma^2}{\text{RSS}_i} \quad \text{for } i = 1, 2, \ldots, k$$

where RSS_i is a residual sum of squares from a regression of x_i on *all* the other $(k - 1)x$'s.

These k regressions are called *auxiliary regressions*. In practice we do not estimate so many regressions. We have given the formula only to show the relationship between simple and multiple regression. This relationship is discussed in the next section.

In results 3 to 5 we have to change the degrees of freedom from $(n - 3)$ to $(n - k - 1)$. In simple regression we have $k = 1$ and hence d.f. $= (n - 2)$. In the case of two explanatory variables $k = 2$ and hence we used d.f. $= (n - 3)$. In all cases one degree of freedom is for the estimation of α.

Result 6 is now that

$$F = \frac{1}{k\hat{\sigma}^2}\left[\sum_{i=1}^{k}\sum_{j=1}^{k} S_{ij}(\hat{\beta}_i - \beta_i)(\hat{\beta}_j - \beta_j)\right]$$

has an *F*-distribution with d.f. k and $(n - k - 1)$. This result is derived in the appendix to this chapter.

Some Illustrative Examples

We will now present a few examples using the multiple regression methods. To facilitate the estimation of alternative models, we are presenting the data sets at the end of the chapter (Tables 4.7 to 4.11). These data are also available on the Web.

Example 1

In Table 4.7 data are given on sales prices of rural land near Sarasota, FL.[1] The variables are listed at the end of the table. Since land values appreciated steadily over time, the variable MO (month in which the parcel was sold) is considered an important explanatory variable. Prices are also expected to be higher for those lots that are wooded and those lots that are closer to transportation facilities (airport, highways, etc.). Finally, the price increases less than proportionately with acreage, and hence price per acre falls with increases in acreage. The estimated equation was (figures in parentheses are standard errors)

$$\log P_t = \underset{(0.204)}{9.213} + \underset{(0.099)}{0.148 WL} - \underset{(0.011)}{0.33 DA} - \underset{(0.0142)}{0.0057 D75} - \underset{(0.0345)}{0.203 \log A}$$

$$+ \underset{(0.0039)}{0.0141 MO} \quad R^2 = 0.559$$

All the coefficients have the expected signs although some of them are not significant (not significantly different from zero) at the 5% level.

Example 2

In Example 1 we had some notions of what signs to expect for the different coefficients in the regression equation. Sometimes, even if the signs are correct, the magnitudes of the coefficients do not make economic sense. In which case one has to examine the model or the data. An example where the magnitude of the coefficient makes sense is the following.

In June 1978, California voters approved what is known as Proposition 13 limiting property taxes. This led to substantial and differential reduction in property taxes, which led to an increase in housing prices. Rosen[2] studied the impact of reduction in property taxes on housing prices in the San Francisco Bay area. Besides property taxes, there are other factors that determine housing prices and these have to be taken into account in the study. Rosen therefore included the characteristics of the house, such as square footage,

---

[1]These data have been provided by J. S. Shonkwiler. They are used in the paper of J. S. Shonkwiler and J. E. Reynolds, "A Note on the Use of Hedonic Price Models in the Analysis of Land Prices at the Urban Fringe," *Land Economics*, February 1986.

[2]Kenneth T. Rosen, "The Impact of Proposition 13 on Housing Prices in Northern California: A Test of the Interjurisdictional Capitalization Hypothesis," *Journal of Political Economy*, February 1982, pp. 191–200.

age of the house, and a quality index. He also included economic factors such as median income and transportation time to San Francisco. The estimated equation was (figures in parentheses are *t-values*, not standard errors)

$$\hat{y} = 0.171 + 7.275x_1 + 0.547x_2 + 0.00073x_3 + 0.0638x_4$$
$$\quad\quad\quad (2.97) \quad\quad (2.32) \quad\quad (1.34) \quad\quad (3.26)$$

$$- 0.0043x_5 + 0.857x_6 \quad R^2 = 0.897 \quad n = 64$$
$$\quad (2.24) \quad\quad (1.80)$$

where y = change in post-Proposition 13 mean house prices
x_1 = post-Proposition 13 decrease in property tax bill on mean house
x_2 = mean square footage of house
x_3 = median income of families in the area
x_4 = mean age of house
x_5 = transportation time to San Francisco
x_6 = housing-quality index as computed by real estate appraisers

All the coefficients have the expected signs.

The coefficient of x_1 indicates that each \$1 decrease in property taxes increases property values by \$7. The question is whether this is about the right magnitude. Assuming that the property tax reduction is expected to be at the same level in future years, the present value of a \$1 return per year is $1/r$, where r is the rate of interest (also expected to remain the same). This is equal to \$7 if $r = 14.29\%$. The interest rates at that time were around this level and thus Rosen concludes: "The capitalization rate implied by this equation is about 7 which is precisely the magnitude that one would expect with an interest rate of 12–15%."

Example 3

In Table 4.8 data are presented on gasoline consumption in the United States for the years 1947–1969. Let us define

$$G = \frac{KC}{M(POP)} = \text{per capita consumption of gasoline in gallons}$$

We will regress G on P_g and y. (The variables are defined in Table 4.8.) The results we get are (figures in parentheses are *t*-ratios)

$$\hat{G} = -117.70 + 0.373P_g + 0.156Y \quad R^2 = 0.953$$
$$\quad\quad (-1.14) \quad\quad (0.44) \quad\quad (12.02)$$

The price P_g has the wrong sign although it is not significant. Only per capita income appears to be the major determinant of demand for gasoline. In log form the equation is

$$\log \hat{G} = - 8.72 + 0.535 \log P_g + 1.541 \log Y \quad R^2 = 0.940$$
$$\quad\quad (-3.00) \quad\quad (1.23) \quad\quad (11.21)$$

Again P_g has the wrong sign. Instead of population, suppose that we use labor force as divisor and define G as $G = KC/ML$. This can be justified on the argument that miles driven would be more related to L than to population. The results we get are

$$\hat{G} = -248.44 + 0.258P_g + 0.406Y \quad R^2 = 0.925$$
$$\underset{(-0.70)}{} \quad \underset{(0.09)}{} \quad \underset{(9.15)}{}$$

The variable P_g still has the wrong sign. In log form the results are

$$\log \hat{G} = -8.53 + 0.541 \log P_g + 1.636 \log Y \quad R^2 = 0.907$$
$$\underset{(-2.18)}{} \quad \underset{(0.92)}{} \quad \underset{(8.82)}{}$$

Gilstein and Leamer[3] estimate the equation using the 1947–1960 data and obtain (figures in parentheses are standard errors)

$$\hat{G} = 799.1 - 2.563P_g + 0.0616Y$$
$$\underset{(77.5)}{} \quad \underset{(0.706)}{} \quad \underset{(0.0015)}{}$$

Also, we get, using the 1947–1960 data (figures in parentheses are *t*-ratios)

$$\hat{G} = -439.4 - 2.241P_g + 0.662Y \quad R^2 = 0.979$$
$$\underset{(-2.92)}{} \quad \underset{(-1.64)}{} \quad \underset{(22.25)}{}$$

In log form we get

$$\log \hat{G} = -10.477 - 0.387 \log P_g + 2.472 \log Y \quad R^2 = 0.974$$
$$\underset{(-5.67)}{} \quad \underset{(-1.16)}{} \quad \underset{(20.04)}{}$$

In summary, the period 1947–1960 shows a price elasticity of demand slightly negative and an income elasticity of demand significantly greater than unity. Estimation of the same equation over 1947–1969 shows no responsiveness to price but an income elasticity of demand again significantly greater than 1.

Further analysis using these data is left as an exercise. Students can experiment with this data set after going through this and the next two chapters.

Example 4

In Table 4.9 data are presented on the demand for food in the United States. Let us try to estimate the price elasticity and income elasticity of demand for food. A regression of Q_D on P_D and Y gave the following results (figures in parentheses are *t*-ratios):

$$\hat{Q}_D = 92.05 - 0.1421P_D + 0.236Y \quad R^2 = 0.7813$$
$$\underset{(15.76)}{} \quad \underset{(-2.13)}{} \quad \underset{(7.56)}{}$$

The coefficients have the right signs. However, someone comes and says that the variables all have trends and we ought to account for this by including T as an extra explanatory variable. The results now are (all variables have the right signs)

$$\hat{Q}_D = 105.1 - 0.325P_D + 0.315Y - 0.224T \quad R^2 = 0.8812$$
$$\underset{(18.47)}{} \quad \underset{(-4.58)}{} \quad \underset{(9.85)}{} \quad \underset{(3.67)}{}$$

---

[3]C. Z. Gilstein and E. E. Leamer, "Robust Sets of Regression Estimates," *Econometrica*, Vol. 51, No. 2, March 1983, p. 330.

Now the price variable is more significant than before. Also, a simple regression of Q_D on P_D gives a wrong sign for P_D:

$$\hat{Q}_D = \underset{(7.89)}{89.97} + \underset{(0.91)}{0.107P_D} \quad R^2 = 0.044$$

We have given four examples, the first two on cross-section data, the other two on time-series data. The results were more straightforward with the cross-section data sets. With the time-series data sets, we have had some trouble obtaining meaningful results. This is a common experience. The problem is that most of the series move together with time.

Example 5

There is an interesting example of predicting the quality of wine and rate of investment in wines in R. P. Byron and O. Ashenfelter, "Predicting the Quality of an Unborn Grange," *Economic Record*, Vol. 71, 1995, pp. 40–53. Grange Hermitage is Australia's premier wine. The results are too lengthy to be discussed here. The data are provided in the paper.

We leave a study of this paper as an exercise.

4.4 Interpretation of the Regression Coefficients

In simple regression we are concerned with measuring the effect of the explanatory variable on the explained variable. Since the regression equation can be written as

$$y - \overline{y} = \hat{\beta}(x - \overline{x}) + \hat{u}_i$$

this effect is measured by $\hat{\beta}$, where

$$\hat{\beta} = \frac{S_{xy}}{S_{xx}} \quad \text{or} \quad \frac{\text{cov}(x,\, y)}{V(x)}$$

In the multiple regression equation with two explanatory variables x_1 and x_2 we can talk of the *joint* effect of x_1 and x_2 and the *partial* effect of x_1 or x_2 upon y. Since the regression equation can be written as

$$y - \overline{y} = \hat{\beta}_1(x_1 - \overline{x}_1) + \hat{\beta}_2(x_2 - \overline{x}_2) + \hat{u}_i$$

the partial effect of x_1 is measured by $\hat{\beta}_1$ and the partial effect of x_2 is measured by $\hat{\beta}_2$. By partial effect we mean holding the other variable constant or eliminating the effect of the other variable. Thus $\hat{\beta}_1$ is to be interpreted as measuring the effect of x_1 on y after eliminating the effect of x_2 on x_1. Similarly, $\hat{\beta}_2$ is to be interpreted as measuring the effect of x_2 on y after eliminating the effect of x_1 on x_2.

This interpretation suggests that we can derive the estimator $\hat{\beta}_1$ of β_1 by estimating two separate simple regressions:

Step 1. Estimate a regression of x_1 on x_2. Let the regression coefficient be denoted by b_{12}. Denoting the residuals from this equation by W_i, we have

$$W_i = x_{1i} - \bar{x}_1 - b_{12}(x_{2i} - \bar{x}_2) \qquad (4.11)$$

Note that W_i is that part of x_1 that is left after removing the effect of x_2 on x_1.

Step 2. Now regress y_i on W_i. The regression coefficient is nothing but $\hat{\beta}_1$, which we derived earlier in the multiple regression [see equation (4.9)]. To see this, note that the regression coefficient of y_i on W_i is nothing but $\text{cov}(y_i, W_i)/\text{var}(W_i)$. From equation (4.11) we have (since $\sum W_i = 0$)

$$n V(W_i) = \sum W_i^2 = S_{11} + b_{12}^2 S_{22} - 2b_{12} S_{12}$$

but $b_{12} = S_{12}/S_{22}$, hence $n V(W_i) = S_{11} - S_{12}^2/S_{22}$. Also,

$$n \, \text{cov}(y_i, W_i) = \sum y_i W_i$$
$$= S_{1y} - b_{12} S_{2y}$$

Now substitute $b_{12} = S_{12}/S_{22}$. We get, on simplification,

$$n \, \text{cov}(y_i, W_i) = S_{1y} - \frac{S_{12} S_{2y}}{S_{22}}$$

Hence we get

$$\frac{n \, \text{cov}(y_i, W_i)}{n V(W_i)} = \frac{S_{22} S_{1y} - S_{12} S_{2y}}{S_{11} S_{22} - S_{12}^2}$$

which is the expression for $\hat{\beta}_1$ we got in equation (4.9).

Suppose that we eliminate the effect of x_2 on y as well. Let V_i be the residual from a regression of y on x_2. If we now regress V_i on W_i, then the regression coefficient we get will be the same as that obtained from a regression of y_i on W_i. This is because

$$V_i = y_i - \bar{y} - b_{y2}(x_{2i} - \bar{x}_2)$$

where b_{y2} is the regression coefficient of y on x_2. However, x_2 will be uncorrelated with W (a residual is uncorrelated with a regressor). Hence

$$\text{cov}(V, W) = \text{cov}(y, W)$$

Thus a regression of V_i on W_i will produce the same estimate $\hat{\beta}_1$ as a regression of y_i on W_i.

This result is important and useful in trend elimination and seasonal adjustment of time-series data. What it implies is that if we have an explained variable y and an explanatory variable x and there is another nuisance variable Z that is influencing both y and x, the "pure" effect of x on y after eliminating the effect of this nuisance variable Z on both x and y can be estimated simply by estimating the multiple regression equation

$$y = \alpha + \beta x + \gamma Z + u$$

The coefficient β gives us the "pure" effect needed. We do not have to run a regression of y on Z and x on Z to eliminate the effect of Z on these variables and then a third regression of "purified" y on "purified" x.

Although we have proved the result for only two variables, the result is general. x and Z can both be sets of variables (instead of single variables).[4]

Finally, the standard error of $\hat{\beta}_1$ obtained from the estimation of the multiple regression (4.1) is also the same as the standard error of the regression coefficient obtained from the simple regression of V_i on W_i. This result is somewhat tedious to prove here, so we will omit the proof.[5]

The correlation coefficient between y and W is called the *partial correlation* between y and x_1. It is partial correlation in the sense that the effect of x_2 has been removed. It will be denoted by $r_{y1\cdot2}$. The subscript after the dot denotes the variable whose effect has been removed. Corresponding to the relationship we have given in Chapter 3 (end of Section 3.6), we have the formula

$$r_{y1\cdot2}^2 = \frac{t_1^2}{t_1^2 + (n-3)}$$

where $t_1 = \hat{\beta}_1/\text{SE}(\hat{\beta}_1)$. The derivation of this formula is also omitted here since it is somewhat tedious.

The interpretation of $\hat{\beta}_2$ and the formulas associated with it are similar. Thus we have

$$r_{y2\cdot1}^2 = \frac{t_2^2}{t_2^2 + (n-3)}$$

where $t_2 = \hat{\beta}_2/\text{SE}(\hat{\beta}_2)$.

Illustrative Example

In the illustrative example in Section 4.3 we have

$$t_1 = \frac{0.7}{0.102} = 6.863 \quad t_2 = \frac{0.2}{0.102} = 1.961$$

Hence

$$r_{y1\cdot2}^2 = \frac{(6.863)^2}{(6.863)^2 + 20} = \frac{47.10}{67.10} = 0.70$$

$$r_{y2\cdot1}^2 = \frac{(1.961)^2}{(1.961)^2 + 20} = \frac{3.846}{23.846} = 0.16$$

---

[4]For a general model this is proved in the appendix to this chapter under the title "prior adjustment."

[5]The proof can easily be constructed using the result in G. S. Maddala, *Econometrics* (New York: McGraw-Hill, 1977), p. 462.

The General Case

In the general case of k regressors we define $t_i = \hat{\beta}_i/\text{SE}(\hat{\beta}_i)$ for $i = 1, 2, \ldots, k$. Then the partial r^2 for the variable x_i is

$$r^2_{yxi} \cdot \text{ other } x\text{'s} = \frac{t_i^2}{t_i^2 + (n - k - 1)}$$

4.5 Partial Correlations and Multiple Correlation

If we have an explained variable y and three explanatory variables x_1, x_2, x_3 and r^2_{y1}, r^2_{y2}, r^2_{y3} are the squares of the simple correlations between y and x_1, x_2, x_3, respectively, then r^2_{y1}, r^2_{y2}, and r^2_{y3} measure the proportion of the variance in y that x_1 *alone*, x_2 *alone*, or x_3 *alone* explain. On the other hand, $R^2_{y \cdot 123}$ measures the proportion of the variance of y that x_1, x_2, x_3 *together* explain. We would also like to measure something else. For instance, how much does x_2 explain *after* x_1 is included in the regression equation? How much does x_3 explain *after* x_1 and x_2 are included? These are measured by the partial coefficients of determination $r^2_{y2 \cdot 1}$ and $r^2_{y3 \cdot 12}$, respectively.[6] The variables after the dot are the variables already included. With three explanatory variables we have the following partial correlations: $r_{y1 \cdot 2}$, $r_{y1 \cdot 3}$, $r_{y2 \cdot 1}$, $r_{y2 \cdot 3}$, $r_{y3 \cdot 1}$, and $r_{y3 \cdot 2}$. These are called partial correlations of the *first order*. We also have three partial correlation coefficients of the *second* order: $r_{y1 \cdot 23}$, $r_{y2 \cdot 13}$, and $r_{y3 \cdot 12}$. The variables after the dot are always the variables already included in the regression equation. The order of the partial correlation coefficient depends on the number of variables after the dot. The usual convention is to denote simple and partial correlations by a small r and multiple correlations by a capital R. For instance, $R^2_{y \cdot 12}$, $R^2_{y \cdot 13}$, and $R^2_{y \cdot 123}$ are all coefficients of multiple determination (their positive square roots are multiple correlation coefficients).

How do we compute the partial correlation coefficients? For this we use the relationship between r^2 and t^2. For example, to compute $r^2_{y2 \cdot 3}$ we have to consider the multiple regression of y on x_2 and x_3. Let the estimated regression equation be

$$\hat{y} = \hat{\alpha} + \hat{\beta}_2 x_2 + \hat{\beta}_3 x_3$$

Let $t_2 = \hat{\beta}_2/\text{SE}(\hat{\beta}_2)$ from this equation. Then

$$r^2_{y2 \cdot 3} = \frac{t_2^2}{t_2^2 + \text{d.f.}}$$

The degrees of freedom d.f. = (number of observations) − (number of regression parameters estimated) = $(n - 3)$ in this case. The variables to be included in the multiple regression equation are all variables that are mentioned in the partial correlation coefficient. For instance, if we want to compute $r^2_{y4 \cdot 237}$, we have to run a regression of y on x_4, x_2, x_3, and x_7. Let $t_4 = \hat{\beta}_4/\text{SE}(\hat{\beta}_4)$, where β_4 is the coefficient of

---

[6]We are using the term *coefficient of determination* to denote the square of the coefficient of correlation.

x_4. Then

$$r^2_{y4 \cdot 237} = \frac{t^2_4}{t^2_4 + \text{d.f.}}$$

and d.f. $= (n - 5)$ in this case (one α and four β's).

Partial correlations are very important in deciding whether or not to include more explanatory variables. For instance, suppose that we have two explanatory variables x_1 and x_2, and r^2_{y2} is very high, say 0.95, but $r^2_{y2 \cdot 1}$ is very low, say 0.01. What this means is that if x_2 alone is used to explain y, it can do a good job. But after x_1 is included, x_2 does not help any more explaining y; that is, x_1 has done the job of x_2. In this case there is no use including x_2. In fact, we can have a situation where, for instance,

$$r^2_{y1} = 0.95 \quad \text{and} \quad r^2_{y2} = 0.96$$

but

$$r^2_{y1 \cdot 2} = 0.1 \quad \text{and} \quad r^2_{y2 \cdot 1} = 0.1$$

In this case each variable is highly correlated with y but the partial correlations are both very low. This is called *multicollinearity* and we will discuss this problem later in Chapter 7. In this example we can use x_1 only or x_2 only or some combination of the two as an explanatory variable. For instance, suppose that x_1 is the amount of skilled labor, x_2 the amount of unskilled labor, and y the output. What the partial correlation coefficients suggest is that the separation of total labor into two components — skilled and unskilled — does not help us much in explaining output. So we might as well use $x_1 + x_2$ or total labor as the explanatory variable.

4.6   Relationships Among Simple, Partial, and Multiple Correlation Coefficients

To study the relationships among the different types of correlation coefficients, we need to make use of the relationship that at each stage the residual sum of squares RSS $= S_{yy}(1 - R^2)$. Suppose that we have two explanatory variables x_1 and x_2. Then

$$S_{yy}(1 - R^2_{y \cdot 12}) = \text{residual sum of squares after } both \text{ } x_1 \text{ and } x_2 \text{ are included}$$

$$S_{yy}(1 - r^2_{y1}) = \text{residual sum of squares after the inclusion of } x_1 \text{ only}$$

Now $r^2_{y2 \cdot 1}$ measures the proportion of this residual sum of squares explained by x_2. Hence the unexplained residual sum of squares after x_2 is also included is

$$(1 - r^2_{y2 \cdot 1})S_{yy}(1 - r^2_{y1})$$

But this is equal to $S_{yy}(1 - R^2_{y \cdot 12})$. Hence we get the result that

$$1 - R^2_{y \cdot 12} = (1 - r^2_{y1})(1 - r^2_{y2 \cdot 1})$$

If we have three explanatory variables we get

$$(1 - R^2_{y \cdot 123}) = (1 - r^2_{y1})(1 - r^2_{y2 \cdot 1})(1 - r^2_{y3 \cdot 12}) \tag{4.12}$$

The subscripts 1, 2, 3 can be interchanged in any required order. Thus if we need to consider them in order 3, 1, 2, we have

$$(1 - R^2_{y \cdot 123}) = (1 - r^2_{y3})(1 - r^2_{y1 \cdot 3})(1 - r^2_{y2 \cdot 31})$$

Note that the partial r^2 can be greater or smaller than the simpler r^2. For instance, the variable x_2 might explain only 20% of the variance of y, but after x_1 is included, it can explain 50% of the residual variance. In this case the simple r^2 is 0.2 and the partial r^2 is 0.5. We are thus talking of the proportions explained of different variances.

On the other hand, the simple r^2 and the partial r^2 can never be greater than R^2 (the square of the multiple correlation coefficient). This is clear from the formulas we have stated.

Two Illustrative Examples

The following examples illustrate simple r^2, partial r^2, and R^2. The first example illustrates some problems in interpreting multiple regression coefficients when the explanatory variables are proportions. The second example illustrates the use of interaction terms.

Example 1: Hospital Costs

Consider the analysis of hospital costs by case mix by Feldstein.[7] The data are for 177 hospitals. The explanatory variables are *proportions* of total patients treated in each category. There are nine categories: M = medical, P = pediatrics, S = general surgery, E = ENT, T = traumatic and orthopedic surgery, OS = other surgery, G = gynecology, Ob = obstetrics, Other = miscellaneous others. The regression coefficients, their standard errors, t-values, partial r^2's, simple r^2's, and average cost per case are given in Table 4.2.

The entries in Table 4.2 need some explanation. The t-values are just the coefficients divided by the respective standard errors. The partial r^2's are obtained by the formula

$$r^2 = \frac{t^2}{t^2 + \text{d.f.}}$$

Thus, for the variable M,

$$\text{partial } r^2 = \frac{(2.38)^2}{(2.38)^2 + 168} = 0.0326$$

---

[7]M. S. Feldstein, *Economic Analysis for the Health Service Industry* (Amsterdam: North-Holland, 1967), Chap. 1.

Table 4.2 Hospital cost regressions

Variable	Regression Coefficient	SE	t-Ratio	Partial r^2	Simple r^2	Average Cost per Case
M	44.97	18.89	2.38	0.0326	0.1423	114.48
P	−44.54	28.51	−1.56	0.0143	0.0074	24.97
S	−36.81	14.88	−2.47	0.0350	0.0343	32.70
E	−54.26	16.52	−3.28	0.0602	0.0947	15.25
T	−29.82	17.18	−1.74	0.0177	0.0062	39.69
OS	28.51	20.27	1.41	0.0117	0.0478	98.02
G	−10.79	21.47	−0.50	0.0015	0.0099	58.72
Ob	−34.63	16.34	−2.12	0.0261	0.0011	34.88
Other	0					69.51
Constant	69.51		$R^2 = 0.3076$			

The simple r^2 is just the square of the correlation of average cost per case and the proportion of the cases in that category. The two are presented together to illustrate how the partial r^2's can be lower or higher than the simple r^2's.

The regression coefficients in this example have to be interpreted in a different way. In the usual case, each regression coefficient measures the change in the dependent variable y for unit increase in that independent variable, *holding other variables constant*. In this example, since the independent variables are proportions in that category, an increase in one variable holding other variables constant does not make sense (in fact, it is impossible to do it). The proper interpretation of the coefficients in this case is: Put the value of $M = 1$, all others 0. Then the estimated value of the dependent variable = (constant + coefficient of M) = $69.51 + 44.97 = 114.48$. This is the average cost of treating a case in M. Similarly, constant + coefficient of $P = 69.51 − 44.54 = 24.97$ is the average cost of treating a case in P. Finally, putting $M, P, \ldots, Ob$ all = 0, we get the constant term = 69.51 as the average cost of treating a case in the "Other" category. These coefficients are all presented in the last column of Table 4.2. What the regression equation enables us to estimate in this case is the average cost of treating a case in each category. The standard errors of these estimates can be calculated as $SE(\hat{\alpha} + \hat{\beta}_i)$ if we know the covariance between the constant term $\hat{\alpha}$ and the other regression coefficient $\hat{\beta}$.

An important point to note is that we have not estimated a coefficient for the category "other." An alternative procedure in which we estimate coefficients for all the categories directly would be to include all the variables and *delete the constant term*. We have to delete the constant term because the sum of all the explanatory variables (which are proportions of cases treated in each category) is equal to 1 for all observations. Since the constant term corresponds to an explanatory variable that is identically equal to 1 for all observations, we cannot include it in the regression equation. If we do, we have a situation where one of the explanatory variables is identically the sum of the other explanatory variables. In this case we cannot estimate all the coefficients.

To see what the problem is, consider the equation

$$y = \alpha + \beta_1 x_1 + \beta_2 x_2 + \beta_3 x_3 + u$$

where $x_3 = x_1 + x_2$. We can easily see that we cannot get separate estimates of β_1, β_2, and β_3 since the equation reduces to

$$y = \alpha + \beta_1 x_1 + \beta_2 x_2 + \beta_3(x_1 + x_2) + u$$
$$= \alpha + (\beta_1 + \beta_3)x_1 + (\beta_2 + \beta_3)x_2 + u$$

Such a situation is known as "perfect multicollinearity" and is discussed in greater detail in Chapter 7.

A regression equation with no constant term is also called "regression through the origin" because if the x variables are all zero, the y variable is also zero. The estimation of such an equation proceeds as before and the normal equations are defined as in equations (4.7) and (4.8) except that we do not apply the "mean corrections." That is, we define

$$S_{11} = \sum x_{1i}^2 \text{ and not } \sum (x_{1i} - \bar{x}_1)^2$$
$$S_{12} = \sum x_{1i} x_{2i} \text{ and not } \sum (x_{1i} - \bar{x}_1)(x_{2i} - \bar{x}_2) \quad \text{etc.}$$

After these changes are made, the solution of the normal equations proceeds as before. The definition of RSS and R^2 also proceeds as before, with the change that in S_{yy} as well, no mean correction be applied.

Cautionary Note: Many regression programs allow the option of including or excluding the constant term. However, some of them may not give the correct R^2 when running a regression equation with no constant term. If the R^2 is computed as $1 - \text{RSS}/S_{yy}$ and S_{yy} is computed using the mean correction, we might get a very small R^2 and sometimes even a negative R^2.

Note that with two explanatory variables, and no constant term, $\text{RSS} = \sum y_i^2 - \hat{\beta}_1(\sum y_i x_{1i}) - \hat{\beta}_2(\sum y_i x_{2i})$ and if S_{yy} is computed (wrongly) with a mean correction, so that $S_{yy} = \sum y_i^2 - n\bar{y}^2$, it can happen that $S_{yy} < \text{RSS}$ and thus we get negative R^2.

The correct R^2 in this case is $1 - \text{RSS}/\sum y_i^2$. Of course, if $\bar{y}$ is very high $\sum y_i^2$ will be very high compared with RSS and we might get a high R^2. But one should not infer from this that the equation with no constant term is better than the one with a constant term. The two R^2 values are not comparable. With a constant term, the R^2 measures the proportion of $\sum (y_i - \bar{y})^2$ explained by the explanatory variables. Without a constant term that R^2 explains the proportion of $\sum y_i^2$ explained by the explanatory variables. Thus we are talking of proportions of two different things, and hence we cannot compare them.

Example 2: Demand for Food

Table 4.3 presents data on per capita food consumption, price of food, and per capita income for the years 1927–1941 and 1948–1962.[8] Two equations are estimated for

---

[8]The data are from Frederick V. Waugh, *Demand and Price Analysis: Some Examples from Agriculture*, U.S.D.A. Technical Bulletin 1316, November 1964, p. 16. The value of y for 1955 has been corrected to 96.5 from 86.5 in that table.

Table 4.3 Indexes of food consumption, food price, and consumer income[a]

Year	Food Consumption per Capita, q	Food Price, p[b]	Consumer Income, y[c]
1927	88.9	91.7	57.7
1928	88.9	92.0	59.3
1929	89.1	93.1	62.0
1930	88.7	90.9	56.3
1931	88.0	82.3	52.7
1932	85.9	76.3	44.4
1933	86.0	78.3	43.8
1934	87.1	84.3	47.8
1935	85.4	88.1	52.1
1936	88.5	88.0	58.0
1937	88.4	88.4	59.8
1938	88.6	83.5	55.9
1939	91.7	82.4	60.3
1940	93.3	83.0	64.1
1941	95.1	86.2	73.7
(World War II years excluded)			
1948	96.7	105.3	82.1
1949	96.7	102.0	83.1
1950	98.0	102.4	88.6
1951	96.1	105.4	88.3
1952	98.1	105.0	89.1
1953	99.1	102.6	92.1
1954	99.1	101.9	91.7
1955	99.8	100.8	96.5
1956	101.5	100.0	99.8
1957	99.9	99.8	99.9
1958	99.1	101.2	98.4
1959	101.0	98.8	101.8
1960	100.7	98.4	101.8
1961	100.8	98.8	103.1
1962	101.0	98.4	105.5

[a] 1957–1959 = 100.
[b] Retail prices of Bureau of Labor Statistics, deflated by dividing by consumer price index.
[c] Per capita disposable income, deflated by dividing by consumer price index.

these data:

$$\text{Equation 1: } \log q = \alpha + \beta_1 \log p + \beta_2 \log y$$

$$\text{Equation 2: } \log q = \alpha + \beta_1 \log p + \beta_2 \log y + \beta_3 \log p \log y$$

The last term in equation 2 is an interaction term that allows the price and income elasticities to vary. Equation 1 implies constant price and income elasticities.

The estimates of α, β_1, β_2, and β_3 for 1927–1942 and 1948–1962 separately and for both periods combined are presented in Table 4.4. *Note that we have presented the t-ratios in parentheses* because this is more convenient to interpret. If we are interested in significance tests, the t-ratios are more convenient and if we are interested in obtaining confidence intervals, it is convenient to have the standard errors.

The interaction term has a very low t-value in the equations for 1927–1942 and 1948–1962 separately. Hence we will consider only the equation for the combined data. For this equation the income coefficient has a low t-value and the sign also appears to be wrong at first sight. However, the equation does give positive income elasticities. The income elasticities are given by

$$\eta_{qy} = \frac{d \log q}{d \log y} = \beta_2 + \beta_3 \log p$$

$$= -0.718 + 0.211 \log p$$

log p ranges from 4.33 to 4.66 in the data. Thus the income elasticity ranges from 0.195 to 0.265.

The price elasticity is given by

$$\eta_{qp} = \frac{d \log q}{d \log p} = \beta_1 + \beta_3 \log y = -0.996 + 0.211 \log y$$

Thus, as income increases, demand for food becomes more price inelastic. For the data in Table 4.3, log y ranges from 3.78 to 4.66. Thus the price elasticity ranges from −0.198 to −0.013.

Table 4.4 Estimates of demand for food equations[a]

	Equation 1			Equation 2[b]		
	1927–1941	1948–1962	All Obs.	1927–1941	1948–1962	All Obs.
α	4.555 (22.67)	5.052 (5.61)	4.050 (29.65)	4.058 (0.54)	16.632 (0.61)	8.029 (4.47)
β_1 (price)	−0.235 (−4.41)	−0.237 (−1.54)	−0.120 (−2.95)	−0.123 (−0.07)	−2.745 (−0.47)	−0.996 (−2.51)
β_2 (income)	0.243 (10.63)	0.141 (3.03)	0.242 (17.85)	0.368 (0.20)	−2.416 (−0.40)	−0.718 (−1.66)
β_3 (interaction)				−0.028 (−0.07)	0.554 (0.43)	0.211 (2.22)
n	15	15	30	15	15	30
R^2	0.9066	0.8741	0.9731	0.9066	0.8762	0.9775
F^c	58.2	41.7	489	35.6	26.0	374.5
$10^2 \times$ RSS	0.1151	0.0544	0.2866	0.1151	0.0535	0.2412
d.f.	12	12	27	11	11	26
$10^4 \times \hat{\sigma}^{2d}$	0.9594	0.4534	1.0613	1.0462	0.4866	0.9278

[a]Figures in parentheses are t-ratios, not standard errors.
[b]From equation 2, all the partial r^2's are very low for 1927–1941 and 1948–1962, although the R^2's are high.
[c]F is an F-statistic for testing overall fit, that is, for R^2. This is discussed in Section 4.8.
[d]$\hat{\sigma}^2 =$ RSS/d.f. The importance of this is discussed in Section 4.9.

4.7   Prediction in the Multiple Regression Model

The formulas for prediction in multiple regression are similar to those in the case of simple regression except that to compute the standard error of the predicted value we need the variances and covariances of all the regression coefficients. Again we will present the expression for the standard error in the case of two explanatory variables and then the expression for the general case of k explanatory variables. But we do not need to compute this general expression because there is an easier way of generating the standard error which we will describe in Chapter 8 (see Section 8.5).

Let the estimated regression equation be

$$\hat{y} = \hat{\alpha} + \hat{\beta}_1 x_1 + \hat{\beta}_2 x_2$$

Now consider the prediction of the value y_0 of y given values x_{10} of x_1, and x_{20} of x_2, respectively. These could be values at some future date.

Then we have

$$y_0 = \alpha + \beta_1 x_{10} + \beta_2 x_{20} + u_0$$

Consider

$$\hat{y}_0 = \hat{\alpha} + \hat{\beta}_1 x_{10} + \hat{\beta}_2 x_{20}$$

The prediction error is

$$\hat{y}_0 - y_0 = \hat{\alpha} - \alpha + (\hat{\beta}_1 - \beta_1)x_{10} + (\hat{\beta}_2 - \beta_2)x_{20} - u_0$$

Since $E(\hat{\alpha} - \alpha)$, $E(\hat{\beta}_1 - \beta_1)$, $E(\hat{\beta}_2 - \beta_2)$, and $E(u_0)$ are all equal to zero, we have $E(\hat{y}_0 - y_0) = 0$. Thus the predictor $\hat{y}_0$ is unbiased. Note that what we are saying is $E(\hat{y}_0) = E(y_0)$ (since both $\hat{y}_0$ and y_0 are random variables). The variance of the prediction error is

$$\sigma^2 \left(1 + \frac{1}{n}\right) + (x_{10} - \bar{x}_1)^2 \ \text{var}(\hat{\beta}_1)$$

$$+ 2(x_{10} - \bar{x}_1)(x_{20} - \bar{x}_2) \ \text{cov}(\hat{\beta}_1, \hat{\beta}_2) + (x_{20} - \bar{x}_2)^2 \ \text{var}(\hat{\beta}_2)$$

In the case of k explanatory variables, this is

$$\sigma^2 \left(1 + \frac{1}{n}\right) + \sum_{i=1}^{k} \sum_{j=1}^{k} (x_{i0} - \bar{x}_i)(x_{j0} - \bar{x}_j) \ \text{cov}(\hat{\beta}_i, \hat{\beta}_j)$$

We estimate σ^2 by $\text{RSS}/(n-3)$ in the case of two explanatory variables and by $\text{RSS}/(n-k-1)$ in the general case.

Illustrative Example

Again consider the illustrative example in Section 4.3. The regression is

$$y = 4.0 + 0.7x_1 + 0.2x_2$$

Consider the prediction of y for $x_{10} = 12$, and $x_{20} = 7$. We have

$$\hat{y}_0 = 4.0 + 0.7(12) + 0.2(7) = 13.8$$

Note that

$$x_{10} - \bar{x}_1 = 12 - 10 = 2$$
$$x_{20} - \bar{x}_2 = 7 - 5 = 2$$

Using the expressions for $\text{var}(\hat{\beta}_1)$, $\text{var}(\hat{\beta}_2)$, $\text{cov}(\hat{\beta}_1, \hat{\beta}_2)$, and $\hat{\sigma}^2$ derived in Section 4.3, we get the estimated variance of the prediction error as

$$0.07 \left(1 + \frac{1}{23} \right) + 4 \left(\frac{3}{20} + \frac{3}{20} - \frac{2}{10} \right) (0.07) = 0.101$$

The standard error of the prediction is 0.318. Thus the 95% confidence interval for the prediction is

$$13.8 \pm 2.086(0.318) \quad \text{or} \quad 13.8 \pm 0.66 \quad \text{or} \quad (13.14, 14.46)$$

Comment

In the case of simple regression we said (in Section 3.7) that the variance of the prediction error increases as we increase the distance of the point x_0 from $\bar{x}$. In the case of multiple regression we cannot say that the variance of the prediction error increases with the Euclidean distance $[(x_{10} - \bar{x}_1)^2 + (x_{20} - \bar{x}_2)^2]^{1/2}$. This is because there is the covariance term as well. For instance, in our example let us change x_{20} to 3. Now $x_{20} - \bar{x}_2 = -2$. The Euclidean distance is the same as before. It is $\sqrt{2^2 + (-2)^2}$. However, the variance of the prediction error is now

$$0.07 \left(1 + \frac{1}{23} \right) + 4 \left(\frac{3}{20} + \frac{3}{20} + \frac{2}{10} \right) (0.7) = 0.213$$

which is higher because of the last term turning positive. If x_1 and x_2 are highly correlated, we will observe wide discrepancies in the variances of the prediction error for the same Euclidean distance of the value of x_0 from the sample mean. Thus the simple relationship we found in the case of simple regression does not hold in multiple regression.

4.8   Analysis of Variance and Tests of Hypotheses

In Section 4.3, result 6, we discussed an F-test to test hypotheses about β_1 *and* β_2. An alternative expression for this test is defined by the statistic

$$F = \frac{(\text{RRSS} - \text{URSS})/r}{\text{URSS}/(n - k - 1)} \tag{4.13}$$

where URSS = unrestricted residual sum of squares

RRSS = restricted residual sum of squares obtained by imposing the restrictions of the hypothesis

r = number of restrictions imposed by the hypothesis

The derivation of this test is given in the appendix to this chapter. A proof in the general case can be found in graduate textbooks in this area.[9]

As an illustration, consider the hypothesis $\beta_1 = 1$, $\beta_2 = 0$ in the illustrative example in Section 4.3. The unrestricted residual sum of squares is URSS = 1.4. To get the restricted residual sum of squares RRSS, we have to minimize

$$\sum (y_i - \alpha - 1.0x_{1i} - 0.0x_{2i})^2$$

Since both β_1 and β_2 are specified, there is only α to be estimated and we get $\hat{\alpha} = \bar{y} - 1.0\bar{x}_1$. Thus

$$\begin{aligned} \text{RRSS} &= \sum [y_i - \bar{y} - (x_{1i} - \bar{x}_1)]^2 \\ &= S_{yy} + S_{11} - 2S_{1y} \\ &= 10.0 + 12.0 - 2(10.0) = 2.0 \end{aligned}$$

Also, we have $r = 2, n = 23, k = 2$. Hence

$$F = \frac{(2.0 - 1.4)/2}{1.4/20} = \frac{0.3}{0.07} = 4.3$$

which is exactly the value we obtained in Section 4.3.

In the special case where the hypothesis is

$$\beta_1 = \beta_2 = \cdots = \beta_k = 0$$

we have URSS = $S_{yy}(1 - R^2)$, and RRSS = S_{yy}. Hence the test is given by

$$F = \frac{[S_{yy} - S_{yy}(1 - R^2)]/k}{S_{yy}(1 - R^2)/(n - k - 1)} = \frac{R^2}{1 - R^2} \cdot \frac{n - k - 1}{k} \tag{4.14}$$

which has an F-distribution with d.f. k and $(n - k - 1)$. What this test does is test the hypothesis that none of the x's influence y; that is, the regression equation is useless. Of course, a rejection of this hypothesis leaves us with the question: Which of the x's are useful in explaining y?

It is customary to present this test in the form of an *analysis of variance* table similar to Table 3.3 we considered for simple regression. This is shown in Table 4.5. What we do is decompose the variance of y into two components: that due to the explanatory variables (i.e., due to regression) and that which is unexplained (i.e., residual).

---

[9]See, for instance, Maddala, *Econometrics*, pp. 457–460.

Table 4.5 Analysis of variance for the multiple regression model

Source of Variation	Sum of Squares, SS	Degrees of Freedom, d.f.	Mean Square, SS/d.f.	F
Regression	$R^2 S_{yy}$	k	$R^2 S_{yy}/k = \mathrm{MS}_1$	$F = \dfrac{\mathrm{MS}_1}{\mathrm{MS}_2}$
Residual	$(1 - R^2)S_{yy}$	$n - k - 1$	$\dfrac{(1 - R^2)S_{yy}}{n - k - 1} = \mathrm{MS}_2$	
Total	S_{yy}	$n - 1$		

Table 4.6 Analysis of variance for the hospital cost regression in Section 4.6

Source of Variation	Sum of Squares, SS	Degrees of Freedom, d.f.	Mean Square, SS/d.f.	F
Regression	10,357	8	1294.625	$F = \dfrac{1294.625}{138.756}$
Residual	23,311	168	138.756	$= 9.33$
Total	33,668	176		

As an illustration, consider the hospital cost regression in Section 4.6. The analysis of variance table is given in Table 4.6. This F value is highly significant. The 1% point from the F-tables with d.f. 8 and 168 is 2.51 and the observed F is much higher.

Of course we reject the hypothesis that $\beta_1 = \beta_2 = \cdots = \beta_k = 0$. All this means is that the case-mix variables are important in explaining the variation in average cost per case between the hospitals. But it does not say which variables are important.

Nested and Nonnested Hypotheses

The hypotheses we are interested in testing can usually be classified under two categories: nested and nonnested. Consider, for instance, the regression models

$$y = \beta_1 x_1 + \beta_2 x_2 + \beta_3 x_3 + u \quad \text{model 1}$$

$$y = \beta_1 x_1 + \beta_2 x_2 \qquad\quad + u \quad \text{model 2}$$

A test of the hypothesis $H_0 : \beta_3 = 0$ versus $H_1 : \beta_3 \neq 0$ is a test of the hypothesis that the data are generated by model 2 versus that the data are generated by model 1. Such a hypothesis is called a *nested hypothesis* because the parameters in model 2 form a subset of the parameters in model 1. A hypothesis

$$H_0 : \beta_1 + \beta_2 + \beta_3 = 0 \quad \text{versus} \quad H_1 : \beta_1 + \beta_2 + \beta_3 \neq 0$$

can also be called a nested hypothesis because we can reparametrize the original equation as

$$y = (\beta_1 + \beta_2 + \beta_3)x_1 + \beta_2(x_2 - x_1) + \beta_3(x_3 - x_1) + u$$

$$= \gamma x_1 + \beta_2(x_2 - x_1) + \beta_3(x_3 - x_1) + u$$

where $\gamma = \beta_1 + \beta_2 + \beta_3$. Now consider the parameter set as $(\gamma, \beta_2, \beta_3)$ and $H_0 : \gamma = 0$ versus $H_1 : \gamma \neq 0$.

Similarly, if we have the hypothesis

$$H_0 : \beta_1 + \beta_2 + \beta_3 = 0, \beta_2 - \beta_3 = 0$$

we reparametrize the original equation by defining $\gamma_1 = \beta_1 + \beta_2 + \beta_3$, $\gamma_2 = \beta_2 - \beta_3$, $\gamma_3 = \beta_3$ so that $\beta_3 = \gamma_3$, $\beta_2 = \gamma_2 + \gamma_3$, $\beta_1 = \gamma_1 - \gamma_2 - 2\gamma_3$ and the original model becomes

$$y = (\gamma_1 - \gamma_2 - 2\gamma_3)x_1 + (\gamma_2 + \gamma_3)x_2 + \gamma_3 x_3 + u$$
$$= \gamma_1 x_1 + \gamma_2(x_2 - x_1) + \gamma_3(x_3 + x_2 - 2x_1) + u$$

Now we consider the parameter set $(\gamma_1, \gamma_2, \gamma_3)$ and H_0 specifies the values of γ_1 and γ_2.

Suppose, on the other hand, that we consider the two regression models:

$$y = \beta_1 x_1 + u_1 \quad \text{model 3}$$

$$y = \beta_2 x_2 + u_2 \quad \text{model 4}$$

$$H_0 : \text{the data are generated by model 3}$$

$$H_1 : \text{the data are generated by model 4}$$

Now the parameter set specified by model 3 is not a subset of the parameter set specified by model 4. Hence we say that hypotheses H_0 and H_1 are *nonnested*.

In the following sections we consider nested hypotheses only. The problem of selection of regressors, for instance, whether to include x_1 only or x_2 only, is a problem in testing nonnested hypotheses. This problem is treated briefly in Chapter 12.

Tests for Linear Functions of Parameters

We have until now discussed tests for parameters. Very often we need tests for functions of parameters. The functions we need to consider can be linear functions or nonlinear functions. We discuss linear functions first.

Suppose that we have estimated a production function in a log-linear form:

$$\log X = \alpha + \beta_1 \log L + \beta_2 \log K + u$$

where X is the output, L the labor input, and K the capital input. Then a test for constant returns to scale is a test of the hypothesis $\beta_1 + \beta_2 = 1$. We can use a t-test to test this hypothesis as follows.

We get the least squares estimates $\hat{\beta}_1$ and $\hat{\beta}_2$ and define

$$\sigma^2 C_{ij} = \text{cov}(\hat{\beta}_i, \hat{\beta}_j) \quad i, j = 1, 2$$

Then, under the null hypothesis $\beta_1 + \beta_2 - 1 = 0$, we have the result that $\hat{\beta}_1 + \hat{\beta}_2 - 1$ is normally distributed with mean 0 and variance $\sigma^2(C_{11} + 2C_{12} + C_{22})$.

Since RSS/σ^2 has an independent χ^2-distribution with d.f. $(n-3)$, the t-statistic to test the hypothesis is given by

$$t = \frac{\hat{\beta}_1 + \hat{\beta}_2 - 1}{\sqrt{C_{11} + 2C_{12} + C_{22}}} \bigg/ \sqrt{\frac{RSS}{n-3}}$$

which has a t-distribution with d.f. $(n-3)$.

An alternative procedure is to derive URSS and RRSS and use the F-test. URSS is the residual sum of squares we obtain when we estimate α, β_1, and β_2. To get RRSS, we have to use the restriction $\beta_1 + \beta_2 - 1 = 0$. The way to do this is to eliminate β_2 since $\beta_2 = 1 - \beta_1$. Thus we get the regression equation as

$$\log X = \alpha + \beta_1 \log L + (1 - \beta_1) \log K + u$$

or

$$(\log X - \log K) = \alpha + \beta_1 (\log L - \log K) + u$$

Thus to get RRSS we regress $(\log X - \log K)$ on $(\log L - \log K)$. The residual sum of squares from this equation gives us the required RRSS.

The same procedure applies if we have two linear restrictions. Consider, for instance, the case of the multiple regression equation

$$y = \alpha + \beta_1 x_1 + \beta_2 x_2 + \beta_3 x_3 + u$$

and we need to test the restrictions

$$\beta_1 + \beta_2 + \beta_3 = 1 \quad \beta_2 - 2\beta_3 = 0$$

Note that these restrictions can be written as

$$\beta_2 = 2\beta_3 \quad \text{and} \quad \beta_1 = 1 - 3\beta_3$$

Substituting these in the original equation, we get

$$y = \alpha + (1 - 3\beta_3)x_1 + 2\beta_3 x_2 + \beta_3 x_3 + u$$

or

$$(y - x_1) = \alpha + \beta_3(-3x_1 + 2x_2 + x_3) + u$$

Thus we get the restricted residual sum of squares RRSS by running a regression of $(y - x_1)$ on $(-3x_1 + 2x_2 + x_3)$ with a constant term.

Illustrative Example

Consider again the illustrative example in Section 4.3. Suppose that the problem is to test the hypothesis:

$$H_0 : \frac{\beta_1}{\beta_2} = \frac{5}{3} \quad \text{against} \quad H_1 : \frac{\beta_1}{\beta_2} \neq \frac{5}{3}$$

at the 5% significance level. The hypothesis is $\beta_2 = 0.6\beta_1$. To compute the restricted estimates, we substitute $\beta_2 = 0.6\beta_1$ and estimate the equation

$$y = \alpha + \beta_1 x + \varepsilon$$

where

$$x = x_1 + 0.6x_2$$

We now have

$$S_{xx} = S_{11} + (0.6)^2 S_{22} + 2(0.6)S_{12}$$
$$= 12 + (0.6)^2(12) + 2(0.6)(8) = 25.92$$
$$S_{xy} = S_{1y} + 0.6S_{2y}$$
$$= 10 + 0.6(8) = 14.8$$

Hence

$$\hat{\beta}_1 = \frac{14.8}{25.92} \simeq 0.57$$

$$\text{RRSS} = S_{yy} - \hat{\beta}_1 S_{xy} = 10 - 8.45 = 1.55$$

Thus RRSS − URSS = 1.55 − 1.40 = 0.15 and the F-statistic is

$$F = \frac{0.15/1}{1.4/20} = \frac{0.15}{0.07} \simeq 2.1$$

which, with d.f. 1 and 20, is not significant at the 5% level.

By the alternative method, we consider $\hat{\beta}_2 - 0.6\hat{\beta}_1$. It is normally distributed with mean zero (under H_0) and using the expression for C we note that its variance is

$$\sigma^2 \left[\frac{12}{80} + (0.6)^2 \frac{12}{80} - 2(0.6)\left(-\frac{1}{10}\right) \right] = 0.324\sigma^2$$

Since

$$\hat{\beta}_2 - 0.6\hat{\beta}_1 = 0.2 - 0.6(0.7) = -0.22$$

we have the F-statistic

$$F = \frac{(-0.22)^2/0.324}{1.4/20} = \frac{0.15}{0.07}$$

which is the same as the one obtained earlier.

4.9 Omission of Relevant Variables and Inclusion of Irrelevant Variables

Until now we have assumed that the multiple regression equation we are estimating includes all the relevant explanatory variables. In practice, this is rarely the case.

Sometimes some relevant variables are not included due to oversight or lack of measurements. At other times some irrelevant variables are included. What we would like to know is how our inferences change when these problems are present.

Omission of Relevant Variables

Let us first consider the omission of relevant variables. Suppose that the true equation is

$$y = \beta_1 x_1 + \beta_2 x_2 + u \tag{4.15}$$

Instead, we omit x_2 and estimate the equation

$$y = \beta_1 x_1 + e$$

This will be referred to as the "misspecified model." The estimate of β_1 we get is

$$\hat{\beta}_1 = \frac{\sum x_1 y}{\sum x_1^2}$$

Substituting the expression for y from equation (4.15) in this, we get

$$\hat{\beta}_1 = \frac{\sum x_1(\beta_1 x_1 + \beta_2 x_2 + u)}{\sum x_1^2} = \beta_1 + \beta_2 \frac{\sum x_1 x_2}{\sum x_1^2} + \frac{\sum x_1 u}{\sum x_1^2}$$

Since $E(\sum x_1 u) = 0$ we get

$$E(\hat{\beta}_1) = \beta_1 + b_{21}\beta_2 \tag{4.16}$$

where $b_{21} = \sum x_1 x_2 / \sum x_1^2$ is the regression coefficient from a regression of x_2 on x_1.

Thus $\hat{\beta}_1$ is a biased estimator for β_1 and the bias is given by

$$\text{bias} = (\text{coefficient of the excluded variable})$$

$$\times \left(\begin{array}{l} \text{regression coefficient in a regression of the} \\ \text{excluded variable on the included variable} \end{array} \right)$$

If we denote the estimator for β_1 from equation (4.15) by $\tilde{\beta}_1$, the variance of $\tilde{\beta}_1$ is given by

$$\text{var}(\tilde{\beta}_1) = \frac{\sigma^2}{S_{11}(1 - r_{12}^2)}$$

where

$$S_{11} = \sum x_1^2$$

On the other hand,

$$\text{var}(\hat{\beta}_1) = \frac{\sigma^2}{S_{11}}$$

Thus $\hat{\beta}_1$ is a biased estimator but has a smaller variance than β_1. In fact, the variance would be considerably smaller if r_{12}^2 is high. However, the estimated standard error need not be smaller for $\hat{\beta}_1$ than for $\tilde{\beta}_1$. This is because σ^2, the estimated variance of the error, can be higher in the misspecified model. It is given by the residual sum of squares divided by degrees of freedom, and this can be higher (or lower) for the misspecified model.

Let us denote the estimated variance by S^2. Then the formula connecting the estimated variances is

$$\frac{S^2(\hat{\beta}_1)}{S^2(\tilde{\beta}_1)} = \frac{1 - r_{12}^2}{1 - r_{y2\cdot1}^2}$$

Thus the standard error of $\hat{\beta}_1$ will be less than the standard error of $\tilde{\beta}_1$ only if $r_{12}^2 > r_{y2\cdot1}^2$.

We have considered the case of only one included and one omitted variable. In the case where we have $k - 1$ included variables and the kth variable omitted, formula (4.16) generalizes to

$$E(\hat{\beta}_i) = \beta_i + b_{ki}\beta_k \quad i = 1, 2, \ldots, k - 1 \tag{4.17}$$

where b_{ki} is the regression coefficient of x_i in the auxiliary regression of x_k on $x_1, x_2, \ldots, x_{k-1}$. That is, we consider the regression of the omitted variable x_k on *all* the included variables.

In the general case[10] where we have several included variables and several omitted variables, we have to estimate the "auxiliary" multiple regressions of *each* of the excluded variables on *all* the included variables. The bias in each of the estimated coefficients of the included variables will be a weighted sum of the coefficients of all the excluded variables with weights obtained from these auxiliary multiple regressions.

Suppose that we have k explanatory variables, of which the first k_1 are included and the remaining $(k - k_1)$ are omitted. Then the formula corresponding to equations (4.16) and (4.17) is

$$E(\hat{\beta}_i) = \beta_i + \sum_{j=k_1+1}^{k} b_{ji}\beta_j \quad i = 1, 2, \ldots, k_1 \tag{4.18}$$

where b_{ji} is the regression coefficient of the ith included variable in a regression of the jth omitted variable on all the included variables. Note that we pick the coefficients of the ith included variable from the $(k - k_1)$ auxiliary multiple regressions.

The formulas (4.16)–(4.18) can be used to get some rough estimates of the direction of the biases in estimated coefficients when some variables are omitted because of lack of observations or because they are not measurable. We will present two examples, one in which the omitted variable is actually measured and the other in which it is not.

Example 1: Demand for Food in the United States

Consider the estimation of the demand for food in the United States based on the data in Table 4.9. Suppose that the "true" equation is

$$Q_D = \alpha + \beta_1 P_D + \beta_2 Y + u$$

---

[10]We will not go through the derivation here because the use of matrix notation is unavoidable. Proofs can be found in many textbooks in econometrics. See, for instance, Maddala, *Econometrics*, p. 461.

However, we omit the income variable. We get (figures in parentheses are standard errors)

$$\hat{Q}_D = 89.97 + \underset{(11.85)}{\,} 0.107 P_D \underset{(0.118)}{\,} \quad \hat{\sigma}^2 = 2.338$$

The coefficient of P_D has the wrong sign. Can this be attributed to the omission of the income variable? The answer is yes, because the coefficient of P_D is a biased estimate with the bias given by

$$\text{bias} = (\text{coefficient of the income variable})$$

$$\times \,(\text{regression coefficient of income on price})$$

The coefficient of income is expected to be positive. Also, given that the data are time-series data, we would expect a positive correlation between P_D and Y. Hence the bias is expected to be positive, and this could turn a negative coefficient to a positive one.

In this case the regression equation with Y included gives the result (figures in parentheses are standard errors)

$$\hat{Q}_D = 92.05 - \underset{(5.84)}{\,} 0.142 P_D \underset{(0.067)}{\,} + 0.236 Y \underset{(0.031)}{\,} \quad \hat{\sigma}^2 = 1.952$$

Note that the coefficient of P_D is now negative. Also, note that the standard error of the coefficient of P_D is higher in the misspecified model than in the "true" model. This is so despite the fact that the variance of β_1 is expected to be smaller in the misspecified model. (Check the relationship between r_{12}^2 and $r_{y2\cdot1}^2$ with the data.)

Example 2: Production Functions and Management Bias

In the estimation of production functions we have to omit the quality of inputs and managerial inputs because of lack of measurement. Consider the estimation of the production function

$$y = \beta_1 x_1 + \beta_2 x_2 + \beta_3 x_3 + u$$

where

$$y = \log \text{ of output}$$

$$x_1 = \log \text{ of labor input}$$

$$x_2 = \log \text{ of capital input}$$

$$x_3 = \log \text{ of managerial input}$$

Now x_3 is not observable. What will be the effect of this on estimates of β_1 and β_2? From the formula (4.17) we have

$$E(\hat{\beta}_1) = \beta_1 + b_{31}\beta_3$$

$$E(\hat{\beta}_2) = \beta_2 + b_{32}\beta_3$$

where b_{31} and b_{32} are the regression coefficients in the regression of x_3 on x_1 and x_2. Now $\beta_1 + \beta_2$ is often referred to as "returns to scale." Let us denote this by S. The estimated returns to scale, $\hat{S}$ is $\hat{\beta}_1 + \hat{\beta}_2$. Thus

$$E(\hat{S}) = S + \beta_3(b_{31} + b_{32})$$

Since β_3 is expected to be positive, the bias in the estimation of returns to scale will depend on the sign of $b_{31} + b_{32}$. If we assume that managerial input does not increase proportionately with measured inputs of labor and capital, we would expect $b_{31} + b_{32}$ to be negative and thus there is a downward bias in the estimates of returns to scale.

Inclusion of Irrelevant Variables

Consider now the case of inclusion of irrelevant variables. Suppose that the true equation is

$$y = \beta_1 x_1 + u$$

but we estimate the equation

$$y = \beta_1 x_1 + \beta_2 x_2 + v$$

The least squares estimators $\tilde{\beta}_1$ and $\tilde{\beta}_2$ from this misspecified equation are given by

$$\tilde{\beta}_1 = \frac{S_{22}S_{1y} - S_{12}S_{2y}}{S_{11}S_{22} - S_{12}^2}$$

$$\tilde{\beta}_2 = \frac{S_{11}S_{2y} - S_{12}S_{1y}}{S_{11}S_{22} - S_{12}^2}$$

where $S_{11} = \sum x_1^2$, $S_{1y} = \sum x_1 y$, $S_{12} = \sum x_1 x_2$, and so on. Since $y = \beta_1 x_1 + u$ we have $E(S_{2y}) = \beta_1 S_{12}$ and $E(S_{1y}) = \beta_1 S_{11}$. Hence we get

$$E(\tilde{\beta}_1) = \beta_1 \quad \text{and} \quad E(\tilde{\beta}_2) = 0$$

Thus we get unbiased estimates for both the parameters. This result, coupled with the earlier results regarding the bias introduced by the omission of relevant variables, might lead us to believe that it is better to include variables (when in doubt) rather than exclude them. However, this is not so, because though the inclusion of irrelevant variables has no effect on the bias of the estimators, it does affect the variances.

The variance of $\hat{\beta}_1$, the estimator of β_1 from the correct equation is given by

$$V(\hat{\beta}_1) = \frac{\sigma^2}{S_{11}}$$

On the other hand, from the misspecified equation we have

$$\text{var}(\tilde{\beta}_1) = \frac{\sigma^2}{(1 - r_{12}^2)S_{11}}$$

where r_{12} is the correlation between x_1 and x_2. Thus $\text{var}(\tilde{\beta}_1) > \text{var}(\hat{\beta}_1)$ unless $r_{12} = 0$. Hence we will be getting unbiased but inefficient estimates by including the irrelevant variable. It can be shown that the estimator for the residual variance we use is an unbiased estimator of σ^2. Thus there is no further bias arising from the use of estimated variance from the misspecified equation.[11]

4.10   Degrees of Freedom and $\overline{R}^2$

If we have n observations and estimate three regression parameters as in equation (4.1), we can see from the normal equations (4.2)–(4.4) that the estimated residuals $\hat{u}_i$ satisfy three linear restrictions:

$$\sum \hat{u}_i = 0 \quad \sum x_{1i}\hat{u}_i = 0 \quad \sum x_{2i}\hat{u}_i = 0 \tag{4.19}$$

or, in essence, there are only $(n - 3)$ residuals to vary because, given any $(n - 3)$ residuals, the remaining three residuals can be obtained by solving equations (4.19). This point we express by saying that there are $(n - 3)$ degrees of freedom.

As we saw earlier, the estimate of the residual variance σ^2 is given by

$$\hat{\sigma}^2 = \frac{\text{RSS}}{\text{degrees of freedom}}$$

As we increase the number of explanatory variables RSS declines but there is a decrease in the degrees of freedom as well. What happens to $\hat{\sigma}^2$ depends on the proportionate decrease in the numerator and the denominator. Thus there will be a point when $\hat{\sigma}^2$ will actually start increasing as we add more explanatory variables. It is often suggested that we should choose the set of variables for which $\hat{\sigma}^2$ is the minimum. We discuss the rationale behind this procedure in Chapter 12.[12]

This is also the reason why, in multiple regression problems, it is customary to report what is known as *adjusted R^2*, denoted by $\overline{R}^2$. The measure R^2 defined earlier keeps on increasing (until it reaches 1.0) as we add extra explanatory variables and thus does not take account of the degrees of freedom problem. $\overline{R}^2$ is simply R^2 adjusted for degrees of freedom. It is defined by the relation

$$1 - \overline{R}^2 = \frac{n - 1}{n - k - 1}(1 - R^2) \tag{4.20}$$

where k is the number of regressors. We subtract $(k + 1)$ from n because we estimate a constant term in addition to the coefficients of these k regressors. We can write equation (4.20) as

$$\frac{(1 - \overline{R}^2)S_{yy}}{n - 1} = \frac{(1 - R^2)S_{yy}}{n - k - 1} = \hat{\sigma}^2 \tag{4.21}$$

---

[11] See Maddala, *Econometrics*, p. 157.

[12] In the limiting case when the number of parameters estimated is equal to the number of observations, we get $\hat{\sigma}^2 = 0/0$.

Since S_{yy} and n are constant, as we increase the number of regressors included in the equation, $\hat{\sigma}^2$ and $(1 - \overline{R}^2)$ move in the same direction as $\hat{\sigma}^2$ and $\overline{R}^2$ move in the opposite direction. Thus the set of variables that gives minimum $\hat{\sigma}^2$ is also the set that maximizes $\overline{R}^2$.

Also, from equation (4.20) we can easily see that if $R^2 < k/(n - 1)$, $1 - R^2 > (n - k - 1)/(n - 1)$ and hence $1 - \overline{R}^2 > 1$. Thus $\overline{R}^2$ is negative! For example, with 2 explanatory variables and 21 observations, if $R^2 < 0.1$, $\overline{R}^2$ will be negative.

There is a relationship between the t-tests and F-tests outlined earlier and $\overline{R}^2$. If the t-ratio for the coefficient of any variable is less than 1, then dropping that variable will increase $\overline{R}^2$. More generally, if the F-ratio for any set of variables is less than 1, then dropping this set of variables from the regression equation will increase $\overline{R}^2$. Since the single-variable problem is a special case of the many-variable problem, we will prove the latter result. Equation (4.21) shows the relationship between $\overline{R}^2$ and $\hat{\sigma}^2$. So, instead of asking the question of whether dropping the variables will increase $\overline{R}^2$, we can as well ask the question of whether $\hat{\sigma}^2$ will decrease.

Let $\hat{\sigma}_1^2$ be the estimate of σ^2 when we drop r regressors. Then

$$\hat{\sigma}_1^2 = \frac{\text{restricted residual sum of squares}}{n - (k - r) - 1}$$

Since the unrestricted residual sum of squares is $(n - k - 1)\hat{\sigma}^2$, the F-test outlined earlier is given by

$$F = \frac{[(n - k + r - 1)\hat{\sigma}_1^2 - (n - k - 1)\hat{\sigma}^2]/r}{[(n - k - 1)\hat{\sigma}^2]/(n - k - 1)}$$

Solving for $\hat{\sigma}_1^2/\hat{\sigma}^2$ yields

$$\frac{\hat{\sigma}_1^2}{\hat{\sigma}^2} = \frac{a + F}{a + 1} \quad \text{where} \quad a = \frac{n - k - 1}{r}$$

Thus $\hat{\sigma}_1^2 \gtrless \hat{\sigma}^2$ according as $F \gtrless 1$. What this says is that if the F-ratio associated with a set of explanatory variables is < 1, we can increase $\overline{R}^2$ by dropping that set of variables. Since for 1 degree of freedom in the numerator, $F = t^2$, what this means is that if the absolute value of the t-ratio for any explanatory variable is less than 1, dropping that variable will increase $\overline{R}^2$. However, we have to be careful about t-ratios for individual coefficients and F-ratios for sets of coefficients and we will discuss the relationships between t and F ratios. There are two cases that create problems:

Case 1. The t-ratios are less than 1 but the F-ratio is greater than 1.
Case 2. The t-ratios are all greater than 1 but the F-ratio for a set of variables is < 1.

Case 1 occurs when the explanatory variables are highly intercorrelated. (This is called *multicollinearity*, which we discuss in Chapter 7.) This case that all the t-ratios are less than 1 does not mean that we can increase $\overline{R}^2$ by dropping *all* the variables. Once we drop one variable the other t-ratios will change.

In case 2, though by dropping any one variable we cannot increase $\overline{R}^2$, it might be possible to get a higher $\overline{R}^2$ by dropping a *set* of explanatory variables. Suppose that we have a regression equation in which all the explanatory variables have t-ratios which are greater than 1. Obviously, we cannot increase $\overline{R}^2$ by dropping any one of the variables. But how do we know whether we can increase $\overline{R}^2$ by dropping some sets of variables without searching over all the sets and subsets?

To answer this question we will state a simple rule that gives the relationship between t and F ratios. Consider a set of k variables that are candidates for exclusion; and let $F(k, n)$ be the F-ratio associated with these variables (n is the sample size). Then the rule says: If $F(k, n) \leq c$, the absolute t-values of each of the k discarded variables must be less than $\sqrt{kc}$, that is, if $F(k, n) \leq 1$, the absolute t-value of each of the k variables is $< \sqrt{k}$. The converse, however, is not true.[13] Thus if we do not have at least k variables with absolute t-values less than $\sqrt{k}$, $\overline{R}^2$ cannot be increased by discarding k independent variables at a time.

However, if there are k or more independent variables with absolute t-values less than $\sqrt{k}$, the F-ratio may or may not be less than 1, and hence we may or may not be able to increase $\overline{R}^2$ by discarding these variables. But if the $\overline{R}^2$ is increased, the variables to be discarded must come from the set of independent variables with absolute t-values less than $\sqrt{k}$.

As an illustration, consider the case $k = 7$. Since $\sqrt{7} = 2.6$, if the F-ratio is less than 1, all we can say about the t-ratios is that the t-ratios are less than 2.6. But this means that we can have all the t-ratios significant and yet have the $\overline{R}^2$ rise by dropping all the variables.

As yet another example, consider a regression equation with five independent variables and t-ratios of 1.2, 1.5, 1.6, 2.3, and 2.7. Note that $\sqrt{2} = 1.414$, $\sqrt{3} = 1.732$, and $\sqrt{5} = 2.236$. We consider $k = 1, 2, 3, 4, 5$ and check whether there are k t-ratios $< \sqrt{k}$. We note that this is the case for only $k = 3$. Thus if we can increase $\overline{R}^2$ at all, it is by dropping the three variables x_1, x_2, x_3. Thus all we have to do is to run the regression with these three variables excluded and check whether $\overline{R}^2$ has increased.

The point in all this discussion is that in multiple regression equations one has to be careful in drawing conclusions from individual t-ratios. In particular, this is so for analyzing the effect on $\overline{R}^2$ of deletion or addition of sets of variables. Often, in applied work it is customary to run a "stepwise" regression where explanatory variables are entered into an equation sequentially (in order determined by the maximum partial r^2 at each stage), and to stop at a point where $\overline{R}^2$ stops increasing. What the previous discussion shows is that it might be possible to increase $\overline{R}^2$ by introducing a set of variables together.

---

[13]Potluri Rao, "On a Correspondence Between t and F Values in Multiple Regression," *American Statistician*, Vol. 30, No. 4, 1976, pp. 190–191. We just present the results here; those interested in the derivation can refer to Potluri Rao's paper.

Thus there are problems with maximizing $\bar{R}^2$. But if one is going to do it, the relationship between t and F ratios we have discussed will be of some help. The rationale behind the maximization of $\bar{R}^2$ is discussed in Chapter 12.

A Cautionary Note on the Omission of Nonsignificant Variables: Finally, there is one other result that needs to be noted regarding the procedure of deleting variables whose coefficients are not "significant." Often researchers are perturbed by some "wrong" signs for some of the coefficients. In an effort to obtain hopefully "right" signs, statistically insignificant variables are dropped. Surprisingly enough, there can be no change in the sign of any coefficient that is more significant than the coefficient of the omitted variable. Leamer[14] shows that the constrained least squares estimate of β_j must lie between $(\hat{\beta}_j - ts_j, \hat{\beta}_j + ts_j)$, where

$$\hat{\beta}_j = \text{unconstrained estimate of } \beta_j$$

$$s_j = \text{standard error of } \hat{\beta}_j$$

$$t = \text{absolute } t\text{-value for the deleted variable}$$

We will not go through the proof here. It can be found in Leamer's article. The result enables us to predict the sign changes in the coefficients of the retained variables when one of the variables is deleted.

As an illustration, consider the problem of estimation of the demand for Ceylonese tea in the United States. This example is discussed in Rao and Miller.[15] The following is the list of variables used:

$$\text{Tea} = \text{demand for Ceylonese tea in the United States}$$

$$Y = \text{disposable income}$$

$$P_C = \text{price of Ceylonese tea}$$

$$P_B = \text{price of Brazilian coffee, considered a substitute}$$

Y, P_C, and P_B are deflated by the price of food commodities in the United States. All equations are estimated in log-linear form. The results are (figures in parentheses are standard errors)

$$\log \text{Tea} = 3.95 + 0.14 \log P_B + 0.75 \log Y + 0.05 \log P_C$$
$$\quad\quad\quad (1.99)\quad\quad (0.14)\quad\quad\quad (0.24)\quad\quad\quad (0.41)$$

The coefficient of $\log P_C$ has the wrong sign, although it is not significantly different from zero. However, dropping the variable P_B, we get

$$\log \text{Tea} = 3.22 + 0.67 \log Y + 0.04 \log P_C$$
$$\quad\quad\quad (2.02)\quad\quad (0.25)\quad\quad\quad (0.42)$$

[14]E. E. Leamer, "A Result on the Sign of the Restricted Least Squares Estimates," *Journal of Econometrics*, Vol. 3, 1975, pp. 387–390.

[15]Potluri Rao and Roger Miller, *Applied Econometrics* (Belmont, CA: Wadsworth, 1971), pp. 38–40.

Another alternative is to drop the variable $\log P_C$ arguing that the demand for Ceylonese tea is price inelastic. This procedure gives us the result

$$\log \text{Tea} = \underset{(0.71)}{3.73} + \underset{(0.13)}{0.14} \log P_B + \underset{(0.14)}{0.73} \log Y$$

However, the correct solution to the problem of a wrong sign for $\log P_C$ is neither to drop that variable nor to drop $\log P_B$ but to see whether some other relevant variables have been omitted. In this case the inclusion of the variable

$$P_I = \text{price of Indian tea which is a close substitute for Ceylonese tea}$$

produces more meaningful results. The results are now

$$\log \text{Tea} = \underset{(2.00)}{2.84} + \underset{(0.13)}{0.19} \log P_B + \underset{(0.37)}{0.26} \log Y - \underset{(0.98)}{1.48} \log P_C + \underset{(0.69)}{1.18} \log P_I$$

Note the coefficient of $\log P_C$ is now negative and the income elasticity has dropped considerably (from 0.73 to 0.26), and is not significant.

Of course, in this case the variable P_I should have been included in the first place rather than as an afterthought. The deletion of $\log Y$ from the last equation will not change the signs of any of the other coefficients by Leamer's rule. The resulting equation is

$$\log \text{Tea} = \underset{(1.39)}{1.85} + \underset{(0.13)}{0.20} \log P_B - \underset{(0.39)}{2.10} \log P_C + \underset{(0.42)}{1.56} \log P_I$$

Now $\log P_C$ and $\log P_I$ are both significant, and have the correct signs.

4.11 Tests for Stability

When we estimate a multiple regression equation and use it for predictions at future points of time we assume that the parameters are constant over the entire time period of estimation and prediction. To test this hypothesis of parameter constancy (or stability) some tests have been proposed. These tests can be described as:

1. Analysis of variance tests.
2. Predictive tests.

The Analysis of Variance Test

Suppose that we have two independent sets of data with sample sizes n_1 and n_2, respectively. The regression equation is

$$y = \alpha_1 + \beta_{11}x_1 + \beta_{12}x_2 + \cdots + \beta_{1k}x_k + u \text{ for the first set}$$
$$y = \alpha_2 + \beta_{21}x_1 + \beta_{22}x_2 + \cdots + \beta_{2k}x_k + u \text{ for the second set}$$

For the β's the first subscript denotes the data set and the second subscript denotes the variable. A test for stability of the parameters between the populations that generated the two data sets is a test of the hypothesis

$$H_0 : \beta_{11} = \beta_{21}, \beta_{12} = \beta_{22}, \ldots, \beta_{1k} = \beta_{2k}, \alpha_1 = \alpha_2$$

If this hypothesis is true, we can estimate a single equation for the data set obtained by pooling the two data sets.

The F-test we use is the F-test described in Section 4.8 based on URSS and RRSS. To get the unrestricted residual sum of squares we estimate the regression model for each of the data sets separately. Define

$$\text{RSS}_1 = \text{residual sum of squares for the first data set}$$

$$\text{RSS}_2 = \text{residual sum of squares for the second data set}$$

$$\frac{\text{RSS}_1}{\sigma^2} \text{ has a } \chi^2\text{-distribution with d.f. } (n_1 - k - 1)$$

$$\frac{\text{RSS}_2}{\sigma^2} \text{ has a } \chi^2\text{-distribution with d.f. } (n_2 - k - 1)$$

Since the two data sets are independent $(\text{RSS}_1 + \text{RSS}_2)/\sigma^2$ has a χ^2-distribution with d.f. $(n_1 + n_2 - 2k - 2)$. We will denote $(\text{RSS}_1 + \text{RSS}_2)$ by URSS. The restricted residual sum of squares RRSS is obtained from the regression with the pooled data. (This imposes the restriction that the parameters are the same.) Thus RRSS/σ^2 has a χ^2-distribution with d.f. $(n_1 + n_2 - k - 1)$.

$$F = \frac{(\text{RRSS} - \text{URSS})/(k + 1)}{\text{URSS}/(n_1 + n_2 - 2k - 2)} \tag{4.22}$$

which has an F-distribution with d.f. $(k + 1)$ and $(n_1 + n_2 - 2k - 2)$. This test is derived in the appendix to this chapter.

Example 1: Stability of the Demand for Food Function

Consider the data in Table 4.3, where we fitted separate demand functions for 1927–1941 and 1948–1962 and for the entire period. Suppose that we want to test the stability of the parameters in the demand function between the two periods. The required numbers are given in Table 4.4.

For equation 1 we have

$$\text{URSS} = \text{sum of RSSs from the two separate regressions}$$
$$\text{for } 1927\text{–}1941 \quad \text{and} \quad 1948\text{–}1962$$
$$= 0.1151 + 0.0544 = 0.1695$$
$$\text{with d.f.} = 12 + 12 = 24$$
$$\text{RRSS} = \text{RSS from a regression for the pooled data}$$
$$= 0.2866 \text{ with d.f.} = 27$$

This regression from the pooled data imposes the restriction that the parameters are the same in the two periods. Hence

$$F = \frac{(0.2866 - 0.1695)/3}{0.1695/24} = 5.53$$

From the F-tables with d.f. 3 and 24 we see that the 5% point is about 3.01 and the 1% point is about 4.72. Thus, even at the 1% level of significance, we reject the hypothesis of stability. Thus there is no case for pooling.

Note that if we look at the individual coefficients, $\hat{\beta}_1$ is almost the same for the two regressions. Thus it appears that the price elasticity has been constant but it is the income elasticity that has changed in the two periods. In Chapter 8 we discuss procedures of testing the stability of individual coefficients using the dummy variable method.

Consider now equation 2. We have

$$\text{URSS} = 0.1151 + 0.0535 = 0.1686 \text{ with d.f. } = 11 + 11 = 22$$

$$\text{RRSS} = 0.2412 \text{ with d.f. } = 26$$

Hence

$$F = \frac{(0.2412 - 0.1686)/4}{0.1686/22} = 2.37$$

From the F-tables with d.f. 4 and 22 we see that the 5% point is about 2.82. So, at the 5% significance level, we do not reject the hypothesis of stability.

One can ask how this result came about. If we look at the individual coefficients for equation 2 for the two periods 1927–1941 and 1948–1962 separately, we notice that the t-ratios are very small, that is, the standard errors are very high relative to the magnitudes of the coefficient estimates. Thus the observed differences in the coefficient estimates between the two periods would not be statistically significant. When we look at the regression for the pooled data we notice that the coefficient of the interaction term is significant, but the estimates for the two periods separately, as well as the rejection of the hypothesis of stability for equation 1, casts doubt on the desirability of including the interaction term.

Example 2: Stability of Production Functions

Consider the data in Table 3.11 on output and labor and capital inputs in the United States for 1929–1967.[16] The variables are:

$X =$ index of gross domestic product (constant dollars)

$L_1 =$ labor input index (number of persons adjusted for hours of work and educational level)

$L_2 =$ persons engaged

$K_1 =$ capital input index (capital stock adjusted for rates of utilization)

$K_2 =$ capital stock in constant dollars

---

[16]The data are from L. R. Christensen and D. W. Jorgenson, "U.S. Real Product and Real Factor Input 1929–67," *Review of Income and Wealth*, March 1970.

We will estimate regression equations of the form

$$\log X = \alpha + \beta_1 \log L + \beta_2 \log K + u \tag{4.23}$$

First, considering the two measures of labor and capital inputs, we obtain the following results (figures in parentheses are standard errors):

$$\log X = -3.938 + \underset{(0.237)}{} 1.451 \log L_1 + 0.384 \log K_1 \tag{4.24}$$
$$\underset{(0.237)}{} \quad \underset{(0.083)}{} \quad \underset{(0.048)}{}$$

$$R^2 = 0.9946 \quad \overline{R}^2 = 0.9943 \quad \text{RSS} = 0.0434 \quad \hat{\sigma}^2 = 0.001205$$

$$\log X = -6.388 + 2.082 \log L_2 + 0.571 \log K_2$$
$$\underset{(0.294)}{} \quad \underset{(0.100)}{} \quad \underset{(0.067)}{}$$

$$R^2 = 0.9831 \quad \text{RSS} = 0.1363$$

Since the dependent variable is the same and the number of independent variables is the same, the R^2's are comparable. A comparison of the R^2's indicates that L_1 and K_1 are better explanatory variables than L_2 and K_2. Hence we will conduct further analysis with L_1 and K_1 only.

One other thing we notice is that all variables increase with time. Regressing each of the variables on time we find:

$$\log X = 4.897 + 0.0395t \quad R^2 = 0.9549$$
$$\underset{(0.032)}{} \quad \underset{(0.0014)}{}$$

$$\log L_1 = 4.989 + 0.0185t \quad R^2 = 0.9238$$
$$\underset{(0.020)}{} \quad \underset{(0.0009)}{}$$

$$\log K_1 = 4.171 + 0.0324t \quad R^2 = 0.9408$$
$$\underset{(0.031)}{} \quad \underset{(0.0013)}{}$$

We can eliminate these time trends from these variables and then estimate the production function with the trend-adjusted data. But this is the same as including t as an extra explanatory variable (see the discussion in Section 4.4).[17]

Thus we get the result

$$\log X = -3.015 + 1.341 \log L_1 + 0.292 \log K_1 + 0.0052t$$
$$\underset{(0.091)}{} \quad \underset{(0.060)}{} \quad \underset{(0.0022)}{}$$

$$R^2 = 0.9954 \quad \overline{R}^2 = 0.9949 \quad \text{RSS} = 0.0375 \quad \hat{\sigma}^2 = 0.001072$$

Comparing this result with equation (4.24), we notice that $\hat{\beta}_1 + \hat{\beta}_2$ has gone down from $1.451 + 0.384 = 1.835$ to $1.341 + 0.292 = 1.633$. $\hat{\beta}_1 + \hat{\beta}_2$ measures returns to scale. Also, the $\overline{R}^2$ has increased, or equivalently, $\hat{\sigma}^2$ has decreased. This is to be expected because the t-value for the last variable is greater than 1.

Although we do not need to test the hypothesis of constant returns to scale, that is $\beta_1 + \beta_2 = 1$, we will illustrate it. The estimated variances and covariances (from the SAS

---

[17]This result is commonly known as the Frisch–Waugh theorem.

regression package used) were

$$\text{estimate of } V(\hat{\beta}_1) = 0.008353 \quad \text{estimate of } V(\hat{\beta}_2) = 0.003581$$

$$\text{estimate of } \text{cov}(\hat{\beta}_1, \hat{\beta}_2) = -0.001552$$

Thus

$$\text{estimate of } V(\hat{\beta}_1 + \hat{\beta}_2 - 1) = 0.008353 + 0.003581 - 2(0.001552)$$

$$= 0.008830$$

Hence

$$\text{SE}(\hat{\beta}_1 + \hat{\beta}_2 - 1) = \sqrt{0.008830} = 0.094$$

The t-statistic to test $\beta_1 + \beta_2 - 1 = 0$ is

$$t = \frac{(\hat{\beta}_1 + \hat{\beta}_2 - 1) - (0)}{\text{SE}(\hat{\beta}_1 + \hat{\beta}_2 - 1)} = \frac{0.633}{0.094} = 6.73$$

From the t-tables with d.f. 34 we find that the 5% significance point is 2.03 and the 1% significance point is 2.73. Thus we reject the hypothesis of constant returns to scale even at the 1% level of significance.

Suppose that we estimate the production function (4.23) for the two periods 1929–1948 and 1949–1967 separately. We get the following results:

1929–1948

$$\log X = -\underset{(0.357)}{4.058} + \underset{(0.209)}{1.617} \log L_1 + \underset{(0.230)}{0.220} \log K_1 \qquad (4.25)$$

$$R^2 = 0.9759 \quad \text{RSS} = 0.03555 \quad \text{d.f.} = 17 \qquad (4.26)$$

1949–1967

$$\log X = -\underset{(0.531)}{2.498} + \underset{(0.144)}{1.009} \log L_1 + \underset{(0.055)}{0.579} \log K_1$$

$$R^2 = 0.9958 \quad \text{RSS} = 0.00336 \quad \text{d.f.} = 16$$

Applying the test for stability (4.22), we get

$$\text{URSS} = 0.03555 + 0.00336 = 0.0389 \text{ with d.f. } = 17 + 16 = 33$$

$$\text{RRSS} = 0.0434 \text{ [from (4.24) earlier] with d.f. } = 36$$

Thus

$$F = \frac{(0.0434 - 0.0389)/3}{0.0389/33} = 1.27$$

From the F-tables with d.f. 3 and 33 we find that the 5% point is 2.9. Thus at the 5% significance level we do not reject the hypothesis of stability.

Again, looking at the individual coefficient estimates for the two periods, this result is perplexing. We will consider some other tests for stability and see whether these tests confirm this result.

Predictive Tests for Stability

The analysis of variance test that we have discussed is also commonly referred to as the Chow test, although it had been known much earlier.[18] Chow suggests another test that can be used even when $n_2 < (k + 1)$. This is the predictive test for stability. The idea behind it is this: We use the first n_1 observations to estimate the regression equation and use it to get predictions for the next n_2 observations. Then we test the hypothesis that the prediction errors have mean zero. If $n_2 = 1$, we just use the method described in Section 4.7. If $n_2 > 1$, the F-test is given by

$$F = \frac{(\text{RRSS} - \text{RSS}_1)/n_2}{\text{RSS}_1/(n_1 - k - 1)} \tag{4.27}$$

which has an F-distribution with d.f. n_2 and $(n_1 - k - 1)$. Here

$$\text{RRSS} = \text{residual sum of squares from the regression based on } n_1 + n_2$$
$$\text{observations; this has d.f. } (n_1 + n_2 - k - 1)$$
$$\text{RSS}_1 = \text{residual sum of squares from the regression based on } n_1$$
$$\text{observations; this has d.f. } (n_1 - k - 1)$$

The proof is given in the appendix to this chapter.[19] In Chapter 8 we give a dummy variable method of applying the same test. We will first illustrate the use of this test and then discuss its advantages and limitations.

Illustrative Example

Consider the example of demand for food that we considered earlier. For equation 1 we have (from Table 4.4):

For 1927–1941: $\text{RSS}_1 = 0.1151$
For 1948–1962: $\text{RSS}_2 = 0.0544$
Combined data: $\text{RRSS} = 0.2866$

Considering the predictions for 1948–1962 using the estimated equation for 1927–1941, we have

$$F = \frac{(\text{RRSS} - \text{RSS}_1)/n_2}{\text{RSS}_1/(n_1 - k - 1)} = \frac{(0.2866 - 0.1151)/15}{0.1151/12} = 1.19$$

---

[18]G. C. Chow, "Tests of Equality Between Subsets of Coefficients in Two Linear Regression Models," *Econometrica*, 1960, pp. 591–605. The paper suggests two tests: the analysis of variance test and the predictive test. The former test, although referred to as the Chow test, was discussed earlier in C. R. Rao, *Advanced Statistical Methods in Biometric Research* (New York: Wiley, 1952), and S. Kullback and H. M. Rosenblatt, "On the Analysis of Multiple Regression in k Categories," *Biometrika*, 1957, pp. 67–83. Thus it is the second test — the predictive test — that should be called the Chow test.

[19]The proof given in the appendix follows Maddala, *Econometrics*, pp. 459–460.

From the F-tables with d.f. 15 and 12 we find that the 5% point is 2.62. Thus at the 5% level of significance, we do not reject the hypothesis of stability. The analysis of variance test led to the opposite conclusion.

For equation 2 we have (from Table 4.4):

$$\text{RRSS} = 0.1151 \quad \text{RSS}_2 = 0.0535 \quad \text{RRSS} = 0.2412$$

The F-test is

$$F = \frac{(0.2412 - 0.1151)/15}{0.1151/11} = 0.80$$

Thus at the 5% significance level we do not reject the hypothesis of stability. Thus the conclusions of the predictive test do not seem to be different from those of the analysis of variance test, for this equation.

However, for the predictive test, we can also reverse the roles of samples 1 and 2. That is, we can also ask the question of how well the equation fitted for the second period predicts for the first period. If the coefficients are stable, we should do well. The F-test for this is now (interchanging 1 and 2)

$$F = \frac{(\text{RRSS} - \text{RSS}_2)/n_1}{\text{RSS}_2/(n_2 - k - 1)} \tag{4.28}$$

which has an F-distribution with d.f. n_1 and $(n_2 - k - 1)$. For equation 2 we have

$$F = \frac{(0.2412 - 0.0535)/15}{0.0535/11} = 2.57$$

From the F-tables with d.f. 15 and 11 we see that the 5% point is 2.72 and the 1% point is 4.25. Thus, even at the 5% significance level, we cannot reject the hypothesis of stability of the coefficients.

Chow suggested the predictive test for the case where n_2 is less than $k + 1$. In this case the regression equation cannot be estimated with the second sample and thus the analysis of variance test cannot be applied. In this case only the predictive test can be used. He also suggested that the predictive test can be used even when $n_2 > (k + 1)$ but that in this case the analysis of variance test should be preferred because it is more powerful.

In our example we have $n_2 > (k + 1)$, but we have also used two predictive tests. In practice it is desirable to use both predictive tests as illustrated in our example.

Comments

1. Wilson[20] argues that though the Chow test (the predictive test) has been suggested only for the case $n_2 < (k + 1)$, that is, for the case when the analysis of variance test cannot be used, the test has desirable power properties when there are some unknown

---

[20] A. L. Wilson, "When Is the Chow Test UMP?," *The American Statistician*, Vol. 32, No. 2, May 1978, pp. 66–68.

specification errors. Hence it should be used even when $n_2 > (k + 1)$, that is, even in those cases where the analysis of variance test can be computed. We have illustrated how the predictive test can be used in two ways in this case.

2. Rea[21] argues that in the case $n_2 < (k + 1)$ the Chow test cannot be considered a test for stability. All it tests is that the prediction error has mean zero, that is, the predictions are unbiased. If the coefficients are stable, the prediction error will have zero mean. But the converse need not be true in the case $n_2 < (k + 1)$. The prediction error can have a zero mean even if the coefficients are not stable, if the explanatory variables have moved in an offsetting manner. Rea's conclusion is that "the Chow test is incapable of testing the hypothesis of equality against that of inequality. It can never be argued from the Chow test itself that the two sets [of regression coefficients] are equal, although at times it may be possible to conclude that they are unequal." This does not mean that the Chow test is not useful. Instead of calling it a test for stability we would call it a test for unbiasedness in prediction. Note that in the case both n_1 and n_2 are greater than $(k + 1)$, the two predictive tests that we have illustrated are tests for stability.

3. Another problem with the application of the tests for stability, which applies to both the analysis of variance and predictive tests, is that the tests are inaccurate if the error variances in the two samples are unequal.[22] The true size of the test (under the null hypothesis) may not equal the prescribed α level. For this reason it would be desirable to test the equality of the variances.

Consider, for instance, the error variances for equation 1 in Table 4.4. The F-statistic to test equality of error variances is

$$F = \left(\frac{\hat{\sigma}_1}{\hat{\sigma}_2}\right)^2 = \frac{0.9594}{0.4534} = 2.12$$

For the F-distribution with d.f. 12 and 12 the 5% point is 2.69. Thus we do not reject the hypothesis of equality at the 5% significance level.

For equation 2 the corresponding test statistic is

$$F = \frac{1.0462}{0.4866} = 2.15$$

Again if we use a 5% significance level, we do not reject the hypothesis of equality of the error variances.

Thus, in both cases we might be tempted to conclude that we can apply the tests for stability. There is, however, one problem with such a conclusion. This is that the F-test for equality of variances is a pretest, that is, it is a test preliminary to the test for stability. There is the question of what significance level we should use for such pretests. The general conclusion is that for pretests one should use a higher significance level than

[21] J. D. Rea, "Indeterminacy of the Chow Test When the Number of Observations Is Insufficient," *Econometrica*, Vol. 46, No. 1, January 1978, p. 229.

[22] This was pointed out in T. Toyoda, "Use of the Chow Test Under Heteroskedasticity," *Econometrica*, 1976, pp. 601–608. The approximations used by Toyoda were found to be inaccurate, but the inaccuracy of the Chow test holds good. See P. Schmidt and R. Sickles, "Some Further Evidence on the Use of the Chow Test Under Heteroskedasticity," *Econometrica*, Vol. 45, No. 5, July 1977, pp. 1293–1298.

5%. In fact, 25 to 50% is a good rule. If this is done, we would reject the hypothesis of equality of variances in the case of both equations 1 and 2.

*4.12   The LR, W, and LM Tests

In the appendix to Chapter 3 we stated large-sample test statistics to test the hypothesis $\beta = 0$. These were

$$LR = n \log_e \left(\frac{1}{1 - r^2} \right)$$

$$W = \frac{nr^2}{1 - r^2}$$

$$LM = nr^2$$

Each has a χ^2-distribution with d.f. 1. In the multiple regression model, to test the hypothesis $\beta_i = 0$ we use these test statistics with the corresponding *partial* r^2 substituted in the place of the simple r^2. The test statistics have a χ^2-distribution with d.f. 1.

To test hypotheses such as

$$\beta_1 = \beta_2 = \cdots = \beta_k = 0$$

we have to substitute the *multiple* R^2 in place of the simple r^2 or partial r^2 in these formulas. The test statistics have a χ^2-distribution with d.f. k.

To test any linear restrictions, we saw (in the appendix to Chapter 3) that the likelihood ratio test statistic was

$$LR = n \log_e \left(\frac{\text{RRSS}}{\text{URSS}} \right)$$

where   RRSS = restricted residual sum of squares
URSS = unrestricted residual sum of squares

LR has a χ^2-distribution with d.f. r, where r is the number of restrictions. The test statistics for the Wald test and the LM test are given by

$$W = \frac{\text{RRSS} - \text{URSS}}{\text{URSS}/n}$$

$$LM = \frac{\text{RRSS} - \text{URSS}}{\text{RRSS}/n}$$

Both W and LM have a χ^2-distribution with d.f. r. The inequality $W \geq LR \geq LM$ again holds and the proof is the same as that given in the appendix to Chapter 3.

Illustrative Example

Consider example 1 in Section 4.11 (stability of the demand for food function). For equation 1 we have

$$\text{URSS} = 0.1695 \quad \text{RRSS} = 0.2866 \quad n = 30$$

and the number of restrictions $r = 3$. We get

$$W = 20.73$$

$$LR = 15.76$$

$$LM = 12.62$$

Looking at the χ^2-tables for d.f. 3 the 0.01 significance point is 11.3. Thus all the test statistics are significant at that level, rejecting the hypothesis of coefficient stability. As we saw earlier, the F-test also rejected the hypothesis at the 1% significance level.

Turning to equation 2, we have

$$\text{URSS} = 0.1686 \quad \text{RRSS} = 0.2397 \quad n = 30 \quad r = 4$$

We now get

$$W = 12.65$$

$$LR = 10.56$$

$$LM = 8.90$$

From the χ^2-tables with d.f. 4 the 5% significance point is 9.49. Thus both the W and LR tests reject the hypothesis of coefficient stability at the 5% significance level, whereas the LM test does not. There is thus a conflict among the three test criteria. We saw earlier that the F-test did not reject the hypothesis at the 5% significance level either.

The conflict between the W, LR, and LM tests has been attributed to the fact that in small samples the actual significance levels may deviate substantially from the normal significance levels. That is, although we said we were testing the hypothesis of coefficient stability at the 5% significance level, we were in effect testing it at different levels for the different tests. Procedures have been developed to correct this problem but a discussion of these procedures is beyond the scope of this book. The suggested formulas are too complicated to be discussed here. However, the elementary introduction of these tests given here will be useful in understanding some other tests discussed in Chapters 4, 5, and 6.

Summary

This chapter is very long and hence summaries will be presented by sections.

(1) Sections 4.2 to 4.5: Model with Two Explanatory Variables

We discuss the model with two explanatory variables in great detail because it clarifies many aspects of multiple regression. Of special interest are the expressions for the variances of the estimates of the regression coefficients given at the beginning of Section 4.3. These expressions are used repeatedly later in the book. Also, it is important to keep in mind the distinction between separate confidence intervals for each individual parameter and joint confidence intervals for sets of parameters (discussed in Section 4.3). Similarly, there can be conflicts between tests for each coefficient separately (*t*-tests) and tests for a set of coefficients (*F*-test). (This is discussed in greater detail in Section 4.10.) Finally, in Section 4.5 it is shown that each coefficient in a multiple regression involving two variables can be interpreted as the regression coefficient in a simple regression involving two variables after removing the effect of all other variables on these two variables. This interpretation is useful in many problems and will be used in other parts of the book.

(2)

The illustrative examples given at the end of Section 4.3 show how sometimes we can get "wrong" signs for some of the coefficients and how this can change with the addition or deletion of variables. (We discuss this in more detail in Section 4.10.) The example of gasoline demand represents one where the results obtained were poor and further analysis with the data was left as an exercise.

(3) Section 4.6: Simple, Partial, and Multiple Correlations

In multiple regression it is important to note that there is no necessary relationship between the simple correlation between two variables y and x and the partial correlation between these variables after allowing for the effect of other variables (see Table 4.2 for an illustration). There is, however, some relationship between R^2 and the simple r^2 and partial r^2's. This is given in equation (4.12). Also partial $r^2 = t^2/(t^2 + \text{d.f.})$ is a useful relationship. Some examples are given to illustrate these relationships.

(4) Section 4.7: Prediction

In the case of the simple regression model (Section 3.7) the variance of the prediction increased with the distance x_0 from $\bar{x}$. In the case of prediction from the multiple regression model this is not necessarily the case. An example is given to illustrate this point. Again, as in the case of the simple regression model, we can consider prediction of y_0 or prediction of $E(y_0)$. The predicted value will be the same in both cases. However, the variance of the prediction error will be different. In the case of prediction of $E(y_0)$ we have to subtract σ^2 from the corresponding expression for the prediction of y_0. Note that we did not discuss the prediction of $E(y_0)$ here as we did this in the simple regression case (Section 3.7).

(5) Section 4.8: Tests of Hypotheses

Tests of single parameters and single linear functions of parameters will be *t*-tests. Tests of several parameters and several linear functions of parameters are *F*-tests. These are both illustrated with examples. Note again that there can be conflicts between the two tests. For instance, the *t*-statistics for each coefficient can be nonsignificant and yet the *F*-statistic for a set of coefficients can be significant.

(6) Section 4.9: Omitted Variables and Irrelevant Variables

The omission of relevant variables produces biased estimates. Expressions are given in equations (4.16)–(4.18) for the omitted variable bias. The variance of the estimated coefficient will be smaller, although the estimated variance (or standard error) need not be. These points are illustrated with examples. The case with the inclusion of irrelevant variables is different. There is no bias. However, the variance of the estimated coefficients increases. Thus we get unbiased but inefficient estimators. These are all only statistical guidelines regarding omission of relevant and inclusion of irrelevant variables.

(7) Section 4.10: $\overline{R}^2$

The addition of explanatory variables always increases R^2. This does not mean that the regression equation is improving. The appropriate thing to look at is the estimate of the error variance. An equivalent measure is $\overline{R}^2$, the value of R^2 adjusted for the loss in degrees of freedom due to the addition of more explanatory variables. It is given by equation (4.20). A procedure usually followed is to keep on adding variables until the $\overline{R}^2$ stops increasing. Apart from the lack of any economic rationale, there are some pitfalls in this procedure. The $\overline{R}^2$ might increase by the addition (or deletion) of two or more variables even though it might not if one variable is added (or dropped) at a time. Some rules are given for the prediction of sign changes in the estimates of the coefficients of the retained variables when a variable is deleted. Although maximization of $\overline{R}^2$ and mechanical deletion of nonsignificant variables have serious pitfalls, these rules provide some useful predictions.

(8) Section 4.11: Tests for Stability

In multiple regression analysis we are often concerned with the stability of the estimated relationships across two samples of sizes n_1 and n_2. We discuss and illustrate two tests: the analysis of variance test (AV test) and the predictive test (Chow test). In practice it is desirable to use both tests. If either n_1 or n_2 is not greater than the number of regression parameters estimated, the AV test cannot be used but the Chow test can be. However, in this case the Chow test is not a test for stability. It is merely a test for unbiasedness of predictions.

Exercises

More difficult exercises are marked with an asterisk.

1. Define the following terms:
   (a) Standard error of the regression.
   (b) R^2 and $\overline{R}^2$.
   (c) Partial r^2.
   (d) Tests for stability.
   (e) Degrees of freedom.
   (f) Linear functions of parameters.
   (g) Nested and nonnested hypotheses.
   (h) Analysis of variance.

2. In a multiple regression equation, show how you can obtain the partial r^2's given the t-ratios for the different coefficients.

3. In the multiple regression equation

$$y = \alpha + \beta_1 x_1 + \beta_2 x_2 + \beta_3 x_3 + u$$

Explain how you will test the joint hypothesis $\beta_1 = \beta_2$ and $\beta_3 = 1$.

4. The following regression equation is estimated as a production function:

$$\log Q = 1.37 + 0.632 \log K + 0.452 \log L \quad R^2 = 0.98$$
$$ {\scriptstyle (0.257)} {\scriptstyle (0.219)}$$

$\text{cov}(b_K, b_L) = -0.044$. The sample size is 40. Test the following hypotheses at the 5% level of significance:

(a) $b_K = b_L$.

(b) There are constant returns to scale.

5. Indicate whether each of the following statements is true (T), false (F), or uncertain (U), and give a brief explanation or proof:

(a) Suppose that the coefficient of a variable in a regression equation is significantly different from zero at the 20% level. If we drop this variable from the regression, both R^2 and $\overline{R}^2$ will necessarily decrease.

(b) Compared with the unconstrained regression, estimation of a least squares regression under a constraint (say, $\beta_2 = \beta_3$) will result in a higher R^2 if the constraint is true and a lower R^2 if it is false.

(c) In a least squares regression of y on x, observations for which x is far from its mean will have more effect on the estimated slope than observations for which x is close to its mean value.

6. The following estimated equation was obtained by ordinary least squares regression using quarterly data for 1960 to 1979 inclusive ($T = 80$):

$$\hat{y}_t = 2.20 + 0.104 x_{1t} + 3.48 x_{2t} + 0.34 x_{3t}$$
$$\phantom{\hat{y}_t =} {\scriptstyle (3.4)} {\scriptstyle (0.005)} {\scriptstyle (2.2)} {\scriptstyle (0.15)}$$

Standard errors are in parentheses, the explained sum of squares was 112.5, and the residual sum of squares was 19.5.

(a) Which of the slope coefficients are significantly different from zero at the 5% significance level?

(b) Calculate the value of R^2 for this regression.

(c) Calculate the value of $\overline{R}^2$ ("adjusted R^2").

7. Suppose that you are given two sets of samples with the following information:

Sample 1	Sample 2
$n = 20$	$n = 25$
$\bar{x} = 20$	$\bar{x} = 23$
$\bar{y} = 25$	$\bar{y} = 28$
$S_{xx} = 80$	$S_{xx} = 100$
$S_{xy} = 120$	$S_{xy} = 150$
$S_{yy} = 200$	$S_{yy} = 250$

(a) Estimate a linear regression equation for each sample separately and for the pooled sample.

(b) State the assumptions under which estimation of the pooled regression is valid.

(c) Explain how you will test the validity of these assumptions using the data provided.

8. A researcher tried two specifications of a regression equation:

$$y = \alpha + \beta x + u$$
$$y = \alpha' + \beta'x + \gamma'z + u'$$

Explain under what circumstances the following will be true. (A "hat" over a parameter denotes its estimate.)

(a) $\hat{\beta} = \hat{\beta}'$.

(b) If $\hat{u}_i$ and $\hat{u}'_i$ are the estimated residuals from the two equations $\sum \hat{u}_i^2 \geq \sum \hat{u}_i'^2$.

(c) $\hat{\beta}$ is statistically significant (at the 5% level) but $\hat{\beta}'$ is not.

(d) $\hat{\beta}'$ is statistically significant (at the 5% level) but $\hat{\beta}$ is not.

9. The model

$$y_t = \beta_0 + \beta_1 x_{1t} + \beta_2 x_{2t} + \beta_3 x_{3t} + u_t$$

was estimated by ordinary least squares from 26 observations. The results were

$$\hat{y}_t = 2 + 3.5x_{1t} - 0.7x_{2t} + 2.0x_{3t}$$
$$\phantom{\hat{y}_t = 2 + }\underset{(1.9)}{} \quad \underset{(2.2)}{} \quad \underset{(1.5)}{}$$

t-ratios are in parentheses and $R^2 = 0.982$. The same model was estimated with the restriction $\beta_1 = \beta_2$. Estimates were

$$\hat{y}_t = 1.5 + 3(x_{1t} + x_{2t}) - 0.6x_{3t} \quad R^2 = 0.876$$
$$\phantom{\hat{y}_t = 1.5 + }\underset{(2.7)}{} \quad \underset{(2.4)}{}$$

(a) Test the significance of the restriction $\beta_1 = \beta_2$. State the assumptions under which the test is valid.

(b) Suppose that x_{2t} is dropped from the equation: would the $\bar{R}^2$ rise or fall?

(c) Would the R^2 rise or fall if x_{2t} is dropped?

10. Suppose that the least squares regression of Y on $x_1, x_2, \ldots, x_k$ yields coefficient estimates b_j ($j = 1, 2, \ldots, k$) none of which exceed their respective standard errors. However, the F-ratio for the equation rejects, at the 0.05 level the hypothesis that $b_1 = b_2 = \cdots = b_k = 0$.

(a) Is this possible?

(b) What do you think is the reason for this?

(c) What further analysis would you perform?

11. What would be your answer to the following queries regarding multiple regression analysis?

(a) I am trying to find out why people go bankrupt. I have gathered data from a sample of people filing bankruptcy petitions. Will these data enable me to find answers to my question?

(b) I want to study the costs of auto accidents. I have collected data from a sample of police auto accident reports. Are these data adequate for my purpose?

(c) I am trying to estimate a consumption function and I suspect that the marginal propensity to consume varies inversely with the rate of interest. Do I run a multiple regression using income and interest rate as explanatory variables?

(d) I am fitting a demand for food function for a sample of 1000 families. I obtain an R^2 of only 0.05 but the regression program indicates that the F-statistic for the equation is very significant and so are the t-statistics. How can this be? Is there a mistake in the program?

(e) In the regression of Y on x and z, should I leave one of them out?

(f) I know that y depends linearly on x but I am not sure whether or not it also depends on another variable z. A friend of mine suggests that I should regress y on x first, calculate the residuals, and then see whether they are correlated with z. Is the correct?

12. A student obtains the following results in several different regression problems. In which cases could you be *certain* that an error has been committed? Explain.

(a) $R^2_{Y \cdot 123} = 0.89$, $R^2_{Y \cdot 1234} = 0.86$

(b) $\overline{R}^2_{Y \cdot 123} = 0.86$, $\overline{R}^2_{Y \cdot 1234} = 0.82$

(c) $r^2_{Y1 \cdot 2} = 0.23$, $r^2_{Y1 \cdot 3} = 0.13$, $R^2_{Y \cdot 123} = 0.70$

(d) Same as part (c) but $r^2_{Y2 \cdot 3} = 0$

13. Given the following estimated regression equations:

$$\hat{C}_t = \text{const.} + 0.92 Y_t$$

$$\hat{C}_t = \text{const.} + 0.84 C_{t-1}$$

$$\hat{C}_{t-1} = \text{const.} + 0.78 Y_t$$

$$\hat{Y}_t = \text{const.} + 0.55 C_{t-1}$$

calculate the regression estimates of β_1 and β_2 for

$$C_t = \beta_0 + \beta_1 Y_t + \beta_2 C_{t-1} + u_t$$

*14. Instead of estimating the coefficients β_1 and β_2 from the model

$$y = \alpha + \beta_1 x_1 + \beta_2 x_2 + u$$

it is decided to use ordinary least squares on the following regression equation:

$$y = \alpha + \beta_1 x_1^* + \beta_2 x_2 + v$$

where x_1^* is the residual from a regression of x_1 and x_2 and v is the disturbance term.

(a) Show that the resulting estimator of β_2 is identical to the regression coefficient of y on x_2.

(b) Obtain an expression for the bias of this estimator.

(c) Prove that the estimators of β_1 obtained from each of the two equations are identical.

*15. Explain how you will estimate a linear regression equation which is piecewise linear with a joint (or knot) at $x = x_0$ if
(a) x_0 is known.
(b) x_0 is unknown.

*16. In the model

$$y_t = \beta_1 x_{1t} + \beta_2 x_{2t} + \beta_3 x_{3t} + u_t$$

the coefficients are known to be related to a more basic economic parameter α according to the equations

$$\beta_1 + \beta_2 = \alpha$$

$$\beta_1 + \beta_3 = -\alpha$$

Assuming that the x's are nonrandom and that $u_t \sim \text{IN}(0, \sigma^2)$, find the best unbiased linear estimator $\hat{\alpha}$ of α and the variance of $\hat{\alpha}$.

17. A study on unemployment in the British interwar period produced the following regression equation (data are given in Table 4.11):

$$U = 5.19 + 18.3(B/W) - 90.0(\log Q - \log Q^*)$$
$$\quad (2.0) \quad (4.46) \quad\quad\quad (-8.3)$$

$$R^2 = 0.8 \quad \text{SER} = 1.9 \quad \text{where SER} = \sqrt{s^2}$$

Sample period 1920–1938 ($n = 19$).

$$U = \text{unemployment rate}$$

$$B/W = \text{ratio of unemployment benefits to average wage}$$

$$Q = \text{actual output}$$

$$Q^* = \text{trend predicted output}$$

$$\log Q - \log Q^* = \text{captures unexpected changes in aggregate demand}$$

The authors[23] conclude that the high benefit levels are partly responsible for the high rates of unemployment. Critics of this study argued that when the single observation for 1920 is dropped the results change dramatically.[24] The equation now is

$$U = 7.9 + 12.9(B/W) - 87.0(\log Q - \log Q^*)$$
$$\quad (3.0) \quad (2.4) \quad\quad\quad (8.3)$$

$$R^2 = 0.82 \quad \text{SER} = 1.7$$

Sample period 1921–1938 ($n = 18$).

Test whether the results are significantly different from each other.

[23] D. K. Benjamin and L. A. Kochin, "Searching for an Explanation of Unemployment in Interwar Britain," *Journal of Political Economy*, June 1979, pp. 441–478.

[24] P. A. Ormerod and G. D. N. Worswick. "Unemployment in Interwar Britain," *Journal of Political Economy*, April 1982, pp. 400–409.

18. In a study on determinants of children born in the Philippines,[25] the following results were obtained:

Variable	Coefficient	SE	t-Ratio	Coefficient	SE	t-Ratio
ED	−0.177	0.026	−6.81	−0.067	0.024	−2.79
LWH	0.476	0.327	1.46	0.091	0.289	0.31
AMAR	—	—	—	−0.296	0.016	−18.50
SURV	−0.006	0.003	−2.00	−0.003	0.003	−1.00
RURAL	0.361	0.193	1.87	0.281	0.171	1.64
Age	0.123	0.024	5.12	0.155	0.021	7.36
Constant	5.650	3.180	1.78	9.440	2.820	3.35
R^2		0.096			0.295	

The variables are:

$$ED = \text{years of schooling of the woman}$$
$$LWH = \text{natural logarithm of present}$$
$$\text{value of husband's earnings at marriage}$$
$$AMAR = \text{age of the woman at marriage}$$
$$SURV = \text{survival probability at}$$
$$\text{age 5 in the province}$$
$$RURAL = \text{residence in rural area (dummy variable);}$$
$$\text{this variable is supposed to}$$
$$\text{capture search and schooling costs}$$
$$\text{Age} = \text{age of the woman}$$

The explained variable is number of children born.

(a) Do the coefficients have the signs you would expect?

(b) Using the t-ratio for AMAR and the R^2 for the two equations, can you tell how many observations were used in the estimation?

(c) Looking at the t-ratio of AMAR, can you predict the signs of the coefficients of the other variables if AMAR is deleted from the equation?

(d) Given that the dependent variable is number of children born, do you think the assumptions of the least squares model are satisfied?

19. In a study of investment plans and realizations in U.K. manufacturing industries since 1955, the following results were obtained:

$$A_t = \text{const.} - \underset{(6.24)}{54.60} C_{t-1} \quad R^2 = 0.89 \quad DW = 2.50$$

$$I_t - A_t = \text{const.} - \underset{(4.44)}{19.96}(C_t - C_{t-1}) \quad R^2 = 0.68 \quad DW = 2.31$$

---

[25]B. L. Boulier and M. R. Rosenzweig, "Schooling, Search and Spouse Selection: Testing Economic Theories of Marriage and Household Behavior," *Journal of Political Economy*, August 1984, p. 729.

$$I_t = \text{const.} + \underset{(0.10)}{0.88A_t} - \underset{(5.15)}{16.32(C_t - C_{t-1})} \quad R^2 = 0.90 \quad DW = 1.65$$

$$I_t = \text{const.} - \underset{(3.64)}{50.08C_{t-1}} - \underset{(3.32)}{14.60(C_t - C_{t-1})} \quad R^2 = 0.96 \quad DW = 2.61$$

A_t = investment that firms anticipate they will complete in year t; these plans are held at the end of year $t - 1$

I_t = actual investment in year t

C_t = measure of average level of underutilization of capacity

Figures in parentheses are standard errors.

(a) Interpret these results and assess whether or not knowledge of firms' anticipated investment is helpful in explaining actual investment.

(b) How many observations have been used in the estimation?

(c) What is the partial correlation coefficient of I_t with A_t after allowing for the effect of $C_t - C_{t-1}$?

20. The demand for Ceylonese tea in the United States is given by the equation

$$\log Q = \beta_0 + \beta_1 \log P_C + \beta_2 \log P_I + \beta_3 \log P_B + \beta_4 \log Y + u$$

where Q = imports of Ceylon tea in the United States

P_c = price of Ceylon tea

P_I = price of Indian tea

P_B = price of Brazilian coffee

Y = disposable income

The following results were obtained from $T = 22$ observations:

$$\log Q = \underset{(2.0)}{2.837} - \underset{(0.987)}{1.481 \log P_C} + \underset{(0.690)}{1.181 \log P_I} + \underset{(0.134)}{0.186 \log P_B}$$

$$+ \underset{(0.370)}{0.257 \log Y} \quad RSS = 0.4277$$

$$\log Q + \log P_C = - \underset{(0.820)}{0.738} + \underset{(0.155)}{0.199 \log P_B} + \underset{(0.165)}{0.261 \log Y} \quad RSS = 0.6788$$

Figures in parentheses are standard errors.

(a) Test the hypothesis $\beta_1 = -1$, $\beta_2 = 0$, and $\beta_3, \beta_4 \neq 0$ against $\beta_i \neq 0$ for $i = 1, 2, 3, 4$.

(b) Discuss the economic implications of these results.

Appendix to Chapter 4

The Multiple Regression Model in Matrix Notation

Consider the multiple regression model with k explanatory variables

$$y_i = \beta_1 x_{1i} + \beta_2 x_{2i} + \cdots + \beta_k x_{ki} + u_i \quad i = 1, 2, \ldots, n$$

This can be written as

$$
\begin{bmatrix} y_1 \\ y_2 \\ \vdots \\ y_n \end{bmatrix} = \begin{bmatrix} x_{11} & x_{21} & & x_{k1} \\ x_{12} & x_{22} & \cdots & x_{k2} \\ \vdots & \vdots & & \vdots \\ x_{1n} & x_{2n} & & x_{kn} \end{bmatrix} \begin{bmatrix} \beta_1 \\ \beta_2 \\ \vdots \\ \beta_k \end{bmatrix} + \begin{bmatrix} u_1 \\ u_2 \\ \vdots \\ u_n \end{bmatrix}
\tag{4A.1}
$$

or $\mathbf{y} = \mathbf{X}\boldsymbol{\beta} + \mathbf{u}$, where

$\mathbf{y} =$ an $n \times 1$ vector of observations on the explained variable

$\mathbf{X} =$ an $n \times k$ matrix of observations on the explanatory variables

$\mathbf{u} =$ an $n \times 1$ vector of errors

$\boldsymbol{\beta} =$ a $k \times 1$ vector of parameters to be estimated

We assume that:

1. The errors are IID$(0, \sigma^2)$, that is, independently and identically distributed with mean 0 and variance σ^2.
2. The x's are nonstochastic and hence independent of the u's.
3. The x's are linearly independent. Hence rank$(\mathbf{X}'\mathbf{X}) = $ rank $\mathbf{X} = k$. This implies that $(\mathbf{X}'\mathbf{X})^{-1}$ exists.

Under these assumptions the best (minimum variance) unbiased linear estimator (BLUE) of β is obtained by minimizing the error sum of squares

$$
Q = \mathbf{u}'\mathbf{u} = (\mathbf{y} - \mathbf{X}\boldsymbol{\beta})'(\mathbf{y} - \mathbf{X}\boldsymbol{\beta})
$$

This is known as the *Gauss–Markoff theorem*.

We shall derive the formula for this estimator and show that it is a linear estimator, that it is unbiased, and that it has minimum variance among the class of linear unbiased estimators. That will complete the proof of the Gauss–Markoff theorem.

Derivation

We have $Q = \mathbf{y}'\mathbf{y} - 2\boldsymbol{\beta}'\mathbf{X}'\mathbf{y} + \boldsymbol{\beta}'\mathbf{X}'\mathbf{X}\boldsymbol{\beta}$. Using the formulas for vector differentiation derived in the appendix to Chapter 2, we get

$$
\frac{\partial Q}{\partial \boldsymbol{\beta}} = 0 \text{ gives} - 2\mathbf{X}'\mathbf{y} + 2\mathbf{X}'\mathbf{X}\boldsymbol{\beta} = 0 \text{ or } \hat{\boldsymbol{\beta}} = (\mathbf{X}'\mathbf{X})^{-1}\mathbf{X}'\mathbf{y}
\tag{4A.2}
$$

Since $(\mathbf{X}'\mathbf{X})^{-1}\mathbf{X}'$ is a matrix of constants, the elements of $\hat{\boldsymbol{\beta}}$ are linear functions of the y's. Hence $\hat{\boldsymbol{\beta}}$ is a *linear estimator*. Also, substituting equation (4A.1) into equation (4A.2), we get

$$
\hat{\boldsymbol{\beta}} = (\mathbf{X}'\mathbf{X})^{-1}\mathbf{X}'(\mathbf{X}\boldsymbol{\beta} + \mathbf{u}) = \boldsymbol{\beta} + (\mathbf{X}'\mathbf{X})^{-1}\mathbf{X}'\mathbf{u}
\tag{4A.3}
$$

Since $E(\mathbf{u}) = 0$, we have $E(\hat{\boldsymbol{\beta}}) = \boldsymbol{\beta}$. Thus $\hat{\boldsymbol{\beta}}$ is an *unbiased estimator*. Also,

$$V(\hat{\boldsymbol{\beta}}) = E(\hat{\boldsymbol{\beta}} - \boldsymbol{\beta})(\hat{\boldsymbol{\beta}} - \boldsymbol{\beta})' = (\mathbf{X}'\mathbf{X})^{-1}\mathbf{X}'E(\mathbf{u}\mathbf{u}')\mathbf{X}(\mathbf{X}'\mathbf{X})^{-1}$$

$$= (\mathbf{X}'\mathbf{X})^{-1}\sigma^2 \text{ since } E(\mathbf{u}\mathbf{u}') = \mathbf{I}\sigma^2$$

The $\hat{\boldsymbol{\beta}}$ is unbiased and has a covariance matrix $(\mathbf{X}'\mathbf{X})^{-1}\sigma^2$.

Now how do we show that this is minimum variance? Any other linear estimator must be of the form $\boldsymbol{\beta}^* = \hat{\boldsymbol{\beta}} + \mathbf{C}\mathbf{y}$. Then $\boldsymbol{\beta}^* = \boldsymbol{\beta} + \mathbf{C}\mathbf{X}\boldsymbol{\beta} + [(\mathbf{X}'\mathbf{X})^{-1}\mathbf{X}' + \mathbf{C}]\mathbf{u}$. Hence $E(\boldsymbol{\beta}^*) = \boldsymbol{\beta} + \mathbf{C}\mathbf{X}\boldsymbol{\beta}$. But if $\boldsymbol{\beta}^*$ is an unbiased estimator for all values of $\boldsymbol{\beta}$, we should have $\mathbf{C}\mathbf{X} = 0$.

$$V(\boldsymbol{\beta}^*) = E(\boldsymbol{\beta}^* - \boldsymbol{\beta})(\boldsymbol{\beta}^* - \boldsymbol{\beta})' = [(\mathbf{X}'\mathbf{X})^{-1}\mathbf{X}' + \mathbf{C}]E(\mathbf{u}\mathbf{u}')[(\mathbf{X}'\mathbf{X})^{-1}\mathbf{X}' + \mathbf{C}]'$$

Since $E(\mathbf{u}\mathbf{u}') = \mathbf{I}\sigma^2$ and $\mathbf{C}\mathbf{X} = 0$, this gives $V(\boldsymbol{\beta}^*) = (\mathbf{X}'\mathbf{X})^{-1}\sigma^2 + (\mathbf{C}\mathbf{C}')\sigma^2$. Hence, $V(\boldsymbol{\beta}^*) \geq V(\hat{\boldsymbol{\beta}})$. Thus $\hat{\boldsymbol{\beta}}$ is BLUE. Note that to prove $\hat{\boldsymbol{\beta}}$ is BLUE, we did not assume that the errors u_i are normal. But to derive the sampling distribution of $\hat{\boldsymbol{\beta}}$ we have to assume normality.

Tests of Significance

We shall now add the assumption that $\mathbf{u} \sim N_n(0, \mathbf{I}\sigma^2)$. We have from equation (4A.3),

$$\mathbf{X}(\hat{\boldsymbol{\beta}} - \boldsymbol{\beta}) = \mathbf{X}(\mathbf{X}'\mathbf{X})^{-1}\mathbf{X}'\mathbf{u} = \mathbf{M}\mathbf{u}$$

and the estimated residual $\hat{\mathbf{u}}$ is given by

$$\hat{\mathbf{u}} = \mathbf{y} - \mathbf{X}\hat{\boldsymbol{\beta}} = \mathbf{X}\boldsymbol{\beta} + \mathbf{u} - \mathbf{X}\hat{\boldsymbol{\beta}} = [\mathbf{I} - \mathbf{X}(\mathbf{X}'\mathbf{X})^{-1}\mathbf{X}]\mathbf{u} = \mathbf{N}\mathbf{u}$$

where $\mathbf{M} = \mathbf{X}(\mathbf{X}'\mathbf{X})^{-1}\mathbf{X}'$ and $\mathbf{N} = \mathbf{I} - \mathbf{M}$. We shall use the properties of idempotent matrices and the χ^2-distribution stated in the appendix to Chapter 2.

1. It can easily be verified that $\mathbf{M}^2 = \mathbf{M}$ and $\mathbf{N}^2 = \mathbf{N}$. Thus $\mathbf{M}$ and $\mathbf{N}$ are idempotent matrices. Also, $\mathbf{M}\mathbf{N} = 0$.
2. Since $\mathbf{M}$ is idempotent, $\text{rank}(\mathbf{M}) = \text{Tr}(\mathbf{M})$. Using the result $\text{Tr}(\mathbf{A}\mathbf{B}) = \text{Tr}(\mathbf{B}\mathbf{A})$, we get

$$\text{Tr}(\mathbf{M}) = \text{Tr } \mathbf{X}(\mathbf{X}'\mathbf{X})^{-1}\mathbf{X}' = \text{Tr}(\mathbf{X}'\mathbf{X})^{-1}(\mathbf{X}'\mathbf{X}) = \text{Tr}(\mathbf{I}_k) = k$$

Thus $\text{rank}(\mathbf{M}) = k$. Similarly, $\text{rank}(\mathbf{N}) = n - k$.
3. Hence $(1/\sigma^2)\mathbf{u}'\mathbf{M}\mathbf{u}$ and $(1/\sigma^2)\mathbf{u}'\mathbf{N}\mathbf{u}$ have independent χ^2-distributions with d.f. k and $(n - k)$, respectively.
4. Now the residual sum of squares

$$\hat{\mathbf{u}}'\hat{\mathbf{u}} = (\mathbf{y} - \mathbf{X}\hat{\boldsymbol{\beta}})'(\mathbf{y} - \mathbf{X}\hat{\boldsymbol{\beta}}) = \mathbf{u}'\mathbf{N}^2\mathbf{u} = \mathbf{u}'\mathbf{N}\mathbf{u}$$

is independent of the regression sum of squares

$$(\hat{\boldsymbol{\beta}} - \boldsymbol{\beta})\mathbf{X}'\mathbf{X}(\hat{\boldsymbol{\beta}} - \boldsymbol{\beta}) = \mathbf{u}'\mathbf{M}\mathbf{M}\mathbf{u} = \mathbf{u}'\mathbf{M}^2\mathbf{u} = \mathbf{u}'\mathbf{M}\mathbf{u}$$

Hence $\dfrac{\text{(regression SS)}/k}{\text{(residual SS)}/(n-k)}$ has an F-distribution with d.f. k and $(n-k)$.

This result can be used to construct confidence regions for $\boldsymbol{\beta}$ and also to apply any tests of significance. To test the hypothesis $\boldsymbol{\beta} = \boldsymbol{\beta}_0$, we substitute the value $\boldsymbol{\beta}_0$ for $\boldsymbol{\beta}$ in the test statistic above and use it as an F-variate. Whether or not the hypothesis is true, the denominator depends on $\hat{\boldsymbol{\beta}}$ only and thus always has a χ^2-distribution. The numerator has a χ^2-distribution only when the null hypothesis is true. When it is false, it has a noncentral χ^2-distribution, and this is used to find the power of the test.

Since regression sum of squares $= S_{yy}R^2$ and residual of sum of squares $= S_{yy}(1-R^2)$, we can also write the F-test as

$$F = \frac{R^2/k}{(1-R^2)/(n-k)} = \frac{R^2(n-k)}{(1-R^2)k}$$

Note that in equation (4.14) we have $(n-k-1)$ because there is also a constant term in addition to the k β's. We can then consider $\boldsymbol{\beta}$ to be a $(k+1)$ vector, and the matrix $\mathbf{X}$ to be $n \times (k+1)$, with the first column of $\mathbf{X}$ consisting of all elements $= 1$.

Tests for Stability

We shall derive the analysis of variance and predictive tests for stability discussed in Section 4.11. Let us write

$$\mathbf{y}_1 = \mathbf{X}_1\boldsymbol{\beta}_1 + \mathbf{u}_1 \text{ for the first } n_1 \text{ observations}$$

$$\mathbf{y}_2 = \mathbf{X}_2\boldsymbol{\beta}_2 + \mathbf{u}_2 \text{ for the second } n_2 \text{ observations}$$

Write

$$\mathbf{u} = \begin{bmatrix} u_1 \\ u_2 \end{bmatrix} \quad \mathbf{X} = \begin{bmatrix} X_1 \\ X_2 \end{bmatrix} \quad \mathbf{y} = \begin{bmatrix} y_1 \\ y_2 \end{bmatrix}$$

We assume the errors to be $\text{IN}(0, \sigma^2)$ in both the equations. If $\boldsymbol{\beta}_1 = \boldsymbol{\beta}_2$, we estimate the pooled regression equation

$$\mathbf{y} = \mathbf{X}\boldsymbol{\beta} + \mathbf{u} \quad \text{for the } n = (n_1 + n_2) \text{ observations}$$

Let RSS_1 and RSS_2 be the residual sum of squares from the two separate regressions and RRSS be the residual sum of squares from the pooled regression. (It is called "restricted" because of the restriction $\boldsymbol{\beta}_1 = \boldsymbol{\beta}_2$.) We shall denote $(\text{RSS}_1 + \text{RSS}_2)$ by URSS (unrestricted residual sum of squares). We have to show that

$$F = \frac{(\text{RRSS} - \text{URSS})/k}{\text{URSS}/(n-2k)}$$

has an F-distribution with d.f. k and $(n-2k)$.

Define

$$\mathbf{N}_1 = \mathbf{I}_1 - \mathbf{X}_1(\mathbf{X}_1'\mathbf{X}_1)^{-1}\mathbf{X}_1'$$

$$\mathbf{N}_2 = \mathbf{I}_2 - \mathbf{X}_2(\mathbf{X}_2'\mathbf{X}_2)^{-1}\mathbf{X}_2'$$

where $\mathbf{I}_1$ and $\mathbf{I}_2$ are identity matrices of order n_1 and n_2, respectively. Then $RSS_1 = \mathbf{u}'_1 \mathbf{N}_1 \mathbf{u}$ and $RSS_2 = \mathbf{u}'_2 \mathbf{N}_2 \mathbf{u}$. If we define $\mathbf{N}_1^* = \begin{bmatrix} \mathbf{N}_1 & \mathbf{0} \\ \mathbf{0} & \mathbf{0} \end{bmatrix}$ and $\mathbf{N}_2^* = \begin{bmatrix} \mathbf{0} & \mathbf{0} \\ \mathbf{0} & \mathbf{N}_2 \end{bmatrix}$ as two $n \times n$ matrices, we can write $RSS_1 = \mathbf{u}'\mathbf{N}_1^*\mathbf{u}$ and $RSS_2 = \mathbf{u}'\mathbf{N}_2^*\mathbf{u}$. Note that $\mathbf{N}_1^*\mathbf{N}_2^* = \mathbf{0}$. Also, $RRSS = \mathbf{u}'\mathbf{N}\mathbf{u}$, where $\mathbf{N} = \mathbf{I} - \mathbf{X}(\mathbf{X}'\mathbf{X})^{-1}\mathbf{X}'$. We can write

$$\mathbf{N} = \begin{bmatrix} \mathbf{I}_1 & \mathbf{0} \\ \mathbf{0} & \mathbf{I}_2 \end{bmatrix} - \begin{bmatrix} \mathbf{X}_1 \\ \mathbf{X}_2 \end{bmatrix} (\mathbf{X}'\mathbf{X})^{-1}[\mathbf{X}'_1 \mathbf{X}'_2] = \begin{bmatrix} \mathbf{N}_{11} & \mathbf{N}_{12} \\ \mathbf{N}_{21} & \mathbf{N}_{22} \end{bmatrix}$$

where

$$\mathbf{N}_{11} = \mathbf{I}_1 - \mathbf{X}_1(\mathbf{X}'\mathbf{X})^{-1}\mathbf{X}'_1$$

$$\mathbf{N}_{12} = -\mathbf{X}_1(\mathbf{X}'\mathbf{X})^{-1}\mathbf{X}'_2$$

$$\mathbf{N}_{21} = -\mathbf{X}_2(\mathbf{X}'\mathbf{X})^{-1}\mathbf{X}'_1$$

$$\mathbf{N}_{22} = \mathbf{I}_2 - \mathbf{X}_2(\mathbf{X}'\mathbf{X})^{-1}\mathbf{X}'_2$$

Define $\mathbf{N}^* = \mathbf{N}_1^* + \mathbf{N}_2^*$ so that we have $URSS = \mathbf{u}'\mathbf{N}^*\mathbf{u}$ and $RRSS = \mathbf{u}'\mathbf{N}\mathbf{u}$. We shall show that:

1. $(\mathbf{N} - \mathbf{N}^*)$ and $\mathbf{N}^*$ are both idempotent.
2. $(\mathbf{N} - \mathbf{N}^*) \cdot \mathbf{N}^* = \mathbf{0}$.
3. $\mathrm{Tr}(\mathbf{N}^*) = n - 2k$ and $\mathrm{Tr}(\mathbf{N} - \mathbf{N}^*) = k$.
4. Hence $(RRSS - URSS)/\sigma^2$ and $URSS/\sigma^2$ have independent χ^2-distributions with d.f. k and $(n - 2k)$, respectively. From this the required F-ratio follows.

Proof: Since $\mathbf{N}_1^*$ and $\mathbf{N}_2^*$ are both idempotent, $\mathbf{N}^*$ is easily seen to be idempotent. If we prove result 2, it is easy to show that $\mathbf{N} - \mathbf{N}^*$ is idempotent. Hence we shall prove result 2. We have

$$(\mathbf{N} - \mathbf{N}_1^*)\mathbf{N}_1^* = \begin{bmatrix} \mathbf{N}_{11} - \mathbf{N}_1 & \mathbf{N}_{12} \\ \mathbf{N}_{21} & \mathbf{N}_{22} \end{bmatrix} \begin{bmatrix} \mathbf{N}_1 & \mathbf{0} \\ \mathbf{0} & \mathbf{0} \end{bmatrix}$$

$$= \begin{bmatrix} (\mathbf{N}_{11} - \mathbf{N}_1)\mathbf{N}_1 & \mathbf{0} \\ \mathbf{N}_{21}\mathbf{N}_1 & \mathbf{0} \end{bmatrix}$$

Since $\mathbf{X}'_1 \mathbf{N}_1 = \mathbf{0}$, we have $\mathbf{N}_{21}\mathbf{N}_1 = \mathbf{0}$ and $\mathbf{N}_{11}\mathbf{N}_1 = \mathbf{N}_1$. Since $\mathbf{N}_1$ is idempotent, it follows that $(\mathbf{N}_{11} - \mathbf{N}_1)\mathbf{N}_1 = \mathbf{0}$. Thus $(\mathbf{N} - \mathbf{N}_1^*)\mathbf{N}_1^* = \mathbf{0}$ or $\mathbf{N}\mathbf{N}_1^* = \mathbf{N}_1^*$. Similarly, $(\mathbf{N} - \mathbf{N}_2^*)\mathbf{N}_2^* = \mathbf{0}$ or $\mathbf{N}\mathbf{N}_2^* = \mathbf{N}_2^*$. Hence it follows that $(\mathbf{N} - \mathbf{N}_1^* - \mathbf{N}_2^*)(\mathbf{N}_1^* + \mathbf{N}_2^*) = \mathbf{0}$ or $(\mathbf{N} - \mathbf{N}^*)\mathbf{N}^* = \mathbf{0}$.

$$\mathrm{Tr}(\mathbf{N}) = n - k$$

$$\mathrm{Tr}(\mathbf{N}^*) = \mathrm{Tr}(\mathbf{N}_1^*) + \mathrm{Tr}(\mathbf{N}_2^*) = (n_1 - k) + (n_2 - k) = n - 2k$$

Hence $\mathrm{Tr}(\mathbf{N} - \mathbf{N}^*) = \mathrm{Tr}(\mathbf{N}) - \mathrm{Tr}(\mathbf{N}^*) = k$. The rest follows from the relationship between idempotent matrices and χ^2-distribution.

Predictive Test for Stability

If $n_2 < k$, the regression equation cannot be estimated with n_2 observations. In this case the predictive test for stability is to use

$$F = \frac{(\text{RRSS} - \text{RSS}_1)/n_2}{\text{RSS}_1/(n_1 - k)}$$

which has an F-distribution with d.f. n_2 and $(n_1 - k)$. We have already derived the expressions to prove this. We have shown that $(\mathbf{N} - \mathbf{N}_1^*)\mathbf{N}_1^* = \mathbf{0}$. Also, $\mathbf{N}_1^*$ is idempotent and of rank $(n_1 - k)$. Hence $(\mathbf{N} - \mathbf{N}_1^*)(\mathbf{N} - \mathbf{N}_1^*) = \mathbf{N}^2 - \mathbf{N}_1^*\mathbf{N} - \mathbf{N}\mathbf{N}_1^* + \mathbf{N}_1^{*2} = \mathbf{N} - \mathbf{N}_1^* - \mathbf{N}_1^* + \mathbf{N}_1^* = \mathbf{N} - \mathbf{N}_1^*$. Thus $\mathbf{N} - \mathbf{N}_1^*$ is idempotent. $\text{Rank}(\mathbf{N} - \mathbf{N}_1^*) = \text{Tr}(\mathbf{N} - \mathbf{N}_1^*) = (n - k) - (n_1 - k) = n_2$.

$$\text{RRSS} - \text{RSS}_1 = \mathbf{u}'(\mathbf{N} - \mathbf{N}_1^*)\mathbf{u}$$

$$\text{RSS}_1 = \mathbf{u}'\mathbf{N}_1^*\mathbf{u}$$

Hence the required result follows.

Omitted Variables and Irrelevant Variables (Section 4.9)

Suppose that the true model is

$$\mathbf{y} = \mathbf{X}\boldsymbol{\beta} + \mathbf{u} \quad \mathbf{X} \text{ is an } n \times k \text{ matrix}$$

Instead, we estimate

$$\mathbf{y} = \mathbf{Z}\boldsymbol{\delta} + \mathbf{v} \quad \mathbf{Z} \text{ is an } n \times r \text{ matrix}$$

r can be less than, equal to, or greater than k. The variables in $\mathbf{Z}$ may include some variables in $\mathbf{X}$. We then have

$$\hat{\boldsymbol{\delta}} = (\mathbf{Z}'\mathbf{Z})^{-1}\mathbf{Z}'\mathbf{y}$$

$$= (\mathbf{Z}'\mathbf{Z})^{-1}\mathbf{Z}'(\mathbf{X}\boldsymbol{\beta} + \mathbf{u})$$

$$= \mathbf{P}\boldsymbol{\beta} + (\mathbf{Z}'\mathbf{Z})^{-1}\mathbf{Z}'\mathbf{u}$$

Since $E(\mathbf{u}) = \mathbf{0}$, we have $E(\hat{\boldsymbol{\delta}}) = \mathbf{P}\boldsymbol{\beta}$. $\mathbf{P} = (\mathbf{Z}'\mathbf{Z})^{-1}\mathbf{Z}'\mathbf{X}$ is the matrix of regression coefficients of the variables $\mathbf{X}$ in the true model on the variables $\mathbf{Z}$ in the misspecified model. As an example, suppose that the true equation is

$$y = \beta_1 x_1 + \beta_2 x_2 + u$$

Instead, we estimate

$$y = \delta_1 x_1 + \delta_2 x_3 + v$$

Then $\mathbf{P}$ is obtained by regressing each of x_1 and x_2 on x_1 and x_3. The regression of x_1 on x_1 and x_3 gives coefficients 1 and 0. The regression of x_2 on x_1 and x_3 gives coefficients (say) b_{21} and b_{23}. These regressions are known as the auxiliary regressions. Hence we get

$$E \begin{bmatrix} \hat{\delta}_1 \\ \hat{\delta}_2 \end{bmatrix} = \begin{bmatrix} 1 & b_{21} \\ 0 & b_{23} \end{bmatrix} \begin{bmatrix} \beta_1 \\ \beta_2 \end{bmatrix}$$

or $E(\hat{\delta}_1) = \beta_1 + b_{21}\beta_2$ and $E(\hat{\delta}_2) = b_{23}\beta_2$.

Suppose that Z includes irrelevant variables, so that the true equation is

$$\mathbf{Y} = \mathbf{X}_1\boldsymbol{\beta}_1 + \mathbf{u}$$

and the misspecified equation is

$$\mathbf{y} = \mathbf{X}_1\boldsymbol{\beta}_1 + \mathbf{X}_2\boldsymbol{\beta}_2 + \mathbf{v}$$

In this case, the matrix $\mathbf{P}$ is the regression coefficients of $\mathbf{X}_1$ on $\mathbf{X}_1$ and $\mathbf{X}_2$. These are $\begin{bmatrix} I \\ 0 \end{bmatrix}$.

Hence $E \begin{bmatrix} \hat{\beta}_1 \\ \hat{\beta}_2 \end{bmatrix} = \begin{bmatrix} I \\ 0 \end{bmatrix} \beta_1$ or $E(\hat{\beta}_1) = \beta_1$ and $E(\hat{\beta}_2) = 0$. Thus even if some "irrelevant" variables are included, we get unbiased estimates for the coefficients of the "relevant" variables.

Prior Adjustment (Section 4.4)

Consider the multiple regression model

$$\mathbf{y} = \mathbf{X}_1\boldsymbol{\beta}_1 + \mathbf{X}_2\boldsymbol{\beta}_2 + \mathbf{u}$$

Let $\hat{\boldsymbol{\beta}}_1$ be the estimator of $\boldsymbol{\beta}_1$ from this equation. Suppose that instead of this, we consider adjusting both $\mathbf{y}$ and $\mathbf{X}_1$ by removing the effect of $\mathbf{X}_2$ on these variables. Let the residuals from a regression of $\mathbf{y}$ on $\mathbf{X}_2$ be denoted by $\mathbf{y}^*$ and the residuals from a regression of $\mathbf{X}_1$ on $\mathbf{X}_2$ be denoted by $\mathbf{X}_1^*$. Now regress the adjusted $\mathbf{y}^*$ on the adjusted $\mathbf{X}_1^*$. Let this regression coefficient be $\mathbf{b}$. We shall show that

$$\mathbf{b} = \hat{\boldsymbol{\beta}}_1$$

That is, if we want to remove the effect of $\mathbf{X}_2$ on $\mathbf{y}$ and $\mathbf{X}_1$ before running a regression on the adjusted variables, we can get the same result by including $\mathbf{X}_2$ as an additional explanatory variable in the regression of $\mathbf{y}$ on $\mathbf{X}_1$. Usually, $\mathbf{X}_2$ is a trend variable or seasonal variable.

Proof: Let $\mathbf{N} = \mathbf{I} - \mathbf{X}_2(\mathbf{X}_2'\mathbf{X}_2)^{-1}\mathbf{X}_2$. Then as we showed earlier, the residual $\mathbf{y}^* = \mathbf{N}\mathbf{y}$ and the residual $\mathbf{X}_1^* = \mathbf{N}\mathbf{X}_1$. Hence $\mathbf{b} = (\mathbf{X}_1^{*'}\mathbf{X}_1^*)^{-1}(\mathbf{X}_1^{*'}\mathbf{y}^*) = (\mathbf{X}_1'\mathbf{N}\mathbf{X}_1)^{-1}\mathbf{X}_1'\mathbf{N}\mathbf{y}$. We have to show that we get the same expression for $\hat{\boldsymbol{\beta}}_1$. We have $(\mathbf{X}'\mathbf{X})\boldsymbol{\beta} = \mathbf{X}'\mathbf{y}$, which can be written as

$$\mathbf{X}'_1\mathbf{X}_1\hat{\boldsymbol{\beta}}_1 + \mathbf{X}'_1\mathbf{X}_2\hat{\boldsymbol{\beta}}_2 = \mathbf{X}'_1\mathbf{y}$$

$$\mathbf{X}'_2\mathbf{X}_1\hat{\boldsymbol{\beta}}_1 + \mathbf{X}'_2\mathbf{X}_2\hat{\boldsymbol{\beta}}_2 = \mathbf{X}'_2\mathbf{y}$$

The second equation gives

$$\hat{\boldsymbol{\beta}}_2 = (\mathbf{X}'_2\mathbf{X}_2)^{-1}[\mathbf{X}'_2\mathbf{y} - \mathbf{X}'_2\mathbf{X}_1\hat{\boldsymbol{\beta}}_1]$$

Substituting this in the first we get

$$\mathbf{X}'_1\mathbf{X}_1\hat{\boldsymbol{\beta}}_1 + \mathbf{X}'_1\mathbf{X}_2(\mathbf{X}'_2\mathbf{X}_2)^{-1}[\mathbf{X}'_2\mathbf{y} - \mathbf{X}'_2\mathbf{X}_1\hat{\boldsymbol{\beta}}_1] = \mathbf{X}'_1\mathbf{y}$$

or $(\mathbf{X}'_1\mathbf{N}\mathbf{X}_1)\hat{\boldsymbol{\beta}}_1 = \mathbf{X}'_1\mathbf{N}\mathbf{y}$. Thus $\hat{\boldsymbol{\beta}}_1 = \mathbf{b}$.

Data Sets

Table 4.7   Sale prices of rural land[a]

N	Price	WL	DA	D75	A	MO
1	5556	1.00	12.1	4.9	36.0	33
2	5236	1.00	12.1	4.9	38.2	30
3	5952	1.00	12.0	4.9	21.0	15
4	7000	0.00	16.0	1.2	40.0	44
5	3750	0.00	15.5	3.2	40.0	43
6	7000	0.00	13.7	3.2	20.0	25
7	5952	0.00	14.5	2.5	21.0	24
8	2009	0.00	16.1	0.1	656.0	19
9	2583	1.00	15.2	3.0	60.0	18
10	2449	0.00	15.5	1.0	156.0	18
11	2500	0.50	15.2	2.0	40.0	3
12	3000	0.00	15.5	3.2	13.0	3
13	3704	0.00	13.5	2.5	27.0	3
14	3500	0.00	15.5	1.0	10.0	3
15	3500	0.00	17.5	5.4	20.0	38
16	4537	1.00	18.0	5.9	38.0	24
17	3700	0.00	17.2	5.1	5.0	3
18	2020	1.00	34.2	22.0	5.0	27
19	5000	0.00	11.1	5.1	3.5	13
20	4764	0.00	14.2	2.0	237.6	40
21	871	1.00	14.2	2.0	237.6	7
22	3500	1.00	11.1	3.1	20.0	41
23	15,200	1.00	14.7	2.4	5.0	36
24	4767	0.00	12.1	4.1	30.0	22
25	16,316	1.00	14.8	2.5	3.8	21
26	9873	1.00	14.8	2.5	7.9	17
27	5175	0.25	14.2	2.0	40.0	13
28	3977	0.00	11.4	2.9	8.8	10
29	5500	0.20	18.5	5.9	10.0	38
30	7500	0.00	16.5	3.9	8.0	42
31	4545	1.00	16.8	4.5	97.0	36
32	3765	0.72	18.7	6.4	178.0	29
33	5000	1.00	18.4	6.1	10.3	25
34	3300	0.00	16.2	4.0	525.7	25
35	5500	0.00	18.0	5.4	6.0	21
36	5172	0.00	15.0	2.4	29.0	20
37	3571	0.00	15.1	2.5	21.0	20

(Continued overleaf)

Table 4.7 (*continued*)

N	Price	WL	DA	D75	A	MO
38	4000	0.00	18.2	6.0	10.0	15
39	4000	0.00	18.4	6.1	15.0	18
40	2625	0.00	15.5	2.9	80.0	10
41	2257	0.00	42.8	30.5	171.0	14
42	15,504	0.00	4.0	4.5	38.7	39
43	5600	0.00	3.8	4.0	30.0	25
44	8000	0.00	3.5	4.2	30.0	27
45	7700	0.00	4.0	3.8	15.0	46
46	6187	0.00	4.2	5.0	69.5	15
47	7018	0.00	3.5	4.0	10.9	23
48	4821	0.60	7.8	2.7	224.0	33
49	6504	0.00	14.9	4.8	6.4	40
50	5225	0.00	16.2	5.0	10.0	40
51	2500	0.00	24.0	14.0	40.0	33
52	4000	1.00	22.5	12.4	10.0	20
53	3638	1.00	5.0	2.2	73.0	2
54	5400	0.00	13.1	3.7	10.0	28
55	4850	0.00	12.4	3.0	10.0	28
56	1628	0.00	22.8	12.8	80.0	23
57	2780	0.00	23.2	13.2	10.0	26
58	4500	0.00	21.0	11.0	5.0	28
59	5600	1.00	21.2	11.2	5.0	22
60	4750	1.00	21.7	11.7	5.0	32
61	1790	0.00	18.8	8.8	375.0	38
62	2750	0.00	23.4	13.4	10.0	22
63	3250	0.00	22.5	12.5	10.0	19
64	8500	1.00	16.8	2.7	5.0	27
65	5357	0.00	16.8	2.7	5.6	26
66	2500	0.00	21.8	7.5	50.0	14
67	8505	1.00	20.5	5.8	9.7	12

[a]Price, observed land price per acre excluding improvements; *WL*, proportion of acreage that is wooded; *DA*, distance from parcel to Sarasota airport; *D75*, distance from parcel to I-75; *A*, acreage of parcel; *MO*, month in which the parcel was sold.

Table 4.8 Data on gasoline consumption in the United States[a]

Year	K	C	M	P_g	P_T	Pop.	L	Y
1947	9732	30.87	14.95	97.0	0.538	145	59.3	1513
1948	9573	33.39	14.96	100.8	0.564	147	60.6	1567
1949	9395	36.35	14.92	105.4	0.633	150	61.3	1547
1950	9015	40.33	14.40	104.3	0.678	152	62.2	1646
1951	9187	42.68	14.50	98.0	0.694	155	62.0	1657
1952	9361	43.82	14.27	97.3	0.723	158	62.1	1678
1953	9370	46.46	14.39	100.0	0.765	160	63.0	1726
1954	9308	48.41	14.57	101.4	0.814	163	63.6	1714
1955	9359	52.09	14.53	101.8	0.840	166	65.0	1795
1956	9348	54.25	14.36	103.3	0.860	170	66.6	1839

(*Continued overleaf*)

Table 4.8 (*continued*)

Year	K	C	M	P_g	P_T	Pop.	L	Y
1957	9391	56.38	14.40	103.2	0.862	172	66.9	1844
1958	9494	57.39	14.30	98.5	0.879	175	67.6	1831
1959	9529	60.13	14.30	98.1	0.897	178	68.4	1881
1960	9446	62.26	14.28	98.6	0.913	181	69.6	1883
1961	9456	63.87	14.38	96.4	0.944	184	70.5	1909
1962	9441	66.64	14.37	95.0	0.965	187	70.6	1968
1963	9240	69.84	14.26	93.2	0.965	189	71.8	2013
1964	9286	72.97	14.25	91.8	0.970	192	73.1	2123
1965	9286	76.63	14.15	92.6	0.972	194	74.5	2235
1966	9384	80.11	14.10	92.7	0.979	196	75.8	2331
1967	9399	82.37	14.05	93.1	1.000	199	77.3	2398
1968	9488	85.79	13.91	90.8	1.004	201	78.7	2480
1969	9633	89.16	13.75	89.0	1.026	203	80.7	2517

[a]K, miles traveled per car per year; C, number of cars (millions); M, miles per gallon; P_g, retail gasoline price index deflated by consumer price index (1953 = 100); P_T, price of public transport (1967 = 100); Pop., population (millions); L, labor force (millions); Y, per capita disposable income in 1958 prices.

Table 4.9 Data on demand for food and supply of food in the United States[a]

Year	Q_D	P_D	Y	Q_S	P_S	t
1922	98.6	100.2	87.4	108.5	99.1	1
1923	101.2	101.6	97.6	110.1	99.1	2
1924	102.4	100.5	96.7	110.4	98.9	3
1925	100.9	106.0	98.2	104.3	110.8	4
1926	102.3	108.7	99.8	107.2	108.2	5
1927	101.5	106.7	100.5	105.8	105.6	6
1928	101.6	106.7	103.2	107.8	109.8	7
1929	101.6	108.2	107.8	103.4	108.7	8
1930	99.8	105.5	96.6	102.7	100.6	9
1931	100.3	95.6	88.9	104.1	81.0	10
1932	97.6	88.6	75.1	99.2	68.6	11
1933	97.2	91.0	76.9	99.7	70.9	12
1934	97.3	97.9	84.6	102.0	81.4	13
1935	96.0	102.3	90.6	94.3	102.3	14
1936	99.2	102.2	103.1	97.7	105.0	15
1937	100.3	102.5	105.1	101.1	110.5	16
1938	100.3	97.0	96.4	102.3	92.5	17
1939	104.1	95.8	104.4	104.4	89.3	18
1940	105.3	96.4	110.7	108.5	93.0	19
1941	107.6	100.3	127.1	111.3	106.6	20

[a]Q_D, food consumption per capita; Q_S, food production per capita; P_D, food prices at retail level/cost of living index; Y, disposable income/cost of living index; P_S, prices received by farmers for food/cost of living; t, time.
Source: M. A. Girschick and T. Haarelmo, "Statistical Analysis of the Demand for Food," *Econometrica*, April 1947.

Table 4.10   Data on housing starts in Canada (1954–4 to 1982–4 quarterly)[a]

T	HS	y	RR	T	HS	y	RR
54 – 4	28.73	101.8	3.92	66 – 2	29.11	185.8	2.73
55 – 1	29.83	103.3	4.25	–3	29.83	191.0	2.44
–2	31.22	107.4	4.42	–4	32.95	186.9	2.38
–3	32.61	113.7	4.63	67 – 1	30.04	190.3	2.29
–4	30.47	110.8	4.90	–2	43.53	193.5	2.14
56 – 1	31.34	117.2	4.63	–3	42.41	194.5	2.13
–2	32.42	118.3	5.16	–4	35.87	194.0	2.39
–3	30.56	116.8	4.64	68 – 1	46.34	197.4	2.83
–4	22.01	121.7	4.09	–2	48.37	202.6	2.70
57 – 1	17.75	122.8	3.12	–3	42.49	208.0	2.40
–2	29.41	122.5	2.79	–4	51.00	209.1	2.53
–3	28.76	118.8	2.96	69 – 1	66.32	211.7	2.93
–4	30.39	121.8	3.47	–2	54.51	213.2	3.42
58 – 1	36.67	121.5	3.71	–3	47.52	218.1	4.06
–2	41.27	124.2	3.38	–4	41.58	218.0	4.09
–3	36.18	123.2	3.04	70 – 1	40.85	218.3	4.25
–4	37.46	127.7	3.07	–2	34.54	220.4	3.77
59 – 1	32.99	127.2	3.42	–3	44.43	222.4	3.29
–2	32.49	128.8	4.52	–4	60.78	221.7	3.62
–3	32.98	128.4	4.87	71 – 1	49.18	227.8	3.36
–4	33.32	131.5	4.59	–2	55.81	233.3	3.76
60 – 1	21.95	133.4	4.41	–3	57.23	239.8	2.97
–2	23.54	130.5	4.52	–4	59.27	242.0	2.02
–3	27.05	133.3	4.54	72 – 1	62.12	243.8	1.93
–4	27.34	133.8	4.55	–2	62.08	250.5	1.68
61 – 1	31.90	132.5	4.54	–3	60.51	249.2	1.60
–2	29.88	137.1	4.36	–4	57.25	257.7	1.05
–3	30.07	135.1	4.47	73 – 1	62.39	264.7	0.88
–4	27.39	141.5	4.45	–2	68.25	267.2	1.65
62 – 1	30.58	143.3	4.34	–3	65.32	267.0	1.92
–2	31.97	143.3	4.05	–4	62.45	278.1	1.46
–3	31.53	148.4	4.38	74 – 1	68.48	280.6	1.21
–4	28.36	148.2	3.96	–2	62.68	279.6	2.34
63 – 1	31.94	148.2	3.72	–3	50.43	274.5	2.50
–2	32.78	150.1	3.63	–4	40.33	281.5	1.37
–3	34.97	157.1	3.84	75 – 1	37.28	278.9	–0.96
–4	39.12	157.7	3.85	–2	51.37	280.4	–1.23
64 – 1	42.82	160.7	3.75	–3	60.49	282.7	–0.09
–2	32.84	162.2	3.69	–4	67.14	286.8	0.78
–3	37.40	165.2	3.81	76 – 1	66.58	294.4	1.42
–4	46.10	166.6	3.90	–2	70.57	298.9	1.87
65 – 1	40.63	169.9	3.68	–3	64.94	299.0	2.54
–2	38.23	172.4	3.47	–4	63.81	299.0	2.88
–3	39.63	177.0	3.34	77 – 1	53.48	301.3	2.36
–4	40.38	179.0	3.28	–2	61.83	302.5	1.65
66 – 1	41.12	183.4	3.17	–3	61.79	304.9	0.71

(Continued overleaf)

Table 4.10   (*continued*)

T	HS	y	RR	T	HS	y	RR
77 − 4	59.81	307.9	0.54	80 − 3	41.39	324.3	2.69
78 − 1	69.51	310.5	0.59	−4	40.57	332.6	4.97
−2	50.31	312.7	1.62	81 − 1	39.14	332.0	7.53
−3	55.22	318.4	2.28	−2	53.69	338.5	8.56
−4	53.05	318.9	4.00	−3	47.06	338.3	11.37
79 − 1	46.19	322.5	4.28	−4	33.87	335.5	8.00
−2	48.53	322.3	3.73	82 − 1	40.71	319.8	6.27
−3	48.29	324.6	3.85	−2	28.61	320.9	7.41
−4	49.24	328.1	5.85	−3	25.43	322.4	6.26
80 − 1	38.24	325.6	6.00	−4	32.20	316.6	3.12
−2	35.33	321.3	5.26				

[a]T, year and quarter; HS, housing starts; y, gross national expenditures (in 1971 dollars); RR, estimated real interest rate.
Source: R. Davidson and J. G. MacKinnon, "Testing Linear and Log-Linear Regressions Against Box–Cox Alternatives," *Canadian Journal of Economics*, August 1985, Table 5, pp. 515–516. Data on HS and y have been rounded to four-digit numbers.

Table 4.11   Wages, benefits, unemployment, and net national product: United Kingdom, 1920–1938

Year	Weekly Wages, W (s.)	Weekly Benefits, B (s.)	Unemployment Rate, U (%)	Benefits/ Wages	NNP, Q^a (£ million at 1938 factor cost)
1920	73.8	11.3	3.9	0.15	3426
1921	70.6	16.83	17.0	0.24	3242
1922	59.1	22.00	14.3	0.37	3384
1923	55.5	22.00	11.7	0.40	3514
1924	56.0	23.67	10.3	0.42	3622
1925	56.4	27.00	11.3	0.48	3840
1926	55.8	27.00	12.5	0.48	3656
1927	56.2	27.00	9.7	0.48	3937
1928	55.7	27.67	10.8	0.50	4003
1929	55.8	28.00	10.4	0.50	4097
1930	55.7	29.50	16.1	0.53	4082
1931	54.9	29.54	21.3	0.54	3832
1932	54.0	27.25	22.1	0.50	3828
1933	53.7	27.25	19.9	0.51	3899
1934	54.3	28.6	16.7	0.53	4196
1935	55.0	30.3	15.5	0.55	4365
1936	56.1	32.00	13.1	0.57	4498
1937	57.2	32.00	10.8	0.56	4665
1938	58.9	32.75	12.9	0.56	4807

[a]NNP, net national product; s., shilling = $\frac{1}{20}$£.

Part II Violation of the Assumptions of the Basic Model

This part consists of seven chapters that deal with the violation of the assumptions made regarding the regression model in Part I.

Chapters 5 and 6 deal, respectively, with the problems of unequal error variances and serially correlated errors in the multiple regression model. Chapter 6, in particular, deals extensively with the commonly used Durbin–Watson statistic, its limitations and several extensions.

Chapter 7 deals with the multicollinearity problem. This problem is commonly misunderstood and the chapter clears up the misunderstandings and discusses the ad hoc solutions proposed to solve this problem.

Chapter 8 discusses the cases where the variables are not continuously observed but are observed as dummy variables and truncated variables. This chapter discusses the logit, probit and tobit models.

Chapter 9 discusses the case where the regressors are correlated with the error term. We discuss the identification problem, and instrumental variable methods of estimating these models.

Chapter 10 relaxes the assumptions of linearity in the regression model and the assumptions of normality of the errors. Some solutions to these problems are outlined. This chapter also discusses models of expectations.

Chapter 11 treats the case where the explanatory variables are observed with error. Again some instrumental variable methods are outlined. Ragnar Frisch, one of the founders of the Econometric Society and *Econometrica*, worked on errors in variables problems. This problem is all pervasive but does not receive much attention in econometrics.

5 Heteroskedasticity

What is in this Chapter?

One of the assumptions made in Chapters 3 and 4 regarding the errors is that they have a common variance. This chapter relaxes this assumption. The issues discussed in this chapter are:

(a) How do we detect this problem?
(b) What are the consequences of this problem?
(c) What are the solutions?

First we discuss tests for detection of heteroskedasticity (nonconstant variance). We discuss tests based on OLS residuals, likelihood ratio test, Goldfeld and Quandt test and the Breusch and Pagan test. The last one is an LM test.

Regarding consequences, we show that the OLS estimators are unbiased but inefficient and the standard errors are also biased, thus invalidating tests of significance.

Regarding solutions, we discuss solutions depending on particular assumptions about the error variance and general solutions. We also discuss transformation of variables to logs and the problems associated with deflators, both of which are commonly used as solutions to the heteroskedasticity problem.

5.1 Introduction

One of the assumptions we have made until now is that the errors u_i in the regression equation have a common variance σ^2. This is known as the *homoskedasticity* assumption. If the errors do not have a constant variance we say they are *heteroskedastic*. There are several questions we might want to ask if the errors do not have a constant variance. These are:

1. How do we detect this problem?
2. What are the consequences on the properties of the least squares estimators, and what are the consequences on the estimated standard errors if we use OLS?
3. What are the solutions to this problem?

We will answer these questions in the following sections. But first, we will consider an example to illustrate the problem.

Illustrative Example

Table 5.1 presents consumption expenditures (y) and income (x) for 20 families. Suppose that we estimate the equation by ordinary least squares. We get (figures in parentheses are standard errors)

$$y = \underset{(0.703)}{0.847} + \underset{(0.0253)}{0.899x} \qquad \begin{array}{l} R^2 = 0.986 \\ \text{RSS} = 31.074 \end{array}$$

We can compute the predicted values and the residuals. In Table 5.2 we present the residuals for the observations which are ordered by their x values. As we can easily see

Table 5.1 Consumption expenditures (y) and income (x) for 20 families (thousands of dollars)

Family	y	x	Family	y	x
1	19.9	22.3	11	8.0	8.1
2	31.2	32.3	12	33.1	34.5
3	31.8	36.6	13	33.5	38.0
4	12.1	12.1	14	13.1	14.1
5	40.7	42.3	15	14.8	16.4
6	6.1	6.2	16	21.6	24.1
7	38.6	44.7	17	29.3	30.1
8	25.5	26.1	18	25.0	28.3
9	10.3	10.3	19	17.9	18.2
10	38.8	40.2	20	19.8	20.1

Table 5.2 Residuals for the consumption function estimated from data in Table 5.1 (ordered by their x values)[a]

Observation	Value of x	Residual	Observation	Value of x	Residual
6	6.2	−0.32	8	26.1	1.18
11	8.1	−0.13	18	28.3	−1.30
9	10.3	0.19	17	30.1	1.38
4	12.1	0.37	2	32.3	1.30
14	14.1	−0.43	12	34.5	1.23
15	16.4	−0.80	3	36.6	−1.96
19	18.2	0.69	13	38.0	−1.52
20	20.1	0.88	10	40.2	1.80
1	22.3	−1.00	5	42.3	1.81
16	24.1	−0.92	7	44.7	−2.45

[a]Residuals are rounded to two decimals.

they are larger (absolutely) for larger values of x. Thus there is some evidence that the error variances are not constant but increase with the value of x. In Figure 5.1 we show the plot of the residuals. This shows graphically (perhaps more than Table 5.2) that there is a heteroskedasticity problem.

Sometimes, the heteroskedasticity problem is solved by estimating the regression in a log-linear form. When we regress log y on log x, the estimated equation is (figures in parentheses are standard errors)

$$\log y = \underset{(0.0574)}{0.0757} + \underset{(0.0183)}{0.9562 \log x} \qquad \begin{array}{l} R^2 = 0.9935 \\ RSS = 0.03757 \end{array}$$

The R^2's are not comparable since the variance of the dependent variable is different. We discuss the problem of comparing R^2's from linear versus log-linear form in Section 5.6. The residuals from this equation are presented in Table 5.3. In this situation there is no

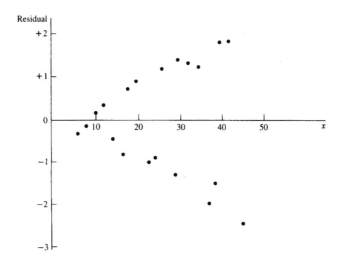

Figure 5.1 Example of heteroskedasticity

Table 5.3 Residuals from the log-linear equation[a]

Observation	Log x	Residual	Observation	Log x	Residual
6	1.82	−0.12	8	3.26	0.44
11	2.09	0.04	18	3.34	−0.53
9	2.33	0.27	17	3.40	0.47
4	2.49	0.34	2	3.48	0.42
14	2.65	−0.33	12	3.54	0.38
15	2.80	−0.56	3	3.60	−0.59
19	2.90	0.35	13	3.64	−0.42
20	3.00	0.41	10	3.69	0.51
1	3.10	−0.54	5	3.74	0.50
16	3.18	−0.46	7	3.80	−0.56

[a]Log x rounded to two decimals and residual multiplied by 10.

perceptible increase in the magnitudes of the residuals as the value of *x* increases. Thus there does not appear to be a heteroskedasticity problem.

In any case, we need formal tests of the hypothesis of homoskedasticity. These are discussed in the following sections.

5.2   Detection of Heteroskedasticity

In the illustrative example in Section 5.1 we plotted the estimated residual $\hat{u}_t$ against x_t to see whether we notice any systematic pattern in the residuals that suggests heteroskedasticity in the errors. Note, however, that by virtue of the normal equation, $\hat{u}_t$ and x_t are uncorrelated though $\hat{u}_t^2$ could be correlated with x_t. Thus if we are using a regression procedure to test for heteroskedasticity, we should use a regression of $\hat{u}_t$ on $x_t^2, x_t^3, \ldots$ or a regression of $|\hat{u}_t|$ or $\hat{u}_t^2$ on $x_t, x_t^2, x_t^3, \ldots$. In the case of multiple regression, we should use powers of $\hat{y}_t$, the predicted value of y_t, or powers of all the explanatory variables.

1. The test suggested by Anscombe[1] and a test called RESET suggested by Ramsey[2] both involve regressing $\hat{u}_t$ on $\hat{y}_t^2, \hat{y}_t^3, \ldots$ and testing whether or not the coefficients are significant.
2. The test suggested by White[3] involves regressing $\hat{u}_t^2$ on all the explanatory variables and their squares and cross products. For instance, with three explanatory variables x_1, x_2, x_3, it involves regressing $\hat{u}_t^2$ on $x_1, x_2, x_3, x_1^2, x_2^2, x_3^2, x_1x_2, x_2x_3$, and x_3x_1.
3. Glejser[4] suggested estimating regressions of the type $|\hat{u}_i| = \alpha + \beta x_i$, $|\hat{u}_i| = \alpha + \beta/x_i, |\hat{u}_i| = \alpha + \beta\sqrt{x_i}$, and so on, and testing the hypothesis $\beta = 0$.

The implicit assumption behind all these tests is that $\text{var}(u_i) = \sigma_i^2 = \sigma^2 f(z_i)$ where z_i is an unknown variable and the different tests use different proxies or surrogates for the unknown function $f(z)$.

Illustrative Example

For the data in Table 5.1, using the residuals in Table 5.2 the Ramsey, White, and Glejser tests produced the following results. Since there is only one explanatory variable *x*, we can use *x* instead of $\hat{y}$ in the application of the Ramsey test. The test thus involves regressing $\hat{u}_i$ on x_i^2, x_i^3, and so on. In our example the test was not very useful. The results were (standard errors are not reported because the R^2 is very low for sample size 20)

$$\hat{u} = -0.379 + 0.236 \times 10^{-2}x^2 - 0.549 \times 10^{-4}x^3 \quad R^2 = 0.034$$

---

[1]F. J. Anscombe, "Examination of Residuals," *Proceedings of the Fourth Berkeley Symposium on Mathematical Statistics and Probability* (Berkeley, CA: University of California Press, 1961), pp. 1–36.

[2]J. B. Ramsey, "Tests for Specification Errors in Classical Linear Least Squares Regression Analysis," *Journal of the Royal Statistical Society, Series B*, Vol. 31, 1969, pp. 350–371.

[3]H. White, "A Heteroskedasticity Consistent Covariance Matrix Estimator and a Direct Test of Heteroskedasticity," *Econometrica*, Vol. 48, 1980, pp. 817–838.

[4]H. Glejser, "A New Test for Homoskedasticity," *Journal of the American Statistical Association*, 1969, pp. 316–323.

None of the coefficients had a t-ratio > 1 indicating that we are unable to reject the hypothesis that the errors are homoskedastic.

The test suggested by White involves regressing $\hat{u}^2$ on x, x^2, x^3, and so on. The results were

$$\hat{u}^2 = -\underset{(0.390)}{1.370} + \underset{(0.014)}{0.116}x \qquad R^2 = 0.7911$$

$$\hat{u}^2 = \underset{(0.620)}{0.493} - \underset{(0.055)}{0.071}x + \underset{(0.0011)}{0.0037}x^2 \qquad R^2 = 0.878$$

The R^2's are highly significant in both cases. Thus the test rejects the hypothesis of homoskedasticity. A suggested procedure to correct for heteroskedasticity is to estimate the regression model assuming that $V(u_i) = \sigma_i^2$, where $\sigma^2 = \gamma_0 + \gamma_1 x + \gamma_2 x^2$. This procedure is discussed in Section 5.4.

Glejser's tests gave the following results:

$$|\hat{u}| = -\underset{(0.094)}{0.209} + \underset{(0.0034)}{0.0512}x \qquad R^2 = 0.927$$

$$|\hat{u}| = -\underset{(0.186)}{1.232} + \underset{(0.037)}{0.475}\sqrt{x} \qquad R^2 = 0.902$$

$$|\hat{u}| = \underset{(0.155)}{1.826} - \underset{(2.39)}{13.78}(1/x) \qquad R^2 = 0.649$$

All the tests reject the hypothesis of homoskedasticity, although on the basis of R^2, the first model is preferable to the others. The suggested model to estimate is the same as that suggested by White's test.

The results are similar for the log-linear form as well, although the coefficients are not as significant. Using the residuals in Table 5.3 we get, for the White test,

$$\hat{u}^2 = -\underset{(0.083)}{0.211} + \underset{(0.026)}{0.129}x \qquad R^2 = 0.572$$

$$\hat{u}^2 = -\underset{(0.385)}{0.620} + \underset{(0.273)}{0.425}x - \underset{(0.047)}{0.051}x^2 \qquad R^2 = 0.600$$

Thus there is evidence of heteroskedasticity even in the log-linear form, although casually looking at the residuals in Table 5.3, we concluded earlier that the errors were homoskedastic. The Goldfeld–Quandt test, to be discussed later in this section, also did not reject the hypothesis of homoskedasticity. The Glejser tests, however, show significant heteroskedasticity in the log-linear form.

Some Other Tests

The Likelihood Ratio Test

If the number of observations is large, one can use a likelihood ratio test. Divide the residuals (estimated from the OLS regression) into k groups with n_i observations in the ith group, $\sum n_i = n$. Estimate the error variances in each group by $\hat{\sigma}_i^2$. Let the estimate of the error variance from the entire sample be $\hat{\sigma}^2$. Then if we define λ as

$$\lambda = \prod_{i=1}^{k} (\hat{\sigma}_i)^{n_i} / \hat{\sigma}^n$$

$-2 \log_e \lambda$ has a χ^2-distribution with d.f. $(k-1)$. If there is only one explanatory variable in the equation, the ordering of the residuals can be based on the absolute magnitude of this variable. But if there are two or more variables and no single variable can provide a satisfactory ordering, then $\hat{y}$, the predicted value of y, can be used.

Feldstein used this LR test for his hospital cost regressions described in Chapter 4 (Section 4.6, Example 1). He divided the total number of observations (177) into four groups of equal size, the residuals being ordered by the predicted values of the dependent variable. The estimates $\hat{\sigma}_i^2$ were 71.47, 114.82, 102.81, and 239.34. The estimate $\hat{\sigma}^2$ for the whole sample was 138.76. Thus $-2 \log \lambda$ was 18.265. The 1% significance point for the χ^2-distribution with d.f. 3 is 11.34. Thus there were significant differences between the error variances. Next Feldstein weighted the observations by weights proportional to $1/\hat{\sigma}_i$. The weights normalized to make their average equal to 1 were 1.2599, 0.9940, 1.0504, and 0.6885. This would make the error variances approximately equal. The equation was estimated by OLS using the transformed data. This procedure is called *weighted least squares* and is often denoted by WLS. The new estimates of the variances from this reestimated equation, for the four groups were 106.34, 110.71, 114.99, and 117.06, which are almost equal. However, the regression parameters did not change much, as shown in Table 5.4. Although the point estimates did not change much, the standard errors could be different. Since Feldstein does not present these, we have no way of comparing them.

Goldfeld and Quandt Test

If we do not have large samples, we can use the Goldfeld and Quandt test.[5] In this test we split the observations into two groups — one corresponding to large values of x and the

Table 5.4   Comparison of OLS and WLS estimates for hospital cost regression

Case Type	Average Cost per Case	
	OLS	WLS
General medicine	114.48	111.81
Pediatrics	24.97	28.35
General surgery	32.70	35.07
ENT	15.25	15.58
Traumatic and orthopedic surgery	39.69	36.04
Other surgery	98.02	101.38
Gynecology	58.72	58.48
Obstetrics	34.88	34.50
Others	69.51	66.26

Source: M. S. Feldstein, *Economic Analysis for Health Service Efficiency* (Amsterdam: North-Holland, 1967), p. 54.

---

[5]S. M. Goldfeld and R. E. Quandt, *Nonlinear Methods in Econometrics* (Amsterdam: North-Holland, 1972), Chap. 3.

other corresponding to small values of x — fit separate regressions for each and then apply an F-test to test the equality of error variances. Goldfeld and Quandt suggest omitting some observations in the middle to increase our ability to discriminate between the two error variances.

Breusch and Pagan Test

Suppose that $V(u_t) = \sigma_t^2$. If there are some variables $z_1, z_2, \ldots, z_r$ that influence the error variance and if $\sigma_t^2 = f(\alpha_0 + \alpha_1 z_{1t} + \alpha_2 z_{2t} + \cdots + \alpha_r z_{rt})$, then the Breusch and Pagan test[6] is a test of the hypothesis

$$H_0 : \alpha_1 = \alpha_2 = \cdots = \alpha_r = 0$$

The function $f(\cdot)$ can be any function. For instance, $f(x)$ can be x, x^2, e^x, and so on. The Breusch and Pagan test does *not* depend on the functional form. Let

$$\hat{\sigma}^2 = \sum \frac{\hat{u}_t^2}{n}$$

S_0 = regression sum of squares from a regression
of $\hat{u}_t^2$ on $z_1, z_2, \ldots, z_r$

Then $\lambda = S_0/2\hat{\sigma}^4$ has a χ^2-distribution with d.f. r.

This test is an asymptotic test. An intuitive justification for the test will be given after an illustrative example.

Illustrative Example

Consider the data in Table 5.1. To apply the Goldfeld–Quandt test we consider two groups of 10 observations each, ordered by the values of the variable x. The first group consists of observations 6, 11, 9, 4, 14, 15, 19, 20, 1, and 16. The second group consists of the remaining 10. The estimated equations were

$$\text{Group 1:} \quad y = 1.0533 + 0.876x \quad R^2 = 0.985$$
$$\underset{(0.616)}{} \quad \underset{(0.038)}{}$$
$$\hat{\sigma}^2 = 0.475$$
$$\text{Group 2:} \quad y = 3.279 + 0.835x \quad R^2 = 0.904$$
$$\underset{(3.443)}{} \quad \underset{(0.096)}{}$$
$$\hat{\sigma}^2 = 3.154$$

The F-ratio for the test is

$$F = \frac{3.154}{0.475} = 6.64$$

The 1% point for the F-distribution with d.f. 8 and 8 is 6.03. Thus the F-value is significant at the 1% level and we reject the hypothesis of homoskedasticity.

---

[6] T. S. Breusch and A. R. Pagan, "A Simple Test for Heteroskedasticity and Random Coefficient Variation," *Econometrica*, Vol. 47, 1979, pp. 1287–1294.

Consider now the logarithmic form. The results are

$$\text{Group 1}: \quad \log y = \underset{(0.079)}{0.128} + \underset{(0.030)}{0.934}x \qquad R^2 = 0.992$$

$$\hat{\sigma}^2 = 0.001596$$

$$\text{Group 2}: \quad \log y = \underset{(0.352)}{0.276} + \underset{(0.099)}{0.902}x \qquad R^2 = 0.912$$

$$\hat{\sigma}^2 = 0.002789$$

The F-ratio for the test is

$$F = \frac{0.002789}{0.001596} = 1.75$$

For d.f. 8 and 8, the 5% point from the F-tables is 3.44. Thus if we use the 5% significance level, we do not reject the hypothesis of homoskedasticity. Hence by the Goldfeld–Quandt test we reject the hypothesis of homoskedasticity if we consider the linear form but do not reject it in the log-linear form. Note that the White test rejected the hypothesis in both the forms.

Turning now to the Breusch and Pagan test, the regression of $\hat{u}_t^2$ on x_t, x_t^2, and x_t^3 gave the following regression sums of squares. For the linear form

$$S = 40.842 \text{ for the regression of } \hat{u}_t^2 \text{ on } x_t, x_t^2, x_t^3$$

$$S = 40.065 \text{ for the regression of } \hat{u}_t^2 \text{ on } x_t, x_t^2$$

Also, $\hat{\sigma}^2 = 1.726$. The test statistic for the χ^2-test is (using the second regression)

$$\frac{S}{2\hat{\sigma}^4} = \frac{40.065}{2(2.979)} = 6.724$$

We use the statistic as a χ^2-distribution with d.f. $\neq 2$ since two slope parameters are estimated. This is significant at the 5% level, thus, rejecting the hypothesis of homoskedasticity.

For the log-linear form, using only x_t and x_t^2 as regressors we get: $S = 0.000011$ and $\hat{\sigma}^2 = 0.00209$. The test statistic is

$$\frac{0.000011}{2(0.00209)^2} = 1.259$$

Using the χ^2-tables with d.f. 2 we see that this is not significant even at the 50% level. Thus, the test does not reject the hypothesis of homoskedasticity in the log-linear form.

An Intuitive Justification for the Breusch–Pagan Test

In Section 4.12 we discussed the LM, W, and LR tests. There we showed that the LM test statistic was $LM = nR^2$, which has a χ^2-distribution. Arguing from analogy, we would get a test statistic nR^2, where R^2 is the multiple correlation coefficient in a regression of $\hat{u}_t^2$ on $z_{1t}, z_{2t}, z_{3t}, \ldots$. To see the relationship between this and the Breusch–Pagan test statistic, note that

$$nR^2 = \frac{\text{regression SS from a regression of } \hat{u}_t^2 \text{ on } z_{1t}, z_{2t}, z_{3t}, \ldots}{\text{var}(\hat{u}_t^2)} = \frac{S}{\text{var}(\hat{u}_t^2)}$$

Now, under the null hypothesis that the errors are homoskedastic, u_t^2/σ^2 has a χ^2-distribution with d.f. 1. Hence $\text{var}(u_t^2/\sigma^2) = 2$ (because the variance of a χ^2 variable is twice the degrees of freedom). Thus

$$\text{var}(u_t^2) = 2\sigma^4$$

In large samples we can write $\text{var}(\hat{u}_t^2) = \text{var}(u_t^2)$ and $\hat{\sigma}^4 = \sigma^4$. Hence we get $\text{var}(\hat{u}_t^2) \simeq 2\hat{\sigma}^4$. Thus the test statistic is $S/2\hat{\sigma}^4$, as described earlier. The statistic can also be viewed as half the regression sum of squares from a regression of $g_t = \hat{u}_t^2/\hat{\sigma}^2$ on $z_{1t}, z_{2t}, z_{3t}, \ldots$. Breusch and Pagan argue that in discussions of heteroskedasticity, *if one is going to plot any quantity*, it is more reasonable to plot g_t than quantities like $\hat{u}_t$.

5.3 Consequences of Heteroskedasticity

Before we attempt solutions to the heteroskedasticity problem, we will study the consequences on the least squares estimators. We will show that

1. The least squares estimators are still unbiased but inefficient.
2. The estimates of the variances are also biased, thus invalidating the tests of significance.

To see this, consider a very simple model with no constant term:

$$y_i = \beta x_i + u_i \quad V(u_i) = \sigma_i^2 \tag{5.1}$$

The least squares estimator of β is

$$\hat{\beta} = \frac{\sum x_i y_i}{\sum x_i^2} = \beta + \frac{\sum x_i u_i}{\sum x_i^2}$$

If $E(u_i) = 0$ and u_i are independent of the x_i, we have $E(\sum x_i u_i / \sum x_i^2) = 0$ and hence $E(\hat{\beta}) = \beta$. Thus $\hat{\beta}$ is unbiased.

If the u_i are mutually independent, denoting $\sum x_i^2$ by S_{xx} we can write

$$V(\hat{\beta}) = V\left(\frac{x_1}{S_{xx}}u_1 + \frac{x_2}{S_{xx}}u_2 + \cdots + \frac{x_n}{S_{xx}}u_n\right)$$

$$= \frac{1}{S_{xx}^2}(x_1^2\sigma_1^2 + x_2^2\sigma_2^2 + \cdots + x_n^2\sigma_n^2)$$

$$= \frac{\sum x_i^2\sigma_i^2}{(\sum x_i^2)^2} \tag{5.2}$$

Suppose that we write $\sigma_i^2 = \sigma^2 z_i^2$, where z_i are known, that is, we know the variances up to a multiplicative constant. Then dividing (5.1) by z_i we have the model

$$\frac{y_i}{z_i} = \beta \frac{x_i}{z_i} + v_i \qquad (5.3)$$

where $v_i = u_i/z_i$ has a constant variance σ^2. Since we are "weighting" the ith observation by $1/z_i$, the OLS estimation of (5.3) is called weighted least squares (WLS). If β^* is the WLS estimator of β, we have

$$\beta^* = \frac{\sum (y_i/z_i)(x_i/z_i)}{\sum (x_i/z_i)^2}$$

$$= \beta + \frac{\sum (x_i/z_i)v_i}{\sum (x_i/z_i)^2}$$

and since the latter term has expectation zero, we have $E(\beta^*) = \beta$. Thus the WLS estimator β^* is also unbiased. We will show that β^* is more efficient than the OLS estimator $\hat{\beta}$.

We have

$$V(\beta^*) = \frac{\sigma^2}{\sum (x_i/z_i)^2}$$

and substituting $\sigma_i^2 = \sigma^2 z_i^2$ in equation (5.2), we have

$$V(\hat{\beta}) = \sigma^2 \frac{\sum x_i^2 z_i^2}{(\sum x_i^2)^2}$$

Thus

$$\frac{V(\beta^*)}{V(\hat{\beta})} = \frac{(\sum x_i^2)^2}{\sum (x_i^2/z_i^2) \sum x_i^2 z_i^2}$$

This expression is of the form $(\sum a_i b_i)^2/\sum a_i^2 \sum b_i^2$, where $a_i = x_i z_i$ and $b_i = x_i/z_i$. Thus it is less than 1 and is equal to 1 only if a_i and b_i are proportional, that is, $x_i z_i$ and x_i/z_i are proportional or z_i^2 is a constant, which is the case if the errors are homoskedastic.

Thus the OLS estimator is unbiased but less efficient (has a higher variance) than the WLS estimator. Turning now to the estimation of the variance of $\hat{\beta}$, it is estimated by

$$\frac{\text{RSS}}{n-1} \frac{1}{\sum x_i^2}$$

where RSS is the residual sum of squares from the OLS model. But

$$E(\text{RSS}) = E\left[\sum (y_i - \hat{\beta} x_i)^2\right]$$

$$= \sum \sigma_i^2 - \frac{\sum x_i^2 \sigma_i^2}{\sum x_i^2}$$

Note that if $\sigma_i^2 = \sigma^2$ for all i, this reduces to $(n-1)\sigma^2$. Thus we would be estimating the variance of $\hat{\beta}$ by an expression whose expected value is

$$\frac{\sum x_i^2 \sum \sigma_i^2 - \sum x_i^2 \sigma_i^2}{(n-1)(\sum x_i^2)^2}$$

whereas the true variance is

$$\frac{\sum x_i^2 \sigma_i^2}{(\sum x_i^2)^2}$$

Thus the estimated variances are also biased. If σ_i^2 and x_i^2 are positively correlated, as is often the case with economic data so that $\sum x_i^2 \sigma_i^2 > (1/n) \sum x_i^2 \sum \sigma_i^2$, then the expected value of the estimated variance is smaller than the true variance. Thus we would be *underestimating* the true variance of the OLS estimator and getting shorter confidence intervals than the true ones. This also affects tests of hypotheses about β.

Estimation of the Variance of the OLS Estimator Under Heteroskedasticity

The solution to the heteroskedasticity problem depends on the assumptions we make about the sources of heteroskedasticity. When we are not sure of this, we can at least try to make corrections for the standard errors, since we have seen that the least squares estimator is unbiased but inefficient, and moreover, the standard errors are also biased.

White[7] suggests that we use the formula (5.2) with $\hat{u}_i^2$ *substituted for* σ_i^2. Using this formula we find that in the case of the illustrative example with data in Table 5.1, the standard error of $\hat{\beta}$, the slope coefficient is 0.027. Earlier, we estimated it from the OLS regression as 0.0253. Thus the difference is really not very large in this example.

5.4   Solutions to the Heteroskedasticity Problem

There are two types of solutions that have been suggested in the literature for the problem of heteroskedasticity:

1. Solutions dependent on particular assumptions about σ_i^2.
2. General solutions.

We first discuss category 1. Here we have two methods of estimation: weighted least squares and maximum likelihood (ML).

---

[7]White, "A Heteroskedasticity." A similar suggestion was made earlier in C. R. Rao, "Estimation of Heteroskedastic Variances in Linear Models," *Journal of the American Statistical Association*, March 1970, pp. 161–172.

If the error variances are known up to a multiplicative constant, there is no problem at all. If $V(u_i) = \sigma^2 z_i^2$, where z_i are known, we divide the equation through by z_i and use ordinary least squares. The only thing to remember is that if the original equation contained a constant term, that is, $y_i = \alpha + \beta x_i + u_i$, the transformed equation will *not* have a constant term. It is

$$\frac{y_i}{z_i} = \alpha \frac{1}{z_i} + \beta \frac{x_i}{z_i} + v_i$$

where $v_i = u_i/z_i$. Now $V(v_i) = \sigma^2$ for all i. Thus we should be running a regression of y_i/z_i on $1/z_i$ and x_i/z_i *without* a constant term.

One interesting case is where $V(u_i) = \sigma^2 x_i$ and $\alpha = 0$. In this case the transformed equation is

$$\frac{y_i}{\sqrt{x_i}} = \beta \frac{x_i}{\sqrt{x_i}} + v_i$$

Hence

$$\beta^* = \frac{\sum(y_i x_i/x_i)}{\sum(\sqrt{x_i})^2} = \frac{\overline{y}}{\overline{x}}$$

that is, the WLS estimator is just the ratio of the means. Another case is where $\sigma_i^2 = \sigma^2 x_i^2$. In this case the transformed equation is

$$\frac{y_i}{x_i} = \alpha \frac{1}{x_i} + \beta + v_i$$

Thus the constant term in this equation is the slope coefficient in the original equation.

Prais and Houthakker[8] found in their analysis of family budget data that the errors from the equation had variance increasing with household income. They considered a model $\sigma_i^2 = \sigma^2[E(y_i)]^2$, that is, $\sigma_i^2 = \sigma^2(\alpha + \beta x_i)^2$. In this case we cannot divide the whole equation by a known constant as before. For this model we can consider a *two-step* procedure as follows. First estimate α and β by OLS. Let these estimators be $\hat{\alpha}$ and $\hat{\beta}$. Now use the WLS procedure as outlined earlier, that is, regress $y_i/(\hat{\alpha} + \hat{\beta} x_i)$ on $1/(\hat{\alpha} + \hat{\beta} x_i)$ and $x_i/(\hat{\alpha} + \hat{\beta} x_i)$ with no constant term. This procedure is called a *two-step weighted least squares* procedure. The standard errors we get for the estimates of α and β from this procedure are valid only asymptotically. They are asymptotic standard errors because the weights $1/(\alpha + \beta x_i)$ have been estimated.

One can iterate this WLS procedure further, that is, use the new estimates of α and β to construct new weights and then use the WLS procedure, and repeat this procedure until convergence. This procedure is called the *iterated weighted least squares procedure.* However, there is no gain in (asymptotic) efficiency by iteration.

If we make some specific assumptions about the errors, say that they are normal, we can use the maximum likelihood method, which is more efficient than the WLS if errors are

---

[8]S. J. Prais and H. S. Houthakker, *The Analysis of Family Budgets* (New York: Cambridge University Press, 1955), p. 55ff.

normal.[9] Under the assumption of normality we can write the log-likelihood function as

$$\log L = -n \log \sigma - \sum \log(\alpha + \beta x_i) - \frac{1}{2\sigma^2} \sum \left(\frac{y_i - \alpha - \beta x_i}{\alpha + \beta x_i} \right)^2$$

Note that maximizing this likelihood function is not the same as the weighted least squares that minimizes the expression

$$\sum \left(\frac{y_i - \alpha - \beta x_i}{\alpha + \beta x_i} \right)^2$$

A more general model is to assume that the variance σ_i^2 is equal to $(\gamma + \delta x_i)^2$. In this case, too, we can consider a WLS procedure, that is, minimize

$$\sum_i \left(\frac{y_i - \alpha - \beta x_i}{\gamma + \delta x_i} \right)^2$$

or if the errors can be assumed to follow a known distribution, use the ML method. For instance, if the errors follow a normal distribution, we can write the log-likelihood function as

$$\log L = \text{const.} - \sum \log(\gamma + \delta x_i) - \frac{1}{2} \sum \left(\frac{y_i - \alpha - \beta x_i}{\gamma + \delta x_i} \right)^2$$

Again, note that the WLS and ML procedures are not the same.[10] A two-step WLS estimation for this model would proceed as follows. Compute the OLS estimates of α and β. Get the estimated residuals and regress the absolute values of these residuals on x to get estimates of γ and δ. Then use WLS.

Illustrative Example

As an illustration, again consider the data in Table 5.1. We saw earlier that regressing the absolute values of the residuals on x (in Glejser's tests) gave the following estimates:

$$\hat{\gamma} = -0.209 \quad \hat{\delta} = 0.0512$$

Now we regress y_i/w_i on $1/w_i$ and x_i/w_i (with no constant term) where $w_i = \hat{\gamma} + \hat{\delta} x_i$. The resulting equation is

$$\frac{y_i}{w_i} = \underset{(0.1643)}{0.4843}(1/w_i) + \underset{(0.0157)}{0.9176}(x_i/w_i) \quad R^2 = 0.9886$$

If we assume that $\sigma_i^2 = \gamma_0 + \gamma_1 x_i + \gamma_2 x_i^2$, the two-step WLS procedure would be as follows.

---

[9]Amemiya discusses the ML estimation for this model when the errors follow a normal, lognormal, and gamma distribution. See T. Amemiya, "Regression Analysis When Variance of the Dependent Variables Is Proportional to Square of Its Expectation," *Journal of the American Statistical Association*, December 1973, pp. 928–934.

[10]The ML estimation of this model is discussed in H. C. Rutemiller and D. A. Bowers, "Estimation in a Heteroskedastic Regression Model," *Journal of the American Statistical Association*, June 1968.

First, we regress $\hat{u}_i^2$ on x_i and x_i^2. Earlier, using this regression we obtained the estimates as

$$\hat{\gamma}_0 = 0.493 \quad \hat{\gamma}_1 = -0.071 \quad \hat{\gamma}_2 = 0.0037$$

Next we compute

$$w_i^2 = 0.493 - 0.071x_i + 0.0037x_i^2$$

and regress y_i/w_i on $1/w_i$ and x_i/w_i. The results were

$$\frac{y_i}{w_i} = \underset{(0.3302)}{0.7296}(1/w_i) + \underset{(0.0199)}{0.9052}(x_i/w_i) \quad R^2 = 0.9982$$

The R^2's in these equations are not comparable. But our interest is in estimates of the parameters in the consumption function

$$y_i = \alpha + \beta x_i$$

Comparing the results with the OLS estimates presented in Section 5.2, we notice that the estimates of β are higher than the OLS estimates, the estimates of α are lower, and the standard errors are lower.

5.5   Heteroskedasticity and the Use of Deflators

There are two remedies often suggested and used for solving the heteroskedasticity problem:

1. Transforming the data to logs.
2. Deflating the variables by some measure of "size."

The first method often does reduce the heteroskedasticity in the error variances, although there are other criteria by which one has to decide between the linear and the logarithmic functional forms. This problem is discussed in greater detail in Section 5.6.

Regarding the use of deflators, one should be careful in estimating the equation with the correct explanatory variables (as explained in the preceding section). For instance, if the original equation involves a constant term, one should not estimate a similar equation in the deflated variables. One should be estimating an equation with the reciprocal of the deflator added as an extra explanatory variable. As an illustration, consider the estimation of railroad cost functions by Griliches[11] where deflation was used to solve the heteroskedasticity problem. The variables are: C = total cost, M = miles of road, and X = output.

If $C = aM + bX$, dividing by M gives $C/M = a + b(X/M)$. But if the true relation is $C = aM + bX + c$, deflation leads to $C/M = a + b(X/M) + c(1/M)$. For 97 observations

[11]Z. Griliches, "Railroad Cost Analysis," *The Bell Journal of Economics and Management Science*, Spring 1972.

using 1957–1969 averages as units, regressions were

$$\frac{C}{M} = \underset{(6218)}{13{,}016} + \underset{(0.871)}{6.431} \frac{X}{M} \qquad R^2 = 0.365$$

$$\frac{C}{M} = \underset{(5115)}{827} + \underset{(0.682)}{6.439} \frac{X}{M} + \underset{(393{,}000)}{3{,}065{,}000} \frac{1}{M} \qquad R^2 = 0.614$$

$$C = \underset{(2.906)}{-1.884M} + \underset{(0.375)}{6.613X} + \underset{(4730)}{3676} \qquad R^2 = 0.945$$

The coefficient c is significant in the second equation but not in the third, and the coefficient a is not significant in either the second or third equation. From this Griliches concludes that there is no evidence that M belongs in the equation in any form. It appears in a significant form in the second equation only because the other variables were divided by it.

Some other equations estimated with the same data are the following:

$$C = \underset{(4524)}{2811} + \underset{(0.18)}{6.39X} \qquad R^2 = 0.944$$

$$\frac{C}{\sqrt{M}} = \underset{(3713)}{3805} \frac{1}{\sqrt{M}} + \underset{(0.51)}{6.06} \frac{X}{\sqrt{M}} \qquad R^2 = 0.826$$

The last equation is the appropriate one to estimate if $C = a + bX + u$ and $V(u) = M\sigma^2$.

One important thing to note is that the purpose in all these procedures of deflation is to get more efficient estimates of the parameters. But once those estimates have been obtained, one should make all inferences — calculation of the residuals, prediction of future values, calculation of elasticities at the means, etc., from the original equation — not the equation in the deflated variables.

Another point to note is that since the purpose of deflation is to get more efficient estimates, it is tempting to argue about the merits of the different procedures by looking at the standard errors of the coefficients. However, this is not correct, because in the presence of heteroskedasticity the standard errors themselves are biased, as we showed earlier. For instance, in the five equations presented above, the second and third are comparable and so are the fourth and fifth. In both cases if we look at the standard errors of the coefficient of X, the coefficient in the undeflated equation has a smaller standard error than the corresponding coefficient in the deflated equation. However, if the standard errors are biased, we have to be careful in making too much of these differences. An examination of the residuals will give a better picture.

In the preceding example we have considered miles M as a deflator and also as an explanatory variable. In this context we should mention some discussion in the literature on "spurious correlation" between ratios.[12] The argument simply is that even if we have two variables X and Y that are uncorrelated, if we deflate both the variables by another variable Z, there could be a strong correlation between X/Z and Y/Z because of the common denominator Z. It is wrong to infer from this correlation that there exists a close

---

[12]See E. Kuh and J. R. Meyer, "Correlation and Regression Estimates When the Data Are Ratios," *Econometrica*, October 1955, pp. 400–416.

relationship between X and Y. Of course, if our interest is in fact the relationship between X/Z and Y/Z, there is no reason why this correlation need be called "spurious." As Kuh and Meyer point out, "The question of spurious correlation quite obviously does not arise when the hypothesis to be tested has initially been formulated in terms of ratios, for instance, in problems involving relative prices. Similarly, when a series such as money value of output is divided by a price index to obtain a 'constant dollar' estimate of output, no question of spurious correlation need arise. Thus, spurious correlation can only exist when a hypothesis pertains to undeflated variables and the data have been divided through by another series for reasons extraneous to but not in conflict with the hypothesis framed as an exact, i.e., nonstochastic relation."

However, even in cases where deflation is done for reasons of estimation, we should note that the problem of "spurious correlation" exists only if we start drawing inferences on the basis of correlation coefficients when we should not be doing so. For example, suppose that the relationship we derive is of the form

$$Y = \alpha Z + \beta X + u \tag{5.4}$$

and we find that the residuals u are heteroskedastic with variance roughly proportional to Z^2. Then we should not hesitate to divide equation (5.4) throughout by Z and estimate the regression equation

$$\frac{Y}{Z} = \alpha + \beta \frac{X}{Z} + u' \tag{5.5}$$

where $u' = u/Z$ has a constant variance σ^2. The estimates of α, β, and σ^2 should be obtained from equation (5.5) and not from equation (5.4). Whether the correlation between Y/Z and X/Z is higher or lower than the correlation between Y and X is irrelevant. The important point to note is that we cannot argue whether (5.4) or (5.5) is a better equation to consider by looking at correlations. As long as we do not base our inferences on correlations, there is nothing wrong with deflation in this case. It should also be noted that if (5.4) is not homogeneous (i.e., it involves a constant term), we end up with an equation of the form

$$\frac{Y}{Z} = \gamma \frac{1}{Z} + \alpha + \beta \frac{X}{Z} + u'$$

which is different from (5.5). The equation will also be different if the variance of u is proportional not to Z^2 but to Z or some other function of Z.

In actual practice, deflation may increase or decrease the resulting correlation. The algebra is somewhat tedious, but with some simplifying assumptions Kuh and Meyer derive the conditions under which the correlation between X/Z and Y/Z is in fact less than that between X and Y.

In summary, often in econometric work deflated or ratio variables are used to solve the heteroskedasticity problem. Deflation can sometimes be justified on pure economic grounds, as in the case of the use of "real" quantities and relative prices. In this case all the inferences from the estimated equation will be based on the equation in the deflated variables. However, if deflation is used to solve the heteroskedasticity problem, any inferences we make have to be based on the original equation, not the equation in the deflated variables. In any case, deflation may increase or decrease the resulting correlations, but this is beside the point. Since the correlations are not comparable anyway, one should not draw any inferences from them.

Illustrative Example: The Density Gradient Model

In Table 5.5 we present data on

$$y = \text{population density}$$

$$x = \text{distance from the central business district}$$

for 39 census tracts on the Baltimore area in 1970. It has been suggested (this is called the "density gradient model") that population density follows the relationship

$$y = Ae^{-\beta x} \quad \beta > 0$$

where A is the density of the central business district. The basic hypothesis is that as you move away from the central business district population density drops off.

For estimation purposes we take logs and write

$$\log y = \log A - \beta x$$

Table 5.5 Data on population density in different census tracts in the Baltimore area in 1970[a]

Observation	y	x	Observation	y	x
1	18,640.0	1.002	21	5485.8	6.748
2	38,275.0	1.403	22	3416.5	6.882
3	2450.3	2.004	23	8194.7	6.948
4	21,969.0	2.138	24	5091.9	6.948
5	9573.7	2.205	25	1183.8	7.082
6	13,751.0	3.608	26	4157.9	7.416
7	38,947.0	3.675	27	2158.3	7.483
8	17,921.0	4.009	28	12,428.0	7.617
9	5050.7	4.276	29	6788.5	7.750
10	4519.0	4.410	30	3277.4	7.750
11	6781.1	4.543	31	3258.2	7.951
12	8246.2	4.810	32	5491.3	8.084
13	5166.4	4.944	33	865.02	11.250
14	7762.4	5.211	34	340.69	13.250
15	11,081.0	5.345	35	507.03	15.500
16	7188.0	5.679	36	323.67	18.000
17	13,753.0	5.813	37	108.36	19.000
18	7492.4	5.813	38	805.66	23.000
19	3620.9	5.879	39	156.84	26.250
20	6390.6	6.080			

[a] y, density of population in the census tract: x, distance of the census tract from the central business district.

Source: I would like to thank Kajal Lahiri for providing me with these data. These data formed the basis of the study in K. Lahiri and R. Numrich, "An Econometric Study of the Dynamics of Urban Spatial Structure," *Journal of Urban Economics*, 1983, pp. 55–79.

Adding an error term u we estimate the model

$$y^* = \alpha - \beta x + u$$

where $y^* = \log y$ and $\alpha = \log A$. Estimation of this equation by OLS gave the following results (figures in parentheses are t-values, not standard errors):

$$\hat{y}^* = \underset{(54.7)}{10.093} - \underset{(-12.28)}{0.2395X} \quad R^2 = 0.803$$

The t-values are very high and the coefficients α and β are significantly different from zero (with a significance level of less than 1%). The sign of β is negative, as expected. With cross-sectional data like these we expect heteroskedasticity, and this could result in an underestimation of the standard errors (and thus an overestimation of the t-ratios). To check whether there is heteroskedasticity, we have to analyze the estimated residuals $\hat{u}_i$. A plot of $\hat{u}_i^2$ against x_i showed a positive relationship and hence Glejser's tests were applied.

Defining $|\hat{u}_i|$ by z_i, the following equations were estimated:

$$z_i = \gamma x_i + v_i$$

$$z_i = \gamma \sqrt{x_i} + v_i$$

$$z_i = \gamma \frac{1}{x_i} + v_i$$

$$z_i = \gamma \frac{1}{\sqrt{x_i}} + v_i$$

We choose the specification that gives the highest R^2 [or equivalently the highest t-value, since $R^2 = t^2/(t^2 + \text{d.f.})$ in the case of only one regressor]. The estimated regressions with t-values in parentheses were

$$\hat{z}_i = \underset{(5.06)}{0.0445}\, x_i$$

$$\hat{z}_i = \underset{(6.42)}{0.1733}\, \sqrt{x_i}$$

$$\hat{z}_i = \underset{(4.50)}{1.390} \left(\frac{1}{x_i} \right)$$

$$\hat{z}_i = \underset{(6.42)}{1.038} \left(\frac{1}{\sqrt{x_i}} \right)$$

All the t-statistics are significant, indicating the presence of heteroskedasticity. Based on the highest t-ratio, we chose the second specification (although the fourth specification is equally valid). Deflating throughout by $\sqrt{x_i}$ gives the regression equations to be estimated as

$$\frac{y_i^*}{\sqrt{x_i}} = \alpha \frac{1}{\sqrt{x_i}} + \beta \sqrt{x_i} + \text{error}$$

The estimates were (figures in parentheses are t-ratios)

$$\hat{\alpha} = \underset{(47.87)}{9.932} \quad \text{and} \quad \hat{\beta} = \underset{(-15.10)}{-0.2258}$$

The estimate of β is negative and highly significant. The estimated density of the central business district is given by $\exp(\hat{\alpha}) = \exp(9.932) = 20,577$. Further analysis of these data is left as an exercise. (What is the R^2 for the equation in the deflated variables? What can you conclude?)

*5.6 Testing the Linear Versus Log-Linear Functional Form

As we mentioned in the introduction, sometimes equations are estimated in log form to take care of the heteroskedasticity problem. In many cases the choice of the functional form is dictated by other considerations like convenience in interpretation and some economic reasoning. For instance, if we are estimating a production function, the linear form

$$X = \alpha + \beta_1 L + \beta_2 K$$

where X is the output, L the labor, and K the capital, implies perfect substitutability among the inputs of production. On the other hand, the logarithmic form

$$\log X = \alpha + \beta_1 \log L + \beta_2 \log K$$

implies a Cobb–Douglas production function with unit elasticity of substitution. Both these formulations are special cases of the CES (constant elasticity of substitution) production function.

For the estimation of demand functions the log form is often preferred because it is easy to interpret the coefficients as elasticities. For instance,

$$\log Q = \alpha + \beta_1 \log P + \beta_2 \log Y$$

where Q is the quantity demanded, P the price, and Y the income, implies that β_1 is the price elasticity and β_2 is the income elasticity. A linear demand function implies that these elasticities depend on the particular point along the demand curve that we are at. In this case we have to consider some methods of choosing statistically between the two functional forms.

When comparing the linear with the log-linear forms, we cannot compare the R^2's because R^2 is the ratio of explained variance to the total variance and the variances of y and log y are different. Comparing R^2's in this case is like comparing two individuals A and B, where A eats 65% of a carrot cake and B eats 70% of a strawberry cake. The comparison does not make sense because there are two different cakes.

The Box–Cox Test

One solution to this problem is to consider a more general model of which both the linear and log-linear forms are special cases. Box and Cox[13] consider the transformation

$$y(\lambda) = \begin{cases} \dfrac{y^\lambda - 1}{\lambda} & \text{for } \lambda \neq 0 \\ \log y & \text{for } \lambda = 0 \end{cases} \tag{5.6}$$

---

[13]G. E. P. Box and D. R. Cox, "An Analysis of Transformations" (with discussion), *Journal of th Statistical Society, Series B*, 1962, pp. 211–243.

This transformation is well defined for all $y > 0$. Also, the transformation is continuous since

$$\lim_{\lambda \to 0} \frac{y^\lambda - 1}{\lambda} = \log \lambda$$

Box and Cox consider the regression model

$$y_i(\lambda) = \beta x_i + u_i \tag{5.7}$$

where $u_i \sim \text{IN}(0, \sigma^2)$. For the sake of simplicity of exposition we are considering only one explanatory variable. Also, instead of considering x_i we can consider $x_i(\lambda)$. For $\lambda = 0$ this is a log-linear model, and for $\lambda = 1$ this is a linear model.

There are two main problems with the specification in equation (5.7):

1. The assumption that the errors u_i in (5.7) are $\text{IN}(0, \sigma^2)$ for *all* values of λ is not a reasonable assumption.
2. Since $y > 0$, unless $\lambda = 0$ the definition of $y(\lambda)$ in (5.6) imposes some constraints on $y(\lambda)$ that depend on the unknown λ. Since $y > 0$, we have, from equation (5.6),

$$y(\lambda) > -\frac{1}{\lambda} \text{ if } \lambda > 0 \quad \text{and} \quad y(\lambda) < -\frac{1}{\lambda} \text{ if } \lambda < 0$$

However, we will ignore these problems and describe the Box–Cox method.

Based on the specification given by equation (5.7) Box and Cox suggest estimating λ by the ML method. We can then test the hypotheses: $\lambda = 0$ and $\lambda = 1$. If the hypothesis $\lambda = 0$ is accepted, we use $\log y$ as the explained variable. If the hypothesis $\lambda = 1$ is accepted, we use y as the explained variable. A problem arises only if both hypotheses are rejected or both accepted. In this case we have to use the estimated λ, and work with $y(\lambda)$.

The ML method suggested by Box and Cox amounts to the following procedure:[14]

1. Divide each y by the geometric mean of the y's.
2. Now compute $y(\lambda)$ for different values of λ and regress it on x. Compute the residual sum of squares and denote it by $\hat{\sigma}^2(\lambda)$.
3. Choose the value of λ for which $\hat{\sigma}^2(\lambda)$ is minimum. This value of λ is the ML estimator of λ.

As a special case, consider the problem of choosing between the linear and log-linear models:

$$y = \alpha + \beta x + u$$

and

$$\log y = \alpha' + \beta' x + u$$

What we do is first divide each y_i by the geometric mean of the y's. Then we estimate the two regressions and choose the one with the smaller residual sum of squares. This is the Box–Cox procedure.

---

[14]G. S. Maddala, *Econometrics* (New York: McGraw-Hill, 1977), pp. 316–317.

We will now describe the two other tests that are based on *artificial regressions*.

The BM Test

This is the test suggested by Bera and McAleer.[15] Suppose the log-linear and linear models to be tested are given by

$$H_0: \quad \log y_t = \beta_0 + \beta_1 x_t + u_{0t} \quad u_{0t} \sim \text{IN}(\sigma_0^2)$$

and

$$H_1: \quad y_t = \beta_0 + \beta_1 x_t + u_{1t} \quad u_{1t} \sim \text{IN}(\sigma_1^2)$$

The BM test involves three steps.

Step 1. Obtain the predicted values $\log \hat{y}_t$ and $\tilde{y}_t$ from the two equations, respectively. The predicted value of y_t from the log-linear equation is $\exp(\log \hat{y}_t)$. The predicted value of $\log y_t$ from the linear equation is $\log \tilde{y}_t$.

Step 2. Compute the artificial regressions

$$\exp(\log \hat{y}_t) = \beta_0 + \beta_1 x_t + v_{1t}$$

and

$$\log \tilde{y}_t = \beta_0 + \beta_1 x_t + v_{0t}$$

Let the estimated residuals from these two regression equations be $\hat{v}_{1t}$ and $\hat{v}_{0t}$, respectively.

Step 3. The tests for H_0 and H_1 are based on θ_0 and θ_1 in the artificial regressions

$$\log y_t = \beta_0 + \beta_1 x_t + \theta_0 \hat{v}_{1t} + \varepsilon_t$$

and

$$y_t = \beta_0 + \beta_1 x_t + \theta_1 \hat{v}_{0t} + u_t$$

We use the usual *t*-tests to test these hypotheses. If $\theta_0 = 0$ is accepted, we choose the log-linear model. If $\theta_1 = 0$ is accepted, we choose the linear model. A problem arises if both these hypotheses are rejected or both are accepted.

The PE Test

The PE test[16] also uses artificial regressions. It involves only two steps. Step 1 is the same as in the BM test.

---

[15] A. K. Bera and M. McAleer, "Further Results on Testing Linear and Log-Linear Regression Models," paper presented at the SSRC Econometric Group Conference on Model Specification and Testing, Warwick, U.K., 1982.

[16] J. G. MacKinnon, H. White, and R. Davidson, "Tests for Model Specification in the Presence of Alternative Hypotheses: Some Further Results," *Journal of Econometrics*, Vol. 21, 1983, pp. 53–70.

Step 2. Test $\theta_0 = 0$ and $\theta_1 = 0$ in the artificial regressions

$$\log y_t = \beta_0 + \beta_1 x_t + \theta_0[\tilde{y}_t - \exp(\log \hat{y}_t)] + \varepsilon_t$$

and

$$y_t = \beta_0 + \beta_1 x_t + \theta_1[\log \hat{y}_t - \log \tilde{y}_t] + u_t$$

There are many other tests for this problem of choosing linear versus log-linear forms.[17] The three tests mentioned here are the easiest to compute. We are not presenting an illustrative example here. The computation of the Box–Cox, BM, and PE tests for the data in Tables 4.7 and 5.5 is left as an exercise.

Summary

1. If the error variance is not constant for all the observations, this is known as the heteroskedasticity problem. The problem is informally illustrated with an example in Section 5.1.

2. First, we would like to know whether the problem exists. For this purpose some tests have been suggested. We have discussed the following tests:
   (a) Ramsey's test.
   (b) Glejser's tests.
   (c) Breusch and Pagan's test.
   (d) White's test.
   (e) Goldfeld and Quandt's test.
   (f) Likelihood ratio test.
Some of these tests have been illustrated with examples (see Section 5.2). Others have been left as exercises. There are two data sets (Tables 4.7 and 5.5) that have been provided for use by students who can experiment with these tests.

3. The consequences of the heteroskedasticity problem are:
   (a) The least squares estimators are unbiased but inefficient.
   (b) The estimated variances are themselves biased.
If the heteroskedasticity problem is detected, we can try to solve it by the use of weighted least squares. Otherwise, we can at least try to correct the error variances (since the estimators are unbiased). This correction (due to White) is illustrated at the end of Section 5.3.

4. There are three solutions commonly suggested for the heteroskedasticity problem:
   (a) Use of weighted least squares.
   (b) Deflating the data by some measure of "size."
   (c) Transforming the data to the logarithmic form.
In weighted least squares, the particular weighting scheme used will depend on the nature of heteroskedasticity. Weighted least squares methods are illustrated in Section 5.4.

---

[17]For instance, L. G. Godfrey and M. R. Wickens, "Testing Linear and Log-Linear Regressions for Functional Form," *Review of Economic Studies*, 1981, pp. 487–496, and R. Davidson and J. G. MacKinnon, "Testing Linear and Log-Linear Regressions Against Box–Cox Alternatives," *Canadian Journal of Economics*, 1985, pp. 499–517.

5. The use of deflators is similar to the weighted least squares method, although it is done in a more ad hoc fashion. Some problems with the use of deflators are discussed in Section 5.5.

6. The question of estimation in linear versus logarithmic form has received considerable attention during recent years. Several statistical tests have been suggested for testing the linear versus logarithmic form. In Section 5.6 we discuss three of these tests: the Box–Cox test, the BM test, and the PE test. All are easy to implement with standard regression packages. We have not illustrated the use of these tests. This is left as an exercise. It would be interesting to see which functional form is chosen and whether the heteroskedasticity problem exists for the functional form chosen.

7. Note that the tests discussed in Section 5.6 start by assuming homoskedastic errors for both functional forms.

Exercises

1. Define the terms "heteroskedasticity" and "homoskedasticity." Explain the effects of heteroskedasticity on the estimates of the parameters and their variances in a normal regression model.

2. Explain the following tests for homoskedasticity:
   (a) Ramsey's test.
   (b) Goldfeld and Quandt's test.
   (c) Glejser's test.
   (d) Breusch and Pagan's test.

   Illustrate each of these tests with the data in Tables 4.7 and 5.5.

3. Indicate whether each of the following statements is true (T), false (F), or uncertain (U), and give a brief explanation:
   (a) Heteroskedasticity in the errors leads to biased estimates of the regression coefficients and their standard errors.
   (b) Deflating income and consumption by the same price results in a higher estimate for the marginal propensity to consume.
   (c) The correlation between two ratios which have the same denominator is always biased upward.

4. Apply the following tests to choose between the linear and log-linear regression models with the data in Tables 4.7 and 5.5:
   (a) Box–Cox test.
   (b) BM test.
   (c) PE test.

5. In the model

$$y_{1t} = a_{11}x_{1t} + a_{12}x_{2t} + u_{1t}$$

$$y_{2t} = a_{21}x_{1t} + a_{22}x_{2t} + u_{2t}$$

you are told that

$$a_{11} + a_{12} = a_{21}$$

$$a_{11} - a_{12} = a_{22}$$

$u_{1t} \sim IN(0, \sigma^2)$, $u_{2t} \sim IN(0, 4\sigma^2)$, and u_{1t} and u_{2t} are independent. Explain how you will estimate the parameters $a_{11}, a_{12}, a_{21}, a_{22}$, and σ^2.

6. Explain how you will choose among the following four regression models:

$$y = \alpha_1 + \beta_1 x + u_1$$

$$y = \alpha_2 + \beta_2 \log x + u_2$$

$$\log y = \alpha_3 + \beta_3 x + u_3$$

$$\log y = \alpha_4 + \beta_4 \log x + u_4$$

7. In the linear regression model

$$y_i = \alpha + \beta x_i + u_i$$

the errors u_i are presumed to have a variance depending on a variable z_i. Explain how you will choose among the following four specifications:

$$\text{var}(u_i) = \sigma^2$$

$$\text{var}(u_i) = \sigma^2 z_i$$

$$\text{var}(u_i) = \sigma^2 z_i^2$$

$$\text{var}(u_i) = \sigma^2 z_i^3$$

8. In a study of 27 industrial establishments of varying size, y = the number of supervisors and x = the number of supervised workers. y varies from 30 to 210 and x from 247 to 1650. The results obtained were as follows:

Variable	Coefficient	SE	t
x	0.115	0.011	9.30
Constant	14.448	9.562	1.51
$n = 27$	$s = 21.73$	$R^2 = 0.776$	

After the estimation of the equation and plotting the residuals against x, it was found that the variance of the residuals increased with x. Plotting the residuals against $1/x$ showed that there was no such relationship. Hence the assumption made was

$$\text{var}(u_i) = \sigma^2 x_i^2$$

The estimated equation was

$$\frac{y}{x} = \underset{(0.009)}{0.121} + \underset{(4.570)}{3.803(1/x)} \quad R^2 = 0.03$$

In terms of the original variables, we have

$$y = 3.803 + 0.121x$$

The estimation gave the following results:

Variable	Coefficient	SE	t
x	0.121	0.009	13.44
Constant	3.803	4.570	0.832
$n = 27$	$s = 22.577$	$R^2 = 0.7587$	

(a) An investigator looks at the drop in R^2 and concludes that the first equation is better. Is this conclusion valid?

(b) What would the equation to be estimated be if $\text{var}(u_i) = \sigma^2 x_i$ instead of $\sigma^2 x_i^2$? How would you determine which of these alternative hypotheses is the better one?

(c) Comment on the computation of R^2 from the transformed equation and the R^2 from the equation in terms of the original variables.

9. In discussion of real estate assessment, it is often argued that the higher-priced houses get assessed at a lower proportion of value than the lower-priced houses. To determine whether such inequity exists, the following equations are estimated:

1. $A_i = \alpha + \beta S_i + u_i$
2. $A_i/S_i = \gamma + \delta S_i + u_i'$
3. $\log A_i = \theta + \lambda \log S_i + u_i''$

where A_i is the assessment for property i and S_i is the observed selling price. In a sample of 416 houses in King County, WA during the period 1977–1979, the following results were obtained:

1. $A_i = 7505.40 + 0.3382 S_i \quad R^2 = 0.597$
   $\quad\ \ (559.2) \qquad\ (0.0136) \qquad$ standard errors
   $\quad\ \ (13.42) \qquad\ (24.79) \qquad\ \ $ t-ratios

2. $A_i/S_i = 0.7374 - 4.5714 \times 10^{-6} S_i \quad R^2 = 0.2917$
   $\qquad\quad (0.0144) \qquad (3.5005 \times 10^{-7}) \qquad$ standard errors
   $\qquad\quad\ \ 51.38 \qquad\qquad -13.06 \qquad\qquad$ t-ratios

3. $\log A_i = 2.8312 + 0.6722 \log S_i \quad R^2 = 0.6547$
   $\qquad\quad (0.2513) \qquad\ \ (0.0240)$

It has been suggested that it is more appropriate to answer this question by estimating a reverse regression

4. $S_i = \gamma_0 + \gamma_1 A_i + \eta_i$
5. $A_i/S_i = \beta_0 + \beta_1 A_i + \eta_i'$

The estimation now gave the results

6. $S_i = 2050.07 + 0.7669 A_i \quad R^2 = 0.597$
   $\quad\ (1527.93) \qquad (0.0713) \qquad$ standard errors
   $\quad\ (1.3417) \qquad\ (24.79) \qquad\ \ $ t-ratios

7. $A_i/S_i = 0.5556 - 3.8288 \times 10^{-7} S_i \quad R^2 = 0.0004$
   $\qquad\quad (0.0203) \qquad (9.506 \times 10^{-7}) \qquad$ standard errors
   $\qquad\quad\ \ 27.26 \qquad\qquad 0.403 \qquad\qquad$ t-ratios

The average value of A/S was 5.6439.

(a) Interpret what the coefficients in each of these equations mean to answer the question of whether there is inequity in real estate assessment.

(b) Given some arguments as to why equations (4) and (5) may be more appropriate to look at than equations (1) to (3).

(c) Also, explain why equations (2) and (5) may be more appropriate than equations (1) and (4), respectively.

(The results are from L. A. Kochin and R. W. Parks, "Testing for Assessment Uniformity: A Reappraisal," *Property Tax Journal*, March 1984, pp. 27–54.)

Appendix to Chapter 5

Generalized Least Squares

In Chapter 4 we assumed that the errors were independent with a common variance σ^2 or $E(\mathbf{uu}') = \mathbf{I}\sigma^2$. This assumption is relaxed in Chapters 5 and 6. We start with the model

$$\mathbf{y} = \mathbf{X}\boldsymbol{\beta} + \mathbf{u} \quad E(\mathbf{uu}') = \boldsymbol{\Omega}$$

where $\boldsymbol{\Omega}$ is an arbitrary positive definite matrix. Premultiplying by $\boldsymbol{\Omega}^{-1/2}$, we get

$$\mathbf{y}^* = \mathbf{X}^*\boldsymbol{\beta} + \mathbf{u}^*$$

where

$$\mathbf{y}^* = \boldsymbol{\Omega}^{-1/2}\mathbf{y}$$

$$\mathbf{X}^* = \boldsymbol{\Omega}^{-1/2}\mathbf{X}$$

$$\mathbf{u}^* = \boldsymbol{\Omega}^{-1/2}\mathbf{u}$$

Then $E(\mathbf{u}^*\mathbf{u}^{*\prime}) = \boldsymbol{\Omega}^{-1/2}E(\mathbf{uu}')\boldsymbol{\Omega}^{-1/2} = \mathbf{I}$. Hence by the result in the appendix to Chapter 4, we get the BLUE of $\boldsymbol{\beta}$ as

$$\boldsymbol{\beta}_{\mathrm{GLS}} = (\mathbf{X}^{*\prime}\mathbf{X}^*)^{-1}(\mathbf{X}^{*\prime}\mathbf{y}^*) = (\mathbf{X}'\boldsymbol{\Omega}^{-1}\mathbf{X})^{-1}\mathbf{X}'\boldsymbol{\Omega}^{-1}\mathbf{y}$$

We use the subscript GLS to denote "generalized least squares." The variance of this estimator is given by

$$V(\hat{\boldsymbol{\beta}}_{\mathrm{GLS}}) = (\mathbf{X}^{*\prime}\mathbf{X}^*)^{-1} = (\mathbf{X}'\boldsymbol{\Omega}^{-1}\mathbf{X})^{-1}$$

By contrast, the ordinary least squares estimator is given by

$$\hat{\boldsymbol{\beta}}_{\mathrm{OLS}} = (\mathbf{X}'\mathbf{X})^{-1}\mathbf{X}'\mathbf{y} = \boldsymbol{\beta} + (\mathbf{X}'\mathbf{X})^{-1}\mathbf{X}'\mathbf{u}$$

Since $E(\mathbf{u}) = \mathbf{0}$ this estimator is still unbiased. But its variance now is given by

$$V(\hat{\boldsymbol{\beta}}_{\mathrm{OLS}}) = (\mathbf{X}'\mathbf{X})^{-1}\mathbf{X}'E(\mathbf{uu}')\mathbf{X}(\mathbf{X}'\mathbf{X})^{-1} = (\mathbf{X}'\mathbf{X})^{-1}\mathbf{X}'\boldsymbol{\Omega}\mathbf{X}(\mathbf{X}'\mathbf{X})^{-1}$$

This is the general expression corresponding to equation (5.2) in Section 5.3. In this chapter we considered the case where $\boldsymbol{\Omega}$ is a diagonal matrix with the ith diagonal element σ_i^2. It is important to note that $\hat{\boldsymbol{\beta}}_{\mathrm{OLS}}$ is not necessarily inefficient if $\boldsymbol{\Omega} \neq \mathbf{I}\sigma^2$. Rao[18] showed

---

[18]C. R. Rao, "Least Squares Theory Using an Estimated Dispersion Matrix," *Proceedings of the Fifth Berkeley Symposium* (Berkeley, CA: University of California Press, 1967), Vol. 1, pp. 355–372.

that a necessary and sufficient condition that the OLS and GLS methods are equivalent is that $\boldsymbol{\Omega}$ be of the form

$$\boldsymbol{\Omega} = \mathbf{XCX'} + \mathbf{ZDZ'} + \mathbf{I}\sigma^2$$

where $\mathbf{Z}$ is a matrix such that $\mathbf{X'Z} = \mathbf{0}$ and $\mathbf{C}$ and $\mathbf{D}$ are arbitrary nonnegative definite matrices. As an example consider the following model:

$$y_i = \alpha + \delta x_i + u_i \quad i = 1, 2, \ldots, n$$
$$\text{var}(u_i) = 1 \quad \text{cov}(u_i, u_j) = \rho \quad \text{for } i \neq j$$

Thus the errors u_i are not independent. They are *equicorrelated*. In matrix form we can write this model as

$$\mathbf{y} = \mathbf{X}\boldsymbol{\beta} + \mathbf{u}$$

where

$$\mathbf{X} = \begin{bmatrix} 1 & x_1 \\ 1 & x_2 \\ \cdot & \cdot \\ \cdot & \cdot \\ 1 & x_n \end{bmatrix} \quad \text{and} \quad \boldsymbol{\beta} = \begin{bmatrix} \alpha \\ \delta \end{bmatrix}$$

$$E(\mathbf{uu'}) = \boldsymbol{\Omega} = \begin{bmatrix} 1 & \rho & \rho & \cdots & \rho \\ \rho & 1 & \rho & \cdots & \rho \\ \cdot & \cdot & \cdot & \cdots & \cdot \\ \cdot & \rho & \rho & \cdots & 1 \end{bmatrix} = (1 - \rho)\mathbf{I} + \rho\mathbf{ee'}$$

where $\mathbf{e}$ is an $n \times 1$ vector with all 1's (first column of $\mathbf{X}$). Thus

$$\boldsymbol{\Omega} = \mathbf{XCX'} + \mathbf{I}\sigma^2$$

with $\sigma^2 = (1 - \rho)$ and $\mathbf{C} = \begin{bmatrix} \rho & 0 \\ 0 & 0 \end{bmatrix}$. Hence, in this model, even if the errors are correlated and $\boldsymbol{\Omega} \neq \mathbf{I}\sigma^2$, the OLS and GLS estimators are identical.

6 Autocorrelation

What is in this Chapter?

In this chapter we relax another assumption made in Chapters 3 and 4 regarding errors that are independent. Again we need to discuss:

(a) How do we detect this problem?
(b) What are the consequences?
(c) What are the solutions?

Things here are more complicated than in the previous chapter.

Regarding the problem of detection, we start with the Durbin–Watson (DW) statistic, and discuss its several limitations and extensions. We discuss Durbin's *h*-test for models with lagged dependent variables and tests for higher-order serial correlation. The final section of the paper reviews some recent work in this area (Sections 6.2, 6.6, 6.7, 6.8, 6.11, 6.12).

We discuss (in Section 6.5) the consequences of serially correlated errors and OLS estimators.

The solutions to the problem of serial correlation are discussed in Section 6.3 (estimation in levels versus first differences), Section 6.9 (strategies when the DW test statistic is significant), and Section 6.10 (trends and random walks). The ideas in this last section are pursued further in Chapters 13 and 14.

This chapter is very important and the several ideas have to be understood thoroughly.

6.1 Introduction

In Chapter 5 we considered the consequences of relaxing the assumption that the variance of the error term is constant. We now come to the next assumption that the error terms in the regression model are independent. In this chapter we study the consequences of relaxing this assumption.

There are two situations under which error terms in the regression model can be correlated. In cross-section data it can arise among contiguous units. For instance, if we are studying consumption patterns of households, the error terms for households in the same neighborhood can be correlated. This is because the error term picks up the effect of omitted variables and these variables tend to be correlated for households in the same neighborhood (because of the "keeping up with the Joneses" effect). Similarly, if our data are on states, the error terms for contiguous states tend to be correlated. All these examples fall in the category of *spatial correlation*. In this chapter we will not be concerned with this type of correlation. Some of the factors that produce this type of correlation among the error terms can be taken care of by the use of dummy variables discussed in Chapter 8.

What we will be discussing in this chapter is the correlation between the error terms arising in time-series data. This type of correlation is called *autocorrelation* or *serial correlation*. The error term u_t at time period t is correlated with error terms $u_{t+1}, u_{t+2}, \ldots$ and $u_{t-1}, u_{t-2}, \ldots$ and so on. Such correlation in the error terms often arises from the correlation of the omitted variables that the error term captures.

The correlation between u_t and u_{t-k} is called an autocorrelation of order k. The correlation between u_t and u_{t-1} is the first-order autocorrelation and is usually denoted by ρ_1. The correlation between u_t and u_{t-2} is called the second-order autocorrelation and is denoted by ρ_2, and so on. There are $(n-1)$ such autocorrelations if we have n observations. However, we cannot hope to estimate all of these from our data. Hence we often assume that these $(n-1)$ autocorrelations can be represented in terms of one or two parameters.

In the following sections we discuss how to:

1. Test for the presence of serial correlation.
2. Estimate the regression equation when the errors are serially correlated.

6.2   Durbin–Watson Test

The simplest and most commonly used model is one where the errors u_t and u_{t-1} have a correlation ρ. For this model one can think of testing hypotheses about ρ on the basis of $\hat{\rho}$, the correlation between the least squares residuals $\hat{u}_t$ and $\hat{u}_{t-1}$. A commonly used statistic for this purpose (which is related to $\hat{\rho}$) is the Durbin–Watson (DW) statistic, which we will denote by d. It is defined as

$$d = \frac{\sum_{2}^{n}(\hat{u}_t - \hat{u}_{t-1})^2}{\sum_{1}^{n}\hat{u}_t^2}$$

where $\hat{u}_t$ is the estimated residual for period t. We can write d as

$$d = \frac{\sum \hat{u}_t^2 + \sum \hat{u}_{t-1}^2 - 2\sum \hat{u}_t\hat{u}_{t-1}}{\sum \hat{u}_t^2}$$

Since $\sum \hat{u}_t^2$ and $\sum \hat{u}_{t-1}^2$ are approximately equal if the sample is large, we have $d \simeq 2(1 - \hat{\rho})$. If $\hat{\rho} = +1$, then $d = 0$, and if $\hat{\rho} = -1$, then $d = 4$. We have $d = 2$ if $\hat{\rho} = 0$. If d is close to 0 or 4, the residuals are highly correlated.

The sampling distribution of d depends on the values of the explanatory variables and hence Durbin and Watson[1] derived upper (d_U) limits and lower (d_L) limits for the significance levels for d. There are tables to test the hypothesis of zero autocorrelation against the hypothesis of first-order positive autocorrelation. (For negative autocorrelation we interchange d_L and d_U.)

If $d < d_L$, we reject the null hypothesis of no autocorrelation.
If $d > d_U$, we do not reject the null hypothesis.
If $d_L < d < d_U$, the test is inconclusive.

Hannan and Terrell[2] show that the upper bound of the DW statistic is a good approximation to its distribution when the regressors are slowly changing. They argue that economic time series are slowly changing and hence one can use d_U as the correct significance point.

The significance points in the DW tables at the end of the book are tabulated for testing $\rho = 0$ against $\rho > 0$. If $d > 2$ and we wish to test the hypothesis $\rho = 0$ against $\rho < 0$, we consider $4 - d$ and refer to the Durbin–Watson tables as if we are testing for positive autocorrelation.

Although we have said that $d \cong 2(1 - \hat{\rho})$ this approximation is valid only in large samples. The mean of d when $\rho = 0$ has been shown to be given approximately by (the proof is rather complicated for our purpose)

$$E(d) \simeq 2 + \frac{2(k - 1)}{n - k}$$

where k is the number of regression parameters estimated (including the constant term) and n is the sample size. Thus, even for zero serial correlation, the statistic is biased upward from 2. If $k = 5$ and $n = 15$, the bias is as large as 0.8. We illustrate the use of the DW test with an example.

Illustrative Example

Consider the data in Table 3.11. The estimated production function is

$$\log X = -3.938 + 1.451 \log L_1 + 0.384 \log K_1$$
$$\quad\quad\,\,(0.237)\quad (0.083)\quad\quad\quad (0.048)$$

$$R^2 = 0.9946 \quad DW = 0.88 \quad \hat{\rho} = 0.559$$

Referring to the DW tables with $k' = 2$ and $n = 39$ for the 5% significance level, we see that $d_L = 1.38$. Since the observed $d = 0.858 < d_L$, we reject the hypothesis $\rho = 0$ at the 5% level.

---

[1] J. Durbin and G. S. Watson, "Testing for Serial Correlation in Least Squares Regression," *Biometrika*, 1950, pp. 409–428; 1951, pp. 159–178.

[2] E. J. Hannan and R. D. Terrell, "Testing for Serial Correlation After Least Squares Regression," *Econometrica*, 1966, pp. 646–660.

Although the DW test is the most commonly used test for serial correlations, it has several limitations.

1. It tests for only first-order serial correlation.
2. The test is inconclusive if the computed value lies between d_L and d_U.
3. The test cannot be applied in models with lagged dependent variables.

At this point it would be distracting to answer all these criticisms. We will present answers to these points in later sections of this chapter. First we discuss some simple solutions to the serial correlation problem.

6.3   Estimation in Levels Versus First Differences

If the DW test rejects the hypothesis of zero serial correlation, what is the next step?

In such cases one estimates a regression by transforming all the variables by ρ-*differencing*, that is, regress $y_t - \hat{\rho} y_{t-1}$ on $x_t - \hat{\rho} x_{t-1}$ where $\hat{\rho}$ is the estimated ρ. However, since $\hat{\rho}$ is subject to sampling errors, one other alternative that is followed if the DW statistic d is small is to use a *first-difference equation*. In fact, a rough rule of thumb is: *Estimate an equation in first differences whenever the DW statistic is $< R^2$.* In first difference equations, we regress $(y_t - y_{t-1})$ on $(x_t - x_{t-1})$ (with all the explanatory variables differences similarly). The implicit assumption is that the first differences of the errors $(u_t - u_{t-1})$ are independent. For instance, if

$$y_t = \alpha + \beta x_t + u_t$$

is the regression equation, then

$$y_{t-1} = \alpha + \beta x_{t-1} + u_{t-1}$$

and we have by subtraction

$$(y_t - y_{t-1}) = \beta(x_t - x_{t-1}) + (u_t - u_{t-1})$$

If the errors in this equation are independent, we can estimate the equation by OLS. However, since the constant term α disappears under subtraction, we should be estimating the regression equation with no constant term. Often, we find a constant term also included in regression equations with first differences. This procedure is valid only if there is a linear trend term in the original equation. If the regression equation is

$$y_t = \alpha + \delta t + \beta x_t + u_t$$

then

$$y_{t-1} = \alpha + \delta(t - 1) + \beta x_{t-1} + u_{t-1}$$

and on subtraction we get

$$(y_t - y_{t-1}) = \delta + \beta(x_t - x_{t-1}) + (u_t - u_{t-1})$$

which is an equation with a constant term.

When comparing equations in levels and first differences, one cannot compare the R^2's because the explained variables are different. One can compare the residual sum of squares but *only after making a rough adjustment*. Note that if $\text{var}(u_t) = \sigma^2$, then the variance of the error term in the first difference equation is

$$\text{var}(u_t - u_{t-1}) = \text{var}(u_t) + \text{var}(u_{t-1}) - 2\,\text{cov}(u_t, u_{t-1})$$
$$\simeq \sigma^2 + \sigma^2 - 2\sigma^2 \rho$$
$$= 2\sigma^2(1 - \rho)$$

where ρ is the correlation coefficient between u_t and u_{t-1}. Since the residual sum of squares divided by the appropriate degrees of freedom gives a consistent estimator for the error variance, the two residual sums of squares can be made roughly comparable if we multiply the residual sum of squares from the levels equation by

$$\left(\frac{n - k - 1}{n - k} \right) 2(1 - \rho)$$

where k is the number of regressors. If $\hat{\rho}$ is an estimate of ρ from the levels equation, since $\hat{\rho} = (2 - d)/2$ where d is the DW test statistic, we get $2(1 - \hat{\rho}) = d$. Thus, we can multiply the residual sum of squares from the levels equation by

$$\left(\frac{n - k - 1}{n - k} \right) d$$

or if n is large, just by d. For instance, if the residual sum of squares is, say, 1.2 by the levels equation, and 0.8 by the first difference equation and $n = 11$, $k = 1$, DW $= 0.9$, then the adjusted residual sum of squares with the levels equation is $(9/10)(0.9)(1.2) = 0.97$ which is the number to be compared with 0.8.

All this discussion, however, assumes that there are no lagged dependent variables among the explanatory variables. If there are lagged dependent variables in the equation, then the estimators of the parameters are not consistent and the above arguments do not hold.

Since we have comparable residual sum of squares, we can get the comparable R^2's as well, using the relationship $\text{RSS} = S_{yy}(1 - R^2)$.

Let

$$R_1^2 = R^2 \text{ from the first difference equation}$$

$$\text{RSS}_0 = \text{residual sum of squares from the levels equation}$$

$$\text{RSS}_1 = \text{residual sum of squares from the first difference equation}$$

$$R_D^2 = \text{comparable } R^2 \text{ from the levels equation}$$

Then

$$\frac{1 - R_D^2}{1 - R_1^2} = \left(\text{RSS}_0 \cdot \frac{n - k - 1}{n - k} \cdot d \right) \Big/ \text{RSS}_1$$

$$= \frac{\text{RSS}_0}{\text{RSS}_1} \left(\frac{n - k - 1}{n - k} \cdot d \right)$$

An alternative formula by Harvey which does not contain the last term will be presented after some illustrative examples.

Some Illustrative Examples

Consider the simple Keynesian model discussed by Friedman and Meiselman.[3] The equation estimated in levels is

$$C_t = \alpha + \beta A_t + \varepsilon_t \quad t = 1, 2, \ldots, T$$

where C_t = personal consumption expenditure (current dollars)
A_t = autonomous expenditures (current dollars)

The model fitted for the 1929–1939 period gave[4] (figures in parentheses are standard errors)

1. $C_t = 58,335.9 + 2.498 A_t$
(0.312)
$\quad R^2 = 0.8771, \quad \text{DW} = 0.89, \quad \text{RSS} = 11,943 \times 10^4$

2. $\Delta C_t = 1.993 \Delta A_t$
(0.324)
$\quad R^2 = 0.8096, \quad \text{DW} = 1.51, \quad \text{RSS} = 8387 \times 10^4$

There is a reduction in the R^2 but the R^2 values are not comparable. The equation in first differences is better because of the larger DW statistic and lower residual sum of squares than for the equation in the levels (even after the adjustments described).

For the production function data in Table 3.11 the first difference equation is

$$\Delta \log X = 0.987 \Delta \log L_1 + 0.502 \Delta \log K_1$$
$$(0.158) (0.134)$$

$$R^2 = 0.8405 \quad \text{DW} = 1.177 \quad \text{RSS} = 0.0278$$

The comparable figures for the levels equation reported earlier in Chapter 4, equation (4.24) are

$$R^2 = 0.9946 \quad \text{DW} = 0.858 \quad \text{RSS} = 0.0434$$

Again, even though the R^2 is larger for the equation in levels, the equation in first differences is better than the equation in levels, because it gives a lower RSS (even after the adjustments described) and a higher DW statistic. The estimate of returns to scale is $0.987 + 0.502 = 1.489$ in the first difference equation compared to $1.451 + 0.384 = 1.835$ in the levels equation.

---

[3] M. Friedman and D. Meiselman, "The Relative Stability of Monetary Velocity and the Investment Multiplier in the U.S., 1897–1958," in *Stabilization Policies* (Commission on Money and Credit) (Englewood Cliffs, NJ: Prentice Hall, 1963).

[4] A. C. Harvey, "On Comparing Regression Models in Levels and First Differences," *International Economic Review*, Vol. 21, No. 3, October 1980, pp. 707–720.

We can also compute R_D^2, the comparable R^2 from the equation in levels and see how it compares with R_1^2, the R^2 from the equation in first differences. In the example with the Friedman–Meiselman data the value of R_D^2 is given by

$$R_D^2 = 1 - \frac{RSS_0}{RSS_1} \left(\frac{n-k-1}{n-k} \right) d(1 - R_1^2)$$

$$= 1 - \frac{11.943}{8.387} \left(\frac{9}{10} \right) (0.89)(1 - 0.8096)$$

$$= 1 - 0.2172 = 0.7828$$

This is to be compared with $R_1^2 = 0.8096$ from the equation in first differences. For the production function data we get

$$R_D^2 = 1 - \left(\frac{0.0434}{0.0278} \right) \left(\frac{36}{37} \right) (0.858)(1 - 0.8405)$$

$$= 1 - 0.2079 = 0.7921$$

This is to be compared with $R^2 = 0.8405$ from the equation in first differences.

Harvey[5] gives a different definition of R_D^2. He defines it as

$$R_D^2 = 1 - \frac{RSS_0}{RSS_1}(1 - R_1^2)$$

This does not adjust for the fact that the error variances in the levels equations and the first difference equation are not the same. The arguments for his suggestion are given in his paper. In the example with the Friedman–Meiselman data his measure of R_D^2 is given by

$$R_D^2 = 1 - \frac{119,430}{83,872}(1 - 0.8096) = 0.7289$$

Although R_D^2 cannot be greater than 1, it can be negative. This would be the case when $\sum(\Delta y_t - \overline{\Delta y})^2 < RSS_0$, that is, when the levels model is giving a poorer explanation than the naive model, which says that Δy_t is a constant.

Usually, with time-series data, one gets high R^2 values if the regressions are estimated with the levels y_t and x_t but one gets low R^2 values if the regressions are estimated in first differences $(y_t - y_{t-1})$ and $(x_t - x_{t-1})$. Since a high R^2 is usually considered as proof of a strong relationship between the variables under investigation, there is a strong tendency to estimate the equations in levels rather than in first differences. This is sometimes called the "R^2 syndrome." However, if the DW statistic is very low, it often implies a misspecified equation, no matter what the value of the R^2 is. In such cases one should estimate the regression equation in first differences and if the R^2 is low, this merely indicates that the variables y and x are not related to each other. Granger and Newbold[6]

---

[5] Harvey, "On Comparing Regression Models," p. 711.

[6] C. W. J. Granger and P. Newbold, "Spurious Regressions in Econometrics," *Journal of Econometrics*, Vol. 2, No. 2, July 1976, pp. 111–120.

present some examples with artificially generated data where y, x, and the error u are each generated independently so that there is no relationship between y and x, but the correlations between y_t and y_{t-1}, x_t and x_{t-1}, and u_t and u_{t-1} are very high. Although there is no relationship between y and x the regression of y on x gives a high R^2 but a low DW statistic. When the regression is run in first differences, the R^2 is close to zero and the DW statistic is close to 2, thus demonstrating that there is indeed no relationship between y and x and that the R^2 obtained earlier is spurious. Thus regressions in first differences might often reveal the true nature of the relationship between y and x. (Further discussion of this problem is in Sections 6.10 and 14.7.)

Finally, it should be emphasized that all this discussion of the Durbin–Watson statistic, first differences, and quasi-first differences is relevant only if we believe that the correlation structure between the errors can be entirely described in terms of ρ, the correlation coefficient between u_t and u_{t-1}. This may not always be the case. We will discuss some general formulations of the correlation structure of the errors in Section 6.9 after we analyze the simple case thoroughly. Also, even if the correlation structure can be described in terms of just one parameter, this need not be the correlation between u_t and u_{t-1}. For instance, suppose that we have quarterly data; then it is possible that the errors in any quarter this year are most highly correlated with the errors in the corresponding quarter last year rather than the errors in the preceding quarter; that is, u_t could be uncorrelated with u_{t-1} but it could be highly correlated with u_{t-4}. If this is the case, the DW statistic will fail to detect it. What we should be using is a modified statistic defined as

$$d_4 = \frac{\sum (\hat{u}_t - \hat{u}_{t-4})^2}{\sum \hat{u}_t^2}$$

Also, instead of using first differences or quasi-first differences in the regressions, we should be using fourth differences or quasi-fourth differences, that is, $y_t - y_{t-4}$ and $x_t - x_{t-4}$ or $y_t - \hat{\rho} y_{t-4}$ and $x_t - \hat{\rho} x_{t-4}$, where $\hat{\rho}$ is the correlation coefficient between the estimated residuals $\hat{u}_t$ and $\hat{u}_{t-4}$.

6.4 Estimation Procedures with Autocorrelated Errors

In Section 6.3 we considered estimation in first differences. We will now consider estimation with *quasi-first differences*, that is, regressing $y_t - \rho y_{t-1}$ on $x_t - \rho x_{t-1}$. As we said earlier, we will be discussing the simplest case where the entire correlation structure of the errors u_t can be summarized in a single parameter ρ. This would be the case if the errors u_t are *first-order autoregressive*, that is,

$$u_t = \rho u_{t-1} + e_t \qquad (6.1)$$

where e_t are serially uncorrelated, with mean zero and common variance σ_e^2. Equation (6.1) is called an autoregression because it is the usual regression model with u_t regressed on u_{t-1}. It is called first-order autoregression because u_t is regressed on its past with only one lag. If there are two lags, it is called second-order autoregression. If there are three lags, it is called third-order autoregression, and so on. If the errors u_t satisfy equation (6.1), we say u_t are AR(1) (i.e., autoregressive of first order). If the errors u_t satisfy the equation

$$u_t = \rho_1 u_{t-1} + \rho_2 u_{t-2} + e_t$$

then we say that u_t are AR(2), and so on.

Now we will derive var(u_t) and the correlations between u_t and lagged values of u_t. From equation (6.1) note that u_t depends on e_t and u_{t-1}, u_{t-1} depends on e_{t-1} and u_{t-2}, and so on. Thus u_t depends on $e_t, e_{t-1}, e_{t-2}, \ldots$. Since e_t are serially independent, and u_{t-1} depends on e_{t-1}, e_{t-2} and so on, but *not* e_t, we have

$$E(u_{t-1}e_t) = 0$$

Since $E(e_t) = 0$, we have $E(u_t) = 0$ for all t.

If we denote var(u_t) by σ^2, we have

$$\sigma^2 = \text{var}(u_t) = E(u_t^2)$$
$$= E(\rho u_{t-1} + e_t)^2$$
$$= \rho^2 \sigma^2 + \sigma_e^2 \quad \text{since cov}(u_{t-1}, e_t) = 0$$

Thus we have

$$\sigma^2 = \frac{\sigma_e^2}{1 - \rho^2}$$

This gives the variance of u_t in terms of the variance of e_t and the parameter ρ.

Let us now derive the correlations. Denoting the correlation between u_t and u_{t-s} (which is called the correlation of lag s) by ρ_s, we get

$$E(u_t u_{t-s}) = \sigma^2 \rho_s$$

But

$$E(u_t u_{t-s}) = \rho E(u_{t-1} u_{t-s}) + E(e_t u_{t-s})$$

Hence

$$\rho_s = \rho \cdot \rho_{s-1} + 0$$

or

$$\rho_s = \rho \cdot \rho_{s-1}$$

Since $\rho_0 = 1$ we get by successive substitution

$$\rho_1 = \rho, \quad \rho_2 = \rho^2, \quad \rho_3 = \rho^3, \ldots$$

Thus the lag correlations are all powers of ρ and decline geometrically.

These expressions can be used to derive the covariance matrix of the errors and using what is known as generalized least squares (GLS).[7] We will not derive the expression for GLS here but will outline the minor changes that it implies. Consider the model

$$y_t = \alpha + \beta x_t + u_t \qquad t = 1, 2, \ldots, T \tag{6.2}$$

$$u_t = \rho u_{t-1} + e_t \tag{6.3}$$

---

[7]The derivation involves the use of matrix algebra, which we have avoided.

Except for the treatment of the first observation in the case of AR(1) errors as in equation (6.3), and the treatment of the first two observations in the case of AR(2) errors, and so on, the GLS procedure amounts to the use of transformed data, which are obtained as follows.[8]

Lagging (6.2) by one period and multiplying it by ρ, we get

$$\rho y_{t-1} = \alpha\rho + \beta\rho x_{t-1} + \rho u_{t-1} \tag{6.4}$$

Subtracting equation (6.4) from (6.2) and using equation (6.3), we get

$$y_t - \rho y_{t-1} = \alpha(1 - \rho) + \beta(x_t - \rho x_{t-1}) + e_t \tag{6.5}$$

Since e_t are serially independent with a constant variance σ_e^2, we can estimate the parameters in this equation by an OLS procedure. Equation (6.5) is often called the *quasi-difference* transformation of (6.4). What we do is transform the variables y_t and x_t to

$$y_t^* = y_t - \rho y_{t-1} \qquad t = 2, 3, \ldots, T$$
$$x_t^* = x_t - \rho x_{t-1} \tag{6.6}$$

and run a regression of y^* on x^*, with or without a constant term depending on whether the original equation has a constant term or not. In this method we use only $(T - 1)$ observations because we lose one observation in the process of taking differences. This procedure is not exactly the GLS procedure. The GLS procedure amounts to using all the T observations with

$$y_1^* = \sqrt{1 - \rho^2}\, y_1$$
$$x_1^* = \sqrt{1 - \rho^2}\, x_1 \tag{6.6'}$$

and regressing y^* on x^* using the T observations.

In actual practice ρ is not known. There are two types of procedures for estimating ρ:

1. Iterative procedures.
2. Grid-search procedures.

Iterative Procedures

Among the iterative procedures, the earliest was the Cochrane–Orcutt procedure.[9] In the Cochrane–Orcutt procedure we estimate equation (6.2) by OLS, get the estimated residuals $\hat{u}_t$, and estimate ρ by $\hat{\rho} = \sum \hat{u}_t \hat{u}_{t-1} / \sum \hat{u}_t^2$.

Durbin[10] suggested an alternative method of estimating ρ. In this procedure, we write equation (6.5) as

$$y_t = \alpha(1 - \rho) + \rho y_{t-1} + \beta x_t - \beta\rho x_{t-1} + e_t \tag{6.7}$$

We regress y_t on y_{t-1}, x_t, and x_{t-1} and take the estimated coefficient of y_{t-1} as an estimate of ρ.

---

[8] If the number of observations is large, the omission of these initial observations does not matter much.

[9] D. Cochrane and G. H. Orcutt, "Application of Least Squares Regressions to Relationships Containing Autocorrelated Error Terms," *Journal of the American Statistical Association*, 1949, pp. 32–61.

[10] J. Durbin, "Estimation of Parameters in Time Series Regression Models," *Journal of the Royal Statistical Society, Series B*, 1960, pp. 139–153.

Once an estimate of ρ is obtained, we construct the transformed variables y^* and x^* as defined in equations (6.6) and (6.6′) and estimate a regression of y^* on x^*. The only thing to note is that the slope coefficient in this equation is β, but the intercept is $\alpha(1 - \rho)$. Thus after estimating the regression of y^* on x^*, we have to adjust the constant term appropriately to get estimates of the parameters of the original equation (6.2). Further, the standard errors we compute from the regression of y^* on x^* are now "asymptotic" standard errors because of the fact that ρ has been estimated. If there are lagged values of y as explanatory variables, these standard errors are not correct even asymptotically. The adjustment needed in this case is discussed in Section 6.7.

If there are many explanatory variables in the equation, Durbin's method involves a regression in too many variables (twice the number of explanatory variables plus y_{t-1}). Hence it is often customary to prefer the Cochrane–Orcutt procedure until it converges. However, there are examples[11] to show that the minimization of $\sum e_t^2$ in equation (6.5) can produce multiple solutions for ρ. In this case the Cochrane–Orcutt procedure, which relies on a single solution for ρ, might give a local minimum, and even when iterated might converge to a local minimum. Hence it is better to use a grid-search procedure, which we will now describe.

Grid-Search Procedures

One of the first grid-search procedures is the Hildreth and Lu procedure[12] suggested in 1960. The procedure is as follows. Calculate y_t^* and x_t^* in equation (6.6) for different values of ρ at intervals of 0.1 in the range $-1 \le \rho \le 1$. Estimate the regression of y_t^* on x_t^* and calculate the residual sum of squares RSS in each case. Choose the value of ρ for which the RSS is minimum. Again repeat this procedure for smaller intervals of ρ around this value. For instance, if the value of ρ for which RSS is minimum is -0.4, repeat this search procedure for values of ρ at intervals of 0.01 in the range $-0.5 < \rho < -0.3$.

This procedure is *not* the same as the ML procedure. If the errors e_t are normally distributed, we can write the log-likelihood function as (derivation is omitted)

$$\log L = \text{const.} - \frac{T}{2} \log \sigma_e^2 + \frac{1}{2} \log(1 - \rho^2) - \frac{Q}{2\sigma_e^2} \tag{6.8}$$

where

$$Q = \sum [y_t - \rho y_{t-1} - \alpha(1 - \rho) - \beta(x_t - \rho x_{t-1})]^2$$

Thus minimizing Q is not the same as maximizing $\log L$. We can use the grid-search procedure to get the ML estimates. The only difference is that after we compute the residual sum of squares RSS(ρ) for each ρ, we choose the value of ρ for which $(T/2) \log$ RSS$(\rho) - (1/2) \log(1 - \rho^2)$ is minimum. If the number of observations is large, the latter term will be small compared to the former, and the ML procedure and the Hildreth–Lu procedure will give almost the same results.

---

[11]J. M. Dufour, M. J. I. Gaudry, and T. C. Lieu, "The Cochrane–Orcutt Procedure: Numerical Examples of Multiple Admissible Minima," *Economics Letters*, 1980 (6), pp. 43–48.

[12]Clifford Hildreth and John Y. Lu, *Demand Relations with Autocorrelated Disturbances*, AES Technical Bulletin 276, Michigan State University, East Lansing, MI, November 1960.

Illustrative Example

Consider the data in Table 3.11 and the estimation of the production function

$$\log X = \alpha + \beta_1 \log L_1 + \beta_2 \log K_1 + u$$

The OLS estimation gave a DW statistic of 0.86, suggesting significant positive autocorrelation. Assuming that the errors were AR(1), two estimation procedures were used: the Hildreth–Lu grid search and the iterative Cochrane–Orcutt (C–O). The other procedures we have described can also be tried, but this is left as an exercise.

The Hildreth–Lu procedure gave $\hat{\rho} = 0.77$. The iterative C–O procedure gave $\hat{\rho} = 0.80$. The DW test statistic implies that $\hat{\rho} = (1/2)(2 - 0.86) = 0.57$.

The estimates of the parameters (with standard errors in parentheses) were as follows:

Estimate of:	OLS	Hildreth–Lu	Iterative C–O
α	-3.938 (0.237)	-2.909 (0.462)	-2.737 (0.461)
β_1	1.451 (0.083)	1.092 (0.151)	1.070 (0.153)
β_2	0.384 (0.048)	0.570 (0.104)	0.558 (0.097)
RSS	0.04338	0.02635	0.02644

In this example the parameter estimates given by Hildreth–Lu and the iterative C–O procedures are pretty close to each other. Correcting for the autocorrelation in the errors has resulted in a significant change in the estimates of β_1 and β_2.

6.5   Effect of AR(1) Errors on OLS Estimates

In Section 6.4 we described different procedures for the estimation of regression models with AR(1) errors. We will now answer two questions that might arise with the use of these procedures:

1. What do we gain from using these procedures?
2. When should we not use these procedures?

First, in the case we are considering (i.e., the case where the explanatory variable x_t is independent of the error u_t), the OLS estimates are unbiased. However, they will not be efficient. Further, the tests of significance we apply, which will be based on the wrong covariance matrix, will be wrong. In the case where the explanatory variables include lagged dependent variables, we will have some further problems, which we discuss in Section 6.7. For the present, let us consider the simple regression model

$$y_t = \beta x_t + u_t \tag{6.9}$$

Let $\text{var}(u_t) = \sigma^2$, $\text{cov}(u_t, u_{t-j}) = \rho_j \sigma^2$. If u_t are AR(1), we have $\rho_j = \rho^j$.

The OLS estimator of β is

$$\hat{\beta} = \frac{\sum x_t y_t}{\sum x_t^2}$$

Hence

$$\hat{\beta} - \beta = \frac{\sum x_t u_t}{\sum x_t^2} \quad \text{and} \quad E(\hat{\beta} - \beta) = 0$$

$$V(\hat{\beta}) = \frac{1}{\left(\sum x_t^2\right)^2} \, \text{var}\left(\sum x_t u_t\right)$$

$$= \frac{\sigma^2}{\left(\sum x_t^2\right)^2} \left(\sum x_t^2 + 2\rho \sum x_t x_{t-1} + 2\rho^2 \sum x_t x_{t-2} + \cdots\right)$$

since $\text{cov}(u_t, u_{t-j}) = \rho^j \sigma^2$. Thus we have

$$V(\hat{\beta}) = \frac{\sigma^2}{\sum x_t^2} \left(1 + 2\rho \frac{\sum x_t x_{t-1}}{\sum x_t^2} + 2\rho^2 \frac{\sum x_t x_{t-2}}{\sum x_t^2} + \cdots\right) \tag{6.10}$$

If we ignore the autocorrelation problem, we would be computing $V(\hat{\beta})$ as $\sigma^2/\sum x_t^2$. Thus we would be ignoring the expression in the parentheses of equation (6.10). To get an idea of the magnitude of this expression, let us assume that the x_t series also follow an AR(1) process with $\text{var}(x_t) = \sigma_x^2$ and $\text{cov}(x_1, x_{t-1}) = r$. Since we are now assuming x_1 to be stochastic, we will consider the asymptotic variance of β. The expression in parentheses in equation (6.10) is now

$$1 + 2\rho r + 2\rho^2 r^2 + \cdots = 1 + \frac{2\rho r}{1 - \rho r} = \frac{1 + \rho r}{1 - \rho r}$$

Thus

$$V(\hat{\beta}) = \frac{\sigma^2}{T\sigma_x^2} \frac{1 + r\rho}{1 - r\rho}$$

where T is the number of observations. If $r = \rho = 0.8$, then

$$\frac{1 + r\rho}{1 - r\rho} = \frac{1.64}{0.36}$$

Thus ignoring the expression in the parentheses of equation (6.10) results in an underestimation by close to 78% for the variance of $\hat{\beta}$.

One further error is also involved. This is that we use $\sum \hat{u}_t^2/(T-1)$ as an estimate of σ^2. If $\rho = 0$, this is an unbiased estimate of σ^2. If $\rho \neq 0$, then under the assumptions we are making, we have approximately[13]

$$E\left(\sum \hat{u}_t^2\right) = \sigma^2 \left(T - \frac{1+r\rho}{1-r\rho}\right)$$

Again if $\rho = r = 0.8$ and $T = 20$, we have

$$E\left(\frac{\sum \hat{u}_t^2}{T-1}\right) = \frac{15.45}{19}\sigma^2 \simeq 0.81\sigma^2$$

Thus there is a further underestimation of 19%. Both these effects result in an underestimation of the standard errors of more than 80%.

We can also derive the asymptotic variance of the ML estimator $\tilde{\beta}$ when both x and u are first-order autoregressive as follows: Note that the ML estimator of β is asymptotically equivalent to the estimator obtained from a regression of $(y_t - \rho y_{t-1})$ on $(x_t - \rho x_{t-1})$. Hence

$$V(\tilde{\beta}) = \text{var} \frac{\sum (x_t - \rho x_{t-1})(u_t - \rho u_{t-1})}{\sum (x_t - \rho x_{t-1})^2}$$

$$= \text{var} \frac{\sum (x_t - \rho x_{t-1})e_t}{\sum (x_t - \rho x_{t-1})^2}$$

$$= \frac{\sigma_e^2}{\sum (x_t - \rho x_{t-1})^2}$$

where $\sigma_e^2 = \text{var}(e_t)$. When x_t is autoregressive we have

$$\lim \frac{1}{T} \sum (x_t - \rho x_{t-1})^2 = \sigma_x^2(1 + \rho^2 - 2r\rho)$$

---

[13]Note that $\hat{u}_t = u_t - x_t(\hat{\beta} - \beta)$. Hence $E(\sum \hat{u}_t^2) = E(\sum u_t^2) + E[(\hat{\beta} - \beta)^2 \sum x_t^2] - 2E[(\hat{\beta} - \beta) \sum x_t u_t]$. The first term is $T\sigma^2$. The second term is

$$\sigma^2 \frac{1+r\rho}{1-r\rho}$$

The last term is

$$-2\sigma^2 \frac{1+r\rho}{1-r\rho}$$

In all this note that we take probability limits rather than expectations, since these results are all asymptotic.

Also,

$$\text{var}(u) = \sigma^2 = \frac{\sigma_e^2}{1 - \rho^2} \quad \text{or} \quad \sigma_e^2 = \sigma^2(1 - \rho^2)$$

Hence by substitution we get the asymptotic variance of $\tilde{\beta}$ as

$$V(\tilde{\beta}) = \frac{\sigma^2}{T\sigma_x^2} \frac{1 - \rho^2}{1 + \rho^2 - 2r\rho}$$

Thus the efficiency of the OLS estimator is

$$\frac{V(\tilde{\beta})}{V(\hat{\beta})} = \frac{1 - r\rho}{1 + r\rho} \frac{1 - \rho^2}{1 + \rho^2 - 2r\rho}$$

One can compute this for different values of r and ρ. For $r = \rho = 0.8$ this efficiency is 0.21.

Thus the consequences of autocorrelated errors are:

1. The least squares estimators are unbiased but are not efficient. Sometimes they are considerably less efficient than the procedures that take account of the autocorrelation.
2. The sampling variances are biased and sometimes likely to be seriously understated. Thus R^2 as well as t and F statistics tend to be exaggerated.

The solution to these problems is to use the maximum likelihood procedure or some other procedure mentioned earlier that takes account of the autocorrelation. However, there are four important points to note:

1. If ρ is known, it is true that one can get estimators better than OLS that take account of autocorrelation. However, in practice ρ is not known and has to be estimated. In small samples it is not necessarily true that one gains (in terms of mean-square error for $\hat{\beta}$) by estimating ρ. This problem has been investigated by Rao and Griliches,[14] who suggest the rule of thumb (for samples of size 20) that one can use the methods that take account of autocorrelation if $|\hat{\rho}| \geq 0.3$, where $\hat{\rho}$ is the estimated first-order serial correlation from an OLS regression.[15] In samples of larger sizes it would be worthwhile using these methods for $\hat{\rho}$ smaller than 0.3.
2. The discussion above assumes that the true errors are first-order autoregressive. If they have a more complicated structure (e.g., second-order autoregressive), it might be thought that it would still be better to proceed on the assumption that the errors are first-order autoregressive rather than ignore the problem completely and use the

---

[14]P. Rao and Z. Griliches, "Some Small Sample Properties of Several Two-Stage Regression Methods in the Context of Autocorrelated Errors," *Journal of the American Statistical Association*, March 1969.

[15]Of course, it is not sufficient to argue in favor of OLS on the basis of mean-square errors of the estimators alone. What is also relevant is how seriously the sampling variances are biased.

OLS method. Engle[16] shows that this is not necessarily true (i.e., sometimes one can be worse off making the assumption of first-order autocorrelation than ignoring the problem completely).

3. In regressions with quarterly (or monthly) data, one might find that the errors exhibit fourth (or twelfth)-order autocorrelation because of not making adequate allowance for seasonal effects. In such cases if one looks for only first-order autocorrelation, one might not find any. This does not mean that autocorrelation is not a problem. In this case the appropriate specification for the error term may be $u_t = \rho u_{t-4} + e_t$ for quarterly data and $u_t = \rho u_{t-12} + e_t$ for monthly data.

4. Finally, and most important, it is often possible to confuse misspecified dynamics with serial correlation in the errors. For instance, a static regression model with first-order autocorrelation in the errors, that is, $y_t = \beta x_t + u_t, u_t = \rho u_{t-1} + e_t$, can be written as

$$y_t = \rho y_{t-1} + \beta x_t - \beta \rho x_{t-1} + e_t \qquad (6.11)$$

This model is the same as

$$y_t = \alpha_1 y_{t-1} + \alpha_2 x_t + \alpha_3 x_{t-1} + e_t \qquad (6.11')$$

with the restriction $\alpha_1 \alpha_2 + \alpha_3 = 0$. We can estimate the model (6.11') and test this restriction. If it is rejected, clearly it is not valid to estimate (6.11). (The test procedure is described in Section 6.8.)

The errors would be serially correlated but not because the errors follow a first-order autoregressive process but because the terms x_{t-1} and y_{t-1} have been omitted. This is what is meant by "misspecified dynamics." Thus a significant serial correlation in the estimated residuals does not necessarily imply that we should estimate a serial correlation model. Some further tests are necessary (like the restriction $\alpha_1 \alpha_2 + \alpha_3 = 0$ in the above-mentioned case). In fact, it is always best to start with an equation like (6.11') and test this restriction before applying any tests for serial correlation.

6.6 Some Further Comments on the DW Test

In Section 6.2 we discussed the Durbin–Watson test for first-order autocorrelation which is based on least squares residuals. There are two other tests that are also commonly used to test first-order autocorrelation. These are:

1. The von Neumann ratio.
2. The Berenblut–Webb test.

We will briefly describe what they are.

---

[16]Robert F. Engle, "Specification of the Disturbance for Efficient Estimation," *Econometrica*, 1973.

The von Neumann Ratio

The von Neumann ratio[17] is defined as

$$\frac{\delta^2}{s^2} = \frac{\sum_{t=2}^{n}(e_t - e_{t-1})^2/(n-1)}{\sum_{t=1}^{n}(e_t - \bar{e})^2/n}$$

where e_t are the residuals. The von Neumann ratio can be used only when e_t are independent (under the null hypothesis) and have a common variance. The least squares residuals $\hat{u}_t$ do not satisfy these conditions and hence one cannot use the von Neumann ratio with least squares residuals.

During recent years there are a large number of alternative residuals that have been suggested for the linear regression model. Many of these residuals, particularly the "recursive residuals," satisfy the properties that they are independent and have a common variance. These different types of residuals are useful for diagnostic checking of the regression model and are discussed in Chapter 12. The recursive residuals, in particular, can easily be computed. Since they are independent and have a common variance, one can use them to compute the von Neumann ratio, as suggested by Phillips and Harvey.[18]

For large samples δ^2/s^2 can be taken as normally distributed with mean and variance given by

$$E\left(\frac{\delta^2}{s^2}\right) = \frac{2n}{n-1} \qquad V\left(\frac{\delta^2}{s^2}\right) = \frac{4n^2(n-2)}{(n+1)(n-1)^3}$$

For finite samples one can use the tables prepared by G. I. Hart, published in *Annals of Mathematical Statistics*, 1962, pp. 207–214.

There are many other residuals suggested in the literature for the purpose of testing serial correlation. These are the Durbin residuals, Sims' residuals, and so on. But all these are more complicated to compute. The recursive residuals, which are useful for analysis of stability of the regression relationships and are easy to compute, can be used for tests for serial correlation in case the Durbin–Watson test is inconclusive.

The Berenblut–Webb Test

The Berenblut–Webb test[19] is based on the statistic

$$g = \sum_{t=2}^{n}\hat{e}_t^2 \Big/ \sum_{t=1}^{n}\hat{u}_t^2$$

---

[17]J. von Neumann, "Distribution of the Ratio of the Mean Square Successive Difference to the Variance," *Annals of Mathematical Statistics*, 1941, pp. 367–395.

[18]G. D. A. Phillips and A. C. Harvey, "A Simple Test for Serial Correlation in Regression Analysis," *Journal of the American Statistical Association*, December 1974, pp. 935–939.

[19]I. I. Berenblut and G. I. Webb, "A New Test for Autocorrelated Errors in the Linear Regression Model," *Journal of the Royal Statistical Society, Series B*, Vol. 35, 1973, pp. 33–50.

where $\hat{e}_t$ are the estimated residuals from a regression of first difference of y on first differences of the explanatory variables (with no constant term). If the original equation contains a constant term, we can use the Durbin–Watson tables on bounds with the g-statistic. The g-statistic is useful when values of $|\rho| \geq 1$ are possible.

The literature on the DW test and the problem of testing for autocorrelation is enormous. We will summarize a few of the important conclusions.

(A) Since the DW statistic is usually printed out from almost all computer programs, and the tables for its use are readily available, one should use this test with least squares residuals. However, with most economic data it is better to use the upper bound as the true significance point (i.e., treat the inconclusive region as a rejection region). For instance, with $n = 25$ and the number of explanatory variables 4, we have $d_L = 1.04$ and $d_U = 1.77$ as the 5% level significance points. Thus if the computed DW statistic is $d = 1.5$, we would normally say that the test is inconclusive at the 5% level. Treating d_U as the 5% significance point, we would reject the null hypothesis $\rho = 0$ at the 5% level. If more accuracy is required when d is in the inconclusive region, there are a number of alternatives suggested but all are computationally burdensome. The whole idea of testing for serial correlation is that if we do not reject the hypothesis $\rho = 0$, we can stay with OLS and avoid excessive computational burden. Thus trying to use all these other tests is more burdensome than estimating the model assuming $\rho \neq 0$. If we generate the recursive residuals for some other purposes, we can apply the von Neumann ratio test using these residuals. Also, if we are estimating the first difference equation, we can use the Berenblut–Webb test as well, without any extra computational burden.

(B) There are many tables other than those reprinted at the end of this book for the DW test that have been prepared to take care of special situations. Some of these are:

1. R. W. Farebrother in *Econometrica*, Vol. 48, September 1980, pp. 1553–1563, gives tables for regression models with no intercept term.
2. N. E. Savin and K. J. White in *Econometrica*, Vol. 45, No. 8, November 1977, pp. 1989–1996, present tables for the DW test for samples with 6 to 200 observations and for as many as 20 regressors.
3. K. F. Wallis in *Econometrica*, Vol. 40, 1972, pp. 617–636, gives tables for regression models with quarterly data. Here one would like to test for fourth-order autocorrelation rather than first-order autocorrelation. In this case the DW statistic is

$$d_4 = \frac{\sum_{t=5}^{n} (\hat{u}_t - \hat{u}_{t-4})^2}{\sum_{t=1}^{n} \hat{u}_t^2}$$

Wallis provides 5% critical values d_L and d_U for two situations: where the k regressors include an intercept (but not a full set of seasonal dummy variables) and another where the regressors include four quarterly seasonal dummy variables. In each case the critical values are for testing $H_0: \rho = 0$ against $H_1: \rho > 0$. For the hypothesis $H_1: \rho < 0$ Wallis suggests that the appropriate critical values are $(4 - d_U)$ and $(4 - d_L)$. M. L.

King and D. E. A. Giles in *Journal of Econometrics*, Vol. 8, 1978, pp. 255–260, give further significance points for Wallis's test.

4. M. L. King in *Econometrica*, Vol. 49, November 1981, pp. 1571–1581, gives the 5% points for d_L and d_U for quarterly time-series data with trend and/or seasonal dummy variables. These tables are for testing first-order autocorrelation.

5. M. L. King in *Journal of Econometrics*, Vol. 21, 1983, pp. 357–366, gives tables for the DW test for monthly data. In the case of monthly data we would want to test for twelfth-order autocorrelation.

(C) All the elaborate tables mentioned in (B) have been prepared for 5% level of significance (and 1% level of significance) and a question arises as to what the appropriate level of significance is for the DW test. Given that the test for serial correlation is a prelude to further estimation and not an end in itself, the theory of pretest estimation suggests that a significance level of, say, 0.35 or 0.4 is more appropriate than the conventional 0.05 significance level.[20]

(D) A significant DW statistic can arise from a lot of different sources. The DW statistic can detect moving average errors, AR(2) errors, or just the effect of omitted variables that are themselves autocorrelated. This raises the question of what the appropriate strategy should be when the DW statistic is significant. It does not necessarily imply that the errors are AR(1). One can proceed in different directions. The different strategies are discussed in Section 6.9.

Finally, the DW test is not applicable if the explanatory variables contain lagged dependent variables. The appropriate tests are discussed in the next section.

6.7 Tests for Serial Correlation in Models with Lagged Dependent Variables

In previous sections we considered explanatory variables that were uncorrelated with the error term. This will not be the case if we have lagged dependent variables among the explanatory variables and we have serially correlated errors. There are several situations under which we would be considering lagged dependent variables as explanatory variables. These could arise through expectations, adjustment lags, and so on. The various situations and models are explained in Chapter 10. For the present we will not be concerned with how the models arise. We will merely study the problem of testing for autocorrelation in these models.

Let us consider a simple model

$$y_t = \alpha y_{t-1} + \beta x_t + u_t \tag{6.12}$$

$$u_t = \rho u_{t-1} + e_t \tag{6.13}$$

e_t are independent with mean 0 and variance σ^2 and $|\alpha| < 1$, $|\rho| < 1$. Because u_t depends on u_{t-1} and y_{t-1} depends on u_{t-1}, the two variables y_{t-1} and u_t will be correlated. The

---

[20] See, for instance, T. B. Fomby and D. K. Guilkey, "On Choosing the Optimal Level of Significance for the Durbin–Watson Test and a Bayesian Alternative," *Journal of Econometrics*, Vol. 8, 1978, pp. 203–214.

least squares estimator $\hat{\alpha}$ will be inconsistent. It can be shown that[21]

$$\text{plim } \hat{\alpha} = \alpha + A$$

and

$$\text{plim } \hat{\rho} = \rho - A$$

where

$$A = \frac{\rho \sigma_x^2 \sigma_u^2}{(1 - \alpha\rho)D}$$

$$D = \text{var}(y_{-1})\text{var}(x) - \text{cov}^2(y_{-1}, x) > 0$$

$$\sigma_x^2 = \text{var}(x) \quad \sigma_u^2 = \text{var}(u)$$

Thus if ρ is positive, the estimate of α is biased upward and the estimate of ρ is biased downward. Hence the DW statistic, which is $\simeq 2(1 - \hat{\rho})$ is biased toward 2 and we would not find any significant serial correlation even if the errors are serially correlated.

Durbin's h-Test

Since the DW test is not applicable in these models, Durbin suggests an alternative test, called the *h*-test.[22] This test uses

$$h = \hat{\rho}\sqrt{\frac{n}{1 - n\hat{V}(\hat{\alpha})}}$$

as a standard normal variable. Here $\hat{\rho}$ is the estimated first-order serial correlation from the OLS residuals, $\hat{V}(\hat{\alpha})$ is the estimated variance of the OLS estimate of α, and n is the sample size. If $n\hat{V}(\hat{\alpha}) > 1$, the test is not applicable. In this case Durbin suggests the following test.

Durbin's Alternative Test

From the OLS estimation of equation (6.12) compute the residuals $\hat{u}_t$. Then regress $\hat{u}_t$ on $\hat{u}_{t-1}$, y_{t-1}, and x_t. The test for $\rho = 0$ is carried out by testing the significance of the coefficient of $\hat{u}_{t-1}$ in the latter regression.

---

[21] The proofs are somewhat long and are omitted. For a first-order autoregressive x, they can be found in G. S. Maddala and A. S. Rao, "Tests for Serial Correlation in Regression Models with Lagged Dependent Variables and Serially Correlated Errors," *Econometrica*, Vol. 47, No. 4, July 1973, Appendix A, pp. 761–774.

[22] J. Durbin, "Testing for Serial Correlation in Least Squares Regression When Some of the Regressors Are Lagged Dependent Variables," *Econometrica*, 1970, pp. 410–421. Durbin's paper was prompted by a note by Nerlove and Wallis that argued that the DW statistic is not applicable when lagged dependent variables are present. See M. Nerlove and K. F. Wallis, "Use of DW Statistic in Inappropriate Situations," *Econometrica*, Vol. 34, 1966, pp. 235–238.

Illustrative Example

An equation of demand for food estimated from 50 observations gave the following results (figures in parentheses are standard errors):

$$\log q_t = \text{const.} - \underset{(0.05)}{0.31} \log P_t + \underset{(0.20)}{0.45} \log y_t + \underset{(0.14)}{0.65} \log q_{t-1}$$

$$R^2 = 0.90 \quad DW = 1.8$$

where q_t = food consumption per capita

p_t = food price (retail price deflated by the consumer price index)

y_t = per capita disposable income deflated by the consumer price index

We have

$$\hat{\alpha} = 0.65 \quad \hat{V}(\hat{\alpha}) = (0.14)^2 = 0.0196$$

$$\hat{\rho} = 0.1 \quad \text{since DW} \simeq 2(1 - \hat{\rho})$$

Hence Durbin's h-statistic is

$$h = 0.1 \sqrt{\frac{50}{1 - 50(0.0196)}} = 5.0$$

This is significant at the 1% level. Thus we reject the hypothesis $\rho = 0$, even though the DW statistic is close to 2 and the estimate $\hat{\rho}$ from the OLS residuals is only 0.1.

Let us keep all the numbers the same and just change the standard error of $\hat{\alpha}$. The following are the results:

SE($\hat{\alpha}$)	$\hat{V}(\hat{\alpha})$	$1 - n\hat{V}(\hat{\alpha})$	h	Conclusion
0.13	0.0169	0.155	1.80	Not significant at the 5% level
0.15	0.0225	−0.125		Test not defined

Thus, other things equal, the precision with which $\hat{\alpha}$ is estimated has significant effect on the outcome of the h-test.

In the case where the h-test cannot be used, we can use the alternative test suggested by Durbin. However, the Monte Carlo study by Maddala and Rao[23] suggests that this test does not have good power in those cases where the h-test cannot be used. On the other hand, in cases where the h-test can be used, Durbin's second test is almost as powerful. It is not often used because it involves more computations. However, we will show that Durbin's second test can be generalized to higher-order autoregressions, whereas the h-test cannot.

---

[23] Maddala and Rao, "Tests for Serial Correlation."

6.8 A General Test for Higher-Order Serial Correlation: The LM Test

The h-test we have discussed is, like the Durbin–Watson test, a test for first-order autoregression. Breusch[24] and Godfrey[25] discuss some general tests that are easy to apply and are valid for very general hypotheses about the serial correlation in the errors. These tests are derived from a general principle — called the Lagrange multiplier (LM) principle. A discussion of this principle is beyond the scope of this book. For the present we will explain what the test is. The test is similar to Durbin's second test that we have discussed.

Consider the regression model

$$y_t = \sum_{i=1}^{k} x_{it}\beta_i + u_t \quad t = 1, 2, \ldots, n \tag{6.14}$$

and

$$u_t = \rho_1 u_{t-1} + \rho_2 u_{t-2} + \cdots + \rho_p u_{t-p} + e_t \quad e_t \sim \text{IN}(0, \sigma^2) \tag{6.15}$$

We are interested in testing $H_0 : \rho_1 = \rho_2 = \cdots = \rho_p = 0$. The x's in equation (6.14) include lagged dependent variables as well. The LM test is as follows.

First, estimate (6.14) by OLS and obtain the least squares residuals $\hat{u}_t$. Next, estimate the regression equation

$$\hat{u}_t = \sum_{t=1}^{k} x_{it}\gamma_i + \sum_{i=1}^{p} \hat{u}_{t-i}\rho_i + \eta_t \tag{6.16}$$

and test whether the coefficients of $\hat{u}_{t-i}$ are all zero. We take the conventional F-statistic and use $p \cdot F$ as χ^2 with d.f. p. We use the χ^2-test rather than the F-test because the LM test is a large sample test.

The test can be used for different specifications of the error process. For instance, for the problem of testing for fourth-order autocorrelation

$$u_t = \rho_4 u_{t-4} + e_t \tag{6.17}$$

we just estimate

$$\hat{u}_t = \sum_{i=1}^{k} x_{it}\gamma_i + \rho_4 \hat{u}_{t-4} + \eta_t \tag{6.18}$$

instead of (6.16) and test $\rho_4 = 0$.

The test procedure is the same for autoregressive or moving average errors. For instance, if we have a moving average (MA) error

$$u_t = e_t + \rho_4 e_{t-4}$$

instead of (6.17), the test procedure is still to estimate (6.18) and test $\rho_4 = 0$.

---

[24]T. S. Breusch, "Testing for Autocorrelation in Dynamic Linear Models," *Australian Economic Papers*, Vol. 17, 1978, pp. 334–355.

[25]L. G. Godfrey, "Testing for Higher Order Serial Correlation in Regression Equations When the Regressors Include Lagged Dependent Variables," *Econometrica*, Vol. 46, 1978, pp. 1303–1310.

Consider the following types of errors:

$$AR(2): u_t = \rho_1 u_{t-1} + \rho_2 u_{t-2} + e_t$$

$$MA(2): u_t = e_t + \rho_1 e_{t-1} + \rho_2 e_{t-2}$$

$$AR(2) \text{ with interaction}: u_t = \rho_1 u_{t-1} + \rho_2 u_{t-2} - \rho_1 \rho_2 u_{t-3} + e_t$$

In all these cases, we just test H_0 by estimating equation (6.16) with $p = 2$ and test $\rho_1 = \rho_2 = 0$. What is of importance is the degree of autoregression, not its nature.

Finally, an alternative to the estimation of (6.16) is to estimate the equation

$$y_t = \sum_{i=1}^{k} x_{it} \beta_i + \sum_{i=1}^{p} \hat{u}_{t-i} \rho_i + \eta_t \tag{6.19}$$

Thus the LM test for serial correlation is:

1. Estimate equation (6.14) by OLS and get the residual $\hat{u}_t$.
2. Estimate equation (6.16) or (6.19) by OLS and compute the F-statistic for testing the hypothesis $H_0: \rho_1 = \rho_2 = \cdots = \rho_p = 0$.
3. Use $p \cdot F$ as χ^2 with p degrees of freedom.

6.9   Strategies When the DW Test Statistic is Significant

The DW test is designed as a test for the hypothesis $\rho = 0$ if the errors follow a first-order autoregressive process $u_t = \rho u_{t-1} + e_t$. However, the test has been found to be robust against other alternatives such as AR(2), MA(1), ARMA(1, 1), and so on. Further, and more disturbingly, it catches specification errors like omitted variables that are themselves autocorrelated, and misspecified dynamics (a term that we will explain). Thus the strategy to adopt, if the DW test statistic is significant, is not clear. We discuss three different strategies:

1. Assume that the significant DW statistic is an indication of serial correlation but may not be due to AR(1) errors.
2. Test whether serial correlation is due to omitted variables.
3. Test whether serial correlation is due to misspecified dynamics.

Errors Not AR(1)

In case 1, if the DW statistic is significant, since it does not necessarily mean that the errors are AR(1), we should check for higher-order autoregressions by estimating equations of the form

$$u_t = \rho_1 u_{t-1} + \rho_2 u_{t-2} + e_t$$

Once the order has been determined, we can estimate the model with the appropriate assumptions about the error structure by the methods described in Section 6.4. Actually, there are two ways of going about this problem of determining the appropriate order of the autoregression. The first is to progressively complicate the model by testing for higher-order autoregressions. The second is to start with an autoregression of sufficiently high order and progressively simplify it. Although the former approach is the one commonly used, the latter approach is better from the theoretical point of view.

One other question that remains is that of moving average errors and ARMA errors. Estimation with moving average errors and ARMA errors is more complicated than with AR errors. Moreover, Hendry[26] and Hendry and Trivedi[27] argue that it is the order of the error process that is more important than the particular form. Thus from the practical point of view, for most economic data, it is just sufficient to determine the order of the AR process. Thus if a significant DW statistic is observed, the appropriate strategy would be to try to see whether the errors are generated by a higher-order AR process than AR(1) and then undertake estimation.

Autocorrelation Caused by Omitted Variables

Case 2, serial correlation being caused by omitted variables, is rather difficult to tackle. It is often asserted that the source of serial correlation in the errors is that some variables that should have been included in the equation are omitted and that these omitted variables are themselves autocorrelated. However, if this is the argument for serial correlation, and it is an appealing one, one should be careful in suggesting the methods that we have discussed until now.

Suppose that the true regression equation is

$$y_t = \beta_0 + \beta_1 x_t + \beta_2 x_t^2 + u_t$$

and instead we estimate

$$y_t = \beta_0 + \beta_1 x_t + v_t \tag{6.20}$$

Then since $v_t = \beta_2 x_t^2 + u_t$, if x_t is autocorrelated, this will produce autocorrelation in v_t. However, v_t is no longer independent of x_t. Thus not only are the OLS estimators of β_0 and β_1 from (6.20) inefficient, they are inconsistent as well.

As yet another example, suppose that the true relation is

$$y_t = \beta_1 x_t + \beta_2 z_t + u_t \tag{6.21}$$

and we estimate

$$y_t = \beta_1 x_t + w_t \tag{6.22}$$

Again, if z_t are autocorrelated, w_t will also be. But if z_t and x_t are independent, the methods we have discussed earlier are applicable. Thus, to justify the methods of estimation we have discussed, we have to argue that the autocorrelated omitted variables that are

[26]D. F. Hendry, "Comments on the Papers by Granger–Newbold and Sargent–Sims," in *New Methods in Business Cycle Research* (Minneapolis: Federal Reserve Bank of Minneapolis, October 1977).

[27]D. F. Hendry and P. K. Trivedi, "Maximum Likelihood Estimation of Difference Equations with Moving Average Errors: A Simulation Study," *The Review of Economic Studies*, Vol. 39, April 1972, pp. 117–145.

producing the autocorrelation in the errors are uncorrelated with the included explanatory variables. Further, if there are any time trends in these omitted variables, they will produce not only autocorrelated errors but also heteroskedastic errors.

In equation (6.21) let us assume that the errors u_t are independent with a common variance σ^2. However, we estimate equation (6.22) and compute the DW statistic d. What can we say about it? Note that since the least squares residuals are always uncorrelated with the included variables (by virtue of the normal equations), the DW statistic d is determined not by the autocorrelation in z_t but the autocorrelation in z_t^*, which is that part of z left unexplained by x_t.

Consider a regression of z_t on x_t. Let the regression coefficient be denoted by b. Then $z_t = bx_t + z_t^*$, where z_t^* is the residual from a regression of z_t on x_t. Equation (6.21) can be written as

$$
\begin{aligned}
y_t &= \beta_1 x_t + \beta_2(bx_t + z_t^*) + u_t \\
&= (\beta_1 + \beta_2 b)x_t + w_t
\end{aligned}
\tag{6.23}
$$

where $w_t = \beta_2 z_t^* + u_t$.

If we estimate equation (6.22) by OLS and $\hat{\beta}_1$ is the OLS estimator of β_1, then $E(\hat{\beta}_1) = \beta_1 + \beta_2 b$ and the residual $\hat{w}_t$ would be estimating $\beta_2 z_t^* + u_t$. Let $\text{var}(z_t^*) = \sigma_*^2$ and $\text{cov}(z_t^*, z_{t-1}^*) = \rho^* \sigma_*^2$. Then since $\text{cov}(z_t^*, u_t) = 0$ we have

$$
\text{cov}(\beta_2 z_t^* + u_t, \beta_2 z_{t-1}^* + u_{t-1}) = \beta_2^2 \rho^* \sigma_*^2
$$

and

$$
\text{var}(\beta_2 z_t^* + u_t) = \beta_2^2 \sigma_*^2 + \sigma^2
$$

The first-order serial correlation in w_t would be[28]

$$
\rho_w = \frac{\rho^*}{1 + \sigma^2/\beta_2^2 \sigma_*^2}
$$

If d is the DW statistic from OLS estimation of equation (6.22), then

$$
\text{plim } d = 2(1 - \rho_w)
$$

Note that the observed serial correlation depends on the serial correlation in z_t^*, not z_t (the omitted variable), *and* the variance ratio $\sigma^2/\beta_2^2 \sigma_*^2$. If this variance ratio is large, then, even if ρ^* is high, ρ_w can be small.

One can test for omitted variables using the RESET test of Ramsey or White's test outlined in Section 5.2. If the DW test statistic is significant but these tests also show significance, the appropriate strategy would be to estimate the model by some general procedure like the procedure described in Section 5.4 rather than use a transformation based on the estimated first-order autocorrelation.

---

[28]This formula has been derived in a more general case in M. Chaudhuri, "Autocorrelated Disturbances in the Light of Specification Analysis," *Journal of Econometrics*, Vol. 5, 1977, pp. 301–313.

Serial Correlation Due to Misspecified Dynamics

In a seminal paper published in 1964, Sargan[29] pointed out that a significant DW statistic does not necessarily imply that we have a serial correlation problem. This point was also emphasized by Henry and Mizon.[30] The argument goes as follows. Consider

$$y_t = \beta x_t + u_t \quad \text{with} \quad u_t = \rho u_{t-1} + e_t \tag{6.24}$$

and e_t are independent with a common variance σ^2. We can write this model as

$$y_t = \rho y_{t-1} + \beta x_t - \beta \rho x_{t-1} + e_t \tag{6.25}$$

Consider an alternative stable dynamic model:

$$y_t = \beta_1 y_{t-1} + \beta_2 x_t + \beta_3 x_{t-1} + e_t \quad |\beta_1| < 1 \tag{6.26}$$

Equation (6.25) is the same as equation (6.26) with the restriction

$$\beta_1 \beta_2 + \beta_3 = 0 \tag{6.27}$$

A test for $\rho = 0$ is a test for $\beta_1 = 0$ (and $\beta_3 = 0$). But before we test this, what Sargan says is that we should first test the restriction (6.27) and test for $\rho = 0$ only if the hypothesis $H_0 : \beta_1 \beta_2 + \beta_3 = 0$ is not rejected. If this hypothesis is rejected, we do not have a serial correlation model and the serial correlation in the errors in (6.24) is due to "misspecified dynamics," that is, the omission of the variables y_{t-1} and x_{t-1} from the equation.

The restriction (6.27) is nonlinear in the β's and hence one has to use the Wald test or the LR or LM tests. If the DW test statistic is significant, a proper approach is to test the restriction (6.27) to make sure that what we have is a serial correlation model before we undertake any autoregressive transformation of the variables. In fact, Sargan suggests starting with the general model (6.26) and testing the restriction (6.27) first, before attempting any tests for serial correlation.[31]

In this case there is, in general, no exact t-test as in the case of linear restrictions. What we do is linearize the restriction by a Taylor series expansion and use what is known as a Wald test, which is an asymptotic test (or use the LR or LM tests).

---

[29] J. D. Sargan, "Wages and Prices in the United Kingdom: A Study in Econometric Methodology," in P. E. Hart, G. Mills, and J. K. Whitaker (eds.), *Econometric Analysis for National Economic Planning*, Colston Papers 16 (London: Butterworth, 1964), pp. 25–54.

[30] D. F. Hendry and G. E. Mizon, "Serial Correlation as a Convenient Simplification, Not a Nuisance: A Comment on a Study of the Demand for Money by the Bank of England," *The Economic Journal*, Vol. 88, September 1978, pp. 549–563.

[31] J. G. Thursby, "A Test Strategy for Discriminating Between Autocorrelation and Misspecification in Regression Analysis," *The Review of Economics and Statistics*, Vol. 63, 1981, pp. 117–123 considers the use of the DW, Ramsey's RESET, and Sargan's test together. This is useful for warning against autoregressive transformations based on the DW statistic but does not tell what the estimation strategy should be after the tests.

The Wald Test

Define

$$f(\beta) = \beta_1\beta_2 + \beta_3$$

Using a first-order Taylor series expansion, we get

$$f(\hat{\beta}) = f(\beta) + \sum_{i=1}^{3} g_i(\hat{\beta}_i - \beta_i)$$

where $g_i = \partial f/\partial\beta_i$. Under the null hypothesis $f(\beta) = 0$ and

$$\text{var}[f(\hat{\beta})] = \sigma^2 \left(\sum_i \sum_j g_i g_j C_{ij} \right) = \psi^2 \text{(say)}$$

since

$$\text{cov}(\hat{\beta}_i, \hat{\beta}_j) = \sigma^2 C_{ij}$$

The Wald test statistic is obtained by substituting $\hat{g}_i$ for g_i and $\hat{\sigma}^2$ for σ^2 in ψ^2. Denoting the resulting expression by $\hat{\psi}^2$, we get the statistic

$$W = \frac{[f(\hat{\beta})]^2}{\hat{\psi}^2}$$

which has (asymptotically) a χ^2-distribution with 1 degree of freedom.

In the particular case we are considering, note that $g_1 = \beta_2$, $g_2 = \beta_1$, and $g_3 = 1$.

However, there are some problems with the Wald test. The restriction (6.27) can as well be written as

$$f_1(\beta) = \beta_1 + \frac{\beta_3}{\beta_2} = 0 \qquad (6.28)$$

or

$$f_2(\beta) = \beta_2 + \frac{\beta_3}{\beta_1} = 0 \qquad (6.28')$$

If we write it as (6.28), we have

$$g_1 = 1 \quad g_2 = -\frac{\beta_3}{\beta_2^2} \quad g_3 = \frac{1}{\beta_2}$$

and if we write it as (6.28'), we have

$$g_1 = -\frac{\beta_3}{\beta_1^2} \quad g_2 = 1 \quad g_3 = \frac{1}{\beta_1}$$

Although, asymptotically, it should not matter how the Wald test is constructed, in practice it has been found that the results differ depending on how we formulate the restrictions.[32] However, formulations (6.28) and (6.28′) implicitly assume that $\beta_2 \neq 0$ or $\beta_1 \neq 0$, respectively, and thus in this case it is more meaningful to use the restriction in the form (6.27) rather than (6.28) or (6.28′).

Note that a hypothesis like $\beta_1/\beta_2 = C$ can be transformed into a linear hypothesis $\beta_1 - C\beta_2 = 0$. Similarly, $\beta_1/(1 - \beta_2) = C$ can be transformed to $\beta_1 + C\beta_2 - C = 0$. On the other hand, if, for some reason, an exact confidence interval was also needed for β_1/β_2, we can use Feiller's method described in Section 3.10. Noting the relationship between confidence intervals and tests of hypotheses, one can construct a test for the hypothesis $\beta_1/\beta_2 = C$.

Illustrative Example

Consider the data in Table 3.11 and the estimation of the production function (4.24). In Section 6.4 we presented estimates of the equation assuming that the errors are AR(1). This was based on a DW test statistic of 0.86. Suppose that we estimate an equation of the form (6.26). The results are as follows (all variables in logs; figures in parentheses are standard errors):

$$X_t = -2.254 + 0.884L_t + 0.710K_t + 0.489X_{t-1}$$
$$\underset{(0.530)}{} \quad \underset{(0.139)}{} \quad \underset{(0.152)}{} \quad \underset{(0.120)}{}$$

$$-0.073L_{t-1} - 0.541K_{t-1} \quad \text{RSS}_0 = 0.01718$$
$$\underset{(0.252)}{} \quad \underset{(0.150)}{}$$

Under the assumption that the errors are AR(1), the residual sum of squares, obtained from the Hildreth–Lu procedure we used in Section 6.4, is $\text{RSS}_1 = 0.02635$.

Since we have two slope coefficients, we have two restrictions of the form (6.27). Note that for the general dynamic model we are estimating six parameters (α and five β's). For the serial correlation model we are estimating four parameters (α, two β's, and ρ). We will use the likelihood ratio test (LR), which is based on (see the appendix to Chapter 3)

$$\lambda = \left(\frac{\text{RSS}_0}{\text{RSS}_1}\right)^{n/2}$$

and $-2\log_e \lambda$ has a χ^2-distribution with d.f. 2 (number of restrictions). In our example

$$-2\log_e \lambda = -39\log_e\left(\frac{0.01718}{0.02635}\right) = 16.7$$

which is significant at the 1% level. Thus the hypothesis of a first-order autocorrelation is rejected. Although the DW statistic is significant, this does not mean that the errors are AR(1).

---

[32] A. W. Gregory and M. R. Veall, "On Formulating Wald Tests of Non-linear Restrictions," *Econometrica*, November 1985. The authors confirm by Monte Carlo studies and an empirical example that these differences can be substantial. See also A. W. Gregory and M. R. Veall, "Wald Tests of Common Factor Restrictions," *Economics Letters*, Vol. 22, 1986, pp. 203–208.

*6.10   Trends and Random Walks

Throughout our discussion we have assumed that $E(u_t) = 0$ and $\text{var}(u_t) = \sigma^2$ for all t, and $\text{cov}(u_t, u_{t-k}) = \sigma^2 \rho_k$ for all t and k, where ρ_k is serial correlation of lag k (this is simply a function of the lag k and does not depend on t). If these assumptions are satisfied, the series u_t is called *covariance stationary* (covariances are constant over time) or just *stationary*. Many economic time series are clearly nonstationary in the sense that the mean and variance depend on time, and they tend to depart ever further from any given value as time goes on. If this movement is predominantly in one direction (up or down) we say that the series exhibits a *trend*. More detailed discussion of the topics covered briefly here can be found in Chapter 14.

Nonstationary time series are frequently de-trended before further analysis is done. There are two procedures used for de-trending:

1. Estimating regressions on time.
2. Successive differencing.

In the regression approach it is assumed that the series y_t is generated by the mechanism

$$y_t = f(t) + u_t$$

where $f(t)$ is the trend and u_t is a stationary series with mean zero and variance σ_u^2. Let us suppose that $f(t)$ is linear so that we have

$$y_t = \alpha + \beta t + u_t \tag{6.29}$$

Note that the trend-eliminated series is $\hat{u}_t$, the least squares residuals that satisfy the relationship $\sum \hat{u}_t = 0$ and $\sum t\hat{u}_t = 0$. If differencing is used to eliminate the trend we get $\Delta y_t = y_t - y_{t-1} = \beta + u_t - u_{t-1}$. We have to take a first difference again to eliminate β and we get $\Delta^2 y_t = \Delta^2 u_t = u_t - 2u_{t-1} + u_{t-2}$ as the de-trended series.

On the other hand, suppose we assume that y_t is generated by the model

$$y_t - y_{t-1} = \beta + \varepsilon_t \tag{6.30}$$

where ε_t is a stationary series with mean zero and variance σ^2. In this case the first difference of y_t is stationary with mean β. This model is also known as the *random-walk model*. Accumulating y_t starting with an initial value y_0 we get from equation (6.30)

$$y_t = y_0 + \beta t + \sum_{j=1}^{t} \varepsilon_j \tag{6.31}$$

which has the same form as (6.29) except for the fact that the disturbance is not stationary, it has variance $t\sigma^2$ that increases over time. Nelson and Plosser[33] call the model (6.29) *trend-stationary processes* (TSP) and model (6.30) *difference-stationary processes* (DSP).

---

[33]C. R. Nelson and C. I. Plosser, "Trends and Random Walks in Macroeconomic Time Series: Some Evidence and Implications," *Journal of Monetary Economics*, Vol. 10, 1982, pp. 139–162.

Both the models exhibit a linear trend. But the appropriate method of eliminating the trend differs. To test the hypothesis that a time series belongs to the TSP class against the alternative that it belongs to the DSP class, Nelson and Plosser use a test developed by Dickey and Fuller.[34] This consists of estimating the model

$$y_t = \alpha + \rho y_{t-1} + \beta t + \varepsilon_t \tag{6.32}$$

which belongs to the DSP class if $\rho = 1$, $\beta = 0$ and the TSP class if $|\rho| < 1$. Thus we have to test the hypothesis $\rho = 1$, $\beta = 0$ against $|\rho| < 1$. The problem here is that we cannot use the usual least squares distribution theory when $\rho = 1$. Dickey and Fuller show that the least squares estimate of ρ is not distributed around unity under the DSP hypothesis (that is, the true value $\rho = 1$) but rather around a value less than one. However, the negative bias diminishes as the number of observations increases. They tabulate the significance points for testing the hypothesis $\rho = 1$ against $|\rho| < 1$. Nelson and Plosser applied the Dickey–Fuller test to a wide range of historical time series for the U.S. economy and found that the DSP hypothesis was accepted in all cases, with the exception of the unemployment rate. They conclude that for most economic time series the DSP model is more appropriate, and that the TSP model would be the relevant one only if we assume that the errors u_t in equation (6.29) are highly autocorrelated.

The problem of testing the hypothesis $\rho = 1$ in the first-order autoregressive equation of the form

$$y_t = \alpha + \rho y_{t-1} + u_t$$

is called "testing for unit roots." There is an enormous literature on this problem but one of the most commonly used tests is the Dickey–Fuller test. The standard expression for the large sample variance of the least squares estimator $\hat{\rho}$ is $(1 - \rho^2)/T$ which would be zero under the null hypothesis. Hence, one needs to derive the limiting distribution of $\hat{\rho}$ under H_0, $\rho = 1$ to apply the test.

For testing the hypothesis $\rho = 1$, $\beta = 0$ in equation (6.32) Dickey and Fuller[35] suggest a LR test, derive the limiting distribution and present tables for the test. The F-values are much higher than those in the usual F-tables. For instance, the 5% significance values from the tables presented in Dickey and Fuller, and the corresponding F-values from the standard F-tables (when the numerator d.f. is 2 as in this test) are as follows:

Sample Size n	F-Ratio from Dickey–Fuller	F-Ratios from Standard F-tables[a]
25	7.24	3.42
50	6.73	3.20
100	6.49	3.10
∞	6.25	3.00

[a]d.f. for denominator $= n - 3$.

---

[34]D. A. Dickey and W. A. Fuller, "Distribution of the Estimators for Autoregressive Time-Series with a Unit Root," *Journal of the American Statistical Association*, Vol. 74, 1979, pp. 427–431.

[35]D. A. Dickey and W. A. Fuller, "Likelihood Ratio Statistics for Autoregressive Time Series with a Unit Root," *Econometrica*, Vol. 49, No. 4, 1981, pp. 1057–1072. See tables on p. 1063.

As an illustration consider the example given by Dickey and Fuller.[36] For the logarithm of the quarterly Federal Reserve Board Production Index 1950–1 through 1977–4 they assume that the time series is adequately represented by the model

$$y_t = \beta_0 + \beta_1 t + \alpha_1 y_{t-1} + \alpha_2 (y_{t-1} - y_{t-2}) + e_t \tag{6.33}$$

where e_t are $IN(0, \sigma^2)$ random variables. The ordinary least squares estimates are

$$y_t - y_{t-1} = \underset{(0.15)}{0.52} + \underset{(0.00034)}{0.00120t} - \underset{(0.033)}{0.119 y_{t-1}} + \underset{(0.081)}{0.498 (y_{t-1} - y_{t-2})}$$

$$RSS = 0.056448$$

$$y_t - y_{t-1} = \underset{(0.0025)}{0.0054} + \underset{(0.083)}{0.447 (y_{t-1} - y_{t-2})}$$

$$RSS = 0.063211$$

where RSS denotes the residual sum of squares and the numbers in parentheses are the "standard errors" as output from the usual regression program.

The F-test for the hypothesis $\beta_1 = 0, \alpha_1 = 1$ is

$$F = \frac{(0.063211 - 0.056448)/2}{0.056448/106} = 6.34$$

If we use the standard F-tables this F-ratio is significant at even the 1% significance level. But the F-ratio tabulated by Dickey and Fuller is 6.49 for the 5% significance level. Thus, the hypothesis that the second-order autoregressive process (6.33) has a unit root is accepted at the 5% significance level, though it is rejected at the 10% significance level.

Spurious Trends

If $\beta = 0$ in equation (6.30) the model is called a trendless random walk or a random walk with zero drift. However, from equation (6.31) note that even though there is no trend in the mean, there is a trend in the variance. Suppose that the true model is of the DSP type with $\beta = 0$. What happens if we estimated a TSP type model? That is, the true model is one with no trend in the mean but only a trend in the variance, and we estimate a model with a trend in the mean but no trend in the variance. It is intuitively clear that the trend in the variance will be transmitted to the mean and we will find a significant coefficient for t even though in reality there is no trend in the mean. How serious is this problem? Nelson and Kang[37] analyze this. They conclude that:

1. Regression of a random walk on time by least squares will produce R^2 values of around 0.44 regardless of sample size when, in fact, the mean of the variable has no relationship with time whatsoever.

---

[36] Dickey and Fuller, "Likelihood Ratio Statistics," pp. 1070–1071.

[37] C. R. Nelson and H. Kang, "Pitfalls in the Use of Time as an Explanatory Variable in Regression," *Journal of Business and Economic Statistics*, Vol. 2, January 1984, pp. 73–82.

2. In the case of random walks with drift, that is $\beta \neq 0$, the R^2 will be higher and will increase with the sample size, reaching one in the limit regardless of the value of β.

3. The residual from the regression on time which we take as the de-trended series, has on the average only about 14% of the true stochastic variance of the original series.

4. The residuals from the regression on time are also autocorrelated being roughly $(1 - 10/N)$ at lag one, where N is the sample size.

5. Conventional t-tests to test the significance of some of the regressors are not valid. They tend to reject the null hypothesis of no dependence on time, with very high frequency.

6. Regression of one random walk on another, with time included for trend, is strongly subject to the spurious regression phenomenon. That is, the conventional t-test will tend to indicate a relationship between the variables when none is present.

The main conclusion is that using a regression on time has serious consequences when, in fact, the time series is of the DSP type and, hence, differencing is the appropriate procedure for trend elimination. Plosser and Schwert[38] also argue that with most economic time series it is always best to work with differenced data rather than data in levels. The reason is that if indeed the data series are of the DSP type, the errors in the levels equation will have variances increasing over time. Under these circumstances many of the properties of least squares estimators as well as tests of significance are invalid. On the other hand, suppose that the levels equation is correctly specified. Then all differencing will do is produce a moving average error and at worst ignoring it will give inefficient estimates. For instance, suppose that we have the model

$$y_t = \alpha + \beta x_t + \gamma t + u_t$$

where u_t are independent with mean zero and common variance σ^2. If we difference this equation, we get

$$\Delta y_t = \beta \cdot \Delta x_t + \gamma + v_t$$

where the error $v_t = \Delta u_t = u_t - u_{t-1}$ is a moving average, and, hence, not serially independent. But estimating the first difference equation by least squares still gives us consistent estimates. Thus, the consequences of differencing when it is not needed are much less serious than those of failing to difference when it is appropriate (when the true model is of the DSP type).

In practice, it is best to use the Dickey–Fuller test to check whether the data are of DSP or TSP type. Otherwise, it is better to use differencing and regressions in first differences, rather than regressions in levels with time as an extra explanatory variable.

Differencing and Long-Run Effects: The Concept of Cointegration

One drawback of the procedure of differencing is that it results in a loss of valuable "long-run information" in the data. Recently, the concept of cointegrated series has

---

[38]C. I. Plosser and G. W. Schwert, "Money, Income and Sunspots: Measuring Economic Relationships and the Effects of Differencing," *Journal of Monetary Economics*, Vol. 4, 1978, pp. 637–660.

been suggested as one solution to this problem.[39] First, we need to define the term "cointegration." Although we do not need the assumption of normality and independence, we will define the terms under this assumption.

If ε_t are IN(0, σ^2) we say ε_t are I(0) that is, integrated of order zero. (More generally, ε_t is a stationary process. This is discussed in Chapter 14.)

If y_t follow a random walk model, that is,

$$y_t = y_{t-1} + \varepsilon_t$$

then we get by successive substitution,

$$y_t = \sum_{j=0}^{t-1} \varepsilon_{t-j} \quad \text{if } y_0 = 0$$

Thus, y_t is a summation of ε_j, and

$$\Delta y_t = \varepsilon_t$$

which is I(0). We say in this case that y_t is I(1) [integrated to order one]. If y_t is I(1) and we add to this z_t which is I(0), then $y_t + z_t$ will be I(1). When we specify regression models in time series, we have to make sure that the different variables are integrated to the same degree. Otherwise, the equation does not make sense. For instance, if we specify the regression model

$$y_t = \beta x_t + u_t \tag{6.34}$$

and we say that $u_t \sim$ IN(0, σ^2), that is u_t is I(0), we have to make sure that y_t and x_t are integrated to the same order. For instance, if y_t is I(1) and x_t is I(0) there will not be any β that will satisfy the relationship (6.34). Suppose y_t is I(1) and x_t is I(1); then if there is a nonzero β such that $y_t - \beta x_t$ is I(0), then y_t and x_t are said to be *cointegrated*.

Suppose that y_t and x_t are both random walks, so that they are both I(1). Then an equation in first differences of the form

$$\Delta y_t = \alpha \Delta x_t + \lambda(y_t - \beta x_t) + v_t \tag{6.35}$$

is a valid equation, since Δy_t, Δx_t, $(y_t - \beta x_t)$, and v_t are all I(0). Equation (6.34) is considered a long-run relationship between y_t and x_t and equation (6.35) describes short-run dynamics. Engle and Granger suggest estimating (6.34) by ordinary least squares, obtaining the estimator $\hat{\beta}$ of β and substituting it in equation (6.35) to estimate the parameters α and λ. This two-step estimation procedure, however, rests on the assumption that y_t and x_t are cointegrated. It is, therefore, important to test for cointegration. Engle and Granger suggest estimating (6.34) by ordinary least squares, getting the residual $\hat{u}_t$

---

[39] A reference which is, however, quite technical for our purpose, is R. F. Engle and C. W. J. Granger, "Co-Integration and Error Correction: Representation, Estimation and Testing," *Econometrica*, Vol. 55, March 1987, pp. 251–276.

and then applying the Dickey–Fuller test (or some other test[40]) based on $\hat{u}_t$. What this test amounts to is testing the hypothesis $\rho = 1$ in

$$u_t = \rho u_{t-1} + e_t$$

that is, testing the hypothesis

$$H_0 : u_t \text{ is I(1)}$$

In essence, we are testing the null hypothesis that y_t and x_t are *not* cointegrated. Note that y_t is I(1) and x_t is I(1), so we are trying to see that u_t is not I(1).

As shown by Bewley and also by Wickens and Breusch,[41] the two-step estimation procedure suggested by Engle and Granger of first estimating the long-run parameter β and then estimating the short-run parameters α and λ in equation (6.35) is unnecessary. They argue that one should estimate both the long-run and short-run parameters simultaneously and one would get more efficient estimates of the long-run parameter β by this procedure. Dividing equation (6.35) by λ and rearranging we get

$$y_t = \beta x_t + \frac{1}{\lambda}\Delta y_t - \frac{\alpha}{\lambda}\Delta x_t - \frac{v_t}{\lambda} \tag{6.36}$$

Since Δy_t will be correlated with the error v_t, equation (6.36) has to be estimated by the instrumental variable method. The coefficients of Δy_t and Δx_t describe the short-run dynamics. Note that if y_t and x_t are I(1), then Δy_t and Δx_t are like v_t, I(0), that is, they are of a lower order. Wickens and Breusch show that misspecification of the short-run dynamics does not have much of an effect on the estimation of the long-run parameters. For instance, in equation (6.36) even if Δx_t is omitted, the estimate of the parameter β will still be consistent. The intuitive reasoning behind this is that Δy_t and Δx_t are of a lower order than y_t and x_t.

*6.11 ARCH Models and Serial Correlation

We saw in Section 6.9 that a significant DW statistic can arise through a number of misspecifications. We will now discuss one other source. This is the ARCH model suggested by Engle[42] which has, in recent years, been found useful in the analysis of speculative prices. ARCH stands for "autoregressive conditional heteroskedasticity."

---

[40]Since $\hat{u}_t$ are estimated residuals, the Dickey–Fuller tables have to be adjusted. An alternative test that is also often suggested for testing unit roots is the Sargan–Bhargava test. See J. D. Sargan and A. Bhargava, "Testing Residuals from Least Squares Regression for Being Generated by the Gaussian Random Walk," *Econometrica*, Vol. 51, 1983, pp. 153–174. This is a Durbin–Watson type test with significance levels corrected.

[41]R. A. Bewley, "The Direct Estimation of the Equilibrium Response in a Linear Dynamic Model," *Economics Letters*, Vol. 3, 1979, pp. 357–361. M. R. Wickens and T. S. Breusch, "Dynamic Specification, the Long Run and the Estimation of Transformed Regression Models," *Economic Journal*, 1988 (supplement), pp. 189–205.

[42]R. F. Engle, "Autoregressive Conditional Heteroskedasticity with Estimates of the Variance of U.K. Inflation," *Econometrica*, Vol. 50, 1982, pp. 987–1007.

When we write the sample autoregressive model

$$y_t = \lambda y_{t-1} + \varepsilon_t \quad \varepsilon_t \sim \text{IN}(0, \sigma^2)$$

we are saying that the conditional mean $E(y_t|y_{t-1}) = \lambda y_{t-1}$ depends on t but the conditional variance $\text{var}(y_t|y_{t-1}) = \sigma^2$ is a constant. The unconditional mean of y_t is zero and the unconditional variance is $\sigma^2/(1 - \lambda^2)$.

The ARCH model is a generalization of this, in that the conditional variance is also made a function of the past. If the conditional density $f(y_t|z_{t-1})$ is normal, a general expression for the ARCH model is

$$y_t|z_{t-1} \sim N(g(z_{t-1}), h(z_{t-1}))$$

To make this operational, Engle specifies the conditional mean $g(z_{t-1})$ as a linear function of the variables z_{t-1} and h as

$$h_t = \alpha_0 + \alpha_1 \varepsilon_{t-1}^2 + \alpha_2 \varepsilon_{t-2}^2 + \cdots + \alpha_p \varepsilon_{t-p}^2$$

where $\varepsilon_t = y_t - g_t$. In the simplest case we can consider the model

$$y_t = \lambda y_{t-1} + \beta x_t + \varepsilon_t \quad \varepsilon_t \sim \text{IN}(0, h_t) \tag{6.37}$$

$$h_t = \text{var } \varepsilon_t = \alpha_0 + \alpha_1 \varepsilon_{t-1}^2 \tag{6.38}$$

Note that ε_t are not autocorrelated. But the fact that the variance of ε_t depends on ε_{t-1}^2 gives a misleading impression of there being a serial correlation. For instance, suppose that in equation (6.37) $\lambda = 0$, that is, we do not have y_{t-1} as an explanatory variable. If we estimate that equation by OLS we will find a significant DW statistic because of the ARCH effect given by equation (6.38). The situation is similar to the one we discussed in Section 6.10 where a trend in the variance was transmitted to a trend in the mean. In this case a simple test for the ARCH effect, that is, a test for the hypothesis $\alpha_1 = 0$ in equation (6.38) is to get the OLS residuals $\hat{\varepsilon}_t$ and regress $\hat{\varepsilon}_t^2$ on $\hat{\varepsilon}_{t-1}^2$ (with a constant term) and test whether the coefficient of $\hat{\varepsilon}_{t-1}^2$ is zero. An LM (Lagrangian multiplier test) is to use nR^2 as χ^2 with d.f. 1. This would enable us to see whether the significant DW test statistic is due to serial correlation in ε_t or due to the ARCH effect. Many empirical studies have found significant ARCH effects.

The estimation of the ARCH model can be carried out by an iterative procedure. First, we estimate (6.37). We then get estimates of α_0 and α_1 in (6.38) by regressing $\hat{\varepsilon}_t^2$ on $\hat{\varepsilon}_{t-1}^2$. Now we estimate (6.37) as a heteroskedastic regression model, since we have an estimate of h_t. This process can be repeated until convergence.

There are, however, problems with this simple procedure that we have ignored. We might get estimates of α_1 less than zero or greater than one. These problems as well as the computation of the asymptotic variances and covariances are discussed in Engle's paper. The purpose of our discussion is to point out one more source for a significant DW test statistic when, in fact, there is no serial correlation.

6.12 Some Comments on the DW Test and Durbin's *h*-Test and *t*-Test

In Sections 6.7 and 6.8 we discussed the problems with the DW test in models with lagged dependent variables and some alternatives that have been suggested: Durbin's *h*-test and *t*-test (Durbin's alternate test) and the LM test.

The study by Maddala and Rao quoted earlier showed that Durbin's *h*-statistic may not be defined when α and R^2 are small. This has been confirmed by Tse,[43] who suggests that some modifications of the *h*-statistic suggested by Sargan and Tse[44] might rectify this situation.

There have been other studies criticizing Durbin's *h*-test. Inder[45] argues that, even in models with lagged dependent variables, the use of the DW test is better than the use of Durbin's *h*-test, if one uses the exact DW critical values from a regression that excludes y_{t-1}. In another paper[46] Inder suggests an alternative test which is, however, not as easily computable as the DW test and *h*-test. Dezhbakhsh and Thursby[47] investigate Inder's tests and an alternative of their own by means of a Monte Carlo study, and find their performance similar.

In summary, there is not much evidence to recommend Durbin's tests in models with lagged dependent variables. It might be better to use the DW test with appropriately determined critical values as in Inder's 1986 paper.

Summary

1. Most economic data consist of time series and there is very often a correlation in the errors corresponding to successive time periods. This is the problem of autocorrelation.

2. The Durbin–Watson (DW) test is the most often used to test for the presence of autocorrelation. If this test detects the presence of autocorrelation, it is customary to transform the data on the basis of the estimated first-order autocorrelation and use least squares with the transformed data.

3. There are several limitations to this procedure. These limitations (discussed in Section 6.9) are:

(a) The serial correlation might be of a higher order.

(b) The serial correlation might be due to omitted variables.

[43]Y. K. Tse, "Some Modified Versions of Durbin's *h*-Statistic," *Review of Economics and Statistics*, Vol. 67, pp. 534–538.

[44]J. D. Sargan and Y. K. Tse, "Edgeworth Approximations to the Distribution of Various Test Statistics," in E. G. Charatsis (ed.), *Proceedings of the Econometric Society European Meeting 1979* (Amsterdam: North-Holland, 1981).

[45]B. A. Inder, "An Approximation to the Null Distribution of the DW Statistic in Models Containing Lagged Dependent Variables," *Econometric Theory*, Vol. 2, pp. 413–428.

[46]B. A. Inder, "A New Test for Autocorrelation in the Disturbances of the Dynamic Linear Regression Model," *International Economic Review*, Vol. 31, pp. 341–354.

[47]H. Dezhbakhsh and J. G. Thursby, "Testing for Autocorrelation in the Presence of Lagged Dependent Variables," *Journal of Econometrics*, Vol. 60, pp. 251–272.

(c) The serial correlation might be due to the noninclusion of lagged values of the explained and explanatory variable, that is, due to misspecification of the dynamic process.

4. Very often, simple solutions are suggested for handling the serial correlation problem, such as estimation in first differences. The issue of estimation of equations in levels versus first differences is discussed in Section 6.3 and also in Section 6.10. Other solutions are discussed in Section 6.4.

5. There have been some extensions and further tables prepared for the DW test. These extensions are outlined in Section 6.6.

6. The DW test is not applicable if there are lagged dependent variables in the model. Durbin suggested an alternative test, known as Durbin's *h*-test. This test is explained and illustrated in Section 6.7. Some problems with its use are also illustrated there. This test again, is for first-order autocorrelation only.

7. A general test which is, however, asymptotic, is the LM test. This test can be used for any specified order of the autocorrelation. It can be applied whether there are lagged dependent variables or not. It can be used with standard regression packages. It is based on omitted variables. This test is discussed in Section 6.8. It consists of two steps:

(a) First estimate the equation by ordinary least squares and get the residual $\hat{u}_t$.

(b) Now introduce appropriate lags of $\hat{u}_t$ in the original equation and reestimate it by least squares. Test that the coefficients of the lagged $\hat{u}_t$'s are zero using the standard tests.

The LM test has not been illustrated with an example. This is left as an exercise. Many of the data sets presented in the book are time-series data, and students can use these to apply the LM test.

8. The effects of autocorrelated errors on least squares estimators are:

(a) If there are no lagged dependent variables among the explanatory variables, the estimators are unbiased but inefficient. However, the estimated variances are biased, sometimes substantially. These problems are discussed in Section 6.5 and the biases are presented for some simple cases.

(b) If there are lagged dependent variables among the explanatory variables, the least squares estimators are not even consistent (see Section 6.7). In this case the DW test statistic is biased as well. This is the reason for the use of Durbin's *h*-test.

9. Obtaining a significant DW test statistic does not necessarily mean that we have a serial correlation problem. In fact, we may not have a serial correlation problem and we may be applying the wrong solution. For this purpose Sargan suggested that we first test for common factors and *then* apply tests for serial correlation if there is a common factor. This argument is explained at the end of Section 6.9 and illustrated with an example.

10. Economic time series can conveniently be classified as belonging to the DSP class or TSP class. The appropriate procedure for trend elimination (whether to use differences or regressions on time) will depend on this classification. One can apply the Dickey–Fuller test (or Sargan–Bhargava test) to test whether the time series is of the DSP type or TSP type. Most economic time series, however, are of the DSP type and, thus, estimation in first differences is appropriate. However, differencing eliminates all information on the long-run properties of the model. One suggestion that has been made is to see whether

the time series are cointegrated. If this is so, then both long-run and short-run parameters can be estimated (either separately or jointly).

11. Sometimes even though the errors in the equation are not autocorrelated, the variance of the error term can depend on the past history of errors. In such models, called ARCH models, one can find a significant DW test statistic even though there is no serial correlation in the errors. A test for the ARCH effect will enable us to judge whether the observed serial correlation is spurious.

Exercises

1. Explain the following:
   (a) The Durbin–Watson test.
   (b) Estimation with quasi-first differences.
   (c) The Cochrane–Orcutt procedure.
   (d) Durbin's h-test.
   (e) Serial correlation due to misspecified dynamics.
   (f) Estimation in levels versus first differences.

2. Use the Durbin–Watson test to test for serial correlation in the errors in Exercises 17 and 19 at the end of Chapter 4.

3. I am estimating an equation in which y_{t-1} is also an explanatory variable. I get the following results:

$$y_t = 2.7 + \underset{(0.4)}{0.4x_t} + \underset{(0.06)}{0.9y_{t-1}} \qquad \begin{array}{l} R^2 = 0.98 \\ \mathrm{DW} = 1.9 \end{array}$$

I find that the R^2 is very high and the Durbin–Watson statistic is close to 2, showing that there is no serial correlation in the errors. My friend tells me that even if the R^2 is high, this is a useless equation. Why is this a useless equation?

4. Examine whether the following statements are true or false. Give an explanation.
   (a) Serial correlation in the errors u leads to biased estimates and biased standard errors when the regression equation $y = \beta x + u$ is estimated by ordinary least squares.
   (b) The Durbin–Watson test for serial correlation is not applicable if the errors are heteroskedastic.
   (c) The Durbin–Watson test for serial correlation is not applicable if there are lagged dependent variables as explanatory variables.
   (d) An investigator estimating a demand function in levels and first differences obtained R^2's of 0.90 and 0.80, respectively. He chose the equation in levels because he got a higher R^2. This is a valid reason for choosing between the two models.
   (e) Least squares techniques when applied to economic time-series data usually yield biased estimates because many economic time series are autocorrelated.
   (f) The Durbin–Watson test can be used to describe whether the errors in a regression equation based on time-series data are serially independent.
   (g) The fact that the Durbin–Watson statistic is significant does not necessarily mean that there is serial correlation in the errors. One has to apply some other tests to come to this conclusion.

(h) Consider the model $y_t = \alpha y_{t-1} + \beta x_t + u_t$, where the errors are autoregressive. Even if the OLS method gives inconsistent estimates of the parameters, we can still use the equation for purposes of prediction if the evolution of x_t during the prediction period is the same as in the estimation period.

(i) Consider the model

$$y_t = \alpha + \beta x_t + u_t$$

$$u_t = \rho u_{t-1} + e_t \quad 0 \le \rho \le 1$$

e_t are IN$(0, \sigma^2)$. By regressing Δy_t on Δx_t, it is possible to get more efficient estimates of β than by regressing y_t on x_t.

(j) The Durbin–Watson test is a useless test because it is inapplicable in almost every situation that we encounter in practice.

5. The phrase "since the model contains a lagged dependent variable, the DW statistic is unreliable" is frequently seen in empirical work.

   (a) What does this phrase mean?

   (b) Is there some way to get around this problem?

6. Apply the LM test to test for first-order and second-order serial correlation in errors for the estimation of some multiple regression models with the data sets presented in Chapter 4. In each case compare the results with those obtained by using the DW test and Durbin's h-test if there are lagged dependent variables in the explanatory variables.

7. Apply Sargan's common factor test to check that the significant serial correlation is not due to misspecified dynamics.

8. In the case of data with housing starts in Table 4.10 illustrate the use of fourth-order autocorrelation using the DW test and the LM test.

7 Multicollinearity

What is in this Chapter?

In Chapter 4 we stated that one of the assumptions in the basic regression model is that the explanatory variables are not exactly linearly related. If they are, then not all parameters are estimable. For instance in the regression

$$y = \beta_1 x_1 + \beta_2 x_2 + \beta_3 x_3 + u$$

if $x_3 = 2x_1 + 3x_2$ then $(\beta_1 + 2\beta_3)$ and $(\beta_2 + 3\beta_3)$ are the linear functions estimable, but β_1, β_2, β_3 separately are not estimable. This is called perfect multicollinearity.

What we are concerned with in this chapter is the case where the individual parameters are not estimable with sufficient precision (because of high standard errors). This often occurs if the explanatory variables are highly intercorrelated (although this condition is not necessary).

This chapter is very important, because multicollinearity is one of the most misunderstood problems in multiple regression. A. S. Goldberger, *A Course in Econometrics* (Harvard University Press, 1991) discusses, in chapter 23 the misconceptions on multicollinearity in several texts in econometrics. There have been several measures for multicollinearity suggested in the literature (variance-inflation factors VIF, condition numbers CN, etc.). This chapter argues that all these are *useless* and *misleading*. They all depend on the correlation structure of the explanatory variables only. It is argued here that this is only one of several factors determining high standard errors. High intercorrelations among the explanatory variables are *neither necessary nor sufficient* to cause the multicollinearity problem. The best indicators of the problem are the *t*-ratios of the individual coefficients.

This chapter also discusses the solutions offered for the multicollinearity problem, such as ridge regression, principal component regression, dropping of variables, and so on, and shows that they are ad hoc and do not help. The only solutions are to get more data or to seek prior information.

7.1   Introduction

Very often the data we use in multiple regression analysis cannot give decisive answers to the questions we pose. This is because the standard errors are very high or the *t*-ratios are very low. The confidence intervals for the parameters of interest are thus very wide. This sort of situation occurs when the explanatory variables display little variation and/or high intercorrelations. The situation where the explanatory variables are highly intercorrelated is referred to as *multicollinearity*. When the explanatory variables are highly intercorrelated, it becomes difficult to disentangle the separate effects of each of the explanatory variables on the explained variable. The practical questions we need to ask are how high these intercorrelations have to be to cause problems in our inference about the individual parameters and what we can do about this problem. We argue in the subsequent sections that high intercorrelations among the explanatory variables need not necessarily create a problem and some solutions often suggested for the multicollinearity problem can actually lead us on a wrong track. The suggested cures are sometimes worse than the disease.

The term "multicollinearity" was first introduced in 1934 by Ragnar Frisch[1] in his book on confluence analysis and referred to a situation where the variables dealt with are subject to two or more relations. In his analysis there was no dichotomy of explained and explanatory variables. It was assumed that all variables were subject to error and given the sample variances and covariances, the problem was to estimate the different linear relationships among the true variables. The problem was thus one of errors in variables. We will, however, be discussing the multicollinearity problem as it is commonly discussed in multiple regression analysis, namely, the problem of high intercorrelations among the explanatory variables.

Multicollinearity or high intercorrelations among the explanatory variables need not necessarily be a problem. Whether or not it is a problem depends on other factors, as we will see presently. Thus the multicollinearity problem cannot be discussed entirely in terms of the intercorrelations among the variables. Further, different parametrizations of the variables will give different magnitudes of these intercorrelations. This point is explained in the next section with some examples. Most of the discussions of the multicollinearity problem and its solutions are based on criteria based on the intercorrelations between the explanatory variables. However, this is an incorrect approach, as will be clear from the examples given in the next section.

7.2   Some Illustrative Examples

We first discuss some examples where the intercorrelationships between the explanatory variables are high and study the consequences.

---

[1] Ragnar Frisch, *Statistical Confluence Analysis by Means of Complete Regression Systems*, Publication 5 (Oslo: University Institute of Economics, 1934).

Consider the model $y = \beta_1 x_1 + \beta_2 x_2 + u$. If $x_2 = 2x_1$, we have

$$y = \beta_1 x_1 + \beta_2 (2x_1) + u = (\beta_1 + 2\beta_2)x_1 + u$$

Thus only $(\beta_1 + 2\beta_2)$ would be estimable. We cannot get estimates of β_1 and β_2 separately. In this case we say that there is "perfect multicollinearity," because x_1 and x_2 are perfectly correlated (with $r_{12}^2 = 1$). In actual practice we encounter cases where r^2 is not exactly 1 but close to 1.

As an illustration, consider the case where

$$\begin{array}{ll} S_{11} = 200 & S_{1y} = 350 \\ S_{12} = 150 & S_{2y} = 263 \\ S_{22} = 113 & \end{array}$$

so that the normal equations are

$$200\hat{\beta}_1 + 150\hat{\beta}_2 = 350$$

$$150\hat{\beta}_1 + 113\hat{\beta}_2 = 263$$

The solution is $\hat{\beta}_1 = 1$ and $\hat{\beta}_2 = 1$. Suppose that we drop an observation and the new values are

$$\begin{array}{ll} S_{11} = 199 & S_{1y} = 347.5 \\ S_{12} = 149 & S_{2y} = 261.5 \\ S_{22} = 112 & \end{array}$$

Now when we solve the equations

$$199\hat{\beta}_1 + 149\hat{\beta}_2 = 347.5$$

$$149\hat{\beta}_1 + 112\hat{\beta}_2 = 261.5$$

we get $\hat{\beta}_1 = -\frac{1}{2}$, $\hat{\beta}_2 = 3$.

Thus very small changes in the variances and covariances produce drastic changes in the estimates of the regression parameters. It is easy to see that the correlation coefficient between the two explanatory variables is given by

$$r_{12}^2 = \frac{(150)^2}{200(113)} = 0.995$$

which is very high.

In practice, addition or deletion of observations would produce changes in the variances and covariances. Thus one of the consequences of high correlation between x_1 and x_2 is that the parameter estimates would be very sensitive to the addition or deletion of observations. This aspect of multicollinearity can be checked in practice by deleting or adding some observations and examining the sensitivity of the estimates to such perturbations.

One other symptom of the multicollinearity problem that is often mentioned is that the standard errors of the estimated regression coefficients will be very high. However, high values of r_{12}^2 need not necessarily imply high standard errors, and conversely, even low values of r_{12}^2 can produce high standard errors. In Section 4.3 we derived the standard errors for the case of two explanatory variables. There we derived the following formulas:

$$V(\hat{\beta}_1) = \frac{\sigma^2}{S_{11}(1 - r_{12}^2)} \tag{7.1}$$

$$V(\hat{\beta}_2) = \frac{\sigma^2}{S_{22}(1 - r_{12}^2)} \tag{7.2}$$

and

$$\text{cov}(\hat{\beta}_1, \hat{\beta}_2) = -\frac{\sigma^2 r_{12}^2}{S_{12}(1 - r_{12}^2)} \tag{7.3}$$

where σ^2 is the variance of the error term. Thus the variance of $\hat{\beta}_1$ will be high if:

1. σ^2 is high.
2. S_{11} is low.
3. r_{12}^2 is high.

Even if r_{12}^2 is high, if σ^2 is low and S_{11} high, we will not have the problem of high standard errors. On the other hand, even if r_{12}^2 is low, the standard errors can be high if σ^2 is high and S_{11} is low (i.e., there is not sufficient variation in x_1). What this suggests is that high values of r_{12}^2 do not tell us anything whether we have a multicollinearity problem or not.

When we have more than two explanatory variables, the simple correlations among them become all the more meaningless. As an illustration, consider the following example with 20 observations on x_1, x_2, and x_3:

$$x_1 = (1, 1, 1, 1, 1, 0, 0, 0, 0, 0, \text{ and } 10 \text{ zeros})$$

$$x_2 = (0, 0, 0, 0, 0, 1, 1, 1, 1, 1, \text{ and } 10 \text{ zeros})$$

$$x_3 = (1, 1, 1, 1, 1, 1, 1, 1, 1, 1, \text{ and } 10 \text{ zeros})$$

Obviously, $x_3 = x_1 + x_2$ and we have perfect multicollinearity. But we can easily see that $r_{12} = -\frac{1}{3}$ and $r_{13} = r_{23} = 1/\sqrt{3} \simeq 0.59$, and thus the simple correlations are not high. In the case of more than two explanatory variables, what we have to consider are multiple correlations of each of the explanatory variables with the other explanatory variables. Note that the standard error formulas corresponding to equations (7.1) and (7.2) are

$$V(\hat{\beta}_i) = \frac{\sigma^2}{S_{ii}(1 - R_i^2)} \tag{7.4}$$

where σ^2 and S_{ii} are defined as before in the case of two explanatory variables and R_i^2 represents the squared multiple correlation coefficient between x_i and the other explanatory variables. Again, it is easy to see that $V(\hat{\beta}_i)$ will be high if:

1. σ^2 is high.
2. S_{ii} is low.
3. R_i^2 is high.

Thus high R_i^2 is neither necessary nor sufficient to get high standard errors and thus multicollinearity by itself need not cause high standard errors.

There are several rules of thumb that have been suggested in the literature to detect when multicollinearity can be considered a serious problem. For instance, Klein says:[2] "Intercorrelation of variables is not necessarily a problem unless it is high relative to the overall degree of multiple correlation." By Klein's rule multicollinearity would be regarded as a problem only if $R_y^2 < R_i^2$ where R_y^2 is the squared multiple correlation coefficient between y and the explanatory variables, and R_i^2 is as defined earlier. However, note that even if $R_y^2 < R_i^2$ we can still have significant partial correlation coefficients (i.e., significant t-ratios for the regression coefficients). For example, suppose that the correlations between y, x_1, and x_2 are given by

	y	x_1	x_2
y	1.00	0.95	0.95
x_1	0.95	1.00	0.97
x_2	0.95	0.97	1.00

Then it can be verified that $R_{y\cdot 12}^2 = 0.916$ and $r_{12}^2 = 0.941$. Thus $R_y^2 < r_{12}^2$. But $r_{y1\cdot 2}^2 = r_{y2\cdot 1}^2 \simeq 0.14$. Since the relationship between the t-ratio and partial r^2 is given by (see Section 4.5)

$$r^2 = \frac{t^2}{t^2 + \text{degrees of freedom}}$$

we will get t-values greater than 3 if the number of observations is greater than 60.

We can summarize the previous discussion as follows:

1. If we have more than two explanatory variables, we should use R_i^2 values to measure the degree of intercorrelations among the explanatory variables, not the simple correlations among the variables.[3]
2. However, whether multicollinearity is a problem or not for making inferences on the parameters will depend on other factors besides R_i^2's, as is clear from equation (7.4). What is relevant is the standard errors and t-ratios. Of course, if R_i^2 is low, we would be better off. But this argument is only a poor consolation. It is not appropriate to make any conclusions about whether multicollinearity is a problem or not just on the basis of R_i^2's. The R_i^2's are useful only as a complaint. Moreover, the R_i^2's depend on the particular parametrization adopted, as we discuss in the next section.

---

[2]L. R. Klein, *An Introduction to Econometrics* (Englewood Cliffs, NJ: Prentice Hall, 1962), p. 101.

[3]Of course, some other measures based on the eigenvalues of the correlation matrix have been suggested in the literature, but a discussion of this is beyond our scope. Further, all these measures are only a "complaint" that the explanatory variables are highly intercorrelated; they do not tell whether the problem is serious.

7.3   Some Measures of Multicollinearity

It is important to be familiar with two measures that are often suggested in the discussion of multicollinearity: the *variance inflation factor* (VIF) and the *condition number* (CN).
   The VIF is defined as

$$\text{VIF}(\hat{\beta}_i) = \frac{1}{1 - R_i^2}$$

where R_i^2 is the squared multiple correlation coefficient between x_i and the other explanatory variables. Looking at the formula (7.4), we can interpret $\text{VIF}(\hat{\beta}_i)$ as the ratio of the actual variance of $\hat{\beta}_i$ to what the variance of $\hat{\beta}_i$ would have been if x_i were to be uncorrelated with the remaining x's. Implicitly, an ideal situation is considered to be one where the x's are all uncorrelated with each other and the VIF_i compares the actual situation with an ideal situation. This comparison is not very useful and does not provide us with guidance as to what to do with the problem. It is more a complaint that things are not ideal. Also, looking at formula (7.4), as we have discussed earlier, $1/(1 - R_i^2)$ is not the only factor determining whether multicollinearity presents a problem in making inferences.
   Whereas the VIF_i is something we compute for each explanatory variable separately, the *condition number* discussed by Raduchel[4] and Belsley, Kuh, and Welsch[5] is an overall measure. The condition number is supposed to measure the sensitivity of the regression estimates to small changes in the data. It is defined as the square root of the ratio of the largest to the smallest eigenvalue of the matrix $\mathbf{X'X}$ of the explanatory variables. Eigenvalues are explained in the appendix to this chapter. For the two-variable case in Section 7.2 it is easily computed. We solve the equation

$$(S_{11} - \lambda)(S_{22} - \lambda) - S_{12}^2 = 0$$
$$(200 - \lambda)(113 - \lambda) - (150)^2 = 0$$

or

$$\lambda^2 - 313\lambda + 100 = 0$$

which gives $\lambda_1 = 312.68$, $\lambda_2 = 0.32$ as the required eigenvalues. The condition number $= \sqrt{\lambda_1/\lambda_2} = 31.26$. The closer the condition number is to 1, the better the condition is.
   Again, there are three problems with this:

1. It looks at only the correlations among the explanatory variables and formula (7.4) shows that this is not the only relevant factor.
2. The condition number can change by a reparametrization of the variables. For instance, if we define $z_1 = x_1 + x_2$ and $z_2 = x_1 - x_2$, the condition number will change. In fact, it can be made equal to 1 with suitable transformations of the variables.

---

[4]W. J. Raduchel, "Multicollinearity Once Again," Paper 205, Harvard Institute of Economic Research, Cambridge, MA, 1971.

[5]D. Belsley, E. Kuh, and R. Welsch, *Regression Diagnostics* (New York: Wiley, 1980).

3. Even if such transformations of variables are not always meaningful (what does 2 apples + 3 oranges mean?), the condition number is merely a complaint that things are not ideal.[6]

In Section 7.4 we consider an example where transformations of variables are meaningful. However, even when they are not, the VIF and CN are only measures of how bad things are relative to some ideal situation, but the standard errors and *t*-ratios will tell a better story of how bad things are. The condition number is actually a "complaint number."

The VIF and CN will be useful for dropping some variables and imposing parameter constraints only in some very extreme cases where $R_i^2 \simeq 1.0$ or the smallest eigenvalue is very close to zero. In this case we estimate the model subject to some constraints on the parameters. This point is illustrated in Section 7.5 with an example.

The major aspect of the VIF and the CN is that they look at only the intercorrelations among the explanatory variables. A measure that considers the correlations of the explanatory variable with the explained variable is Theil's measure,[7] which is defined as

$$m = R^2 - \sum_{i=1}^{k}(R^2 - R_{-i}^2)$$

where R^2 = squared multiple correlation from a regression of y on $x_1, x_2, \ldots, x_k$
R_{-i}^2 = squared multiple correlation from a regression of y on $x_1, x_2, \ldots, x_k$ with x_i omitted

The quantity $(R^2 - R_{-i}^2)$ is termed the "incremental contribution" to the squared multiple correlation by Theil. If $x_1, x_2, \ldots, x_k$ are mutually uncorrelated, then m will be 0 because the incremental contributions all add up to R^2. In other cases m can be negative as well as highly positive. This makes it difficult to use it for any guidance.

To see what this measure means and how it is related to the *t*-ratios, let us consider the case of two explanatory variables. Following the notation in Section 4.6, we will write R^2 as $R_{y\cdot12}^2$. R_{-i}^2 are now just the squared simple correlations r_{y1}^2 and r_{y2}^2. Thus

$$m = R_{y\cdot12}^2 - (R_{y\cdot12}^2 - r_{y1}^2) - (R_{y\cdot12}^2 - r_{y2}^2)$$

The *t*-ratios are related to the partial r^2's, $r_{y1\cdot2}^2$ and $r_{y2\cdot1}^2$. We also derived in Section 4.6 the relation that

$$(1 - R_{y\cdot12}^2) = (1 - r_{y1}^2)(1 - r_{y2\cdot1}^2)$$
$$= 1 - r_{y1}^2 - (1 - r_{y1}^2)r_{y2\cdot1}^2$$

Hence

$$(R_{y\cdot12}^2 - r_{y1}^2) = (1 - r_{y1}^2)r_{y2\cdot1}^2$$

---

[6]E. E. Leamer, "Model Choice and Specification Analysis," in Z. Griliches and M. D. Intrilligator (eds.), *Handbook of Econometrics*, Vol. 1 (Amsterdam: North-Holland, 1983), pp. 286–330.

[7]H. Theil, *Principles of Econometrics* (New York: Wiley, 1971), p. 179.

Thus

$$m = \text{(squared multiple correlation coefficient)}$$
$$\quad - \text{(weighted sum of the partial } r^2\text{'s)}$$

This weighted sum is $w_1 \cdot r_{y2\cdot1}^2 + w_2 \cdot r_{y1\cdot2}^2$, where $w_1 = 1 - r_{y1}^2$ and $w_2 = 1 - r_{y2}^2$. If the partial r^2's are all very low, m will be very close to multiple R^2. In the earlier example that we gave to illustrate Klein's measure of multicollinearity, we had $R_{y\cdot12}^2 = 0.916$, $r_{y2}^2 = 0.9025$, and $r_{y1\cdot2}^2 = r_{y2\cdot1}^2 = 0.14$. Thus Theil's measure of multicollinearity is

$$m = 0.916 - 2(1 - 0.9025)(0.14)$$
$$\quad = 0.888$$

Of course, m is not zero. But is multicollinearity serious or not? One can never tell. If the number of observations is greater than 60, we will get significant t-ratios. Thus Theil's measure is even less useful than VIF and CN.

We have discussed several measures of multicollinearity and they are all of limited use from the practical point of view. As Leamer puts it, they are all merely complaints that things are not ideal. The standard errors and t-ratios give us more information about how serious things are. It is relevant to remember formula (7.4) while assessing any measures of multicollinearity.

Leamer suggests some measures of multicollinearity based on the sensitivity of inferences to different forms of prior information. Since a discussion of these measures involves a knowledge of Bayesian statistical inference and multivariate statistics, we have to omit these measures.

7.4   Problems with Measuring Multicollinearity

In Section 7.3 we talked of measuring multicollinearity in terms of the intercorrelations among the explanatory variables. However, there is one problem with this. The intercorrelations can change with a redefinition of the explanatory variables. Some examples will illustrate this point.

Let us define

$$C = \text{real consumption per capita}$$
$$Y = \text{real per capita current income}$$
$$Y_P = \text{real per capita permanent income}$$
$$Y_T = \text{real per capita transitory income}$$
$$Y = Y_T + Y_P \text{ and } Y_P \text{ and } Y_T \text{ are uncorrelated}$$

Suppose that we formulate the consumption function as

$$C = \alpha Y + \beta Y_P + u \tag{7.5}$$

This equation can alternatively be written as

$$C = \alpha Y_T + (\alpha + \beta)Y_P + u \qquad (7.6)$$

or

$$C = (\alpha + \beta)Y - \beta Y_T + u \qquad (7.7)$$

All these equations are equivalent. However, the correlations between the explanatory variables will be different depending on which of the three equations is considered. In equation (7.5), since Y and Y_P are often highly correlated, we would say that there is high multicollinearity. In equation (7.6), since Y_T and Y_P are uncorrelated, we would say that there is no multicollinearity. However, the two equations are essentially the same. What we should be talking about is the precision with which α and β or $(\alpha + \beta)$ are estimable.

Consider, for instance, the following data:[8]

$$\begin{array}{llll}
\text{var}(C) = 7.3 & \text{cov}(C, Y) = 8.3 & \text{cov}(Y, Y_P) = 9.0 & \\
\text{var}(Y) = 10.0 & \text{cov}(C, Y_P) = 8.0 & \text{cov}(Y, Y_T) = 1.0 & \\
\text{var}(Y_P) = 9.0 & \text{cov}(C, Y_T) = 0.3 & \text{cov}(Y_P, Y_T) = 0 & \text{by definition} \\
\text{var}(Y_T) = 1.0 & & &
\end{array}$$

For these data the estimation of equation (7.5) gives (all variables measured as deviations from their means) (figures in parentheses are standard errors)

$$C = \underset{(0.32)}{0.30}Y + \underset{(0.33)}{0.59}Y_P \qquad \hat{\sigma}_u^2 = 0.1$$

One reason for the imprecision in the estimates is that Y and Y_P are highly correlated (the correlation coefficient is 0.95).

For equation (7.6) the correlation between the explanatory variables is zero and for equation (7.7) it is 0.32. The least squares estimates of α and β are no more precise in equation (7.6) or (7.7).

Let us consider the estimation of equation (7.6). We get

$$C = \underset{(0.32)}{0.30}Y_T + \underset{(0.11)}{0.89}Y_P$$

The estimate at $(\alpha + \beta)$ is thus 0.89 and the standard error is 0.11. Thus $(\alpha + \beta)$ is indeed more precisely estimated than either α or β. As for α, it is not precisely estimated even though the explanatory variables in this equation are uncorrelated. The reason is that the variance of Y_T is very low [see formula (7.1)].

We can summarize the conclusions from this illustrative example as follows:

1. It is difficult to define multicollinearity in terms of the correlations between the explanatory variables because the explanatory variables can be redefined in a number of different ways and these can give drastically different measures of intercorrelations. In

---

[8] The data are those used in an illustrative example by Gary Smith, "An Example of Ridge Regression Difficulties," *Canadian Journal of Statistics*, Vol. 8, No. 2, 1980, pp. 217–225.

some cases, these redefinitions may not make sense, but in the example above involving measured income, permanent income, and transitory income, these redefinitions make sense.

2. Just because the explanatory variables are uncorrelated it does not mean that we have no problems with inference. Note that the estimate of α and its standard error are the same in equation (7.5) (with the correlation among the explanatory variables equal to 0.95) and in equation (7.6) (with the explanatory variables uncorrelated).

3. Often, though the individual parameters are not precisely estimable, some linear combinations of the parameters are. For instance, in our example, $(\alpha + \beta)$ is estimable with good precision. Sometimes, these linear combinations do not make economic sense. But at other times they do.

We will present yet another example to illustrate some problems in judging whether multicollinearity is serious or not and also to illustrate the fact that even if individual parameters are not estimable with precision, some linear functions of the parameters are.

In Table 7.1 we present data on C, Y, and L for the period from the first quarter of 1952 to the second quarter of 1961. C is consumption expenditures, Y is disposable income, and L is liquid assets at the end of the previous quarter. All figures are in billions of 1954 dollars.[9] Using the 38 observations we get the following regression equations (figures in

Table 7.1   Data on consumption, income, and liquid assets

Year, Quarter		C	Y	L	Year, Quarter		C	Y	L
1952	I	220.0	238.1	182.7	1957	I	268.9	291.1	218.2
	II	222.7	240.9	183.0		II	270.4	294.6	218.5
	III	223.8	245.8	184.4		III	273.4	296.1	219.8
	IV	230.2	248.8	187.0		IV	272.1	293.3	219.5
1953	I	234.0	253.3	189.4	1958	I	268.9	291.3	220.5
	II	236.2	256.1	192.2		II	270.9	292.6	222.7
	III	236.0	255.9	193.8		III	274.4	299.9	225.0
	IV	234.1	255.9	194.8		IV	278.7	302.1	229.4
1954	I	233.4	254.4	197.3	1959	I	283.8	305.9	232.2
	II	236.4	254.8	197.0		II	289.7	312.5	235.2
	III	239.0	257.0	200.3		III	290.8	311.3	237.2
	IV	243.2	260.9	204.2		IV	292.8	313.2	237.7
1955	I	248.7	263.0	207.6	1960	I	295.4	315.4	238.0
	II	253.7	271.5	209.4		II	299.5	320.3	238.4
	III	259.9	276.5	211.1		III	298.6	321.0	240.1
	IV	261.8	281.4	213.2		IV	299.6	320.1	243.3
1956	I	263.2	282.0	214.1	1961	I	297.0	318.4	246.1
	II	263.7	286.2	216.5		II	301.6	324.8	250.0
	III	263.4	287.7	217.3					
	IV	266.9	291.0	217.3					

[9]The data are from Z. Griliches et al., "Notes on Estimated Aggregate Quarterly Consumption Functions," *Econometrica*, July 1962.

parentheses are t-ratios, not standard errors):

$$C = -7.160 + 0.95213Y \qquad\qquad r^2 = 0.9933 \qquad\qquad (7.8)$$
$$\underset{(-1.93)}{} \underset{(73.25)}{}$$

$$C = -10.627 + 0.68166Y + 0.37252L \qquad R^2 = 0.9953 \qquad (7.9)$$
$$\underset{(-3.25)}{} \underset{(9.60)}{} \underset{(3.96)}{}$$

$$L = 9.307 + 0.76207Y \qquad\qquad r^2_{LY} = 0.9758 \qquad\qquad (7.10)$$
$$\underset{(1.80)}{} \underset{(37.20)}{}$$

Equation (7.10) shows that L and Y are very highly correlated. In fact, substituting the value of L in terms of Y from (7.10) into equation (7.9) and simplifying, we get equation (7.8) correct to four decimal places! However, looking at the t-ratios in equation (7.9) we might conclude that multicollinearity is not a problem.

Are we justified in this conclusion? Let us consider the stability of the coefficients with deletion of some observations. Using only the first 36 observations we get the following results:

$$C = -6.980 + 0.95145Y \qquad\qquad r^2 = 0.9925 \qquad\qquad (7.11)$$
$$\underset{(-1.74)}{} \underset{(67.04)}{}$$

$$C = -13.391 + 0.63258Y + 0.45065L \qquad R^2 = 0.9951 \qquad (7.12)$$
$$\underset{(-3.71)}{} \underset{(8.32)}{} \underset{(4.24)}{}$$

$$L = 14.255 + 0.70758Y \qquad\qquad r^2_{LY} = 0.9768 \qquad\qquad (7.13)$$
$$\underset{(2.69)}{} \underset{(37.80)}{}$$

Comparing equation (7.11) with (7.8) and equation (7.12) with (7.9) we see that the coefficients in the latter equation show far greater changes than in the former equation. Of course, if one applies the tests for stability discussed in Section 4.11, one might conclude that the results are not statistically significant at the 5% level. Note that the test for stability that we use is the "predictive" test for stability.

Finally, we might consider predicting C for the first two quarters of 1961 using equations (7.11) and (7.12). The predictions are:

		Equation (7.11)	Equation (7.12)
1961	I	295.96	298.93
	II	302.05	304.73

Thus the prediction from the equation including L is further off from the true value than the predictions from the equations excluding L. Thus if prediction was the sole criterion, one might as well drop the variable L.

The example above illustrates four different ways of looking at the multicollinearity problem:

1. Correlation between the explanatory variables L and Y, which is high. This suggests that the multicollinearity may be serious. However, we explained earlier the fallacy in looking at just the correlation coefficients between the explanatory variables.
2. Standard errors or t-ratios for the estimated coefficients: In this example the t-ratios are significant, suggesting that multicollinearity might not be serious.

3. Stability of the estimated coefficients when some observations are deleted. Again one might conclude that multicollinearity is not serious, if one uses a 5% level of significance for this test.
4. Examining the predictions from the model: If multicollinearity is a serious problem, the predictions from the model would be worse than those from a model that includes only a subset of the set of explanatory variables.

The last criterion should be applied if prediction is the object of the analysis. Otherwise, it would be advisable to consider the second and third criteria. The first criterion is not useful, as we have so frequently emphasized.

7.5 Solutions to the Multicollinearity Problem: Ridge Regression

One of the solutions often suggested for the multicollinearity problem is to use what is known as ridge regression first introduced by Hoerl and Kennard.[10] Simply stated, the idea is to add a constant λ to the variances of the explanatory variables before solving the normal equations. For instance, in the example in Section 7.2, we add 5 to S_{11} and S_{22}. It is easy to see that the squared correlation now drops to

$$r_{12}^2 = \frac{(150)}{205(118)} = 0.930$$

Thus the intercorrelations are decreased. One can easily see what a mechanical solution this is. However, there is an enormous literature on ridge regression.

The addition of λ to the variances produces biased estimators but the argument is that if the variance can be decreased, the mean-squared error will decline. Hoerl and Kennard show that there always exists a constant $\lambda > 0$ such that

$$\sum_{i=1}^{k} \text{MSE}(\tilde{\beta}_i) < \sum_{i=1}^{k} \text{MSE}(\hat{\beta}_i)$$

where $\tilde{\beta}_i$ are the estimators of β_i from the ridge regression and $\hat{\beta}_i$ are the least squares estimators and k is the number of regressors. Unfortunately, λ is a function of the regression parameters β_i and error variance σ^2, which are unknown. Hoerl and Kennard suggest trying different values of λ and picking the value of λ so that "the system will stabilize" or the "coefficients do not have unreasonable values." Thus subjective arguments are used. Some others have suggested obtaining initial estimates of β_i and σ^2 and then using the estimated λ. This procedure can be iterated and we get the iterated ridge estimator. The usefulness of these procedures has also been questioned.[11]

---

[10]A. E. Hoerl and R. W. Kennard, "Ridge Regression: Biased Estimation for Non-orthogonal Problems," and "Ridge Regression: Applications to Non-orthogonal Problems," *Technometrics*, Vol. 12, 1977, pp. 55–67 and 69–82.
[11]These methods are all reviewed in N. R. Draper and R. Craig Van Nostrand, "Ridge Regression and James–Stein Estimation: Review and Comments," *Technometrics*, Vol. 21, No. 4, November 1979, pp. 451–466. The authors do not approve of these methods and discuss the shortcomings of each.

One other problem about ridge regression is the fact that it is not invariant to units of measurement of the explanatory variables and to linear transformations of variables. If we have two explanatory variables x_1 and x_2 and we measure x_1 in tens and x_2 in thousands, it does not make sense to add the same value of λ to the variances of both. This problem can be avoided by normalizing each variable by dividing it by its standard deviation. Even if x_1 and x_2 are measured in the same units, in some cases there are different linear transformations of x_1 and x_2 that are equally sensible. For instance, as discussed in Section 7.4, equations (7.5), (7.6), (7.7) are all equivalent and they are all sensible. The ridge estimators, however, will differ depending on which of these forms is used.

There are different situations under which the ridge regression arises naturally. These will throw light on the matter of the circumstances under which the method will be useful. We mention three of them.

1. *Constrained least squares.* Suppose that we estimated the regression coefficients subject to the condition that

$$\sum_{i=1}^{k} \beta_i^2 = c \tag{7.14}$$

Then we would get something like the ridge regression. The λ that we use is the Lagrangian multiplier in the minimization. To see this, suppose that we have two explanatory variables.

We get the constrained least squares estimator by minimizing

$$\sum (y - \beta_1 x_1 - \beta_2 x_2)^2 + \lambda(\beta_1^2 + \beta_2^2 - c)$$

where λ is the Lagrangian multiplier. Differentiating this expression with respect to β_1 and β_2 and equating the derivatives to zero, we get the normal equations

$$2 \sum (y - \beta_1 x_1 - \beta_2 x_2)(-x_1) + 2\lambda\beta_1 = 0$$

$$2 \sum (y - \beta_1 x_1 - \beta_2 x_2)(-x_2) + 2\lambda\beta_2 = 0$$

These equations can be written as

$$(S_{11} + \lambda)\beta_1 + S_{12}\beta_2 = S_{1y}$$

$$S_{12}\beta_1 + (S_{22} + \lambda)\beta_2 = S_{2y}$$

where $S_{11} = \sum x_1^2$, $S_{12} = \sum x_1 x_2$, and so on. Thus we get the ridge regression and λ is the Lagrangian multiplier. The value of λ is decided by the criterion $\beta_1^2 + \beta_2^2 = c$. In this case there is a clear-cut procedure for choosing λ.

It is rarely the case that we would have prior knowledge about the β_i that are in the form $\sum \beta_i^2 = c$. But some other less concrete information can also be used to choose the value of λ in ridge regression. Brown and Beattie's[12] ridge regression on

---

[12]W. G. Brown and B. R. Beattie, "Improving Estimates of Economic Parameters by the Use of Ridge Regression with Production Function Applications," *American Journal of Agricultural Economics*, Vol. 57, 1975, pp. 21–32.

production function data used their prior knowledge on the relationship between the signs of the β_i's.

2. *Bayesian interpretation.* We have not discussed the Bayesian approach to statistics in this book. However, roughly speaking, what the approach does is to combine systematically some prior information on the regression parameters with sample information. Under this approach we get the ridge regression estimates of the β_i's if we assume that the prior information is of the form that $\beta_i \sim \text{IN}(0, \sigma_\beta^2)$. In this case the ridge constant λ is equal to σ^2/σ_β^2. Again, σ^2 is not known but has to be estimated. However, in almost all economic problems, this sort of prior information (that the means of the β_i's are zero) is very unreasonable. This suggests that the simple ridge estimator does not make sense in econometrics (with the Bayesian interpretation). Of course, the assumption that β_i has mean zero can be relaxed. But then we will get more complicated estimators (generalized ridge estimators).

3. *Measurement error interpretation.* Consider the two-variable model we discussed under constrained least squares. Suppose that we add random errors with zero mean and variance λ to both x_1 and x_2. Since these errors are random, the covariance between x_1 and x_2 will be unaffected. The variances of x_1 and x_2 will both increase by λ. Thus we get the ridge regression estimator. This interpretation makes the ridge estimator somewhat suspicious. Smith and Campbell[13] say that a one-liner summary of this is: "Use less precise data to get more precise estimates."

These are situations in which the ridge regression can be easily justified. In almost all other cases, there is subjective judgment involved. This subjective judgment is sometimes equated to "vague prior information." The Bayesian methods allow a systematic analysis of the data with "vague prior information" but a discussion of these methods is beyond the scope of this book.

Because of the deficiencies of ridge regression discussed above, the method is not recommended as a general solution to the multicollinearity problem. Particularly the simplest form of the method (where a constant λ is added to each variance) is not very useful. Nevertheless, for the sake of curiosity, we will present some results on the method. For the consumption function data in Table 7.1 we estimated the regression equation

$$c_t = \beta_0 y_t + \beta_1 y_{t-1} + \beta_2 y_{t-2} + \cdots + \beta_8 y_{t-8} + u_t$$

Needless to say, the y_t's are highly intercorrelated. The results are presented in Table 7.2. Note that as λ increases, there is a smoothing of the coefficients and the estimate of β_0 declines. The OLS coefficients, of course, are very erratic. But the estimates of β_0 (portion of current income going into current consumption) are implausibly low with the ridge regression method. The sudden pickup of coefficients after the fifth quarter is also something very implausible. Maybe we can just estimate the effects only up to four lags. The OLS estimates are erratic even with four lags. The computation of the ridge regression estimates with four lags is left as an exercise.

---

[13]Gary Smith and Frank Campbell, "A Critique of Some Ridge Regression Methods" (with discussion), *Journal of the American Statistical Association*, Vol. 75, March 1980, pp. 74–103.

Table 7.2 Ridge estimates for consumption function data

	Value of λ					
Lag	0.0	0.0002	0.0006	0.0010	0.0014	0.0020
0	0.70974	0.42246	0.29302	0.24038	0.21096	0.18489
1	0.20808	0.28187	0.22554	0.19578	0.17773	0.16096
2	0.27463	0.15615	0.14612	0.13865	0.13324	0.12764
3	−0.48068	−0.06079	0.03052	0.05761	0.07060	0.08088
4	0.25129	−0.00301	0.02429	0.04473	0.05736	0.06902
5	−0.23845	−0.06461	−0.00562	0.02304	0.04010	0.05578
6	0.12432	0.01705	0.03600	0.05116	0.06135	0.07138
7	−0.11278	0.06733	0.07964	0.08491	0.08862	0.09254
8	0.19838	0.12632	0.11941	0.11563	0.11367	0.11220
Sum	0.93453	0.94277	0.94892	0.95189	0.95363	0.95529

7.6 Principal Component Regression

Another solution that is often suggested for the multicollinearity problem is the *principal component regression*, which is as follows. Suppose that we have k explanatory variables. Then we can consider linear functions of these variables

$$z_1 = a_1 x_1 + a_2 x_2 + \cdots + a_k x_k$$

$$z_2 = b_1 x_1 + b_2 x_2 + \cdots + b_k x_k \quad \text{etc.}$$

Suppose we choose the a's so that the variance of z_1 is maximized subject to the condition that

$$a_1^2 + a_2^2 + \cdots + a_k^2 = 1$$

This is called the normalization condition. (It is required or else the variance of z_1 can be increased indefinitely.) z_1 is then said to be the first principal component. It is the linear function of the x's that has the highest variance (subject to the normalization rule).

The detailed derivation of the principle components is given in the appendix. We will discuss the main features and uses of the method which are easy to understand without the use of matrix algebra. Further, for using the method there are computer programs available that give the principal components (z's) given any set of variables $x_1, x_2, \ldots, x_k$.

The process of maximizing the variance of the linear function z subject to the condition that the sum of squares of the coefficients of the x's is equal to 1, produces k solutions. Corresponding to these we construct k linear functions $z_1, z_2, \ldots, z_k$. These are called the principal components of the x's. They can be ordered so that

$$\text{var}(z_1) > \text{var}(z_2) > \cdots > \text{var}(z_k)$$

z_1, the one with the highest variance, is called the first principal component, z_2, with the next highest variance, is called the second principal component, and so on. These principal components have the following properties:

1. $\mathrm{var}(z_1) + \mathrm{var}(z_2) + \cdots + \mathrm{var}(z_k) = \mathrm{var}(x_1) + \mathrm{var}(x_2) + \cdots + \mathrm{var}(x_k)$.
2. Unlike the x's, which are correlated, the z's are orthogonal or uncorrelated. Thus there is zero multicollinearity among the z's.

Sometimes it is suggested that instead of regressing y on $x_1, x_2, \ldots, x_k$, we should regress y on $z_1, z_2, \ldots, z_k$. But this is *not* a solution to the multicollinearity problem. If we regress y on the z's and then substitute the values of z's in terms of x's, we finally get the same answers as before. This is similar to the example we considered in Section 7.4. The fact that the z's are uncorrelated does not mean that we will get better estimates of the coefficients in the original regression equation. So there is a point in using the principal components *only* if we regress y on a subset of the z's. But there are some problems with this procedure as well. They are:

1. The first principal component z_1, although it has the highest variance, need not be the one that is most highly correlated with y. In fact, there is no necessary relationship between the order of the principal components and the degree of correlation with the dependent variable y.
2. One can think of choosing only those principal components that have high correlation with y and discard the rest, but the same sort of procedure can be used with the original set of variables $x_1, x_2, \ldots, x_k$ by first choosing the variable with the highest correlation with y, then the one with the highest partial correlation, and so on. This is what "stepwise regression programs" do.
3. The linear combinations z's often do not have economic meaning. For example, what does 2(income) + 3(price) mean? This is one of the most important drawbacks of the method.
4. Changing the units of measurement of the x's will change the principal components. This problem can be avoided if all variables are standardized to have unit variance.

However, there are some uses for the principal component method in exploratory stages of the investigation. For instance, suppose that there are many interest rates in the model (since all are measured in the same units, there is no problem of choice of units of measurement). If the principal component analysis shows that two principal components account for 99% of the variation in the interest rates and if, by looking at the coefficients, we can identify them as short-term component and long-term component, we can argue that there are only two "latent" variables that account for all variations in the interest rates. Thus the principal component method will give us some guidance as to the question: "How many independent sources of variation are there?" In addition, if we can give an economic interpretation to the principal components, this is useful.

We illustrate the method with reference to a data set from Malinvaud.[14] We have chosen this data set because it has been used by Chatterjee and Price[15] to illustrate the principal

---

[14]E. Malinvaud, *Statistical Methods of Econometrics*, 2nd ed. (Amsterdam: North-Holland, 1970).

[15]S. Chatterjee and B. Price, *Regression Analysis by Example* (New York: Wiley, 1977).

Table 7.3 Imports, production, stock formation, and consumption in France (millions of new francs at 1959 prices)

Years	Imports, y	Gross Domestic Production, x_1	Stock Formation, x_2	Consumption, x_3
1949	15.9	149.3	4.2	108.1
1950	16.4	161.2	4.1	114.8
1951	19.0	171.5	3.1	123.2
1952	19.1	175.5	3.1	126.9
1953	18.8	180.8	1.1	132.1
1954	20.4	190.7	2.2	137.7
1955	22.7	202.1	2.1	146.0
1956	26.5	212.4	5.6	154.1
1957	28.1	226.1	5.0	162.3
1958	27.6	231.9	5.1	164.3
1959	26.3	239.0	0.7	167.6
1960	31.1	258.0	5.6	176.8
1961	33.3	269.8	3.9	186.6
1962	37.0	288.4	3.1	199.7
1963	43.3	304.5	4.6	213.9
1964	49.0	323.4	7.0	223.8
1965	50.3	336.8	1.2	232.0
1966	56.6	353.9	4.5	242.9

Source: E. Mallinvaud, *Statistical Methods of Econometrics*, 2nd ed. (Amsterdam: North-Holland, 1970), p. 19.

component method. We will also be using this same data set in Chapter 11 to illustrate the errors in variables methods.

The data are presented in Table 7.3. First let us estimate an import demand function. The regression of y on x_1, x_2, x_3 gives the following results:

Variable	Coefficient	SE	t
x_1	0.032	0.187	0.17
x_2	0.414	0.322	1.29
x_3	0.243	0.285	0.85
Constant	−19.73	4.125	−4.78
$n = 18$	$R^2 = 0.973$	$F_{3.14} = 168.4$	

The R^2 is very high and the F-ratio is highly significant but the individual t-ratios are all insignificant. This is evidence of the multicollinearity problem. Chatterjee and Price argue that before any further analysis is made, we should look at the residuals from this equation. They find (we are omitting the residual plot here) a distinctive pattern — the residuals declining until 1960 and then rising. Chatterjee and Price argue that the difficulty with the model is that the European Common Market began operations in 1960, causing changes in import–export relationships. Hence they drop the years after 1959 and consider only the 11 years 1949–1959. The regression results now are as follows:

Variable	Coefficient	SE	t
x_1	−0.051	0.070	−0.731
x_2	0.587	0.905	6.203
x_3	0.287	0.102	2.807
Constant	−10.13	1.212	−8.355
$n = 11$		$R^2 = 0.992$	

The residual plot (not shown here) is now satisfactory (there are no systematic patterns), so we can proceed. Even though the R^2 is very high, the coefficient of x_1 is not significant. There is thus a multicollinearity problem.

To see what should be done about it, we first look at the simple correlations among the explanatory variables. These are $r_{12}^2 = 0.026$, $r_{13}^2 = 0.99$, and $r_{23}^2 = 0.036$. We suspect that the high correlation between x_1 and x_3 could be the source of the trouble.

Does principal component analysis help us? First, the principal components (obtained from a principal components program)[16] are

$$z_1 = 0.7063X_1 + 0.0435X_2 + 0.7065X_3$$

$$z_2 = -0.0357X_1 + 0.9990X_2 - 0.0258X_3$$

$$z_3 = -0.7070X_1 - 0.0070X_2 + 0.7072X_3$$

X_1, X_2, X_3 are the normalized values of x_1, x_2, x_3. That is, $X_1 = (x_1 - m_1)/\sigma_1$, $X_2 = (x_2 - m_2)/\sigma_2$, and $X_3 - (x_3 - m_3)/\sigma_3$, where m_1, m_2, m_3 are the means and σ_1, σ_2, σ_3 are the standard deviations of x_1, x_2, x_3, respectively. Hence

$$\text{var}(X_1) = \text{var}(X_2) = \text{var}(X_3) = 1$$

The variances of the principal components are

$$\text{var}(z_1) = 1.999 \qquad \text{var}(z_2) = 0.998 \qquad \text{var}(z_3) = 0.003$$

Note that $\sum \text{var}(z_i) = \sum \text{var}(X_i) = 3$. The fact that $\text{var}(z_3) = 0$ identifies that linear function as the source of multicollinearity. In this example there is only one such linear function. In some examples there could be more. Since $E(X_1) = E(X_2) = E(X_3) = 0$ because of normalization, the z's have mean zero. Thus z_3 has mean zero and its variance is also close to zero. Thus we can say that $z_3 \simeq 0$. Looking at the coefficients of the X's, we can say that (ignoring the coefficients that are very small)

$$z_1 \simeq 0.706(X_1 + X_3)$$

$$z_2 \simeq X_2$$

$$z_3 \simeq 0.707(X_3 - X_1)$$

$$z_3 \simeq 0 \text{ gives us } X_1 \simeq X_3$$

---

[16]These are from Chatterjee and Price, *Regression Analysis*, p. 161. The details of how the principal components are computed need not concern us here.

Actually, we would have got the same result from a regression of X_3 on X_1. The regression coefficient is $r_{13} = 0.9984$. (Note that X_1 and X_3 are in standardized form. Hence the regression coefficient is r_{13}.)

In terms of the original (nonnormalized) variables the regression of x_3 on x_1 is (figure in parentheses is standard error)

$$x_3 = 6.258 + \underset{(0.0077)}{0.686 x_1} \qquad r^2 = 0.998$$

In a way we have got no more information from the principal component analysis than from a study of the simple correlations in this example. Anyway, what is the solution now? Given that there is an almost exact relationship between x_3 and x_1, we cannot hope to estimate the coefficients of x_1 and x_3 separately. If the original equation is

$$y = \beta_0 + \beta_1 x_1 + \beta_2 x_2 + \beta_3 x_3 + u$$

then substituting for x_3 in terms of x_1 we get

$$y = (\beta_0 + 6.258\beta_3) + (\beta_1 + 0.686\beta_3) x_1 + \beta_2 x_2 + u$$

This gives the linear functions of the β's that are estimable. They are $(\beta_0 + 6.258\beta_3)$, $(\beta_1 + 0.686\beta_3)$, and β_2. The regression of y on x_1 and x_2 gave the following results:

Variable	Coefficient	SE	t
x_1	0.145	0.007	20.67
x_2	0.622	0.128	4.87
Constant	−8.440	1.435	−5.88
	$R^2 = 0.983$		

Of course, we can estimate a regression of x_1 and x_3. The regression coefficient is 1.451. We now substitute for x_1 and estimate a regression of y on x_1 and x_3. The results we get are slightly better (we get a higher R^2). The results are:

Variable	Coefficient	SE	t
x_2	0.596	0.091	6.55
x_3	0.212	0.007	29.18
Constant	−9.743	1.059	−9.20
	$R^2 = 0.991$		

The coefficient of x_3 now is $(\beta_3 + 1.451\beta_1)$.

We can get separate estimates of β_1 and β_3 only if we have some prior information. As this example as well as the example in Section 7.3 indicate, what multicollinearity implies is that we cannot estimate individual coefficients with good precision but can estimate some linear functions of the parameters with good precision. If we want to estimate the individual parameters, we would need some prior information. We will show that the use of principal components implies the use of some prior information about the restrictions on the parameters.

Suppose that we consider regressing y on the principal components z_1 and z_2 (z_3 is omitted because it is almost zero). We saw that $z_1 = 0.7(X_1 + X_3)$ and $z_2 = X_2$. We have to transform these to the original variables. We get

$$z_1 = 0.7 \left(\frac{x_1 - m_1}{\sigma_1} + \frac{x_3 - m_3}{\sigma_3} \right)$$

$$= \frac{0.7}{\sigma_1} \left(x_1 + \frac{\sigma_1}{\sigma_3} x_3 \right) + \text{ a constant}$$

$$z_2 = \frac{1}{\sigma_2}(x_2 - m_2)$$

Thus, using z_2 as a regressor is equivalent to using x_2, and using z_1 is equivalent to using $(x_1 + (\sigma_1/\sigma_3)x_3)$. Thus the principal component regression amounts to regressing y on $(x_1 + (\sigma_1/\sigma_3)x_3)$ and x_2. In our example $\sigma_1/\sigma_3 = 1.4536$. The results are

Variable	Coefficient	SE	t
$x_1 + 1.4536x_3$	0.073	0.003	25.12
x_2	0.609	0.106	5.77
Constant	-9.129	1.207	-7.56
	$R^2 = 0.988$		

This is the regression equation *we would have* estimated if we assumed that $\beta_3 = (\sigma_1/\sigma_3)\beta_1 = 1.4536\beta_1$. Thus the principal component regression amounts, in this example, to the use of the prior information $\beta_3 = 1.4536\beta_1$.

If all principal components are used, it is exactly equivalent to using all the original set of explanatory variables. If some principal components are omitted, this amounts to using some prior information on the β's. In our example the question is whether the assumption $\beta_3 = 1.45\beta_1$ makes economic sense. Without having more disaggregated data that break down imports into consumption and production goods we cannot say anything. Anyway, with 11 observations we cannot hope to answer many questions. The purpose of our analysis has been merely to show what principal component regression is and to show that it implies some prior information.

7.7 Dropping Variables

The problem with multicollinearity is essentially lack of sufficient information in the sample to permit accurate estimation of the individual parameters. In some cases it may be the case that we are not interested in all the parameters. In such cases we can get estimators for the parameters we are interested in that have smaller mean-square errors than the OLS estimators, by dropping some variables.

Consider the model

$$y = \beta_1 x_1 + \beta_2 x_2 + u \tag{7.15}$$

and the problem is that x_1 and x_2 are very highly correlated. Suppose that our main interest is in β_1. Then we drop x_2 and estimate the equation

$$y = \beta_1 x_1 + v \tag{7.16}$$

Let the estimator of β_1 from the complete model (7.15) be denoted by $\hat{\beta}_1$ and the estimator of β_1 from the omitted variable model be denoted by β_1^*. $\hat{\beta}_1$ is the OLS estimator and β_1^* is the OV (omitted variable) estimator. For the OLS estimator we know that

$$E(\hat{\beta}_1) = \beta_1 \quad \text{and} \quad \text{var}(\hat{\beta}_1) = \frac{\sigma^2}{S_{11}(1 - r_{12}^2)}$$

[see formula (7.1)]. For the OV estimator we have to compute $E(\beta_1^*)$ and $\text{var}(\beta_1^*)$. Now

$$\beta_1^* = \frac{\sum x_1 y}{\sum x_1^2}$$

substituting for y from (7.15) we get

$$\beta_1^* = \frac{\sum x_1 (\beta_1 x_1 + \beta_2 x_2 + u)}{\sum x_1^2}$$

$$= \beta_1 + \frac{S_{12}}{S_{11}} \beta_2 + \frac{\sum x_1 u}{S_{11}}$$

(Note that we used $S_{11} = \sum x_1^2$ and $S_{12} = \sum x_1 x_2$.) Hence

$$E(\beta_1^*) = \beta_1 + \beta_2 \frac{S_{12}}{S_{11}}$$

and

$$\text{var}(\beta_1^*) = \text{var}\left(\frac{\sum x_1 u}{S_{11}}\right) = \frac{\sigma^2 S_{11}}{S_{11}^2} = \frac{\sigma^2}{S_{11}}$$

Thus β_1^* is biased but has a smaller variance than $\hat{\beta}_1$. We have

$$\frac{\text{var}(\beta_1^*)}{\text{var}(\hat{\beta}_1)} = 1 - r_{12}^2$$

and if r_{12} is very high, then $\text{var}(\beta_1^*)$ will be considerably less than $\text{var}(\hat{\beta}_1)$. Now

$$\frac{(\text{bias in } \beta_1^*)^2}{\text{var}(\hat{\beta}_1)} = \left(\frac{\beta_2 S_{12}}{S_{11}}\right)^2 \frac{S_{11}(1 - r_{12}^2)}{\sigma^2}$$

$$= \frac{S_{12}^2}{S_{11} S_{22}} \beta_2^2 \frac{S_{22}(1 - r_{12}^2)}{\sigma^2}$$

The first term in this expression is r_{12}^2. The last term is the reciprocal of $\text{var}(\hat{\beta}_2)$ [see formula (7.2)]. Thus the whole expression can be written as $r_{12}^2 t_2^2$, where

$$t_2^2 = \frac{\beta_2^2}{\text{var}(\hat{\beta}_2)}$$

t_2 is the "true" t-ratio for x_2 in equation (7.15), not the "estimated" t-ratio.

Noting that $\text{MSE} = (\text{bias})^2 + \text{variance}$, and that for $\hat{\beta}_1$, $\text{MSE} = \text{variance}$, we get

$$\frac{\text{MSE}(\beta_1^*)}{\text{MSE}(\hat{\beta}_1)} = \frac{(\text{bias in } \beta_1^*)^2}{\text{var}(\hat{\beta}_1)} + \frac{\text{var}(\beta_1^*)}{\text{var}(\hat{\beta}_1)}$$

$$= r_{12}^2 t_2^2 + (1 - r_{12}^2)$$

$$= 1 + r_{12}^2(t_2^2 - 1) \tag{7.17}$$

Thus if $|t_2| < 1$, then $\text{MSE}(\beta_1^*) < \text{MSE}(\hat{\beta}_1)$. Since t_2 is not known, what is usually done is to use the estimated t-value $\hat{t}_2$ from equation (7.15). As an estimator of β_1, we use the conditional omitted variable (COV) estimator, defined as

$$\tilde{\beta}_1 = \begin{cases} \hat{\beta}_1 & \text{the OLS estimator if } |\hat{t}_2| \geq 1 \\ \beta_1^* & \text{the OV estimator if } |\hat{t}_2| < 1 \end{cases}$$

Also, instead of using $\hat{\beta}_1$ or β_1^*, depending on $\hat{t}_2$ we can consider a linear combination of both, namely

$$\lambda \hat{\beta}_1 + (1 - \lambda)\beta_1^*$$

This is called the weighted (WTD) estimator and it has minimum mean-square error if $\lambda = t_2^2/(1 + t_2^2)$. Again t_2 is not known and we have to use its estimated value $\hat{t}_2$. This weighted estimator was first suggested by Huntsberger. The COV estimator was first suggested by Bancroft. Feldstein[17] studied the mean-squared error of these two estimators for different values of t_2 and $\hat{t}_2$. He argues that:

1. Omitting a collinear nuisance variable on the basis of its sample t-statistic $\hat{t}_2$ is generally not advisable. OLS is preferable to any COV estimator unless one has a strong prior notion that $|t_2|$ is < 1.
2. The WTD estimator is generally better than the COV estimator.
3. The WTD estimator is superior to OLS for $|t_2| \leq 1.25$ and only slightly inferior for $1.5 \leq |t_2| \leq 3.0$.
4. The inadequacy of collinear data should not be disguised by reporting results from the omitted variable regressions. Even if a WTD estimator is used, one should report the OLS estimates and their standard errors to let readers judge the extent of multicollinearity.

---

[17]M. S. Feldstein, "Multicollinearity and the Mean Square Error of Alternative Estimators," *Econometrica*, Vol. 41, March 1973, pp. 337–345. References to the papers by Bancroft, Huntsberger, and others can be found in that paper.

What all this discussion shows is that even in the use of the COV or WTD estimators prior information on t_2 is very important. This brings us back to the same story as our discussion of the ridge regression and principal components regression, namely, the importance of prior information. The prior information regarding the omission of nuisance variables pertains to the *true t*-values for the coefficients of these variables.

Leamer[18] suggests studying the sensitivity of estimates of the coefficients to different specifications about prior information on the coefficients. Although his approach is Bayesian and is beyond the scope of this book, one can do a simple sensitivity analysis in each problem to assess the impact on the estimates of the coefficients of interest of changes in the assumptions about the coefficients of the nuisance parameters. Such sensitivity analysis would be more useful than using one solution like ridge regression, principal component regression, omitting variables, and so on, each of which implies some particular prior information in a concealed way. Very often, this may not be the prior information you would want to consider.

7.8 Miscellaneous Other Solutions

There have been several other solutions to the multicollinearity problem that one finds in the literature. All these, however, should be used only if there are other reasons to use them — not for solving the collinearity problem as such. We will discuss them briefly.

Using Ratios or First Differences

We have discussed the method of using ratios in our discussion of heteroskedasticity (Chapter 5) and first differences in our discussion of autocorrelation (Chapter 6). Although these procedures might reduce the intercorrelations among the explanatory variables, they should be used on the basis of the considerations discussed in those chapters, not as a solution to the collinearity problem.

Using Extraneous Estimates

This method was followed in early demand studies. It was found that in time-series data income and price were both highly correlated. Hence neither the price nor income elasticity could be estimated with precision. What was done was to get an estimate of the income elasticity from budget studies (where prices do not vary much), use this estimate to "correct" the quantity series for income variation and then estimate the price elasticity.[19] For example, if the equation to be estimated is

$$\log Q = \alpha + \beta_1 \log p + \beta_2 \log y + u$$

---

[18]E. E. Leamer, "Multicollinearity: A Bayesian Interpretation," *Review of Economics and Statistics*, Vol. 55, 1973, pp. 371–380; "Regression Selection Strategies and Revealed Priors," *Journal of the American Statistical Association*, Vol. 73, 1978, pp. 580–587.

[19]An example of this is J. Tobin, "A Statistical Demand Function for Food in the U.S.A.," *Journal of the Royal Statistical Society, Series A*, 1950, pp. 113–141.

we first get $\hat{\beta}_2$ from budget studies and then regress $(\log Q - \hat{\beta}_2 \log y)$ on $\log p$ to get estimates of α and β_1. Here $\hat{\beta}_2$ is known as the "extraneous estimate." There are two main problems with this procedure. First, the fact that β_2 is estimated should be taken into account in computing the variances of $\hat{\alpha}$ and $\hat{\beta}_1$. This is not usually done, but it can be. Second, and this is the more important problem, the cross-section estimate of β_2 may be measuring something entirely different from what the time-series estimate is supposed to measure. As Meyer and Kuh[20] argue, the "extraneous" estimate can be really extraneous.

Suppose that we want to use an estimate for a parameter from another data set. What is the best procedure for doing this? Consider the equation

$$y_1 = \beta_1 x_1 + \beta_2 x_2 + u \tag{7.18}$$

Suppose that because of the high correlation between x_1 and x_2, we cannot get good estimates of β_1 and β_2. We try to get an estimate of β_1 from another data set and another equation

$$y_2 = \beta_1 x_1 + \gamma z + v \tag{7.19}$$

In this equation x_1 and z are not highly correlated and we get a good estimate of β_1, say $\hat{\beta}_1$. Now we substitute this in equation (7.18) and regress $(y_1 - \hat{\beta}_1 x_1)$ on x_2 to get an estimate $\hat{\beta}_2$ of β_2. This is the procedure we mentioned earlier. The estimate of $\hat{\beta}_2$ is a *conditional estimate*, conditional on $\beta_1 = \hat{\beta}_1$. Also, we have to make corrections for the estimated variance of $\hat{\beta}_2$ because the error in the equation now is

$$(y - \hat{\beta}_1 x_1) = \beta_2 x_2 + W$$

where $W = u + (\beta_1 - \hat{\beta}_1)x_1$ is not the same as u. This procedure is advisable only when the data behind the estimation of (7.19) are not available to us (the study is done by somebody else).

On the other hand, if the two sets of data are available to us, there is no reason to use this conditional estimation procedure. A better procedure would be to estimate equations (7.18) and (7.19) jointly. This is what was done by Maddala[21] for the data used by Tobin in his study on demand for food. It is also possible to test, by using the joint estimation of equations (7.18) and (7.19) and separate estimation of the equations, whether the coefficient of x_1 is the same in the two equations.[22]

In summary, as a solution to the multicollinearity problem, it is not advisable to substitute extraneous parameter estimates in the equation. One can, of course, pool the different data sets to get more efficient estimates of the parameters, but one should also perform some tests to see whether the parameters in the different equations are indeed the same.

---

[20] John Meyer and Edwin Kuh, "How Extraneous Are Extraneous Estimates?," *Review of Economics and Statistics*, November 1957.

[21] G. S. Maddala, "The Likelihood Approach to Pooling Cross-Section and Time-Series Data," *Econometrica*, Vol. 39, November 1971, pp. 939–953.

[22] In the case of Tobin's demand for food example, this test done by Maddala showed that there were significant differences between the two parameters.

Getting More Data

One solution to the multicollinearity problem that is often suggested is to "go and get more data." Actually, the extraneous estimators case we have discussed also falls in this category (we look for another model with common parameters and the associated data set). Sometimes using quarterly or monthly data instead of annual data helps us in getting better estimates. However, we might be adding more sources of variation like seasonality. In any case, since weak data and inadequate information are the sources of our problem, getting more data will help matters.

Summary

1. In multiple regression analysis it is usually difficult to interpret the estimates of the individual coefficients if the variables are highly intercorrelated. This problem is often referred to as the multicollinearity problem.

2. However, high intercorrelations among the explanatory variables by themselves need not necessarily cause any problems in inference. Whether or not this is a problem will depend on the magnitude of the error variance and the variances of the explanatory variables. If there is enough variation in the explanatory variables and the variance of the error term is sufficiently small, high intercorrelations among the explanatory variables need not cause a problem. This is illustrated by using formulas (7.1)–(7.4) in Section 7.2.

3. Measures of multicollinearity based solely on high intercorrelations among the explanatory variables are useless. These are discussed in Section 7.3. Also, as shown in Section 7.4, these correlations can change with simple transformations of the explanatory variables. This does not mean that the problem has been solved.

4. There have been several solutions to the multicollinearity problem. These are:
   (a) Ridge regression, on which an enormous amount of literature exists.
   (b) Principal component regression—this amounts to transforming the explanatory variables to an uncorrelated set, but mere transformation does not solve the problem. (It appears through the back door.)
   (c) Dropping variables.

All of these so-called solutions are really ad hoc procedures. Each implies the use of some prior information and it is better to examine this before undertaking a mechanical solution that has been suggested by others.

5. The basic problem is lack of enough information to answer the questions posed. The only solutions are:
   (a) To get more data.
   (b) To ask what questions are answerable with the data at hand.
   (c) To examine what prior information will be most helpful [in fact, this should precede solution (a)].

Exercises

1. Define the term "multicollinearity." Explain how you would detect its presence in a multiple regression equation you have estimated. What are the consequences of multicollinearity, and what are the solutions?

2. Explain the following methods:
   (a) Ridge regression.
   (b) Omitted variable regression.
   (c) Principle component regression.
   What are the problems these methods are supposed to solve?

3. Examine whether the following statements are true or false. Give an explanation.
   (a) In multiple regression, a high correlation in the sample among the regressors (multicollinearity) implies that the least squares estimators of the coefficients are biased.
   (b) Whether or not multicollinearity is a problem cannot be decided by just looking at the intercorrelations between the explanatory variables.
   (c) If the coefficient estimates in an equation have high standard errors, this is evidence of high multicollinearity.
   (d) The relevant question to ask if there is high multicollinearity is not what variables to drop but what other information will help.

4. In a study analyzing the determinants of faculty salaries, the results shown below were obtained.[23] The dependent variable is 1969–1970 academic year salary. We have omitted eight more other explanatory variables.
   (a) Do any of the coefficients have unexpected signs?
   (b) Is there a multicollinearity problem? What variables do you expect to be highly correlated?
   (c) Teacher rating is the only nonsignificant variable among the variables presented. Can you explain why? Note that T is a dummy variable indicating whether or not the professor ranked in the top 50% of all instructors by a vote of the students.
   (d) Would dropping the variable T from the equation change the signs of any of the other variables?

Explanatory Variable	Coefficient	Standard Error	F
Books, B	230	86	7.21
Articles, A	18	8	5.37
Excellent articles, E	102	28	13.43
Dissertations, F	489	60	66.85
Public Service, P	89	38	5.65
Committees, C	156	49	10.02
Experience, Y	189	17	126.92
Teacher rating, T	53	370	0.01
English professors, D_4	−2293	529	18.75

(Continued overleaf)

[23]David A. Katz, "Faculty Salaries, Promotions and Productivity at a Large University," *The American Economic Review*, June 1973, pp. 469–477.

(*continued*)

Explanatory Variable	Coefficient	Standard Error	F
Female, X	−2410	528	20.80
Ph.D. degree, R	1919	607	10.01

Constant = 11,155; $R^2 = 0.68$; $n = 596$
Standard error of regression = 2946
Mean of the dependent variable = 15,679
SD of the dependent variable = 5093

(e) The variable F is the number of dissertations supervised since 1964. B is the number of books published. How do you explain the high coefficient for F relative to that of B?

(f) Would you conclude from the coefficient of X that there is sex discrimination?

(g) Compute the partial r^2 for experience.

5. Estimate demand for food functions on the basis of the data in Table 4.9. Discuss if there is a multicollinearity problem and what you are going to do about it.

6. Estimate demand for gasoline on the basis of the data in Table 4.8. Are the wrong signs for P_g a consequence of multicollinearity?

Appendix to Chapter 7

Linearly Dependent Explanatory Variables

In Chapter 4 we assumed that the explanatory variables were linearly independent and hence that $(\mathbf{X}'\mathbf{X})^{-1}$ exists. What happens if the explanatory variables are linearly dependent? This is the case of perfect multicollinearity. In this case $(\mathbf{X}'\mathbf{X})$ will be a singular matrix (its rank will be less than k). Hence we do not have a unique solution to the normal equations. However, consider two different solutions, $\hat{\boldsymbol{\beta}}_1$ and $\hat{\boldsymbol{\beta}}_2$, to the normal equations. We then have

$$(\mathbf{X}'\mathbf{X})\hat{\boldsymbol{\beta}}_1 = \mathbf{X}'\mathbf{y}$$

and

$$(\mathbf{X}'\mathbf{X})\hat{\boldsymbol{\beta}}_2 = \mathbf{X}'\mathbf{y}$$

Premultiply the first equation by $\hat{\boldsymbol{\beta}}_2'$ and the second equation by $\hat{\boldsymbol{\beta}}_1'$ and subtract. Since $\hat{\boldsymbol{\beta}}_2'\mathbf{X}'\mathbf{X}\hat{\boldsymbol{\beta}}_1 = \hat{\boldsymbol{\beta}}_1'\mathbf{X}'\mathbf{X}\hat{\boldsymbol{\beta}}_2$ (the transpose of a scalar is the same), we get the result that $\hat{\boldsymbol{\beta}}_1'\mathbf{X}'\mathbf{y} = \hat{\boldsymbol{\beta}}_2'\mathbf{X}'\mathbf{y}$; that is, the regression sum of squares is the same. Hence the residual sum of squares will be the same whatever solution we take.

If $(\mathbf{X}'\mathbf{X})$ is singular, it means that not all the regression parameters β_i are estimable, but only certain linear functions of the β_i are estimable. The question is: What linear functions are estimable?

Let $\boldsymbol{\alpha}$ be a $k \times 1$ vector that is a linear combination of the columns of $(\mathbf{X}'\mathbf{X})$. Thus $\boldsymbol{\alpha} = (\mathbf{X}'\mathbf{X})\boldsymbol{\lambda}$. Then the linear function $\boldsymbol{\alpha}'\boldsymbol{\beta}$ is uniquely estimable. To see this consider *any* solution $\hat{\boldsymbol{\beta}}$ of the normal equations. Then

$$\boldsymbol{\alpha}'\boldsymbol{\beta} = \boldsymbol{\lambda}'\mathbf{X}'\mathbf{X}\hat{\boldsymbol{\beta}} = \boldsymbol{\lambda}'\mathbf{X}'\mathbf{y}$$

Thus $\boldsymbol{\alpha}'\hat{\boldsymbol{\beta}}$ is a unique linear function of $\mathbf{y}$. Since $E(\boldsymbol{\lambda}'\mathbf{X}'\mathbf{y}) = \boldsymbol{\lambda}'\mathbf{X}'\mathbf{X}\boldsymbol{\beta} = \boldsymbol{\alpha}'\boldsymbol{\beta}$, we get the result that $\boldsymbol{\alpha}'\hat{\boldsymbol{\beta}}$ is a unique unbiased linear estimator of $\boldsymbol{\alpha}'\boldsymbol{\beta}$. It can also be shown that it has minimum variance among all linear unbiased estimators (the proof is similar to the one in the appendix to Chapter 4). Thus it is BLUE.

In case $(\mathbf{X}'\mathbf{X})$ is nonsingular, every $k \times 1$ vector can be expressed as a linear combination of the columns of $(\mathbf{X}'\mathbf{X})$. Thus *all* linear functions $\boldsymbol{\alpha}'\boldsymbol{\beta}$ are uniquely estimable. Hence all the β_i are uniquely estimable. As an illustration of perfect multicollinearity, consider the example in Section 7.2, where $x_3 = x_1 + x_2$. In this case we have

$$y = \beta_1 x_1 + \beta_2 x_2 + \beta_3 x_3 + u$$
$$= (\beta_1 + \beta_3)x_1 + (\beta_2 + \beta_3)x_2 + u$$

Thus we can see that only $\beta_1 + \beta_3$ and $\beta_2 + \beta_3$ are estimable. In this case we have

$$(\mathbf{X}'\mathbf{X}) = \begin{bmatrix} 5 & 0 & 5 \\ 0 & 5 & 5 \\ 5 & 5 & 10 \end{bmatrix}$$

Take $\boldsymbol{\alpha} = \frac{1}{5}$ (first column). Then $\boldsymbol{\alpha}' = (1, 0, 1)$ and $\boldsymbol{\alpha}'\boldsymbol{\beta} = \beta_1 + \beta_3$. Hence $\beta_1 + \beta_3$ is estimable. If we take $\boldsymbol{\alpha} = \frac{1}{5}$ (second column). Then $\boldsymbol{\alpha}' = (0, 1, 1)$ and $\boldsymbol{\alpha}'\boldsymbol{\beta} = \beta_2 + \beta_3$. Hence $\beta_2 + \beta_3$ is estimable. Can we estimate $\beta_1 + \beta_2 + \beta_3$? No, because we cannot get $\boldsymbol{\alpha}' = (1, 1, 1)$ by taking any linear combination of the columns of $(\mathbf{X}'\mathbf{X})$.

Exercise

As yet another example, consider the case

$$\mathbf{X}'\mathbf{X} = \begin{bmatrix} 5 & 2 & 17 \\ 2 & 3 & 9 \\ 17 & 9 & 60 \end{bmatrix}$$

Show that $\beta_1 + 3\beta_3$ and $\beta_2 + \beta_3$ are estimable. Is $\beta_1 - \beta_2 + 2\beta_3$ estimable? Is $\beta_1 + \beta_2 + \beta_3$ estimable?

The "Condition Number" Measure of Multicollinearity (Section 7.3)

The preceding discussion referred to the case where $(\mathbf{X}'\mathbf{X})$ was singular. In actual practice the variables are not exactly linearly dependent but almost are. That is, $(\mathbf{X}'\mathbf{X})$ is close to singularity. The question is: How do we measure closeness? For this purpose the *condition number* has been suggested. It is defined as the square root of the ratio of the largest to the smallest *eigenvalues* (or *characteristic roots*) of the matrix $(\mathbf{X'X})$. To understand this we have to define characteristic roots.

Characteristic Roots and Vectors

Let $\mathbf{A}$ be an $n \times n$ symmetric matrix. Consider minimizing the quadratic form $\mathbf{x'Ax}$ subject to the condition $\mathbf{x'x} = 1$. Introducing the Lagrangian multiplier λ, we minimize

$$\mathbf{x'Ax} - \lambda(\mathbf{x'x} - 1)$$

Differentiating with respect to $\mathbf{x}$ and equating the derivatives to zero, we get

$$2\mathbf{Ax} - 2\lambda\mathbf{x} = 0 \qquad \text{or} \qquad (\mathbf{A} - \lambda\mathbf{I})\mathbf{x} = 0$$

In order that this set of equations should have a nonnull solution, we should have

$$\text{rank}(\mathbf{A} - \lambda\mathbf{I}) < n \qquad \text{or} \qquad |\mathbf{A} - \lambda\mathbf{I}| = 0$$

The roots of this determinantal equation, which is called the *characteristic equation*, are called the *characteristic roots* of $\mathbf{A}$ (alternative terms are *latent roots* or *eigenvalues*). The determinantal equation $|\mathbf{A} - \lambda\mathbf{I}| = 0$ is an nth-degree equation in λ and has n roots. Corresponding to each solution λ_i there is a vector $\mathbf{x}_i$ that is a solution of $(\mathbf{A} - \lambda_i\mathbf{I})\mathbf{x} = 0$. These vectors are called *characteristic vectors* (or *latent vectors* or *eigenvectors*). For instance, if $\mathbf{A}$ is a 3×3 matrix, we have to solve the equation

$$\begin{vmatrix} a_{11} - \lambda & a_{12} & a_{13} \\ a_{21} & a_{22} - \lambda & a_{23} \\ a_{31} & a_{32} & a_{33} - \lambda \end{vmatrix} = 0$$

which is a cubic in λ and has three roots. In the text we showed the calculation of the characteristic roots and the condition number for a 2×2 matrix.

As an example, consider the matrix

$$\mathbf{A} = \begin{bmatrix} 4 & 2 & 2 \\ 2 & 1 & 1 \\ 3 & -4 & 4 \end{bmatrix}$$

Before we go to the characteristic roots of this 3×3 matrix, let us consider the 2×2 submatrix $\begin{bmatrix} 4 & 2 \\ 2 & 1 \end{bmatrix}$. The characteristic equation is

$$\begin{vmatrix} 4 - \lambda & 2 \\ 2 & 1 - \lambda \end{vmatrix} = 0$$

or $(4 - \lambda)(1 - \lambda) - 4 = 0 \Rightarrow \lambda^2 - 5\lambda = 0 \Rightarrow \lambda(\lambda - 5) = 0$. Thus, the two roots are $\lambda = 0$ and $\lambda = 5$. Note that the sum of the roots is equal to the sum of the diagonal elements.

For $\lambda = 0$, the characteristic vector is obtained by solving the equations

$$\begin{bmatrix} 4 & 2 \\ 2 & 1 \end{bmatrix} \begin{bmatrix} x_1 \\ x_2 \end{bmatrix} = \begin{bmatrix} 0 \\ 0 \end{bmatrix} \qquad \text{or} \qquad \begin{matrix} 4x_1 + 2x_2 = 0 \\ 2x_1 + x_2 = 0 \end{matrix}$$

This gives $x_2 = -2x_1$. Normalizing this by taking $x_1^2 + x_2^2 = 1$ or $x_1^2 + 4x_1^2 = 1$, we get $x_1 = 1/\sqrt{5}$, $x_2 = -2/\sqrt{5}$. Thus, the characteristic vector is $(1/\sqrt{5}, -2\sqrt{5})$. For the root $\lambda = 5$, we have to solve the equations

$$\begin{bmatrix} 4-5 & 2 \\ 2 & 1-5 \end{bmatrix} \begin{bmatrix} x_1 \\ x_2 \end{bmatrix} = \begin{bmatrix} 0 \\ 0 \end{bmatrix} \quad \text{or} \quad \begin{matrix} -x_1 + 2x_2 = 0 \\ 2x_1 - 4x_2 = 0 \end{matrix}$$

This gives $x_1 = 2x_2$. Again normalizing using $x_1^2 + x_2^2 = 1$ or $4x_2^2 + x_2^2 = 1$, we get $x_2 = 1/\sqrt{5}$, $x_1 = 2/\sqrt{5}$. Hence, the characteristic vector is $(2/\sqrt{5}, 1/\sqrt{5})$. Thus, we have the characteristic roots and vectors as

$$\lambda = 0 \Rightarrow \text{vector} \left(\frac{1}{\sqrt{5}}, \frac{-2}{\sqrt{5}} \right)$$

$$\lambda = 5 \Rightarrow \text{vector} \left(\frac{2}{\sqrt{5}}, \frac{1}{\sqrt{5}} \right)$$

Note that the two vectors are orthogonal. Returning to the 3×3 matrix we have the characteristic equation

$$\begin{vmatrix} 4-\lambda & 2 & 2 \\ 2 & 1-\lambda & 1 \\ 3 & -4 & 4-\lambda \end{vmatrix} = 0$$

This gives $\lambda(\lambda - 3)(\lambda - 6) = 0$. Thus $\lambda = 0$, 3, and 6 are the characteristic roots. To get the characteristic vectors, we solve the equation $(\mathbf{A} - \lambda \mathbf{I})\mathbf{x} = 0$. For $\lambda = 0$ we have

$$\begin{bmatrix} 4 & 2 & 2 \\ 2 & 1 & 1 \\ 3 & -4 & 4 \end{bmatrix} \begin{bmatrix} x_1 \\ x_2 \\ x_3 \end{bmatrix} = \begin{bmatrix} 0 \\ 0 \\ 0 \end{bmatrix}$$

We get the equations

$$2x_1 + x_2 + x_3 = 0$$

$$3x_1 - 4x_2 + 4x_3 = 0$$

This gives $x_2 = \frac{5}{8}x_1$ and $x_3 = -\frac{11}{8}x_1$ or $x_1 = 1$, $x_2 = \frac{5}{8}$, and $x_3 = -\frac{11}{8}$. We have to normalize this vector by taking $x_1^2 + x_2^2 + x_3^2 = 1$. This gives the normalized vector as

$$\mathbf{x} = \left(\frac{8}{\sqrt{210}}, \frac{5}{\sqrt{210}}, -\frac{11}{\sqrt{210}} \right)$$

For $\lambda = 3$ we solve

$$\begin{bmatrix} 4-3 & 2 & 2 \\ 2 & 1-3 & 1 \\ 3 & -4 & 4-3 \end{bmatrix} \begin{bmatrix} x_1 \\ x_2 \\ x_3 \end{bmatrix} = \begin{bmatrix} 0 \\ 0 \\ 0 \end{bmatrix}$$

We get

$$x_1 + 2x_2 + 2x_3 = 0$$

$$2x_1 - 2x_2 + x_3 = 0$$

$$3x_1 - 4x_2 + x_3 = 0$$

This gives $x_2 = \frac{1}{2}x_1$ and $x_3 = -x_1$. Taking $x_1 = 1$ and normalizing, we get the characteristic vector as $\mathbf{x}' = \left(\frac{2}{3}, \frac{1}{3}, -\frac{2}{3}\right)$. For $\lambda = 6$ we proceed similarly and get

$$\mathbf{x}' = \left(\frac{2}{\sqrt{6}}, \frac{1}{\sqrt{6}}, -\frac{1}{\sqrt{6}}\right)$$

The example we have considered is that of a singular matrix (the first row is twice the second row). Hence one of the characteristic roots is zero. The matrix is also *nonsymmetric*. In this case the characteristic vectors are *not* orthogonal to each other. In the case of a symmetric matrix, they are orthogonal (as proved later). As an example, consider the symmetric matrix

$$\mathbf{A} = \begin{bmatrix} 9 & 3 & 3 \\ 3 & 1 & 1 \\ 3 & 1 & 7 \end{bmatrix}$$

Using the previous procedure we get the characteristic roots as $\lambda = 0, 5$, and 12. The corresponding characteristic vectors are

$$\text{For } \lambda = 0: \quad \mathbf{x}_1' = \left(\frac{1}{\sqrt{10}}, -\frac{3}{\sqrt{10}}, 0\right)$$

$$\text{For } \lambda = 5: \quad \mathbf{x}_2' = \left(\frac{3}{\sqrt{35}}, \frac{1}{\sqrt{35}}, -\frac{5}{\sqrt{35}}\right)$$

$$\text{For } \lambda = 12: \quad \mathbf{x}_3' = \left(\frac{3}{\sqrt{14}}, \frac{1}{\sqrt{14}}, \frac{2}{\sqrt{14}}\right)$$

Note that these vectors are orthogonal to each other. That is, $\mathbf{x}_1'\mathbf{x}_2 = \mathbf{x}_1'\mathbf{x}_3 = \mathbf{x}_2'\mathbf{x}_3 = 0$.

Properties of Characteristic Roots and Vectors

Let $\lambda_1, \lambda_2, \ldots, \lambda_n$ be the n characteristic roots and $x_1, x_2, \ldots, x_n$ be the corresponding characteristic vectors of the matrix $\mathbf{A}$. We shall state some important properties of the characteristic roots and vectors.

1. The maximum value of $\mathbf{x}'\mathbf{A}\mathbf{x}$ is the maximum characteristic root.
   Proof: $\mathbf{x}_i'\mathbf{A}\mathbf{x}_i = \lambda_i\mathbf{x}_i'\mathbf{x}_i = \lambda_i$. Hence the result follows.
2. If λ_1 and λ_2 are two distinct characteristic roots, then $\mathbf{x}_1'\mathbf{x}_2 = 0$ or the corresponding characteristic vectors are orthogonal.
   Proof: $\mathbf{A}\mathbf{x}_1 = \lambda_1\mathbf{x}_1$. Hence $\mathbf{x}_2'\mathbf{A}\mathbf{x}_1 = \lambda_1\mathbf{x}_2'\mathbf{x}_1$. $\mathbf{A}\mathbf{x}_2 = \lambda_2\mathbf{x}_2$. Hence $\mathbf{x}_1'\mathbf{A}\mathbf{x}_2 = \lambda_2\mathbf{x}_1'\mathbf{x}_2$. By subtraction we get $0 = (\lambda_1 - \lambda_2)\mathbf{x}_1'\mathbf{x}_2$. But since $\lambda_1 \neq \lambda_2$ we have $\mathbf{x}_1'\mathbf{x}_2 = 0$.
3. $|\mathbf{A}| = \lambda_1\lambda_2\ldots\lambda_n$ and $\text{Tr}(\mathbf{A}) = \lambda_1 + \lambda_2 + \cdots + \lambda_n$.
   Proof: Let $\mathbf{X}$ be the matrix whose columns are the characteristic vectors of $\mathbf{A}$. That is, $\mathbf{X} = [\mathbf{x}_1, \mathbf{x}_2, \ldots, \mathbf{x}_n]$. If the λ_i are all distinct, the columns of $\mathbf{X}$ are orthogonal. Also, $\mathbf{x}_i'\mathbf{x}_i = 1$ for all i. Thus $\mathbf{X}$ is an orthogonal matrix. Hence $\mathbf{X}^{-1} = \mathbf{X}'$ (see the appendix to Chapter 2) and $\mathbf{X}'\mathbf{X} = \mathbf{I}$. Now $\mathbf{A}(\mathbf{x}_1, \mathbf{x}_2, \ldots, \mathbf{x}_n) = (\lambda_1\mathbf{x}_1, \lambda_2\mathbf{x}_2, \ldots, \lambda_n\mathbf{x}_n)$

or $\mathbf{AX} = \mathbf{XD}$, where $\mathbf{D}$ is the diagonal matrix

$$
\begin{bmatrix}
\lambda_1 & & & \\
& \lambda_2 & & \\
& & \ddots & \\
& & & \lambda_n
\end{bmatrix}
$$

with all nondiagonal terms zero. Therefore, $\mathbf{X'AX} = \mathbf{X'XD} = \mathbf{D}$. $|\mathbf{X'AX}| = |\mathbf{D}|$ or $|\mathbf{X'}| \cdot |\mathbf{A}| \cdot |\mathbf{X}| = \lambda_1 \lambda_2 \dots \lambda_n$. But since $\mathbf{X}$ is an orthogonal matrix, $|\mathbf{X'}| \cdot |\mathbf{X}| = 1$. Hence we get $|\mathbf{A}| = \lambda_1 \lambda_2 \dots \lambda_n$. Also, $\mathrm{Tr}(\mathbf{D}) = \lambda_1 + \lambda_2 + \dots + \lambda_n$ and $\mathrm{Tr}(\mathbf{X'AX}) = \mathrm{Tr}(\mathbf{AXX'}) = \mathrm{Tr}(\mathbf{A})$ since $\mathbf{XX'} = \mathbf{I}$. Hence $\mathrm{Tr}(\mathbf{A}) = \lambda_1 + \lambda_2 + \dots + \lambda_n$.

Note: Although we have proved the results above for distinct roots, the results are valid for even repeated roots. That is, given a symmetric matrix $\mathbf{A}$, there exists an orthogonal matrix $\mathbf{X}$ (whose columns are the characteristic vectors of $\mathbf{A}$) such that $\mathbf{X'AX} = \mathbf{D}$, where $\mathbf{D}$ is a diagonal matrix whose elements are the characteristic roots of $\mathbf{A}$.

4. $\mathrm{Rank}(\mathbf{A}) = \mathrm{rank}(\mathbf{D}) =$ the number of nonzero characteristic roots of $\mathbf{A}$.

   Proof: Since rank is unaltered by pre- or postmultiplication by a nonsingular matrix, $\mathrm{rank}(\mathbf{A}) = \mathrm{rank}(\mathbf{X'AX}) = \mathrm{rank}(\mathbf{D})$.

5. The characteristic roots of $\mathbf{A}^2$ are the squares of the characteristic roots of $\mathbf{A}$, but the characteristic vectors are the same.

   Proof: $\mathbf{X'AX} = \mathbf{D}$ or $\mathbf{A} = \mathbf{XDX'}$. $\mathbf{A}^2 = (\mathbf{XDX'})(\mathbf{XDX'}) = \mathbf{XD}^2\mathbf{X'}$ since $\mathbf{X'X} = \mathbf{I}$. Thus the characteristic roots are given by the diagonal elements of $\mathbf{D}^2$ (i.e., λ_i^2) and the characteristic vectors are given by the columns of $\mathbf{X}$.

6. If $\mathbf{A}$ is a positive definite matrix, all the characteristic roots are positive.

   Proof: Consider $\mathbf{Ax}_j = \lambda_j \mathbf{x}_j$. $\mathbf{x}_j'\mathbf{Ax}_j > 0$ if $\mathbf{A}$ is positive definite. Since $\mathbf{x}_j'\mathbf{x}_j = 1$, we have $\lambda_j > 0$. By a similar argument we can show that if $\mathbf{A}$ is positive semidefinite, $\lambda_j \geq 0$. If $\mathbf{A}$ is negative definite, $\lambda_j < 0$ for all j. If $\mathbf{A}$ is negative semidefinite, $\lambda_j \leq 0$ for all j. Note that for the symmetric matrix we considered earlier, the roots were 0, 5, and 12. Thus it is positive semidefinite.

The Case of a Nonsymmetric Matrix

The preceding results are for symmetric matrices. In econometrics we encounter nonsymmetric matrices as well (the case of VAR models in Chapter 14). For these matrices the characteristic vectors are not orthogonal, as we saw earlier. However, some of the other results are still valid. For example, the result sum of the characteristic roots of $\mathbf{A} = \mathrm{Tr}(\mathbf{A})$ is valid.

Consider the equations $\mathbf{Ax}_1 = \lambda_1 \mathbf{x}_1$, $\mathbf{Ax}_2 = \lambda_2 \mathbf{x}_2$, and so on, which we solve to get the characteristic vectors $\mathbf{x}_1, \mathbf{x}_2, \dots$. We can write these as

$$
\mathbf{A}(\mathbf{x}_1 \mathbf{x}_2 \dots \mathbf{x}_n) = (\lambda_1 \mathbf{x}_1, \lambda_2 \mathbf{x}_2, \dots, \lambda_n \mathbf{x}_n) \Rightarrow \mathbf{AX} = \mathbf{XD}
$$

where $\mathbf{X}$ is the matrix whose columns are the characteristic vectors and $\mathbf{D}$ is a diagonal matrix with $\lambda_1, \lambda_2, \dots, \lambda_n$ as the diagonal elements. Premultiplying both sides by $\mathbf{X}^{-1}$, we get

$$
\mathbf{X}^{-1}\mathbf{AX} = \mathbf{D}
$$

(We have assumed that $\mathbf{X}$ is nonsingular. This can be proved, but we omit the proof here.) Thus given a square matrix $\mathbf{A}$, we can find a nonsingular matrix $\mathbf{X}$ such that $\mathbf{X}'\mathbf{A}\mathbf{X}$ is a diagonal matrix with the characteristic roots of $\mathbf{A}$ as the diagonal elements. The columns of $\mathbf{X}$ are the corresponding characteristic vectors. Also, $\mathrm{Tr}(\mathbf{X}^{-1}\mathbf{A}\mathbf{X}) = \mathrm{Tr}(\mathbf{D}) = \sum_{i=1}^{n} \lambda_i$. But $\mathrm{Tr}(\mathbf{X}^{-1}\mathbf{A}\mathbf{X}) = \mathrm{Tr}(\mathbf{A}\mathbf{X}\mathbf{X}^{-1}) = \mathrm{Tr}(\mathbf{A})$. Hence $\mathrm{Tr}(\mathbf{A}) = \sum \lambda_i$. This can be checked with the two examples considered earlier. In the case of the nonsymmetric matrix, $\sum \lambda_i = 9$ and $\mathrm{Tr}(\mathbf{A}) = 9$. In the case of the symmetric matrix, $\sum \lambda_i = 17$ and $\mathrm{Tr}(\mathbf{A}) = 17$.

Principal Components

Consider a set of variables $x_1, x_2, \ldots, x_n$ with covariance matrix $\mathbf{V}$. We want to find a linear function $\boldsymbol{\alpha}'\mathbf{x}$ that has maximum variance subject to $\boldsymbol{\alpha}'\boldsymbol{\alpha} = 1$. The problem is similar to the one we considered earlier. We have to solve $|\mathbf{V} - \lambda\mathbf{I}| = 0$. The maximum characteristic root of $\mathbf{V}$ is the required maximum value and the corresponding characteristic vector is the required $\boldsymbol{\alpha}$.

Let us order the characteristic roots $\lambda_1, \lambda_2, \ldots, \lambda_n$ in decreasing order; let the corresponding vectors be $\mathbf{x}_1, \mathbf{x}_2, \ldots, \mathbf{x}_n$. Consider the linear functions $\mathbf{z}_1 = \boldsymbol{\alpha}_1'\mathbf{X}$, $\mathbf{z}_2 = \boldsymbol{\alpha}_2'\mathbf{X}, \ldots, \mathbf{z}_n = \boldsymbol{\alpha}_n'\mathbf{X}$. Then $\mathbf{V}(\mathbf{z}_1) = \boldsymbol{\alpha}_1'\mathbf{V}\boldsymbol{\alpha}_1 = \lambda_1$, $\mathbf{V}(\mathbf{z}_2) = \lambda_2, \ldots$. The $\mathbf{z}$'s are called the principal components of the $\mathbf{x}$'s.

They have the following properties:

1. $\mathrm{var}(\mathbf{z}_1) + \mathrm{var}(\mathbf{z}_2) + \cdots + \mathrm{var}(\mathbf{z}_n) = \lambda_1 + \lambda_2 + \cdots + \lambda_n = \mathrm{Tr}(\mathbf{V}) = \mathrm{var}(\mathbf{x}_1) + \mathrm{var}(\mathbf{x}_2) + \cdots + \mathrm{var}(\mathbf{x}_n)$.
2. Since $(\boldsymbol{\alpha}_1 \boldsymbol{\alpha}_2 \ldots \boldsymbol{\alpha}_n)$ are orthogonal vectors, $\mathbf{z}_1, \mathbf{z}_2, \ldots, \mathbf{z}_n$ are orthogonal or uncorrelated. The drawbacks of principal component analysis have been discussed in the text.

Ridge Regression

If $(\mathbf{X}'\mathbf{X})$ is close to singularity, the problem can be solved by adding positive elements to the diagonals. The simple ridge estimator is

$$\hat{\boldsymbol{\beta}}_R = (\mathbf{X}'\mathbf{X}' + \lambda\mathbf{I})^{-1}\mathbf{X}'\mathbf{y}$$

There are several interpretations of this estimator (discussed in the text). One is to obtain the least squares estimator when $\sum \beta_i^2 = c$. Introducing the Lagrangian multiplier λ, we minimize

$$(\mathbf{y} - \mathbf{X}\boldsymbol{\beta})'(\mathbf{y} - \mathbf{X}\boldsymbol{\beta}) + \lambda(\boldsymbol{\beta}'\boldsymbol{\beta} - c)$$

Differentiating with respect to $\boldsymbol{\beta}$, we get

$$-2\mathbf{X}'\mathbf{y} + 2\mathbf{X}'\mathbf{X}\boldsymbol{\beta} + 2\lambda\boldsymbol{\beta} = 0 \qquad \text{or} \qquad (\mathbf{X}'\mathbf{X} + \lambda\mathbf{I})\boldsymbol{\beta} = \mathbf{X}'\mathbf{y}$$

This gives the ridge estimator. λ is the Lagrangian multiplier or the "shadow price" of the constraint.

8 Dummy Variables and Truncated Variables

What is in this Chapter?

This chapter relaxes the assumption made in Chapter 4 that the variables in the regression are observed as continuous variables.

First we start with dummy explanatory variables and show their use in taking account of differences in intercepts and/or slope coefficients, estimation of equations with cross-equation restrictions and tests for stability of regression coefficients. The dummy variable method is useful in computing predicted and studentized residuals (Chapter 12) and the fixed effects model in panel data analysis (Chapter 15).

We next turn to dummy dependent variable models: the linear probability model and the logit and probit models. These are very often used in econometric applications where the explained variable is observed as a qualitative variable (e.g., employed or unemployed).

Finally we discuss models with truncated variables. We explain the difference between the censored regression model (the tobit model) and the truncated regression model and discuss limitations of the tobit model, very often used in empirical applications.

> *Let us remember the unfortunate econometrician who, in one of the major functions of his system, had to use a proxy for risk and a dummy for sex.*
>
> Fritz Machlup
> Journal of Political Economy
> *July/August 1974*

8.1 Introduction

In the preceding chapters we discussed the estimation of multiple regression equations and several associated problems such as tests of significance, R^2, heteroskedasticity, autocorrelation, and multicollinearity. In this chapter we discuss some special kinds of variables occurring in multiple regression equations and the problems caused by them. The variables we will be considering are:

1. Dummy variables.
2. Truncated variables.

We start with dummy explanatory variables and then discuss dummy dependent variables and truncated variables. Proxy variables referred to in Machlup's quotation are discussed in Chapter 11.

Dummy explanatory variables can be used for several purposes. They can be used to

1. Allow for differences in intercept terms.
2. Allow for differences in slopes.
3. Estimate equations with cross-equation restrictions.
4. Test for stability of regression coefficients.

We discuss each of these uses in turn.

8.2 Dummy Variables for Changes in the Intercept Term

Sometimes there will be some explanatory variables in our regression equation that are only qualitative (e.g., presence or absence of college education and racial, sex, or age differences). In such cases one often takes account of these effects by a dummy variable. The implicit assumption is that the regression lines for the different groups differ only in the intercept term but have the same slope coefficients. For example, suppose that the relationship between income y and years of schooling x for two groups is as shown in Figure 8.1. The dots are for group 1 and circles for group 2.

Note that the slopes of the regression lines for both groups are roughly the same but the intercepts are different. Hence the regression equations we fit will be

$$y = \begin{cases} \alpha_1 + \beta x + u & \text{for the first group} \\ \alpha_2 + \beta x + u & \text{for the second group} \end{cases} \qquad (8.1)$$

These equations can be combined into a single equation

$$y = \alpha_1 + (\alpha_2 - \alpha_1)D + \beta x + u \qquad (8.2)$$

where

$$D = \begin{cases} 1 & \text{for group 2} \\ 0 & \text{for group 1} \end{cases}$$

The variable D is the dummy variable. The coefficient of the dummy variable measures the differences in the two intercept terms.

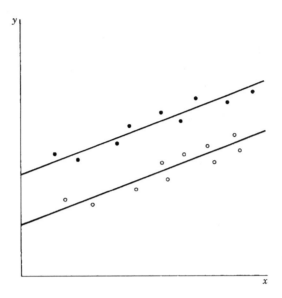

Figure 8.1 Regression lines with a common slope and different intercepts

If there are more groups, we have to introduce more dummies. For three groups we have

$$y = \begin{cases} \alpha_1 + \beta x + u & \text{for group 1} \\ \alpha_2 + \beta x + u & \text{for group 2} \\ \alpha_3 + \beta x + u & \text{for group 3} \end{cases}$$

These can be written as

$$y = \alpha_1 + (\alpha_2 - \alpha_1)D_1 + (\alpha_3 - \alpha_1)D_2 + \beta x + u \tag{8.3}$$

where

$$D_1 = \begin{cases} 1 & \text{for group 2} \\ 0 & \text{for groups 1 and 3} \end{cases}$$

$$D_2 = \begin{cases} 1 & \text{for group 3} \\ 0 & \text{for groups 1 and 2} \end{cases}$$

It can be easily checked that by substituting the values for D_1 and D_2 in equation (8.3), we get the intercepts $\alpha_1, \alpha_2, \alpha_3$, respectively for the three groups. Note that in combining the three equations, we are assuming that the slope coefficient β is the same for all groups *and* that the error term u has the same distribution for the three groups.

If there is a constant term in the regression equation, the number of dummies defined should always be one less than the number of groupings by that category because the constant term is the intercept for the base group and the coefficients of the dummy variables measure differences in intercepts, as can be seen from equation (8.3). In that equation the constant term measures the intercept for the first group, the constant term plus the coefficient of D_1 measures the intercept for the second group, and the constant term plus the coefficient of D_2 measures the intercept for the third group. We have chosen group 1 as the base group, but any one group may be chosen. The coefficients of the dummy variables measure the differences in the intercepts from that of the base group. If we do not introduce a constant term in the regression equation, we can define a dummy variable for each group, and in this case the coefficients of the dummy variables measure the intercepts for the respective groups. If we include both the constant term and three dummies, we will be introducing perfect multicollinearity and the regression program will not run (or will omit one of the dummies automatically).

As yet another example, suppose that we have data on consumption C and income Y for a number of households. In addition, we have data on

1. S: the sex of the head of the household.
2. A: the age of the head of the household, which is given in three categories, < 25 years, 25 to 50 years, and > 50 years.
3. E: the education of the head of the household, also in three categories, $<$ high school, $\geq$ high school but $<$ college degree, $\geq$ college degree.

We include these qualitative variables in the form of dummy variables

$$D_1 = \begin{cases} 1 & \text{if sex is male} \\ 0 & \text{if female} \end{cases}$$

$$D_2 = \begin{cases} 1 & \text{if age } <25 \text{ years} \\ 0 & \text{otherwise} \end{cases}$$

$$D_3 = \begin{cases} 1 & \text{if age between 25 and 50 year} \\ 0 & \text{otherwise} \end{cases}$$

$$D_4 = \begin{cases} 1 & \text{if } < \text{ high school} \\ 0 & \text{otherwise} \end{cases}$$

$$D_5 = \begin{cases} 1 & \text{if } \geq \text{ high school but } < \text{ college degree} \\ 0 & \text{otherwise} \end{cases}$$

For each category the number of dummy variables is one less than the number of classifications.

Then we run the regression equation

$$C = \alpha + \beta Y + \gamma_1 D_1 + \gamma_2 D_2 + \gamma_3 D_3 + \gamma_4 D_4 + \gamma_5 D_5 + u$$

The assumption made in the dummy variable method is that it is only the intercept that changes for each group but not the slope coefficients (i.e., coefficients of Y).

The intercept term for each individual is obtained by substituting the appropriate values for D_1 through D_5. For instance, for a male, age < 25, with a college degree, we have $D_1 = 1$, $D_2 = 1$, $D_3 = 0$, $D_4 = 0$, $D_5 = 0$ and hence the intercept is $\alpha + \gamma_1 + \gamma_2$. For a female, age > 50, with a college degree, we have $D_1 = 0$, $D_2 = 0$, $D_3 = 0$, $D_4 = 0$, $D_5 = 0$ and hence the intercept term is just α.

The dummy variable method is also used if one has to take care of seasonal factors. For example, if we have quarterly data on C and Y, we fit the regression equation

$$C = \alpha + \beta Y + \lambda_1 D_1 + \lambda_2 D_2 + \lambda_3 D_3 + u$$

where $D_1, D_2,$ and D_3 are seasonal dummies defined by

$$D_1 = \begin{cases} 1 & \text{for the first quarter} \\ 0 & \text{for others} \end{cases}$$

$$D_2 = \begin{cases} 1 & \text{for the second quarter} \\ 0 & \text{for others} \end{cases}$$

$$D_3 = \begin{cases} 1 & \text{for the third quarter} \\ 0 & \text{for others} \end{cases}$$

If we have monthly data, we use 11 seasonal dummies

$$D_1 = \begin{cases} 1 & \text{for January} \\ 0 & \text{for others} \end{cases}$$

$$D_2 = \begin{cases} 1 & \text{for February} \\ 0 & \text{for others} \end{cases} \quad \text{etc.}$$

If we feel that, say, December (because of Christmas shopping) is the only month with strong seasonal effect, we use only one dummy variable

$$D = \begin{cases} 1 & \text{for December} \\ 0 & \text{for other months} \end{cases}$$

Illustrative Example

The Environmental Protection Agency (EPA) publishes auto mileage estimates that are designed to help car buyers compare the relative fuel efficiency of different models. Does the EPA estimate provide all the information necessary for comparing the relative fuel efficiency of the different models? To investigate this problem Lovell[1] estimated the following regressions (figures in parentheses are standard errors):

$$\hat{y} = 7.952 + 0.693\text{EPA} \qquad \bar{R}^2 = 0.74$$
$$\underset{(1.735)}{} \quad \underset{(0.061)}{}$$

$$\hat{y} = 22.008 - 0.002W - 2.760S/A + 3.280G/D + 0.415\text{EPA} \qquad \bar{R}^2 = 0.82$$
$$\underset{(5.349)}{} \quad \underset{(0.001)}{} \quad \underset{(0.708)}{} \quad \underset{(1.413)}{} \quad \underset{(0.097)}{}$$

where
$y =$ miles per gallon as reported by Consumer Union based on road tests
$W =$ weight of the vehicle (pounds)
$S/A =$ dummy variable equal to 0 for standard transmission and 1.0 for automatic transmission
$G/D =$ dummy variable equal to 0 for gas and 1.0 for diesel power
$\text{EPA} =$ mileage estimate by the EPA

The variables $W, S/A, G/D$ all have correct signs and are significant, showing that the EPA did not use all the information available in giving its estimates on fuel efficiency.

---

[1]M. C. Lovell, "Tests of the Rational Expectations Hypothesis," *The American Economic Review*, March 1986, p. 120.

Two More Illustrative Examples

We will discuss two more examples using dummy variables. They are meant to illustrate two points worth noting, which are as follows:

1. In some studies with a large number of dummy variables it becomes somewhat difficult to interpret the signs of the coefficients because they seem to have the wrong signs. The first example illustrates this problem.
2. Sometimes the introduction of dummy variables produces a drastic change in the slope coefficient. The second example illustrates this point.

The examples are rather old and outdated but they establish the points we wish to make.

The first example is a study of the determinants of automobile prices. Griliches[2] regressed the logarithm of new passenger car prices on various specifications. The results are shown in Table 8.1. Since the dependent variable is the logarithm of price, the regression coefficients can be interpreted as the estimated percentage change in the price for a unit change in a particular quality, *holding other qualities constant*. For example, the coefficient of H indicates that an increase in 10 units of horsepower, *ceteris paribus*, results in a 1.2% increase in price. However, some of the coefficients have to be interpreted with caution. For example, the coefficient of P in the equation for 1960 says that the presence of power steering as "standard equipment" led to a 22.5% higher price in 1960. In this case the variable P is obviously not measuring the effect of power steering alone but is measuring the effect of "luxuriousness" of the car. It is also picking up the effects of A and B. This explains why the coefficient of A is so low in 1960. In fact, A, P, and B together can perhaps be replaced by a single dummy that measures "luxuriousness." These variables appear to be highly intercorrelated. Another coefficient, at first sight puzzling, is the coefficient of V, which, though not significant, is consistently negative. Though a V-8 costs more than a six-cylinder engine on a "comparable" car, what this coefficient says is that, holding horsepower and other variables constant, a V-8 is cheaper by about 4%. Since the V-8's have higher horsepower, what this coefficient is saying is that higher horsepower can be achieved more cheaply if one shifts to V-8 than by using the six-cylinder engine. It measures the decline in price per horsepower as one shifts to V-8's even though the total expenditure on horsepower goes up. This example illustrates the use of dummy variables and the interpretation of seemingly wrong coefficients.

As another example consider the estimates of liquid-asset demand by manufacturing corporations. Vogel and Maddala[3] computed regressions of the form $\log C = \alpha + \beta \log S$, where C is the cash and S the sales, on the basis of data from the Internal Revenue Service, "Statistics of Income," for the year 1960–1961. The data consisted of 16 industry subgroups and 14 size classes, size being measured by total assets. When the regression

---

[2]Z. Griliches, "Hedonic Price Indexes for Automobiles: An Econometric Analysis of Quality Change," *Government Price Statistics*, Hearings, U.S. Congress, Joint Economic Committee (Washington, DC: U.S. Government Printing Office, 1961). Further results on this problem can be found in M. Ohta and Z. Griliches, "Automobile Prices Revisited: Extensions of the Hedonic Hypothesis," in N. Terleckyj (ed.), *Household Behavior and Consumption* (New York: National Bureau of Economic Research, 1975).

[3]R. C. Vogel and G. S. Maddala, "Cross-Section Estimates of Liquid Asset Demand by Manufacturing Corporations," *The Journal of Finance*, December 1967.

Table 8.1 Determinants of prices of automobiles[a]

Coefficient of:[b]	1960	1959	1957
H	0.119 (0.029)	0.118 (0.029)	0.117 (0.030)
W	0.136 (0.046)	0.238 (0.034)	0.135 (0.010)
L	0.015 (0.017)	−0.016 (0.015)	0.039 (0.013)
V	−0.039 (0.025)	−0.070 (0.039)	−0.025 (0.023)
T	0.058 (0.016)	0.027 (0.019)	0.028 (0.012)
A	0.003 (0.040)	0.063 (0.038)	0.114 (0.025)
P	0.225 (0.037)	0.188 (0.041)	0.078 (0.030)
B			0.159 (0.026)
C	0.048 (0.039)		
R^2	0.951	0.934	0.966

[a]Figures in parentheses are standard errors.
[b]H, advertised brake horsepower (hundreds); W, shipping weight (thousands of pounds); L, overall length (tens of inches); V, 1 if the car has a V-8 engine, 0 if it has a six-cylinder engine; T, 1 if the car is hard top, 0 if not; A, 1 if automatic transmission is "standard" (i.e., included in price), 0 if not; P, 1 if power steering is "standard," 0 if not; B, 1 if power brakes are "standard," 0 if not; C, 1 if car is designated as a "compact," 0 if not.

equations were estimated separately for each industry, the estimates of β ranged from 0.929 to 1.077. The R^2's were uniformly high, ranging from 0.985 to 0.998. Thus one might conclude that the sales elasticity of demand for cash is close to 1. Also, when the data were pooled and a single equation estimated for the entire set of 224 observations, the estimate of β was 0.992 and $R^2 = 0.897$. When industry dummies were added, the estimate of β was 0.995 and $R^2 = 0.992$. From the high R^2's and relatively constant estimate of β one might be reassured that the sales elasticity is very close to 1. However, when asset-size dummies were introduced, the estimate of β fell to 0.334 with R^2 of 0.996. Also, all asset-size dummies were highly significant. The situation is described in Figure 8.2. That the sales elasticity is significantly less than 1 is also confirmed by other evidence. This example illustrates how one can be very easily misled by high R^2's and apparent constancy of the coefficients.

8.3 Dummy Variables for Changes in Slope Coefficients

In Section 8.2 we considered dummy variables to allow for differences in the intercept term. These dummy variables assume the values zero or 1. Not all dummy variables are

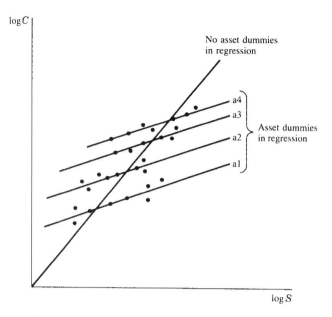

Figure 8.2   Bias due to omission of dummy variables

of this form. We can use dummy variables to allow for differences in slope coefficients as well. For example, if the regression equations are

$$y_1 = \alpha_1 + \beta_1 x_1 + u_1 \qquad \text{for the first group}$$

and

$$y_2 = \alpha_2 + \beta_2 x_2 + u_2 \qquad \text{for the second group}$$

we can write these equations together as

$$y_1 = \alpha_1 + (\alpha_2 - \alpha_1) \cdot 0 + \beta_1 x_1 + (\beta_2 - \beta_1) \cdot 0 + u_1$$
$$y_2 = \alpha_1 + (\alpha_2 - \alpha_1) \cdot 1 + \beta_1 x_2 + (\beta_2 - \beta_1) \cdot x_2 + u_2$$

or

$$y = \alpha_1 + (\alpha_2 - \alpha_1)D_1 + \beta_1 x + (\beta_2 - \beta_1)D_2 + u \qquad (8.4)$$

where $D_1 = \begin{cases} 0 & \text{for all observations in the first group} \\ 1 & \text{for all observations in the second group} \end{cases}$

$\quad\quad\ D_2 = \begin{cases} 0 & \text{for all observations in the first group} \\ x_2 & \text{i.e., the respective value of } x \text{ for the second group} \end{cases}$

The coefficient of D_1 measures the difference in the intercept terms and the coefficient of D_2 measures the difference in the slope. Estimation of equation (8.4) amounts to estimating the two equations separately if we assume that the errors have an identical distribution. If we delete D_2 from equation (8.4), this amounts to allowing for different intercepts but not different slopes, and if we delete D_1, it amounts to allowing for different slopes but not different intercepts.

Suitable dummy variables can be defined when there are changes in slopes and intercepts at different times. Suppose that we have data for three periods and in the second period only the intercept changed (there was a parallel shift). In the third period the intercept and the slope changed. Then we write

$$y_1 = \alpha_1 + \beta_1 x_1 + u_1 \qquad \text{for period 1}$$
$$y_2 = \alpha_2 + \beta_1 x_2 + u_2 \qquad \text{for period 2} \qquad (8.5)$$
$$y_3 = \alpha_3 + \beta_2 x_3 + u_3 \qquad \text{for period 3}$$

Then we can combine these equations and write the model as

$$y = \alpha_1 + (\alpha_2 - \alpha_1)D_1 + (\alpha_3 - \alpha_1)D_2 + \beta_1 x + (\beta_2 - \beta_1)D_3 + u \qquad (8.6)$$

where $D_1 = \begin{cases} 1 & \text{for observations in period 2} \\ 0 & \text{for other periods} \end{cases}$

$D_2 = \begin{cases} 1 & \text{for observations in period 3} \\ 0 & \text{for other periods} \end{cases}$

$D_3 = \begin{cases} 0 & \text{for observations in periods 1 and 2} \\ x_3 & \text{or the respective value of } x \text{ for} \\ & \text{all observations in period 3} \end{cases}$

Note that in all these examples we are assuming that the error terms in the different groups all have the same distribution. That is why we combine the data from the different groups and write an error term u as in (8.4) or (8.6) and estimate the equation by least squares.

An alternative way of writing the equations (8.5), which is very general, is to stack the y variables and the error terms in columns. Then write all the parameters α_1, α_2, α_3, β_1, β_2 down with their multiplicative factors stacked in columns as follows:

$$\begin{pmatrix} y_1 \\ y_2 \\ y_3 \end{pmatrix} = \alpha_1 \begin{pmatrix} 1 \\ 0 \\ 0 \end{pmatrix} + \alpha_2 \begin{pmatrix} 0 \\ 1 \\ 0 \end{pmatrix} + \alpha_3 \begin{pmatrix} 0 \\ 0 \\ 1 \end{pmatrix} + \beta_1 \begin{pmatrix} x_1 \\ x_2 \\ 0 \end{pmatrix} + \beta_2 \begin{pmatrix} 0 \\ 0 \\ x_3 \end{pmatrix} + \begin{pmatrix} u_1 \\ u_2 \\ u_3 \end{pmatrix} \qquad (8.7)$$

What this says is

$$y_1 = \alpha_1(1) + \alpha_2(0) + \alpha_3(0) + \beta_1(x_1) + \beta_2(0) + u_1$$
$$y_2 = \alpha_1(0) + \alpha_2(1) + \alpha_3(0) + \beta_1(x_2) + \beta_2(0) + u_2$$
$$y_3 = \alpha_1(0) + \alpha_2(0) + \alpha_3(1) + \beta_1(0) + \beta_2(x_3) + u_3$$

where ( ) is used for multiplication, e.g., $\alpha_3(0) = \alpha_3 \times 0$.

Now we can write these equations as

$$y = \alpha_1 D_1 + \alpha_2 D_2 + \alpha_3 D_3 + \beta_1 D_4 + \beta_2 D_5 + u \tag{8.8}$$

where the definitions of D_1, D_2, D_3, D_4, D_5 are clear from equation (8.7). For instance,

$$D_2 = \begin{cases} 1 & \text{for observations in period 2} \\ 0 & \text{for other periods} \end{cases}$$

$$D_4 = \begin{cases} x_i & \text{corresponding values of } x \text{ for observations in periods 1 and 2} \\ 0 & \text{for all observations in period 3} \end{cases}$$

Note that equation (8.8) has to be estimated without a constant term.

In this method we define as many dummy variables as there are parameters to estimate and we estimate the regression equation with no constant term. We will give an illustrative example in the next section, where this method is extended to take care of cross-equation constraints.

Note that equations (8.6) and (8.8) are equivalent. The method of writing the equation in terms of differences in the parameters is useful in tests for stability discussed in Section 8.5.

8.4 Dummy Variables for Cross-Equation Constraints

The method described in Section 8.3 can be extended to the case where some parameters across equations are equal. As an illustration, consider the joint estimation of the demand for beef, pork, and chicken on the basis of data presented in Table 8.2.[4] Waugh estimates a set of demand equations of the form

$$p_1 = \alpha_1 + \beta_{11}x_1 + \beta_{12}x_2 + \beta_{13}x_3 + \gamma_1 y + u_1$$
$$p_2 = \alpha_2 + \beta_{12}x_1 + \beta_{22}x_2 + \beta_{23}x_3 + \gamma_2 y + u_2 \tag{8.9}$$
$$p_3 = \alpha_3 + \beta_{13}x_1 + \beta_{23}x_2 + \beta_{33}x_3 + \gamma_3 y + u_3$$

where
$p_1 =$ retail price of beef
$p_2 =$ retail price of pork
$p_3 =$ retail price of chicken
$x_1 =$ consumption of beef per capita
$x_2 =$ consumption of pork per capita
$x_3 =$ consumption of chicken per capita
$y =$ disposable income per capita

x_1, x_2, and x_3 are given in Table 8.2. The prices in Table 8.2 are, however, retail prices divided by a consumer price index. Hence we multiplied them by the consumer

---

[4]The data are from F. V. Waugh, *Demand and Price Analysis: Some Examples from Agriculture*, U.S.D.A. Technical Bulletin 1316, November 1964, Table 5-1, p. 39.

Table 8.2 Per capita consumption and deflated prices of selected meats, 1948–1963

Year	Beef Consumption per Capita[a] (lb)	Beef Price per Pound[b] (cents)	Pork Consumption per Capita[a] (lb)	Pork Price per Pound[b] (cents)	Lamb Consumption per Capita[a] (lb)	Lamb Price per Pound[b] (cents)	Veal Consumption per Capita[a] (lb)	Veal Price per Pound[b] (cents)	Chicken Consumption per Capita[a] (lb)	Chicken Price per Pound[b] (cents)
1948	63.1	82.9	67.8	67.6	5.1	77.8	9.5	77.1	18.3	75.4
1949	63.9	76.3	67.7	61.5	4.1	82.4	8.9	75.7	19.6	71.8
1950	63.4	88.3	69.2	60.4	4.0	84.2	8.0	81.1	20.6	68.0
1951	56.1	90.0	71.9	60.6	3.4	86.7	6.6	87.6	21.7	66.0
1952	62.2	85.4	72.4	57.3	4.2	86.2	7.2	86.3	22.1	65.0
1953	77.6	66.2	63.5	62.9	4.7	70.0	9.5	68.7	21.9	62.8
1954	80.1	64.1	60.0	63.7	4.6	71.0	10.0	65.8	22.8	56.4
1955	82.0	63.2	66.8	54.6	4.6	69.0	9.4	65.8	21.3	58.7
1956	85.4	60.9	67.3	51.4	4.5	68.3	9.5	63.6	24.4	50.4
1957	84.6	63.1	61.1	57.6	4.2	69.9	8.8	65.5	25.5	47.6
1958	80.5	72.0	60.2	60.5	4.2	74.1	6.7	76.1	28.2	45.8
1959	81.4	73.3	67.6	52.8	4.8	69.6	5.7	79.8	28.9	41.4
1960	85.2	70.4	65.2	51.6	4.8	67.6	6.2	77.8	28.2	41.4
1961	88.0	68.3	62.2	53.3	5.1	63.3	5.7	77.3	30.3	37.0
1962	89.1	69.8	64.0	52.9	5.1	67.1	5.5	79.5	30.2	38.6
1963[c]	95.2	67.8	64.9	50.5	4.9	68.0	5.0	79.2	30.6	37.6

[a]Carcass weight equivalent.
[b]Divided by consumer price index (1957–1959 = 100).
[c]1963 data are preliminary and were not used in the analysis.

price index p to get p_1, p_2, p_3. This index p and disposable income y are as follows:

	p	y		p	y		p	y
1948	0.838	1291	1953	0.932	1582	1958	1.007	1826
1949	0.830	1271	1954	0.936	1582	1959	1.015	1904
1950	0.838	1369	1955	0.934	1660	1960	1.031	1934
1951	0.906	1473	1956	0.947	1742	1961	1.041	1980
1952	0.925	1520	1957	0.981	1804	1962	1.054	2052

The special thing about the system of equations (8.9) is the symmetry in the β coefficients. We have

$$\frac{dp_1}{dx_2} = \frac{dp_2}{dx_1} = \beta_{12} \qquad \frac{dp_1}{dx_3} = \frac{dp_3}{dx_1} = \beta_{13} \qquad \frac{dp_2}{dx_3} = \frac{dp_3}{dx_2} = \beta_{23}$$

Thus there are cross-equation restrictions on the coefficients. If we assume that $V(u_1) = V(u_2) = V(u_3)$, we can minimize $(\sum u_1^2 + \sum u_2^2 + \sum u_3^2)$, obtain the normal equations, and estimate the regression coefficients. This is the method used by Waugh. This method involves working out the necessary algebraic expressions and programming things afresh. Instead, we can use the standard regression programs by using the dummy variable method. We can write equations (8.9) as a single equation

$$\begin{pmatrix} p_1 \\ p_2 \\ p_3 \end{pmatrix} = \alpha_1 \begin{pmatrix} 1 \\ 0 \\ 0 \end{pmatrix} + \alpha_2 \begin{pmatrix} 0 \\ 1 \\ 0 \end{pmatrix} + \alpha_3 \begin{pmatrix} 0 \\ 0 \\ 1 \end{pmatrix} + \beta_{11} \begin{pmatrix} x_1 \\ 0 \\ 0 \end{pmatrix} + \beta_{12} \begin{pmatrix} x_2 \\ x_1 \\ 0 \end{pmatrix}$$

$$+ \beta_{13} \begin{pmatrix} x_3 \\ 0 \\ x_1 \end{pmatrix} + \beta_{22} \begin{pmatrix} 0 \\ x_2 \\ 0 \end{pmatrix} + \beta_{23} \begin{pmatrix} 0 \\ x_3 \\ x_2 \end{pmatrix} + \beta_{33} \begin{pmatrix} 0 \\ 0 \\ x_3 \end{pmatrix}$$

$$+ \gamma_1 \begin{pmatrix} y \\ 0 \\ 0 \end{pmatrix} + \gamma_2 \begin{pmatrix} 0 \\ y \\ 0 \end{pmatrix} + \gamma_3 \begin{pmatrix} 0 \\ 0 \\ y \end{pmatrix} + \begin{pmatrix} u_1 \\ u_2 \\ u_3 \end{pmatrix}$$

We ran this equation with 45 observations and the 12 dummies (no constant term). The values of the dummy variables are easily generated; for example, the set of observations for β_{12} consists of the 15 observations of x_2 followed by the 15 observations of x_1 and 15 zeros. The results (with t-ratios in parentheses) are[5]

$$\hat{p}_1 = \underset{(12.00)}{118.98} - \underset{(14.55)}{1.534x_1} - \underset{(4.31)}{0.474x_2} - \underset{(3.01)}{0.445x_3} + \underset{(12.61)}{0.0650y}$$

---

[5]The results are almost the same as those obtained by Waugh. Part of the difference could be that our program is in double precision.

$$\hat{p}_2 = 149.79 - 0.474x_1 - 1.189x_2 - 0.319x_3 + 0.0162y$$
$$\quad\;\; (9.18) \qquad (4.31) \qquad\; (6.20) \qquad\; (1.54) \qquad\;\; (2.83)$$

$$\hat{p}_3 = 131.06 - 0.445x_1 - 0.319x_2 - 2.389x_3 + 0.0199y$$
$$\quad\;\; (7.36) \qquad (3.01) \qquad\; (1.54) \qquad\; (4.32) \qquad\;\; (1.66)$$

One can raise questions about the appropriateness of the specification of the system of demand functions (8.9). Our purpose here has been merely to illustrate the use of dummy variable methods to estimate equations where some parameters in different equations are the same.

8.5 Dummy Variables for Testing Stability of Regression Coefficients

Dummy variables can also be used to test for stability of regression coefficients as discussed in Section 4.11. The definition of the appropriate dummy variables depends on whether we are using the analysis of covariance test or the predictive test for stability. We will first discuss the analysis of covariance test.

Consider, for instance, the two equations

$$y_1 = \alpha_1 + \beta_1 x_1 + \gamma_1 z_1 + u_1 \qquad \text{for the first period}$$
$$y_2 = \alpha_2 + \beta_2 x_2 + \gamma_2 z_2 + u_2 \qquad \text{for the second period}$$

We may be interested in testing the hypothesis that none of the coefficients changed between the two time periods; only the intercept coefficients changed, or only the intercept and the coefficient of the x variable changed, and so on. As discussed in Section 4.11, the analysis of variance test depends on obtaining the unrestricted and restricted residual sums of squares. Both these residual sums of squares can be obtained from the same dummy variable regression if we define enough dummy variables.

For instance, we can write the equations for the two periods as

$$y = \alpha_1 + (\alpha_2 - \alpha_1)D_1 + \beta_1 x + (\beta_2 - \beta_1)D_2 + \gamma_1 z + (\gamma_2 - \gamma_1)D_3 + u \qquad (8.10)$$

Note that we write the equation in terms of differences in the parameters and define the dummy variables accordingly

$$D_1 = \begin{cases} 1 & \text{for period 2} \\ 0 & \text{for period 1} \end{cases}$$

$$D_2 = \begin{cases} x_2 & \text{i.e., the corresponding value of } x \text{ for observations in period 2} \\ 0 & \text{for all observations in period 1} \end{cases}$$

$$D_3 = \begin{cases} z_2 & \text{i.e., the corresponding value of } z \text{ for observations in period 2} \\ 0 & \text{for all observations in period 1} \end{cases}$$

The unrestricted residual sum of squares is the one from estimating equation (8.10). As for the restricted residual sum of squares, it is obtained by deleting the dummy variables corresponding to that hypothesis:

Hypothesis	Variables Deleted
(1) All coefficients same	D_1, D_2, D_3
$\alpha_1 = \alpha_2,\ \beta_1 = \beta_2,\ \gamma_1 = \gamma_2$	
(2) Only intercepts change	D_2, D_3
$\beta_1 = \beta_2,\ \gamma_1 = \gamma_2$	
(3) Only intercepts and	D_2
coefficients of z change	
$\beta_1 = \beta_2$	

There are some who argue in favor of estimating equations like (8.10) and checking which of the dummy variables is significant in preference to the Chow test discussed in Chapter 4.[6] However, we should be cautious in making inferences about stability and instability of the coefficients by looking at the t-ratios of the dummy variables alone. As we pointed out in our discussion of R^2 (Section 4.10) it is possible that the t-ratios for each of a set of coefficients are all insignificant and still the F-ratio for the entire set of coefficients is significant. What one should do in any particular example is to use the F-tests and then use the t-tests on individual dummy variables only if they correspond to economically meaningful hypotheses.

As discussed in Section 4.11, the analysis of covariance test cannot be used if $n_2 < k$. In this case the predictive test suggested by Chow is to use

$$F = \frac{(\text{RSS} - \text{RSS}_1)/n_2}{\text{RSS}_1/(n_1 - k - 1)}$$

as an F-variate with d.f. n_2 and $(n_1 - k - 1)$. Here RSS is the residual sum of squares with $(n_1 + n_2)$ observations and RSS_1 is the residual sum of squares with n_1 observations.

The F-test, however, does not tell us which of the n_2 observations contribute to the instability of the coefficients or are outliers. To do this, we can define a set of n_2 dummy variables as[7]

$$D_i = \begin{cases} 1 & \text{for observation } n_1 + i \\ 0 & \text{for other observations} \end{cases} \qquad i = 1, 2, \ldots, n_2$$

and test whether the coefficients of the dummy variables are zero. Since one can get the standard error for each of these dummy variables separately from the standard regression packages, one can easily check for outliers and see which of the observations are significantly outside the regression line estimated from the first n_1 observations.

---

[6]D. Gujarati, "Use of Dummy Variables in Testing for Equality of Sets of Coefficients in Two Linear Regressions: A Note," *American Statistician*, February 1970. Gujarati argues that the Chow test might reject the hypothesis of stability but not tell us which particular coefficients are unstable, whereas the dummy variable method gives this information.

[7]D. S. Salkever, "The Use of Dummy Variables to Compute Predictions, Prediction Errors and Confidence Intervals," *Journal of Econometrics*, Vol. 4, 1976, pp. 393–397.

The common regression parameters will be estimated from the first n_1 observations, the coefficient of the ith dummy variable for $i = n_1 + 1, \ldots, n_2$ will measure the prediction error for the prediction of this observation based on the coefficients estimated from the first n_1 observations, and the standard error of this coefficient will measure the standard error of this prediction error.

Consider, for instance,

$$Y = \begin{cases} \alpha + \beta_1 x_1 + \beta_2 x_2 + u & \text{for the first } n_1 \text{ observations} \\ \alpha + \beta_1 x_1 + \beta_2 x_2 + \gamma_1 + u & \text{for the } (n_1 + 1)\text{th observation} \\ \alpha + \beta_1 x_1 + \beta_2 x_2 + \gamma_2 + u & \text{for the } (n_1 + 2)\text{th observation} \end{cases}$$

Then minimizing the sum of squares

$$\sum_{i=1}^{n1} u_i^2 + u_{n1+1}^2 + u_{n2+1}^2$$

we get $\hat{\alpha}$, $\hat{\beta}_1$, and $\hat{\beta}_2$ from the minimization of $\sum_{i=1}^{n1} u_i^2$ and

$$\hat{\gamma}_j = Y_j - \hat{\alpha} - \hat{\beta}_1 x_{1j} - \hat{\beta}_2 x_{2j} \qquad \text{for } j = n_1 + 1 \text{ and } n_1 + 2$$

What we have considered here for tests for stability is the use of dummy variables to get within-sample predictions. We can use the dummy variable method to generate out-of-sample predictions and their standard errors as well (a problem we discussed in Section 4.7). Suppose we have n observations on Y, x_1, and x_2. We are given the $(n+1)$th observations on x_1 and x_2 and asked to get the predicted value of Y and a standard error for the prediction. The way we proceed is as follows.

Set the value of Y for the $(n+1)$th observation at zero. Define a dummy variable D as

$$D = \begin{cases} 0 & \text{for the first } n \text{ observations} \\ -1 & \text{for the } (n+1)\text{th observation} \end{cases}$$

Now run a regression of Y on x_1, x_2, and D using the $(n+1)$ observations. The coefficient of D is the prediction $\overline{Y}_{n+1}$ needed and its standard error is the standard error of the prediction. To see this is so, note that the model says

$$Y = \alpha + \beta_1 x_1 + \beta_2 x_2 + u \qquad \text{for the } n \text{ observations}$$

$$0 = \alpha + \beta_1 x_1 + \beta_2 x_2 - \gamma + u \qquad \text{for the } (n+1)\text{th observation}$$

Minimizing the residual sum of squares amounts to obtaining the least squares estimators $\hat{\alpha}$, $\hat{\beta}_1$, $\hat{\beta}_2$ from the first n observations, and

$$\hat{\gamma} = \hat{\alpha} + \hat{\beta}_1 x_1 + \hat{\beta}_2 x_2 \text{ for the } (n+1)\text{th observation}$$

Thus, $\hat{\gamma} = \hat{Y}_{n+1}$ and its standard error gives us the required standard error of $\hat{Y}_{n+1}$.

This method has been extended by Pagan and Nicholls[8] to the case of nonlinear models and simultaneous equation models.

8.6 Dummy Variables Under Heteroskedasticity and Autocorrelation

In the preceding sections we discussed the use of dummy variables but we need to exercise some caution in the use of these variables when we have heteroskedasticity or autocorrelation.

Consider first the case of heteroskedasticity. Suppose that we have the two equations

$$y = \begin{cases} \alpha_1 + \beta_1 x + u_1 & \text{for the first group} \\ \alpha_2 + \beta_2 x + u_2 & \text{for the second group} \end{cases}$$

Let $\text{var}(u_1) = \sigma_1^2$ and $\text{var}(u_2) = \sigma_2^2$. When we pool the data and estimate an equation like (8.4), we are implicitly assuming that $\sigma_1^2 = \sigma_2^2$. If σ_1^2 and σ_2^2 are widely different, then, even if α_2 is not significantly different from α_1 and β_2 is not significantly different from β_1, the coefficients of the dummy variables in (8.4) can turn out to be significant. One can easily demonstrate this by generating data for the two groups imposing $\alpha_1 = \alpha_2$ and $\beta_1 = \beta_2$ but $\sigma_1^2 = 16\sigma_2^2$ (σ_1^2 being chosen suitably), and estimating equation (8.4). The reverse situation can also arise; that is, ignoring heteroskedasticity can make significant differences appear to be insignificant. Suppose that we take $\alpha_1 = 2\alpha_2$ and $\beta_1 = 2\beta_2$. Then by taking $\sigma_1^2 = 16\sigma_2^2$ (or a multiple around that) we can make the dummy variables appear nonsignificant. The problem is just the same as that of applying tests for stability under heteroskedasticity.

Regarding autocorrelation, suppose that the errors in the equations for the two groups are first-order autoregressive so that we use a first-order autoregressive transformation, that is, write

$$y_t^* = y_t - \rho y_{t-1} \qquad \text{for } y_t$$

$$x_t^* = x_t - \rho x_{t-1} \qquad \text{for } x_t$$

The question is: What happens to the dummy variables in equation (8.4)? These variables *should not* be subject to the autoregressive transformation and care should be taken if the computer program we use does this automatically.[9] We can easily derive the appropriate dummy variables in this case.

Consider the case with n_1 observations in the first group and n_2 observations in the second group. We will introduce the time subscript t for each observation later when needed.

---

[8] A. R. Pagan and D. F. Nicholls, "Estimating Predictions, Prediction Errors and Their Standard Deviations Using Constructed Variables," *Journal of Econometrics*, Vol. 24, 1984, pp. 293–310.

[9] This point was brought to my attention by Ben-Zion Zilberfarb through a manuscript "On the Use of Autoregressive Transformation in Equations Containing Dummy Variables."

Define

$$\alpha_1^* = \alpha_1(1 - \rho)$$
$$\alpha_2^* = \alpha_2(1 - \rho)$$

Then equation (8.4) can be rewritten as

$$y^* = \alpha_1^* + (\alpha_2^* - \alpha_1^*)D_1 + \beta_1 x^* + (\beta_2 - \beta_1)D_2 + e$$

where D_2 will be defined as before with x_2^* in place of x_2 and the random errors e_t are defined by

$$u_t - \rho u_{t-1} = e_t$$

This equation, however, is all right for the observations in the first group and the last $(n_2 - 1)$ observations in the second group. However, the problem is with the first observation in the second group. For this observation, the ρ-differenced equation turns out to be

$$y_t - \rho y_{t-1} = \alpha_2 - \rho\alpha_1 + (\beta_2 x_t - \rho\beta_1 x_{t-1}) + e_t$$

or

$$y_t^* = \alpha_1^* + \frac{1}{1 - \rho}(\alpha_2^* - \alpha_1^*) + \beta_1 x_t^* + (\beta_2 - \beta_1)x_t + e_t$$

This means that the dummy variables D_1 and D_2 have to be defined as follows:

$$D_1 = \begin{cases} 0 & \text{for all observations in the first group} \\ \dfrac{1}{1 - \rho} & \text{for the first observation in the second group} \\ 1 & \text{for all other observations in the second group} \end{cases}$$

$$D_2 = \begin{cases} 0 & \text{for all observations in the first group} \\ x_t & \text{for the first observation in the second group} \\ x_t^* & \text{for all other observations in the second group} \end{cases}$$

8.7 Dummy Dependent Variables

Until now we have been considering models where the explanatory variables are dummy variables. We now discuss models where the explained variable is a dummy variable. This dummy variable can take on two or more values but we consider here the case where it takes on only two values, zero or 1. Considering the other cases is beyond the scope of this book.[10] Since the dummy variable takes on two values, it is called a dichotomous

---

[10]This is a complete area by itself, so we give only an elementary introduction. A more detailed discussion of this topic can be found in G. S. Maddala, *Limited-Dependent and Qualitative Variables in Econometrics* (Cambridge: Cambridge University Press, 1983), Chap. 2, "Discrete Regression Models;" T. Amemiya, "Qualitative Response Models: A Survey," *Journal of Economic Literature*, December 1981, pp. 483–536; and D. R. Cox, *Analysis of Binary Data* (London: Methuen, 1970).

variable. There are numerous examples of dichotomous explained variables. For instance,

$$y = \begin{cases} 1 & \text{if a person is in the labor force} \\ 0 & \text{otherwise} \end{cases}$$

or

$$y = \begin{cases} 1 & \text{if a person owns a home} \\ 0 & \text{otherwise} \end{cases}$$

There are several methods to analyze regression models where the dependent variable is a zero or 1 variable. The simplest procedure is to just use the usual least squares method. In this case the model is called the *linear probability* model. Another method, called the "linear discriminant function," is related to the linear probability model. The other alternative is to say that there is an underlying or latent variable y^* which we do not observe. What we observe is

$$y = \begin{cases} 1 & \text{if } y^* > 0 \\ 0 & \text{otherwise} \end{cases}$$

This is the idea behind the *logit* and *probit* models. First we discuss these methods and then give an illustrative example.

8.8   The Linear Probability Model and the Linear Discriminant Function

The Linear Probability Model

The term *linear probability model* is used to denote a regression model in which the dependent variable y is a dichotomous variable taking the value 1 or zero. For the sake of simplicity we consider only one explanatory variable, x.

The variable y is an indicator variable that denotes the occurrence or nonoccurrence of an event. For instance, in an analysis of the determinants of unemployment, we have data on each person that shows whether or not the person is employed, and we have some explanatory variables that determine the state of employment. Here the event under consideration is employment. We define the dichotomous variable

$$y = \begin{cases} 1 & \text{if the person is employed} \\ 0 & \text{otherwise} \end{cases}$$

Similarly, in an analysis of bankruptcy of firms, we define

$$y = \begin{cases} 1 & \text{if the firm is bankrupt} \\ 0 & \text{otherwise} \end{cases}$$

We write the model in the usual regression framework as

$$y_i = \beta x_i + u_i \tag{8.11}$$

with $E(u_i) = 0$. The conditional expectation $E(y_i|x_i)$ is equal to βx_i. This has to be interpreted in this case as the probability that the event will occur given the x_i. The calculated value of y from the regression equation (i.e., $\hat{y}_i = \hat{\beta} x_i$) will then give the estimated probability that the event will occur given the particular value of x. In practice these estimated probabilities can lie outside the admissible range $(0, 1)$.

Since y_i takes the value 1 or zero, the errors in equation (8.11) can take only two values, $(1 - \beta x_i)$ and $(-\beta x_i)$. Also, with the interpretation we have given equation (8.11), and the requirement that $E(u_i) = 0$, the respective probabilities of these events are βx_i and $(1 - \beta x_i)$. Thus we have

u_i	$f(u_i)$
$1 - \beta x_i$	βx_i
$-\beta x_i$	$1 - \beta x_i$

Hence

$$\text{var}(u_i) = \beta x_i (1 - \beta x_i)^2 + (1 - \beta x_i)(-\beta x_i)^2$$
$$= \beta x_i (1 - \beta x_i)$$
$$= E(y_i)[1 - E(y_i)]$$

Because of this heteroskedasticity problem the OLS estimates of β from equation (8.11) will not be efficient. We can use the following two-step procedure:[11]

First estimate (8.11) by least squares.

Next compute $\hat{y}_i(1 - \hat{y}_i)$ and use weighted least squares, that is, defining

$$w_i = \sqrt{\hat{y}_i(1 - \hat{y}_i)}$$

we regress y_i/w_i on x_i/w_i. The problems with this procedure are

1. $\hat{y}_i(1 - \hat{y}_i)$ in practice may be negative, although in large samples this will be so with a very small probability[12] since $\hat{y}_i(1 - \hat{y}_i)$ is a consistent estimator for $E(y_i)([1 - E(y_i)])$.
2. Since the errors u_i are obviously not normally distributed, there is a problem with the application of the usual tests of significance. As we will see in the next section, on the linear discriminant function, they can be justified only under the assumption that the explanatory variables have a multivariate normal distribution.
3. The most important criticism is with the formulation itself: that the conditional expectation $E(y_i|x_i)$ be interpreted as the probability that the event will occur. In many cases $E(y_i|x_i)$ can lie outside the limits $(0, 1)$.

The limitations of the linear probability model are shown in Figure 8.3, which shows the bunching up of points[13] along $y = 0$ and $y = 1$. The predicted values can easily lie outside the interval $(0, 1)$ and the prediction errors can be very large.

---

[11] A. S. Goldberger, *Econometric Theory* (New York: Wiley, 1964), p. 250.

[12] R. G. McGilvray, "Estimating the Linear Probability Function," *Econometrica*, 1970, pp. 775–776.

[13] This bunching of points is described in M. Nerlove and S. J. Press, "Univariate and Multivariate Log-Linear and Logistic Models," Report R-1306-EDA/NIH, Rand Corporation, Santa Monica, CA, December 1973.

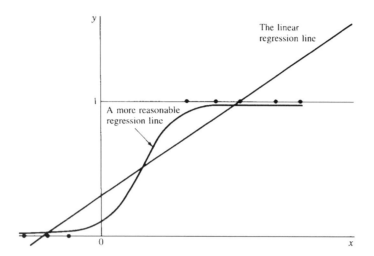

Figure 8.3   Predictions from the linear probability model

In the 1960s and early 1970s the linear probability model was widely used mainly because it is a model that can be easily estimated using multiple regression analysis. Some others used discriminant analysis, not noting that this method is very similar to the linear probability model. For instance, Meyer and Pifer[14] analyzed bank failures using the linear probability model and Altman[15] analyzed bankruptcy of manufacturing corporations using discriminant analysis. In both studies the bankrupt banks or corporations were taken and a paired sample of nonbankrupt banks or corporations was chosen (i.e., for each bankrupt bank or corporation, a similarly situated nonbankrupt bank or corporation was found). Then the linear probability model or linear discriminant function was estimated.

Since the linear probability model and linear discriminant function are closely related, we will discuss the latter here.

The Linear Discriminant Function

Suppose that we have n individuals for whom we have observations on k explanatory variables and we observe that n_1 of them belong to a group π_1 and n_2 of them belong to a second group π_2 where $n_1 + n_2 = n$. We want to construct a linear function of the k variables that we can use to predict that a new observation belongs to one of the two groups. This linear function is called the *linear discriminant function*.

As an example suppose that we have data on a number of loan applicants and we observe that n_1 of them were granted loans and n_2 of them were denied loans. We also have the socioeconomic characteristics on the applicants. Now given a new applicant with

---

[14]Paul A. Meyer and Howard W. Pifer, "Prediction of Bank Failures," *Journal of Finance*, 1970, pp. 853–868.

[15]Edward I. Altman, "Financial Ratios, Discriminant Analysis and the Prediction of Corporate Bankruptcy," *Journal of Finance*, September 1968.

specified socioeconomic characteristics, we would want to predict whether the applicant will get a loan or not.

Let us define a linear function

$$Z = \lambda_0 + \sum_{i=1}^{k} \lambda_i x_i$$

Then it is intuitively clear that to get the best discrimination between the two groups, we would want to choose the λ_i so that the ratio

$$\frac{\text{between-group variance of } Z}{\text{within-group variance of } Z} \quad \text{is maximum}$$

Fisher[16] suggested an analogy between this problem and multiple regression analysis. He suggested that we define a dummy variable

$$y = \begin{cases} \dfrac{n_2}{n_1 + n_2} & \text{if the individual belongs to } \pi_1 \text{ (first group)} \\[2mm] -\dfrac{n_1}{n_1 + n_2} & \text{if the individual belongs to } \pi_2 \text{ (second group)} \end{cases}$$

Now estimate the multiple regression equation

$$y = \beta_0 + \beta_1 x_1 + \beta_2 x_2 + \cdots + \beta_k x_k + u$$

Get the residual sum of squares RSS. Then

$$\hat{\beta}_i = \hat{\lambda}_i \frac{\text{RSS}}{n_1 + n_2 - 2}$$

Thus, once we have the regression coefficients and the residual sum of squares from the dummy dependent variable regression, we can very easily obtain the discriminant function coefficients.[17]

The linear probability model is only slightly different from the formulation of Fisher. In the linear probability model we define

$$y = \begin{cases} 1 & \text{if the individual belongs to } \pi_1 \\ 0 & \text{if the individual belongs to } \pi_2 \end{cases}$$

This merely amounts to adding $n_1/(n_1 + n_2)$ to each observation of y as defined by Fisher. Thus only the estimate of the constant term changes.

---

[16]R. A. Fisher, "The Use of Multiple Measurements in Taxonomic Problems," *Annals of Eugenics*, 1936, pp. 179–188.

[17]We are omitting the algebraic details here. They can be found in Maddala, *Limited-Dependent*, pp. 18–21. Also, the tests of significance for the coefficients of the linear discriminant function or the linear probability model discussed later are described there.

8.9 The Probit and Logit Models

An alternative approach is to assume that we have a regression model

$$y_i^* = \beta_0 + \sum_{j=1}^{k} \beta_j x_{ij} + u_i \tag{8.12}$$

where y_i^* is not observed. It is commonly called a "latent" variable. What we observe is a dummy variable y_i defined by

$$y_i = \begin{cases} 1 & \text{if } y_i^* > 0 \\ 0 & \text{otherwise} \end{cases} \tag{8.13}$$

The probit and logit models differ in the specification of the distribution of the error term u in equation (8.12). The difference between the specification (8.12) and the linear probability model is that in the linear probability model we analyze the dichotomous variables as they are, whereas in (8.12) we assume the existence of an underlying latent variable for which we observe a dichotomous realization. For instance, if the observed dummy variable is whether or not the person is employed, y_i^* would be defined as "propensity or ability to find employment." Similarly, if the observed dummy variable is whether or not the person has bought a car, then y_i^* would be defined as "desire or ability to buy a car." Note that in both the examples we have given, there is "desire" and "ability" involved. Thus the explanatory variables in (8.12) would contain variables that explain both these elements.

Note from system (8.13) that multiplying y_i^* by any positive constant does not change y_i. Hence if we observe y_i, we can estimate the β's in (8.12) only up to a positive multiple. Hence it is customary to assume var$(u_i) = 1$. This fixes the scale of y_i^*. From the relationships (8.12) and (8.13) we get

$$P_i = \text{Prob}(y_i = 1) = \text{Prob}\left[u_i > -\left(\beta_0 + \sum_{j=1}^{k} \beta_j x_{ij}\right)\right]$$

$$= 1 - F\left[-\left(\beta_0 + \sum_{j=1}^{k} \beta_j x_{ij}\right)\right]$$

where F is the cumulative distribution function of u.

If the distribution of u is symmetric, since $1 - F(-Z) = F(Z)$, we can write

$$P_i = F\left(\beta_0 + \sum_{j=1}^{k} \beta_j x_{ij}\right) \tag{8.14}$$

Since the observed y_i are just realizations of a binomial process with probabilities given by equation (8.14) and varying from trial to trial (depending on x_{ij}), we can write the likelihood function as

$$L = \prod_{y_i=1} P_i \prod_{y_i=0} (1 - P_i) \tag{8.15}$$

The functional form for F in equation (8.14) will depend on the assumption made about the error term u. If the cumulative distribution of u_i is logistic we have what is known as the *logit* model. In this case

$$F(Z_i) = \frac{\exp(Z_i)}{1 + \exp(Z_i)} \tag{8.16}$$

Hence

$$\log \frac{F(Z_i)}{1 - F(Z_i)} = Z_i$$

Note that for the logit model

$$\log \frac{P_i}{1 - P_i} = \beta_0 + \sum_{j=1}^{k} \beta_j x_{ij}$$

The left-hand side of this equation is called the *log-odds ratio*. Thus the log-odds ratio is a linear function of the explanatory variables. For the linear probability model it is P_i that is assumed to be a linear function of the explanatory variables.

If the errors u_i in (8.12) follow a normal distribution, we have the *probit* model (it should more appropriately be called the *normit* model, but the word *probit* was used in the biometrics literature). In this case

$$F(Z_i) = \int_{-\infty}^{Z_i/\sigma} \frac{1}{\sqrt{2\pi}} \exp\left(-\frac{t^2}{2}\right) dt \tag{8.17}$$

Maximization of the likelihood function (8.15) for either the probit or the logit model is accomplished by nonlinear estimation methods. There are now several computer programs available for probit and logit analysis, and these programs are very inexpensive to run.

The likelihood function (8.15) is concave[18] (does not have multiple maxima), and hence any starting values of the parameters would do. It is customary to start the iterations for the logit and probit models with the estimates from the linear probability model.

Since the cumulative normal and the logistic distributions are very close to each other except at the tails, we are not likely to get very different results using equations (8.16) or (8.17), that is, the logit or the probit method, unless the samples are large (so that we have enough observations at the tails). However, the estimates of the parameters β_i from the two methods are not directly comparable. Since the logistic distribution has a variance $\pi^2/3$, the estimates of β_i obtained from the logit model have to be multiplied by $\sqrt{3}/\pi$ to be comparable to the estimates obtained from the probit model (where we normalize σ to be equal to 1).

Amemiya[19] suggests that the logit estimates be multiplied by $1/1.6 = 0.625$ instead of $\sqrt{3}/\pi$, saying that this transformation produces a closer approximation between the logistic distribution and the distribution function of the standard normal. He also suggests

---

[18] This is proved for a general model in J. W. Pratt, "Concavity of the Log-Likelihood," *Journal of the American Statistical Association*, 1981, pp. 137–159.

[19] T. Amemiya, "Qualitative Response Model: A Survey," *Journal of Economic Literature*, 1981, p. 1488.

that the coefficients of the linear probability model $\hat{\beta}_{Lp}$ and the coefficients of the logit model $\hat{\beta}_L$ are related by

$$\hat{\beta}_{Lp} \simeq 0.25\hat{\beta}_L \text{ except for the constant term}$$

$$\hat{\beta}_{Lp} \simeq 0.25\hat{\beta}_L + 0.5 \text{ for the constant term}$$

Thus if we need to make $\hat{\beta}_{Lp}$ comparable to the probit coefficients, we need to multiply them by 2.5 and subtract 1.25 from the constant term.

Alternative ways of comparing the models would be:

1. To calculate the sum of squared deviations from predicted probabilities.
2. To compare the percentages correctly predicted.
3. To look at the derivatives of the probabilities with respect to a particular independent variable.

Illustrative Example

As an illustration, we consider data on a sample of 750 mortgage applications in the Columbia, SC, metropolitan area.[20] There were 500 loan applications accepted and 250 loan applications rejected. We define

$$y = \begin{cases} 1 & \text{if the loan application was accepted} \\ 0 & \text{if the loan application was rejected} \end{cases}$$

Three models were estimated: the linear probability model, the logit model, and the probit model. The explanatory variables were:

$$AI = \text{applicant's and coapplicant's income } (10^3 \text{ dollars})$$

$$XMD = \text{debt minus mortgage payment } (10^3 \text{ dollars})$$

$$DF = \text{dummy variable, 1 for female, 0 for male}$$

$$DR = \text{dummy variable, 1 for nonwhite, 0 for white}$$

$$DS = \text{dummy variable, 1 for single, 0 otherwise}$$

$$DA = \text{age of house } (10^2 \text{ years})$$

$$NNWP = \text{percent nonwhite in the neighborhood } (\times 10^3)$$

$$NMFI = \text{neighborhood mean family income } (10^5 \text{ dollars})$$

$$NA = \text{neighborhood average age of homes } (10^2 \text{ years})$$

The results are presented in Table 8.3.

---

[20]This example is from G. S. Maddala and R. P. Trost, "On Measuring Discrimination in Loan Markets," *Housing Finance Review*, 1982, pp. 245–268.

Table 8.3 Comparison of the probit, logit, and linear probability models: loan data from South Carolina[a]

Variable	Linear Probability Model	Logit Model	Probit Model
AI	1.489 (4.69)	2.254 (4.60)	2.030 (4.73)
XMD	−1.509 (5.74)	−1.170 (5.57)	−1.773 (5.67)
DF	0.140 (0.78)	0.563 (0.87)	0.206 (0.95)
DR	−0.266 (1.84)	−0.240 (1.60)	−0.279 (1.66)
DS	−0.238 (1.75)	−0.222 (1.51)	−0.274 (1.70)
DA	−1.426 (3.52)	−1.463 (3.34)	−1.570 (3.29)
NNWP	−1.762 (0.74)	−2.028 (0.80)	−2.360 (0.85)
NMFI	0.150 (0.23)	0.149 (0.20)	0.194 (0.25)
NA	−0.393 (1.34)	−0.386 (1.25)	−0.425 (1.26)
Constant	0.501	0.363	0.488

[a]Figures in parentheses are t-ratios, not standard errors.

The coefficients of the probit model were left as they were computed. The other coefficients were adjusted as follows:[21]

1. The coefficients of the logit model were multiplied by 0.625.
2. The coefficients of the linear probability model were multiplied by 2.5 throughout and then 1.25 was subtracted from the constant term.

These are the adjustments described in the text. The three sets of coefficients reported in Table 8.3 are not much different from each other (particularly those of the logit and the probit models).

One can compare the three models by comparing the R^2's. We will illustrate this with another example in the next section after defining the different measures of R^2's for the qualitative dependent variable models.

The Problem of Disproportionate Sampling

In many applications of the logit, probit, or linear probability models it happens that the number of observations in one of the groups is much smaller than the number in the other group. For instance, in an analysis of bank failures, the number of failed banks would be much smaller than the number of solvent banks. In a study of unemployment, the number of unemployed persons is much smaller than the number of employed persons. Thus either we have to get a very large data set (which is what is done in the studies of unemployment based on census tapes) or we have to sample the two groups at

---

[21]After getting the estimates from the three models, it is always desirable to adjust the coefficients so that they are all on a comparable level. The linear probability model can be estimated by any multiple regression program. As for the logit and probit models, there are many computer programs available now (TSP, RATS, LIMDEP, etc.).

different sampling rates. For instance, in an analysis of bank failures, all the failed banks are considered in the analysis, but only a small percentage of the solvent banks are sampled. Thus the two groups are sampled at different rates. In the example of loan applications in Columbia, SC (we have presented estimates in Table 8.3) the sampling was actually at different rates. There were 4600 applications in the accepted category and 250 applications in the rejected category. To have enough observations on females and blacks in the rejected category, it was decided to include all the 250 observations from the rejected category and get a random sample of 500 observations from the accepted category. Thus the sampling rate was 100% for the rejected group and 10.87% for the accepted group.

In such cases a question arises as to how one should analyze the data. It has been commonly suggested that one should use a weighted logit (or probit or linear probability) model similar to the weighted least squares method we discussed under heteroskedasticity in Chapter 5. For instance, Avery and Hanweck argue:[22] "In addition, because failed and non-failed banks were sampled at different rates, it was also necessary to weight observations in estimation" (p. 387). However, this is not a correct procedure. The usual logit model can be used without any change even with unequal sampling rates. Thus the results presented in Table 8.3 are based on the usual estimation procedures with no weighting used.

Regarding the estimation of the coefficients of the explanatory variables, if we use the logit model, the coefficients are not affected by the unequal sampling rates for the two groups. It is only the constant term that is affected.[23] In Table 8.3 the logit coefficients are all correct, except for the constant term which needs to be decreased by $\log p_1 - \log p_2$, where p_1 and p_2 are the proportions of observations chosen from the two groups for which $y = 1$ and 0, respectively, and the logarithm is the natural logarithm. In the example in Table 8.3, the constant term for the logit model has to be decreased by $\log (0.1087) - \log(1.0) \simeq -2.22$. Since the coefficients in Table 8.3 have been adjusted (as described earlier), we have to multiply this by 0.625. Thus the decrease in the constant terms is -1.39, that is an increase of 1.39.

Note that this result is valid for the logit model, not for the probit model or the linear probability model. However, even for these models, although one cannot derive the results analytically, it appears that the slope coefficients are not much affected by unequal sampling rates.

Weighting the observations is the correct procedure if there is a heteroskedasticity problem. There is no reason why the unequal sampling proportions should cause a heteroskedasticity problem. Thus weighting the observations is clearly not a correct solution. If our interest is mainly in examining which variables are significant, we need not make any changes in the estimated coefficients for the logit model. On the other hand, if the estimated model is going to be used for prediction purposes, an adjustment in the constant term, as suggested earlier, is necessary.

---

[22]Robert B. Avery and Gerald A. Hanweck, "A Dynamic Analysis of Bank Failures," *Bank Structure and Competition* (Chicago: Federal Reserve Bank of Chicago, 1984), pp. 380–395.

[23]For a discussion of this point, see Maddala, *Limited-Dependent*, pp. 90–91. On p. 91 there is an error. The constant term should be decreased (not increased).

Prediction of Effects of Changes in the Explanatory Variables

After estimating the parameters β_i, we would like to know the effects of changes in any of the explanatory variables on the probabilities of any observation belonging to either of the two groups. These effects are given by

$$\frac{\partial P_i}{\partial x_{ij}} = \begin{cases} \beta_j & \text{for the linear probability model} \\ \beta_j P_i (1 - P_i) & \text{for the logit model} \\ \beta_j \phi(Z_i) & \text{for the probit model} \end{cases}$$

where

$$Z_i = \beta_0 + \sum_{i=1}^{k} \beta_i x_{ij}$$

and $\phi(\cdot)$ is the density function of the standard normal.

In the case of the linear probability model these derivatives are constant. In the case of the logit and probit models, we need to calculate them at different levels of the explanatory variables to get an idea of the range of variation of the resulting changes in probabilities. If one is interested in the prediction of the effect on the log-odds ratio, then for the logit model, this effect is constant since

$$\frac{\partial}{\partial x_{ij}} \left(\log \frac{P_i}{1 - P_i} \right) = \beta_j$$

Measuring Goodness of Fit

There is a problem with the use of conventional R^2-type measures when the explained variable y takes on only two values.[24] The predicted values $\hat{y}$ are probabilities and the actual values y are either 0 or 1. For the linear probability model and the logit model we have $\sum y = \sum \hat{y}$, as with the linear regression model, if a constant term is also estimated. For the probit model there is no such exact relationship although it is approximately valid. We will see this in the illustrative example presented later.

There are several R^2-type measures that have been suggested for models with qualitative dependent variables. The following are some of them. In the case of the linear regression model, they are all equivalent. However, they are not equivalent in the case of models with qualitative dependent variables.

1. $R^2 = $ squared correlation between y and $\hat{y}$.
2. *Measures based on residual sum of squares.* For the linear regression model we have

$$R^2 = 1 - \left[\frac{\sum_{i=1}^{n} (y_i - \hat{y}_i)^2}{\sum_{i=1}^{n} (y_i - \overline{y})^2} \right]$$

---

[24]These are summarized in Maddala, *Limited-Dependent*, pp. 37–41.

We can use this same measure if we can use $\sum_{i=1}^{n}(y_i - \hat{y}_i)^2$ as the measure of residual sum of squares. Effron[25] argued that we can use it.

Note that in the case of a binary dependent variable

$$\sum(y_i - \bar{y})^2 = \sum y_i^2 - n\bar{y}^2 = n_1 - n\left(\frac{n_1}{n}\right)^2 = \frac{n_1 n_2}{n}$$

Hence Effron's measure of R^2 is

$$R^2 = 1 - \frac{n}{n_1 n_2}\sum_{i=1}^{n}(y_i - \bar{y}_i)^2$$

Amemiya[26] argues that it makes more sense to define the residual sum of squares as

$$\sum_{i=1}^{n}\frac{(y_i - \hat{y}_i)^2}{\hat{y}_i(1 - \hat{y}_i)}$$

that is, to weight the squared error $(y_i - \hat{y}_i)^2$ by a weight that is inversely proportional to its variance.

3. *Measures based on likelihood ratios.* For the standard linear regression model

$$y = \beta_0 + \sum_{i=1}^{k}\beta_i x_i + u \qquad u \sim \text{IN}(0, \sigma^2)$$

let L_{UR} be the maximum of the likelihood function when maximized with respect to all the parameters and L_{R} be the maximum when maximized with the restriction $\beta_i = 0$ for $i = 1, 2, \ldots, k$. Then

$$R^2 = 1 - \left(\frac{L_{\text{R}}}{L_{\text{UR}}}\right)^{2/n}$$

One can use an analogous measure for the logit and probit model as well. However, for the qualitative dependent variable model, the likelihood function (8.15) attains an absolute maximum of 1. This means that

$$L_{\text{R}} \leq L_{\text{UR}} \leq 1$$

or

$$L_{\text{R}} \leq \frac{L_{\text{R}}}{L_{\text{UR}}} \leq 1$$

or

$$L_{\text{R}}^{2/n} \leq 1 - R^2 \leq 1$$

or

$$0 \leq R^2 \leq 1 - L_{\text{R}}^{2/n}$$

[25] B. Effron, "Regression and ANOVA with Zero–One Data: Measures of Residual Variation," *Journal of the American Statistical Association*, May 1978, pp. 113–121.

[26] Amemiya, "Qualitative Response Models," p. 1504.

Hence Cragg and Uhler[27] suggest a pseudo R^2 (it lies in [0, 1]):

$$\text{pseudo } R^2 = \frac{L_{UR}^{2/n} - L_R^{2/n}}{(1 - L_R^{2/n})L_{UR}^{2/n}}$$

Another measure of R^2 is that of McFadden,[28] who defines it as

$$\text{McFadden's } R^2 = 1 - \frac{\log L_{UR}}{\log L_R}$$

However, this measure does not correspond to any R^2 measure in the linear regression model.

4. Finally, we can also think of R^2 in terms of the *proportion* of correct predictions. Since the dependent variable is a zero or 1 variable, after we compute the $\hat{y}_i$ we classify the ith observation as belonging to group 1 if $\hat{y}_i < 0.5$ and group 2 if $\hat{y}_i < 0.5$. We can then count the number of correct predictions. We can define a predicted value $\hat{y}_i^*$, which is also a zero−one variable such that

$$\hat{y}_i^* = \begin{cases} 1 & \text{if } \hat{y}_i > 0.5 \\ 0 & \text{if } \hat{y}_i < 0.5 \end{cases}$$

(Provided that we calculate y_i to enough decimals, ties will be very unlikely.) Now define

$$\text{count } R^2 = \frac{\text{number of correct predictions}}{\text{total number of observations}}$$

Although this is a useful measure worth reporting in all problems, it might not have enough discriminatory power. In the illustrative example in the next section, we found that the logit model predicted 41 of the total 44 cases correctly, whereas the probit and linear probability models each predicted 40 of the 44 correctly. However, looking at $\hat{y}_i$, the linear probability model had five observations with $\hat{y}_i$ substantially greater than 1, thus outside the range of (0, 1). Also, this measure did not appear to help us much in discriminating between the three models as the other measures of R^2's did. It is, however, possible that this measure has better discriminatory power in other problems. In any case, it is a measure worth reporting in every problem.

8.10   Illustrative Example

Consider the data in Table 8.4. The data refer to a study on the deterrent effect of capital punishment by McManus.[29] The data are cross-sectional data for 44 states in

---

[27]J. G. Cragg and R. Uhler, "The Demand for Automobiles," *Canadian Journal of Economics*, 1970, pp. 386–406. See also Maddala, *Limited-Dependent*, pp. 39–40 for a discussion of this pseudo R^2.

[28]D. McFadden, "The Measurement of Urban Travel Demand," *Journal of Public Economics*, 1974, pp. 303–328.

[29]Walter S. McManus, "Estimates of the Deterrent Effect of Capital Punishment: The Importance of the Researcher's Prior Beliefs," *Journal of Political Economy*, Vol. 93, April 1985, pp. 417–425.

Table 8.4   Determinants of murder rates in the United States (cross-section data on states in 1950)[a]

N	M	PC	PX	D_1	T	Y	LF	NW	D_2
1	19.25	0.204	0.035	1	47	1.10	51.2	0.321	1
2	7.53	0.327	0.081	1	58	0.92	48.5	0.224	1
3	5.66	0.401	0.012	1	82	1.72	50.8	0.127	0
4	3.21	0.318	0.070	1	100	2.18	54.4	0.063	0
5	2.80	0.350	0.062	1	222	1.75	52.4	0.021	0
6	1.41	0.283	0.100	1	164	2.26	56.7	0.027	0
7	6.18	0.204	0.050	1	161	2.07	54.6	0.139	1
8	12.15	0.232	0.054	1	70	1.43	52.7	0.218	1
9	1.34	0.199	0.086	1	219	1.92	52.3	0.008	0
10	3.71	0.138	0	0	81	1.82	53.0	0.012	0
11	5.35	0.142	0.018	1	209	2.34	55.4	0.076	0
12	4.72	0.118	0.045	1	182	2.12	53.5	0.299	0
13	3.81	0.207	0.040	1	185	1.81	51.6	0.040	0
14	10.44	0.189	0.045	1	104	1.35	48.5	0.069	1
15	9.58	0.124	0.125	1	126	1.26	49.3	0.330	1
16	1.02	0.210	0.060	1	192	2.07	53.9	0.017	0
17	7.52	0.227	0.055	1	95	2.04	55.7	0.166	1
18	1.31	0.167	0	0	245	1.55	51.2	0.003	0
19	1.67	0.120	0	0	97	1.89	54.0	0.010	0
20	7.07	0.139	0.041	1	177	1.68	52.2	0.076	0
21	11.79	0.272	0.063	1	125	0.76	51.1	0.454	1
22	2.71	0.125	0	0	56	1.96	54.0	0.032	0
23	13.21	0.235	0.086	1	85	1.29	55.0	0.266	1
24	3.48	0.108	0.040	1	199	1.81	52.9	0.018	0
25	0.81	0.672	0	0	298	1.72	53.7	0.038	0
26	2.32	0.357	0.030	1	145	2.39	55.8	0.067	0
27	3.47	0.592	0.029	1	78	1.68	50.4	0.075	0
28	8.31	0.225	0.400	1	144	2.29	58.8	0.064	0
29	1.57	0.267	0.126	1	178	2.34	54.5	0.065	0
30	4.13	0.164	0.122	1	146	2.21	53.5	0.065	0
31	3.84	0.128	0.091	1	132	1.42	48.8	0.090	1
32	1.83	0.287	0.075	1	98	1.97	54.5	0.016	0
33	3.54	0.210	0.069	1	120	2.12	52.1	0.061	0
34	1.11	0.342	0	0	148	1.90	56.0	0.019	0
35	8.90	0.133	0.216	1	123	1.15	56.2	0.389	1
36	1.27	0.241	0.100	1	282	1.70	53.3	0.037	0
37	15.26	0.167	0.038	1	79	1.24	50.9	0.161	1
38	11.15	0.252	0.040	1	34	1.55	53.2	0.127	1
39	1.74	0.418	0	0	104	2.04	51.7	0.017	0
40	11.98	0.282	0.032	1	91	1.59	54.3	0.222	1
41	3.04	0.194	0.086	1	199	2.07	53.7	0.026	0
42	0.85	0.378	0	0	101	2.00	54.7	0.012	0
43	2.83	0.757	0.033	1	109	1.84	47.0	0.057	1
44	2.89	0.356	0	0	117	2.04	56.9	0.022	0

[a]N, observation number; M, murder rate per 100,000 (FBI estimate 1950); PC, number of convictions/number of murders in 1950; PX, average number of executions during 1946–1950 divided by convictions in 1950; Y, median family income of families in 1949 (thousands of dollars); LF, labor force participation rate in 1950 (expressed as a percentage); NW, proportion of population that is nonwhite in 1950; D_2, dummy variable (1 for southern states, 0 for others); D_1, dummy variable which is 1 if the state has capital punishment, 0 otherwise ($D_1 = 1$ if $PX > 0$, 0 otherwise); T, median time served in months of convicted murderers released in 1951.

the United States in 1950. There are two dummy variables in the data. D_2, which is a South–North dummy, is clearly an explanatory variable. But D_1 can be both an explained and explanatory variable. If it is an explained variable we would consider it as "a propensity to have capital punishment."

Let us first consider the regression of M on all the other variables. The results are as follows (figures in parentheses are t-ratios, not standard errors):

$$\hat{M} = \underset{(-0.82)}{-8.50} - \underset{(-1.38)}{3.696PC} - \underset{(-0.54)}{3.568PX} + \underset{(2.11)}{2.598D_1}$$

$$\underset{(2.62)}{-0.018T} - \underset{(-2.3)}{4.095Y} + \underset{(1.82)}{0.400LF}$$

$$+ \underset{(1.17)}{6.444NW} + \underset{(1.93)}{2.541D_2} \qquad R^2 = 0.7746$$

Some of the coefficients have signs opposite to those we would expect.

Let us now consider treating D_1 as an explained variable. We will consider T, Y, LF, NW, and D_2 as the explanatory variables.

The linear probability model gave the following results (figures in parentheses are t-ratios obtained from an ordinary regression program that ignores the zero–one characteristic of the dependent variable):

$$\hat{D}_1 = \underset{(1.50)}{1.993} + \underset{(1.46)}{0.00146T} + \underset{(2.74)}{0.658Y} - \underset{(-1.93)}{0.055LF}$$

$$+ \underset{(2.62)}{1.988NW} + \underset{(1.81)}{0.343D_2} \qquad R^2 = 0.3376$$

What these results indicate is that southern states and states with higher percentages of nonwhites have a positive effect on the probability of having capital punishment. The percentage of labor force employed has a negative effect on the probability of having capital punishment. What is perplexing is the coefficient of Y (median family income), which is significantly positive. One possible explanation for this is that states with high incomes (New York, California, etc.) also have big cities where crime rates are high.

Let us now look at the logit and probit estimates.[30] The logit model gave (figures in parentheses are asymptotic t-ratios)

$$D_1 = \underset{(0.53)}{10.99} + \underset{(1.87)}{0.0194T} + \underset{(1.88)}{10.61Y} - \underset{(-1.40)}{0.668LF} + \underset{(1.95)}{70.99NW} + \underset{(0.02)}{13.33D_2}$$

The results of the probit model were (figures in parentheses are asymptotic t-ratios)

$$\hat{D}_1 = \underset{(0.61)}{6.92} + \underset{(2.00)}{0.0113T} + \underset{(2.05)}{6.46Y} - \underset{(-1.59)}{0.409LF} + \underset{(2.05)}{42.50NW} + \underset{(0.04)}{4.63D_2}$$

As mentioned earlier, the logit coefficients have to be divided by 1.6 to be comparable to the probit coefficients. Such division produces the coefficients 6.87, 0.0121, 6.63, −0.418, 44.37, and 8.33, respectively which are close to the probit coefficients. Surprisingly, D_2 is

---

[30]The logit and probit estimates were computed using William Greene's LIMDEP program.

Table 8.5   Different R^2 measures for the logit, probit, and linear probability models

	Logit	Probit	Linear Probability
Squared correlation between D_1 and $\hat{D}_1$	0.6117	0.6099	0.3376
Effron's R^2	0.6116	0.6095	0.3376
Cragg–Uhler's R^2	0.7223	0.7258	0.5273
McFadden's R^2	0.6083	0.6124	0.4029

not significant, but all the other coefficients have the same signs as in the linear probability model. The coefficient of Y is still positive and is significant.

One other problem is that, as mentioned in Section 8.9, the coefficients of the logit model should be approximately four times the coefficients of the linear probability model, but the coefficients we have obtained are much higher than that. One possible reason for this is the poor fit given by the linear probability model. To investigate this we computed the different measures of R^2's discussed in the preceding section, and the R^2's for the linear probability model are significantly lower than those for the logit and probit models.

In Table 8.5 we present four different measures of R^2's.[31] The first two are easy to compute and are reasonable measures of R^2's. The measures suggested by Cragg and Uhler and by McFadden both depend on the computation of L_R and L_{UR}. The results indicate that there is not much to choose between the logit and probit models and that both are better than the linear probability model. From the practical point of view it appears that the squared correlation between D_1 and $\hat{D}_1$ and Effron's R^2 are sufficient for many problems.

Since we decided on the probit and logit models and D_2 was not significant in these models, we decided to drop that variable and reestimate the probit and logit models. The revised estimates were as follows (figures in parentheses are asymptotic t-ratios).

Logit

$$\hat{D}_1 = \underset{(0.84)}{16.57} + \underset{(1.72)}{0.0165T} + \underset{(1.81)}{9.13Y} - \underset{(-1.49)}{0.715LF} + \underset{(2.38)}{85.36NW}$$

$$R^2(D_1, \hat{D}_1) = 0.5982 \qquad \text{Effron's } R^2 = 0.5982$$
$$\text{Cragg–Uhler's } R^2 = 0.7077 \qquad \text{McFadden's } R^2 = 0.5914$$

Probit

$$\hat{D}_1 = \underset{(0.98)}{10.27} + \underset{(1.86)}{0.0094T} + \underset{(1.97)}{5.55Y} - \underset{(-1.7)}{0.437LF} + \underset{(2.50)}{50.25NW}$$

$$R^2(D_1, \hat{D}_1) = 0.5950 \qquad \text{Effron's } R^2 = 0.5947$$
$$\text{Cragg–Uhler's } R^2 = 0.7113 \qquad \text{McFadden's } R^2 = 0.5955$$

---

[31] We did not compute Amemiya's R^2's. Although he has given an expression for the residual sum of squares, he has not given an expression for the total sum of squares (which should also be appropriately weighted). Using the unweighted total sum of squares $\sum(y_i - \bar{y})^2$ produces a negative R^2.

Again, to make the logit coefficients comparable to the probit coefficients, we have to divide the former by 1.6. This gives 10.36, 0.0103, 5.71, −0.447, and 53.35, respectively, which are close to the probit coefficients.

8.11 Truncated Variables: The Tobit Model

In our discussion of the logit and probit models we talked about a latent variable y_i^* which was not observed, for which we could specify the regression model

$$y_i^* = \beta x_i + u_i \tag{8.18}$$

For simplicity of exposition we are assuming that there is only one explanatory variable. In the logit and probit models, what we observe is a dummy variable

$$y_i = \begin{cases} 1 & \text{if } y_i^* > 0 \\ 0 & \text{if } y_i^* \le 0 \end{cases}$$

Suppose, however, that y_i^* is observed if $y_i^* > 0$ and is not observed if $y_i^* \le 0$. Then the observed y_i will be defined as

$$y_i = \begin{cases} y_i^* = \beta x_i + u_i & \text{if } y_i^* > 0 \\ 0 & \text{if } y_i^* \le 0 \end{cases} \tag{8.19}$$

$$u_i \sim \text{IN}(0, \sigma^2)$$

This is known as the *tobit model* (Tobin's probit) and was first analyzed in the econometrics literature by Tobin.[32] It is also known as a *censored normal regression model* because some observations on y^* (those for which $y^* \le 0$) are censored (we are not allowed to see them). Our objective is to estimate the parameters β and σ.

Some Examples

The example that Tobin considered was that of automobile expenditures. Suppose that we have data on a sample of households. We wish to estimate, say, the income elasticity of demand for automobiles. Let y^* denote expenditures on automobiles and x denote income, and we postulate the regression equation

$$y_i^* = \beta x_i + u_i \qquad u_i \sim \text{IN}(0, \sigma^2)$$

However, in the sample we would have a large number of observations for which the expenditures on automobiles are zero. Tobin argued that we should use the censored regression model. We can specify the model as

$$y_i = \begin{cases} \beta x_i + u_i & \text{for those with positive automobile expenditures} \\ 0 & \text{for those with no expenditures} \end{cases} \tag{8.20}$$

The structure of this model thus appears to be the same as that in (8.19).

---

[32]J. Tobin, "Estimation of Relationships for Limited Dependent Variables," *Econometrica*, Vol. 26, 1958, pp. 24–36.

There have been a very large number of applications of the tobit model.[33] Take, for instance, hours worked (H) or wages (W). If we have observations on a number of individuals, some of whom are employed and others not, we can specify the model for hours worked as

$$H_i = \begin{cases} \beta x_i + u_i & \text{for those working} \\ 0 & \text{for those not working} \end{cases} \tag{8.21}$$

Similarly, for wages we can specify the model

$$W_i = \begin{cases} \gamma z_i + v_i & \text{for those working} \\ 0 & \text{for those not working} \end{cases} \tag{8.22}$$

The structure of these models again appears to be the same as in (8.19). However, there are some limitations in the formulation of the models in (8.20)–(8.22) that we will presently outline after discussing the estimation of the model in (8.19).

Method of Estimation

Let us consider the estimation of β and σ by the use of ordinary least squares. We cannot use OLS with the positive observations y_i because when we write the model

$$y_i = \beta x_i + u_i$$

the error term u_i does not have a zero mean. Since observations with $y_i^* \le 0$ are omitted, it implies that only observations for which $u_i > -\beta x_i$ are included in the sample. Thus the distribution of u_i is a *truncated normal distribution* shown in Figure 8.4 and its mean is not zero. In fact, it depends on β, σ, and x_i and is thus different for each observation. A method of estimation commonly suggested is the maximum likelihood method, which is as follows.

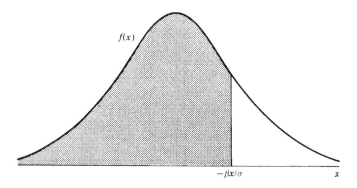

Figure 8.4   Truncated normal distribution

[33] See T. Amemiya, "Tobit Models: A Survey," *Journal of Econometrics*, Vol. 24, 1984, pp. 3–61, which lists a large number of applications of the tobit model.

Note that we have two sets of observations:

1. The positive values of y, for which we can write down the normal density function as usual. We note that $(y_i - \beta x_i)/\sigma$ has a standard normal distribution.
2. The zero observations of y for which all we know is that $y_i^* \leq 0$ or $\beta x_i + u_i \leq 0$. Since u_i/σ has a standard normal distribution, we will write this as $u_i/\sigma \leq -(\beta x_i)/\sigma$. The probability of this can be written as $F(-(\beta x_i)/\sigma)$, where $F(z)$ is the cumulative distribution function of the standard normal.

Let us denote the density function of the standard normal by $f(\cdot)$ and the cumulative distribution function by $F(\cdot)$. Thus

$$f(t) = \frac{1}{\sqrt{2\pi}} \exp\left(-\frac{t^2}{2}\right)$$

and

$$F(z) = \int_{-\infty}^{z} f(t)\, dt$$

Using this notation we can write the likelihood function for the tobit model as

$$L = \prod_{y_i > 0} \frac{1}{\sigma} f\left(\frac{y_i - \beta x_i}{\sigma}\right) \prod_{y_i \leq 0} F\left(-\frac{\beta x_i}{\sigma}\right)$$

Maximizing this likelihood function with respect to β and σ, we get the ML estimates of these parameters. We will not go through the algebraic details of the ML method here.[34] Instead, we discuss the situations under which the tobit model is applicable and its relationship to other models with truncated variables.

Limitations of the Tobit Model

Consider the models of automobile expenditures in (8.20), of hours worked in (8.21), and of wages in (8.22). In each case there are zero observations on some individuals in the sample and thus the structure of the model looks very similar to that in (8.19). But is it really? Every time we have some zero observations in the sample, it is tempting to use the tobit model. However, it is important to understand what the model in (8.19) really says. What we have in model (8.19) is a situation where y_i^* can, *in principle*, take on negative values. However, we do not observe them because of censoring. Thus the zero values are due to nonobservability. This is *not* the case with automobile expenditures, hours worked, or wages. These variables cannot, in principle, assume negative values. The observed zero values are due not to censoring, but to the decisions of individuals. In this case the appropriate procedure would be to model the decisions that produce the zero observations rather than use the tobit model mechanically.

---

[34]For details see Maddala, *Limited-Dependent*, Chap. 6. There are many convenient computer programs that estimate tobit models: SHAZAM, TSP, SAS, LIMDEP. See Appendix C.

Consider, for instance, the model of wages in (8.22). We can argue that each person has a reservation wage W_1 below which the person would not want to work. If W_2 is the market wage for this person (i.e., the wage that employers are willing to pay) and $W_2 \geq W_1$, then we will observe the person as working and the observed wage W is equal to W_2. On the other hand, if $W_1 > W_2$, we observe the person as not working and the observed wage is zero.

If this is the story behind the observed zero wages (one can construct other similar stories), we can formulate the model as follows. Let the reservation wages W_{1i} and market wages W_{2i} be given by

$$W_{1i} = \beta_1 x_{1i} + u_{1i}$$

$$W_{2i} = \beta_2 x_{2i} + u_{2i}$$

The observed W_i is given by

$$W_i = \begin{cases} W_{2i} & \text{if } W_{2i} \geq W_{1i} \\ 0 & \text{otherwise} \end{cases}$$

We can write this as

$$W_i = \begin{cases} \beta_2 x_{2i} + u_{2i} & \text{if } u_{2i} - u_{1i} \geq \beta_i x_{1i} - \beta_2 x_{2i} \\ 0 & \text{otherwise} \end{cases} \tag{8.23}$$

Note the difference between this formulation and the one in equation (8.19). The criterion that $W_i = 0$ is not given by $u_{2i} \leq -\beta_2 x_{2i}$ as in the simple tobit model but by $u_{2i} - u_{1i} < \beta_1 x_{1i} - \beta_2 x_{2i}$. Hence estimation of a simple tobit model in this case produces inconsistent estimates of the parameters.

Estimation of the model given by (8.23) is somewhat complicated to be discussed here.[35] However, the purpose of the example is to show that every time we have some zero observations, we should not use the tobit model. In fact, we can construct similar models for automobile expenditures and hours worked wherein the zero observations are a consequence of decisions by individuals. The simple censored regression model (or the tobit model) is applicable only in those cases where the latent variable can, in principle, take negative values and the observed zero values are a consequence of censoring and nonobservability.

The Truncated Regression Model

The term *truncated regression model* refers to a situation where samples are drawn from a truncated distribution. It is important to keep in mind the distinction between this model and the tobit model. In the censored regression model (tobit model) we have observations on the explanatory variable x_i for all individuals. It is only the dependent variable y_i^* that is missing for some individuals. In the truncated regression model, we have no data on either y_i^* or x_i for some individuals because no samples are drawn if y_i^* is below or above a certain level. The New Jersey negative income tax experiment was an example in which

---

[35]It is discussed in Maddala, *Limited-Dependent*, Section 6.11.

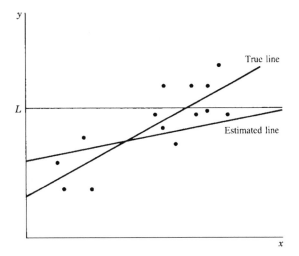

Figure 8.5 Truncated regression model

high-income families were not sampled at all. Families were selected at random but those with incomes higher than 1.5 times the 1967 poverty line were eliminated from the study. If we are estimating earnings functions from these data, we cannot use the OLS method. We have to take account of the fact that the sample is from a truncated distribution. Figure 8.5 illustrates this point. The observations above $y = L$ are omitted from the sample. If we use OLS, the estimated line gives a biased estimate of the true slope. A method of estimation often suggested is, again, the maximum likelihood method.[36]

Suppose that the untruncated regression model is

$$y_i^* = \beta x_i + u_i \qquad u_i \sim \text{IN}(0, \sigma^2)$$

Now, only observations with $y_i^* \leq L$ are included in the sample. The total area under the normal curve up to $y_i^* < L$, that is, $u_i/\sigma < (L - \beta x_i)/\sigma$ is $F[(L - \beta x_i)/\sigma]$, where $F(\cdot)$ is the cumulative distribution function of the standard normal. The density function of the observed y_i is the standard normal density except that its total area is $F[(L - \beta x_i)/\sigma]$. Since the total area under a probability density function should be equal to 1, we have to normalize by this factor. Thus the density function of the observations y_i from the truncated normal is

$$g(y_i) = \begin{cases} \dfrac{1}{\sigma} f\left(\dfrac{y_i - \beta x_i}{\sigma}\right) \Big/ F\left(\dfrac{L - \beta x_i}{\sigma}\right) & \text{if } y_i \leq L \\ 0 & \text{otherwise} \end{cases}$$

The log-likelihood is, therefore,

$$\log L = -n \log \sigma - \frac{1}{2\sigma^2} \sum (y_i - \beta x_i)^2 - \sum \log F\left(\frac{L - \beta x_i}{\sigma}\right)$$

---

[36]Maddala, *Limited-Dependent*, Chap. 6.

Table 8.6 Earnings equations estimated from the New Jersey negative income tax experiment[a]

Variable	OLS	ML
Constant	8.203 (0.091)	9.102 (0.026)
Education	0.010 (0.006)	0.015 (0.007)
IQ	0.002 (0.002)	0.006 (0.005)
Training	0.002 (0.001)	0.006 (0.003)
Union	0.090 (0.030)	0.246 (0.089)
Illness	−0.076 (0.038)	−0.226 (0.107)
Age (linear)	−0.003 (0.002)	−0.016 (0.005)

[a]Figures in parentheses are standard errors.

Maximizing this with respect to β and σ, we get the ML estimates of β and σ. Again, we need not be concerned with the details of the ML estimation method. As an illustration of how different the OLS and ML estimates can be, we present the estimates obtained by Hausman and Wise[37] in Table 8.6. The dependent variable was log earnings. The results show how the OLS estimates are biased. In this particular case they are all biased toward zero.

Summary

1. In this chapter we discussed:
(a) Dummy explanatory variables.
(b) Dummy dependent variables.
(c) Truncated dependent variables.

2. Dummy explanatory variables can be used in tests for coefficient stability in the linear regression models, for obtaining predictions in the linear regression models, and for imposing cross-equation constraints. These uses have been illustrated with examples.

3. One should exercise caution in using the dummy variables when there is heteroskedasticity or autocorrelation. In the presence of autocorrelated errors, the dummy variables for testing stability have to be defined suitably. The proper definitions are given in Section 8.6.

4. Regarding the dummy dependent variables, there are three different models that one can use: the linear probability model, the logit model, and the probit model. The linear discriminant function is closely related to the linear probability model. The coefficients of

---

[37]J. A. Hausman and D. A. Wise, "Social Experimentation, Truncated Distributions, and Efficient Estimation," *Econometrica*, Vol. 45, 1977, pp. 319–339.

the discriminant function are just proportional to those of the linear probability model (see Section 8.8). Thus there is nothing new in linear discriminant analysis. The linear probability model has the drawback that the predicted values can be outside the permissible interval (0, 1).

5. In the analysis of models with dummy dependent variables, we assume the existence of a latent (unobserved) continuous variable which is specified as the usual regression model. However, the latent variable can be observed only as a dichotomous variable. The difference between the logit and probit models is in the assumptions made about the error term. If the error term has a logistic distribution, we have the logit model. If it has a normal distribution, we have the probit model. From the practical point of view, there is not much to choose between the two. The results are usually very similar. If both the models are computed, one should make some adjustments in the coefficients to make them comparable. These adjustments have been outlined in Section 8.9.

6. For comparing the linear probability, logit, and probit models, one can look at the number of cases correctly predicted. However, this is not enough. It is better to look at some measures of R^2's. In Section 8.9 we discuss several measures of R^2: squared correlation between y and $\hat{y}$, Effron's R^2, Cragg and Uhler's R^2, and McFadden's R^2. For practical purposes the first two are descriptive enough. The computation of the different R^2's is illustrated with an example in Section 8.10.

7. The tobit model is a censored regression model. Observations on the latent variable y^* are missing (or censored) if y^* is below (or above) a certain threshold level. This model has been used in a large number of applications where the dependent variable is observed to be zero for some individuals in the sample (automobile expenditures, medical expenditures, hours worked, wages, etc.). However, on careful scrutiny we find that the censored regression model (tobit model) is inappropriate for the analysis of these problems. The tobit model is, strictly speaking, applicable in only those situations where the latent variable can, in principle, take negative values, but these negative values are not observed because of censoring. Where the zero observations are a consequence of individual decisions, these decisions should be modeled appropriately and the tobit model should not be used mechanically.

8. Sometimes samples are drawn from truncated distributions. In this case the truncated regression model should be used. This model is different from the censored regression model (tobit model).

9. The LIMDEP program can be used to compute the logit, probit, tobit, truncated regression, and related models discussed here.

Exercises

1. Explain the meaning of each of the following terms:
   (a) Seasonal dummy variables.
   (b) Dummy dependent variables.
   (c) Linear probability model.
   (d) Linear discriminant function.
   (e) Logit model.
   (f) Probit model.

(g) Tobit model.

(h) Truncated regression model.

2. What would be your answer to the following queries?

(a) My regression program refuses to estimate four seasonal coefficients when I enter the quarterly data including a zero–one dummy for each quarter. What am I supposed to do?

(b) I estimated a model with a zero–one dependent variable using the logit and probit programs. The coefficients I got from the probit program were all smaller than the corresponding coefficients estimated by the logit program. Is there something wrong with my programs?

(c) I have data on medical expenditures on a sample of individuals. Some of them, who did not have any ailments, or did not bother to go to the doctor even if they had ailments, had no expenditures. I wish to estimate the income elasticity of medical expenditures. I am thinking of dropping the individuals with zero expenditures and estimating the model by OLS. My friend says that I would be overestimating the income elasticity by doing this. Is she correct?

3. Explain how you would use dummy variables for generating predictions from a regression model.

4. In the model

$$Y_t = \beta_1 x_{1t} + \beta_2 x_{2t} + \beta_3 x_{3t} + u_t$$

the coefficients are known to be related to a more basic economic parameter α according to the equations

$$\beta_1 + \beta_2 = \alpha$$

$$\beta_1 + \beta_3 = -\alpha$$

Explain how you would estimate α and the variance of $\hat{\alpha}$.

5. In the model

$$Y_{1t} = \alpha x_{1t} + \beta x_{2t} + u_{1t}$$

$$Y_{2t} = \alpha x_{2t} + u_{2t}$$

$$Y_{3t} = \beta x_{1t} + u_{3t}$$

where $u_{1t} \sim \text{IN}(0, 2\sigma^2)$, $u_{2t} \sim \text{IN}(0, \sigma^2)$, $u_{3t} \sim \text{IN}(0, \sigma^2)$, and u_{1t}, u_{2t}, u_{3t} are mutually independent, explain how you will estimate α, β, and σ^2.

6. The following equation was estimated to explain a short-term interest rate (figures in parentheses are standard errors):

$$Y_t = 5.5 + 0.93 x_t - 0.38 x_{t-1} - 5.2 (P_t/P_{t-4}) + 0.50 Y_{t-1}$$
$$ (1.3) \quad (0.04) \quad\quad (0.09) \quad\quad (1.3) \quad\quad\quad (0.07)$$

$$- 0.05 (D_1 - D_4) + 0.08 (D_2 - D_4) + 0.06 (D_3 - D_4)$$
$$ (0.04) \quad\quad\quad (0.04) \quad\quad\quad (0.04)$$

$$R^2 = 0.90 \qquad \bar{R}^2 = 0.89 \qquad \text{SEE} = 0.19 \qquad \text{DW} = 1.3 \qquad T = 92$$

where $Y =$ interest rate on 4 to 6-month commercial paper (percent)

$x =$ interest rate on 90-day Treasury bills (percent)

$D_1 =$ seasonal dummy $= \begin{cases} 1 & \text{for first quarter} \\ 0 & \text{otherwise} \end{cases}$

$D_2 =$ seasonal dummy $= \begin{cases} 1 & \text{for second quarter} \\ 0 & \text{otherwise} \quad \text{etc.} \end{cases}$

$\text{SEE} = \hat{\sigma}$

(a) What is the estimated seasonal pattern in the commercial paper rate?

(b) About how much would R^2 drop if P_t/P_{t-4} were dropped from the equation?

(c) Will $\bar{R}^2$ increase or decrease if P_t/P_{t-4} is dropped?

(d) Instead of using P_t/P_{t-4}, suppose that we use the percentage rate of inflation $\prod_t$ defined by

$$\prod_t = 100 \left(\frac{P_t - P_{t-4}}{P_{t-4}} \right)$$

What will be the new coefficients and their standard errors?

7. You are asked to estimate the coefficients in a linear discriminant function. You do not have a computer program for this. All you have is a program for multiple regression analysis. How will you compute the linear discriminant function?

8. Consider a model with a zero–one dependent variable. You have a multiple regression program and a program for the logit and probit models. You have computed the coefficients of the linear probability model and the logit and probit models:

(a) How will you transform the coefficients of the three models so that they are comparable?

(b) How will you compute the R^2's for the three models?

(c) By what criteria will you choose the best model?

9. Explain how you will formulate a model explaining the following. In each case the sample consists of some observations for which the dependent variable is zero. Suggest a list of explanatory variables in each case.

(a) Automobile expenditures (in a year) of a number of families.

(b) Hours worked by a group of married women.

(c) Amount of child support received by a number of working wives.

(d) Medical expenditures of a number of families.

(e) Amount of loan granted by a bank to a number of applicants.

(f) Amount of financial aid received by a group of students at a college.

*10. Table 8.7 (available on the Web) presents data on bride–groom characteristics and dowries for marriages in rural south-central India.[38] The variable definitions follow the table:

(a) Estimate an equation explaining the determinants of the dowry.

(b) Estimate probit and tobit equations explaining the determinants of bride's years of schooling and groom's years of schooling.

---

[38]The data have kindly been provided by Anil B. Deolalikar. They have been analyzed in A. B. Deolalikar and V. Rao, "The Demand for Dowries and Bride Characteristics in Marriage: Empirical Estimates for Rural South Central India," Manuscript, University of Washington, September 1990.

9 Simultaneous Equations Models

What is in this Chapter?

In Chapter 4 we mentioned that one of the assumptions in the basic regression model is that the explanatory variables are uncorrelated with the error term. In this chapter we relax that assumption and consider the case where several variables are jointly determined. A different source of violation of this basic assumption, due to errors in variables, is discussed in Chapter 11.

This chapter first discusses the conditions under which equations are estimable in the case of jointly determined variables (the "identification problem") and methods of estimation. One major method is that of "instrumental variables," a method we shall also discuss in Chapter 11.

This chapter also discusses the application of OLS (ordinary least squares) in these models—a topic not often mentioned. This topic is important because the earliest discussion of the identification problem by Working was in terms of OLS.

Finally, this chapter also discusses recent work on exogeneity and causality.

9.1 Introduction

In the usual regression model y is the dependent or determined variable and $x_1, x_2, \ldots$ are the independent or determining variables. The crucial assumption we make is that the x's are independent of the error term u. Sometimes, this assumption is violated: for example, in demand and supply models. It is also violated in the case where the x's are measured with error, but we postpone discussion of this case to Chapter 11. We illustrate here the case of a demand and supply model.

Suppose that we write the demand function as

$$q = \alpha + \beta p + u \tag{9.1}$$

where q is the quantity demanded, p the price, and u the disturbance term, which denotes random shifts in the demand function. In Figure 9.1 we see that a shift in the demand function produces a change in *both* price and quantity if the supply curve has an upward slope. If the supply curve is horizontal (i.e., completely price inelastic), a shift in the demand curve produces a change in price only, and if the supply curve is vertical (infinite price elasticity), a shift in the demand curve produces a change in quantity only.

Thus in equation (9.1) the error term u is correlated with p when the supply curve is upward sloping or perfectly horizontal. Hence an estimation of the equation by ordinary least squares produces inconsistent estimates of the parameters.

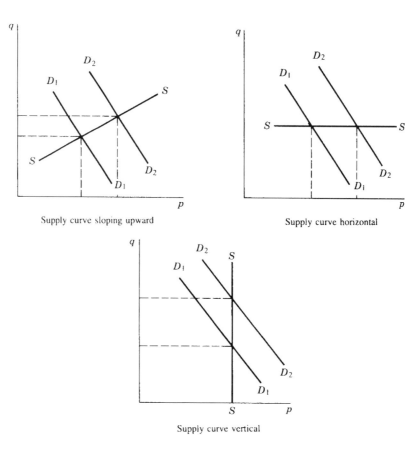

Figure 9.1   Effects of shifts in the demand function on price

We could have written the demand function as

$$p = \alpha' + \beta' q + u' \qquad (9.1')$$

But, again, u' will be correlated with q if the supply function is upward sloping or perfectly vertical. There is the question of whether the demand function should be written as in equation (9.1) or (9.1'). If it is written as in (9.1), we say that the equation is *normalized with respect to q* (i.e., the coefficient of q is unity). If it is written as in (9.1'), we say that the equation is *normalized with respect to p*. Since price and quantity are determined by the interaction of demand and supply, it should not matter whether we normalize the equations with respect to p or with respect to q.

The estimation methods we use should produce identical estimates whatever normalization we adopt. However, the preceding discussion and Figure 9.1 suggest that if quantity supplied is not responsive to price, the demand function should be normalized with respect to p, that is, it should be written as in (9.1'). On the other hand, if quantity supplied is highly responsive to price, the demand function should be normalized with respect to q as in (9.1). An empirical example will be given in Section 9.3 to illustrate this point. The question of normalization is discussed in greater detail in Section 9.7.

Returning to the demand and supply model, the problem is that we cannot consider the demand function in isolation when we are studying the relationship between quantity and price as in (9.1). The solution is to bring the supply function into the picture, and estimate the demand and supply functions together. Such models are known as *simultaneous equations models*.

9.2   Endogenous and Exogenous Variables

In simultaneous equations models variables are classified as endogenous and exogenous. The traditional definition of these terms is that endogenous variables are variables that are determined by the economic model and exogenous variables are those determined from outside.

Endogenous variables are also called *jointly determined* and exogenous variables are called *predetermined*. (It is customary to include past values of endogenous variables in the predetermined group.) Since the exogenous variables are predetermined, they are independent of the error terms in the model. They thus satisfy the assumptions that the x's satisfy in the usual regression model of y on x's.

The foregoing definition of exogeneity has recently been questioned in the econometric literature, but we have to postpone this discussion to a later section (Section 9.10). We will discuss this criticism and its implications after going through the conventional methods of estimation for simultaneous equation models.

Consider now the demand and supply model

$$q = a_1 + b_1 p + c_1 y + u_1 \quad \text{demand function}$$
$$q = a_2 + b_2 p + c_2 R + u_2 \quad \text{supply function} \qquad (9.2)$$

q is the quantity, p the price, y the income, R the rainfall, and u_1 and u_2 are the error terms. Here p and q are the endogenous variables and y and R are the exogenous variables. Since the exogenous variables are independent of the error terms u_1 and u_2 and satisfy the usual requirements for ordinary least squares estimation, we can estimate regressions of p and q on y and R by ordinary least squares, although we cannot estimate equations (9.2) by ordinary least squares. We will show presently that from these regressions of p and q on y and R we can recover the parameters in the original demand and supply equations (9.2). This method is called *indirect least squares* — it is indirect because we do not apply least squares to equations (9.2). The indirect least squares method does not always work, so we will first discuss the conditions under which it works and how the method can be simplified. To discuss this issue, we first have to clarify the concept of identification.

9.3   The Identification Problem: Identification Through Reduced Form

We have argued that the error terms u_1 and u_2 are correlated with p in equations (9.2), and hence if we estimate the equation by ordinary least squares, the parameter estimates are inconsistent. Roughly speaking, the concept of identification is related to consistent estimation of the parameters. Thus if we can somehow obtain consistent estimates of the parameters in the demand function, we say that the demand function is *identified*. Similarly, if we can somehow get consistent estimates of the parameters in the supply function, we say that the supply function is *identified*. Getting consistent estimates is just a necessary condition for identification, not a sufficient condition, as we show in the next section.

If we solve the two equations in (9.2) for q and p in terms of y and R, we get

$$q = \frac{a_1 b_2 - a_2 b_1}{b_2 - b_1} + \frac{c_1 b_2}{b_2 - b_1} y - \frac{c_2 b_1}{b_2 - b_1} R + \text{an error}$$

$$p = \frac{a_1 - a_2}{b_2 - b_1} + \frac{c_1}{b_2 - b_1} y - \frac{c_2}{b_2 - b_1} R + \text{an error} \tag{9.3}$$

These equations are called the *reduced-form equations*. Equations (9.2) are called the *structural equations* because they describe the structure of the economic system. We can write equations (9.3) as

$$q = \pi_1 + \pi_2 y + \pi_3 R + v_1$$

$$p = \pi_4 + \pi_5 y + \pi_6 R + v_2 \tag{9.4}$$

where v_1 and v_2 are error terms and

$$\pi_1 = \frac{a_1 b_2 - a_2 b_1}{b_2 - b_1}, \quad \pi_2 = \frac{c_1 b_2}{b_2 - b_1} \quad \text{etc.}$$

The π's are called *reduced-form parameters*. The estimation of the equations (9.4) by ordinary least squares gives us consistent estimates of the reduced form parameters. From these we have to obtain consistent estimates of the parameters in equations (9.2). These parameters are called *structural parameters*. Comparing (9.3) with (9.4) we get

$$\hat{b}_1 = \frac{\hat{\pi}_3}{\hat{\pi}_6} \quad \hat{b}_2 = \frac{\hat{\pi}_2}{\hat{\pi}_5}$$

$$\hat{c}_2 = \hat{\pi}_6(\hat{b}_1 - \hat{b}_2) \quad \hat{c}_1 = -\hat{\pi}_5(\hat{b}_1 - \hat{b}_2)$$

$$\hat{a}_1 = \hat{\pi}_1 - \hat{b}_1\hat{\pi}_4 \quad \hat{a}_2 = \hat{\pi}_1 - \hat{b}_2\hat{\pi}_4$$

Since $\hat{a}_1$, $\hat{a}_2$, $\hat{b}_1$, $\hat{b}_2$, $\hat{c}_1$, $\hat{c}_2$ are all single-valued functions of the $\hat{\pi}$, they are consistent estimates of the corresponding structural parameters. As mentioned earlier, this method is known as the *indirect least squares method*.

It may not be always possible to get estimates of the structural coefficients from the estimates of the reduced-form coefficients, and sometimes we get multiple estimates and we have the problem of choosing between them. For example, suppose that the demand and supply model is written as

$$q = a_1 + b_1 p + c_1 y + u_1 \quad \text{demand function}$$
$$q = a_2 + b_2 p + u_2 \quad\quad\quad \text{supply function} \tag{9.5}$$

Then the reduced form is

$$q = \frac{a_1 b_2 - a_2 b_1}{b_2 - b_1} + \frac{c_1 b_2}{b_2 - b_1} y + v_1$$

$$p = \frac{a_1 - a_2}{b_2 - b_1} + \frac{c_1}{b_2 - b_1} y + v_2$$

or

$$q = \pi_1 + \pi_2 y + v_1$$
$$p = \pi_3 + \pi_4 y + v_2$$

In this case $\hat{b}_2 = \hat{\pi}_2/\hat{\pi}_4$ and $\hat{a}_2 = \hat{\pi}_1 - \hat{b}_2\hat{\pi}_3$. But there is no way of getting estimates of a_1, b_1, and c_1. Thus the supply function is identified but the demand function is not. On the other hand, suppose that we have the model

$$q = a_1 + b_1 p + u_1 \quad\quad\quad \text{demand function}$$
$$q = a_2 + b_2 p + c_2 R + u_2 \quad \text{supply function}$$

Now we can check that the demand function is identified but the supply function is not.

Finally, suppose that we have the system

$$q = a_1 + b_1 p + c_1 y + d_1 R + u_1 \quad \text{demand function}$$
$$q = a_2 + b_2 p + u_2 \quad\quad\quad\quad\quad \text{supply function} \tag{9.6}$$

Rainfall affects demand (if there is rain, people do not go shopping), but not supply. The reduced-form equations are

$$q = \frac{a_1 b_2 - a_2 b_1}{b_2 - b_1} + \frac{c_1 b_2}{b_2 - b_1} y + \frac{d_1 b_2}{b_2 - b_1} R + v_1$$

$$p = \frac{a_1 - a_2}{b_2 - b_1} + \frac{c_1}{b_2 - b_1} y + \frac{d_1}{b_2 - b_1} R + v_2$$

or

$$q = \pi_1 + \pi_2 y + \pi_3 R + v_1$$

$$p = \pi_4 + \pi_5 y + \pi_6 R + v_2$$

Now we get two estimates of b_2. One is $\hat{b}_2 = \hat{\pi}_2 / \hat{\pi}_5$ and the other is $\hat{b}_2 = \hat{\pi}_3 / \hat{\pi}_6$, and these need not be equal. For each of these we get an estimate of a_2, which is $\hat{a}_2 = \hat{\pi}_1 - \hat{b}\hat{\pi}_4$.

On the other hand, we get no estimates for the parameters a_1, b_1, c_1, and d_1 of the demand function. Here we say that the supply function is *overidentified* and the demand function is *underidentified*. When we get unique estimates for the structural parameters of an equation from the reduced-form parameters, we say that the equation is *exactly identified*. When we get multiple estimates, we say that the equation is *overidentified*, and when we get no estimates, we say that the equation is *underidentified* (or *not identified*).

There is a simple counting rule available in the linear systems that we have been considering. This counting rule is also known as the *order condition* for identification. This rule is as follows: Let g be the number of endogenous variables in the system and k the total number of variables (endogenous and exogenous) missing from the equation under consideration. Then:

1. If $k = g - 1$, the equation is exactly identified.
2. If $k > g - 1$, the equation is overidentified.
3. If $k < g - 1$, the equation is underidentified.

This condition is *only necessary but not sufficient*. In Section 9.4 we will give a necessary and sufficient condition.

Let us apply this rule to the equation systems we are considering. In equations (9.2), g, the number of endogenous variables, is 2, and there is only one variable missing from each equation. Hence both equations are identified exactly. In equations (9.5), again $g = 2$. There is no variable missing from the first equation; hence it is underidentified. There is one variable missing in the second equation; hence it is exactly identified. In equation (9.6), there is no variable missing in the first equation; hence it is not identified. In the second equation there are two variables missing; thus $k > g - 1$ and the equation is overidentified.

Illustrative Example

The indirect least squares method we have described is rarely used. In the following sections we describe a more popular method of estimating simultaneous equation models.

This is the method of two-stage least squares (2SLS). However, if some coefficients in the reduced-form equations are close to zero, this gives us some information about what variables to omit in the structural equations. We will provide a simple example of a two-equation demand and supply model where the estimates from OLS, reduced-form least squares, and indirect least squares provide information on how to formulate the model. The example also illustrates some points we have raised in Section 9.1 regarding normalization.

The model is from Merrill and Fox.[1] In Table 9.1 data are presented for demand and supply of pork in the United States for 1922–1941. The model estimated by Merrill and Fox is

$$Q = a_1 + b_1 P + c_1 Y + u \quad \text{demand function}$$

$$Q = a_2 + b_2 P + c_2 Z + v \quad \text{supply function}$$

Table 9.1 Demand and supply of pork, United States, 1922–1941[a]

Year	P_t	Q_t	Y_t	Z_t
1922	26.8	65.7	541	74.0
1923	25.3	74.2	616	84.7
1924	25.3	74.0	610	80.2
1925	31.1	66.8	636	69.9
1926	33.3	64.1	651	66.8
1927	31.2	67.7	645	71.6
1928	29.5	70.9	653	73.6
1929	30.3	69.6	682	71.2
1930	29.1	67.0	604	69.6
1931	23.7	68.4	515	68.0
1932	15.6	70.7	390	74.8
1933	13.9	69.6	364	73.6
1934	18.8	63.1	411	70.2
1935	27.4	48.4	459	46.5
1936	26.9	55.1	517	57.6
1937	27.7	55.8	551	58.7
1938	24.5	58.2	506	58.0
1939	22.2	64.7	538	67.2
1940	19.3	73.5	576	73.7
1941	24.7	68.4	697	66.5

[a]P_t, retail price of pork (cents per pound); Q_t, consumption of pork (pounds per capita); Y_t, disposable personal income (dollars per capita); Z_t, "predetermined elements in pork production."
Source: William C. Merrill and Karl A. Fox, *Introduction to Economic Statistics* (New York: Wiley, 1971), p. 539.

[1]William C. Merrill and Karl A. Fox, *Introduction to Economic Statistics* (New York: Wiley, 1971).

The equations were fitted for 1922–1941. The reduced-form equations were (standard errors in parentheses)

$$\hat{P} = -0.0101 + \underset{(0.1339)}{1.0813}Y - \underset{(0.1159)}{0.8320}Z \quad R^2 = 0.893$$

$$\hat{Q} = 0.0026 - \underset{(0.0673)}{0.0018}Y + \underset{(0.0582)}{0.6839}Z \quad R^2 = 0.898$$

The coefficient of Y in the second equation is very close to zero and the variable Y can be dropped from this equation. This would imply that $b_2 = 0$, or supply is not responsive to price. In any case, solving from the reduced form to the structural form, we get the estimates of the structural equation as

$$Q = -0.0063 - 0.8220P + 0.8870Y \quad \text{demand function}$$

$$Q = 0.0026 - 0.0017P + 0.6825Z \quad \text{supply function}$$

The least squares estimates of the demand function are:
Normalized with respect to Q

$$\hat{Q} = -0.0049 - \underset{(0.0594)}{0.7205}P + \underset{(0.0967)}{0.7646}Y \quad R^2 = 0.903$$

Normalized with respect to P

$$\hat{P} = -0.0070 - \underset{(0.1032)}{1.2518}Q + \underset{(0.0861)}{1.0754}Y \quad R^2 = 0.956$$

The structural demand function can also be written in the two forms:
Normalized with respect to Q

$$\hat{Q} = -0.0063 - 0.8220P + 0.8870Y$$

Normalized with respect to P

$$\hat{P} = -0.0077 - 1.2165Q + 1.0791Y$$

The estimates of the parameters in the demand function are almost the same with the direct least squares method as with the indirect least squares method when the demand function is normalized with respect to P.

Which is the correct normalization? We argued in Section 9.1 that if quantity supplied is not responsive to price, the demand function should be normalized with respect to P. We saw that the fact that the coefficient of Y in the reduced-form equation for Q was close to zero implied that $b_2 = 0$ or quantity supplied is not responsive to price. This is also confirmed by the structural estimate of b_2, which shows a wrong sign for b_2 as well but a coefficient close to zero.

Dropping P from the supply function and using OLS, we get the supply function as

$$\hat{Q} = 0.0025 + \underset{(0.0857)}{0.6841}Z \quad R^2 = 0.898$$

Thus we normalize the demand function with respect to P, drop the variable P from the supply function, and estimate both equations by OLS.

9.4 Necessary and Sufficient Conditions for Identification

In Section 9.3 our discussion was in terms of obtaining estimates for the structural parameters from estimates of the reduced-form parameters. An alternative way of looking at the identification problem is to see whether the equation under consideration can be obtained as a linear combination of the other equations.

Consider, for instance, equations (9.5). Take a weighted average of the two equations with weights w and $(1 - w)$. Then we get

$$q = w(a_1 + b_1 p + c_1 y) + (1 - w)(a_2 + b_2 p) + u'1$$
$$= a_1^* + b_1^* p + c_1^* y + u_1' \tag{9.7}$$

where $a_1^* = wa_1 + (1 - w)a_2$

$b_1^* = wb_1 + (1 - w)b_2$

$c_1^* = wc_1$ and $u_1' = wu_1 + (1 - w)u_2$

Equation (9.7) looks like the first equation in (9.5). Thus when we estimate the parameters of the demand function, we do not know whether we are getting estimates of the parameters in the demand function or in some weighted average of the demand and supply functions. Thus the parameters in the demand function are not identified. The same cannot be said about the supply function because the only way that equation (9.7) can look like the supply function in (9.5) is if $c_1^* = 0$ (i.e., $wc_1 = 0$). But since $c_1 \neq 0$, we must have $w = 0$. That is, the weighted average gives zero weight to the demand function. Hence when we estimate the supply function, we are sure that the estimates we have are of the supply function. Thus the parameters of the supply function are identified.

Checking this condition has been easy with two equations. But when we have many equations, we need a more systematic way of checking this condition. For illustrative purposes consider the case of three endogenous variables y_1, y_2, y_3 and three exogenous variables z_1, z_2, z_3. We will mark with a cross $\times$ if a variable occurs in an equation and a 0 if not. Suppose that the equation system is the following:

Equation	y_1	y_2	y_3	z_1	z_2	z_3
1	$\times$	0	$\times$	$\times$	0	$\times$
2	$\times$	0	0	$\times$	0	$\times$
3	0	$\times$	$\times$	$\times$	$\times$	0

The rule for identification of any equation is as follows:

1. Delete the particular row.
2. Pick up the columns corresponding to the elements that have zeros in that row.
3. If from this array of columns we can find $(g - 1)$ rows and columns that are not all zeros, where g is the number of endogenous variables and no column (or row) is

proportional to another column (or row) for all parameter values, then the equation is identified. Otherwise, not. If there is one such column (or row) delete that column (or row).

This condition is called the *rank condition* for identification and is a necessary and sufficient condition.[2]

We will now apply the order and rank conditions to the illustrative example we have. The number of equations is $g = 3$. Hence the number of missing variables is 2 for the first equation, 3 for the second, and 2 for the third. Thus, by the order condition, the first and third equations are exactly identified and the second equation is overidentified. We will see that the rank condition gives us a different answer.

To check the rank condition for equation 1, we delete the first row and pick up the columns corresponding to the missing variables y_2 and z_2. The columns are

$$
\begin{array}{cc}
0 & 0 \\
\times & \times
\end{array}
$$

Note that we have only one row with not all elements zero. Thus, by the rank condition the equation is not identified. For equation 2, we delete row 2, and pick up the columns corresponding to y_2, y_3, and z_2. We get

$$
\begin{array}{ccc}
0 & \times & 0 \\
\times & \times & \times
\end{array}
$$

We now have two rows (and two columns) with not all elements zero. Thus the equation is identified. Similarly, for the third equation deleting the third row, the columns for y_1 and z_3 give

$$
\begin{array}{cc}
\times & \times \\
\times & \times
\end{array}
$$

Again we have two rows with not all elements zero. Hence the equation is identified. Note that the rank condition states whether the equation is identified or not. From the order condition we know whether it is exactly identified or overidentified.

In summary the second and third equations are estimable. The first one is not, and the order condition misleads us into thinking that it is so. There are many estimation methods for simultaneous equations models that break down if the order condition is not satisfied but do give us estimates of the parameters if the order condition is satisfied even if the rank condition is not. In such cases these estimates are meaningless. Thus it is desirable to check the rank condition. In our example, for equation 1, the rank condition is not satisfied. What this means is that the estimates we obtain for the parameters in equation 1 are actually estimates of some linear combinations of the parameters in all the equations

---

[2]The array of columns is called a *matrix* and the condition that we have stated is that the rank of this matrix be $(g - 1)$: hence the use of the term *rank condition*. We have avoided the use of matrix notation and stated the condition in an alternative fashion. A derivation using matrix notation is presented in the appendix to this chapter.

and thus have no special economic interpretation. This is what we mean when we say that equation 1 is not estimable.

Illustrative Example

As an illustration, consider the following macroeconomic model with seven endogenous variables and three exogenous variables. The endogenous and exogenous variables are:

Endogenous	*Exogenous*
C = real consumption	G = real government purchases
I = real investment	T = real tax receipts
N = employment	M = nominal money stock
P = price level	
R = interest rate	
Y = real income	
W = money wage rate	

The equations are:

(1) $C = a_1 + b_1 Y - c_1 T + d_1 R + u_1$ (consumption function)
(2) $I = a_2 + b_2 Y + c_2 R + u_2$ (investment function)
(3) $Y = C + I + G$ (identity)
(4) $M = a_3 + b_3 Y + c_3 R + d_3 P + u_3$ (liquidity preference function)
(5) $Y = a_4 + b_4 N + u_4$ (production function)
(6) $N = a_5 + b_5 W + c_5 P + u_5$ (labor demand)
(7) $N = a_6 + b_6 W + c_6 P + u_6$ (labor supply)

The question is which of these equations are underidentified, exactly identified, and overidentified. To answer this question, we prepare the following table. A 1 denotes that the variable is present, a 0 denotes that it is missing:

Equation	C	I	N	P	R	Y	W	G	T	M
1	1	0	0	0	1	1	0	0	1	0
2	0	1	0	0	1	1	0	0	0	0
3	1	1	0	0	0	1	0	1	0	0
4	0	0	0	1	1	1	0	0	0	1
5	0	0	1	0	0	1	0	0	0	0
6	0	0	1	1	0	0	1	0	0	0
7	0	0	1	1	0	0	1	0	0	0

Note that equation 3 is an identity and does not have any parameters to be estimated. Hence we do not need to discuss its identification. The number of endogenous variables minus one is 6 in this model. By the order condition we get the result that equations 1 and 4 are exactly identified and equations 2, 5, 6, and 7 are overidentified.

Let us look at the rank condition for equation 1. The procedure is similar for other equations. Delete the first row and gather the columns for the missing variables I, N, P, W, G, M. We get

$$
\begin{array}{cccccc}
1 & 0 & 0 & 0 & 0 & 0 \\
1 & 0 & 0 & 0 & 1 & 0 \\
0 & 0 & 1 & 0 & 0 & 1 \\
0 & 1 & 0 & 0 & 0 & 0 \\
0 & 1 & 1 & 1 & 0 & 0 \\
0 & 1 & 1 & 1 & 0 & 0
\end{array}
$$

Since we have six rows (and six columns) whose elements are not all zero, the equation is identified. It can be checked that the same is true for equations 2, 4, and 5. However, for equations 6 and 7, we cannot find six rows whose elements are not all zero. Thus, equations 6 and 7 are not identified by the rank condition even though they are overidentified by the order condition.

9.5 Methods of Estimation: The Instrumental Variable Method

In previous sections we discussed the identification problem. Now we discuss some methods of estimation for simultaneous equations models. Actually, we have already discussed one method of estimation: the indirect least squares method. However, this method is very cumbersome if there are many equations and hence it is not often used. Here we discuss some methods that are more generally applicable. These methods of estimation can be classified into two categories:

1. Single-equation methods (also called "limited-information methods").
2. System methods (also called "full-information methods").

We will not discuss the full-information methods here because they involve algebraic detail beyond the scope of this book. We discuss single-equation methods only. In these methods we estimate each equation separately using only the information about the restrictions on the coefficients of that particular equation. For instance, in the illustrative example in Section 9.4 when we estimate the consumption function (the first equation), we just make use of the fact that the variables I, N, P, W, G, M are missing and that the last two variables are exogenous. We are not concerned about what variables are missing from the other equations. The restrictions on the other equations are used only to check identification, not for estimation. This is the reason these methods are called limited-information methods. In full-information methods we use information on the restrictions on all equations.

A general method of obtaining consistent estimates of the parameters in simultaneous equations models is the *instrumental variable method*. Broadly speaking, an instrumental variable is a variable that is uncorrelated with the error term but correlated with the explanatory variables in the equation.

For instance, suppose that we have the equation

$$
y = \beta x + u
$$

where x is correlated with u. Then we cannot estimate this equation by ordinary least squares. The estimate of β is inconsistent because of the correlation between x and u. If we can find a variable z that is uncorrelated with u, we can get a consistent estimator for β. We replace the condition $\text{cov}(z, u) = 0$ by its sample counterpart

$$\frac{1}{n} \sum z(y - \beta x) = 0$$

This gives

$$\hat{\beta} = \frac{\sum zy}{\sum zx} = \frac{\sum z(\beta x + u)}{\sum zx} = \beta + \frac{\sum zu}{\sum zx}$$

But $\sum zu / \sum zx$ can be written as $(1/n)\sum zu / (1/n)\sum zx$. The probability limit of this expression is

$$\frac{\text{cov}(z, u)}{\text{cov}(z, x)} = 0$$

since $\text{cov}(z, x) \neq 0$. Hence plim $\hat{\beta} = \beta$, thus proving that $\hat{\beta}$ is a consistent estimator for β. Note that we require z to be correlated with x so that $\text{cov}(z, x) \neq 0$.

Now consider the simultaneous equations model

$$y_1 = b_1 y_2 + c_1 z_1 + c_2 z_2 + u_1$$
$$y_2 = b_2 y_1 + c_3 z_3 + u_2$$
(9.8)

where y_1, y_2 are endogenous variables, z_1, z_2, z_3 are exogenous variables, and u_1, u_2 are error terms. Consider the estimation of the first equation. Since z_1 and z_2 are independent of u_1, we have $\text{cov}(z_1, u_1) = 0$ and $\text{cov}(z_2, u_1) = 0$. However, y_2 is not independent of u_1. Hence $\text{cov}(y_2, u_1) \neq 0$. Since we have three coefficients to estimate, we have to find a variable that is independent of u_1. Fortunately, in this case we have z_3 and $\text{cov}(z_3, u_1) = 0$. z_3 is the instrumental variable for y_2. Thus, writing the sample counterparts of these three covariances, we have the three equations

$$\frac{1}{n} \sum z_1(y_1 - b_1 y_2 - c_1 z_1 - c_2 z_2) = 0$$

$$\frac{1}{n} \sum z_2(y_1 - b_1 y_2 - c_1 z_1 - c_2 z_2) = 0$$
(9.8')

$$\frac{1}{n} \sum z_3(y_1 - b_1 y_2 - c_1 z_1 - c_2 z_2) = 0$$

The difference between the normal equations for the ordinary least squares method and the instrumental variable method is only in the last equation.

Consider the second equation of our model. Now we have to find an instrumental variable for y_1 but we have a choice of z_1 and z_2. This is because this equation is overidentified (by the order condition).

Note that the order condition (counting rule) is related to the question of whether or not we have enough exogenous variables elsewhere in the system to use as instruments for the endogenous variables in the equation with unknown coefficients. If the equation is underidentified we do not have enough instrumental variables. If it is exactly identified, we have just enough instrumental variables. If it is overidentified, we have more than enough instrumental variables. In this case we have to use weighted averages of the instrumental variables available. We compute these weighted averages so that we get the most efficient (minimum asymptotic variance) estimators.

It has been shown (proving this is beyond the scope of this book) that the efficient instrumental variables are constructed by regressing the endogenous variables on *all* the exogenous variables in the system (i.e., estimating the reduced-form equations). In the case of the model given by equations (9.8), we first estimate the reduced-form equations by regressing y_1 and y_2 on z_1, z_2, z_3. We obtain the predicted values $\hat{y}_1$ and $\hat{y}_2$ and use these as instrumental variables. For the estimation of the first equation we use $\hat{y}_2$, and for the estimation of the second equation we use $\hat{y}_1$. We can write $\hat{y}_1$ and $\hat{y}_2$ as linear functions of z_1, z_2, z_3. Let us write

$$\hat{y}_1 = a_{11}z_1 + a_{12}z_2 + a_{13}z_3$$

$$\hat{y}_2 = a_{21}z_1 + a_{22}z_2 + a_{23}z_3$$

where the a's are obtained from the estimation of the reduced-form equations by OLS. In the estimation of the first equation in (9.8) we use $\hat{y}_2$, z_1, and z_2 as instruments. This is the same as using z_1, z_2, and z_3 as instruments because

$$\sum \hat{y}_2 u_1 = 0 \Rightarrow \sum (a_{21}z_1 + a_{22}z_2 + a_{23}z_3)u_1 = 0$$

$$\Rightarrow a_{21} \sum z_1 u_1 + a_{22} \sum z_2 u_1 + a_{23} \sum z_3 u_1 = 0$$

But the first two terms are zero by virtue of the first two equations in (9.8'). Thus $\sum \hat{y}_2 u_1 = 0 \Rightarrow \sum z_3 u_1 = 0$. Hence using $\hat{y}_2$ as an instrumental variable is the same as using z_3 as an instrumental variable. This is the case with exactly identified equations where there is no choice in the instruments.

The case with the second equation in (9.8) is different. Earlier, we said that we had a choice between z_1 and z_2 as instruments for y_1. The use of $\hat{y}_1$ gives the optimum weighting. The normal equations now are

$$\sum \hat{y}_1 u_2 = 0 \quad \text{and} \quad \sum z_3 u_2 = 0$$

$$\sum \hat{y}_1 u_2 = 0 \Rightarrow \sum (a_{11}z_1 + a_{12}z_2 + a_{13}z_3)u_2 = 0$$

$$\Rightarrow \sum (a_{11}z_1 + a_{12}z_2)u_2 = 0$$

since $\sum z_3 u_2 = 0$. Thus the optimal weights for z_1 and z_2 are a_{11} and a_{12}.

Measuring R^2

When we are estimating an equation with instrumental variables, a question arises as to how to report the goodness of fit measure R^2. This question also arises with the two-stage least squares (2SLS) method described in Section 9.6. We can think of two measures:

1. R^2 = squared correlation between y and $\hat{y}$.

2. Measures based on residual sum of squares:

$$R^2 = 1 - \frac{\displaystyle\sum_{i=1}^{n}(y_i - \hat{y}_i)^2}{\displaystyle\sum(y_i - \overline{y})^2}$$

In the results we present we will be reporting the second measure.

Note that the R^2 from the instrumental variable method will be lower than the R^2 from the OLS method. It is also conceivable that the R^2 would be negative, but this is an indication that something is wrong with the specification — perhaps the equation is not identified. We illustrate this point with an example.

Many computer programs present an R^2 for simultaneous equations models. But since there is no unique measure of R^2 in such models, it is important to check the formula that the program uses. For instance, the SAS program gives an R^2, but it appears to be neither one of the above-mentioned measures.

Illustrative Example[3]

Table 9.2 provides data on some characteristics of the wine industry in Australia for 1955–1956 to 1974–1975. It is assumed that a reasonable demand–supply model for the

Table 9.2   Data for wine industry in Australia[a]

Year	Q	S	P^w	P^b	A	Y
1955–1956	0.91	85.4	77.5	35.7	89.1	1056
1956–1957	1.05	88.4	80.2	37.4	83.3	1037
1957–1958	1.18	89.1	79.5	37.7	84.4	1006
1958–1959	1.27	90.5	84.9	37.1	90.1	1047
1959–1960	1.27	93.1	94.9	36.2	89.4	1091
1960–1961	1.37	97.2	92.7	35.0	89.3	1093
1961–1962	1.46	100.3	92.5	37.6	89.8	1102
1962–1963	1.59	100.3	92.7	40.1	96.7	1154
1963–1964	1.86	101.5	97.1	39.7	99.9	1234
1964–1965	1.96	104.8	93.9	38.3	103.2	1254
1965–1966	2.32	107.5	102.7	37.0	102.2	1241
1966–1967	2.86	111.8	100.0	36.1	100.0	1299
1967–1968	3.50	114.9	119.5	35.4	103.0	1287
1968–1969	3.96	117.9	119.7	35.1	104.2	1369
1969–1970	4.21	122.3	125.2	34.5	113.0	1443
1970–1971	4.54	128.2	134.1	34.5	132.5	1517
1971–1972	4.93	134.1	124.3	34.3	143.6	1562
1972–1973	5.40	145.1	119.0	34.3	176.2	1678
1973–1974	6.13	174.9	108.5	31.9	159.9	1769
1974–1975	6.29	237.2	107.9	31.0	182.1	1847

[a]Data are not in logs.

---

[3]I would like to thank Kim Sawyer for providing me with these data and the example.

industry would be (where all variables are in *logs*)

$$Q_t = a_0 + a_1 P_t^w + a_2 P_t^b + a_3 Y_t + a_4 A_t + u_t \quad \text{demand}$$

$$Q_t = b_0 + b_1 P_t^w + b_2 S_t + v_t \qquad\qquad \text{supply}$$

where Q_t = real per capita consumption of wine

P_t^w = price of wine relative to CPI

P_t^b = price of beer relative to CPI

Y_t = real per capita disposable income

A_t = real per capita advertising expenditure

S_t = index of storage costs

Q_t and P_t^w are the two endogenous variables. The other variables are exogenous. For the estimation of the demand function we have only one instrumental variable S_t. But for the estimation of the supply function we have available three instrumental variables: P_t^b, Y_t, and A_t.

The OLS estimation of the demand function gave the following results (all variables are in logs and figures in parentheses are t-ratios):

$$\hat{Q} = -23.651 + 1.158 P_w - 0.275 P_B - 0.603 A + 3.212 Y \quad R^2 = 0.9772$$
$$\underset{(-6.04)}{} \quad \underset{(4.0)}{} \quad \underset{(-0.45)}{} \quad \underset{(-1.3)}{} \quad \underset{(4.50)}{}$$

All the coefficients except that of Y have the wrong signs. The coefficient of P_w not only has the wrong sign but is also significant.

Treating P_w as endogenous and using S as an instrument, we get the following results:

$$\hat{Q} = -26.195 + 0.643 P_w - 0.140 P_B - 0.985 A + 4.082 Y \quad R^2 = 0.9724$$
$$\underset{(-5.09)}{} \quad \underset{(0.98)}{} \quad \underset{(-0.20)}{} \quad \underset{(-1.51)}{} \quad \underset{(3.28)}{}$$

The coefficient of P_w still has a wrong sign but it is at least not significant. In any case the conclusion we arrive at is that the quantity demanded is not responsive to prices and advertising expenditures but is responsive to income. The income elasticity of demand for wine is about 4.0 (significantly greater than unity).

Turning next to the supply function, there are three instrumental variables available for P_w: P_B, A, and Y. Also, the efficient instrumental variable is obtained by regressing P_w on P_B, A, Y, and S. The results obtained by using the OLS method and the different instrumental variables are as follows (figures in parentheses are asymptotic t-ratios for the instrumental variable methods; the R^2's for the IV methods are computed as explained earlier):

Method	OLS	Instrumental Variables			
		P_B	A	Y	$\hat{P}_w$
Constant	-15.57 (-18.36)	-10.76 (-0.28)	-17.65 (-6.6)	-16.98 (-14.56)	-16.82 (-15.57)
P_w	2.145 (8.99)	0.336 (0.02)	2.928 (3.02)	2.676 (7.30)	2.616 (7.89)
S	1.383 (8.95)	2.131 (0.36)	1.058 (2.47)	1.163 (5.72)	1.188 (6.24)
R^2	0.9632	0.8390	0.9400	0.9525	0.9548

There are considerable differences between the estimates obtained by the different instrumental variables methods. Particularly, the use of P_B seems to produce very different results. Y appears to be the best of all the instrumental variables.

The IV estimates can be obtained by the procedures outlined earlier. But an easier way is to note that the IV estimator and the two-stage least squares (2SLS) estimator (which we will describe in Section 9.6) are the same if the equation is exactly identified. This implies that we can get the IV estimator by the 2SLS method by changing the model so that the supply function is exactly identified. In this case, a standard computer program like the SAS can be used to get the estimates as well as their standard errors. In fact, this is the procedure we have followed.

For instance, to get the IV estimator of the supply function using Y as the instrumental variable, we can specify the model as

$$Q = \beta_0 + \beta_1 P_w + \beta_2 Y + u \quad \text{demand function}$$

$$Q = \alpha_0 + \alpha_1 P_w + \alpha_2 S + v \quad \text{supply function}$$

Now the supply function is identified exactly.

In this particular case, this does not seem to be an unreasonable model.

Before we leave this example, we will present a case where the R^2 from the IV method is negative. Consider the model

$$Q = \beta_0 + \beta_1 P_w + \beta_2 A + u \quad \text{demand function}$$

$$Q = \alpha_0 + \alpha_1 P_w + \alpha_2 S + u \quad \text{supply function}$$

The first equation is exactly identified. We will use S as the instrumental variable for P_w. (The IV estimator is the same as the 2SLS estimator.) The OLS estimation of the demand function gave the following results (figures in parentheses are t-ratios):

$$\hat{Q} = \underset{(-14.50)}{-\ 15.30} + \underset{(6.60)}{2.064 P_w} + \underset{(6.76)}{1.418 A} \quad R^2 = 0.9431$$

The IV estimation gave the following results:

$$\hat{Q} = \underset{(-0.03)}{-\ 304.13} + \underset{(0.03)}{119.035 P_w} - \underset{(-0.03)}{52.177 A} \quad R^2 = -467.3$$

What is the problem? To see what the problem is, let us look at the reduced-form equations

$$\hat{Q} = \underset{(-8.12)}{-\ (10.42)} + \underset{(1.75)}{1.316 A} + \underset{(1.50)}{1.085 S} \quad R^2 = 0.8208$$

$$\hat{P}_w = \underset{(4.40)}{2.47} + \underset{(1.37)}{0.449 A} + \underset{(0.03)}{0.00912 S} \quad R^2 = 0.4668$$

The coefficient of S in the equation for P_w is almost zero. From the relationships (9.3) and (9.4) between the parameters in the reduced and structural forms discussed in Section 9.3, we note that this implies that $\beta_1 \to \infty$ and α_2 is indeterminate. Thus the demand function is not identified. Whenever the R^2 from the IV estimator (or the 2SLS estimator) is negative or very low and the R^2 from the OLS estimation is high, it should be concluded that something is wrong with the specification of the model or the identification of that particular equation.

9.6 Methods of Estimation: The Two-Stage Least Squares Method

The 2SLS method differs from the IV method described in Section 9.5 in that the $\hat{y}$'s are used as regressors rather than as instruments, but the two methods give identical estimates.

Consider the equation to be estimated:

$$y_1 = b_1 y_2 + c_1 z_1 + u_1 \tag{9.9}$$

The other exogenous variables in the system are z_2, z_3, and z_4.

Let $\hat{y}_2$ be the predicted value of y_2 from a regression on y_2 on z_1, z_2, z_3, z_4 (the reduced-form equation). Then

$$y_2 = \hat{y}_2 + v_2$$

where v_2, the residual, is uncorrelated with each of the regressors z_1, z_2, z_3, z_4 and hence with $\hat{y}_2$ as well. (This is the property of least squares regression that we discussed in Chapter 4.)

The normal equations for the efficient IV method are

$$\sum \hat{y}_2 (y_1 - b_1 y_2 - c_1 z_1) = 0$$
$$\sum z_1 (y_1 - b_1 y_2 - c_1 z_1) = 0 \tag{9.10}$$

Substituting $y_2 = \hat{y}_2 + v_2$ we get

$$\sum \hat{y}_2 (y_1 - b_1 \hat{y}_2 - c_1 z_1) - b_1 \sum \hat{y}_2 v_2 = 0$$
$$\sum z_1 (y_1 - b_1 \hat{y}_2 - c_1 z_1) - b_1 \sum z_1 v_2 = 0 \tag{9.11}$$

But $\sum z_1 v_2 = 0$ and $\sum \hat{y}_2 v_2 = 0$ since z_1 and $\hat{y}_2$ are uncorrelated with v_2. Thus equations (9.11) give

$$\sum \hat{y}_2 (y_1 - b_1 \hat{y}_2 - c_1 z_1) = 0$$
$$\sum z_1 (y_1 - b_1 \hat{y}_2 - c_1 z_1) = 0 \tag{9.12}$$

But these are the normal equations if we replace y_2 by $\hat{y}_2$ in (9.9) and estimate the equation by OLS. This method of replacing the endogenous variables on the right-hand side by their predicted values from the reduced form and estimating the equation by OLS is called the *two-stage least squares* (2SLS) method. The name arises from the fact that OLS is used in two stages:

Stage 1. Estimate the reduced-form equations by OLS and obtain the predicted $\hat{y}$'s.
Stage 2. Replace the right-hand side endogenous variables by $\hat{y}$'s and estimate the equation by OLS.

Note that the estimates do not change even if we replace y_1 by $\hat{y}_1$ in equation (9.9). Take the normal equations (9.12). Write

$$y_1 = \hat{y}_1 + v_1$$

where v_1 is again uncorrelated with each of z_1, z_2, z_3, z_4. Thus it is also uncorrelated with $\hat{y}_1$ and $\hat{y}_2$, which are both linear functions of the z's. Now substitute $y_1 = \hat{y}_1 + v_1$ in equations (9.12). We get

$$\sum \hat{y}_2(\hat{y}_1 - b_1\hat{y}_2 - c_1z_1) + \sum \hat{y}_2 v_1 = 0$$

$$\sum z_1(\hat{y}_1 - b_1\hat{y}_2 - c_1z_1) + \sum z_1 v_1 = 0$$

The last terms of these two equations are zero and the equations that remain are the normal equations from the OLS estimation of the equation

$$\hat{y}_1 = b_1\hat{y}_2 + c_1z_1 + w$$

Thus in stage 2 of the 2SLS method we can replace *all* the endogenous variables in the equation by their predicted values from the reduced forms and then estimate the equation by OLS.

What difference does it make? The answer is that the estimated standard errors from the second stage will be different because the dependent variable is $\hat{y}_1$ instead of y_1. However, the estimated standard errors from the second stage are the wrong ones anyway, as we will show presently. Thus it does not matter whether we replace the endogenous variables on the right-hand side or all the endogenous variables by $\hat{y}$'s in the second stage of the 2SLS method.

The preceding discussion has been in terms of a simple model, but the arguments are general because all the $\hat{y}$'s are uncorrelated with the reduced-form residual $\hat{v}$'s. Since our discussion has been based on replacing y by $\hat{y} + \hat{v}$, the arguments all go through for the general models.

Computing Standard Errors

We will now show how the standard errors we obtain from the second stage of the 2SLS method are not the correct ones and how we can obtain the correct standard errors. Consider the very simple model

$$y_1 = \beta y_2 + u \tag{9.13}$$

where y_1 and y_2 are endogenous variables. There are some (more than one) exogenous variables in the system. We first estimate the reduced-form equation for y_2 and write

$$y_2 = \hat{y}_2 + v_2$$

The IV estimator of β is obtained by solving $\sum \hat{y}_2(y_1 - \beta y_2) = 0$, or

$$\hat{\beta}_{IV} = \frac{\sum \hat{y}_2 y_1}{\sum \hat{y}_2 y_2}$$

The 2SLS estimator of β is obtained by solving $\sum \hat{y}_2(y_1 - \beta\hat{y}_2) = 0$, or

$$\hat{\beta}_{2SLS} = \frac{\sum \hat{y}_2 y_1}{\sum \hat{y}_2^2}$$

Since $\sum \hat{y}_2 y_2 = \sum \hat{y}_2 (\hat{y}_2 + v_2) = \sum \hat{y}_2^2$ the two estimators are identical and we will drop the subscripts IV and 2SLS and just write $\hat{\beta}$:

$$\hat{\beta} = \frac{\sum \hat{y}_2 y_1}{\sum \hat{y}_2^2} = \frac{\sum \hat{y}_2 (\beta y_2 + u)}{\sum \hat{y}_2^2}$$

$$= \beta + \frac{\sum \hat{y}_2 u}{\sum \hat{y}_2^2}$$

(*Note:* $\sum \hat{y}_2 y_2 = \sum \hat{y}_2^2$.) Hence

$$\hat{\beta} - \beta = \frac{(1/n) \sum \hat{y}_2 u}{(1/n) \sum \hat{y}_2^2}$$

where n is the sample size. Since u is independent of the exogenous variables in the system and $\hat{y}_2$ is a linear function of the exogenous variables, we have

$$\text{plim } \frac{1}{n} \sum \hat{y}_2 u = 0$$

If we assume that

$$\text{plim } \frac{1}{n} \sum \hat{y}_2^2 \neq 0$$

we see that plim $\hat{\beta} = \beta$ and thus $\hat{\beta}$ is a consistent estimator for β.

To compute the asymptotic variance of $\hat{\beta}$, note that as $n \to \infty$, var$(\hat{\beta}) \to 0$. Hence it is customary to consider n var$(\hat{\beta})$. We have

$$n \text{ var}(\hat{\beta}) = n \text{ plim}(\hat{\beta} - \beta)^2$$

$$= n \text{ plim} \frac{[(1/n) \sum \hat{y}_2 u][(1/n) \sum \hat{y}_2 u]}{[(1/n) \sum \hat{y}_2^2]^2}$$

$$= \text{plim} \frac{(1/n)(\sum \hat{y}_2 u)(\sum \hat{y}_2 u)}{[(1/n) \sum \hat{y}_2^2]^2}$$

$$= \frac{\sigma_u^2 \text{ plim } [(1/n) \sum \hat{y}_2^2]}{\{\text{plim } [(1/n) \sum \hat{y}_2^2]\}^2}$$

$$= \sigma_u^2 / \text{plim } \left(\frac{1}{n} \sum \hat{y}_2^2 \right) \qquad (9.14)$$

where $\sigma_u^2 = \text{var}(u)$. In practice, we get an estimate of var$(\hat{\beta})$ as $\hat{\sigma}_u^2 / \sum \hat{y}_2^2$, where $\hat{\sigma}_u^2$ is a consistent estimator of σ_u^2. This is obtained by plugging in the consistent estimator $\hat{\beta}$ of

β in equation (9.13) and computing the sum of squares of residuals. Thus

$$\hat{\sigma}_u^2 = \frac{1}{n} \sum (y_1 - \hat{\beta} y_2)^2$$

There is the question of whether we should use n as divisor or $(n-1)$. Since the expression is asymptotic, the choice does not matter. Note that if we ignored the fact that $\hat{y}_2$ is a random variable, then using equation (9.14) we would have written

$$\text{var}(\hat{\beta}) = \text{var}\left(\frac{\sum \hat{y}_2 u}{\sum \hat{y}_2^2}\right) = \frac{\sigma_u^2}{\sum \hat{y}_2^2} \tag{9.15}$$

as in a simple regression model. In effect, this is the expression we use in getting the asymptotic standard errors (after substituting $\hat{\sigma}_u^2$ for σ_u^2), but the correct derivation will have to use probability limits.

Now what is wrong with the standard errors obtained at the second stage of the 2SLS method? To see what is wrong, let us write equation (9.13) as

$$y_1 = \beta \hat{y}_2 + (u + \beta v_2)$$
$$= \beta \hat{y}_2 + w \tag{9.16}$$

When we estimate this equation by OLS, the standard error of $\hat{\beta}$ is obtained as

$$\left(\frac{\hat{\sigma}_w^2}{\sum \hat{y}_2^2}\right)^{1/2}$$

Comparing this with equation (9.15), we note that what we need is $\hat{\sigma}_u^2$ and what we get from the second stage of 2SLS is $\hat{\sigma}_w^2$. The denominator is correct. It is the estimate of the error variance that is wrong. We can correct this by multiplying the standard errors obtained by $\hat{\sigma}_u/\hat{\sigma}_w$, where

$$\hat{\sigma}_u^2 = \frac{1}{n} \sum (y_1 - \hat{\beta} y_2)^2$$

$$\hat{\sigma}_w^2 = \frac{1}{n} \sum (y_1 - \hat{\beta} \hat{y}_2)^2$$

The latter is the expression we get from the OLS program at the second stage. Most computer programs make this correction anyway, so when using the standard programs we do not have to worry about this problem. The discussion above is meant to show how the correct standard errors are obtained.

The preceding results are also valid when there are exogenous variables in equation (9.13). We have considered a simple model for ease of exposition.

Illustrative Example

In Table 9.3 data are provided on commercial banks' loans to business firms in the United States for 1979–1984. The following demand–supply model has been estimated.[4]

---

[4]The model postulated here is not necessarily the right model for the problem of analyzing the commercial loan market. It is adequate for our purpose of a two-equation model with both equations overidentified.

Table 9.3   Data for U.S. commercial loan market January
1979–December 1984 (monthly)

N	Q	R	RD	X	RS	y
1	251.8	11.75	9.25	150.8	9.35	994.3
2	255.6	11.75	9.26	151.5	9.32	1002.5
3	259.8	11.75	9.37	152.0	9.48	994.0
4	264.7	11.75	9.38	153.0	9.46	997.4
5	268.8	11.75	9.50	150.8	9.61	1013.2
6	274.6	11.65	9.29	152.4	9.06	1015.6
7	276.9	11.54	9.20	152.6	9.24	1012.3
8	280.5	11.91	9.23	152.8	9.52	1020.9
9	288.1	12.90	9.44	151.6	10.26	1043.6
10	288.3	14.39	10.13	152.4	11.70	1062.6
11	287.9	15.55	10.76	152.4	11.79	1058.5
12	295.0	15.30	11.31	152.1	12.64	1076.3
13	295.1	15.25	11.86	152.2	13.50	1063.1
14	298.5	15.63	12.36	152.7	14.35	1070.0
15	301.7	18.31	12.96	152.6	15.20	1073.5
16	302.0	19.77	12.04	152.1	13.20	1101.1
17	298.1	16.57	10.99	148.3	8.58	1097.1
18	297.8	12.63	10.58	144.0	7.07	1088.7
19	301.2	11.48	11.07	141.5	8.06	1099.9
20	304.7	11.12	11.64	140.4	9.13	1111.1
21	308.1	12.23	12.02	141.8	10.27	1122.2
22	315.6	13.79	12.31	144.1	11.62	1161.4
23	323.1	16.06	11.94	146.9	13.73	1200.6
24	330.6	20.35	13.21	149.4	15.49	1239.9
25	330.9	20.16	12.81	151.0	15.02	1223.5
26	331.3	19.43	13.35	151.7	14.79	1207.1
27	331.6	18.04	13.33	151.5	13.36	1190.6
28	336.2	17.15	13.88	152.1	13.69	1206.0
29	340.9	19.61	14.32	151.9	16.30	1221.4
30	345.5	20.03	13.75	152.7	14.73	1236.7
31	350.3	20.39	14.38	152.9	14.95	1221.5
32	354.2	20.50	14.89	153.9	15.51	1250.3
33	366.3	20.08	15.49	153.6	14.70	1293.7
34	361.7	18.45	15.40	151.6	13.54	1224.6
35	365.5	16.84	14.22	149.1	10.86	1254.1
36	361.4	15.75	14.23	146.3	10.85	1288.7
37	359.8	15.75	15.18	143.4	12.28	1251.5
38	364.6	16.56	15.27	140.7	13.48	1258.3
39	372.4	16.50	14.58	142.7	12.68	1295.0
40	374.7	16.50	14.46	141.5	12.70	1272.1
41	379.3	16.50	14.26	140.2	12.09	1286.1
42	386.7	16.50	14.81	139.2	12.47	1325.8
43	384.4	16.26	14.61	138.7	11.35	1307.3
44	384.5	14.39	13.71	138.8	8.68	1321.7
45	395.0	13.50	12.94	138.4	7.92	1335.5
46	393.7	12.52	12.12	137.3	7.71	1345.2
47	398.9	11.85	11.68	135.7	8.07	1358.1
48	395.3	11.50	11.83	134.9	7.94	1409.7
49	392.4	11.16	11.79	135.2	7.86	1385.4

(Continued overleaf)

Table 9.3 (*continued*)

N	Q	R	RD	X	RS	y
50	392.3	10.98	12.01	137.4	8.11	1412.6
51	395.9	10.50	11.73	138.1	8.35	1419.5
52	393.5	10.50	11.51	140.0	8.21	1411.0
53	391.7	10.50	11.46	142.6	8.19	1413.1
54	395.3	10.50	11.74	144.4	8.79	1443.8
55	397.7	10.50	12.15	146.4	9.08	1438.1
56	400.6	10.89	12.51	149.7	9.34	1461.4
57	402.7	11.00	12.37	151.8	9.00	1448.9
58	405.3	11.00	12.25	153.8	8.64	1459.0
59	412.0	11.00	12.41	155.0	8.76	1499.4
60	420.1	11.00	12.57	155.3	9.00	1508.9
61	424.4	11.00	12.20	156.2	8.90	1504.1
62	428.8	11.00	12.08	158.5	9.09	1499.3
63	433.1	11.21	12.57	160.0	9.52	1494.5
64	439.7	11.93	12.81	160.8	9.69	1501.5
65	447.3	12.39	13.28	162.1	9.83	1541.3
66	452.9	12.60	13.55	162.8	9.87	1532.9
67	454.4	13.00	13.44	164.4	10.12	1535.5
68	455.2	13.00	12.87	165.9	10.47	1539.0
69	459.9	12.97	12.66	166.0	10.37	1549.9
70	467.7	12.58	12.63	165.0	9.74	1578.9
71	468.7	11.77	12.29	164.4	8.61	1578.2
72	476.8	11.06	12.13	164.8	8.06	1631.2

Source: Several issues of the *Federal Reserve Bulletin*. I would like to thank Walter Mayer for providing me with the data.

Demand for loans by business firms:

$$Q_t = \beta_0 + \beta_1 R_t + \beta_2 RD_t + \beta_3 X_t + u_t$$

and supply by banks of commercial loans:

$$Q_t = \alpha_0 + \alpha_1 R_t + \alpha_2 RS_t + \alpha_3 y_t + v_t$$

where Q_t = total commercial loans (billions of dollars)
  R_t = average prime rate charged by banks
  RS_t = 3-month Treasury bill rate (represents an alternative) rate of return for banks)
  RD_t = AAA corporate bond rate (represents the price of alternative financing to firms)
  X_t = industrial production index and represents firms' expectation about future economic activity
  y_t = total bank deposits (represents a scale variable) (billions of dollars)

Both the equations are overidentified. So we chose to estimate them by 2SLS. R_t is expected to have a negative sign in the demand function and a positive sign in the supply function. The coefficient of RS_t is expected to be negative. The coefficients of RD_t, X_t,

Table 9.4   OLS and 2SLS estimates for the demand–supply
model of the commercial loan market

	OLS		2SLS[a]	
	Coefficient	*t*-Ratio	Coefficient	*t*-Ratio
	Demand function			
β_0	−203.70	−2.9	−210.53	−2.8
β_1	−15.99	−12.0	−20.19	−12.6
β_2	−2.29	5.4	2.34	5.2
β_3	36.07	14.2	40.76	14.4
R^2	0.7804		0.7485	
	Supply function			
α_0	−77.41	−6.9	−87.97	−6.3
α_1	2.41	2.9	6.90	3.6
α_2	−1.89	−1.8	−7.08	−3.1
α_3	0.33	51.3	0.33	42.9
R^2	0.9768		0.9666	

[a]For the 2SLS, the "*t*-ratio" is coefficient/asymptotic SE.

and y_t are expected to be positive. Both the OLS and 2SLS estimates of the parameters had the expected signs. These estimates are presented in Table 9.4. Note that the R^2 might increase or decrease when we use 2SLS as compared to OLS.

There are only minor changes in the 2SLS estimates compared to the OLS estimates for the demand function. As for the supply function, the only changes we see are in the parameters α_1 and α_2 (coefficients of R_t and RS_t). In this example this is quite important because what this shows is that quantity supplied is more responsive to changes in interest rates than is evidenced from the OLS estimates.

If the R^2 values from the reduced-form equations are very high, the 2SLS and OLS estimates will be almost identical. This is because the $\hat{y}$'s that we substitute in the 2SLS estimation procedure are very close to the corresponding y's in case the R^2's are very high. This is often the case in large econometric models with a very large number of exogenous variables. An example of this is the quarterly model of T. C. Liu.[5] Liu presents 2SLS and OLS estimates side by side and for some equations they are identical to three decimals. Many studies, however, do not report OLS and 2SLS estimates at the same time.

9.7   The Question of Normalization

Going back to equations (9.8), we notice that the coefficient of y_1 in the first equation and that of y_2 in the second equation are both unity. This is expressed by saying

---

[5]T. C. Liu, "An Exploratory Quarterly Model of Effective Demand in the Post-war U.S. Economy," *Econometrica*, Vol. 31, July 1963.

that the first equation is normalized with respect to y_1 and the second equation with respect to y_2. Sometimes this is taken to mean that y_1 is the "dependent" variable in the first equation and y_2 is the "dependent" variable in the second equation. This is particularly so in the 2SLS method. Strictly speaking, this goes contrary to the spirit of simultaneous equation models because by definition y_1 and y_2 are jointly determined and we cannot label any single variable as the dependent variable in any equation. Of course, we have to assume the coefficient of one of the variables as 1 (i.e., normalize with respect to one variable). But the method of estimation should be such that it should not matter which variable we choose for normalization. The early methods of estimation like full-information maximum likelihood (FIML) and limited-information maximum likelihood (LIML) satisfied this requirement. But the more popular methods like 2SLS do not and are, strictly speaking, not in the spirit of simultaneous equations estimation. A discussion of FIML is beyond the scope of this book, but we discuss LIML in Section 9.8.

In practice, normalization is determined by the way the economic theories are formulated. For instance, in a macro model of income determination, although consumption C and income y are considered as jointly determined, we write the consumption function as

$$C = \alpha + \beta y + u$$

and not as

$$y = \alpha' + \beta' C + u'$$

This is because, at the level of individuals, consumption C is determined by income y. At the back of our minds there is a causal relationship from y to C at the micro level, and we carry this to the macro level as well.

In an exactly identified system normalization does not matter. To see this, consider the first equation in (9.8). We saw earlier that we use z_1, z_2, z_3 as instrumental variables. Since there is no problem of weighting these instrumental variables, it does not matter how the equation is normalized. On the other hand, for the second equation in (9.8) we have the choice between z_1 and z_2 as instruments and the optimum instrumental variable is a weighted average of z_1 and z_2. We saw that these weights were obtained from the reduced-form equation for y_1. On the other hand, if the equation is normalized with respect to y_1 and written as

$$y_1 = b_2' y_2 + c_3' z_3 + u_2'$$

then the weights for z_1 and z_2 are obtained from the reduced-form equations for y_2. Thus 2SLS and IV estimators are different for different normalizations in overidentified systems.

*9.8 The Limited-Information Maximum Likelihood Method

The LIML method, also known as the least variance ratio (LVR) method is the first of the single-equation methods suggested for simultaneous equations models. It was suggested by Anderson and Rubin[6] in 1949 and was popular until the advent of the 2SLS introduced by Theil[7] in the late 1950s. The LIML method is computationally more cumbersome, but for the simple models we are considering, it is easy to use.

Consider again the equations in (9.8). We can write the first equation as

$$y_1^* = y_1 - b_1 y_2 = c_1 z_1 + c_2 z_2 + u_1 \qquad (9.17)$$

For each b_1 we can construct a y_1^*. Consider a regression of y_1^* on z_1 and z_2 only and compute the residual sum of squares (which will be a function of b_1). Call it RSS_1. Now consider a regression of y_1^* on all the exogenous variables z_1, z_2, z_3 and compute the residual sum of squares. Call it RSS_2. What equation (9.17) says is that z_3 is not important in determining y_1^*. Thus the extra reduction in RSS by adding z_3 should be minimal. The LIML or LVR method says that we should choose b_1 so that $(RSS_1 - RSS_2)/RSS_1$ or RSS_1/RSS_2 is minimized. After b_1 is determined, the estimates of c_1 and c_2 are obtained by regressing y_1^* on z_1 and z_2. The procedure is similar for the second equation in (9.8).

There are some important relationships between the LIML and 2SLS methods. (We will omit the proofs, which are beyond the scope of this book.)

1. The 2SLS method can be shown to minimize the *difference* $(RSS_1 - RSS_2)$, whereas the LIML minimizes the *ratio* (RSS_1/RSS_2).
2. If the equation under consideration is exactly identified, then 2SLS and LIML give identical estimates.
3. The LIML estimates are invariant to normalization.
4. The asymptotic variances and covariances of the LIML estimates are the same as those of the 2SLS estimates. However, the standard errors will differ because the error variance σ_u^2 is estimated from different estimates of the structural parameters.
5. In the computation of LIML estimates we use the variances and covariances among the endogenous variables as well. But the 2SLS estimates do not depend on this information. For instance, in the 2SLS estimation of the first equation in (9.8), we regress y_1 on $\hat{y}_2$, z_1, and z_2. Since $\hat{y}_2$ is a linear function of the z's we do not make any use of $cov(y_1, y_2)$. This covariance is used only in the computation of $\hat{\sigma}_u^2$.

Illustrative Example

Consider the demand and supply model of the Australian wine industry discussed in Section 9.5. Since the demand function is exactly identified, the 2SLS and LIML estimates would be identical and they are also identical to the instrumental variable estimates (using S as an instrument) presented earlier in Section 9.5.

As for the supply function, since it is overidentified, the 2SLS and LIML estimates will be different. The following are the 2SLS and LIML estimates of the parameters of

---

[6]T. W. Anderson and H. Rubin, "Estimation of the Parameters of a Single Equation in a Complete System of Stochastic Equations," *Annals of Mathematical Statistics*, Vol. 20, No. 1, March 1949.
[7]H. Theil, *Economic Forecasts and Policy* (Amsterdam: North-Holland, 1958).

the supply function (as computed from the SAS program). All variables are in logs:

Variable	2SLS			LIML		
	Coefficient	SE	t-Ratio	Coefficient	SE	t-Ratio
Intercept	-16.820	1.080	-15.57	-16.849	1.087	-15.49
P_w	2.616	0.331	7.89	2.627	0.334	7.86
S	1.188	0.190	6.24	1.183	0.191	6.18
R^2 (as computed by the SAS program)		0.9548			0.9544	

Actually, in this particular example, the LIML and 2SLS estimates are not much different. But this is not usually the experience in many studies of overidentified models.

*9.9   On the Use of OLS in the Estimation of Simultaneous Equations Models

Although we know that the simultaneity problem results in inconsistent estimators of the parameters, when the structural equations are estimated by ordinary least squares, this does not mean that OLS estimation of simultaneous equations models is useless. In some instances we may be able to say something about the direction of the (large-sample) bias, and this would be useful information. Also, if an equation is underidentified, it does not necessarily mean that nothing can be said about the parameters in that equation.

Consider the demand and supply model

$$q_t = \beta p_t + u_t \quad \text{demand function}$$

$$q_t = \alpha p_t + v_t \quad \text{supply function}$$

q_t and p_t are in log form and are measured in deviations from their means. Thus β and α are the price elasticities of demand and supply respectively. Let $\text{var}(u_t) = \sigma_u^2$, $\text{var}(v_t) = \sigma_v^2$, and $\text{cov}(u_t, v_t) = \sigma_{uv}$. The OLS estimator of β is

$$\hat{\beta} = \frac{\sum p_t q_t}{\sum p_t^2} = \beta + \frac{\sum p_t u_t}{\sum p_t^2}$$

$$= \beta + \frac{(1/n) \sum p_t u_t}{(1/n) \sum p_t^2}$$

where n is the sample size. Now

$$\beta p_t + u_t = \alpha p_t + v_t$$

or

$$p_t = \frac{v_t - u_t}{\beta - \alpha}$$

Hence we have

$$\text{plim}\left(\frac{1}{n}\sum p_t u_t\right) = \text{cov}(p_t, u_t) = \frac{\sigma_{uv} - \sigma_u^2}{\beta - \alpha}$$

and

$$\text{plim}\left(\frac{1}{n}\sum p_t^2\right) = \text{var}(p_t) = \frac{\sigma_v^2 + \sigma_u^2 - 2\sigma_{uv}}{(\beta - \alpha)^2}$$

Thus

$$\text{plim}\,\hat{\beta} = \beta + (\beta - \alpha)\frac{\sigma_{uv} - \sigma_u^2}{\sigma_v^2 + \sigma_u^2 - 2\sigma_{uv}}$$

This expression is not very useful, but if $\sigma_{uv} = 0$ (i.e., the shifts in the demand and supply functions are unrelated), we get

$$\text{plim}\,\hat{\beta} = \beta + (\beta - \alpha)\left(-\frac{\sigma_u^2}{\sigma_v^2 + \sigma_u^2}\right)$$

Now β is expected to be negative and α positive. Thus the bias term is expected to be positive. Hence if we find a price elasticity of demand of -0.8, the true price elasticity is < -0.8.

We can show by a similar reasoning that if we estimate the supply function by OLS we get

$$\hat{\alpha} = \frac{\sum p_t q_t}{\sum p_t^2}$$

and if $\sigma_{uv} = 0$, then

$$\text{plim}\,\hat{\alpha} = \alpha + (\beta - \alpha)\frac{\sigma_v^2}{\sigma_v^2 + \sigma_u^2}$$

The bias is now negative since $(\beta - \alpha)$ is expected to be negative. Again, suppose that the supply elasticity is estimated to be 0.6; then we know that the true price elasticity is > 0.6.

In practice, when we regress q on p we do not know whether we are estimating the demand function or the supply function. However, if the regression coefficient is, say, $+0.3$, we know that the supply elasticity is $0.3 +$ a positive number and the demand elasticity is $0.3 +$ a negative number. Thus the practically useful conclusion is that the supply elasticity is > 0.3. On the other hand, if the regression coefficient is -0.9, we know that the supply elasticity is $-0.9 +$ a positive number and the demand elasticity is $-0.9 +$ a negative number. Thus the practically useful conclusion is that the demand elasticity < -0.9 (or greater than 0.9 in absolute value).

In the example above we also note that

$$\text{plim}\left(\frac{\sum p_t q_t}{\sum p_t^2}\right) \to \beta \text{ as } \sigma_u^2 \to 0$$

$$\to \alpha \text{ as } \sigma_v^2 \to 0$$

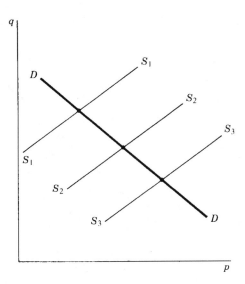

Figure 9.2 Stable demand and shifting supply

Since σ_u^2 is the variance of the random shift in the demand function, $\sigma_u^2 \to 0$ means that the demand function does not shift or is stable. Thus the regression of q on p will estimate the demand elasticity if the demand function is stable and the supply elasticity if the supply function is stable.

Figure 9.2 gives the case of a supply curve shifting and the demand curve not shifting. What we observe in practice are the points of intersection of the demand curve and the supply curve. As can be seen, the locus of these points of intersection traces out the demand curve. In Figure 9.3, where the demand curve shifts and the supply curve does not, this locus determines the supply curve.[8]

Working's Concept of Identification

After concluding that if the demand curve did not shift much, but the supply curve did, then the locus of the points of intersection would come close to tracing a demand curve, Working added that by "correcting" for the influence of an additional important determining variable (such as income) in the demand curve, we could reduce its shifts and hence get a better approximation of the price elasticity of demand. If we add income to the demand function, we get the equation system

$$q_t = \beta p_t + \gamma y_t + u_t \quad \text{demand function}$$

$$q_t = \alpha p_t + v_t \qquad \text{supply function}$$

---

[8]This was the main conclusion of the article by E. J. Working, "What Do Statistical Demand Curves Show?," *Quarterly Journal of Economics*, February 1927.

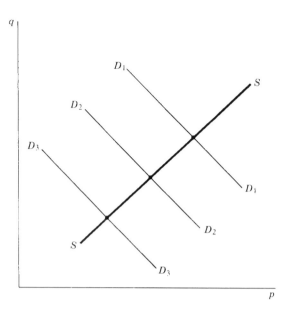

Figure 9.3   Stable supply and shifting demand

What Working said was that by introducing y_t in the demand function, we can get a better estimate of β. What he had in mind was that the introduction of y_t reduced the variance of u_t.

If we use the results on identification discussed in Sections 9.3 and 9.4, we come to the conclusion that the supply equation is identified (it has one missing variable) but the demand function is not. *This is exactly the opposite of what Working said.* The problem here is that the concept of identification we have discussed is in terms of our ability to get consistent estimates. What Working was concerned about is the least squares bias. His argument is that if σ_u^2 is somehow reduced, we get good estimates by OLS (i.e., the bias would be negligible). Consider two estimates $\hat{\beta}_1$ and $\hat{\beta}_2$ for β. Suppose that

$$\text{plim } \hat{\beta}_1 = \beta \quad \text{and} \quad \text{plim } \hat{\beta}_2 = 0.999\beta$$

then $\hat{\beta}_1$ is consistent but $\hat{\beta}_2$ is not. But for all practical purposes $\hat{\beta}_2$ is also consistent.

Suppose that we include all the relevant explanatory variables in the demand function so that σ_u^2 is very small, whereas the supply function includes only price as the "explanatory" variable. Then, even if the demand equation is not identified by the rules we discussed earlier, we are still justified in estimating the equation by OLS. On the other hand, even if the supply function is overidentified, if σ_v^2 is very large, we get a poor estimate of the supply elasticity α. We can get a consistent estimator for α, but its variance will be very high.

In summary, it is not true that if an equation is underidentified we have to give up all hopes of estimating it. Nor does it follow that an equation that is overidentified can be better estimated than one that is exactly identified or underidentified. Further discussion of the demand–supply model considered here can be found in Maddala[9] and Leamer.[10]

In simultaneous equations models the classification of variables as endogenous and exogenous is quite arbitrary. Often, current values of some variables are treated as endogenous and lagged values of these same variables are treated as exogenous even when the current and lagged values are very highly correlated. In addition, some equations are regarded as identified (overidentified or exactly identified) and others are not identified by merely looking at how many variables are missing from the equation, and the underidentified equations are regarded as nonestimable. The discussion above illustrates that least squares estimation of underidentified equations can still be worthwhile. Also, instead of simply counting the number of exogenous variables, one should also look at how high their intercorrelations are.

Recursive Systems

Not all simultaneous equations models give biased estimates when estimated by OLS. An important class of models for which OLS estimation is valid is that of recursive models. These are models in which the errors from the different equations are independent and the coefficients of the endogenous variables show a triangular pattern. For example, consider a model with three endogenous variables, y_1, y_2, and y_3, and three exogenous variables, z_1, z_2, and z_3, which has the following structure:

$$y_1 + \beta_{12} y_2 + \beta_{13} y_3 + \alpha_1 z_1 = u_1$$

$$y_2 + \beta_{23} y_3 + \alpha_2 z_2 = u_2$$

$$y_3 + \alpha_3 z_3 = u_3$$

where u_1, u_2, u_3 are independent. The coefficients of the endogenous variables are

$$\begin{matrix} 1 & \beta_{12} & \beta_{13} \\ & 1 & \beta_{23} \\ & & 1 \end{matrix}$$

which form a triangular structure. In such systems, each equation can be estimated by ordinary least squares. Suppose that in the example above u_2 and u_3 are correlated but they are independent of u_1; then the model is said to be *block-recursive*. The second and third equations have to be estimated jointly, but the first equation can be estimated by OLS. Note that y_2 and y_3 depend on u_2 and u_3 only and hence are independent of the error term u_1.

Estimation of Cobb–Douglas Production Functions

In the estimation of production functions, output, labor input, and capital input are usually considered the endogenous variables and wage rate and price of capital the exogenous variables.

---

[9]G. S. Maddala, *Econometrics* (New York: McGraw-Hill, 1977), pp. 244–249.

[10]E. E. Leamer, "Is It a Demand Curve or Is It a Supply Curve: Partial Identification Through Inequality Constraints," *The Review of Economics and Statistics*, Vol. 63, No. 3, August 1981, pp. 319–327.

Suppose that we use the Cobb–Douglas production function

$$X_i = AL_i^{\alpha}K_i^{\beta}e^{u_{1i}} \tag{9.18}$$

where u_{1i} is the error term; then taking logs we can write it as

$$y_{1i} - \alpha y_{2i} - \beta y_{3i} = c_1 + u_{1i} \tag{9.19}$$

where $y_{1i} = \log X_i$, $y_{2i} = \log L_i$, $y_{3i} = \log K_i$, and $c_1 = \log A$.

Since y_{2i} and y_{3i} are endogenous variables, we cannot estimate this equation by OLS. We have to add the equations for y_{2i} and y_{3i} and these are obtained from the marginal productivity conditions. However, Zellner, Kmenta, and Dreze[11] argue that in this case we can estimate equation (9.19) by OLS. Their argument is that since output given (9.18) is stochastic, the firm should be maximizing expected profits (not profits). If $u_{1i} \sim \text{IN}(0, \sigma^2)$, then

$$E(e^{u_{1i}}) = \exp(\tfrac{1}{2}\sigma^2)$$

Hence

$$E(X_i) = AL_i^{\alpha}K_i^{\beta}\exp(\tfrac{1}{2}\sigma^2)$$

Expected profits $= R_i = p_iE(X_i) - w_iL_i - r_iK_i$, where p is the price of output, w the price of labor input, and r the price of capital input. Maximization of expected profits gives us the following conditions:

$$\frac{\partial R_i}{\partial L_i} = 0 \Rightarrow \frac{X_i}{L_i} = \frac{w_i}{\alpha p_i}\exp\left(u_{1i} - \frac{1}{2}\sigma^2\right)$$

$$\frac{\partial R_i}{\partial K_i} = 0 \Rightarrow \frac{X_i}{K_i} = \frac{r_i}{\beta p_i}\exp\left(u_{1i} - \frac{1}{2}\sigma^2\right)$$

Taking logs and adding error terms u_{2i} and u_{3i} to these equations, we get (the errors depict errors in maximization of expected profits)

$$y_{1i} - y_{2i} = c_{2i} + u_{1i} + u_{2i}$$

$$y_{1i} - y_{3i} = c_{3i} + u_{1i} + u_{3i}$$

where

$$c_{2i} = \log\left(\frac{w_i}{\alpha p_i}\right) - \frac{1}{2}\sigma^2 \tag{9.20}$$

$$c_{3i} = \log\left(\frac{r_i}{\beta p_i}\right) - \frac{1}{2}\sigma^2$$

Now we can solve equations (9.19) and (9.20) to get the reduced forms for y_{1i}, y_{2i}, y_{3i}. We can easily see that when we substitute for y_{1i} from equation (9.19) into equations (9.20), the u_{1i} term cancels. Thus y_{2i} and y_{3i} involve only the error terms u_{2i} and u_{3i}.

---

[11] A. Zellner, J. Kmenta, and J. Dreze, "Specification and Estimation of Cobb–Douglas Production Function Models," *Econometrica*, October 1966, pp. 786–795.

It is reasonable to assume that u_{1i} are independent of u_{2i} and u_{3i} because u_{1i} are errors due to "acts of nature" like weather and u_{2i} and u_{3i} are "human errors." Under these assumptions y_{2i} and y_{3i} (which depend on u_{2i} and u_{3i} only) are independent of u_{1i}. Hence OLS estimation of the production function (9.19) yields consistent estimates of the parameters α and β. We thus regress y_{1i} on y_{2i} and y_{3i}.

Here is an example where there is no simultaneity bias by using the OLS method. The model is not recursive either, but from the peculiar way the error terms entered the equations we could show that in the first equation the included endogenous variables are independent of the error term in that equation.

*9.10   Exogeneity and Causality

The approach to simultaneous equations models that we have discussed until now is called the *Cowles Foundation approach*. Its name derives from the fact that it was developed during the late 1940s and early 1950s by the econometricians at the Cowles Foundation at the University of Chicago. The basic premise of this approach is that the data are assumed to have been generated by a system of simultaneous equations. The classification of variables into "endogenous" and "exogenous," and the causal structure of the model are both given *a priori* and are untestable. The main emphasis is on the estimation of the unknown parameters for which the Cowles Foundation devised several methods (limited-information and full-information methods).

This approach has, in recent years, been criticized on several grounds:

1. The classification of variables into endogenous and exogenous is sometimes arbitrary.
2. There are usually many variables that should be included in the equation that are excluded to achieve identification. This argument was made by T. C. Liu[12] in 1960 but did not receive much attention. It is known as the *Liu critique*.
3. One of the main purposes of simultaneous equations estimation is to forecast the effect of changes in the exogenous variables on the endogenous variables. However, if the exogenous variables are changed and profit-maximizing agents see the change coming, they would modify their behavior accordingly. Thus the coefficients in the simultaneous equations models cannot be assumed to be independent of changes in the exogenous variables. This is now called the *Lucas critique*.[13]

One solution to the Lucas critique is to make the coefficients of the simultaneous equations system depend on the exogenous policy variables. Since this makes the model a varying parameter model, which is beyond the scope of this book, we will not pursue it here.[14]

---

[12]T. C. Liu, "Under-Identification, Structural Estimation, and Forecasting," *Econometrica*, Vol. 28, 1960, pp. 855–865.

[13]R. E. Lucas, "Econometric Policy Evaluation: A Critique," in Karl L. Brunner (ed.), *The Phillips Curve and Labor Markets* (supplement to the *Journal of Monetary Economics*), 1976, pp. 19–46.

[14]This is the solution suggested in Maddala, *Econometrics*, Chap. 17, "Varying Parameter Models."

Leamer[15] suggests redefining the concept of exogeneity. He suggests defining the variable x as exogenous if the conditional distribution of y given x is invariant to modifications that alter the process generating x. What this says is that a variable is defined as exogenous if the Lucas critique does not apply to it. It is, however, not clear whether such a redefinition solves the problem raised by Lucas.

There are two concepts of exogeneity that are usually distinguished:

1. *Predeterminedness.* A variable is predetermined in a particular equation if it is independent of the *contemporaneous and future* errors in that equation.
2. *Strict exogeneity.* A variable is strictly exogenous if it is independent of the *contemporaneous, future, and past* errors in the relevant equation.

To explain these concepts we have to consider a model with lagged variables. Consider[16]

$$y_t = \alpha_1 x_t + \beta_{11} y_{t-1} + \beta_{12} x_{t-1} + u_{1t}$$
$$x_t = \alpha_2 y_t + \beta_{21} y_{t-1} + \beta_{22} x_{t-1} + u_{2t}$$

$$(9.21)$$

with u_{1t} and u_{2t} mutually and serially independent. If $\alpha_2 = 0$, x_t is predetermined for y_t in the first equation. On the other hand, x_t is strictly exogenous for y_t only if $\alpha_2 = 0$ and $\beta_{21} = 0$, because if $\beta_{21} \neq 0$, x_t depends on $u_{1 \cdot t-1}$ through y_{t-1}. That is, in the first equation x_t is not independent of past errors.

In nondynamic models, and models with no serial correlation in the errors, we do not have to make this distinction. For instance, in Section 9.9 we considered an example of estimation of the Cobb–Douglas production function under the hypothesis of maximization of expected profit. We saw that y_2 and y_3 were independent of the error term u_1. Thus these variables are exogenous for the estimation of the parameters in the production function. Similarly, in a recursive system, the (nonnormalized) endogenous variables in each equation can be treated as exogenous for the purpose of estimation of the parameters in that equation.

Engle, Hendry, and Richard[17] are not satisfied with the foregoing definitions of exogeneity and suggest three more concepts:

1. Weak exogeneity.
2. Superexogeneity.
3. Strong exogeneity.

Since these concepts are often used and they are not difficult to understand anyway, we will discuss them briefly. The concept of strong exogeneity is linked to another concept: "Granger causality." There is a proliferation of terms here, but they occur frequently in recent econometric literature.

---

[15] E. E. Leamer, "Vector Autoregressions for Causal Inference," in K. Brunner and A. Meltzer (eds.), *Understanding Monetary Regimes* (supplement to *Journal of Monetary Economics*), 1985, pp. 255–304.

[16] This example and the discussion that follows are from R. L. Jacobs, E. E. Leamer, and M. P. Ward, "Difficulties with Testing for Causation," *Economic Inquiry*, 1979, pp. 401–413.

[17] R. F. Engle, D. F. Hendry, and J. F. Richard, "Exogeneity," *Econometrica*, Vol. 51, March 1983.

One important point to note is that whether a variable is exogenous or not depends on the parameter under consideration. Consider the equation[18]

$$y = bx + u$$

where b is the unknown parameter and u is a variable that is unknown and unnamed. This equation can also be written as

$$y = b^*x + v$$

where $b^* = b + 1$ and $v = u - x$. Again, b^* is an unknown parameter and v is an unknown variable. If $E(u|x) = 0$, it cannot be true that $E(v|x) = 0$. So is x exogenous or not? It clearly depends on the parameter value. This points to the importance of the question: "Exogenous for what?"

As yet another example, consider the case where y_t and x_t have a bivariate normal distribution with means $E(y_t) = \mu_1$, $E(x_t) = \mu_2$ and variances and covariance given by $\text{var}(y_t) = \sigma_{11}$, $\text{var}(x_t) = \sigma_{22}$, and $\text{cov}(y_t, x_t) = \sigma_{12}$. The conditional distribution of y_t given x_t is

$$y_t|x_t \sim \text{IN}(\alpha + \beta x_t, \sigma^2)$$

where $\beta = \sigma_{12}/\sigma_{22}$, $\alpha = \mu_1 - \beta\mu_2$, and $\sigma^2 = \sigma_{11} - \sigma_{12}^2/\sigma_{22}$.

We can write the joint distribution of y_t and x_t as

$$f(y_t, x_t) = g(y_t|x_t)h(x_t)$$

and we can write the model as

$$\begin{aligned} y_t &= \alpha + \beta x_t + u_{1t} & u_{1t} &\sim \text{IN}(0, \sigma^2) \\ x_t &= \mu_2 + v_{2t} & v_{2t} &\sim \text{IN}(0, \sigma_{22}) \end{aligned} \tag{9.22}$$

where $\text{cov}(x_t, u_{1t}) = 0$ and $\text{cov}(u_{1t}, v_{2t}) = 0$ by construction. If we consider this set of equations, x_t is "exogenous."

On the other hand, we can similarly write

$$f(y_t, x_t) = h(x_t|y_t)g(y_t)$$

and write the model as

$$\begin{aligned} x_t &= \gamma + \delta y_t + u_{2t} & u_{2t} &\sim \text{IN}(0, \omega^2) \\ y_t &= \mu_1 + v_{1t} & v_{1t} &\sim \text{IN}(0, \sigma_{11}) \end{aligned} \tag{9.23}$$

where $\text{cov}(y_t, u_{2t}) = \text{cov}(u_{2t}, v_{1t}) = 0$ by construction and $\delta = \sigma_{12}/\sigma_{11}$, $\gamma = \mu_2 - \delta\mu_1$, $\omega^2 = \sigma_{22} - \sigma_{12}^2/\sigma_{11}$. Now y_t is "exogenous" in this model. So which of x_t and y_t is exogenous, if at all? The answer depends on the parameters of interest. If we are interested

---

[18]The example is from J. W. Pratt and R. Schlaifer, "On the Nature and Discovery of Structure," *Journal of the American Statistical Association*, Vol. 79, March 1984, pp. 9–21. It is also discussed in Leamer, "Vector Autoregressions."

in the parameters α, β, σ^2, then x_t is exogenous and equations (9.22) are the ones to estimate. If we are interested in the parameters γ, δ, ω^2, then y_t is exogenous and equations (9.23) are the ones to estimate.

The considerations above led to the following definitions of weak exogeneity by Engle, Hendry, and Richard.

Weak Exogeneity

A variable x_t is said to be weakly exogenous for estimating a set of parameters λ if inference on λ conditional on x_t involves no loss of information. That is, if we write

$$f(y_t, x_t) = g(y_t | x_t) h(x_t)$$

where $g(y_t | x_t)$ involves the parameters λ, weak exogeneity implies that the marginal distribution $h(x_t)$ does not involve the parameters λ. Essentially, the parameters in $h(x_t)$ are nuisance parameters.

In the example where y_t and x_t have a bivariate normal distribution, there are five parameters: $\mu_1, \mu_2, \sigma_{11}, \sigma_{22}, \sigma_{12}$. These can be transformed by a one-to-one transformation into $(\alpha, \beta, \sigma^2)$ and (μ_2, σ_{22}). The two sets are separate. Thus for the estimation of $(\alpha, \beta, \sigma^2)$ we do not need information on (μ_2, σ_{22}). Hence x_t is weakly exogenous for the estimation of $(\alpha, \beta, \sigma^2)$.

Superexogeneity

The concept of superexogeneity is related to the Lucas critique. If x_t is weakly exogenous and the parameters in $f(y_t | x_t)$ remain invariant to changes in the marginal distribution of x_t, then x_t is said to be *superexogenous*. In the example we have been considering, namely that of y_t and x_t having a bivariate normal distribution, x_t is weakly exogenous for the estimation of $(\alpha, \beta, \sigma^2)$ in model (9.22). But it is *not* superexogenous because if we change μ_2 and σ_{22}, the parameters in the marginal distribution of x_t, this will produce changes in $(\alpha, \beta, \sigma^2)$. Note that weak exogeneity is a condition required for efficient estimation. Superexogeneity is a condition required for policy purposes.

Leamer finds it unnecessary to require weak exogeneity as a condition for superexogeneity. He argues that this confounds the problem of efficient estimation with that of policy analysis. His definition of exogeneity is the same as the definition of superexogeneity by Engle, Hendry, and Richard without the requirement of weak exogeneity.

Strong Exogeneity

If x_t is weakly exogenous and x_t *is not preceded* by any of the endogenous variables in the system, x_t is defined to be strongly exogenous. As an example, consider the model

$$y_t = \beta x_t + u_{1t}$$

$$x_t = \alpha_1 x_{t-1} + \alpha_2 y_{t-1} + u_{2t}$$

(u_{1t}, u_{2t}) have a bivariate normal distribution and are serially independent; $\text{var}(u_{1t}) = \sigma_{11}$, $\text{var}(u_{2t}) = \sigma_{22}$, and $\text{cov}(u_{1t}, u_{2t}) = \sigma_{12}$. If $\sigma_{12} = 0$, then x_t is weakly exogenous because the marginal distribution of x_t does not involve β and σ_{11}. However, the second equation shows that y_t precedes x_t (x_t depends on y_{t-1}). Hence x_t is not strongly exogenous.

We have used the word "precedence" following Leamer but the definition by Engle, Hendry, and Richard is in terms of a concept called *Granger causality* and is as follows. If x_t is weakly exogenous and x_t is *not caused* in the sense of Granger by any of the endogenous variables in the system, then x_t is defined to be *strongly exogenous*. Simply stated the term "Granger causality" means "precedence" but we will discuss it in greater detail.

Granger Causality

Granger starts from the premise that the future cannot cause the present or the past. If event A occurs after event B, we know that A cannot cause B. At the same time, if A occurs before B, it does not necessarily imply that A causes B. For instance, the weatherman's prediction occurs before the rain. This does not mean that the weatherman causes the rain. In practice, we observe A and B as time series and we would like to know whether A precedes B, or B precedes A, or they are contemporaneous. For instance, do movements in prices precede movements in interest rates, or is it the opposite, or are the movements contemporaneous? This is the purpose of Granger causality. It is not causality as it is usually understood.

Granger[19] devised some tests for causality (in the limited sense discussed above) which proceed as follows. Consider two time series, $\{y_t\}$ and $\{x_t\}$. The series x_t *fails to Granger cause* y_t if in a regression of y_t on lagged y's and lagged x's, the coefficients of the latter are zero. That is, consider

$$y_t = \sum_{i=1}^{k} \alpha_i y_{t-i} + \sum_{i=1}^{k} \beta_i x_{t-i} + u_t$$

Then if $\beta_i = 0$ ($i = 1, 2, \ldots, k$), x_t fails to cause y_t. The lag length k is, to some extent, arbitrary.

An alternative test provided by Sims[20] is as follows: x_t fails to cause y_t in the Granger sense if in a regression of y_t on lagged, current, and future x's, the latter coefficients are zero. Consider the regression

$$y_t = \sum_{j=-k_1}^{k_2} \beta_j x_{t-1} + u_t$$

Test $\beta_{-j} = 0$ ($j = 1, 2, \ldots, k_1$). What this says is that the prediction of y from current and past x's would not be improved if future values of x are included. There are some

---

[19]C. W. J. Granger, "Investigating Causal Relations by Econometric Models and Cross-Spectral Methods," *Econometrica*, Vol. 37, January 1969, pp. 24–36.

[20]C. A. Sims, "Money, Income and Causality," *American Economic Review*, Vol. 62, 1972, pp. 450–552.

econometric differences between the two tests, but the two tests basically test the same hypothesis.[21]

As mentioned earlier, Leamer suggests using the simple word "precedence" instead of the complicated words Granger causality since all we are testing is whether a certain variable precedes another and we are not testing causality as it is usually understood. However, it is too late to complain about the term since it has already been well established in the econometrics literature. Hence it is important to understand what it means.

Granger Causality and Exogeneity

As we defined earlier, Granger noncausality is necessary for strong exogeneity as defined by Engle, Hendry, and Richard. Sims also regards tests for Granger causality as tests for exogeneity.[22] However, Granger noncausality is neither necessary nor sufficient for exogeneity as understood in the usual simultaneous equations literature.[23] This point can be illustrated with the example in equations (9.21). We said that x_t is predetermined for y_t in the first equation if $\alpha_2 = 0$, and x_t is strictly exogenous for y_t if $\alpha_2 = 0$ and $\beta_{21} = 0$.

Now to see what the Granger test does, write the reduced forms for y_t and x_t:

$$y_t = \pi_{11} y_{t-1} + \pi_{12} x_{t-1} + v_{1t}$$

$$x_t = \pi_{21} y_{t-1} + \pi_{22} x_{t-1} + v_{2t}$$

For Granger noncausality, we have to have $\pi_{21} = 0$. But

$$\pi_{21} = \frac{\alpha_2 \beta_{11} + \beta_{21}}{1 - \alpha_1 \alpha_2}$$

Thus $\pi_{21} = 0$ implies that $\alpha_2 \beta_{11} + \beta_{21} = 0$. From this it does not follow that $\alpha_2 = 0$. Thus Granger noncausality does not necessarily imply that x_t is predetermined. Conversely, $\alpha_2 = 0$ does not imply that $\pi_{21} = 0$. However, $\alpha_2 = 0$ and $\beta_{21} = 0$ implies that $\pi_{21} = 0$, although the converse is not true.

Thus a test for Granger noncausality is not useful as a test for exogeneity. Some argue that it is, nevertheless, useful as a descriptive device for time-series data.

Tests for Exogeneity

The Cowles Foundation approach to simultaneous equations held the view that causality and exogeneity cannot be tested. These are things that have to be specified *a priori*. In recent years it has been argued that if some variables are specified as exogenous and the equation is identified, one can test whether some other variables considered endogenous are indeed endogenous or not.

---

[21]G. Chamberlain, "The General Equivalence of Granger and Sims Causality," *Econometrica*, Vol. 50, 1982, pp. 569–582.

[22]Sims, "Money," p. 550.

[23]T. F. Cooley and S. F. LeRoy, "A-theoretical Macroeconometrics," *Journal of Monetary Economics*, Vol. 16, No. 3, November 1985, pp. 283–308, see Section 5 on Granger causality and Cowles causality.

As an illustration, consider the following. We have a simultaneous equations model with three endogenous variables y_1, y_2, and y_3, and three exogenous variables z_1, z_2, and z_3. Suppose that the first equation of the model is

$$y_1 = \beta_2 y_2 + \beta_3 y_3 + \alpha_1 z_1 + u_1$$

We want to test whether y_2 and y_3 can be treated as exogenous for the estimation of this equation. To test this hypothesis, we obtain the predicted values $\hat{y}_2$ and $\hat{y}_3$ of y_2 and y_3, respectively, from the reduced-form equations for y_2 and y_3. We then estimate the model

$$y_1 = \beta_2 y_2 + \beta_3 y_3 + \alpha_1 z_1 + \gamma_2 \hat{y}_2 + \gamma_3 \hat{y}_3 + u_1$$

by OLS and test the hypothesis: $\gamma_2 = \gamma_3 = 0$ (using the F-test described in Chapter 4). If the hypothesis is rejected, y_2 and y_3 cannot be treated as exogenous. If it is not rejected, y_2 and y_3 can be treated as exogenous.[24]

9.11 Some Problems with Instrumental Variable Methods

Earlier, in Section 9.5 we introduced the instrumental variable (IV) method of estimation. This is a general method of wide applicability in all cases where the explanatory variables are correlated with the errors (see Section 11.5). An earlier book-length discussion of IV methods is in Bowden and Turkington.[25]

Recall that we defined an instrumental variable as a variable that is uncorrelated with the error term but highly correlated with the relevant endogenous variable. In practice both these assumptions are likely to be violated, and the instrument is then said to be poor. The problem of poor instruments, and testing the validity of available instruments, has received considerable attention during recent years. The literature is voluminous but an example of the argument that the "cure can be worse than the disease," that is, IV estimators can be worse than the ordinary least squares (OLS) estimators, is the paper by Bound, Jaeger, and Baker.[26] They argue that there are two problems associated with IV estimation that are not fully appreciated. First, if the correlation between the IV and the endogenous explanatory variable is low, then even if the IV is weakly correlated with the error term, there can be large inconsistencies in the IV estimators. Second, in finite samples the IV estimators are biased in the same direction as the OLS estimators.[27] The bias in the IV estimators approaches the bias in the OLS estimators if the R^2 between the instrument and the potential endogenous variable approaches zero.

---

[24]The test procedure described here is Hausman's test discussed in greater detail in Section 12.10. It is equivalent to some other tests suggested in the literature. Two references are D. Wu, "Alternative Tests of Independence Between Stochastic Regressors and Disturbances," *Econometrica*, Vol. 41, 1973, pp. 733–750, and N. S. Revankar, "Asymptotic Relative Efficiency Analysis of Certain Tests of Independence in Structural Systems," *International Economic Review*, Vol. 19, 1978, pp. 165–179.

[25]R. J. Bowden and D. A. Turkington, *Instrumental Variables* (Cambridge University Press, 1984).

[26]J. Bound, D. A. Jaeger, and R. Baker, "Problems With Instrumental Variable Estimation When the Correlation Between the Instruments and the Endogenous Explanatory Variable is Weak," *Journal of the American Statistical Association*, Vol. 90, 1996, pp. 443–450.

[27]A. Buse, "The Bias of Instrumental Variable Estimators," *Econometrica*, Vol. 60, 1992, pp. 173–180.

They illustrate these two problems with reference to a study by Angrist and Krueger[28] on the effect of compulsory school attendance on schooling and earnings, arguing that the results are very sensitive to these problems of IV estimation.

Summary

1. In simultaneous equations models, each equation is normalized with respect to one endogenous variable. Strictly speaking, since the endogenous variables are all jointly determined, it should not matter which variable is chosen for normalization. However, some commonly used methods of estimation (like the two-stage least squares) do depend on the normalization rule adopted. In practice, normalization is determined by the way economic theories are formulated.

2. In a demand and supply model, if quantity supplied is not responsive to price, the demand function should be normalized with respect to price. On the other hand, if quantity supplied is highly responsive to price, the demand function should be normalized with respect to quantity. (See Section 9.1 for a graphical discussion and Section 9.3 for an empirical illustration.)

3. Before a simultaneous equations model is estimated, one should check whether each equation is identified or not. In linear simultaneous equations systems, a necessary condition for the identification of an equation is the order condition which says that the number of variables missing from the equation should be greater than or equal to the number of endogenous variables in the equation minus one. This counting rule is only a necessary condition. One also has to check the rank condition which is based on the structure of the missing variables in the other equations. This is illustrated with some examples in Section 9.4.

4. It is customary to classify an equation into the overidentified, exactly identified, and underidentified categories according as the number of variables missing from the equation is, respectively, greater than, equal to, or less than the number of endogenous variables minus one. It is not possible to get consistent estimates of the parameters in the underidentified equations. The difference between overidentified and exactly identified equations is simply that the latter are easier to estimate than the former.

5. We have discussed only single-equation methods, that is, estimation of each equation at a time. The methods we have discussed are:
(a) The instrumental variable (IV) method (Section 9.5).
(b) The two-stage least squares (2SLS) method (Section 9.6).
(c) The limited-information maximum likelihood (LIML) method (Section 9.8).
For an exactly identified equation, all the methods are equivalent and give the same answers. For an overidentified equation the IV method gives different estimates depending on which of the missing exogenous variables are chosen as instruments. The 2SLS method is a weighted instrumental variable method.

---

[28]J. B. Angrist and A. B. Krueger, "Does Compulsory School Attendance Affect Schooling and Earnings," *Quarterly Journal of Economics*, Vol. 106, 1991, pp. 979–1014. See also C. Gao and K. Lahiri, "Further Consequences of Viewing LIML as an Iterated Aitken Estimator," *Journal of Econometrics*, Vol. 98, 2000, pp. 187–202.

6. In overidentified equations, the 2SLS estimates depend on the normalization rule adopted. The LIML estimates do not depend on the choice of normalization. The LIML method is thus a truly simultaneous estimation method, but the 2SLS is not because, strictly speaking, since the endogenous variables are jointly determined, normalization should not matter.

7. It is not always true that we can say nothing about the parameters of an underidentified equation. In some cases the OLS estimates, even if they are not consistent, do give us some information about the parameters. Some examples are given in Section 9.9. It is also interesting to note that the concept of identification as discussed by Working in 1927 is quite different from the current discussion which is concentrated on getting consistent estimators for the parameters (see Section 9.9).

8. There are some cases where the simultaneous equations model can be estimated by using the OLS method. One such example is the recursive model. We also give another example — that of estimation of the Cobb–Douglas production function under uncertainty where the OLS method is the appropriate one (see Section 9.9).

9. In recent years, the usual definition of exogeneity has been questioned. Some new terms have been introduced, such as weak exogeneity, strong exogeneity, and superexogeneity. One important question that has been raised is: "Exogenous for what?" If it is for efficient estimation of the parameters (this is the concept of weak exogeneity), a variable can be treated as endogenous in one equation and exogenous in another (as in a recursive system). Also, whether a variable is exogenous or not depends on the parameter to be estimated (see Pratt's example).

10. Strong exogeneity is weak exogeneity plus Granger causality. The term "Granger causality" has nothing to do with causality as it is usually understood. A better term for it is "precedence." Some econometricians have equated the concept of exogeneity with Granger causality. The example in Section 9.10 shows that linking Granger causality to exogeneity has some pitfalls. It is better to keep the two concepts separate.

11. A variable is considered superexogenous if interventions in that variable leave the parameters in the system unaltered. It is a concept that has to do with Lucas's critique of econometric policy evaluation. As a definition, the concept is all right. But from the practical point of view its use is questionable.

12. There have been some tests of exogeneity suggested in the context of simultaneous equations systems. These tests depend on the availability of extra instrumental variables. The tests are easy to apply because they depend on the addition of some constructed variables to the usual models, and testing that the coefficients of these added variables are zero.

Exercises

1. Explain the meaning of each of the following terms:
   (a) Endogenous variables.
   (b) Exogenous variables.
   (c) Structural equations.
   (d) Reduced-form equations.
   (e) Order condition for identification.

(f) Rank condition for identification.
(g) Indirect least squares.
(h) Two-stage least squares.
(i) Instrumental variable methods.
(j) Normalization.
(k) Simultaneity bias.
(l) Recursive systems.

2. Explain concisely what is meant by "the identification problem" in the context of the linear simultaneous equations model.

3. Consider the three-equation model

$$y_1 = \beta_{13}y_3 + \gamma_{12}x_2 + u_1$$
$$y_2 = \beta_{21}y_1 + \beta_{23}y_3 + \gamma_{21}x_1 + \gamma_{22}x_2 + u_2$$
$$y_3 = \gamma_{33}x_3 + u_3$$

where y_1, y_2, and y_3 are endogenous, and x_1, x_2, and x_3 are exogenous. Discuss the identification of each of the equations of the model, based on the order and rank conditions.

   Now suppose that you want to estimate the first equation by two-stage least squares, but you have only an ordinary least squares program available. Explain carefully, step by step, how you would estimate β_{13}, γ_{12}, and $\mathrm{var}(u_1)$.

4. Consider the model

$$y_1 = \alpha y_2 + \delta x + u_1$$
$$y_2 = \beta y_1 + \gamma x + u_2$$

where x is exogenous, and the error terms u_1 and u_2 have mean zero and are serially uncorrelated.

(a) Write down the equations expressing the reduced-form coefficients in terms of the structural parameters.
(b) Show that if $\gamma = 0$, then β can be identified. Are the parameters α and δ identified in this case? Why or why not?
(c) In the case of $\gamma = 0$, what formula would you use to estimate β? What is the asymptotic variance of your estimator of β?

5. What is meant by the phrase: "The estimator is invariant to normalization"? Do any problems arise if an estimator is not invariant to normalization? Which of the following estimation methods gives estimators that are invariant to normalization?
(a) Indirect least squares.
(b) 2SLS.
(c) Instrumental variable methods.
(d) LIML.

Explain how you would choose the appropriate normalization (with respect to quantity or price) in a demand and supply model.

6. The structure of a model with four endogenous and three exogenous variables is as follows (1 indicates presence and 0 absence of the variable in the equation):

$$
\begin{array}{ccccccc}
1 & 0 & 1 & 1 & 1 & 0 & 0 \\
1 & 1 & 1 & 0 & 0 & 1 & 1 \\
0 & 0 & 1 & 0 & 1 & 0 & 0 \\
1 & 0 & 1 & 1 & 0 & 1 & 0
\end{array}
$$

Which of the four equations are identified?

7. Explain how you would compute R^2 in simultaneous equations estimation methods.

8. Examine whether each of the following statements is true (T), false (F), or uncertain (U), and give a short explanation:

 (a) In a simultaneous equation system, the more the number of exogenous variables the better.

 (b) If the multiple correlations of the reduced-form equations are nearly 1, the OLS and 2SLS estimates of the parameters will be very close to each other.

 (c) In the 2SLS method we should replace only the endogenous variables on the right-hand side of the equation by their fitted values from the reduced form. We should not replace the endogenous variable on the left-hand side by its fitted value.

 (d) Which variables should be treated as exogenous and which as endogenous cannot be determined from the data.

 (e) An estimation of the demand function for steel gave the price elasticity of steel as +0.3. This finding should be interpreted to mean that the price elasticity of supply is at least +0.3.

 (f) Any equation can be made identified by deleting enough exogenous variables from the equation or adding enough exogenous variables to the other equations.

 (g) Any variable can be endogenous in one equation and exogenous in another equation.

 (h) Some simultaneous equation systems can be estimated by ordinary least squares.

 (i) If the R^2 from the 2SLS method is negative or very low and the R^2 from the OLS method is high, it should be concluded that something is wrong with the specification of the model or the identification of that particular equation.

 (j) The R^2 from the OLS method will always be higher than the R^2 from the 2SLS method, but this does not mean that the OLS method is better.

 (k) In exactly identified equations, the choice of which variable to normalize does not matter.

 (l) In exactly identified equations, we can normalize the equation with respect to an exogenous variable as well.

9. Consider the model

$$Q = \beta_0 + \beta_1 P_w + \beta_2 Y + u \quad \text{demand function}$$

$$Q = \alpha_0 + \alpha_1 P_w + \alpha_2 S + u \quad \text{supply function}$$

Estimate this model by 2SLS, instrumental variable, and indirect least squares methods using the data in Table 9.2 (transform all variables to logs). Would you get different results using the three methods?

How would you choose the appropriate normalization (with respect to Q or P_w)? Does normalization matter in this model?

10. Estimate the supply equation in the model of the Australian wine industry in Section 9.5 if it is normalized with respect to P_w.

Appendix to Chapter 9

Necessary and Sufficient Conditions for Identification (Section 9.4)

Consider a simultaneous equations model with g endogenous variables and k exogenous variables. In matrix notation we can write the model as

$$\mathbf{By}_t + \mathbf{\Gamma x}_t = \mathbf{u}_t \quad t = 1, 2, \ldots, T \tag{9A.1}$$

where $\mathbf{y}_t$ = a $g \times 1$ vector of observations on the endogenous variables
$\mathbf{x}_t$ = a $k \times 1$ vector of observations on the exogenous variables
$\mathbf{u}_t$ = a $g \times 1$ vector of errors
$\mathbf{B}$ = a $g \times g$ matrix of coefficients of the endogenous variables
$\mathbf{\Gamma}$ = a $g \times k$ matrix of coefficients of the exogenous variables

In the example given in Section 9.4, $g = 7$ and $k = 3$. $\mathbf{B}$ is the 7×7 matrix consisting of the first seven columns, and $\mathbf{\Gamma}$ is the 7×3 matrix consisting of the last three columns.

We assume that the matrix $\mathbf{B}$ is nonsingular. Hence we can solve equation (9A.1) for $\mathbf{y}_t$ to get

$$\begin{aligned} \mathbf{y}_t &= -\mathbf{B}^{-1}\mathbf{\Gamma x}_t + \mathbf{B}^{-1}\mathbf{u}_t \\ &= \mathbf{\Pi x}_t + \mathbf{v}_t \end{aligned} \tag{9A.2}$$

This equation is called the *reduced form*. Equation (9A.1) is called the *structural form*. From equation (9A.2) we have

$$-\mathbf{B}^{-1}\mathbf{\Gamma} = \mathbf{\Pi} \quad \text{or} \quad \mathbf{B\Pi} + \mathbf{\Gamma} = 0 \quad \text{and} \quad \mathbf{v}_t = \mathbf{B}^{-1}\mathbf{u}_t \tag{9A.3}$$

We assume that the errors $\mathbf{u}_t$ have zero mean, are independent, and have a common covariance matrix $E(\mathbf{u}_t \mathbf{u}_{t'}) = \mathbf{\Sigma}$.

To discuss identification, without any loss of generality, consider the first equation in (9A.1). Let $\boldsymbol{\beta}'$ be the first row of $\mathbf{B}$ and $\boldsymbol{\gamma}'$ the first row of $\mathbf{\Gamma}$. Partition these vectors each into two components corresponding to the included and excluded variables in this equation. We have

$$\boldsymbol{\beta}' = [\boldsymbol{\beta}_1' \boldsymbol{\beta}_2']$$
$$\boldsymbol{\gamma}' = [\boldsymbol{\gamma}_1' \boldsymbol{\gamma}_2']$$

$\boldsymbol{\beta}_1'$ corresponds to g_1 included and $\boldsymbol{\beta}_2'$ corresponds to g_2 excluded endogenous variables $(g_1 + g_2 = g)$. Similarly, $\boldsymbol{\gamma}_1'$ corresponds to k_1 included and $\boldsymbol{\gamma}_2'$ to k_2 excluded exogenous variables $(k_1 + k_2 = k)$. In the first equation in the example in Section 9.4, we have $g_1 = 3$, $g_2 = 4$, $k_1 = 1$, and $k_2 = 2$.

Now partition the matrices **B** and **Γ** also conformably to the partitioning of **β** and **γ**. We have

$$\mathbf{B} = \begin{bmatrix} \boldsymbol{\beta}_1' & 0 \\ \mathbf{B}_1 & \mathbf{B}_2 \end{bmatrix} \quad \text{and} \quad \boldsymbol{\Gamma} = \begin{bmatrix} \boldsymbol{\gamma}_1' & 0 \\ \boldsymbol{\Gamma}_1 & \boldsymbol{\Gamma}_2 \end{bmatrix}$$

Consider the matrix

$$\mathbf{D} = \begin{bmatrix} 0 & 0 \\ \mathbf{B}_2 & \boldsymbol{\Gamma}_2 \end{bmatrix}$$

D is the matrix corresponding to the missing endogenous and exogenous variables. The necessary and sufficient condition for identification, also known as the rank condition, is

$$\text{rank}(\mathbf{D}) = g - 1$$

The proof of this proposition follows from noting that if rank$[\mathbf{B}_2 \ \boldsymbol{\Gamma}_2] < g - 1$, there will exist a nonnull vector $\boldsymbol{\alpha}'[\mathbf{B}_2 \ \boldsymbol{\Gamma}_2] = [0 \ 0]$. In this case we can find a linear combination of the $(g - 1)$ equations, with coefficients given by the elements of $\boldsymbol{\alpha}$, which, when added to the first equation, results in an equation that "looks like" it. Thus it is not possible to identify the parameters of the first equation.

Methods of Estimation (Sections 9.4 and 9.5)

We shall consider the estimation of a single equation by least squares methods. Let the particular equation consisting of g_1 endogenous variables and k_1 exogenous variables be written as

$$\mathbf{y} = \mathbf{Y}_1\boldsymbol{\beta} + \mathbf{X}_1\boldsymbol{\gamma} + \mathbf{u} = \mathbf{Z}_1\boldsymbol{\delta} + \mathbf{u} \tag{9A.4}$$

where $\mathbf{y} = T \times 1$ vector of observations on the endogenous variable chosen for normalization (i.e., to have coefficient 1)

$\mathbf{Y}_1 = T \times (g_1 - 1)$ matrix of observations on the included endogenous variables

$\mathbf{X}_1 = T \times k_1$ matrix of observations on the included exogenous variables

$\boldsymbol{\delta}' = [\boldsymbol{\beta}'\boldsymbol{\gamma}']$ is the vector of parameters to be estimated

$\mathbf{Z}_1 = [\mathbf{Y}_1\mathbf{X}_1]$

$\mathbf{u} = T \times 1$ vector of errors

We assume that $E(\mathbf{u}\mathbf{u}') = \sigma^2\mathbf{I}_T$.

Let **X** be the $T \times k$ matrix of observations on *all* the exogenous variables in the system. Equation (4) is identified by the order condition only if the number of excluded variables is $\geq g - 1$; that is, $g_2 + k_2 \geq (g - 1)$. We shall assume that this is satisfied.

Since $\mathbf{Y}_1$ and **u** are correlated, the OLS estimators of the parameters in equation (9A.4) are not consistent. To get consistent estimates, we use instrumental variables for $\mathbf{Y}_1$. Let us consider $\hat{\mathbf{Y}}_1$ where $\hat{\mathbf{Y}}_1$ is the predicted value of $\mathbf{Y}_1$ from the reduced-form equations. Then

$$\hat{\mathbf{Y}}_1 = \mathbf{X}(\mathbf{X}'\mathbf{X})^{-1}\mathbf{X}'\mathbf{Y}_1 \tag{9A.5}$$

Also let $\hat{\mathbf{V}}_1$ be the estimated residuals from the reduced form, so that $\mathbf{Y}_1 = \hat{\mathbf{Y}}_1 + \hat{\mathbf{V}}_1$. Then we have $\mathbf{X}'\hat{\mathbf{V}}_1 = 0$ (the residuals from an OLS estimation are uncorrelated with the regressors). Hence we get

$$\mathbf{X}'\hat{\mathbf{Y}}_1 = \mathbf{X}'\mathbf{Y}_1 \quad \text{and} \quad \hat{\mathbf{Y}}_1'\hat{\mathbf{V}}_1 = \mathbf{0} \tag{9A.6}$$

We assume that the exogenous variables are independent of the errors so that plim $[(1/T)\mathbf{X}'\mathbf{u}] = \mathbf{0}$ and also that plim $[(1/T)\mathbf{X}'\mathbf{X}]$ is a positive definite matrix (i.e., there are no linear dependencies among the x's and no degeneracies).

These assumptions now enable us to prove that the instrumental variable (IV) estimator is consistent and also enable us to derive its asymptotic distribution.

Define $\hat{\mathbf{Z}}_1 = [\hat{\mathbf{Y}}_1 \mathbf{X}_1]$.

Then using the relations (9A.6) we can check that $\hat{\mathbf{Z}}_1'\hat{\mathbf{Z}}_1 = \hat{\mathbf{Z}}_1'\mathbf{Z}_1$. The IV estimator of δ in equation (9A.4) is

$$\hat{\delta}_{\mathrm{IV}} = (\hat{\mathbf{Z}}_1'\mathbf{Z}_1)^{-1}\hat{\mathbf{Z}}_1'\mathbf{y} = (\hat{\mathbf{Z}}_1'\mathbf{Z}_1)^{-1}\hat{\mathbf{Z}}_1'(\mathbf{Z}_1\delta + \mathbf{u}) = \delta + (\hat{\mathbf{Z}}_1'\mathbf{Z}_1)^{-1}\hat{\mathbf{Z}}_1'\mathbf{u} \tag{9A.7}$$

plim $\hat{\delta}_{\mathrm{IV}} = \delta + $ plim $[(1/T)\hat{\mathbf{Z}}_1'\mathbf{Z}_1]^{-1}$. plim $[(1/T)\hat{\mathbf{Z}}_1'\mathbf{u}] = \delta$, since plim $[(1/T)\hat{\mathbf{Z}}_1\mathbf{u}] = \mathbf{0}$ and plim $[(1/T)\hat{\mathbf{Z}}_1'\mathbf{Z}_1]^{-1}$ is finite. These relations follow from the assumptions that plim $[(1/T)\mathbf{X}'\mathbf{u}] = \mathbf{0}$ and plim $[(1/T)\mathbf{X}'\mathbf{X}]$ is a positive definite matrix.

Thus, as expected, the IV estimator is consistent. The asymptotic covariance matrix of $\hat{\delta}_{\mathrm{IV}}$ is given by

$$\mathrm{AE}\ T(\hat{\delta}_{\mathrm{IV}} - \delta)(\hat{\delta}_{\mathrm{IV}} - \delta)'$$

where AE denotes asymptotic expectation. It is customary to assume that we can substitute plim for AE. This gives the asymptotic covariance matrix as

$$\mathrm{plim}\ T(\hat{\delta}_{\mathrm{IV}} - \delta)(\hat{\delta}_{\mathrm{IV}} - \delta)'$$

and using equation (9A.7) we get this $= \mathrm{plim}\ [(1/T)\hat{\mathbf{Z}}_1\mathbf{Z}_1]^{-1}$. plim $[(1/T)\hat{\mathbf{Z}}_1'\mathbf{u}\mathbf{u}'\hat{\mathbf{Z}}_1]$

$$\mathrm{plim}\ \left(\frac{1}{T}\mathbf{Z}_1'\hat{\mathbf{Z}}_1\right)^{-1} = \sigma^2 \mathrm{plim}\ \left(\frac{1}{T}\hat{\mathbf{Z}}_1'\hat{\mathbf{Z}}_1\right)^{-1} \tag{9A.8}$$

since $E(\mathbf{u}\mathbf{u}') = \sigma^2\mathbf{I}_T$ and $\hat{\mathbf{Z}}_1'\mathbf{Z}_1 = \hat{\mathbf{Z}}_1'\hat{\mathbf{Z}}_1$. In practice we estimate σ^2 by

$$\hat{\sigma}^2 = \frac{(\mathbf{y} - \mathbf{Y}_1\hat{\beta} - \mathbf{X}_1\hat{\gamma})'(\mathbf{y} - \mathbf{Y}_1\hat{\beta} - \mathbf{X}_1\hat{\gamma})}{T - g_1 - k_1} \tag{9A.9}$$

Also, note that $\mathbf{Y}_1'\hat{\mathbf{Y}}_1 = \mathbf{Y}_1'\mathbf{M}\mathbf{M}\mathbf{Y}_1 = \mathbf{Y}_1'\mathbf{M}\mathbf{Y}_1$, where $\mathbf{M} = \mathbf{X}(\mathbf{X}'\mathbf{X})^{-1}\mathbf{X}'$ is an idempotent matrix and $\hat{\mathbf{Y}}_1'\mathbf{X} = \mathbf{Y}_1'\mathbf{X}$. Also, in practice we estimate plim $[(1/T)\hat{\mathbf{Z}}_1'\hat{\mathbf{Z}}_1]$ by

$$\left(\frac{1}{T}\hat{\mathbf{Z}}_1'\hat{\mathbf{Z}}_1\right)^{-1} = T\begin{bmatrix} \mathbf{Y}_1'\mathbf{M}\mathbf{Y}_1 & \mathbf{Y}_1'\mathbf{X}_1 \\ \mathbf{X}_1'\mathbf{Y}_1 & \mathbf{X}_1'\mathbf{X}_1 \end{bmatrix}^{-1}$$

In practice, we consider the variance of $\hat{\delta}_{\mathrm{IV}}$ (not $\sqrt{T}\hat{\delta}_{\mathrm{IV}}$) and we write

$$\mathrm{var}(\hat{\delta}_{\mathrm{IV}}) = \sigma^2 \begin{bmatrix} \mathbf{Y}_1'\mathbf{M}\mathbf{Y}_1 & \mathbf{Y}_1'\mathbf{X}_1 \\ \mathbf{X}_1'\mathbf{Y}_1 & \mathbf{X}_1'\mathbf{X}_1 \end{bmatrix}^{-1}$$

and estimate σ^2 by $\hat{\sigma}^2$ given by equation (9A.9).

In the 2SLS estimation method, we use $\hat{\mathbf{Y}}_1$ as regressors rather than instrumental variables; that is, we substitute $\hat{\mathbf{Y}}_1$ for $\mathbf{Y}_1$ on the right-hand side of (9A.4) and estimate the equation by OLS. The equation is

$$\mathbf{y} = \hat{\mathbf{Y}}_1\boldsymbol{\beta} + \mathbf{X}_1\boldsymbol{\gamma} + (\mathbf{u} + \hat{\mathbf{V}}_1\boldsymbol{\beta})$$

$$= \hat{\mathbf{Z}}_1\boldsymbol{\delta} + (\mathbf{u} + \hat{\mathbf{V}}_1\boldsymbol{\beta})$$

$$\hat{\boldsymbol{\delta}}_{2SLS} = (\hat{\mathbf{Z}}_1'\hat{\mathbf{Z}}_1)^{-1}\hat{\mathbf{Z}}_1\mathbf{y}$$

$$= (\hat{\mathbf{Z}}_1'\hat{\mathbf{Z}}_1)^{-1}\hat{\mathbf{Z}}_1'(\hat{\mathbf{Z}}_1\boldsymbol{\delta} + \mathbf{u} + \hat{\mathbf{V}}_1\boldsymbol{\beta})$$

$$= \boldsymbol{\delta} + (\hat{\mathbf{Z}}_1'\hat{\mathbf{Z}}_1)^{-1}\hat{\mathbf{Z}}_1'\mathbf{u} \quad \text{since} \quad \hat{\mathbf{Z}}_1'\hat{\mathbf{V}}_1 = 0$$

Since $\hat{\mathbf{Z}}_1'\mathbf{Z}_1 = \hat{\mathbf{Z}}_1'\hat{\mathbf{Z}}_1$, it follows from equation (9A.7) that

$$\hat{\boldsymbol{\delta}}_{IV} \equiv \hat{\boldsymbol{\delta}}_{2SLS}$$

That is, it does not make any difference whether $\hat{\mathbf{Y}}_1$ is used as a regressor or as an instrument. This shows that the 2SLS estimator is also an IV estimator.

We can also show that the 2SLS estimator is the best IV estimator. We shall, however, omit the proof here.[29]

---

[29]For a proof, see Maddala, *Econometrics*, p. 477.

10 NONLINEAR REGRESSIONS, MODELS OF EXPECTATIONS, AND NONNORMALITY

What is in this Chapter?

In this chapter we first discuss nonlinear estimation methods: the Newton–Raphson method, and the Gauss–Newton method for nonlinear least squares. We then discuss grid-search methods and illustrate them with respect to partial adjustment models with adaptive expectations.

We next discuss expectations models, and tests for rationality. The estimation of rational expectations models is illustrated with a simple demand and supply model under rational expectations. The problems of serial correlation in the errors in these models are also outlined.

Finally, we consider the nonnormality of errors. We discuss tests for normality and estimation methods under the assumption of nonnormality. We discuss Huber's robust methods, least absolute residual (LAR) method, and some other alternatives to least squares.

The methods described in this chapter can all be estimated using the SHAZAM computer package.

10.1 Introduction

Often, we have n observations $(y_1, y_2, \ldots, y_n)$, each of which depends on a set of m parameters $\theta_1, \theta_2, \ldots, \theta_m$, so that we can write

$$y_j = f_j(\theta_1, \theta_2, \ldots, \theta_m) \quad j = 1, 2, \ldots, n$$

The functions f_j are not necessarily linear functions. We are required to obtain estimates of the parameters θ_j which satisfy a criterion function. In the maximum likelihood method, we obtain estimates of the parameters that maximize the likelihood function. (We discuss the maximum likelihood method in detail in Chapter 16.) In the nonlinear least squares procedure we obtain the estimates that minimize the sum of squares

$$\sum_i [y_i - f_i(\theta_1, \theta_2, \ldots, \theta_m)]^2$$

In all these cases, so far as the numerical problem is concerned, we have the problem of maximizing a function of the form $F(x_1, x_2, \ldots, x_m)$ where the x's are the parameters. One of the most widely used methods is the Newton–Raphson method (and variants of this method). We shall, therefore, discuss this method. Other methods can be found in books on nonlinear parameter estimation but we need not be concerned with them here.[1]

10.2   The Newton–Raphson Method

The Newton–Raphson method depends on a Taylor series expansion to the second order. Let

$$G_{ij} = \frac{\partial^2 F}{\partial x_i \partial x_j} \quad i, j = 1, 2, \ldots, m$$

Then the Taylor expansion to the second order gives

$$F(x_1 + d_1, x_2 + d_2, \ldots, x_m + d_m) - F(x_1, x_2, \ldots, x_m) \approx \sum_i d_i g_i + \sum_i \sum_j G_{ij} d_i d_j$$

At the maximum, the first derivatives are all zero, and hence if the quadratic approximation is exact, the point $(x_1 + d_1, x_2 + d_2, \ldots, x_m + d_m)$ is the required optimum only if

$$g_i + \sum_j G_{ij} d_j = 0 \quad i = 1, 2, \ldots, m$$

Thus, if

$$\mathbf{d} = \begin{bmatrix} d_1 \\ d_2 \\ d_m \end{bmatrix} \quad \mathbf{g} = \begin{bmatrix} g_1 \\ g_2 \\ g_m \end{bmatrix} \quad \text{and} \quad \mathbf{G} = [G_{ij}]$$

---

[1]See for instance, Y. Bard, *Non-Linear Parameter Estimation* (New York: Academic Press, 1972).

then $\mathbf{d} = -\mathbf{G}^{-1}\mathbf{g}$. This technique is applied iteratively, changing the starting values of x_i at each state to $x_i + d_i$ and computing $\mathbf{G}$ and $\mathbf{g}$ at the new values to get the new step. If the function F is quadratic, the quadratic approximation is exact and we get the maximum in a single step. If F is not quadratic but the starting point $(x_1, x_2, \ldots, x_m)$ is close to the maximum, the approximation is likely to be good and the iterative process can be expected to converge rapidly. If the starting value is far from the maximum, the Newton–Raphson method may not converge and can keep moving in the wrong direction. One well-known strategy to avoid going in the wrong direction is not to take the entire step $\mathbf{d}$ but to choose a value λ and take a step $\lambda\mathbf{d}$ so that $\phi(\lambda) = F(x_1 + \lambda d_1, x_2 + \lambda d_2, \ldots, x_m + \lambda d_m)$ is maximum. This "extended Newton–Raphson method" has been found to be very successful in practice.

There have been several modifications of the Newton–Raphson method in practice. See, for instance, the quadratic hill climbing method by Goldfeld and Quandt.[2]

10.3   Nonlinear Least Squares

In nonlinear least squares we have a set of n observations $y_1, y_2, \ldots, y_n$ where

$$y_i = f_i(\theta_1, \theta_2, \ldots, \theta_m) + u_i$$

and we choose the parameters $\theta_1, \theta_2, \ldots, \theta_m$ so as to minimize

$$\sum_{i=1}^{n} \left[y_i - f_i(\theta_1, \theta_2, \ldots, \theta_m) \right]^2$$

The functions f_i will, of course, involve some explanatory variables in regression problems, but we need not consider them here. Written compactly in vector and matrix notation, we minimize

$$\mathbf{S}(\theta) = [\mathbf{y} - \mathbf{f}(\theta)]'[\mathbf{y} - \mathbf{f}(\theta)]$$

Let $\mathbf{F}$ be an $n \times m$ matrix of partial derivatives

$$\frac{\partial f_i}{\partial \theta_j} \quad \begin{matrix} i = 1, 2, \ldots, n \\ j = 1, 2, \ldots, m \end{matrix}$$

The ith row of $\mathbf{F}$ gives the derivatives of f_i with respect to $\theta_1, \theta_2, \ldots, \theta_m$. Let $\mathbf{F}_0$ be the value of $\mathbf{F}$ evaluated at the initial value $\theta_0 = (\theta_{10}, \theta_{20}, \ldots, \theta_{m0})$.

The Gauss–Newton Method

This method consists of taking a linear expansion of $\mathbf{f}(\theta)$ around θ_0 and then using ordinary least squares. We therefore minimize with respect to θ

$$[\mathbf{y} - \mathbf{f}(\theta_0) - \mathbf{F}_0(\theta - \theta_0)]'[\mathbf{y} - \mathbf{f}(\theta_0) - \mathbf{F}_0(\theta - \theta_0)]$$

[2]S. M. Goldfeld and R. E. Quandt, *Non-linear Methods in Econometrics* (Amsterdam: North-Holland, 1972), Chap. 1.

This gives $\mathbf{F}_0'[\mathbf{y} - \mathbf{f}(\boldsymbol{\theta}_0) - \mathbf{F}_0(\boldsymbol{\theta} - \boldsymbol{\theta}_0)] = \mathbf{0}$. Or the change $\mathbf{d} = \boldsymbol{\theta} - \boldsymbol{\theta}_0$ is given by

$$\mathbf{d} = (\mathbf{F}_0'\mathbf{F}_0)^{-1}\mathbf{F}_0'[\mathbf{y} - \mathbf{f}(\boldsymbol{\theta}_0)]$$

This procedure is repeated with the new value as the starting value. As an illustration suppose the regression model is $y_i = \theta_i + \theta_2 x_i^{\theta_3} + u_i$ and we minimize the sum of squares $\sum[y_i - f_i(\theta)]^2$. Here $f_i(\theta) = \theta_1 + \theta_2 x_i \theta_i^{\theta_3}$. The ith row of the matrix $\mathbf{F}$ is

$$\left[\frac{\partial f_i}{\partial \theta_j}\right] = \begin{bmatrix} 1 & x_i^{\theta_3} & \theta_2 x_i^{\theta_3} & \log x_i \end{bmatrix}$$

Hence

$$\mathbf{F}'\mathbf{F} = \begin{bmatrix} n & \sum x_i^{\theta_3} & \sum \theta_2 x_i^{\theta_3} \log x_i \\ \sum x_i^{\theta_3} & \sum x_i^{2\theta_3} & \sum \theta_2 x_i^{2\theta_3} \log x_i \\ \sum \theta_2 x_i^{\theta_3} \log x_i & \sum \theta_2 x_i^{2\theta_3} \log x_i & \sum \theta_2^2 x_i^{2\theta_3} (\log x_i)^2 \end{bmatrix}$$

(all summations are from 1 to n). Also

$$\mathbf{F}'[\mathbf{y} - \mathbf{f}(\boldsymbol{\theta})] = \begin{bmatrix} \sum (y_i - \theta_1 - \theta_2 x_i^{\theta_3}) \\ \sum x_i^{\theta_3}(y_i - \theta_1 - \theta_2 x_i^{\theta_3}) \\ \sum (\theta_2 x_i^{\theta_3} \log x_i)(y_i - \theta_1 - \theta_2 x_i^{\theta_3}) \end{bmatrix}$$

At each iteration we have to evaluate these two expressions at the starting values. The correction factor is given by $(\mathbf{F}'\mathbf{F})^{-1}\mathbf{F}'[\mathbf{y} - \mathbf{f}(\boldsymbol{\theta})]$.

Hartley[3] suggests a modification of the Gauss–Newton method where instead of taking the step $\mathbf{d}$, we take the step $\lambda\mathbf{d}$, where λ is between 0 and 1 and $\text{SSE}(\boldsymbol{\theta}_0 + \lambda\mathbf{d}) < \text{SSE}(\boldsymbol{\theta}_0)$ where SSE is the sum of squares of errors

$$\text{SSE}(\boldsymbol{\theta}_0) = [\mathbf{y} - \mathbf{f}(\boldsymbol{\theta}_0)]'[\mathbf{y} - \mathbf{f}(\boldsymbol{\theta}_0)]$$

The value of λ changes from iteration to iteration.

If we assume that the errors u_i are independently and identically distributed with mean 0 and variance σ^2 and if $\hat{\theta}$ is the final estimate of θ, then

$$\hat{\sigma}^2 = \frac{1}{n}\text{SSE}(\hat{\theta})$$

and the nonlinear least squares estimator $\hat{\theta}$ is approximately normally distributed with mean θ and covariance matrix $\sigma^2[\mathbf{F}(\hat{\theta})'\mathbf{F}(\hat{\theta})]^{-1}$.

10.4 Models of Expectations

Expectations play a crucial role in almost every economic activity. Production depends on expected sales, investment depends on expected profits, long-term interest rates depend

---

[3]See H. O. Hartley, "The Modified Gauss–Newton Method for the Fitting of Non-Linear Regression Functions by Least Squares," *Technometrics*, 1961, pp. 269–280. Also H. O. Hartley and A. Booker, "Non-Linear Least Squares Estimation," *Annals of Mathematical Statistics*, 1965, pp. 638–650.

on expected short-term rates, expected inflation rates, and so on. It is, therefore, important to study models of expectations and how these models are estimated.

In the following sections we study three different models of expectation formation:

1. Naive models of expectation.
2. Adaptive models of expectation.
3. Rational expectations models.

In each case we concentrate on the econometric problems involved.

Since expectations play an important role in economic activity, there are many surveys conducted by different organizations to find out what consumers' expectations are regarding different economic variables. For instance, the Survey Research Center at the University of Michigan conducts surveys regarding consumers' attitudes toward purchases of different durable goods and their forecasts about future inflation rates. There are now survey data available on forecasts of a number of economic variables: wages, interest rates, exchange rates, and so on. An important question arises regarding how we can make use of these survey data. Many econometricians have also investigated the question of how well these survey data forecast the relevant economic variables. After discussing the three models of expectations mentioned above, we discuss the usefulness of survey data on expectations.

10.5 Naive Models of Expectations

The earliest models of expectations involved using past values of the relevant variables or simple extrapolations of the past values, as measures of the expected variables. Consider, for instance, an investment equation

$$y_t = a + bx_{t+1}^* + u_t \tag{10.1}$$

where y_t = investment in period t
  x_{t+1}^* = expected profits during period $t + 1$
  u_t = error term

Unless otherwise noted, expectations are formed in the previous time period. Thus x_t^* denotes expectations of profits for period t as formed at period $t - 1$. Let x_t be the actual profits for period t. Then a naive model for x_{t+1}^* is

$$x_{t+1}^* = x_t \tag{10.2}$$

That is, the firm believes that the profits next period will be the same as the profits this period. A simple extrapolative model would be to say that profits next period will increase by the same amount as the latest increase. This gives

$$x_{t+1}^* - x_t = x_t - x_{t-1}$$

or

$$x_{t+1}^* = 2x_t - x_{t-1} \tag{10.3}$$

Another extrapolative model would be to say that profits will increase by the same percentage as the latest rate of increase. This gives

$$\frac{x_{t+1}^*}{x_t} = \frac{x_t}{x_{t-1}}$$

or

$$x_{t+1}^* = \frac{x_t^2}{x_{t-1}} \tag{10.4}$$

In all these cases we estimate equation (10.1) after substituting the relevant formula for x_t^* from equation (10.2), (10.3), or (10.4). Since the formula for x_t^* is derived from outside and does not consider the equation (10.1) to be estimated, these expectations are considered *exogenous* (derived from outside the economic model under consideration). We will, in the following sections, discuss cases where expectations are *endogenous* (i.e., derived by taking account of the economic model we are considering).

The previous formulas for x_t^* need to be changed suitably if we have quarterly data or monthly data. In these cases there are quarterly or monthly fluctuations, called seasonal fluctuations. For instance, December sales this year would be comparable to December sales last year because of the Christmas season. Hence formula (10.4) would be written as

$$\frac{x_{t+1}^*}{x_{t-3}} = \frac{x_t}{x_{t-4}} \quad \text{for quarterly data}$$

$$\frac{x_{t+1}^*}{x_{t-11}} = \frac{x_t}{x_{t-12}} \quad \text{for monthly data} \tag{10.5}$$

where, again, x_t^* denotes expected profits and x_t actual profits. Note that we compare the corresponding quarters or months and take the most recent percentage gain as the benchmark.

Formulas like (10.5) were used by Ferber[4] to check the predictive accuracy of railroad shipper's forecasts with actual values. He compared the shipper's forecasts with actual values and also forecasts given by formula (10.5) with the actual values and found that the railroad shipper's forecasts were worse than those given by the naive formula. For the comparison he used average absolute error AAE given by

$$\text{AAE} = \frac{1}{n} \sum |\text{actual} - \text{predicted}|$$

Hirsch and Lovell[5] did a similar study based on the Manufacturers' Inventory and Sales Expectations Survey of the Office of Business Economics, U.S. Department of Commerce. However, they found that the anticipations data were more accurate than predictions from naive models.

---

[4]Robert Ferber, *The Railroad Shipper's Forecasts* (Urbana, IL: Bureau of Economic Research, University of Illinois, 1953).

[5]A. A. Hirsch and M. C. Lovell, *Sales Anticipations and Inventory Behavior* (New York: Wiley, 1969).

Yet another naive formula that is often used, and used by Ferber, is that of *regressive expectations*. In this formula there are two components:

1. A growth component based on recent growth rates as in equation (10.5).
2. A return-to-normal component, also called the regressivity component.

Formula (10.5) would now be written as

$$x_{t+1}^* = x_{t-3} \left[\beta \frac{x_t}{x_{t-1}} - \alpha \left(\frac{x_t}{x_{t-1}} - 1 \right) \right] \qquad (10.6)$$

where α is the "reversal coefficient." Ferber estimated an equation like (10.6) using the railroad shipper's forecasts for x_t^* and the actual values for x_t. He found an estimate of $\beta = 0.986$ and $\alpha = 0.556$ and concluded that expectations were regressive. Hirsch and Lovell also found that the data they considered also showed regressivity in expectations, but they argue that this is because the actual data are also regressive.

The naive models that we have considered are by no means recommended. However, they are often used as benchmarks by which we judge any survey data on expectations.

10.6   The Adaptive Expectations Model

The models considered in Section 10.5 use only a few of the past values in forming expectations. Some other models use the entire past history, with the past values receiving declining weights as we go farther into the distant past. These models are called *distributed lag models* of expectations. Consider

$$x_{t+1}^* = \beta_0 x_t + \beta_1 x_{t-1} + \cdots + \beta_\lambda x_{t-k} \qquad (10.7)$$

This is called a *finite* distributed lag since the number of lagged (past) values is finite. $\beta_0, \beta_1, \ldots, \beta_k$ are the weights that we give to these past values. The naive model (10.2) corresponds to $\beta_0 = 1$ and $\beta_1 = \beta_2 = \cdots = \beta_k = 0$. Distributed lags like equation (10.7) have a long history. Irving Fisher[6] was perhaps the first one to use them. He suggested arithmetically declining weights

$$\beta_i = \begin{cases} (k+1-i)\beta & \text{for } 0 \le i \le k \\ 0 & \text{for } i > k \end{cases}$$

Thus the weights are $(k+1)\beta$, $k\beta$, $(k-1)\beta$, $(k-2)\beta$, and so on. The sum of the weights is

$$\beta \frac{(k+1)(k+2)}{2}$$

We might want to restrict this sum to 1. The only problem with this is that if there is a trend in x_t, say x_t is increasing over time, then x_{t+1}^* given by equation (10.7) will continuously

---

[6]I. Fisher, "Our Unstable Dollar and the So-Called Business Cycle," *Journal of the American Statistical Association*, Vol. 20, 1925; also I. Fisher, "Note on a Short-Cut Method for Calculating Distributed Lags," *Bulletin of the International Statistical Institute*, Vol. 29, 1937, pp. 323–327.

underpredict the actual values. We can make adjustment for this by multiplying x_{t+1}^* by $(1 + g)$, where g is the average growth rate of x_t. Thus in using distributed lag models we make adjustments for the growth rate observed in the past [which is actually the idea in formulas like (10.4)].

The distributed lag models received greater attention in the 1950s when Koyck,[7] Cagan,[8] and Nerlove[9] suggested using an infinite lag distribution with geometrically declining weights. Equation (10.7) will now be written as

$$x_{t+1}^* = \sum_{i=0}^{\infty} \beta_i x_{t-i} \tag{10.8}$$

If β_i are geometrically decreasing we can write

$$\beta_i = \beta_0 \lambda^i \quad 0 < \lambda < 1$$

The sum of the infinite series is $\beta_0/1 - \lambda$, and if this sum is equal to 1 we should have $\beta_0 = 1 - \lambda$. Thus we get

$$x_{t+1}^* = \sum_{i=0}^{\infty} (1 - \lambda)\lambda^i x_{t-i} \tag{10.9}$$

Figure 10.1 shows the graph of successive values of β_i. There is one interesting property with this relationship. Lag equation (10.9) by one time period and multiply by λ. We get

$$\lambda x_t^* = \lambda \sum_{i=0}^{\infty} (1 - \lambda)\lambda^i x_{t-i-1} = \sum_{i=0}^{\infty} (1 - \lambda)\lambda^{i+1} x_{t-i-1}$$

Substituting $j = i + 1$, we get

$$\lambda x_t^* = \sum_{j=1}^{\infty} (1 - \lambda)\lambda^j x_{t-j} \tag{10.10}$$

Subtracting equation (10.10) from (10.9) we are left with only the first term on the right-hand side of (10.9). We thus get

$$x_{t+1}^* - \lambda x_t^* = (1 - \lambda)x_t \tag{10.11}$$

or

$$\underbrace{x_{t+1}^* - x_t^*}_{\substack{\text{revision in} \\ \text{expectation}}} = (1 - \lambda) \underbrace{(x_t - x_t^*)}_{\substack{\text{last period's} \\ \text{error}}} \tag{10.12}$$

---

[7] L. M. Koyck, *Distributed Lags and Investment Analysis* (Amsterdam: North-Holland, 1954). A thorough discussion of the Koyck model can be found in M. Nerlove, *Distributed Lags and Demand Analysis*, U.S.D.A. Handbook 141 (Washington, DC: U.S. Government Printing Office, 1958).

[8] Phillip D. Cagan, "The Monetary Dynamics of Hyperinflations," in M. Friedman (ed.), *Studies in the Quantity Theory of Money* (Chicago: University of Chicago Press, 1956), pp. 25–117.

[9] Marc Nerlove, *The Dynamics of Supply: Estimation of Farmers' Response to Price* (Baltimore, MD: The John Hopkins Press, 1958).

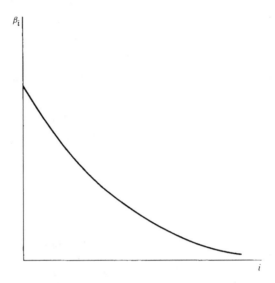

Figure 10.1   Geometric or Koyck lag

Equation (10.12) says that expectations are revised (upward or downward) based on the most recent error. Suppose that x_t^* was 100 but x_t was 120. The error in prediction or expectation is 20. The prediction for $(t + 1)$ will be revised upward but by less than the last period's error. The prediction will, therefore, be > 100 but < 120 (since $0 < \lambda < 1$). This is the reason why the model given by equation (10.9) is called the *adaptive expectations* model (adaptive based on the most recent error).

Again, since the coefficients in equation (10.9) sum to 1, if there is a trend in x_t, the formula for x_{t+1}^* has to be adjusted so that x_{t+1}^* is multiplied by $(1 + g)$, where g is the average growth rate in x_t. Otherwise, the adaptive expectations model can continuously underpredict the true value.

10.7   Estimation with the Adaptive Expectations Model

Consider now the estimation of the investment equation (10.1) where the expected profits x_{t+1}^* are given by the adaptive expectations model (10.9). We can substitute (10.9) in (10.1) and try to estimate the equation in that form. This is called *estimation in the distributed lag form.*

Alternatively, we can try to use equation (10.11) to eliminate the unobserved x_{t+1}^* and estimate the resulting equation. This is called estimation in the *autoregressive form.* Since this is easier, we will discuss this first.

Estimation in the Autoregressive Form

Consider equation (10.1), which we want to estimate:

$$y_t = a + bx_{t+1}^* + u_t \tag{10.1}$$

Lag this equation by one time period and multiply throughout by λ. We get

$$\lambda y_{t-1} = a\lambda + b\lambda x_t^* + \lambda u_{t-1} \tag{10.13}$$

Subtracting equation (10.13) from (10.1) and using the definition of the adaptive expectations model as given in (10.11), we get

$$y_t - \lambda y_{t-1} = a(1 - \lambda) + b(x_{t+1}^* - \lambda x_t^*) + u_t - \lambda u_{t-1}$$
$$= a(1 - \lambda) + b(1 - \lambda)x_t + u_t - \lambda u_{t-1}$$

or

$$y_t = a' + \lambda y_{t-1} + b'x_t + v_t \tag{10.14}$$

where $a' = a(1 - \lambda)$, $b' = b(1 - \lambda)$, and $v_t = u_t - \lambda u_{t-1}$. We have eliminated the unobserved x_{t+1}^* and obtained an equation in the observed variable x_t.

Since equation (10.14) involves a regression of y_t on y_{t-1}, we call this the autoregressive form. One can think of estimating equation (10.14) by ordinary least squares and, in fact, this is what was done in the 1950s and that accounted for the popularity of the adaptive expectations model. However, notice that the error term v_t is equal to $u_t - \lambda u_{t-1}$ and is thus autocorrelated. Since y_{t-1} involves u_{t-1}, we see that y_{t-1} is correlated with the error term v_t. Thus estimation of equation (10.14) by ordinary least squares gives us inconsistent estimates of the parameters.

What is the solution? We can use the instrumental variable method. Use x_{t-1} as an instrument for y_{t-1}. Thus the normal equations will be

$$\sum x_t v_t = 0 \quad \text{and} \quad \sum x_{t-1} v_t = 0$$

The other alternative is to take the error structure of v_t explicitly into account (note that it depends on λ). But this amounts to not making the transformation we have made and thus is exactly the same as estimation in the distributed lag form, which is as follows.

Estimation in the Distributed Lag Form

Substituting the expression (10.9) in (10.1), we get

$$y_t = a + b\left[\sum_{i=0}^{\infty}(1 - \lambda)\lambda^i x_{t-i}\right] + u_t$$

Since this involves an infinite series and we do not observe the infinite past values of x_t, we have to tackle this problem somehow. What we do is to break up the series into the observed and unobserved past. We will write the infinite series as

$$\sum_{i=0}^{t-1}(1 - \lambda)\lambda^i x_{t-i} + \sum_{i=t}^{\infty}(1 - \lambda)\lambda^i x_{t-i}$$

The first part is observed and we will denote it by $z_{1t}(\lambda)$. We use λ since it depends on λ. The second part can be written as

$$\lambda^t \sum_{i=t}^{\infty}(1-\lambda)\lambda^{i-t}x_{t-i} = \lambda^t \sum_{j=0}^{\infty}(1-\lambda)\lambda^j x_{-j} \quad \text{(writing } j = i - t)$$

Notice that the second part of this expression is nothing but equation (10.9) with $t = 0$, that is x_1^* (the expected price for the first period). If we treat this as an unknown parameter c and define $z_{2t} = \lambda^t$, we can write

$$x_{t+1}^* = z_{1t} + cz_{2t}$$

Thus equation (10.1) that we wish to estimate can be written as

$$\begin{aligned} y_t &= a + bx_{t+1}^* + u_t \\ &= a + b(z_{1t} + cz_{2t}) + u_t \\ &= a + bz_{1t} + c'z_{2t} + u_t \end{aligned} \qquad (10.15)$$

with $c' = bc$. Note that z_{1t} and z_{2t} depend on λ. Actually, we are not interested in the parameter c'. The estimation proceeds as follows.

For each value of λ in the range $(0, 1)$ we construct the variables

$$z_{1t} = \sum_{i=0}^{t-1}(1-\lambda)\lambda^i x_{t-i}$$

and $z_{2t} = \lambda^t$. Thus

$$\begin{aligned} z_{11} &= (1-\lambda)x_1 \\ z_{12} &= (1-\lambda)(x_2 + \lambda x_1) \\ z_{13} &= (1-\lambda)(x_3 + \lambda x_2 + \lambda^2 x_1) \end{aligned}$$

and so on. We estimate equation (10.15) by ordinary least squares and obtain the residual sum of squares. Call this $\text{RSS}(\lambda)$. We choose the value of λ for which $\text{RSS}(\lambda)$ is minimum and obtain the corresponding estimates of a and b as the desired least squares estimates.

Note that since z_{1t} and z_{2t} are nonlinear functions of λ, the estimation of (10.15) involves nonlinear least squares. What we have done is to note that *for given* λ we have a linear least squares model. Thus we are using a *search procedure* over λ. In practice one can choose λ in intervals of 0.1 in the first stage and then intervals of 0.01 in the second stage.

10.8   Two Illustrative Examples

As mentioned earlier, the adaptive expectations model was used by (among others) Nerlove for the analysis of agricultural supply functions, and by Cagan for the analysis of hyperinflations. The hyperinflation model involves more problems than have been noted in the literature, and hence we will discuss it in greater detail. In the analysis of agricultural supply functions, we have to deal with the expectation of a current endogenous variable p_t, whereas in the hyperinflation model, we have to deal with the expectation of a future endogenous variable p_{t+1}.

Consider the supply function

$$Q_t = \alpha + \beta p_t^* + \gamma z_t + u_t$$

where p_t^* is the price expected to prevail at time t (as expected in the preceding period), Q_t the quantity supplied, z_t an exogenous variable, and u_t a disturbance term. The adaptive expectations model implies that

$$p_t^* - \lambda p_{t-1}^* = (1 - \lambda)p_{t-1}$$

Thus

$$Q_t - \lambda Q_{t-1} = \alpha - \alpha\lambda + \beta(p_t^* - \lambda p_{t-1}^*) + \gamma(z_t - \lambda z_{t-1}) + u_t - \lambda u_{t-1}$$

Eliminating p_t^*, we get

$$Q_t = \alpha(1 - \lambda) + \lambda Q_{t-1} + \beta(1 - \lambda)p_{t-1} + \gamma z_t - \lambda\gamma z_{t-1} + u_t - \lambda u_{t-1}$$

This equation can be estimated by the methods described in Section 10.7. Computation of the estimates for this model using the data in Table 9.1 is left as an exercise. We will consider Cagan's hyperinflation model in greater detail because it involves more problems than the agricultural supply model.

The hyperinflation model says that the demand for real cash balances is inversely related to the expected rate of inflation. That is, the higher the expected rate of inflation, the lower the real cash balances that individuals would want to hold. Of course, the demand for real cash balances depends on other variables like income, but during a hyperinflation the expected inflation rate is the more dominant variable. We specify the demand for money function as

$$m_t - p_t = a + b(p_{t+1}^* - p_t) + u_t \quad b < 0$$

where m_t is the log of the money supply, p_t the log of the price level, p_{t+1}^* the expectation of p_{t+1} as expected at time t, and u_t the error term. Since the variables are in logs, $p_{t+1}^* - p_t$ is the expected inflation rate. We will denote it by π_{t+1}^*. The actual rate of inflation is $\pi_{t+1} = p_{t+1} - p_i$. Let us define $y_t = m_t - p_t$. Then the demand for money model can be written as

$$y_t = a + b\pi_{t-1}^* + u_t$$

This is similar to equation (10.1) and the estimable equation we derived in Section 10.7 is equation (10.14). This equation applies here with π_t in place of x_t. The equation we get is

$$y_t = a(1 - \lambda) + \lambda y_{t-1} + b(1 - \lambda)\pi_t + v_t \tag{10.14'}$$

where $v_t = u_t - \lambda u_{t-1}$. Cagan estimated this equation by OLS but the problem with the OLS estimation of this equation is that it gives inconsistent estimators because the equation involves the lagged dependent variable y_{t-1} and the errors are serially correlated. One can use Klein's method or estimation in the distributed lag form to avoid this problem. The equation we estimate is similar to equation (10.15) and is

$$y_t = a + bz_{1t} + cz_{2t} + u_t \qquad (10.15')$$

where

$$z_{1t} = \sum_{i=0}^{t-1}(1 - \lambda)\lambda^i \pi_{t-i}$$

and $z_{2t} = \lambda^t$. Thus for each value of λ we generate z_{1t} and z_{2t} and estimate (10.15') by OLS. We choose the value of λ for which the residual sum of squares is minimum, and the corresponding estimates of a, b, and c.

However, even though this is the correct method of estimation for the agricultural supply functions, it is *not* the correct method for the hyperinflation model. The reason is that the model is one where money supply m_t is the exogenous variable and price level p_t is the endogenous variable. By defining the variable $y_t = m_t - p_t$ and writing the equation in a form similar to (10.1) we have missed this point. Equation (10.15') cannot be estimated by OLS because $\pi_t = p_t - p_{t-1}$ in z_{1t} is correlated with the error term u_t.

We can solve this problem by moving the variable p_t to the left-hand side. Let us define $W_t = z_{1t} - (1 - \lambda)p_t$. Now W_t involves p_{t-1} and higher-order lagged values of p_t and does not involve current p_t. We can write equation (10.15') as

$$m_t - p_t = a + b(1 - \lambda)p_t + bW_t + cz_{2t} + u_t$$

Collecting the coefficients of p_t and simplifying, we can write this equation as

$$p_t = \theta_0 + \theta_1 m_t + \theta_2 W_t + \theta_3 z_{2t} + v_t \qquad (10.15'')$$

where

$$\theta_0 = \frac{-a}{1 + b(1 - \lambda)} \qquad \theta_1 = \frac{1}{1 + b(1 - \lambda)} \qquad \theta_2 = \frac{-b}{1 + b(1 - \lambda)}$$

$$\theta_3 = \frac{-c}{1 + b(1 - \lambda)} \qquad v_t = \frac{-u_t}{1 + b(1 - \lambda)}$$

Thus the appropriate equation to estimate for the estimation of the hyperinflation model under adaptive expectations is equation (10.15'') and not equation (10.15') or the simple OLS estimation of the autoregressive form (10.14'). Both equations (10.14') and (10.15') ignore the fact that the same endogenous variable p_t occurs on both the left-hand side and the right-hand side of the equation. Equation (10.14') can also be rearranged similarly. We rewrite it as

$$m_t - p_t = a(1 - \lambda) + \lambda(m_{t-1} - p_{t-1}) + b(1 - \lambda)(p_t - p_{t-1}) + v_t$$

We have to gather the coefficients of p_t, normalize the equation with respect to p_t, and estimate it using p_t as the dependent variable and m_t, m_{t-1}, and p_{t-1} as the explanatory variables. The problem of lagged dependent variables and serially correlated errors still remains and we have to estimate the equation by instrumental variables using, say, m_{t-2} as an instrument.

In summary, the estimation of the hyperinflation model under adaptive expectations is not as straightforward as it appears at first sight looking at equation (10.14′) or (10.15′). An important aspect of the model under adaptive expectations (and also some naive expectations) that has not been noticed often is the occurrence of the endogenous variable p_t on the right-hand side of the equation, which makes OLS estimation inapplicable unless some rearranging of the variables is made. The appropriate dependent variable should be p_t, and the explanatory variables are m_t and lagged values of m_t and p_t.

Since the estimation of the hyperinflation model under adaptive expectations is only of historic interest, we will not present the results here. The estimation of equations (10.14′), (10.14″), (10.15′), and (10.15″) is left as an exercise for students. Tables 10.1 and 10.2 on this and the following pages present the data for Hungary and Germany, respectively. The last periods (particularly since June 1924) can be omitted in the analysis. The data have been provided here because the same data can be used for the estimation of the rational expectations model discussed in Section 10.13.

Table 10.1   Price index and money supply for Hungary, 1921–1925[a]

	Notes in Circulation	Current Accounts and Deposits	Price Index
1921			
January	15.21	3.85	—
February	15.57	5.53	—
March	15.65	5.25	—
April	13.12	6.80	—
May	13.69	5.76	—
June	18.10	1.16	—
July	15.80	3.53	4.20
August	17.33	2.98	5.40
September	20.84	2.41	6.25
October	23.64	2.15	6.75
November	24.74	2.35	8.30
December	25.18	2.24	8.25
1922			
January	25.68	2.49	8.10
February	26.76	2.35	8.50
March	29.33	2.22	9.90
April	30.58	2.90	10.75
May	31.93	3.29	11.00
June	33.60	3.74	12.90
July	38.36	3.93	17.40
August	46.24	5.42	21.40
September	58.46	5.93	26.60
October	70.00	5.19	32.90
November	72.02	6.41	32.60
December	75.89	4.76	33.40

(Continued overleaf)

Table 10.1 (*continued*)

	Notes in Circulation	Current Accounts and Deposits	Price Index
1923			
January	73.72	5.89	38.50
February	75.14	6.60	41.80
March	82.21	11.15	66.00
April	100.10	9.79	83.50
May	119.29	10.61	94.00
June	155.00	12.74	144.50
July	226.29	21.98	286.00
August	399.49	23.63	462.50
September	588.81	60.25	554.00
October	744.93	60.18	587.00
November	853.99	74.97	635.00
December	931.34	84.79	714.00
1924			
January	1084.70	105.48	1026.00
February	1278.40	164.84	1839.10
March	1606.90	253.90	2076.70
April	2098.10	308.10	2134.60
May	2486.30	527.10	2269.60
June	2893.70	1135.70	2207.80
July	3277.90	1424.60	2294.50
August	3659.80	1473.20	2242.00
September	4115.90	1416.40	2236.60
October	4635.10	1465.30	2285.20
November	4442.60	1929.80	2309.50
December	4514.00	2069.50	2346.60
1925			
January	4449.60	2138.60	2307.50
February	4238.00	2542.30	2218.70
March	4270.10	2552.80	2177.80
April	4526.20	2470.50	—

[a]Money supply in 10^9 kronen.

Source: John Parke Young, *European Currency and Finance*, Commission of Gold and Silver Inquiry, U.S. Senate, Serial 9, Vol. 2, U.S. Government Printing Office, Washington, DC, 1925.

10.9 Expectational Variables and Adjustment Lags

In previous sections we discussed models in which the expectational variables were functions of lagged values of the relevant variables for which expectations were formed. There is another source of lagged relationships. This is lags in adjustment to desired levels. In practice both these lags will be present and there is an econometric problem of isolating (or identifying) the separate effects of these two sources.

A simple model incorporating adjustment lags is the *partial adjustment model*, which says that firms adjust their variables (say, capital stock) only partially toward their desired

Table 10.2 Prices and money supply in Germany, 1921–1924[a]

	Notes in Circulation	Total Demand Deposits	Wholesale Price Index
1921			
January	66.62	15.83	1.44
February	67.43	17.36	1.38
March	69.42	28.04	1.34
April	70.84	20.86	1.33
May	71.84	14.09	1.31
June	75.32	20.39	1.37
July	77.39	15.82	1.43
August	80.07	13.65	1.92
September	86.38	19.98	2.07
October	91.53	18.30	2.46
November	100.90	25.31	3.42
December	113.60	32.91	3.49
1922			
January	115.40	23.42	3.67
February	120.00	26.53	4.10
March	130.70	33.36	5.43
April	140.40	31.62	6.36
May	151.90	33.13	6.46
June	169.20	37.17	7.03
July	189.80	39.98	10.16
August	238.10	56.12	19.20
September	316.90	110.00	28.70
October	469.50	140.80	56.60
November	754.10	241.00	115.10
December	1280.00	530.50	147.50
1923			
January	1984.00	763.30	278.50
February	3513.00	1583.00	588.50
March	5518.00	2272.00	488.80
April	6546.00	3854.00	521.20
May	8564.00	5063.00	817.00
June	17,290.00	9953.00	1938.50
July	43,600.00	27,857.00	7478.70
August	663,200.00	591,080.00	94,404.00
September	2823×10^4	1697×10^4	2395×10^3
October	2497×10^6	3868×10^6	709.5×10^6
November	4003×10^8	3740×10^8	72.6×10^9
December	4965×10^8	5480×10^8	126×10^9
1924			
January	4837×10^8	2813×10^8	117×10^9
February	5879×10^8	6505×10^8	116×10^9
March	6899×10^8	7047×10^8	121×10^9
April	7769×10^8	8050×10^8	124×10^9
May	9269×10^8	8046×10^8	122×10^9
June	$10,970 \times 10^8$	7739×10^8	116×10^9

(Continued overleaf)

Table 10.2 (*continued*)

	Notes in Circulation	Total Demand Deposits	Wholesale Price Index
July	$12,110 \times 10^8$	7430×10^8	115×10^9
August	$13,920 \times 10^8$	5619×10^8	120×10^9
September	$15,210 \times 10^8$	6701×10^8	127×10^9
October	$17,810 \times 10^8$	7087×10^8	131×10^9
November	$18,630 \times 10^8$	7039×10^8	129×10^9
December	$19,410 \times 10^8$	8209×10^8	131×10^9

[a]Money supply is for end of the month and in 10^9 marks. Since January 1924 the Reischsbank reported money supply in reischmarks. 1 reischmark $= 10^{12}$ old marks. All figures have been converted to old marks and rounded to four significant digits. Thus the money supply is all on a comparable basis for the whole period.
Source: John Parke Young, *European Currency and Finance*, Commission of Gold and Silver Inquiry, U.S. Senate, Serial 9, Vol. 1, U.S. Government Printing Office, Washington, DC, 1925.

levels. Suppose that a firm anticipates some change in the demand for its product. In anticipation of that, it has to adjust its productive capacity or capital stock denoted by y_t. But it cannot do this immediately. Let y_t^d be the "desired" capital stock. Then $y_t^d - y_{t-1}$ is the desired change. The partial adjustment model says that the actual change is only a fraction of the desired change, that is,

$$y_t - y_{t-1} = \delta(y_t^d - y_{t-1}) \quad \text{where } 0 < \delta < 1 \quad (10.16)$$

Note that this equation is similar to the adaptive expectations model (10.12) with $y_t = x_{t+1}^*$ and $y_t^d = x_t$. Thus y_t will be a distributed lag of y_t^d with geometrically declining weights. Now suppose that y_t^d is a function of anticipated sales x_t; then we can write

$$y_t^d = \alpha x_t + \varepsilon_t \quad \text{where } \varepsilon_t \sim \text{IID}(0, \sigma_0^2)$$

and combining the two equations we get

$$y_t - y_{t-1} = \delta(\alpha x_t + \varepsilon_t - y_{t-1})$$

or

$$y_t = (1 - \delta)y_{t-1} + \alpha\delta x_t + \delta\varepsilon_t$$

which can be written as

$$y_t = \beta_1 y_{t-1} + \beta_2 x_t + u_t$$

with $\beta_1 = 1 - \delta$, $\beta_2 = \alpha\delta$, and $u_t = \delta\varepsilon_t$. Note that $0 < \beta_1 < 1$ and we need this extra condition for a partial adjustment model. Also note that the properties of the error term u_t are the same as those of ε_t. Thus the partial adjustment model does not change the properties of the error term.

A simple explanation as to why firms make only a partial adjustment to the desired level is as follows. The firm faces two costs: the cost of making the adjustment and the cost of being in disequilibrium. If the two costs are quadratic and additive, we can write total cost C_t as

$$C_t = a_1(y_t - y_{t-1})^2 + a_2(y_t^d - y_t)^2$$

Given y_{t-1} and y_t^d we have to choose y_t so that total cost C_t is minimum.

$$\frac{dC_t}{dy_t} = 0 \quad \text{gives} \quad 2a_1(y_t - y_{t-1}) = 2a_2(y_t^d - y_t)$$

$$= 2a_2[y_t^d - y_{t-1} - (y_t - y_{t-1})]$$

Thus we get

$$(y_t - y_{t-1}) = \delta(y_t^d - y_{t-1})$$

where

$$\delta = \frac{a_2}{a_1 + a_2}$$

Note that $0 < \delta < 1$ and δ is close to 1 if the cost of being in disequilibrium is much higher than the cost of adjustment. δ is close to zero if the cost of adjustment is much higher than the cost of disequilibrium.

Partial adjustment models were popular in the 1950s and 1960s but were criticized as being ad hoc.[10] The desired level y_t^* is derived independently by some optimization rule and then the adjustment equation is tagged on to it. However, the cost of adjustment and the cost of being in disequilibrium should be incorporated in the optimization rule. There have been many attempts along these lines but they have not resulted in any tractable estimable equations.[11]

One refinement that can easily be done is to make the partial adjustment parameter δ a function of some explanatory variables that are considered important in determining the speed of adjustment (e.g., interest rates). Denoting the interest rate by r_t, since δ_t is supposed to be between 0 and 1 we can write

$$\delta_t = \frac{\exp(\alpha_0 + \alpha_1 r_t)}{1 + \exp(\alpha_0 + \alpha_1 r_t)}$$

(we use a subscript t for δ since it changes over time).

However, there is no reason that the adjustment parameter be between 0 and 1 at all times. In this case we can make δ_t a linear function of r_t. There are many empirical studies that use partial adjustment models with varying coefficients. Since we have explained the basic idea we will not review them here.

---

[10]Z. Griliches, "Distributed Lags: A Survey," *Econometrica*, January 1967, pp. 16–49, Section 5, "Theoretical Ad-Hockery."

[11]See M. Nerlove, "Lags in Economic Behavior," *Econometrica*, March 1972, pp. 221–251, for a survey of the work on adjustment costs and the development of a model with adjustment costs. There are, however, no empirical results in the paper. Nerlove says, "current research on lags in economic behavior is not 'good' because neither is the empirical research soundly based in economic theory nor is the theoretical research very strongly empirically oriented" (p. 246).

A more generalized version of the partial adjustment model is the *error correction model*. This model says that

$$y_t - y_{t-1} = \underbrace{\delta(y_t^d - y_{t-1}^d)}_{\substack{\text{change in the} \\ \text{desired values}}} + \underbrace{\gamma(y_{t-1}^d - y_{t-1})}_{\substack{\text{past period's} \\ \text{disequilibrium}}} \qquad (10.17)$$

where $0 < \delta < 1$ and $0 < \gamma < 1$. If $\delta = \gamma$, we have the partial adjustment model. Unlike the partial adjustment model, however, this model generates serially correlated errors in the final equation we estimate. Suppose that, as before, we write

$$y_t^d = \alpha x_t + \varepsilon_t$$

where x_t is anticipated sales. Then substituting this in equation (10.17), we get

$$(y_t - y_{t-1}) = \alpha\delta(x_t - x_{t-1}) + \alpha\gamma x_{t-1} - \gamma y_{t-1} + \delta\varepsilon_t - (\delta - \gamma)\varepsilon_{t-1} \qquad (10.18)$$

The error term is now correlated with y_{t-1} and we cannot estimate this equation by ordinary least squares. Again, we can think of using an instrumental variable (say, x_{t-2} for y_{t-1}) and estimate this equation by instrumental variable methods.

10.10 Partial Adjustment with Adaptive Expectations

When adjustment and expectational lags are combined we may have some problems of identifying their separate effects. We can see the problem by considering the partial adjustment model with adaptive expectations. We can consider the error correction model as well but the partial adjustment model is simpler.

Suppose that

$$K_t^d = \text{desired capital stock at the beginning of period } t$$
$$S_t^* = \text{expected sales in period } t$$
$$K_t^d = \beta_0 + \beta_1 S_t^* + u_t \qquad (10.19)$$

The partial adjustment model states that

$$K_t - K_{t-1} = \delta(K_t^d - K_{t-1}) \quad 0 < \delta < 1$$

and substituting for K_t^d, we get

$$K_t = \beta_0\delta + (1 - \delta)K_{t-1} + \beta_1\delta S_t^* + \delta u_t \qquad (10.20)$$

If we use the adaptive expectations model

$$S_t^* - S_{t-1}^* = \lambda(S_{t-1} - S_{t-1}^*) \quad 0 < \lambda < 1$$

then, lagging equation (10.20) by one period, multiplying it by $(1 - \lambda)$, subtracting this from (10.20), and simplifying, we get

$$K_t = \delta\lambda\beta_0 + (1 - \delta + 1 - \lambda)K_{t-1} \tag{10.21}$$
$$- (1 - \delta)(1 - \lambda)K_{t-2} + \lambda\beta_1\delta S_{t-1} + v_t$$

where

$$v_t = \delta[u_t - (1 - \lambda)u_{t-1}]$$

Now if we added the error term to the final simplified equation (10.21) rather than (10.20), it is easy to see from (10.21) that δ and λ occur symmetrically and hence there is some ambiguity in their estimates, which have to be obtained from the coefficients of K_{t-1} and K_{t-2}.

Note that this ambiguity arises only if an error term is superimposed on the final simplified equation (10.21), and the equation is estimated by ordinary least squares assuming that the error terms are serially uncorrelated. On the other hand, we can estimate equation (10.20) in its distributed lag version.[12] For this we use the procedures for the estimation of adaptive expectations models in the distributed lag form as described in Section 10.7. Thus if the model is estimated in the distributed lag form, there is no ambiguity in the estimates of δ and λ.

The preceding discussion on partial adjustment models with adaptive expectations illustrates the point that specification of the error term cannot be done in a cavalier fashion. The estimation procedures and whether any parameters (like δ and λ in our example) are unambiguously estimable or not, depend on the specification of the error term at different stages of the modeling process.

Of course, one can argue that there is no reason why the errors u_t in equation (10.19) should be assumed serially independent. If for some reason one starts with equation (10.21) and a general specification for the error term v_t, the ambiguity in the estimation of δ, the speed of adjustment, and λ, the reaction of expectations, remains. However, in this case, if equation (10.19) has some other explanatory variables, the parameters λ and δ are identified, for example, suppose that (ignoring the error term which we will introduce at the end after all simplifications)

$$K_t^d = \beta_0 + \beta_1 S_t^* + \beta_2 L_t$$

where L_t is the amount of labor hired. Then, on simplification, and adding an error term v_t at the end, we get

$$K_t = \beta_0\delta\lambda + (1 - \delta + 1 - \lambda)K_{t-1} - (1 - \delta)(1 - \lambda)K_{t-2}$$
$$+ \beta_1\delta\lambda S_{t-1} + \delta\beta_2 L_t - \delta\beta_2(1 - \lambda)L_{t-1} + v_t \tag{10.22}$$

In this equation δ and λ do not occur symmetrically.

---

[12] This is equivalent to estimating equation (10.21) with a moving average error that depends on λ, as specified in the equation for v_t.

Suppose that we write the equation as

$$K_t = \alpha_1 + \alpha_2 K_{t-1} + \alpha_3 K_{t-2} + \alpha_4 S_{t-1} + \alpha_5 L_t + \alpha_6 L_{t-1} + v_t \tag{10.23}$$

Then

$$\lambda = 1 + \frac{\alpha_6}{\alpha_5}$$

But the problem is that we get two estimates of δ. From the coefficient of K_{t-1} we get

$$\delta = 2 - \alpha_2 - \lambda$$

and from the coefficient of K_{t-2} we get

$$\delta = 1 + \frac{\alpha_3}{1 - \lambda}$$

The problem is that equation (10.23) has six parameters and our model has only five parameters, $\beta_0, \beta_1, \beta_2, \lambda$, and δ. Note, however, that *given* λ, equation (10.22) can be written as

$$\overline{K}_t = \beta_0 \delta \lambda + (1 - \delta)\overline{K}_{t-1} + \beta_1 \delta \lambda S_{t-1} + \beta_2 \delta \overline{L}_t + v_t \tag{10.24}$$

where

$$\overline{K}_t = K_t - (1 - \lambda)K_{t-1}$$
$$\overline{L}_t = L_t - (1 - \lambda)L_{t-1}$$

The estimation of equation (10.24) gives us unique estimates of δ, β_0, β_1, and β_2. Thus we can use the following *two-step procedure*:

1. Estimate equation (10.23) and get an estimate of λ.
2. Use this to construct $\overline{K}_t$ and $\overline{L}_t$ and then estimate equation (10.24) to get unique estimates of δ, β_0, β_1, and β_2.

An alternative *search method* is the following. Choose different values of λ in the interval (0, 1). For each value of λ run the regression of $\overline{K}_t$ on $\overline{K}_{t-1}, S_{t-1}$, and $\overline{L}_t$. Then the value of λ for which the residual sum of squares is minimum is the best estimate of λ and the corresponding estimates of δ, β_0, β_1, and β_2 are the desired estimates of the parameters. Actually, we can conduct the search in two steps, first at steps of 0.1 and then at steps of 0.01 around the minimum given in the first step. We have discussed a similar procedure in Section 10.7. These are all examples where an equation that is nonlinear in the parameters can be reduced to an equation linear in the parameters conditional on one of the parameters being given.

10.11   Alternative Distributed Lag Models: Polynomial Lags

We saw in previous sections that the adaptive expectations model (10.11) implies that the expectation x_{t+1}^* is a weighted average of x_t and past values of x_t, with geometrically declining weights. We also saw that the partial adjustment model (10.16) implies that y_t is a weighted average of y_t^d and past values of y_t^d again with geometrically declining weights. Since the weights of the lagged variables all sum to 1, and they are usually all positive, it is customary to compare these weights to the successive terms in a probability distribution. The weights β_i in equations like (10.7) and (10.8) are said to form a *lag distribution*. The geometrically declining weights correspond to the geometric distribution. As we mentioned in Section 10.6, this type of lag is also called the *Koyck lag*, named after L. M. Koyck, who first used it.

In addition to the geometric lag distribution, there are some alternative forms of lag distributions that have been suggested in the literature. We will discuss these with reference to:

1. The finite lag distribution (10.7).
2. The infinite lag distribution (10.8).

Finite Lags: The Polynomial Lag

Consider the estimation of the equation

$$y_t = \beta_0 x_t + \beta_1 x_{t-1} + \cdots + \beta_k x_{t-k} + u_t \tag{10.25}$$

The problem with the estimation of this equation is that because of the high correlations between x_t and its lagged values (multicollinearity), we do not get reliable estimates of the parameters β_i. As we discussed in Section 10.6, Irving Fisher assumed the β_i to be declining arithmetically. Almon[13] generalized this to the case where the β_i follow a polynomial of degree r in i. This is known as the Almon lag or the polynomial lag. We denote this by PDL(k, r), where PDL denotes polynomial distributed lag, k is the length of the lag, and r the degree of the polynomial. For instance, if $r = 2$, we write

$$\beta_i = \alpha_0 + \alpha_1 i + \alpha_2 i^2 \tag{10.26}$$

Substituting this in equation (10.25), we get

$$y_t = \sum_{i=0}^{k} (\alpha_0 + \alpha_1 i + \alpha_2 i^2) x_{t-i} + u_t \tag{10.27}$$

$$= \alpha_0 z_{0t} + \alpha_1 z_{1t} + \alpha_2 z_{2t} + u_t$$

where

$$z_{0t} = \sum_{i=0}^{k} x_{t-i} \quad z_{1t} = \sum_{i=0}^{k} i x_{t-i} \quad z_{2t} = \sum_{i=0}^{k} i^2 x_{t-i}$$

Thus we regress y_t on the constructed variables z_{0t}, z_{1t}, and z_{2t}. After we get the estimates of the α's we use equation (10.26) to get estimates of the β_i.

---

[13]S. Almon, "The Distributed Lag Between Capital Appropriations and Net Expenditures," *Econometrica*, January 1965, pp. 178–196.

Following the suggestion of Almon, often some "endpoint constraints" are used. For instance, if we use the constraints $\beta_{-1} = 0$ and $\beta_{k+1} = 0$ in equation (10.26), we have the following two linear relationships between the α's [substituting $i = -1$ and $i = k + 1$ in (10.26)]:

$$\alpha_0 - \alpha_1 + \alpha_2 = 0 \quad \text{and} \quad \alpha_0 + \alpha_1(k + 1) + \alpha_2(k + 1)^2 = 0 \tag{10.28}$$

These give the conditions

$$\alpha_0 = -\alpha_2(k + 1) \quad \text{and} \quad \alpha_1 = -\alpha_2 k \tag{10.29}$$

Thus we can simplify equation (10.27) to

$$y_t = \alpha_2 z_t + u_t$$

where

$$z_t = \sum (i^2 - ki - k - 1)x_{t-i}$$

We get an estimate of α_2 by regressing y_t on z_t and we get estimates of α_0 and α_1 from equation (10.29). Using these we get estimates of β_i from equation (10.26).

Figure 10.2 shows a polynomial distributed lag. The curve shown is that where β_i is a quadratic function of i. A quadratic function can take many shapes and it has been argued that the imposition of the endpoint restrictions (10.29) is often responsible for the "plausible" shapes of the lag distribution fitted by the Almon method.[14] Instead of imposing endpoint constraints *a priori*, one can actually test them because once equation (10.27) has been estimated, tests of the hypotheses like (10.28) are standard tests of linear hypotheses (discussed in Section 4.8).

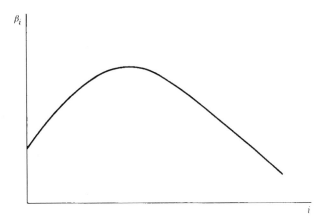

Figure 10.2 Polynomial distributed lag

[14]P. Schmidt and R. N. Waud. "The Almon Lag Technique and the Monetary Versus Fiscal Policy Debate," *Journal of the American Statistical Association*, March 1973, pp. 11–19.

Many of the problems related to polynomial lags can be analyzed in terms of the number of restrictions they impose on β_i in equation (10.25). For instance, with a quadratic polynomial we estimate three α's, whereas we have $(k + 1)$ β's in equation (10.27). Thus there are $k + 1 - 3 = k - 2$ restrictions on the β's. With an rth-degree polynomial, we have $(k - r)$ restrictions.

Suppose that we fit a quadratic polynomial for lag length k and lag length $(k + 1)$. The residual sum of squares may increase or decrease.[15] The reason is that linear restrictions are being imposed on two different parameter sets: $(\beta_1, \beta_2, \ldots, \beta_k)$ and $(\beta_1, \beta_2, \ldots, \beta_k, \beta_{k+1})$.

Apart from the problem of endpoint restrictions, there are three other problems with polynomial lags:

1. *Problems of long-tailed distributions.* It is difficult to capture long-tailed lag distributions like the one shown in Figure 10.3. This problem can be solved by using a piecewise polynomial. Another procedure is to have a polynomial for the initial β_i and a Koyck or geometric lag for the latter part.

2. *Problem of choosing the lag length k.* Schmidt and Waud suggest choosing k on the basis of maximum $\overline{R}^2$: Frost[16] did a simulation experiment using this criterion and found that a substantial upward bias in the lag length occurs. As we discussed in Chapter 4, the $\overline{R}^2$ criterion implies that a regressor is retained if the F-ratio is > 1. The bias that Frost suggests can be corrected by using F-ratios greater than 1, say $F = 2$.

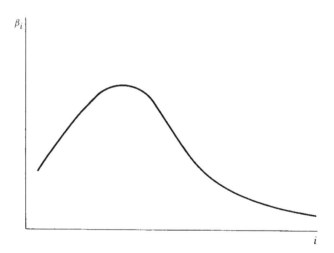

Figure 10.3   Long-tailed lag distribution

---

[15]This is demonstrated with an empirical example in J. J. Thomas, "Some Problems in the Use of Almon's Technique in the Estimation of Distributed Lags," *Empirical Economics*, Vol. 2, 1977, pp. 175–193.

[16]P. A. Frost, "Some Properties of the Almon Lag Technique When One Searches for Degree of Polynomial and Lag," *Journal of the American Statistical Association*, Vol. 70, 1975, pp. 606–612.

3. *Problem of choosing r, the degree of the polynomial.* If the lag length k is correctly specified, then choosing the degree of the polynomial r is straightforward. What we do is start with a sufficiently high-degree polynomial as in equation (10.27). Construct $z_{0t}, z_{1t}, z_{2t}, z_{3t}, \ldots$ as defined in (10.27) and start dropping the higher terms sequentially. Note that the proper way of testing is to start with the highest-degree polynomial possible and then go backward, until one of the hypotheses is rejected. This sequential test was suggested by Anderson,[17] who showed that the resulting sequence of tests are independent and that the significance level for the jth test is

$$1 - \prod_{i=1}^{j}(1 - \gamma_i)$$

where γ_i is the significance level chosen at the ith step in the sequence. If $\gamma_i = 0.05$ for all i, the significance levels for four successive tests are 0.05, 0.0975, 0.1426, and 0.1855, respectively. Godfrey and Poskitt[18] use this procedure suggested by Anderson to choose the degree of the polynomial for the Almon lag.

We will now illustrate this procedure with an example.

Illustrative Example

Consider the data in Table 10.3. The data are on capital expenditures (Y) and approximations (X) for the years 1953–1967 on a quarterly basis. These data are from the National Industrial Conference Board. Since they have been used very often (in fact, too often) in the illustration of different distributed lag models, they are being reproduced here. It is a good data set for some beginning exercises in distributed lag estimation.

Before we impose any functional forms on the data, it would be interesting to see what some OLS estimates of unrestricted distributed lag equations look like. There are a total of 60 observations and it was decided to estimate 12 lagged coefficients. The implicit assumption is that the maximum time lag between appropriations and expenditures is 3 years. To make the estimated σ^2 comparable, the equations were all estimated using the last 48 observations of the dependent variable Y. The results are presented in Table 10.4.

There are several features of the lag distributions in Table 10.4 that are interesting. The $\overline{R}^2$ steadily increases until we use seven lags. The sum of the coefficients also increases steadily. Overall, from the results presented there, it appears that a lag distribution using seven lags is appropriate. This corresponds to a maximum of a 1.75-year lag between capital appropriations and expenditures. Further, about 98.6% of all appropriations are eventually spent.

One disturbing feature of the OLS estimates is that no matter how many lags we include, the DW test statistic shows significant positive correlation. For instance, the following

---

[17]T. W. Anderson, "The Choice of the Degree of a Polynomial Regression as a Multiple Decision Problem," *Annals of Mathematical Statistics*, Vol. 33, No. 1, 1966, pp. 255–265. This test is also discussed in T. W. Anderson, *The Statistical Analysis of Time Series* (New York: Wiley, 1971), pp. 34–43.

[18]L. G. Godfrey and D. S. Poskitt, "Testing the Restrictions of the Almon Lag Technique," *Journal of the American Statistical Association*, Vol. 70, March 1975, pp. 105–108.

are the DW test statistics for different lengths of the lag distribution:

Length of Lag	DW
0	0.38
4	0.58
8	0.35
12	0.44

This suggests that we should be estimating some more general dynamic models, allowing for autocorrelated errors.

Choosing the Degree of the Polynomial

Consider the data in Table 10.3. We will consider a lag length of 12 and consider the choice of the degrees of the polynomial by the sequential testing method outlined here. We start with a fourth-degree polynomial.

The results are as follows (figures in parentheses are t-ratios, not standard errors):

	Equation			
Coefficient of:	1	2	3	4
z_{0t}	0.1150 (5.78)	0.1108 (5.80)	0.1468 (14.20)	0.1637 (33.06)
$10^{-1} \times z_{1t}$	0.2003 (0.82)	0.3305 (1.83)	−0.0507 (−0.97)	−0.1463 (−16.70)
$10^{-2} \times z_{2t}$	−0.2681 (−0.33)	−0.8549 (−2.42)	−0.0824 (−1.86)	
$10^{-3} \times z_{3t}$	−0.4517 (−0.41)	0.4011 (2.20)		
$10^{-4} \times z_{4t}$	0.3951 (0.79)			
$\hat{\sigma}^2$	15,520	15,389	16,702	17,590
DW	0.514	0.465	0.518	0.536
$\overline{R}^2$	0.9988	0.9988	0.9987	0.9986

First we test the coefficient of z_{4t} at the 5% level and do not reject the hypothesis that it is zero. Next we test the coefficient of z_{3t}, and we reject the hypothesis that its coefficient is zero. Since this is the first hypothesis rejected, we use a polynomial of the third degree. The results of the other lower-degree polynomials are not needed and are just presented for the sake of curiosity. Actually, for the fourth-degree polynomial, the high R^2 and the low t-ratios indicate that there is high multicollinearity among the variables.

We now estimate the coefficients of the lag distribution using the formula

$$\beta_i = 0.1108 + 0.3305 \times 10^{-1}i - 0.8549 \times 10^{-2}i^2 + 0.4011 \times 10^{-3}i^3$$

Table 10.3 Capital expenditures (Y) and appropriations (X) for 1953–1967
(quarterly data)

N	Y	X	N	Y	X	N	Y	X
1	2072	1660	21	2697	1511	41	2601	2629
2	2077	1926	22	2338	1631	42	2648	3133
3	2078	2181	23	2140	1990	43	2840	3449
4	2043	1897	24	2012	1993	44	2937	3764
5	2062	1695	25	2071	2520	45	3136	3983
6	2067	1705	26	2192	2804	46	3299	4381
7	1964	1731	27	2240	2919	47	3514	4786
8	1981	2151	28	2421	3024	48	3815	4094
9	1914	2556	29	2639	2725	49	4093	4870
10	1991	3152	30	2733	2321	50	4262	5344
11	2129	3763	31	2721	2131	51	4531	5433
12	2309	3903	32	2640	2552	52	4825	5911
13	2614	3912	33	2513	2234	53	5160	6109
14	2896	3571	34	2448	2282	54	5319	6542
15	3058	3199	35	2429	2533	55	5574	5785
16	3309	3262	36	2516	2517	56	5749	5707
17	3446	3476	37	2534	2772	57	5715	5412
18	3466	2993	38	2494	2380	58	5637	5465
19	3435	2262	39	2596	2568	59	5383	5550
20	3183	2011	40	2572	2944	60	5467	5465

The coefficients are:

Lag	Coefficient	Lag	Coefficient	Lag	Coefficient
0	0.1108				
1	0.1357	5	0.1125	9	0.0082
2	0.1459	6	0.0880	10	−0.0125
3	0.1438	7	0.0608	11	−0.0262
4	0.1319	8	0.0334	12	−0.0306

The sum of the coefficients is 0.9017, and furthermore, the last three coefficients are negative. This is the reason that, as mentioned earlier, some endpoint restrictions are often imposed in estimating the polynomial distributed lags. Comparing these results with the unrestricted OLS estimates in Table 10.4, it appears that not much is to be gained (in this particular example) by using the polynomial lag.

In any case, the example illustrates the procedure of choice of the degree of the polynomial for given lag length.

10.12 Rational Lags

In Section 10.11 we discussed finite lag distributions. We will now discuss infinite lag distributions. Actually, we considered one earlier: the geometric or Koyck lag. A straightforward generalization of this is the rational lag distribution.[19]

---

[19]D. W. Jorgenson, "Rational Distributed Lag Functions," *Econometrica*, Vol. 34, January 1966, pp. 135–149.

Table 10.4 Unrestricted least squares estimates of distributed lags

Coefficient of:	Equation									
	1	2	3	4	5	6	7	8	9	10
x_t	0.081 (1.3)	0.093 (1.6)	0.088 (1.6)	0.067 (1.3)	0.106 (1.9)	0.163 (1.9)	0.113 (1.0)	0.050 (0.3)	−0.011 (0.1)	0.915 (42.1)
x_{t-1}	0.092 (0.9)	0.090 (1.0)	0.094 (1.2)	0.137 (1.8)	0.100 (1.2)	0.056 (0.5)	0.063 (0.4)	0.075 (0.3)	0.940 (5.0)	
x_{t-2}	0.236 (2.2)	0.228 (2.5)	0.229 (3.1)	0.210 (2.8)	0.229 (2.8)	0.139 (1.1)	0.131 (0.8)	0.817 (5.5)		
x_{t-3}	0.183 (1.7)	0.183 (2.1)	0.172 (2.3)	0.186 (2.5)	0.139 (1.8)	0.131 (1.1)	0.648 (5.9)			
x_{t-4}	0.142 (1.2)	0.130 (1.6)	0.133 (1.7)	0.100 (1.3)	0.118 (1.5)	0.476 (5.8)				
x_{t-5}	−0.042 (0.4)	−0.006 (0.1)	−0.002 (0.0)	0.011 (0.1)	0.003 (0.0)					
x_{t-6}	0.137 (1.3)	0.123 (1.4)	0.133 (1.7)	0.119 (1.5)	0.285 (5.2)					
x_{t-7}	0.058 (0.4)	0.059 (0.6)	0.057 (0.6)	0.156 (2.8)						
x_{t-8}	0.147 (1.1)	0.110 (1.1)	0.084 (1.4)							
x_{t-9}	−0.010 (0.1)	0.010 (0.1)								
x_{t-10}	−0.069 (0.5)	−0.032 (0.5)								
x_{t-11}	−0.045 (0.3)									
x_{t-12}	0.081 (1.1)									
Sum of coefficients	0.991	0.988	0.988	0.986	0.980	0.965	0.955	0.942	0.929	0.915
$\overline{R}^2$	0.9988	0.9988	0.9988	0.9988	0.9985	0.9965	0.9941	0.9896	0.9829	0.9742

Consider equation (10.11). One way of generalizing it is to add more lags on the left-hand side and right-hand side of the equation, and have the parameters different. If p is the number of lags on the right-hand side and q the number of lags on the left-hand side, we have a rational distributed lag model which we denote by RDL(p, q). For instance, the RDL(3, 2) model corresponding to (10.11) is

$$x_{t+1}^* + \beta_0 x_t^* + \beta_1 x_{t-1}^* = \alpha_0 x_{t-1} + \alpha_2 x_{t-2} + \alpha_3 x_{t-3}$$

A similar generalization can be given for the partial adjustment model (10.16). We have

$$y_t + \beta_1 y_{t-1} + \beta_2 y_{t-2} = \alpha_0 y_t^d + \alpha_1 y_{t-1}^d + \alpha_2 y_{t-2}^d + \alpha_3 y_{t-3}^d$$

As before, we have to somehow eliminate the unobserved variables x_t^* and y_t^d. Since the algebraic details are similar to those in Section 10.10, we will not pursue them here.[20] Lucas and Rapping[21] use the RDL model for price expectations, instead of the adaptive expectations model, but they estimate it in the autoregressive form ignoring serial correlation.

The rational distributed lag model and its use in expectations should not be confused with the rational expectations models we discuss in the next section.

10.13 Rational Expectations

In Sections 10.5 and 10.6 we discussed some naive models of expectations and the adaptive expectations model. We also saw how the latter can be generalized using some polynomial lags. During the last decade a new theory, that of "rational expectations," has taken a strong hold in almost all econometric work on expectations.

The basic idea of "rational expectations" comes from a pathbreaking paper by John Muth,[22] who observed that the various expectational formulas that were used in the analysis of dynamic economic models had little resemblance to the way the economy works. If the economic system changes, the way expectations are formed should change, but the traditional models of expectations do not permit any such changes. The adaptive expectations formula, for instance, says that economic agents revise their expectations upward or downward based on the most recent error. The formula says

$$y_t^* - y_{t-1}^* = \lambda(y_{t-1} - y_{t-1}^*) \quad 0 < \lambda < 1$$

where y_t^* is the expectation for y_t as formed at time $t - 1$. In this formula λ is a constant. Of course, one can modify this formula so that λ depends on whatever variables produce changes in the economic system.

---

[20]The estimation of the RDL model in the distributed lag form is discussed in G. S. Maddala, *Econometrics* (New York: McGraw-Hill, 1977), pp. 366–367.

[21]R. E. Lucas, Jr. and L. A. Rapping, "Price Expectations and the Phillips Curve," *The American Economic Review*, Vol. 59, 1969, pp. 342–350. They warn that this should not be confused with the "rational expectations" model as defined by Muth (which we discuss in the next section).

[22]John F. Muth, "Rational Expectations and the Theory of Price Movements," *Econometrica*, Vol. 29, 1961, pp. 315–335.

There are some reasonable requirements that y_t^* or the predicted value of y_t should satisfy. Consider the prediction error

$$\varepsilon_t = y_t - y_t^*$$

It is reasonable to require that expectations be unbiased, that is,

$$E(\varepsilon_t) = 0$$

Otherwise, there is a systematic component in the forecast error which forecasters should be able to correct.

Muth also required that the prediction error be uncorrelated with the entire information set that is available to the forecaster at the time the prediction is made. If we denote by I_{t-1} the information available at time $(t - 1)$ and write

$$y_t = y_t^* + \varepsilon_t \tag{10.30}$$

then y_t^* depends on I_{t-1} and y_t^* is uncorrelated with ε_t. One implication of this equation is that $\text{var}(y_t) = \text{var}(y_t^*) + \text{var}(\varepsilon_t)$ and hence $\text{var}(y_t) \geq \text{var}(y_t^*)$. If the prediction error is correlated with any variables in I_{t-1}, it implies that the forecaster has not used all the available information. Taking (mathematical) expectations of all variables in equation (10.30), we get

$$y_t^* = E(y_t | I_{t-1}) \tag{10.31}$$

The left-hand side of equation (10.31) should be interpreted as the *subjective* expectation and the right-hand side of equation (10.31) as the *objective* expectation conditional on data available when the expectation was formed. Thus there is a connection between the subjective beliefs of economic agents and the actual behavior of the economic system.

Formula (10.31) forms the basis of almost all the econometric work on rational expectations. There are three assumptions involved in the use of formula (10.31):

1. There exists a unique mathematical expectation of the random variable y_t based on the given set of information I_{t-1}.
2. Economic agents behave *as if* they know this conditional expectation and equate their own subjective expectation of y_t to this conditional expectation. Note that this implies that the economic agents behave *as if they have full knowledge* about the model that the econometrician is estimating, that is, they behave as if they know not only the structure of the model but the parameters as well.
3. The econometrician, however, does not know the parameters of the model but has to make inferences about them based on assumption 2 about the behavior of economic agents and the resulting stochastic behavior of the system.

There have been many criticisms of the rational expectations hypothesis as implied by equation (10.31). The basic argument is that "rational" economic agents need not behave this way. We will not go through these criticisms here. The whole controversy surrounding the rational expectations hypothesis could have been avoided if the term "rational" was not used to describe the mechanism of expectation formation given by equation (10.31). A more appropriate term to characterize (10.31) is *model consistent*, because the expression for y_t^* derived from (10.31) depends on the particular model we start with. The coinage of the term "rational" is rather unfortunate. We will, however, continue to use the word "rational" to describe "model consistent" or Muthian expectations formed using (10.31).

The requirement that y_t^* should completely summarize the information in I_{t-1} has led Lovell[23] to suggest the term "sufficient expectations" because it is related to the statistical concept of a "sufficient estimator" which may be loosely defined as an estimator that utilizes all the information available in the sample.

There are, basically, two methods of estimation for rational expectations models. The first method involves using the definition (10.31) and writing

$$y_t^* = y_t - v_t$$

where v_t is uncorrelated with all the variables in the information set I_{t-1}. We then estimate this model using the instrumental variable methods with the appropriate instruments. This method is very easy to apply and gives consistent, though not efficient estimators. We will illustrate this using the hyperinflation model discussed in Section 10.8.

The second method uses information on the structure of the model to derive an explicit expression for y_t^*. This method involves the following steps:

1. Derive the equation for y_t from the model you start with.
2. Take expectations of y_t conditional on I_{t-1} and substitute the resulting expression for y_t^* in the model.
3. Reestimate the model with this substitution.

We will illustrate this with a simple demand and supply model in Section 10.15. We will also present the results from the instrumental variable method for purposes of comparison.

The instrumental variable method, although not efficient, gives consistent estimators of the parameters in all rational expectations models and is worth using at least as an initial step. Consider, for instance, Cagan's model of hyperinflation. The model is

$$m_t - p_t = a + b(p_{t+1}^* - p_t) + u_t$$

Now substitute $p_{t+1} - v_{t+1}$ for p_{t+1}^*, where v_{t+1} is uncorrelated with all variables in the information set I_t. We can write the model as

$$m_t - p_t = a + b(p_{t+1} - p_t) + u_t - bv_{t+1}$$

This equation cannot be estimated by OLS because p_{t+1} is correlated with v_{t-1} and p_t with u_t. If m_t and p_t are known at time t, then v_{t+1} will be uncorrelated with these variables. One needs an instrument that is uncorrelated with u_t and v_{t+1}. Valid instruments

---

[23]M. C. Lovell, "Tests of the Rational Expectations Hypothesis," *The American Economic Review*, Vol. 76, March 1986, pp. 110–124.

are m_{t-1}, p_{t-1}, and higher-order lags of m_t and p_t. One can regress $p_{t+1} - p_t$ on lagged values of m_t and p_t and use the 2SLS method.

The estimation of the hyperinflation model under rational expectations using the above-mentioned instrumental variable method using the data in Tables 10.1 and 10.2 is left as an exercise.

10.14 Tests for Rationality

There is a considerable amount of literature on what is known as "tests for rationality." In this literature we do not start with any economic model. Usually, we have observations on y_t^* from survey data or other sources and we test whether the forecast error $y_t - y_t^*$ is uncorrelated with variables in the information set I_{t-1}. It is customary to start with a test of unbiasedness by estimating the regression equation

$$y_t = \beta_0 + \beta_1 y_t^* + \varepsilon_t$$

and testing the hypothesis $\beta_0 = 0$, $\beta_1 = 1$.

Further, since y_{t-1} is definitely in the information set I_{t-1}, the following equation is estimated:

$$y_t - y_t^* = \alpha_0 + \alpha_1 y_{t-1} + \varepsilon_t$$

and the hypothesis $\alpha_0 = 0$, $\alpha_1 = 0$ is tested. Rationality implies that $\alpha_1 = 0$. An alternative equation that can be estimated is

$$y_t - y_t^* = \alpha_0 + \alpha_1 (y_{t-1} - y_{t-1}^*) + \varepsilon_t$$

Again, rationality implies that $\alpha_1 = 0$. If the forecast errors exhibit a significant nonzero mean and serial correlation (significant α_1), then this implies that the information contained in past forecast errors was not fully utilized in forming future predictions.

Tests based on y_{t-1} and $(y_{t-1} - y_{t-1}^*)$ examine what is known as the *weak version of the rational expectations hypotheses* and are tests for weak rationality. The strong version says that the forecast error $(y_t - y_t^*)$ is uncorrelated with all the variables known to the forecaster.

Yet another test for rationality is that $\text{var}(y_t) > \text{var}(y_t^*)$. As we saw earlier if

$$y_t = y_t^* + \varepsilon_t$$

and ε_t is uncorrelated with y_t^*, then $\text{var}(y_t) = \text{var}(y_t^*) + \text{var}(\varepsilon_t)$. Hence $\text{var}(y_t) \geq \text{var}(y_t^*)$.

Lovell[24] considers these two tests:

1. Tests based on y_{t-1}.
2. Tests based on $\text{var}(y_t) > \text{var}(y_t^*)$.

He examines the evidence from a number of surveys on sales and inventory expectations, price expectations, wage expectations, data revisions, and so on, and argues that in a majority of cases the tests for rationality reject the hypothesis of rationality.

---

[24]Lovell, "Tests."

Some studies that test for rationality of survey forecasts like those by Pesando, Carlson, and Mullineaux for price expectations[25] and tests by Friedman for interest-rate expectations[26] use a different procedure. What they do is the following:

1. Regress y on the variables in the information set I_{t-1}.
2. Regress y^* on the same variables in the information set I_{t-1}.
3. Test the equality of coefficients in the two regressions using the Chow test described in Chapter 4.

However, note that the variance of the error terms in the two equations is likely to be unequal, since $\text{var}(y_t)$ is expected to be greater than $\text{var}(y_t^*)$. Hence some adjustment should be made for this before applying the Chow test. (Divide each data set by the estimated standard deviation of the error term.)

This test is formally identical to the test suggested earlier of regressing the forecast error $y_t - y_t^*$ on the variables in I_{t-1} and checking that their coefficients are zero. Without any loss of generality, suppose that there are two variables z_1 and z_2 in the information set I_{t-1} (z_1 and z_2 can be sets of variables). We can write

$$y = \beta_1 z_1 + \beta_2 z_2 + u$$
$$y^* = \beta_1^* z_1 + \beta_2^* z_2 + u^*$$

Then

$$(y - y^*) = (\beta_1 - \beta_1^*)z_1 + (\beta_2 - \beta_2^*)z_2 + (u - u^*) \tag{10.32}$$

Thus a regression of $(y - y^*)$ on z_1 and z_2 and testing whether the coefficients of z_1 and z_2 are significantly different from zero is the same as testing the equality of the coefficients of z_1 and z_2 in the regressions of y and y^* on these variables. There is something to be said in favor of the test based on equation (10.32) instead of the one based on separate regressions for y and y^*. With the test based on (10.32), the fact that $\text{var}(u)$ and $\text{var}(u^*)$ are different does not matter.

What happens if in the tests for rationality we use only a subset of the variables in the information set I_{t-1}? For instance, in equation (10.32) we just regress $y - y^*$ on z_1 only and test whether the coefficient of z_1 is significantly different from zero. Recall that this is what we do in tests for weak rationality where we regress $y_t - y_t^*$ on y_{t-1}.

Suppose that $(y - y^*)$ is uncorrelated with z_1 but not with z_2, so that in equation (10.32), $\beta_2 - \beta_2^* \neq 0$. This implies that the expectations y^* are not rational. Now suppose that z_1 and z_2 are uncorrelated. We can still get the result that the coefficient of z_1 in a regression of $y - y^*$ on z_1 is zero. Thus if we do not reject the hypothesis that this coefficient is

[25] J. E. Pesando, "A Note on the Rationality of the Livingston Price Expectations," *Journal of Political Economy*, Vol. 83, August 1975, pp. 849–858; J. A. Carlson, "A Study of Price Forecasts," *Annals of Economic and Social Measurement*, Vol. 6, Winter 1977, pp. 27–56; D. J. Mullineaux, "On Testing for Rationality: Another Look at the Livingston Price Expectations Data," *Journal of Political Economy*, Vol. 86, April 1978, pp. 329–336.

[26] B. M. Friedman, "Survey Evidence on the 'Rationality' of Interest Rate Expectations," *Journal of Monetary Economics*, Vol. 6. October 1980, pp. 453–466.

zero, it does not necessarily mean that we can accept the hypothesis of rationality.[27] This implies that tests of weak rationality are indeed weak. However, in practice, it is highly unlikely that the variables in the information set I_{t-1} are uncorrelated. Hence one can have sufficient confidence in the weak tests and need not worry that all the variables in the information set I_{t-1} are not included in the tests.

10.15   Estimation of a Demand and Supply Model Under Rational Expectations

We will illustrate the estimation of econometric models with rational expectations using equations (10.30) and (10.31) by considering a simple demand and supply model. Consider the following model (all variables considered as deviations from their means):

$$q_t = \beta_1 p_t + \gamma_1 z_{1t} + u_{1t} \quad \text{demand function} \tag{10.33}$$

$$q_t = \beta_2 p_t^* + \gamma_2 z_{2t} + u_{2t} \quad \text{supply function} \tag{10.34}$$

where q_t = quantity demanded or supplied (both are the same by the assumption of equilibrium)

p_t = market price

p_t^* = market price at time t as expected at time $(t-1)$; we assume that there is one period lag between production decisions and market supply

z_{1t}, z_{2t} = exogenous variables

u_{1t}, u_{2t} = serially uncorrelated disturbances with the usual properties (zero mean, constant variances, and constant covariance)

We consider two cases: z_{1t} and z_{2t} known, and unknown, at time $(t-1)$.

Case 1

z_{1t} and z_{2t} are known at time $(t-1)$, that is, they are in the information set I_{t-1}. In this case the estimation of the model is very simple. The rational expectations hypothesis implies that

$$p_t = p_t^* + \varepsilon_t$$

where $E(\varepsilon_t) = 0$ and $\text{cov}(\varepsilon_1, z_{1t}) = \text{cov}(\varepsilon_t, z_{2t}) = 0$. Thus ε_t has the same stochastic properties as u_{1t} and u_{2t}. Now substituting $p_t^* = p_t - \varepsilon_t$ in equation (10.34) we get

$$q_t = \beta_2 p_t + \gamma_2 z_{2t} + (u_{2t} - \beta_2 \varepsilon_t) \tag{10.34'}$$

The composite error in this equation has the same properties as the error term in (10.34) (zero mean, and zero correlation with z_{1t} and z_{2t}).

---

[27] A. Abel and F. S. Mishkin, "An Integrated View of Tests of Rationality, Market Efficiency and Short-Run Neutrality of Monetary Policy," *Journal of Monetary Economics*, Vol. 11, 1983, pp. 3–24.

Thus the implication of the "rational" expectations hypothesis is that all we have to do is to substitute p_t for p_t^* and proceed with the estimation as usual. Thus the rational expectations hypothesis greatly simplifies the estimation procedures. This conclusion holds good in any simultaneous equations model involving expectations of current endogenous variables if the current exogenous variables are assumed to be known at time $(t-1)$ (or at the time expectations are formed), and the errors are serially independent.

There is, however, one problem that the "rational" expectations hypothesis creates. Suppose that the variable z_{2t} is missing in equation (10.34). Then with any exogenous specification of the expectational variable p_t^* (as in the adaptive expectations formulation), the equation system would be identified. On the other hand, under the "rational" expectations hypothesis the demand function is not identified. Thus, in the general simultaneous equations model with expectations of current endogenous variable, the identification properties will depend on the identification properties of the simultaneous equations model resulting from the substitution of y_t for y_t^*, where y_t^* is the expectation of the endogenous variable y_t. This result makes intuitive sense since what the rational expectations hypothesis does is to make the expectations endogenous.

Case 2

z_{1t} and z_{2t} are not known at time $(t-1)$. That is, the exogenous variables at time t have to be forecast at time $(t-1)$. What will happen if we just substitute $p_t^* = p_t - \varepsilon_t$ as before? Since ε_t is not uncorrelated with z_{1t} and z_{2t} [they are not in the information set at time $(t-1)$], the composite error term in equation (10.34′) will be correlated with z_{1t} and z_{2t}.

How do we estimate this model, then? What we have to do is to add equations for z_{1t} and z_{2t}. A common procedure is to specify them as autoregressions. For simplicity we will specify them as first-order autoregressions. Then we have

$$z_{1t} = \alpha_1 z_{1,t-1} + v_{1t}$$

$$z_{2t} = \alpha_2 z_{2,t-1} + v_{2t}$$

(10.35)

We now estimate equations (10.33), (10.34′), and (10.35) together.[28]

An alternative way of looking at this is to say that we estimate the demand and supply model given by equations (10.33) and (10.34) by replacing p_t^* by p_t and using lagged values of z_{1t} and z_{2t} as instrumental variables.

There is an alternative method of estimating the model with rational expectations which is somewhat more complicated. This is called the *substitution method* (SM). In this method we derive an expression for p_t^* using the relationship

$$p_t^* = E(p_t | I_{t-1})$$

---

[28] See M. R. Wickens, "The Efficient Estimation of Econometric Models with Rational Expectations," *Review of Economic Studies*, Vol. 49, 1982, pp. 55–67, who calls this method the "errors in variables method" (EVM).

and substitute it in the model and then estimate the model. For this we proceed as follows.

Equating demand and supply we get the equilibrium condition

$$\beta_1 p_t + \gamma_1 z_{1t} + u_{1t} = \beta_2 p_t^* + \gamma_2 z_{2t} + u_{2t} \tag{10.36}$$

Now take expectations throughout, conditional on the information set I_{t-1}. Note that $E(u_{1t}|I_{t-1}) = 0$ and $E(u_{2t}|I_{t-1}) = 0$. Hence we get

$$\beta_1 p_t^* + \gamma_1 z_{1t}^* = \beta_2 p_t^* + \gamma_2 z_{2t}^* \tag{10.37}$$

where

$$z_{1t}^* = E(z_{1t}|I_{t-1}) \quad \text{and} \quad z_{2t}^* = E(z_{2t}|I_{t-1})$$

These are, respectively, the expectations of z_{1t} and z_{2t} as of time $(t-1)$. Let us define

$$z_{1t} = z_{1t}^* + w_{1t}$$

$$z_{2t} = z_{2t}^* + w_{2t}$$

Subtracting equation (10.37) from (10.36), we get

$$\beta_1(p_t - p_t^*) + \gamma_1 w_{1t} + u_{1t} = \gamma_2 w_{2t} + u_{2t}$$

or

$$p_t^* = p_t + \frac{1}{\beta_1}(\gamma_1 w_{1t} - \gamma_2 w_{2t} + u_{1t} - u_{2t}) \tag{10.38}$$

We now substitute this expression in equation (10.34) and get

$$q_t = \beta_2 p_t + \gamma_2 z_{2t} + \frac{\gamma_1 \beta_2}{\beta_1} w_{1t} - \frac{\gamma_2 \beta_2}{\beta_1} w_{2t} + u_{2t}^* \tag{10.39}$$

where

$$u_{2t}^* = u_{2t} + \frac{\beta_2}{\beta_1}(u_{1t} - u_{2t})$$

The error term u_{2t}^* has the same properties as the error term u_{2t} except in the special case where u_{1t} and u_{2t} are independent. Thus the consequence of the Muthian rational expectations hypothesis is the inclusion of the extra variables w_{1t} and w_{2t} in the supply function and the constraints on the parameters. (Note that the coefficients of w_{1t} and w_{2t} involve no new parameters.) This is an omitted variable interpretation of the rational expectations models.

If the nature of the autoregressions for z_{1t} and z_{2t} is specified, one can derive an alternative expression for p_t^*. For the purpose of simplicity of exposition, let us assume that z_{1t} and z_{2t} are first-order autoregressive as in equations (10.35). We then have

$$z_{1t}^* = \alpha_1 z_{1,t-1}$$

$$z_{2t}^* = \alpha_2 z_{2,t-1}$$

Substituting these in equation (10.37), we get

$$p_t^* = \frac{1}{\beta_1 - \beta_2}(\gamma_2\alpha_2 z_{2,t-1} - \gamma_1\alpha_1 z_{1,t-1})$$

Now we substitute this expression in equation (10.34) and get

$$q_t = \frac{\beta_2\gamma_2\alpha_2}{\beta_1 - \beta_2} z_{2,t-1} - \frac{\beta_2\gamma_1\alpha_1}{\beta_1 - \beta_2} z_{1,t-1} + \gamma_2 z_{2t} + u_{2t} \qquad (10.40)$$

We now estimate this equation along with equation (10.33) and equations (10.35). Again, note that the coefficients of $z_{1,t-1}$ and $z_{2,t-1}$ in equation (10.40) do not involve any new parameters. If higher-order autoregressions are used for z_{1t} and z_{2t}, then p_t^* will involve more of the lagged values of these variables.

Note that even if estimates α_1 and α_2 are obtained from equations (10.35) and substituted in equation (10.40), we still have to deal with cross-equation constraints. Tests of these cross-equation constraints have been often referred to as "tests for the rational expectations hypothesis."[29] The restrictions, however, arise because the exogenous variables z_{1t} and z_{2t} are not known at time $(t-1)$ and not from the rational expectations hypothesis as such. Moreover, the number of restrictions depends on the specification of the order of autoregression of the exogenous variables z_{1t} and z_{2t}. In view of this, it might be inappropriate to name the tests for the restrictions as tests of the rational expectations hypothesis. Note also that if equation (10.39) is used, the restrictions do not depend on the specification of the order of autoregression of the exogenous variables.

We have used a simple demand and supply model to outline the problems that are likely to arise in the Muthian rational expectations models if the exogenous variables are not known at time $(t-1)$.

Summary

There are three procedures we have outlined:

1. Just substitute p_t for p_t^* and use lagged exogenous variables as instruments. This can be done for all expectational variables.
2. Estimate autoregressions for z_{1t} and z_{2t}. Get the estimated residuals $\hat{w}_{1t}$ and $\hat{w}_{2t}$. Use these as additional regressors as in equation (10.39) after substituting p_t for p_t^*. Estimate the equations using the parameter constraints (computer programs like TSP do this).
3. Get an expression for p_t^* based on the structure of the model *and* the structure of the exogenous variables as in equation (10.40). Estimate the equations using the parameter constraints.

---

[29]K. F. Wallis, "Econometric Implications of the Rational Expectations Hypotheses," *Econometrica*, Vol. 48, 1980, pp. 49–74; N. S. Revankar, "Testing of the Rational Expectations Hypothesis," *Econometrica*, Vol. 48, 1980, pp. 1347–1663; D. L. Hoffman and P. Schmidt, "Testing the Restrictions Implied by the Rational Expectations Hypothesis," *Journal of Econometrics*, February 1981, pp. 265–288; K. Lahiri and Y. H. Lee, "An Empirical Study on the Econometric Implications of Rational Expectations Hypothesis," *Empirical Economics*, Vol. 6, 1981, pp. 111–127.

Note that method 1 uses equation (10.30), which says that $p_t = p_t^* + \varepsilon_t$. Methods 2 and 3 use equation (10.31), which says that

$$p_t^* = E(p_t | I_{t-1})$$

The latter methods use the structure of the model in deriving an expression for p_t^*. Method 3 uses the structure of the exogenous variables as well.

Illustrative Example[30]

We will illustrate the methods we have described, with the estimation of a demand and supply model. In Table 10.5 we present data for the 1964–1984 growing seasons on fresh strawberries in Florida. The variables in the table are:

P_t = price (cents per flat)

Q_t = number of flats (thousands)

d_t = food price deflator (1972 = 1.00)

C_t = production cost index (1977 = 100)

N_t = U.S. population (millions)

X_t = real per capita food expenditures (dollars per year)

Table 10.5   Data on Florida fresh strawberries, 1964–1984

Year	P_t	Q_t	d_t	C_t	N_t	X_t
1964	378	2134	0.74	78.97	192	651.04
1965	397	1742	0.76	77.84	194	675.26
1966	395	1467	0.79	81.16	197	685.28
1967	346	1267	0.80	81.89	199	688.44
1968	391	1333	0.84	78.97	201	706.47
1969	553	1200	0.88	79.76	203	719.21
1970	419	1467	0.93	74.67	205	731.71
1971	379	1667	0.95	72.31	208	725.96
1972	516	1575	1.00	67.41	210	738.10
1973	457	1467	1.12	68.66	212	721.70
1974	508	1650	1.28	82.98	214	710.28
1975	506	1750	1.37	100.69	216	722.22
1976	493	1817	1.41	98.93	218	752.29
1977	689	2417	1.46	100.00	220	777.27
1978	692	3200	1.60	98.90	223	771.30
1979	706	3958	1.77	99.50	225	782.22
1980	498	5600	1.91	103.87	228	793.86
1981	644	8125	2.07	108.58	230	786.96
1982	614	8550	2.16	112.89	232	784.48
1983	538	7225	2.20	118.63	234	807.69
1984	694	8833	2.28	121.03	237	818.57

---

[30]I would like to thank my colleague, J. Scott Shonkwiler, for the data, model, and computations.

The model estimated was the following:

$$Q_t = \alpha_0 + \alpha_1(P_t^* - C_t) + \alpha_2 Q_{t-1} + u_{1t} \qquad \text{supply}$$

$$P_t - d_t = \beta_0 + \beta_1(Q_t - N_t) + \beta_2 X_t + \beta_3 t + u_{2t} \quad \text{demand}$$

All variables are in logs except the time trend t. (Note that the data in Table 10.5 are *not* in logs.) P_t^* is the expected price (as expected at time $t - 1$). The different estimation methods depend on different specifications of P_t^*.

Five different models have been estimated (except for the first model, the other models assume rational expectations):

1. *The Cobweb model.* In this model we substitute P_{t-1} for P_t^* and estimate the demand and supply functions by OLS.
2. *The 2SLS (two-stage least squares) method.* This is the procedure for the rational expectations model if the exogenous variables are assumed to be known at time $t - 1$ and the errors are not serially correlated. Since the rational expectations hypothesis implies

$$P_t^* = P_t - v_t$$

where v_t is an error uncorrelated with the variables in the information set I_{t-1}, we just substitute $P_t - v_t$ for P_t^* and combine the error v_t with the error in the supply function. Since v_t has the same properties as u_{1t}, we just estimate the model by 2SLS.
3. *The IV (instrumental variable) method.* This is the method we use to get consistent estimators of the parameters under rational expectations when the exogenous variables at time t are not known at time $(t - 1)$. In this case, the error v_t can be correlated with the exogenous variables. We used the lagged exogenous variables as instruments.
4. *The OV (omitted variable) method.* In this method we first estimated first-order autoregressions for the exogenous variables and used the residuals as additional explanatory variables in the supply function [estimating an equation like (10.39)], imposing no parameter constraints. After obtaining initial estimates of the parameters in the demand and supply functions the predicted value of P_t^* was obtained as in equation (10.38). This was introduced in the supply function which was then reestimated by OLS. This is just a two-stage method of imposing the parameter constraints in (10.39).
5. *The joint estimation method.* In this model the explicit expression for the rational expectation P_t^* is derived and then equation (10.40) is estimated jointly with the demand function imposing parameter constraints.

The results from these five methods of estimation are presented in Tables 10.6 and 10.7. Regarding the estimates of the supply function, the price coefficient is significant only when the estimation is done by the 2SLS method or the joint estimation method. The IV and OV methods which are less efficient methods for the estimation of rational expectations models gave rather worse results (the results, however, for the two methods are very close to each other). The Cobweb model gave the worst results. Of some concern is the fact that the coefficient α_2 of Q_{t-1} is not significantly different from 1, and the DW

Table 10.6   Estimates of the parameters of the supply function[a]

	Cobweb	2SLS	IV	OV	Joint Estimation
α_0	−0.997 (0.594)	−1.593 (0.741)	−1.427 (0.762)	−1.371 (0.726)	−1.815 (0.747)
α_1	0.310 (0.213)	0.604 (0.301)	0.520 (0.318)	0.515 (0.308)	0.713 (0.315)
α_2	1.070 (0.057)	1.080 (0.058)	1.078 (0.057)	1.071 (0.075)	1.085 (0.054)
DW[b]	1.573	1.642	1.326	1.440	—

[a]Figures in parentheses are standard errors.
[b]DW is the Durbin–Watson test statistic.

Table 10.7   Estimates of the parameters of the demand function[a]

	Cobweb	2SLS	IV	OV	Joint Estimation
β_0	−9.796 (9.848)	−9.476 (9.871)	−14.896 (11.643)	−9.561 (9.860)	−9.531 (9.720)
β_1	−0.121 (0.075)	−0.139 (0.079)	−0.136 (0.078)	−0.134 (0.077)	−0.133 (0.077)
β_2	2.513 (1.513)	2.468 (1.516)	3.302 (1.789)	2.480 (1.515)	2.477 (1.493)
β_3	−0.047 (0.017)	−0.045 (0.018)	−0.053 (0.020)	−0.045 (0.017)	−0.046 (0.017)
DW[b]	2.286	2.315	2.306	2.245	—

[a]Figures in parentheses are standard errors.
[b]DW is the Durbin–Watson test statistic.

statistic is low for a model with a lagged dependent variable. Both these results indicate that the model is misspecified.

Regarding the estimates of the demand function (presented in Table 10.7), the Cobweb model and the 2SLS, OV, and joint estimation methods for the rational expectations model, all gave very similar results. It is only the IV method that gives slightly different results. The results are not very encouraging, although β_1 and β_2 both have expected signs. The negative coefficient of β_3 implies a gradual downward shift of the demand function.

Overall, we cannot say that the data are very informative about the models. All we can say, perhaps, is that the rational expectations model appears to be more appropriate than the Cobweb model. Many coefficients are not significant (although they have signs that one would expect *a priori*). The computations, however, illustrate the methods described. In estimating the rational expectations models, we used progressively more information about the models in the four methods described. Although the results are not much different in this case, one would be able to find differences in other cases. The estimation of the hyperinflation model described in Section 10.8 is left as an exercise.

10.16 The Serial Correlation Problem in Rational Expectations Models

Until now we have assumed that the errors are serially uncorrelated. If they are serially correlated, we cannot use variables in the information set I_{t-1} as instruments. The following example illustrates the problem. Consider the model

$$y_t = \alpha x_t^* + \beta z_t + u_t \tag{10.41}$$

z_t is an exogenous variable, but x_t can be an exogenous or endogenous variable. We will assume that z_t is *not* a part of the information set I_{t-1}. This means that z_t should also be treated as endogenous if we substitute x_t for x_t^*. Finally, u_t follow a first-order autoregressive process

$$u_t = \rho u_{t-1} + v_t \quad |\rho| < 1 \quad \text{and} \quad v_t \sim \text{IN}(0, \sigma^2)$$

Let us write, as usual, equation (10.41) as

$$y_t = \rho y_{t-1} + \alpha x_t^* - \alpha \rho x_{t-1}^* + \beta z_t - \beta \rho z_{t-1} + v_t$$

Using the rational expectations assumption and substituting $x_t^* = x_t - \varepsilon_t$, we get

$$y_t = \rho y_{t-1} + \alpha x_t - \alpha \rho x_{t-1} + \beta z_t - \beta \rho z_{t-1} + w_t \tag{10.42}$$

where $w_t = v_t - \alpha(\varepsilon_t - \rho \varepsilon_{t-1})$.

We would like to estimate this equation by instrumental variables. Note that x_{t-1} is correlated with ε_{t-1} and hence w_t. Thus although y_{t-1}, x_{t-1}, and z_{t-1} are definitely in the information set I_{t-1}, we cannot use them as instrumental variables.

The solution to the problem is to use the set of variables in I_{t-2} rather than I_{t-1}. Thus we obtain the predicted values $\bar{x}_t, \bar{x}_{t-1}, \bar{z}_t, \bar{z}_{t-1}, \bar{y}_{t-1}$ by regressing each of these variables on the variables in the information set I_{t-2} and use these as instruments for estimating equation (10.42). Note that if the degree of autoregression in u_t is of a higher order, we have to use the variables in the information set of a higher order of lag. For instance, if u_t is a second-order autoregression, we use I_{t-3}, and so on.

Thus with serial correlation in errors we should not use the variables in the information set I_{t-1} to construct the instrumental variables in models with rational expectations.[31]

10.17 Nonnormality of Errors

A major assumption we have made throughout the previous chapters is that the errors in the equations are all normally distributed. We shall now discuss the issues arising from relaxing this assumption.

---

[31] A concise discussion of methods of obtaining consistent estimates of the parameters in single-equation models with rational expectations can be found in B. T. McCallum. "Topics Concerning the Formulation, Estimation and Use of Macroeconomic Models with Rational Expectations," *Proceedings of the Business and Economic Statistics Section*, American Statistical Association, 1979, pp. 65–72.

First, we need to test the normality assumption. Next there is the issue of what to do about it if the tests indicate nonnormality.

Tests for Normality

For a normal distribution, the measure of skewness S is zero and the measure of kurtosis K is 3. The definitions of S and K are:

$$S = \mu_3^2/\mu_2^3 \quad \text{and} \quad K = \mu_4/\mu_2^2$$

where μ_2, μ_3, and μ_4 are the second, third and fourth moments about the mean respectively.

A recent test using S and K based on least squares residuals is the Jarque–Bera test[32] with statistic

$$\text{JB} = n\left[\frac{S^2}{6} + \frac{(K-3)^2}{24}\right]$$

The JB test is an asymptotic test that is applicable in large samples only.

An earlier test is the Shapiro–Wilk test statistic discussed in Huang and Bolch[33] who compared it with several other tests for normality and recommend it. But it is more cumbersome to use than the JB statistic.

Turning next to the question "What are the consequences?" we need to know what happens to the significance levels and the powers of the tests we apply on the assumption of normality if the assumption is not satisfied. Box and Watson[34] studied the "robustness" of tests for regression coefficients when the errors are nonnormal. They argue that if the empirical distribution of the explanatory variable x is approximately normal, the usual tests have the assumed significance levels. In the case of simple regression they suggest using the usual t and F tests but with d.f. $k(T-2)$ instead of $(T-2)$ where

$$\frac{1}{k} = 1 + \frac{(K_u - 3)(K_x - 3)}{2T}$$

with K_u and K_x the values of K (measuring kurtosis) defined earlier for the error u and the explanatory variable x, respectively. Note that for the lognormal distribution K is very high and the degrees of freedom correction will indeed be very large.

Some nonparametric tests are suggested in the statistical literature, but these are cumbersome to use and are also applicable in only very simple models. Hence we will not discuss them here.

Finally, we come to the question of what to do if indeed we find the errors to be nonnormal. If we have a specific distribution in mind — such as gamma, lognormal, etc. — we should carry out the analysis under these assumptions. The assumption of lognormal errors is possibly quite justified in econometric work. Unfortunately, the nature of the errors affecting economic relations has not been investigated to any great extent.

---

[32]C. M. Jarque and A. K. Bera, "A Test for Normality of Observations and Regression Residuals," *International Statistical Review*, Vol. 55, 1987, pp. 163–172.

[33]C. H. Huang and B. W. Bolch, "On the Testing of Regression Disturbances for Normality," *Journal of the American Statistical Association*, 1974, pp. 330–335.

[34]G. E. P. Box and G. S. Watson, "Robustness to Non-Normality of Regression Tests", *Biometrika*, 1962.

Hence one has to proceed with some plausible assumptions like gamma, χ^2, lognormal, and Pareto distributions. The Pareto distribution is given by

$$f(u) = k(u - u_0)^{-\alpha - 1}$$

10.18 Data Transformations

Another alternative to the new methods suggested earlier is to transform the data so that the assumption of normality holds good. If we have reason to believe that the distribution is skew, it may be possible to symmetrize the distribution, usually by raising y to a power (or taking logs). On the other hand, if the distribution of the errors is symmetric but different from normal, it is usually not possible to bring the distribution closer to normality by making a simple transformation of the y's. In this case the previously suggested alternatives to least squares should be used. Thus the solutions we discuss here are specifically to be used if we believe that the error distributions are skew.

Tukey,[35] who first gave a detailed discussion of transformations, suggested that transformations of data will help in making the model more nearly linear, the errors more homoskedastic and normal. A transformation is good if it achieves all these objectives simultaneously. On the other hand, it might achieve one of these objectives at the expense of the others: e.g., if the model was linear to start with, transformations to produce normality in the errors might make the model nonlinear. Tukey considers a wide family of transformations $(x + c)^\lambda$, but he assumes c and λ are known.

Box and Cox[36] consider transformations of the dependent variables (and also of the independent variables). Their transformation is defined as

$$y^{(\lambda)} = \frac{y^\lambda - 1}{\lambda} \quad \lambda \neq 0$$
$$= \log y \quad \lambda = 0$$

The advantage with this transformation as compared with the simple power transformation $y \to y^\lambda$ is that it is continuous at $\lambda = 0$, since

$$Lt_{\lambda \to 0} \frac{y^\lambda - 1}{\lambda} = \log y$$

Summary

1. Two assumptions we made in Chapters 3 and 4 regarding the basic model are that the relationships are linear and that the errors are normally distributed. This chapter discusses the consequences of relaxing these assumptions.

2. First, we discuss methods of nonlinear optimization, in particular the Newton–Raphson method. Next, we discuss the nonlinear least squares (NLLS) method. In all these

---

[35]J. W. Tukey, "On the Comparative Anatomy of Transformations," *Annals of Mathematical Statistics*, 1957, pp. 602–632.

[36]G. E. P. Box and D. R. Cox, "An Analysis of Transformations" (with discussion), *Journal of the Royal Statistical Society, Series B*, 1962, pp. 211–243.

nonlinear methods, the first step is to start with a linear approximation using a Taylor series expansion of the nonlinear functions. We discussed some nonlinear models in earlier chapters: the Box–Cox model in Chapter 5 (Section 5.6) and the logit, probit, and tobit models in Chapter 8. But this chapter talks of general methods for nonlinear models.

3. A class of important nonlinear models is that of models of expectations. In this chapter we discuss estimation of adaptive expectations models with partial adjustment, estimation of models under rational expectations, and tests for rationality.

4. We have discussed three types of models of expectations:

(a) Naive models of expectations.

(b) The adaptive expectations model.

(c) The rational expectations model.

Naive models merely serve as benchmarks against which other models or survey data on expectations are judged.

5. Two methods of estimation of the adaptive expectations model have been discussed:

(a) Estimation in the autoregressive form.

(b) Estimation in the distributed lag form.

The first method is easy to use because one can use an OLS regression program. However, this method is not advisable. The second method is the better one. It can be implemented with an OLS regression program by using a search method (see Section 10.7).

6. Many economic variables when disturbed from their equilibrium position do not adjust instantly to their new equilibrium position. There are some lags in adjustment. The partial equilibrium model has been suggested to handle this problem. Recently, a generalization of this model, the error correction model, has been found to be more useful (see Section 10.9). One can combine these partial adjustment models with the adaptive (or any other) model of expectations (see Section 10.10).

7. Besides the partial adjustment and error correction models, two other models are commonly used in the literature on adjustment lags. These are:

(a) The polynomial lag (also known as the Almon lag) (Section 10.11).

(b) The rational lags (Section 10.12).

The latter should not be confused with the rational expectations model. Rational here means the ratio of two polynomials.

8. In the polynomial lags one has to choose the length of the lag and the degree of the polynomial. Given the lag length, some procedures have been suggested for these two choices. All lag distributions imply some restrictions on the coefficients. Before imposing these restrictions, it is always best to estimate unconstrained lag models by OLS.

9. The rational expectations model suggested by Muth has been very popular. The idea behind the rational expectations hypothesis is that the specification of expectations should be consistent with the rest of the model rather than being ad hoc. A proper terminology for this is "model-consistent expectations" rather than "rational expectations." Two investigators starting with two different models can arrive at two different expressions of the "rational expectation" of the same variable. However, we continued to use the word "rational" rather than "model consistent" because the former is the commonly used term.

10. The essence of the rational expectations hypothesis is that the difference between the realized value and the expected value should be uncorrelated with all the variables in the information set at the time the expectation is formed. Based on this, several tests for

"rationality" have been applied to survey data on expectations. These tests are described in Section 10.14. In a large number of cases these tests reject the "rationality" of survey data on expectations.

11. There are, broadly speaking, two methods of estimation for rational expectations models. One procedure involves substitution of the realized value for the expected value and using some appropriate instrumental variables. The other procedure involves obtaining an explicit expression for the expected value from the model, substituting this in the model, and then estimating the model using any parameter constraints that are implied. These procedures are illustrated with reference to a demand and supply model in Section 10.15.

12. With serially correlated errors one has to be careful in the choice of appropriate instruments when estimating rational expectations models. A careful examination of which variables are correlated or uncorrelated with errors will reveal what variables are valid instruments. This is illustrated with a first-order autoregression in Section 10.16.

13. Some empirical examples are provided for the Almon lag, but computation of the Koyck model and some rational expectations models are left as exercises.

14. Next, we come to the normality assumption. We discuss tests for normality, the consequences if the normality fails, and some robust estimation methods in the presence of nonnormality.

Exercises

1. Explain the meaning of each of the following terms:
   (a) Adaptive expectations.
   (b) Regressive expectations.
   (c) Rational expectations.
   (d) Koyck lag.
   (e) Almon lag.
   (f) Rational lags.
   (g) Partial adjustment model.
   (h) Error correction model.
   (i) Testing rationality.
   (j) Estimation in autoregressive form.
   (k) Estimation in distributed lag form.

2. What are the problems one encounters in the OLS estimation under adaptive expectations in the following models?
   (a) Models of agricultural supply.
   (b) Models of hyperinflation.
   (c) Partial adjustment models.
   (d) Error correction models.

3. Answer Exercise 2 if, instead of assuming adaptive expectations, we assume the following:
   (a) Naive expectations $y_t^* = y_{t-1}$.
   (b) Rational expectations.

4. In the demand and supply model for pork discussed in Section 9.3 (data are in Table 9.1), assume that supply depends on expected price, P_t^*. Estimate the model assuming the following:

    (a) Naive expectations $P_t^* = P_{t-1}$. This is the Cobweb model.

    (b) Adaptive expectations.

    (c) Rational expectations.

5. Estimate the hyperinflation model for Hungary and Germany using the data in Tables 10.1 and 10.2 and assuming the following:

    (a) Naive expectations $P_{t+1}^* = P_t$.

    (b) Adaptive expectations.

    (c) Rational expectations.

6. Answer Exercise 4 with the Australian wine data discussed in Section 9.5 (data are in Table 9.2). Assume that the supply depends on expected price.

7. Explain tests for rationality based on

    (a) y_{t-1}.

    (b) var y_t^* and var y_t.

    (c) Tests for equality of coefficients.

8. What is meant by weak tests for rationality? Are these tests really weak?

9. Future prices have often been used as a proxy for expected prices in the cases of estimation of supply functions for agricultural commodities. How do you test whether the expectations implied in the future prices are rational?

11 Errors in Variables

What is in this Chapter?

This chapter discusses another source that causes correlation between the errors and the regressors (Chapter 9 was a case considered earlier). This is the errors in variables problem. Ragnar Frisch and Koopmans worked on this problem in the 1930s. Since then this problem has been put on a back burner except for a spurt of activity in the 1970s.

Most textbooks do not discuss this problem but it is very important from the practical point of view and hence it is discussed here.

This chapter covers first the single-equation model with an explanatory variable and two explanatory variables. It then discusses the reverse regression methods and instrumental variable estimation. Next there is a discussion of proxy variables, when to use them and when to ignore them. Next there is a discussion of how the errors in variables problem can be solved in multiple equation models. Finally, there is a brief discussion of correlated measurement errors.

This chapter is a very elementary introduction to the errors in variables problems.

11.1 Introduction

Since the early 1970s there has been a resurgence of interest in the topic of errors in variables models and models involving latent variables.[1] This late interest is perhaps surprising since there is no doubt that almost all economic variables are measured with error.

---

[1] Three early papers that sparked interest in this area are: A. Zellner, "Estimation of Regression Relationships Containing Unobservable Independent Variables," *International Economic Review*, October 1970, pp. 441–454; A. S. Goldberger, "Maximum Likelihood Estimation of Regression Models Containing Unobservable Variables," *International Economic Review*, January 1972, pp. 1–15; and Zvi Griliches, "Errors in Variables and Other Unobservables," *Econometrica*, November 1974, pp. 971–998.

Part of the neglect of errors in variables is due to the fact that consistent estimation of parameters is rather difficult. During the 1970s this attitude changed because of the following developments:

1. It was realized that sometimes we can use some extra information available in the dynamics of the equation or the structure of other equations in the model to get consistent estimates of the parameters.
2. The fact that we cannot get consistent point estimates of the parameters does not imply that no inference is possible. It was realized that one can obtain expressions for the direction of the biases and one can also obtain consistent "bounds" for the parameters.

We will now discuss how consistent estimation of equations which contain variables that are measured with errors can be accomplished. We start our discussion with a single-equation model with one explanatory variable measured with error. This is known as the "classical" errors in variable model. We then consider a single equation with two explanatory variables. Next we apply these results to the problem of "reverse regression," which has been a suggested technique in the analysis of wage discrimination by race and sex.

Before we proceed, we should make it clear what we mean by "errors in variables." Broadly speaking, there are two types of errors that we can talk about:

1. Recording errors.
2. Errors due to using an imperfect measure of the true variable. Such imperfect measures are known as "proxy" variables. The true variables are often not measurable and are called "latent" variables.

What we will be concerned with in this chapter are errors of type 2.

A commonly cited example of a proxy variable is years of schooling (S), which is a proxy for education (E). In this case, however, the error $S - E$ is likely to be independent of S rather than of E. Another example is that of expectational variables, which must be replaced by proxies (either estimates generated from the past or measures obtained from survey data). Examples of this were given in Chapter 10.

We start our discussion with the classical errors in variables model and then progressively relax at least some of the restrictive assumptions of this model.

11.2   The Classical Solution for a Single-Equation Model with One Explanatory Variable

Suppose that the true model is

$$y = \beta x + e \tag{11.1}$$

Instead of y and x, we measure

$$Y = y + v \quad \text{and} \quad X = x + u$$

where u and v are measurement errors, x and y are called the systematic components. We will assume that the errors have zero means and variances σ_u^2 and σ_v^2, respectively. We will also assume that they are mutually uncorrelated and are uncorrelated with the systematic components. That is,

$$E(u) = E(v) = 0 \quad \text{var}(u) = \sigma_u^2 \quad \text{var}(v) = \sigma_v^2$$

$$\text{cov}(u, x) = \text{cov}(u, y) = \text{cov}(v, x) = \text{cov}(v, y) = 0$$

Equation (11.1) can be written in terms of the observed variables as

$$Y - v = \beta(X - u) + e$$

or

$$Y = \beta X + w \tag{11.2}$$

where $w = e + v - \beta u$. The reason we cannot apply the OLS method to equation (11.2) is that $\text{cov}(w, X) \neq 0$. In fact,

$$\text{cov}(w, X) = \text{cov}(-\beta u, x + u) = -\beta \sigma_u^2$$

Thus one of the basic assumptions of least squares is violated. If only y is measured with error and x is measured without error, there is no problem because $\text{cov}(w, X) = 0$ in this case. Thus given the specification (11.1) of the true relationship, it is errors in x that cause a problem.

If we estimate β by OLS applied to equation (11.2) we have

$$b_{YX} = \frac{\sum XY}{\sum X^2} = \frac{\sum (x + u)(y + v)}{\sum (x + u)^2}$$

$$\text{plim } b_{YX} = \frac{\text{cov}(xy)}{\text{var}(x) + \text{var}(u)} = \frac{\sigma_{xy}}{\sigma_x^2 + \sigma_u^2}$$

since all cross products vanish. Since $\beta = \sigma_{xy}/\sigma_x^2$, we have

$$\text{plim } b_{YX} = \frac{\beta}{1 + \sigma_u^2/\sigma_x^2} \tag{11.3}$$

Thus b_{YX} will underestimate β. The degree of underestimation depends on σ_u^2/σ_x^2.

If we run a reverse regression (i.e., regress X on Y), we have

$$b_{XY} = \frac{\sum XY}{\sum Y^2} = \frac{\sum (x + u)(y + v)}{\sum (y + v)^2}$$

Hence

$$\text{plim } b_{XY} = \frac{\sigma_{xy}}{\sigma_y^2 + \sigma_v^2}$$

But from equation (11.1)

$$\sigma_y^2 = \beta^2 \sigma_x^2 + \sigma_e^2 \quad \text{and} \quad \sigma_{xy} = \beta \sigma_x^2$$

Hence

$$\text{plim } \frac{1}{b_{XY}} = \frac{\beta^2 \sigma_x^2 + \sigma_e^2 + \sigma_v^2}{\beta \sigma_x^2} = \beta \left(1 + \frac{\sigma_e^2 + \sigma_v^2}{\beta^2 \sigma_x^2} \right) \tag{11.3'}$$

Thus $1/b_{XY}$ overestimates β, and we have

$$\text{plim } b_{YX} \le \beta \le \frac{1}{\text{plim } b_{XY}}$$

We can use the two regression coefficients b_{YX} and b_{XY} to get bounds on β (at least in large samples).

In the preceding discussion we have implicitly assumed that $\beta > 0$. If $\beta < 0$, then

$$\text{plim } b_{YX} > \beta \quad \text{and} \quad (\text{plim } b_{XY})^{-1} < \beta$$

and thus the bounds have to be reversed, that is,

$$(\text{plim } b_{XY})^{-1} < \beta < \text{plim } b_{YX}$$

Note that since $b_{XY} \cdot b_{YX} = R_{XY}^2$, the higher the value of R^2 the closer these bounds are. Consider, for instance, the data in Table 7.3.[2] We have the equation

$$Y = 0.193X_1 - 15.86 \quad R^2 = 0.969$$
$$X_1 = 5.088Y + 86.87 \quad R^2 = 0.969$$

The second equation when solved for Y gives

$$Y = 0.199X_1 - 17.32$$

Hence we have the bounds $0.193 < \beta_1 < 0.199$. Such consistent estimates of the bounds have been studied by Frisch and Schultz.[3]

The general conclusion from equation (11.3) is that the least squares estimator of β is biased toward zero and if equation (11.1) has a constant term, α, the least squares estimator of α is biased away from zero.[4]

If we define

$$\lambda = \frac{\sigma_u^2}{\sigma_u^2 + \sigma_x^2}$$

then from equation (11.3) we get the result that the asymptotic bias in the least squares estimator of β is $-\beta\lambda$.

---

[2]These data are from E. Malinvaud, *Statistical Methods of Econometrics*, 3rd ed. (Amsterdam: North-Holland, 1980), p. 19.

[3]R. Frisch, *Statistical Confluence Analysis by Means of Complete Regression Systems*, Publication 5 (Oslo: University Economics Institute, 1934); H. Schultz, *The Theory and Measurement of Demand* (Chicago: University of Chicago Press, 1938).

[4]In the discussion that follows we mean by bias, asymptotic bias or more precisely plim $\hat{\theta} - \theta$, where $\hat{\theta}$ is the estimator of θ.

11.3 The Single-Equation Model with Two Explanatory Variables

In Section 11.2 we derived the bias in the least squares estimator and also some consistent bounds for the true parameter. We will now see how these two results can be extended to the case of several explanatory variables. Since it is instructive to consider some simple models, we discuss a model with two explanatory variables in some detail.

Two Explanatory Variables: One Measured with Error

Let us consider the case of two explanatory variables only one of which is measured with error. The equation is

$$y = \beta_1 x_1 + \beta_2 x_2 + e$$

The observed variables are

$$Y = y + v \quad X_1 = x_1 + u \quad X_2 = x_2$$

As before we will assume that the errors u, v, e are mutually uncorrelated and also uncorrelated with y, x_1, x_2. Note that we can combine the errors e and v into a single composite error in Y. Let $\text{var}(u) = \sigma_u^2$ and $\text{var}(v + e) = \sigma^2$. The regression equation we can estimate in terms of observables is

$$Y = \beta_1 X_1 + \beta_2 X_2 + w$$

where

$$w = e + v - \beta_1 u$$

To save on notation (and without any loss in generality) we will normalize the observed variables X_1 and X_2 so that $\text{var}(X_1) = 1$, $\text{var}(X_2) = 1$, and $\text{cov}(X_1, X_2) = \rho$. Note that

$$\text{cov}(X_1, w) = -\beta_1 \sigma_u^2 = -\beta_1 \lambda$$

where

$$\lambda = \frac{\sigma_u^2}{\text{var}(X_1)} = \sigma_u^2 \quad \text{since} \quad \text{var}(X_1) = 1$$

Hence we get

$$\text{var}(Y) = \beta_1^2 + \beta_2^2 + 2\rho\beta_1\beta_2 + \sigma^2 - \beta_1^2 \lambda$$

$$\text{cov}(X_1, Y) = \beta_1 + \beta_2 \rho - \beta_1 \lambda$$

$$\text{cov}(X_2, Y) = \beta_1 \rho + \beta_2$$

It is important to note that in this model there are some limits on λ that need to be imposed for the analysis to make sense. This is because the condition

$$\text{var}(x_1)\text{var}(x_2) - [\text{cov}(x_1, x_2)]^2 \geq 0$$

needs to be satisfied.

Since $\text{var}(X_1) = 1$ we have $\text{var}(x_1) = 1 - \lambda$. Also, $\text{var}(X_2) = \text{var}(x_2) = 1$ and $\text{cov}(x_1, x_2) = \text{cov}(X_1, X_2) = \rho$. Hence we have the condition

$$1 - \lambda - \rho^2 \geq 0 \quad \text{or} \quad \lambda \leq 1 - \rho^2$$

This condition will turn out to be very stringent if ρ^2 is large or there is high collinearity between X_1 and X_2. For instance, if $\rho^2 = 0.99$, we cannot assume that $\lambda > 0.01$. If $\lambda = 0.01$, this implies that x_1 and x_2 are perfectly correlated.

What this implies is that we cannot use the classical errors in variables model if X_1 and X_2 are highly correlated and we believe that the variance of the error in x_1 is high.

We will see the implications of this condition when we derive the probability limits of the least squares estimators $\hat{\beta}_1$ and $\hat{\beta}_2$. The least squares estimators $\hat{\beta}_1$ and $\hat{\beta}_2$ of β_1 and β_2 are obtained by solving the equations

$$\sum X_1^2 \hat{\beta}_1 + \sum X_1 X_2 \hat{\beta}_2 = \sum X_1 Y$$

$$\sum X_1 X_2 \hat{\beta}_1 + \sum X_2^2 \hat{\beta}_2 = \sum X_2 Y$$

Dividing by the sample size throughout and taking probability limits, we get

$$\text{var}(X_1) \, \text{plim} \, \hat{\beta}_1 + \text{cov}(X_1, X_2) \, \text{plim} \, \hat{\beta}_2 = \text{cov}(X_1, Y)$$

$$\text{cov}(X_1, X_2) \, \text{plim} \, \hat{\beta}_1 + \text{var}(X_2) \, \text{plim} \, \hat{\beta}_2 = \text{cov}(X_2, Y)$$

That is,

$$\text{plim} \, \hat{\beta}_1 + \rho \, \text{plim} \, \hat{\beta}_2 = \beta_1 + \beta_2 \rho - \beta_1 \lambda$$

$$\rho \, \text{plim} \, \hat{\beta}_1 + \text{plim} \, \hat{\beta}_2 = \beta_1 \rho + \beta_2$$

Solving these equations, we get[5]

$$\text{plim} \, \hat{\beta}_1 = \beta_1 - \frac{\beta_1 \lambda}{1 - \rho^2} = \beta_1 \left(1 - \frac{\lambda}{1 - \rho^2} \right)$$

$$\text{plim} \, \hat{\beta}_2 = \beta_2 + \frac{\beta_1 \lambda \rho}{1 - \rho^2}$$

(11.4)

Thus bias in $\hat{\beta}_2 = -\rho(\text{bias in } \hat{\beta}_1)$. This result also applies if there is more than one explanatory variable with no errors. For instance, if the regression equation is

$$y = \beta_1 x_1 + \beta_2 x_2 + \cdots + \beta_k x_k + e$$

and only x_1 is measured with error, the first formula in (11.4) remains the same except that ρ^2 is now the square of the multiple correlation coefficient between X_1 and

---

[5]These results are derived in Z. Griliches and V. Ringstad, *Economies of Scale and the Form of the Production Function* (Amsterdam: North-Holland, 1971), Appendix C.

$(X_2, X_3, \ldots, X_k)$. As for the biases in the other coefficients, we have

$$\text{bias in } \hat{\beta}_j = -\gamma_j(\text{bias in } \hat{\beta}_1)$$

where γ_j are the regression coefficients from the "auxiliary" regression of X_1 on $X_2, X_3, \ldots, X_k$:

$$E(X_1|X_2, X_3, \ldots, X_k) = \gamma_2 X_2 + \gamma_3 X_3 + \cdots + \gamma_k X_k$$

Note that we are normalizing all the observed variables to have a unit variance.[6]

Returning to equations (11.4), note that if $\rho = 0$, the bias in β_1 is $-\beta_1\lambda$ as derived in equation (11.3). Whether or not $\hat{\beta}_1$ is biased toward zero as before depends on whether or not $\lambda < (1 - \rho^2)$. As we argued earlier, this condition has to be imposed for the classical errors in variables model to make sense. Thus, even in this model we can assume that $\hat{\beta}_1$ is biased toward zero. As for $\hat{\beta}_2$ the direction of bias depends on the sign of $\beta_1\rho$. The sign of ρ is known from the data and the sign of β_1 is the same as the sign of $\hat{\beta}_1$.

Consider now the regression of X_1 on Y and X_2. Let the equation be

$$X_1 = \gamma_1 Y + \gamma_2 X_2 + w^*$$

Then

$$\gamma_1 = \frac{1}{\beta_1} \quad \gamma_2 = \frac{-\beta_2}{\beta_1} \quad w^* = -\frac{w}{\beta_1}$$

The least squares estimators $\hat{\gamma}_1$ and $\hat{\gamma}_2$ for γ_1 and γ_2 are obtained from the equations

$$\left(\sum Y^2\right)\hat{\gamma}_1 + \left(\sum YX_2\right)\hat{\gamma}_2 = \left(\sum X_1 Y\right)$$

$$\left(\sum YX_2\right)\hat{\gamma}_1 + \left(\sum X_2^2\right)\hat{\gamma}_2 = \left(\sum X_1 X_2\right)$$

Divide throughout by the sample size and take probability limits. That is, we substitute population variances for sample variances and covariances. We get

$$(\beta_1^2 + \beta_2^2 + 2\rho\beta_1\beta_2 + \sigma^2 - \beta_1^2\lambda) \text{ plim } \hat{\gamma}_1 + (\beta_1\rho + \beta_2) \text{ plim } \hat{\gamma}_2 = \beta_1 + \beta_2\rho - \beta_1\lambda$$

$$(\beta_1\rho + \beta_2) \text{ plim } \hat{\gamma}_1 + \text{ plim } \hat{\gamma}_2 = \rho$$

---

[6]Similar formulas have been derived in M. D. Levi, "Errors in Variables Bias in the Presence of Correctly Measured Variables," *Econometrica*, Vol. 41, 1973, pp. 985–986, and Steven Garber and Steven Klepper, "Extending the Classical Normal Errors in Variables Model," *Econometrica*, Vol. 48, No. 6, 1980, pp. 1541–1546. However, these papers discuss the biases in terms of the variances and covariances of the *true* variables, $x_1, x_2, \ldots, x_k$ as well as auxiliary regression of the *true* variable x_1 on $x_2, \ldots, x_k$. The formulas stated here are in terms of the correlations of the *observed* variables. The only unknown parameter is thus λ. The formulas presented here are practically more useful since they are in terms of the correlations of the *observed* variables.

Hence

$$\text{plim } \hat{\gamma}_1 = \frac{1}{\Delta}[\beta_1(1 - \rho^2 - \lambda)]$$

$$\text{plim } \hat{\gamma}_2 = \frac{1}{\Delta}[-\beta_1\beta_2(1 - \rho^2 - \lambda) + \rho\sigma^2]$$

where

$$\Delta = \beta_1^2(1 - \rho^2 - \lambda) + \sigma^2$$

Hence the estimates $(\tilde{\beta}_1, \tilde{\beta}_2)$ of (β_1, β_2) from the equations

$$\tilde{\beta}_1 = \frac{1}{\hat{\gamma}_1} \quad \tilde{\beta}_2 = -\frac{\hat{\gamma}_2}{\hat{\gamma}_1}$$

have the probability limits

$$\text{plim } \tilde{\beta}_1 = \beta_1 + \frac{\sigma^2}{\beta_1(1 - \rho^2 - \lambda)} = \beta_1\left[1 + \frac{\sigma^2}{\beta_1^2(1 - \rho^2 - \lambda)}\right]$$

$$\text{plim } \tilde{\beta}_2 = \beta_2 - \frac{\rho\sigma^2}{\beta_1(1 - \rho^2 - \lambda)}$$

(11.5)

Again the bias in $\tilde{\beta}_2 = -\rho(\text{bias in } \tilde{\beta}_1)$. Also, if $\lambda < (1 - \rho^2)$ or $(1 - \rho^2 - \lambda) > 0$, we have the result that $\tilde{\beta}_1$ is biased away from zero. Hence

$$\text{plim } \hat{\beta}_1 < \beta_1 < \text{plim } \tilde{\beta}_1 \quad \text{if } \beta_1 > 0$$

(11.6)

and

$$\text{plim } \hat{\beta}_1 > \beta_1 > \text{plim } \tilde{\beta}_1 \quad \text{if } \beta_1 < 0$$

As for $\tilde{\beta}_2$ the bias will depend on the sign of $\rho\beta_1$.
   If $\rho\beta_1 > 0$, we have

$$\text{plim } \tilde{\beta}_2 < \beta_2 < \text{plim } \hat{\beta}_2$$

(11.7a)

and if $\rho\beta_1 < 0$, we have

$$\text{plim } \tilde{\beta}_2 > \beta_2 > \text{plim } \hat{\beta}_2$$

(11.7b)

Illustrative Example

Consider the data in Table 7.3 and a regression of imports (Y) on domestic production (X_1) and consumption (X_3). Note that X_1 and X_3 are very highly correlated, $\rho^2 = 0.99789$ or $1 - \rho^2 = 0.00211$. Let us assume that X_3 has no measurement error but that there is measurement error in X_1. As mentioned earlier, we have to have $\lambda \leq 1 - \rho^2$ or $\lambda \leq 0.00211$. This implies that the variance of the measurement error in X_1 cannot be greater than 0.211% of the variance of X_1. Thus we have to make a very stringent assumption on λ to carry out any sensible analysis of the data.

The regression equation in this case is (figures in parentheses are standard errors)

$$Y = \underset{(0.1907)}{0.043X_1} + \underset{(0.2913)}{0.230X_3} - 18.63 \quad R^2 = 0.970$$

The reverse regression is

$$X_1 = 0.078Y + 1.503X_3 - 16.37 \quad R^2 = 0.998$$

which, when normalized with respect to Y, gives

$$Y = 12.81X_1 - 19.28X_3 + 2.09$$

If $\lambda < 0.00211$, we come to the conclusion that $\beta_1 > 0$, and hence from equation (11.6) the consistent estimates of bounds are

$$0.043 < \beta_1 < 12.81$$

Also, from equation (11.7) the consistent bounds for β_2 are (since $\rho\beta_1 > 0$)

$$-19.28 < \beta_2 < 0.23$$

All this merely indicates that the coefficients β_1 and β_2 are not estimable with any precision, which is what one would also learn from the high multicollinearity between X_1 and X_2 and the large standard errors reported. What the errors in variables analysis shows is that even very small errors in measurement can make a great deal of difference to the results, that is, the multicollinearity may be even more serious than it appears to be, and the confidence intervals are perhaps wider than those reported.

Note that the consistent bounds are not comparable to a confidence interval. The estimated bounds themselves have standard errors since $\hat{\beta}_1$ and $\tilde{\beta}_1$ are both subject to sampling variation. If there are no errors in variables, even with multicollinearity, the least squares estimators are unbiased. But with errors in measurement they are not, and the estimated bounds yield (for a large sample) estimates of the biases.

One important thing to note is that the bounds are usually much too wide and making some special assumptions about the errors, one can get a range of consistent estimates of the parameters. We will illustrate this point.

Consider the regression of Y on X_1 and X_2 with the data in Table 7.3. Let us assume that stock formation is subject to error but X_1 is not.[7]

In this case we have $r_{12}^2 = 0.046$. The regression of Y on X_1 and X_2 gives

$$Y = \underset{(0.0087)}{0.191X_1} + \underset{(0.319)}{0.405X_2} - 16.78 \quad R^2 = 0.972$$

$$\hat{\sigma}^2 = 155.8$$

The reverse regression gives (note we use X_2 as the regressand)

$$X_2 = 0.239Y - 0.040X_1 + 6.07 \quad R^2 = 0.139$$

---

[7]We will apply the formulas in (11.6) and (11.7) except that we have to interchange the subscripts 1 and 2.

which, when normalized with respect to Y, gives

$$Y = 0.169X_1 + 4.184X_2 - 25.35$$

We thus get the bounds

$$0.169 < \beta_1 < 0.191 \quad \text{and} \quad 0.405 < \beta_2 < 4.184$$

The bounds for β_2 are very wide and we can learn more by studying the first equation in (11.4).[8] Suppose that $\lambda = 0.477$, that is, the error variance is 47.7% of the variance of X_2, which is a very generous assumption. In this case, a consistent estimate of β_2 is $2 \times 0.405 = 0.81$, which is far below the upper bound of 4.184. If $\lambda = 0$, that is, there is no error in X_2 a consistent estimate of β_2 is, of course, 0.405. Since $(1 - \rho^2) = 0.954$ in this case, we have to have $\lambda \simeq 0.86$ or the error variance about 86% of the variance of X_2 to say that a consistent estimate of β_2 is 4.184.

Thus, in many problems, any analysis of bounds should be supplemented by some estimates based on some plausible assumptions of error variances, especially when the bounds are very wide. Many of the comments made here regarding the use of bounds in errors in variables models apply to more general models. The purpose of analyzing a specialized model is to show some of the uses and shortcomings of the analysis in terms of bounds and these would not be as transparent when we consider a k-variable model with all variables measured with error.[9]

Two Explanatory Variables: Both Measured with Error

Consider the case where both x_1 and x_2 are measured with error. Let the observed variables be

$$Y = y + v \quad X_1 = x_1 + u_1 \quad X_2 = x_2 + u_2$$

We continue to make the same assumptions as before, that is, u_1, u_2, v are mutually uncorrelated and uncorrelated with x_1, x_2, y. As before, we use the normalization $\text{var}(X_1) = 1$, $\text{var}(X_2) = 1$, and $\text{cov}(X_1, X_2) = \rho$. Define

$$\lambda_1 = \frac{\text{var}(u_1)}{\text{var}(X_1)} \quad \lambda_2 = \frac{\text{var}(u_2)}{\text{var}(X_2)} \quad \sigma^2 = \text{var}(e + v)$$

We have the equation in observable variables:

$$Y = \beta_1 X_1 + \beta_2 X_2 + w$$

---

[8]Note that since it is x_2 that we are assuming to have an error, we have to interchange the subscripts 1 and 2.

[9]The case of only one variable measured with error has also been considered by M. D. Levi, "Measurement Errors and Bounded OLS Estimates," *Journal of Econometrics*, Vol. 6, 1977, pp. 165–171. However, considering the two-variable case discussed here, it is easy to see that the formulas he gives depend on the variances and covariance of the true variables x_1 and x_2, and σ_u^2. We have presented the results in terms of the sample variances and covariance of X_1 and X_2, as done by Griliches and Ringstad. In this case all we have to do is to make some assumption about λ, the proportion of error variance to total variance in X_1 to derive the bounds.

where

$$w = e + v - \beta_1 u_1 - \beta_2 u_2$$

Thus

$$\text{cov}(X_1, w) = -\beta_1 \lambda_1$$

$$\text{cov}(X_2, w) = -\beta_2 \lambda_2$$

We thus have

$$\sigma_{1y} = \text{cov}(Y, X_1) = \beta_1 + \beta_2 \rho - \beta_1 \lambda_1$$

$$\sigma_{2y} = \text{cov}(Y, X_2) = \beta_1 \rho + \beta_2 - \beta_2 \lambda_2 \tag{11.8}$$

$$\sigma_y^2 = \text{var}(Y) = \beta_1^2 + \beta_2^2 + 2\rho\beta_1\beta_2 + \sigma^2 - \beta_1^2\lambda_1 - \beta_2^2\lambda_2$$

As before, we can derive the probability limits of $\hat{\beta}_1$ and $\hat{\beta}_2$, the least squares estimators of β_1 and β_2. We get

$$\text{plim } \hat{\beta}_1 = \beta_1 - \frac{\beta_1 \lambda_1 - \rho\beta_2\lambda_2}{1 - \rho^2}$$

$$\tag{11.9}$$

$$\text{plim } \hat{\beta}_2 = \beta_2 - \frac{\beta_2 \lambda_2 - \rho\beta_1\lambda_1}{1 - \rho^2}$$

These equations correspond to equations (11.4) considered earlier (which were for $\lambda_2 = 0$).

We will not present the detailed calculations here (because they are tedious), but the equations corresponding to (11.5) obtained from a regression of X_1 on Y and X_2 and normalizing with respect to Y are

$$\text{plim } \tilde{\beta}_1 = \beta_1 + \frac{1}{\Delta}[\beta_2\lambda_2(\beta_2 + \rho\beta_1 - \beta_2\lambda_2) + \sigma^2]$$

$$\tag{11.10}$$

$$\text{plim } \tilde{\beta}_2 = \beta_2 - \frac{1}{\Delta}[\beta_2\lambda_2(\beta_1 - \rho\beta_2 - \beta_1\lambda_1) + \rho\sigma^2]$$

where

$$\Delta = \beta_1(1 - \rho^2 - \lambda_1) + \beta_2\lambda_2\rho = \beta_1(1 - \rho^2) - (\beta_1\lambda_1 - \rho\beta_2\lambda_2)$$

[substituting $\lambda_2 = 0$, we get the results in (11.5)].

If $\tilde{\beta}_1$ and $\tilde{\beta}_2$ are the estimators of β_1 and β_2 obtained from a regression of X_2 on X_1 and Y, then plim $\tilde{\beta}_1$ and plim $\tilde{\beta}_2$ are obtained by just interchanging the subscripts 1 and 2 in equations (11.10).

It is easy to see from equations (11.9) and (11.10) that the direction of biases are rather difficult to evaluate. Further, we saw earlier in the case of equations (11.4) and (11.5) that the derived bounds are in many cases rather too wide to be of any practical use and it is better to use equations (11.4) to get a range of consistent estimates based on different assumptions about λ. The problem with equations (11.5) or (11.10) is that they depend on a further unknown parameter σ^2.

In this case, we cannot get any bounds on the parameters using the procedures of calculating probability limits as in equations (11.9) and (11.10). There is an alternative procedure due to Klepper and Leamer[10] but its discussion is beyond our scope.

Here we will illustrate the range of consistent estimates of β_1 and β_2 using equations (11.8) or (11.9) with different assumptions about λ_1 and λ_2. This method is useful when we have some rough idea about the range of possible values for λ_1 and λ_2. There is the problem, however, that not all these estimates are valid because the implied estimate of σ^2 obtained from the third equation in (11.8) should be positive and also $\text{var}(x_1)\text{var}(x_2) - [\text{cov}(x_1, x_2)]^2 \geq 0$. This last condition implies that $(1 - \lambda_1)(1 - \lambda_2) - \rho^2 > 0$. Using equations (11.9) we obtain consistent estimates β_1^* and β_2^* of β_1 and β_2 by solving the equations

$$(1 - \rho^2 - \lambda_1)\beta_1^* + \rho\lambda_2\beta_2^* = (1 - \rho^2)\hat{\beta}_1$$

$$\rho\lambda_1\beta_1^* + (1 - \rho^2 - \lambda_2)\beta_2^* = (1 - \rho^2)\hat{\beta}_2 \tag{11.11}$$

The estimate of σ^2 is obtained from the last equation in (11.8). It is

$$\hat{\sigma}^2 = \hat{\sigma}_y^2 - (\beta_1^{*2} + \beta_2^{*2} + 2\rho\beta_1^*\beta_2^* - \lambda_1\beta_1^{*2} - \lambda_2\beta_2^{*2}) \tag{11.12}$$

As an example, let us consider the data in Table 7.3 and a regression of Y on X_1 and X_2. The correlation coefficient between X_1 and X_2 is 0.2156. Hence $\rho = 0.2156$. Also, $\hat{\sigma}_{1y} = 11.9378$ and $\hat{\sigma}_{2y} = 3.2286$.

It is reasonable to assume that X_1 (gross domestic production) has smaller measurement errors than X_2 (stock formation). Hence we consider

$$\lambda_1 = 0.01, 0.02, 0.05, 0.10$$

$$\lambda_2 = 0.10, 0.20, 0.30, 0.40$$

Note that for all these values, the condition $(1 - \lambda_1)(1 - \lambda_2) - \rho^2 > 0$ is satisfied. The results of solving equations (11.11) are presented in Table 11.1. The range of consistent estimates of β_1 is (0.128, 0.201) and the range of consistent estimates of β_2 is (0.447, 0.697). Note that the OLS estimates were $\hat{\beta}_1 = 0.191$ and $\hat{\beta}_2 = 0.405$. Thus with the assumptions about error variances we have made, the OLS estimate $\hat{\beta}_2$ is not within the consistent bounds for β_2 that we have obtained.

Note that assuming only X_2 (and not X_1) was measured with error we obtained earlier the bounds

$$0.169 < \beta_1 < 0.191 \quad \text{and} \quad 0.405 < \beta_2 < 4.184$$

The OLS estimates are at the extremes of these bounds. With the assumptions about error variances we have made, the bounds for β_1 are wider but the bounds for β_2 are much narrower.

The important conclusion that emerges from all this discussion and illustrative calculations is that in errors in variables models, making the most general assumptions

---

[10]S. Klepper and E. E. Leamer, "Consistent Sets of Estimates for Regressions with Errors in All Variables," *Econometrica*, Vol. 52, 1984, pp. 163–183.

Table 11.1 Estimates of regression parameters and error variance based on different assumptions about error variances

λ_1	λ_2	β_1	β_2	σ^2
0.01	0.10	0.1817	0.4519	155.5
0.01	0.20	0.1687	0.5119	155.5
0.01	0.30	0.1516	0.5903	155.5
0.01	0.40	0.1284	0.6970	155.4
0.02	0.10	0.1837	0.4514	155.5
0.02	0.20	0.1705	0.5114	155.5
0.02	0.30	0.1533	0.5898	155.5
0.02	0.40	0.1298	0.6965	155.4
0.05	0.10	0.1898	0.4500	155.5
0.05	0.20	0.1762	0.5099	155.5
0.05	0.30	0.1585	0.5882	155.5
0.05	0.40	0.1343	0.6949	155.4
0.10	0.10	0.2010	0.4473	155.5
0.10	0.20	0.1867	0.5071	155.5
0.10	0.30	0.1680	0.5853	155.5
0.10	0.40	0.1424	0.6920	155.4

about error variances leads to very wide bounds for the parameters, thus making no inference possible. On the other hand, making some plausible assumptions about the variances of the errors in the different variables, one could get more reasonable bounds for the parameters. A sensitivity analysis based on reasonable assumptions about error variances would be more helpful than obtaining bounds on very general assumptions.

11.4 Reverse Regression

In Sections 11.2 and 11.3 we considered two types of regressions. When we have the variables y and x both measured with error (the observed values being Y and X), we consider two regression equations:

1. Regression of Y on X, which is called the "direct" regression.
2. Regression of X on Y, which is called the "reverse" regression.

Reverse regression has been frequently advocated in the case of analysis of salary discrimination.[11] Since the problem is one of the usual errors in variables, both regressions need to be computed and whether reverse regression alone gives the correct estimates depends on the assumptions one makes.

The usual model, in its simplest form, is that of two explanatory variables, one of which is measured with error

$$y = \beta_1 x_1 + \beta_2 x_2 + u \tag{11.13}$$

---

[11]There is a large amount of literature on this issue, many papers arguing in favor of "reverse regression." For a survey and different alternative models, see A. S. Goldberger, "Reverse Regression and Salary Discrimination," *Journal of Human Resources*, Vol. 19, No. 3, 1984, pp. 293–318.

where y = salary

x_1 = true qualifications

x_2 = gender (in sex discrimination)

= race (in race discrimination)

What we are interested in is the coefficient of x_2. The problem is that x_1 is measured with error. Let

$$X_1 = \text{measured qualifications}$$

$$X_1 = x_1 + v$$

Suppose we adopt the notation that

$$x_2 = \begin{cases} 1 & \text{for men} \\ 0 & \text{for women} \end{cases}$$

Then $\hat{\beta}_2 > 0$ implies that men are paid more than women with the same qualifications and thus there is sex discrimination. A direct least squares estimation of equation (11.13) with X_1 substituted for x_1, and $\hat{\beta}_2 > 0$ has been frequently used as evidence of sex discrimination.

In the reverse regression

$$X_1 = \gamma_1 y + \gamma_2 x_2 + w \tag{11.14}$$

we are asking whether men are more or less qualified than women having the same salaries. The proponents of the reverse regression argue that to establish discrimination, one has to have $\hat{\gamma}_2 < 0$ in equation (11.14); that is, among men and women receiving equal salaries, the men possess lower qualifications.

The evidence from the reverse regression has been mixed. In some cases $\hat{\gamma}_2 < 0$ but not significant and in some others $\hat{\gamma}_2 > 0$. Conway and Roberts[12] consider data for 274 employees of a Chicago bank in 1976. In their analysis $y = \log$ salary and they get $\hat{\beta}_2 = 0.148$ (standard error 0.036), thus indicating that men are overpaid by about 15% compared with women with the same qualifications. In the reverse regression they get $\hat{\gamma} = -0.0097$ (standard error 0.0202), thus showing no evidence of discrimination one way or the other. In another study by Abowd, Abowd, and Killingsworth,[13] who compare wages for whites and several ethnic groups, the direct regression gave $\hat{\beta}_2 > 0$ and the indirect regression gave $\hat{\gamma}_2 > 0$ (indicating that whites are disfavored). Thus the direct regression showed discrimination and the reverse regression showed reverse discrimination.

Of course, in all these studies, there is no single measure of qualifications and x_1 is a set of variables rather than a single variable. In this case what they do in reverse regression is take the estimated coefficients from the direct regression and take the linear combination of these variables based on these estimated coefficients as the dependent

[12] Delores A. Conway and Harry V. Roberts, "Reverse Regression, Fairness and Employment Discrimination," *Journal of Business and Economic Statistics*, Vol. 1, January 1983, pp. 75–85.

[13] A. M. Abowd, J. M. Abowd, and M. R. Killingsworth, "Race, Spanish Origin and Earnings Differentials Among Men: The Demise of Two Stylized Facts," NORC Discussion Paper 83-11, The University of Chicago, Chicago, May 1983.

variable and regress it on y and x_2. Since the direct regression gives biased estimates of these coefficients, what we have here is a biased index of qualifications.

The usual errors in variables results in equations (11.4) and (11.5) show that one should not make inferences on the basis of $\hat{\beta}_2$ and $\hat{\gamma}_2$ but obtain bounds for β_2, from the direct regression and reverse regression estimates. As shown in equation (11.7), these bounds depend on the sign of $\rho\beta_1$, where $\rho = $ correlation between X_1 and x_2. Normally, one would expect $\rho > 0$ and $\beta_1 > 0$ and hence we have

$$\text{plim } \tilde{\beta}_2 < \beta_2 < \text{plim } \hat{\beta}_2$$

where $\tilde{\beta}_2$ is the implied estimate of β_2 from the reverse regression.

Note also from equations (11.4) and (11.5) that the (asymptotic) biases depend on two factors: $\lambda = \sigma_u^2/\text{var}(X_1)$ and $\rho = $ correlation between X_1 and x_2. λ is unknown but ρ can be computed from the data. Thus one can generate different estimates of β_2 from these equations based on different assumptions about the value of λ. We will not, however, undertake this exercise here.

11.5 Instrumental Variable Methods

Consider equation (11.2). The reason we cannot use OLS is because the error w_i is correlated with x_i. The instrumental variable method consists of finding a variable z_i that is uncorrelated with w_i but correlated with x_i, and estimating β by $\hat{\beta}_{IV} = \sum y_i z_i / \sum x_i z_i$. The variable z_i is called an "instrumental variable."

Note that in the usual regression model $y = \beta x + w$, the normal equation for the OLS estimation of β is

$$\sum x(y - \hat{\beta}x) = 0 \tag{11.15}$$

This is the sample analog of the assumption we make that $\text{cov}(x, u) = 0$. If this assumption is violated, we cannot use the normal equation (11.15). However, if we have a variable z such that $\text{cov}(z, w) = 0$, we replace the normal equation (11.15) by

$$\sum z(y - \hat{\beta}x) = 0$$

or

$$\hat{\beta}_{IV} = \frac{\sum yz}{\sum xz}$$

which is the instrumental variable (IV) estimator. We can show that the IV estimator is consistent.

$$\text{plim } \hat{\beta}_{IV} = \text{plim } \frac{\sum(\beta x_i + w_i)z_i}{\sum x_i z_i}$$

$$= \beta + \text{plim } \left[\left(\frac{1}{n}\sum w_i z_i\right) \bigg/ \frac{1}{n}\sum x_i z_i\right]$$

$$= \beta + \frac{\text{cov}(z, w)}{\text{cov}(z, x)} = \beta$$

since $\text{cov}(z, w) = 0$ and $\text{cov}(z, x) \neq 0$. The reason we want z to be uncorrelated with w but correlated with x is that we want $\text{cov}(z, w) = 0$ but $\text{cov}(z, x) \neq 0$. It is often suggested that z is a "good" instrument if it is highly correlated with x.

In practice it is rather hard to find valid instrumental variables. Usually, the instrumental variables are some variables that are "around," that is, whose data are available but do not belong in the equation. An illustration of this is the study by Griliches and Mason[14] who estimate an earnings function of the form

$$y = \alpha + \beta s + \gamma a + \delta x + u$$

where y is the log wages, s the schooling, a the ability, x the other variables, and u the error term. They substituted an observed test score t for the unobserved ability variable and assumed that it was measured with a random error. They then used a set of instrumental variables such as parental status, regions of origin, and so on. The crucial assumption is that these variables do not belong in the earnings function explicitly, that is, they enter only through their influence on the ability variable. Some such assumption is often needed to justify the use of instrumental variables.

In the Griliches–Mason study the OLS estimation (the coefficients of the "other variables" x are not reported) gave (figures in parentheses are standard errors)

$$y = \text{const.} + \underset{(0.0458)}{0.1982}(\text{race}) + \underset{(0.0067)}{0.0331}(\text{schooling}) + \underset{(0.00038)}{0.00298}(\text{test score})$$

The IV estimation gave

$$y = \text{const.} + \underset{(0.0468)}{0.0730}(\text{race}) + \underset{(0.0065)}{0.0483}(\text{schooling}) + \underset{(0.00078)}{0.00889}(\text{test score})$$

The IV estimation thus gave a much higher estimate of the ability coefficient and lower estimate of the race coefficient.

In the case of time-series data, lagged values of the measured X_t are often used as instrumental variables. If $X_t = x_t + u_t$ and the measurement errors u_t are serially uncorrelated but the true x_t are serially correlated, then X_{t-1} can be used as an instrumental variable. This suggestion was made as early as 1941 by Riersol.[15]

As an illustration, consider the model

$$Y_t = \beta x_t + e_t$$

$$X_t = x_t + u_t$$

$$x_t = \rho x_{t-1} + v_t$$

(there is no error of observation in Y_t). Then

$$\text{var}(X_t) = \sigma_{xx} + \sigma_{uu}$$

$$\text{var}(Y_t) = \beta^2 \sigma_{xx} + \sigma_{ee}$$

[14]Z. Griliches and W. M. Mason, "Education, Income and Ability," *Journal of Political Economy*, Vol. 80, No. 3, Part 2, May 1972, pp. S74–S103.

[15]O. Riersol, "Confluence Analysis by Means of Lag Moments and Other Methods of Confluence Analysis," *Econometrica*, 1941, pp. 1–24.

$$\text{cov}(X_t, Y_t) = \beta \sigma_{xx}$$

$$\text{cov}(X_t, X_{t-1}) = \rho \sigma_{xx}$$

$$\text{cov}(Y_t, Y_{t-1}) = \beta^2 \rho \sigma_{xx}$$

$$\text{cov}(Y_t, X_{t-1}) = \text{cov}(X_t, Y_{t-1}) = \beta \rho \sigma_{xx}$$

Thus we can estimate β by

$$\hat{\beta}_1 = \frac{\text{cov}(Y_t, X_{t-1})}{\text{cov}(X_t, X_{t-1})} \quad \text{or} \quad \hat{\beta}_2 = \frac{\text{cov}(Y_t, Y_{t-1})}{\text{cov}(X_t, Y_{t-1})}$$

The former amounts to using X_{t-1} as the instrumental variable, and the latter amounts to using Y_{t-1} as the instrumental variable.

One other instrumental variable method is the *method of grouping*. Three main grouping methods have been suggested in the literature, by Wald, Bartlett, and Durbin.[16] In Wald's method we rank the X's and form those above the median X into one group and those below the median X into another group. If the means in the two groups are, respectively, $\overline{Y}_1, \overline{X}_1$ and $\overline{Y}_2, \overline{X}_2$, we estimate the slope β by

$$\beta^* = (\overline{Y}_2 - \overline{Y}_1)/(\overline{X}_2 - \overline{X}_1)$$

This amounts to using the instrumental variable

$$Z_i = \begin{cases} +1 & \text{if } X_i > \text{median} \\ -1 & \text{if } X_i < \text{median} \end{cases}$$

and using the estimator $\beta^* = \sum Y_i Z_i / \sum X_i Z_i$. Bartlett suggested ranking X's, forming three groups, and discarding the $n/3$ observations in the middle group. His estimator of β is

$$\beta^* = \frac{\overline{Y}_3 - \overline{Y}_1}{\overline{X}_3 - \overline{X}_1}$$

This amounts to using the instrumental variable

$$Z_i = \begin{cases} +1 & \text{for the top } n/3 \text{ observations} \\ -1 & \text{for the bottom } n/3 \text{ observations} \end{cases}$$

Durbin suggests using the ranks of X_i as the instrumental variables. Thus

$$\beta^* = \frac{\sum i Y_i}{\sum i X_i}$$

where the X_i are ranked in ascending order and the Y_i are the values of Y corresponding to the X_i. If the errors are large, the ranks will be correlated with the errors and the estimators given by Durbin's procedure will be inconsistent. Since the estimators given by Wald's

---

[16] A. Wald, "The Fitting of Straight Lines If Both Variables Are Subject to Errors," *Annals of Mathematical Statistics*, 1940, pp. 284–300; M. S. Bartlett, "Fitting of Straight Lines When Both Variables Are Subject to Error," *Biometrics*, 1949, pp. 207–212; J. Durbin, "Errors in Variables," *Review of International Statistical Institute*, 1954, pp. 23–32.

procedure and Bartlett's procedure also depend on the ranking of the observations, these estimators can also be expected to be inconsistent. Pakes[17] investigates the consistency properties of the grouping estimators in great detail and concludes that except in very few cases they are inconsistent, quite contrary to the usual presumption that they are consistent (although inefficient).

Thus the grouping estimators are of not much use in errors in variable models.

11.6 Proxy Variables

Often, the variables we measure are surrogates for the variables we really want to measure. It is customary to call the measured variable a "proxy" variable — it is a proxy for the true variable. Some commonly used proxies are years of schooling for level of education, test scores for ability, and so on. If we treat the proxy variable as the true variable with a measurement error satisfying the assumptions of the errors in variables model we have been discussing, the analysis of proxy variables is just the same as the one we have been discussing. However, there are some other issues associated with the use of proxy variables that we need to discuss.

Sometimes, in multiple regression models it is not the coefficient of the proxy variable that we are interested in but the other coefficients. An example of this is the earnings function in Section 11.5, where our interest may be in estimating the effect of years of schooling on income and not the coefficient of ability (for which we use the test score as a proxy). In such cases one question that is often asked is whether it is not better to omit the proxy variable altogether. To simplify matters, consider the two-regressor case:

$$y = \beta x + \gamma z + u \tag{11.16}$$

where x is observed but z is unobserved. We make the usual assumption about x, z, and the error term u. Instead of z we observe a proxy $p = z + e$. As in the usual errors in variables literature, we assume that e is uncorrelated with z, x, and u. Let the population variances and covariances be denoted by M_{xx}, M_{xz}, M_{xp}, and so on.

If we omit the variable z altogether from equation (11.16) and the estimator of β is $\hat{\beta}_{ov}$, then using the omitted variable formula [equation (4.16)], we get

$$\text{plim } \hat{\beta}_{ov} = \beta + \gamma \frac{M_{xz}}{M_{xx}} \tag{11.17}$$

On the other hand, if we substitute the proxy p for z in equation (11.16) and the estimator of β is $\hat{\beta}_p$, it can be shown that[18]

$$\text{plim } \hat{\beta}_p = \beta + \gamma \frac{M_{xz}}{M_{xx}} \left[\frac{\sigma_e^2}{\sigma_e^2 + M_{zz}(1 - \rho^2)} \right] \tag{11.18}$$

[17] Ariel Pakes, "On the Asymptotic Bias of Wald-Type Estimators of a Straight Line When Both Variables Are Subject to Error," *International Economic Review*, Vol. 23, 1982, pp. 491–497.

[18] G. S. Maddala, *Econometrics* (New York: McGraw-Hill, 1977), p. 160. This result was derived in B. T. McCallum, "Relative Asymptotic Bias from Errors of Omission and Measurement," *Econometrica*, July 1972, pp. 757–758, and M. R. Wickens, "A Note on the Use of Proxy Variables," *Econometrica*, July 1972, pp. 365–372.

where ρ is the correlation between x and z. The bias due to omission of the variable z is $\gamma(M_{xz}/M_{xx})$. The bias due to the use of the proxy p for z is the same multiplied by the ratio in brackets of (11.18). Since this ratio is less than 1, it follows that the bias is reduced by using the proxy. McCallum and Wickens have argued on the basis of this result that it is desirable to use even a poor proxy.

However, there are four major qualifications to this conclusion:

1. One should look at the variances of the estimators as well and not just at bias. Aigner[19] studied the mean-squared errors of the two estimators $\hat{\beta}_{ov}$ and $\hat{\beta}_p$ and derived a sufficient condition under which $\text{MSE}(\hat{\beta}_p) \geq \text{MSE}(\hat{\beta}_{ov})$. This condition is

$$\frac{1 - (1 - \lambda n)\rho^2}{[1 - (1 - \lambda)\rho^2]^2} \frac{\lambda}{n} > \rho^2$$

where

$$\lambda = \frac{\sigma_e^2}{\sigma_e^2 + M_{zz}}$$

and ρ is defined earlier. From this he concludes that the use of a proxy, although generally advisable may not be a superior strategy to dropping the error-ridden variable altogether. Kinal and Lahiri[20] analyze this problem in greater detail and generality. They give several alternative expressions to Aigner's. They conclude that including even a poor proxy is advisable under a wide range of empirical situations when the alternative is to discard it altogether.

2. The second major qualification is that the proxy variable does not always fall in the pure errors in variables case. Usually, the proxy variable is "some variable" that also depends on the same factors, that is, p is of the form

$$p = \alpha x + \delta z + \varepsilon$$

Since z is unobserved and does not have any natural units of measurement, we will assume that $\delta = 1$. We can then write

$$p = \alpha x + z + e \tag{11.19}$$

We will also assume that M_{ue} is not zero. Now it does not necessarily follow that including the proxy p leads to a smaller bias in the estimator of β in equation (11.16).[21] Thus, except in cases where the proxies fall in the category of pure errors in variables, it does not follow that using even a poor proxy is better than using none at all.

3. The third qualification is that the reduction in bias argument does not apply if the proxy variable is a dummy variable.[22] This is the case where we do not observe z but

[19]D. J. Aigner, "MSE Dominance of Least Squares with Errors of Observation," *Journal of Econometrics*, Vol. 2, 1974, pp. 365–372.

[20]T. Kinal and K. Lahiri, "Specification Error Analysis with Stochastic Regressors," *Econometrica*, Vol. 51, 1983, pp. 1209–1219.

[21]Maddala, *Econometrics*, p. 161.

[22]See Maddala, *Econometrics*, pp. 161–162, for an example due to D. M. Grether.

we know when it is in different ranges. For instance, we do not know how to measure "effective education" but we use dummies for the amount of education (e.g., grade school, high school, college). In this case it does not necessarily follow that using the proxy results in a smaller bias compared with the omission of z altogether.

4. The reduction in bias argument also does not apply if the other explanatory variables are measured with error.[23] In equation (11.16) suppose that the variable x is measured with error so that what we observe is $X = x + v$. We will assume that $cov(x, v) = cov(x, z) = cov(v, e) = 0$. We can consider two estimates of β, one using the proxy p and the other omitting it. Now we cannot say anything about the direction of the biases, nor about whether the bias will increase or decrease with the introduction of p.[24]

Coefficient of the Proxy Variable

The preceding discussion referred to a situation where our interest was in the coefficients of variables other than the proxy variable. There are also many situations where our interest is in γ, the coefficient of the unobserved variable in equation (11.16). Since z is not observed, we cannot think of any natural units of measurement for z. Thus it is not the magnitude of γ but the sign of γ with which we are concerned. A question we would like to ask is under what conditions the use of the proxy p will give us the correct sign for γ. To answer this question we need a method of combining subjective assessments of how good the proxies are with objective information on the observed variables.

This problem has been analyzed by Krasker and Pratt.[25] Consider equation (11.16). Let the correlation coefficient between the unobserved variable z and the proxy variable p be r^*. The condition that the coefficient of the proxy variables has the same sign as γ, the coefficient of the unobserved variable in equation (11.16) is

$$(r^*)^2 > R_{p \cdot x} + 1 - R_{p \cdot yx}^2 \tag{11.20}$$

As an example they consider the determinants of motor vehicle deaths. The data are cross-section data in 1960 for the 48 contiguous states in the United States. The variables are:

$y_i = $ logarithm of the number of motor vehicle deaths per capita in the ith state in 1960

$x_{1i} = $ dummy variable defined to be 1 if the ith state had mandatory motor vehicle inspection, 0 otherwise

$x_{2i} = $ logarithm of per capita gasoline consumption in state i in 1960

$x_{3i} = $ logarithm of the fraction of the ith state's population that was 18–24 in 1960

$x_{4i} = $ logarithm of the number of automobiles (per capita) older than 9 years in state i in 1960

---

[23] See Maddala, *Econometrics*, pp. 304–305, referring to the results from the papers by Welch and Griliches on estimation of the effects of schooling on income.

[24] Finis Welch, "Human Capital Theory: Education, Discriminations and Life Cycles," *American Economic Review*, May 1975, p. 67; Zvi Griliches, "Estimating the Returns to Schooling: Some Econometric Problems," *Econometrica*, Vol. 45, 1977, p. 12.

[25] W. S. Krasker and J. W. Pratt, "Bounding the Effects of Proxy Variables on Regression Coefficients," *Econometrica*, Vol. 54, 1986, pp. 641–655.

The estimated regression equation (with standard errors in parentheses) is

$$\hat{y}_i = -4.53 - 0.23x_{1i} + 1.17x_{2i} + 1.49x_{3i} + 0.04x_{4i}$$
$$\quad\;\;(1.77)\quad\;(0.06)\qquad(0.23)\qquad(0.37)\qquad(0.12)$$

x_{2i} is considered a proxy variable for an unobserved variable z which is "per capita exposure to situations that create the possibility of fatal accidents." The question is whether the proxy has the same sign as the coefficient of this unobserved variable z. The R^2 from a regression of x_{2i} on x_{1i}, x_{3i}, x_{4i} is 0.3895. The R^2 from a regression of x_{2i} on y_i, x_{1i}, x_{3i}, x_{4i} is 0.6193. Hence, according to equation (11.20), we can be sure that the coefficient of x_{2i} has the same sign as the coefficient of z, regardless of other correlations if we are sure that the correlation between x_{2i} and z exceeds

$$(0.3895 + 1 - 0.6193)^{1/2} = 0.878$$

Krasker and Pratt conclude that "To ensure that the signs of the coefficients coincide with the signs of the unobservable true variables, the proxies must be of much higher quality than could be hoped for in the actual context."

Krasker and Pratt also give alternative formulas and methods of determining the correctness of the sign for the other coefficient β in equation (11.16) as well. Since these expressions are somewhat complicated, we will not reproduce them here. The condition given in equation (11.20) would enable us to judge the sign of γ. One reason why they get such a stringent condition is that they relax the usual assumptions made in the errors in variables models. They do not make the assumption that the error e in p is independent of z, x, or u.

To compute the Krasker–Pratt criterion (11.20) we have to compute the R^2's from a regression of the proxy on the other explanatory variables, and a regression of the proxy on the other explanatory variables *and* the dependent variable.

11.7 Some Other Problems

We introduced the simple errors in variables model in Section 11.2 as a starting point of our analysis. This simple model may not be applicable with most economic data because of the violation of some of the assumptions implied in this simple model. The crucial assumptions made in that model are:

1. The errors have zero mean.
2. The covariances between the errors and the systematic parts are zero.
3. The covariances between the errors themselves are zero.

Based on these conclusions, we showed that the OLS estimator $\hat{\beta}$ is not consistent and is biased toward zero. We will now show that:

1. The problem of obtaining consistent estimators can be solved in some cases if we have more equations in which the same error-ridden variable occurs.

2. If we consider correlated errors, the least squares estimators need not be biased toward zero. In fact, the OLS estimator $\hat{\beta}$ may overestimate (rather than underestimate) β.

Thus the conclusions derived in Section 11.2 will not be correct.

The Case of Multiple Equations

The case of multiple equations can be illustrated as follows. Suppose that

$$y_1 = \beta_1 x + e_1$$

$$y_2 = \beta_2 x + e_2$$

x is not observed. Instead, we observe $X = x + u$. Suppose that e_1, e_2, and u are mutually uncorrelated and also uncorrelated with x. Also, let $\text{var}(e_1) = \sigma_1^2$, $\text{var}(e_2) = \sigma_2^2$, $\text{var}(u) = \sigma_u^2$, and $\text{var}(x) = \sigma_x^2$. Then we have

$$\text{var}(y_1) = \beta_1^2 \sigma_x^2 + \sigma_1^2$$

$$\text{var}(y_2) = \beta_2^2 \sigma_x^2 + \sigma_2^2$$

$$\text{cov}(y_1, y_2) = \beta_1 \beta_2 \sigma_x^2$$

$$\text{cov}(y_1, X) = \beta_1 \sigma_x^2$$

$$\text{cov}(y_2, X) = \beta_2 \sigma_x^2$$

$$\text{var}(X) = \sigma_x^2 + \sigma_u^2$$

These six equations can be solved to get estimates of β_1, β_2, σ_x^2, σ_u^2, σ_1^2, and σ_2^2. Specifically, we have

$$\hat{\beta}_1 = \frac{\text{cov}(y_1, y_2)}{\text{cov}(X, y_2)} \quad \text{and} \quad \hat{\beta}_2 = \frac{\text{cov}(y_2, y_1)}{\text{cov}(X, y_1)}$$

In effect, this is like using y_2 as an instrumental variable in the equation $y_1 = \beta_1 X + w_1$ and y_1 as an instrumental variable in the equation $y_2 = \beta_2 X + w_2$. Further elaboration of this approach of solving the errors in variables (and unobservable variables) problem by increasing the number of equations can be found in Goldberger.[26]

As an illustration, suppose that

$$y_1 = \text{expenditures on automobiles}$$

$$y_2 = \text{expenditures on other durables}$$

$$x = \text{permanent income}$$

$$X = \text{measured income}$$

If we are given only y_1 and X (or y_2 and X), we are in the single-equation errors in variables problem and we cannot get consistent estimators for β_1 (or β_2). But if we are given y_1, y_2, and X, we can get consistent estimators for both β_1 and β_2.

---

[26]A. S. Goldberger, "Structural Equation Methods in the Social Sciences," *Econometrica*, 1972, pp. 979–1002.

Correlated Errors

Until now we have assumed that the errors of observation are mutually uncorrelated and also uncorrelated with the systematic parts. If we drop these assumptions, things will get more complicated. For example, consider the model $y = \beta x + e$.

The observed values are $X = x + u$ and $Y = y + v$, where u and v are the measurement errors. Let σ_{xy} denote the covariance between x and y, with a similar notation for all the other covariances. If the least squares estimate of β from a regression of Y on X is $\hat{\beta}$, then

$$\text{plim } \hat{\beta} = \frac{\text{cov}(Y, X)}{\text{var}(X)} = \frac{\text{cov}(x + u, y + v)}{\text{var}(x + u)}$$

$$= \frac{\sigma_{xy} + \sigma_{xv} + \sigma_{yu} + \sigma_{uv}}{\sigma_{xx} + 2\sigma_{xu} + \sigma_{uu}}$$

$$= \frac{\beta\sigma_{xx} + \sigma_{xv} + \sigma_{yu} + \sigma_{uv}}{\sigma_{xx} + 2\sigma_{xu} + \sigma_{uv}}$$

Since $\sigma_{yu} = \beta\sigma_{xu}$ and $\sigma_{xv} = \text{cov}[(y - e)/\beta, v] = \sigma_{yv}/\beta$, we have

$$\text{plim } \hat{\beta} = \frac{\beta(\sigma_{xx} + \sigma_{xu}) + \sigma_{yv}/\beta + \sigma_{uv}}{\sigma_{xx} + 2\sigma_{xu} + \sigma_{uu}}$$

Now even if there is no error in x (i.e., $u = 0$), we find that $\hat{\beta} \neq \beta$ since $\sigma_{yv} \neq 0$. Thus it is not just errors in x that create a problem as in the earlier case.

One can calculate the nature of the bias in $\hat{\beta}$ making different assumptions about the different covariances. We need not pursue this further here. What is important to note is that one can get either underestimation or overestimation of β. With economic data where such correlations are more the rule than the exception, it is important not to believe that the slope coefficients are always underestimated in the presence of errors in observations, as is suggested by the classical analysis of errors in variables models.

We have all along omitted the intercept term. If there is an intercept term α, i.e., our true relationship is $y = \alpha + \beta x + e$, and instead we estimate $Y = \alpha + \beta X + w$, then the least squares estimator $\hat{\beta}$ underestimates β and consequently the least squares estimator $\hat{\alpha}$ will overestimate α. If, however, the errors do not have a zero mean [i.e., $X = x + u$ and $E(u) \neq 0$], these conclusions need not hold.

A recent empirical example of correlated measurement error is in Ashenfelter and Krueger.[27] The paper also discusses the effects of correlated measurement errors on instrumental variable estimators. The details of the procedures are too complicated to be discussed here.

Summary

1. In the single-equation model with a single explanatory variable that is measured with error, the least squares estimator of β underestimates the true β. Specifically, the bias is

---

[27]O. Ashenfelter and A. Krueger, "Estimates of the Economic Returns to Schooling from a New Sample of Twins," *American Economic Review*, Vol. 84, 1994, pp. 1157–1173.

$-\beta\lambda$, where λ is the proportion of the error variance in the variance of x. This result is based on the assumption that the errors have zero means and have zero covariance with the systematic parts and among themselves.

2. We can obtain bounds for the true coefficient β by computing the regression coefficient of y on x and the reciprocal of the regression coefficient of x on y (Section 11.2).

3. In a model with two explanatory variables x_1 and x_2 with coefficients of β_1 and β_2 where only x_1 is measured with error, we can show that the bias in the estimator of β_1 is $(-\beta_1\lambda)/(1 - \rho^2)$, where ρ is the correlation between the *measured* values of x_1 and x_2. Also, the bias in the estimator of $\beta_2 = -\rho$ (the bias in the estimator of β_1). Similar results can be derived when there are many explanatory variables. Some papers in the literature derive the expressions for the bias in terms of the correlations between the true unobserved variables. These expressions are not very useful in practice. Here we derive the expressions in terms of the correlations of the observed variables. The only unknown factor is λ, the proportion of error variance in the variance of the error-ridden variable (Section 11.3).

4. As with the model with a single explanatory variable, we can derive bounds for the true coefficients by running two regressions. These bounds are given in equations (11.6) and (11.7). However, these bounds are not comparable to confidence intervals. The estimated bounds themselves have standard errors. We have illustrated with an example that these bounds can sometimes be so wide as to be almost useless. In many problems, therefore, it is better to supplement them with estimates based on some plausible assumptions about the error variances.

5. In the model with two explanatory variables, if both the variables are measured with error, the direction of biases in the OLS estimators cannot be easily evaluated [see equations (11.9) and (11.10)]. Making the most general assumptions about error variances often leads to wide bounds for the parameters, thus making no inference possible. On the other hand, making some plausible assumptions about the error variances, one can get more reasonable bounds for the parameters. This point is illustrated with an example.

6. In the application of the errors in variables model to problems of discrimination, the "reverse regression" has often been advocated. The arguments for and against this procedure are reviewed in Section 11.4.

7. One method for obtaining consistent estimators for the parameters in errors in variables models is the instrumental variable method. In practice it is rather hard to find valid instrumental variables. In time-series data lagged values of the measured x_t are often used as instrumental variables. Some grouping methods are often suggested for the estimation of errors in variables models. These methods can be viewed as instrumental variable methods. However, their use is not recommended. Except in special cases, the estimators they yield are not consistent.

8. Often in econometric work it is customary to use some surrogate variables for the variables we cannot measure. These surrogate variables are called proxy variables. In an equation like

$$y = \beta x + \gamma z + u$$

where we use a proxy p for z, a question that has often been asked is whether it is better to leave out p completely if we are interested in estimating β. Assuming that p falls in the category of the usual errors in variables, it has been shown that the bias in the estimator for β is reduced if we leave p in the equation. On the basis of this result it has been argued that even a poor proxy is better than none. However, this conclusion does not necessarily hold good if we take into account the variances of the estimators, or if the proxy is a dummy variable, or if the proxy does not fall in the category of the usual errors in variables. The conclusion also does not follow if x itself is measured with error.

9. In case we are interested in the coefficient γ, a question often arises whether the use of the proxy p gives us the correct sign. A criterion for determining this is given in equation (11.20).

10. If there are many explanatory variables that depend on the same error-ridden variable, sometimes we can use the dependent variables in the other equations as instrumental variables for the estimation of the parameters in each equation. An example of this is given in Section 11.7. Furthermore, all these assumptions about bias are invalid in the presence of correlated errors (see Section 11.7).

Exercises

1. Explain the meaning of each of the following terms:
   (a) Errors in variable bias.
   (b) Bounds for parameters.
   (c) Reverse regression.
   (d) Grouping methods.
   (e) Proxy variables.

2. Examine whether the following statements are true, false, or uncertain. Give a short explanation. If a statement is not true in general but is true under some conditions, state the conditions.
   (a) Errors in variables lead to estimates of the regression coefficients that are biased toward zero.
   (b) In errors in variables models we can always get two estimators $\hat{\beta}_1$ and $\hat{\beta}_2$ such that

$$\text{plim } \hat{\beta}_1 < \beta < \text{plim } \hat{\beta}_2$$

   Thus, even though we cannot get a confidence interval, we can get bounds for the parameters that will serve the same purpose.
   (c) Grouping methods give consistent (although inefficient) estimators for the regression parameters in errors in variables models. Since they are very easy to compute, they should be used often.
   (d) It is always desirable to use even a poor proxy rather than to drop an error-ridden variable from an equation.
   (e) If we have an unobserved variable in an equation and we are interested in the sign of its coefficient, we should always use a proxy, since the estimated coefficient of the proxy variable will give us the correct sign.
   (f) In regressions of income on schooling where schooling is measured with error, omitting variables that measure ability will overestimate the effect of schooling on income.

(g) In part (f) the bias in the estimator of the effect of schooling on income can be reduced if we include a proxy like test score for ability.

(h) In part (g), if ability is measurable, then we should *always* include the measure available, in the earnings function.

(i) In an analysis of discrimination in salaries an investigator finds that the direct regression shows discrimination, whereas the reverse regression shows reverse discrimination. This proves that there is no evidence of discrimination in salaries.

3. Consider a regression model

$$y = \alpha_0 + \alpha_1 x_1 + \alpha_2 x_2 + \alpha_3 x_3 + u$$

The variable x_1 is not observed, but we use a proxy p for it. Let $\hat{\alpha}_1$ be the estimator of α_1 obtained from the multiple regression equation. If you are told that the correlation between x_1 and p is at least 0.8, explain how you will determine whether $\hat{\alpha}_1$ has the correct sign (same sign as α_1).

4. Consider the regression model

$$y = \beta_1 x_1 + \beta_2 x_2 + u$$

x_1 is not observed. The observed value is $X_1 = x_1 + e$, where e is uncorrelated with x_1, x_2, and u. Let $\gamma = \text{var}(e)/\text{var}(X_1)$. Suppose that we drop x_2 from the equation. Let the OLS estimator of β_1 be $\hat{\beta}_1$. Show that

$$\text{plim } \hat{\beta}_1 = \beta_1 - \gamma \beta_1 + \beta_2 b_{21}$$

where b_{21} is the regression coefficient from a regression of x_2 on X_1. If $\tilde{\beta}_1$ is the estimator of β_1 from a regression of y on X_1 and x_2, show that

$$\text{plim } \tilde{\beta}_1 = \beta_1 - \frac{\gamma \beta_1}{1 - r^2}$$

where r is the correlation between X_1 and x_2. [This is equation (11.4) derived in the text.]

5. In Exercise 4 compute the two probability limits if the true equation is

$$y = 1.0x_1 + 0.5x_2 + u$$

$$\gamma = 0.1 \quad \text{var}(X_1) = \text{var}(x_2) = 9 \quad r = 0.5$$

What do you conclude from these results?

Part III Special Topics

This part consists of six chapters. Chapter 12 discusses recent work on diagnostic checking, specification testing, and model selection. It discusses the different types of residuals, different criteria of model selection, and Hausman's specification error test.

Chapter 13 is an introduction to time-series analysis and Box–Jenkins methods.

Chapter 14 is on unit roots and cointegration — the major developments in modern time-series analysis.

Chapter 15 is on panel data. It discusses fixed effects, random effects and random coefficient models, dynamic panel data models and issues about pooling.

Chapter 16 is on large-sample theory. It discusses maximum likelihood (ML) and generalized method of moments (GMM). It also discusses three asymptotic tests: likelihood ratio (LR), Wald (W), and score of Lagrangian multiplier (LM) tests.

Chapter 17 is on small-sample theory. It discusses Monte Carlo methods and bootstrap methods for making small-sample inferences.

Bayesian methods are not discussed in great detail. But in Chapter 12, Section 12.8 we explain the basics of the Bayesian approach and the posterior odds approach to model selection.

12 Diagnostic Checking, Model Selection, and Specification Testing

What is in this Chapter?

This chapter presents some advances in econometrics in the 1980s. Diagnostic tests have become popular, starting around 1980, and several computer programs (SHAZAM, MICROFIT, TSP, etc. reviewed in Appendix C) have built in diagnostics — to diagnose what is wrong with the model. Several diagnostic tests have already been discussed in Chapter 4 (tests for stability), Chapter 5 (tests for heteroskedasticity), and Chapter 6 (tests for serial correlation).

In this chapter we discuss the use of different kinds of residuals to detect outliers, the DFFITS criterion, and bounded influence estimation.

We also discuss the Hausman specification error test, the differencing test, and nonnested tests.

Another problem discussed in this chapter is the problem of model selection, selection of regressors, and the implied F-ratios for the different model selection criteria. The difference between hypothesis testing and model selection as research alternatives is emphasized.

12.1 Introduction

The early developments in econometrics were concerned with the problems of estimation of an econometric model once the model was specified. The major preoccupation of econometricians was with devising methods of estimation that produced consistent and efficient estimates of the parameters. These are the methods we discussed in the previous chapters. Sometimes more simplified methods like two-stage least squares were suggested because some other methods like limited-information maximum likelihood (LIML) were complicated to compute. With the recent developments in computer technology, such search for simplified methods of estimation is no longer worthwhile, at least in a majority of problems.

During recent years the attention of econometricians has been diverted to the problems of:

1. Checking the adequacy of the specification of the model. This is called "diagnostic checking" and "specification testing."
2. Choosing between alternative specifications of the model. This is called "model selection."
3. Devising methods of estimation based on weaker assumptions about the error distributions. This is called "semiparametric estimation."

The last area is well beyond the scope of this book and will not be discussed at all. The first two areas are also very vast in scope. Hence what we will do is to consider only a few of the major developments.

It is, of course, true that the problem of diagnostic checking has not been completely ignored. In fact, we discussed some tests for this purpose in the earlier chapters. For instance:

1. Tests for parameter stability in Chapter 4.
2. Tests for heteroskedasticity in Chapter 5.
3. Tests for autocorrelation in Chapter 6.

However, these tests are all based on least squares residuals, and during recent years some alternative residuals have been suggested. Also, tests for diagnostic checking have been more systematized (and incorporated in computer programs like the SAS regression program). The limitations of some standard tests have been noticed and further modifications have been suggested. For instance, in Chapter 6 we discussed the limitations of the DW test, which has been the most commonly used "diagnostic test" for many years.

We begin our discussion with diagnostic tests based on the least squares residuals. Here we summarize the tests discussed in the earlier chapters and discuss some other tests. We will then present some alternatives to least squares residuals and the diagnostic tests based on them. Next, we discuss some problems in model selection and specification testing. Many of the specification tests involve "expanded regressions," that is, the addition of residuals or some other constructed variables as regressors to the original model and testing for the significance of the coefficients of these added variables. Thus most of these tests can be easily implemented using the standard regression packages.

12.2 Diagnostic Tests Based on Least Squares Residuals

Diagnostic tests are tests that are meant to "diagnose" some problems with the models that we are estimating. The least squares residuals play an important role in many diagnostic tests. We have already discussed some of these tests, such as tests for parameter stability in Chapter 4, tests for heteroskedasticity in Chapter 5, and tests for autocorrelation in Chapter 6. Here we discuss two other tests using least squares residuals.

Tests for Omitted Variables

Consider the linear regression model

$$y_t = \beta x_t + u_t$$

To test whether the model is misspecified by the omission of a variable z_t, we have to estimate the model

$$y_t = \beta x_t + \gamma z_t + v_t$$

and test the hypothesis $\gamma = 0$.

If data on z_t are available, there is no problem. All we do is regress y_t on x_t and z_t and test whether the coefficient of z_t is zero. Suppose, on the other hand, that we use the following procedure:

1. Regress y_t on x_t and get the residual $\bar{u}_t$.
2. Regress $\bar{u}_t$ on z_t. Let the regression coefficient be $\tilde{\gamma}$. Test the hypothesis $\gamma = 0$ using this regression equation.

What is wrong with this procedure?

The answer is that $\tilde{\gamma}$ is an inconsistent estimator of γ unless $\gamma = 0$. Furthermore, the distribution of $\tilde{\gamma}$ is complex and the standard errors provided by the least squares estimation of step 2 will not be the correct ones. If the least squares residuals at step 1 are to be used, we should regress them on z_t *and* x_t and then test whether the coefficient of z_t is zero.[1]

Thus if we are to use the residuals $\bar{u}_t$ from a regression of y_t on x_t for testing specification errors caused by omitted variables, it is advisable to regress $\bar{u}_t$ on z_t *and* x_t and not z_t only, and test the hypothesis that the coefficient of z_t is zero.

When observations on z are not available, we use a proxy $\bar{z}$ for z. The preceding results apply to this case as well.[2] That is, an appropriate test for omitted variables is to estimate the model

$$y_t = \beta x_t + \gamma \tilde{z}_t + v_t$$

and test the hypothesis $\gamma = 0$. Alternatively, if we are using the residuals $\bar{u}_t$ from a regression of y_t on x_t, we have to regress $\bar{u}_t$ on $\tilde{z}_t$ and x_t and then test whether the coefficient of $\tilde{z}_t$ is zero. Of course, we need not go through this circuitous procedure, but the reason for discussing this is to make clear the distinction between tests for heteroskedasticity discussed in Chapter 5 and tests for omitted variables.

---

[1] We are omitting the detailed proofs. They can be found in the paper by A. R. Pagan and A. D. Hall, "Diagnostic Tests as Residual Analysis" (with discussion), *Econometric Reviews*, Vol. 2, 1983, pp. 159–218.

[2] The only problem is that if $\tilde{z}$ is uncorrelated with z, the test would have low power, but cases where $\tilde{z}$ is uncorrelated with z are rare.

Ramsey[3] suggests the use of $\hat{y}_t^2$, $\hat{y}_t^3$, and $\hat{y}_t^4$ as proxies for z_t, where $\hat{y}_t$ is the predicted value of y_t from a regression of y_t on x_t.

The test procedure is as follows:

1. Regress y_t on x_t and get $\hat{y}_t$.
2. Regress y_t on x_t, $\hat{y}_t^2$, $\hat{y}_t^3$, and $\hat{y}_t^4$ and test the hypothesis that the coefficients of the powers of $\hat{y}_t$ are zero.

Note that this test is slightly different from Ramsey's test for heteroskedasticity discussed in Section 5.2. That test proceeds as follows:

1. Regress y_t on x_t and get the residual $\hat{u}_t$.
2. Regress $\hat{u}_t$ on $\hat{y}_t^2$, $\hat{y}_t^3$, and $\hat{y}_t^4$ and test that the coefficients of these variables are zero.

As explained earlier, if we want to use $\hat{u}_t$ to test for omitted variables, we have to include x_t as an extra explanatory variable. This is the difference between the two Ramsey tests.

Tests for ARCH Effects

In econometric models, the uncertainty in the economic relationship is captured by the variance σ^2 of the error term u_t. It has been found that it is important to model this error variance because it affects the behavior of economic agents. One such model is the ARCH model (Autoregressive Conditionally Heteroskedastic model) suggested by Engle.[4] In this model the unconditional variance $E(u_t^2)$ is constant but the conditional variance $E(u_t^2|x_t)$ is not. Denoting this conditional variance by σ_t^2, the model suggested by Engle is

$$\sigma_t^2 = \sigma^2 + \gamma u_{t-1}^2 \quad \gamma > 0$$

that is, the variance of the current error term u_t is higher if the past error term is higher. An unusually high disturbance term in one period results in an increase in uncertainty for the next period. If $\gamma = 0$, there is no ARCH effect and the usual methods of estimation apply. If $\gamma \neq 0$, we have to use more complicated maximum likelihood procedures to estimate the model.

A test for ARCH effect using the least squares residuals proceeds as follows:

1. Regress y_t on x_t. Obtain $\hat{u}_t$.
2. Regress $\hat{u}_t^2$ on $\hat{u}_{t-1}^2$ and test whether the regression coefficient is zero.

A large number of studies, particularly those of speculative prices, have reported significant ARCH effects. However, one has to be careful in interpreting the results because $\hat{u}_{t-1}^2$ might be acting as a proxy for omitted lagged values of y_t and x_t from the

---

[3] J. B. Ramsey, "Tests for Specification Errors in Classical Linear Least Squares Regression Analysis," *Journal of the Royal Statistical Society, Series B*, Vol. 31, 1969, pp. 350–371.

[4] R. F. Engle, "Autoregressive Conditional Heteroscedasticity with Estimates of the Variance of United Kingdom Inflation," *Econometrica*, Vol. 50, 1982, pp. 987–1007. See also Section 6.11.

equation. (Note that $\hat{u}_{t-1} = y_{t-1} - \hat{\beta}x_{t-1}$.) Thus the ARCH test should be performed after including a sufficient number of lagged values of y_t and x_t in the equation.[5]

12.3 Problems with Least Squares Residuals

In our discussion of heteroskedasticity in Chapter 5 and autocorrelation in Chapter 6, we considered only the least squares residuals $\hat{u}_i$ obtained from the least squares regression. The problem with these residuals, as we will demonstrate, is that they are heteroskedastic and autocorrelated *even if* the true errors have a common variance and are serially independent. This heteroskedasticity and autocorrelation depends on the particular values of the explanatory variables in the sample. That is why the Durbin–Watson test gives an inconclusive region. Durbin and Watson obtained lower and upper bounds for their test statistic that are valid irrespective of what values the explanatory variables take. Presumably, the bounds can be improved with a knowledge of the explanatory variables. In fact, we argued that with most economic variables, the upper limit is the one to use. An alternative solution is to construct residuals that have the same properties as the true errors. That is, if the errors have mean zero and constant variance σ^2 and are serially independent, the residuals also exhibit these same properties. One such set of residuals is the "recursive residuals" which are discussed in Section 12.4. First we demonstrate the problems with the least squares residuals.

During recent years separate books have been written on just the topic of residuals.[6] This is because an analysis of residuals is very important for all diagnostic tests. Consider the regression model

$$\mathbf{y} = \mathbf{x}\boldsymbol{\beta} + \mathbf{u}$$

The least squares residuals are

$$\hat{\mathbf{u}} = \mathbf{y} - \mathbf{x}\hat{\boldsymbol{\beta}} = \mathbf{y} - \mathbf{X}(\mathbf{X}'\mathbf{X})^{-1}\mathbf{X}'\mathbf{y}$$

Let us define the "hat matrix" $\mathbf{H}$ by

$$\mathbf{H} = \mathbf{X}(\mathbf{X}'\mathbf{X})^{-1}\mathbf{X} \tag{12.1}$$

Then $\hat{\mathbf{u}} = (\mathbf{I} - \mathbf{H})\mathbf{y} = (\mathbf{I} - \mathbf{H})\mathbf{u}$ since $\mathbf{HX} = \mathbf{X}$.

The covariance matrix of $\hat{\mathbf{u}}$ is

$$E(\hat{\mathbf{u}}) = (\mathbf{I} - \mathbf{H})\sigma^2 \tag{12.2}$$

Note that $\mathbf{I} - \mathbf{H}$ is an idempotent matrix (see p. 55 for a definition of an idempotent matrix).

Hence, if h_i is the ith diagonal element of $\mathbf{H}$ and $\hat{u}_i$ is the ith element of $\hat{\mathbf{u}}$, then

$$\text{var}(\hat{u}_i) = (1 - h_i)\sigma^2 \tag{12.3}$$

---

[5]The point is similar to the one made in Section 6.9, where it was argued that sometimes the observed serial correlation in the residuals could be a consequence of misspecified dynamics (i.e., omission of lagged values of y_t and x_t from the equation).

[6]For instance, C. Dubbelman, *Disturbances in the Linear Model: Estimation and Hypothesis Testing* (The Hague: Martinus Nihjoff, 1978), and R. D. Cook and S. Weisberg, *Residuals and Influence in Regression* (London: Chapman & Hall, 1982).

This shows that the least squares residuals are heteroskedastic. Also, equation (12.2) shows that they are correlated, since $\mathbf{H}$ is in general a nondiagonal matrix.

12.4   Some Other Types of Residuals

We will discuss four other types of residuals:

1. Predicted residuals.
2. Studentized residuals.
3. BLUS residuals.
4. Recursive residuals.

The predicted and studentized residuals both have the same problems as the least squares residuals. However, some statisticians have found the predicted and studentized residuals useful in choosing between different regression models and detection of outliers, respectively. Hence we will discuss them briefly. The BLUS and recursive residuals both have the property that they have mean zero and constant variance σ^2 and are serially independent. Thus they solve the problems of least squares residuals. However, the BLUS residuals are more difficult to compute and have been found to be less useful than recursive residuals. Hence we will discuss them only briefly.

Predicted Residuals and Studentized Residuals

Suppose that we take sample data of n observations and estimate the regression equation with $(n-1)$ observations at a time by omitting one observation and then use this estimated equation to predict the y value for the omitted observation. Let us denote the prediction error by $u_i^* = y_i - \hat{y}(i)$. The u_i^* are the *predicted residuals*.

By $\hat{y}(i)$ we mean a prediction of y_i from a regression equation that is estimated from all observations except the ith observation. This is in contrast to $\hat{y}_i$, which is the predicted value of y_i from a regression equation that is estimated using all the observations.

There is a simple relationship between the least squares residuals $\hat{u}_i$ and the predicted residuals u_i^*. This is[7]

$$u_i^* = \frac{\hat{u}_i}{1 - h_i}$$

Since $V(\hat{u}_i) = (1 - h_i)\sigma^2$, we have

$$V(u_i^*) = \frac{\sigma^2}{1 - h_i}$$

Thus the predicted residuals are also heteroskedastic. It has also been proved that the predicted residuals have the same correlation structure as the least squares residuals.

Although the predicted residuals have properties similar to the least squares residuals, some statisticians have found them more useful than the least squares residuals in problems

---

[7]We will not be concerned with the proof here. Proofs can be found in Cook and Weisberg, *Residuals*.

of choosing between different regression models.[8] The criterion they use is that of the *predicted residual sum of squares* (PRESS), which is defined as

$$\text{PRESS} = \sum (u_i^*)^2$$

The more common criterion used is (the rationale for this is discussed in Section 12.6)

$$\text{RSS} = \sum \hat{u}_i^2$$

Since $u_i^* = \hat{u}_i/(1 - h_i)$, from the definition of h_i we note that PRESS as a criterion for selection of regression models results in a preference for models that fit relatively well at remote values of the explanatory variables.

The predicted residuals can be computed by using the dummy variable method described in Chapter 8 (see Section 8.6). We will describe it after discussing studentized residuals, because the two are closely related.

One can compute the "hat matrix" and h_i. Then using $\hat{u}_i$ and h_i we get the predicted residual u_i^*. The studentized residual $\tilde{u}_i$ is the predicted residual divided by its standard error. Thus

$$\tilde{u}_i = \hat{u}_i / S(i)(1 - h_i)^{1/2}$$

where $[S(i)]^2$ is the estimate of σ^2 from the regression with the ith observation deleted. If S^2 is the estimate of σ^2 from the complete regression, then there is a relationship between the two error variances:

$$(n - k)S^2 - (n - k - 1)S^2(i) = \hat{u}_i^2/(1 - h_i)$$

(proof can be found in the book by Cook and Weisberg).

Thus, $S(i)$ can be calculated from the OLS regression and hence the studentized residual as well. However, we shall describe a dummy variable method for computing the studentized residuals.

Dummy Variable Method for Studentized Residuals

The studentized residual is just the predicted residual divided by its standard error. Thus if we are using the dummy variable method to get the ith studentized residual, we do the following. Estimate the regression equation with an extra variable D defined as

$$D = \begin{cases} 1 & \text{for the } i\text{th observation} \\ 0 & \text{for all other observations} \end{cases}$$

Then the estimate of the coefficient of D is the predicted residual and the t-ratio for this coefficient is the studentized residual. Thus to generate predicted and studentized residuals,

---

[8]See, for instance, R. L. Anderson, D. M. Allen, and F. Cady, "Selection of Predictor Variables in Multiple Linear Regression," in T. A. Bancroft (ed.), *Statistical Papers in Honor of George W. Snedecor* (Ames, IA: Iowa State University Press, 1972). Also N. T. Quan, "The Prediction Sum of Squares as a General Measure for Regression Diagnostics," *Journal of Business and Economic Statistics*, Vol. 6, 1988, pp. 501–504.

the regressions involve all the observations in the sample and we create dummy variables in succession for the first, second, third, ... observations. Studentized residuals are usually used in the detection of outliers. Suppose that there is an outlier. In the case of the least squares residual, it might not be detected because we use the outlier as well in computing the regression equation. In the case of predicted and studentized residuals, we use all the other observations in computing the regression equation and try to use it in predicting this particular (outlying) observation. Thus there is a better chance of detecting outliers with this method.

The least squares and the predicted residuals both suffer from two problems. They are correlated and heteroskedastic even if the errors u_i are uncorrelated and have the same variance. There have been several methods suggested for the construction of residuals that do not have these shortcomings. We discuss only two of them: the BLUS residuals suggested by Theil[9] and recursive residuals.

BLUS Residuals

The BLUS (which stands for "best linear unbiased scalar") residuals are constructed from the least squares residuals so that they have the same properties as the errors u_i; that is, they have zero mean (they are unbiased), are uncorrelated, and have the same variance σ^2 as the errors u_i.

The computation of BLUS residuals is too complicated to be described here. However, we need not be concerned with this because it has been found that in tests for heteroskedasticity and autocorrelation, there is not much to be gained by using the BLUS residuals as compared with the least squares residuals.[10] Hence we will not discuss the BLUS residuals further.

Recursive Residuals

Recursive residuals have been suggested by Brown, Durbin, and Evans,[11] for testing the stability of regression relationships. However, these residuals can be used for other problems as well, such as tests for autocorrelation and tests for heteroskedasticity. Phillips and Harvey[12] use recursive residuals for testing serial correlation. Since the recursive residuals are serially uncorrelated and have a common variance σ^2, we can use the von Neumann ratio tests (described in Chapter 6). There is no inconclusive region as with the Durbin–Watson test.

[9]H. Theil, "The Analysis of Disturbances in Regression Analysis," *Journal of the American Statistical Association*, Vol. 60, 1965, pp. 1067–1079.

[10]Cook and Weisberg, *Residuals*, p. 35.

[11]R. L. Brown, J. Durbin, and J. M. Evans, "Techniques for Testing the Constancy of Regression Relationships" (with discussion), *Journal of the Royal Statistical Society, Series B*, Vol. 37, 1975, pp. 149–163. This paper gives algorithms for the construction of recursive residuals. Farebrother gives algorithms for the construction of BLUS and recursive residuals. See R. W. Farebrother, "BLUS Residuals: Algorithm A5104" and "Recursive Residuals: A Remark on Algorithm A75: Basic Procedures for Large, Sparse or Weighted Least Squares Problems," *Applied Statistics*, Vol. 25, 1976, pp. 317–319 and 323–324.

[12]G. D. A. Phillips and A. C. Harvey, "A Simple Test for Serial Correlation in Regression Analysis," *Journal of the American Statistical Association*, Vol. 69, 1974, pp. 935–939.

We will now describe the construction of recursive residuals. First, we order observations sequentially. This is not a problem with time-series data. The recursive residual can be computed by forward recursion or backward recursion. We describe forward recursion only. Backward recursion is similar. The idea behind recursive residuals is this: Let us say that we have T observations and the regression equation is

$$y_t = \beta x_t + u_t \quad t = 1, 2, \ldots, T$$

Let $\hat{\beta}_i$ be the estimate of β from the first i observations. Then we use this to predict the next observation y_{i+1}. The prediction is

$$\tilde{y}_{i+1} = \hat{\beta}_i x_{i+1}$$

The prediction error is

$$e_{i+1} = y_{i+1} - \tilde{y}_{i+1}$$

Let us denote $V(e_{i+1})$ by $d_{i+1}^2 \sigma^2$. (The variance of prediction error in multiple regression has been discussed in Section 4.7.) Then the recursive residuals, which we denote by $\tilde{u}_{i+1}$, are

$$\tilde{u}_{i+1} = \frac{e_{i+1}}{d_{i+1}}$$

Note that $\text{var}(\tilde{u}_{i+1}) = \sigma^2$. Now we add one more observation, estimate β using $(i+1)$ observations, and use this to predict the next observation, y_{i+2}. Thus

$$\tilde{y}_{i+2} = \hat{\beta}_{i+1} x_{i+2}$$

and if $e_{i+2} = y_{i+2} - \tilde{y}_{i+2}$ and $V(e_{i+2}) = d_{i+2}^2 \sigma^2$, then

$$\tilde{u}_{i+2} = \frac{e_{i+2}}{d_{i+2}}$$

We continue this process until we get to the last observation. If we have k explanatory variables, since we have to estimate $k+1$ parameters (including the constant term) and obtain their variances, we need at least $(k+2)$ observations. Thus the recursive residuals start with the observation $(k+3)$ and we have $T - k - 2$ recursive residuals.

The recursive residuals have been shown to have the following properties:[13]

1. They are uncorrelated.
2. They have a common variance σ^2.
3. Their sum of squares is equal to RSS, the residual sum of squares from the least squares regression.

The third property is useful in checking the accuracy of the calculations.

There are algorithms for calculating the regression coefficients $\hat{\beta}_i$ and also the prediction variance $d_i^2 \sigma^2$, in a recursive fashion.[14] There is, however, an alternative method that we

---

[13]Proofs are omitted. These properties are proved in Brown, Durbin, and Evans, "Techniques for Testing."
[14]Phillips and Harvey, "A Simple Test."

can use for the recursive residuals as we have done for the predicted residuals described earlier. Note that recursive residuals are similar to predicted residuals except that the predictions are sequential.

Suppose that we use n observations and want to get the prediction error and the variance of the prediction error for the $(n + 1)$th observation. Then all we have to do is to create a dummy variable D which is defined as

$$D = \begin{cases} 1 & \text{for the } (n+1)\text{th observation} \\ 0 & \text{for all other observations} \end{cases}$$

We have discussed this procedure in Chapter 8.

Now we just run a multiple regression with all the $(n + 1)$ observations and this extra variable D. The estimate of the coefficient of this variable D is the prediction error e_{n+1} and its standard error is $\hat{\sigma} d_{n+1}$. This result has been proved in Chapter 8. Thus we get from the regression program e_{n+1} and $d_{n+1}\hat{\sigma}$ or t_{n+1} the t-ratio, which is $e_{n+1}/d_{n+1}\hat{\sigma}$. But for the recursive residuals we need e_{n+1}/d_{n+1}. Thus all we have to do is multiply the t-ratio we get for the coefficient of D by $\hat{\sigma}$. This gives us the recursive residual.

The calculation of recursive residuals by the dummy variable method is similar to that for predicted residuals except that the regressions for predicted residuals involve all the observations in the sample and for recursive residuals the observation set is sequential and the dummy variable is also sequential.

Illustrative Example

In Table 12.1 we present the OLS residual, the forward recursive, and the backward recursive residuals for the production function (4.24). The sum of squares of the recursive residuals should be equal to the sum of squares of the OLS residuals, but there are small discrepancies which are due to rounding errors.

The recursive residuals are useful for:

1. Tests for heteroskedasticity described in Chapter 5.
2. Tests for autocorrelation described in Chapter 6.
3. Tests for stability described in Chapter 4.

For stability analysis, Brown, Durbin, and Evans suggest computing the cumulative sums (CUSUM) and cumulative sums of squares (CUSUMSQ) of the recursive residuals and comparing them with some percentage points that they have tabulated. A discussion of this is beyond the scope of this book.[15] Instead, we will apply some simple t-tests. If a test of the hypothesis that the mean of the recursive residual is zero gives us a significant t-statistic, this is an indication of instability of the coefficients. In Table 12.1 we present these t-ratios. With the forward recursive residuals we do not reject the hypothesis of zero mean. With the backward recursive residuals, we do reject at the 5% level the hypothesis of zero mean. Thus the conclusions from the recursive residuals are similar to the conclusions we arrived at earlier in Chapter 4 from the predictive tests for stability.

---

[15]Those interested in this detail can refer to the paper by Brown, Durbin, and Evans, "Techniques for Testing."

Table 12.1 Different residuals for the production function (4.25) (multiplied by 100)

Year	OLS Residual	Forward Recursive	Backward Recursive
1929	−1.27		−1.304
1930	−4.29		−4.530
1931	−3.99		−4.710
1932	−1.30		−3.044
1933	−3.04	−1.975	−6.187
1934	−1.99	−0.809	−6.476
1935	−0.79	0.512	−6.440
1936	1.04	1.115	−4.246
1937	−0.26	−1.040	−4.359
1938	4.55	3.824	−2.900
1939	4.93	4.163	−2.224
1940	4.37	4.182	−2.668
1941	1.84	1.335	−2.971
1942	−1.74	−1.456	−4.775
1943	0.13	1.609	−3.110
1944	6.59	6.065	3.502
1945	11.11	8.487	8.844
1946	1.34	−4.811	5.452
1947	−6.59	−10.322	−1.531
1948	−5.90	−7.172	−1.884
1949	−2.06	−1.601	−0.132
1950	0.12	1.343	2.331
1951	−2.68	−0.884	0.273
1952	−3.24	−0.667	−0.702
1953	−2.38	0.883	−0.716
1954	1.10	4.137	1.293
1955	1.48	3.540	2.917
1956	−1.52	0.186	0.826
1957	−1.00	0.772	0.764
1958	1.43	2.917	0.912
1959	0.00	1.083	0.989
1960	−1.39	−0.367	−0.854
1961	0.38	1.400	−2.372
1962	1.21	1.963	−1.994
1963	2.51	2.865	−1.793
1964	2.31	2.297	
1965	1.85	1.561	
1966	0.00	−0.328	
1967	−2.97	−3.160	
Mean	0.00	0.618	−1.252
SD	3.379	3.506	3.338
Range	17.70	18.81	15.32
SS	433.8	431.3	433.6
t	0.00	1.04	−2.22

12.5   DFFITS and Bounded Influence Estimation

In Section 3.8 we discussed briefly the problem of outliers. The usual approach to outliers based on least squares residuals is as follows:

1. Look at the OLS residuals.
2. Delete the observations with large residuals.
3. Reestimate the equation.

Two major problems with this approach are that the OLS residuals (as we showed earlier) do not all have the same variance and furthermore the OLS residuals do not give us any idea of how important this particular observation is for the overall results. The idea behind the studentized residual is to allow for these differences in the variances and to look at the prediction error resulting from the deletion of this observation. Using a plus or minus 2σ rule of thumb, the studentized residuals shown in Table 12.2 suggest that the observations for the years 1945 and 1947 are outliers. With the OLS residuals in Table 12.1 we might have included 1944 and 1948 as well.

One other measure that is used to detect outliers is to see the change in the fitted value $\hat{y}$ of y that results from dropping a particular observation. Let $\hat{y}_{(i)}$ be the fitted value of y if the ith observation is dropped. The quantity $(\hat{y}_i - \hat{y}_{(i)})$ divided by the scaling factor $h_i S_i$, where S_i^2 is the estimator of σ^2 from a regression with the ith observation omitted is called DFFITS$_i$.

It has been shown that[16]

$$\text{DFFITS}_i = \left(\frac{h_i}{1 - h_i} \right)^{1/2} \tilde{u}_i$$

where $\tilde{u}_i$ is the ith studentized residual.

There are many computer programs available to compute studentized residuals and DFFITS. For instance, the SAS regression program gives these statistics. The results in Table 12.2 have been obtained from the SAS regression program.

A rough value of DFFITS $> 2\sqrt{k/n}$ is considered "significant." Belsley, Kuh, and Welsch, hereafter referred to as BKW, suggest using DFFITS to distinguish between outliers and "influential observations." An outlier need not be influential ($\tilde{u}_i$ the studentized residual significant but DFFITS$_i$ not), and an influential observation need not be an outlier (DFFITS$_i$ significant but $\tilde{u}_i$ not).

Unfortunately, this criterion has been built into several computer programs (e.g., SAS) and it is in widespread use. However, *this criterion is not useful* and the supposed conflict it detects is spurious. To see this, examine how it was derived. BKW divide the change in prediction by what they call the "scaling factor" which is the SE of $\hat{y}_i = x_i\hat{\beta}$. Note that $\text{var}(\hat{y}_i) = h_i\sigma^2$ and the change in prediction is $x_i'(\hat{\beta} - \hat{\beta}(i)) = h_i u_i^*$. If we divide this by the correct standard error, instead of the arbitrary "scaling factor" used by BKW, we

---

[16]D. A. Belsley, E. Kuh, and R. E. Welsch, *Regression Diagnostics: Identifying Influential Data and Sources of Collinearity* (New York: Wiley, 1980).

Table 12.2 Regression diagnostics for detecting outliers for the production function (4.24)

Year	Studentized Residual	DFFITS	Year	Studentized Residual	DFFITS
1929	−0.38	−0.08	1949	−0.61	−0.16
1930	−1.28	−0.35	1950	0.04	0.01
1931	−1.21	−0.39	1951	−0.79	−0.19
1932	−0.42	−0.21	1952	−0.96	−0.22
1933	−0.97	−0.46	1953	−0.70	−0.15
1934	−0.61	−0.22	1954	0.32	0.06
1935	−0.24	−0.07	1955	0.43	0.08
1936	0.31	0.08	1956	−0.45	−0.09
1937	−0.08	−0.02	1957	−0.29	−0.06
1938	1.36	0.37	1958	0.42	0.10
1939	1.46	0.37	1959	0.01	0.00
1940	1.29	0.29	1960	−0.41	−0.11
1941	0.54	0.12	1961	0.11	0.03
1942	−0.51	−0.12	1962	0.37	0.11
1943	0.04	0.01	1963	0.75	0.23
1944	1.94	0.46	1964	0.70	0.22
1945	3.28	0.88	1965	0.56	0.18
1946	0.42	0.17	1966	0.02	0.01
1947	−2.04	−0.85	1967	−0.91	−0.33
1948	−1.80	−0.66			

end up with the studentized residual. *Thus, DFFITS is a different criterion because the change in fit is divided by the wrong standard error.*

The same argument applies to another criterion suggested by BKW (and also incorporated in several computer programs). This is DFBETAS. This is supposed to measure the influence of the ith observation on the estimate of β_j, the jth component of β. However, we have

$$\hat{\beta}_j - \hat{\beta}_j(i) = (\mathbf{X'X})_j^{-1} x_i u_i^*$$

where $(\mathbf{X'X})_j^{-1}$ is the jth row of $(\mathbf{X'X})^{-1}$. Again a test of significance of this is exactly equivalent to a test of significance of u_i^* and this is done by using the studentized residual. BKW arrive at a different answer because they use the wrong standard error (they use an arbitrary "scaling factor").

Belsley, Kuh, and Welsch suggest that DFFITS is a better criterion to detect outliers and influential observations. DFFITS is a standardized measure of the difference in the fitted value of y due to deleting this particular observation. Further, they suggest that observations with large studentized residuals or DFFITS should not be deleted. Their influence should be minimized. This method of estimation is called *bounded influence estimation*. The details of this method are complicated but a simple one-step bounded influence estimator is suggested by Welsch[17] as follows: Minimize

---

[17]Roy E. Welsch, "Regression Sensitivity Analysis and Bounded Influence Estimation," in J. Kmenta and J. B. Ramsay (eds.), *Evaluation of Econometric Models* (New York: Academic Press, 1980), pp. 153–167.

$\sum w_i(y_i - \beta x_i)^2$, where

$$w_i = \begin{cases} 1 & \text{if } |\text{DFFITS}_i| \leq 0.34 \\ \dfrac{0.34}{|\text{DFFITS}_i|} & \text{if } |\text{DFFITS}_i| > 0.34 \end{cases}$$

Illustrative Example

As an illustration, consider again the production function (4.24). The values of DFFITS are shown in Table 12.2. There are nine observations (all before 1948) that have $|\text{DFFITS}_i| > 0.34$. These observations receive a weight <1 in the bounded influence estimation.

Using this weighting scheme, we obtained the following results:

Estimate of:	Bounded Influence	OLS	OLS with Outlier Deletion
α	−3.987	−3.938	−3.980
β_1	1.468	1.451	1.466
β_2	0.375	0.384	0.376

For comparison we also present the estimates from the OLS regression (4.24) and also estimates using OLS after deleting the observations for 1944, 1945, 1947, and 1948, the years for which the OLS residuals in Table 12.1 are large.

In this example there was not much difference in the estimated coefficients. In fact, the bounded influence method and OLS with outlier deletion gave almost identical results. The data set we have used is perhaps not appropriate for the illustration of the bounded influence method. The problem of parameter instability and autocorrelated errors seems to be more important with this data set than that of detection of outliers.

In any case the preceding discussion gives an idea of what "bounded influence estimation" is about. The basic point is that the OLS residuals are not appropriate for detection of outliers. Further, outliers should not all be discarded. Their influence on the least squares estimates should be reduced (bounded) based on their magnitude.

As mentioned earlier, the data set we have used has not turned out to be appropriate for illustrating the method. Other data sets in the book can be used to check out the usefulness of the method.

Krasker[18] gives an interesting example of the use of bounded influence estimation. The problem is a forecasting problem faced by Korvett's Department Stores in 1975. The company has to choose between two locations, A and B to start a new store. Data are

---

[18]W. S. Krasker, "The Role of Bounded Influence Estimation in Model Selection," *Journal of Econometrics*, Vol. 16, 1981, pp. 131–138.

available for 25 existing stores on the following variables:

$$y = \text{sales per capita}$$

$$x_1 = \text{medium home value } (\times 10^{-6})$$

$$x_2 = \text{average family size } (\times 10^{-2})$$

$$x_3 = \text{percent of population which is black or hispanic } (\times 10^{-4})$$

The regression results were (dependent variable: sales) (figures in parentheses are standard errors) as follows:

	Constant	x_1	x_2	x_3	$\hat{\sigma}$
OLS	−0.13 (0.05)	2.70 (0.51)	2.5 (1.1)	0.22 (3.1)	0.014
WLS	−0.05 (0.04)	1.00 (0.52)	1.7 (1.0)	−4.1 (2.9)	0.010

Note the change in the coefficient for x_3. The WLS estimator is the weighted least squares.[19] Krasker argues that there are two outliers (observations 2 and 11 in this sample). The other 23 observations are "well described by an OLS regression whose estimates are essentially those of the WLS." Thus again in this example the bounded influence estimator does not appear to be different from the OLS with the two outliers omitted. (Results from OLS with 23 observations are not presented here.)

Krasker suggests that site A is similar to observation 2 and if the model cannot be used to predict observation 2, it should not be used to make predictions for site A (with 50.8% of the population from minorities). The model (OLS with 23 observations or WLS with all observations) can be used to make predictions for site B.

12.6 Model Selection

In the usual textbook econometrics, the statistical model underlying the data is assumed to be known at the outset and the problem is merely one of obtaining good estimates of the parameters in the model. In reality, however, the choice of a model is almost always made after some preliminary data analysis. For instance, in the case of a regression model, we start with a specification that seems most reasonable *a priori*. But after examining the coefficients, their standard errors and the residuals, we change the specification of the model. Purists would consider this "data mining" as an illegitimate activity, but it is equally unreasonable to assume that we know the model exactly at the very outset.

The area of model selection comprises:

1. Choice between some models specified before any analysis.
2. Simplification of complicated models based on the data (data-based simplification).
3. Post-data model construction.

---

[19]The weighting scheme is slightly different from the weighting scheme discussed in Welsch, "Regression Sensitivity."

The area of model selection is quite vast in its scope and includes diagnostic checking and specification testing (the other two areas we are discussing in this chapter). There are many references on the topic, some of which are a book by Leamer,[20] a paper by Mizon,[21] the dissertation by Sawyer,[22] and a special volume of the *Journal of Econometrics*.[23] Since it is impossible to cover this vast area, we discuss Leamer's classification of the different types of model searches usually attempted, and also Hendry's ideas behind data-based simplification of models. In Sections 12.7 to 12.9 we go through two particular aspects of model selection:

1. Selection of regressors.
2. Use of cross-validation techniques.

Leamer talks of six types of specification searches that are usually undertaken in the process of model selection. The differences between the different searches are very minor. However, they are useful for organization of our ideas. The different searches are:

Type of Search	Purpose
(1) Hypothesis-testing search	Choosing a "true model"
(2) Interpretive search	Interpreting the sample evidence on many intercorrelated variables
(3) Simplification search	Constructing a "fruitful" model
(4) Proxy variable search	Choosing between different measures of the same set of hypothetical variables
(5) Data selection search	Selecting the appropriate data set for estimation and prediction
(6) Post-data model construction	Improving an existing model

Many of these searches have been discussed in previous chapters. But we will give further examples.

Hypothesis-Testing Search

Suppose that we estimate a Cobb–Douglas production function as in Section 4.11, and test the hypothesis of constant returns to scale ($\beta_1 + \beta_2 = 1$ in that example). If the hypothesis is rejected, as in that example, we do not change the specification of the model. If it is not rejected, we change the specification and estimate a production function with constant returns to scale.

[20]E. E. Leamer, *Specification Searches* (New York: Wiley, 1978).

[21]G. E. Mizon, "Model Selection Procedures," in M. J. Artis and A. R. Nobay (eds.), *Studies in Current Economic Analysis* (Oxford: Basil Blackwell, 1977), Chap. 4.

[22]K. R. Sawyer, "The Theory of Econometric Model Selection," unpublished doctoral dissertation, Australian National University, 1980.

[23]G. S. Maddala (ed.), "Model Selection," *Journal of Econometrics*, Vol. 16, 1981.

Interpretive Search

Sometimes the coefficients of the model do not make economic sense but the imposition of some constraints does. For instance, based on data for 150 households, Leamer[24] estimated the demand for oranges as (figures in parentheses are standard errors)

$$\log D_i = \underset{(1.0)}{3.1} + \underset{(0.20)}{0.83 \log E_i} + \underset{(0.15)}{0.01 \log P_i} - \underset{(0.60)}{0.56 \log \pi_i} \quad R^2 = 0.20$$

where D_i = purchases of oranges by household i
   E_i = total expenditures by household i
   P_i = price of oranges
   π_i = price of grapefruit (a substitute commodity)

The coefficients of the price variables are insignificant and have the "wrong" sign. Also, the sum of the coefficients ($0.83 + 0.01 - 0.56 = 0.28$) is rather far from zero. If there is no money illusion, then multiplying E_i, P_i, and π_i by the same factor should not produce any change in D_i. This implies that the sum of the coefficients of these variables should be zero. (This is known as the "homogeneity postulate.") Imposing this condition, Leamer gets the result

$$\log D_i = \underset{(0.9)}{4.2} + \underset{(0.19)}{0.52 \log E_i} - \underset{(0.14)}{0.61 \log P_i} + \underset{(0.31)}{0.09 \log \pi_i} \quad R^2 = 0.19$$

The R^2 has fallen only slightly and the coefficients all have the right signs. Expenditure E_i and price P_i are significant. The constraint has improved the specifications, and the interpretation.

Simplification Search

In the equation above the coefficient of $\log \pi_i$ is not significant. Dropping this variable and imposing the homogeneity constraint, that is, assuming the other two coefficients to be equal in value and opposite in sign, we get

$$\log D_i = \underset{(0.8)}{3.7} + \underset{(0.18)}{0.58 \log(E_i/P_i)} \quad R^2 = 0.18$$

The R^2 is only slightly smaller and we have a simplified equation. This is called a simplification search. The purpose of this search is to find a simple but useful model.

Proxy Variable Search

In econometric work an investigator is faced with several definitions of the same variable. There are several definitions of money supply, several definitions of income, and so on. Further, some variables like education, ability, and risk are not directly measurable and we have to use some proxies for them. We are thus left with the problem of choosing among the different proxies. In the example of demand for oranges that Leamer considered, one has to choose between money income Y_i and expenditures E_i as measures of the

---

[24]Leamer, *Specification Searches*, p. 8.

household's true income. The estimated equations he gets are

$$\log D_i = 6.2 + 0.85 \log Y_i - 0.67 \log P_i \quad R^2 = 0.15$$
$${\scriptstyle (1.1)} {\scriptstyle (0.21)} {\scriptstyle (0.13)}$$

and

$$\log D_i = 5.2 + 1.1 \log E_i - 0.45 \log P_i \quad R^2 = 0.18$$
$${\scriptstyle (1.0)} {\scriptstyle (0.18)} {\scriptstyle (0.16)}$$

The R^2 has increased with the use of E_i, suggesting that E_i is a better proxy than Y_i for "true income."

Data Selection Search

Often, in econometric work we have different data sets from which we can estimate the same relationship. A question often arises as to whether we can pool the different data sets and get more efficient estimates of the parameters. In Section 4.6 we gave some examples where the data sets referred to prewar and postwar years. There we found significant differences in the coefficients between the two periods which suggested that the data should not be pooled. This is an example of a data selection search.

Post-Data Model Construction

This is what Leamer calls "Sherlock Holmes" inference. In response to a question by Dr. Watson about the likely perpetrators of the crime, Sherlock Holmes replied: "No data yet. . . . It is a capital mistake to theorize before you have all the evidence. It biases the judgments." According to the traditional statistical theory, on the other hand, it is a "capital mistake to view the facts before you have all the theories. It biases the judgments." Any theory that is postulated after looking at a particular data set cannot be tested using the same data set, because doing so would amount to double counting. On the other hand, Sherlock Holmes would argue that the set of viable alternative hypotheses is immense and the set of hypotheses formulated before the data set is observed can be incomplete. There is always the risk that the data favor some unspecified hypothesis. Hence the data evidence is used to construct a set of "empirically relevant" hypotheses, thereby reducing the cost of formulating a comprehensive set of hypotheses and the risk of not identifying the "best" hypothesis.

In almost all econometric work investigators do something similar to what Sherlock Holmes does. They formulate some hypotheses, then observe that the coefficients of some variables have wrong signs or implausible magnitudes or that the residuals have a peculiar pattern. Then they introduce more explanatory variables or impose some constraints on the parameters. A question arises as to whether this type of Sherlock Holmes inference can be brought within the scope of statistical inference.

Leamer's answer to this is that we have to view this new "data-instigated hypothesis" as something that was in the back of our mind all the time. We did not consider it explicitly because we thought it to be unimportant but now we change our mind after observing the data. Suppose that the model we want to consider is $y = \beta x + \gamma z + u$. Initially, we consider z to be uncorrelated with x or that γ is negligibly small. So we start with the model $y = \beta x + u$. If the resulting estimate of β has the wrong sign or the pattern of estimated residuals is peculiar, we change our mind and observe z. If the problem is viewed in this form of a decision problem, Leamer argues that we can attach the appropriate standard errors to the coefficients when the model $y = \beta x + \gamma z + u$ is estimated.

In all cases of specification searches, there is the question of what the appropriate standard errors should be for the final model estimated. There is no easy answer to this question except that the standard errors are higher than those obtained from the estimation of the final model. The inference problem is more straightforward in the case of a simplification search. That is why David Hendry suggests starting with an extremely general model and then simplifying it progressively. We will, therefore, discuss this approach in greater detail.

Hendry's Approach to Model Selection

The approach to model building suggested by David Hendry,[25] which is mainly applicable to dynamic time-series models, can be summarized as: *intended overparametrization with data-based simplification*. By contrast most of empirical econometric work can be characterized as *excessive presimplification with inadequate diagnostic testing*. The latter method consists of the following steps:

1. Commence from theories which are drastic abstractions of reality.
2. Formulate highly parsimonious relationships to represent the theories.
3. Estimate the equations from the available data using techniques which are "optimal" only on the assumptions that the highly restricted model is correctly specified.
4. Test a few of the assumptions explicitly or implicitly (such as the conventional Durbin–Watson test for autocorrelation).
5. Revise the specification in the light of evidence acquired.
6. Reestimate accordingly.

According to Hendry, this approach to model building, which is a "specific to general" approach or a "bottom-up" approach, has three main drawbacks:

1. Every test is conditional on arbitrary assumptions which are to be tested *later*, and if these are rejected, all earlier inferences are invalidated.
2. The significance levels of the unstructured sequence of tests actually conducted are unknown. For instance, suppose that we estimate an equation by OLS, find a significant DW statistic, and then reestimate the equation adjusting for the serial correlation. What are the significance levels for the estimated coefficients from this transformed equation? This is not very clear.
3. It is not always possible to end up with the best model by using this iterative method. We might get sidetracked by using the wrong (or inadequate) diagnostic tests. For instance, we might start with the equation $y = \beta x + u$ and observing a significant DW test statistic, we reestimate the equation in a ρ-differenced form. If we now find that the

---

[25] This approach is originally due to J. D. Sargan but has been popularized and expounded by David Hendry. Some representative papers are: D. F. Hendry, "Predictive Failure and Econometric Modelling in Macroeconomics: The Transactions Demand for Money," in Paul Ormerod (ed.), *Economic Modelling* (London: Heinemann, 1979), Chap. 9, pp. 217–242; and Mizon, "Model Selection Procedures."

coefficients of our equation are of the correct sign, we might rest satisfied. However, this procedure might lead us to the wrong model because as discussed in Section 6.9 the DW statistic could be significant not because of serial correlation in errors but because of misspecified dynamics. The model with serially correlated errors

$$y_t = \beta x_t + u_t \quad u_t = \rho u_{t-1} + e_t$$

implies the model

$$y_t = \rho y_{t-1} + \beta x_t - \beta \rho x_{t-1} + e_t$$

which is the same as

$$y_t = \beta_1 y_{t-1} + \beta_2 x_t + \beta_3 x_{t-1} + e_t$$

with the restriction $\beta_1 \beta_2 = -\beta_3$. Now the true model could be the last one but with the restriction $\beta_1 \beta_2 = -\beta_3$ *not* satisfied. But there is no way of our arriving at this model by the modeling approach adopted. When we estimate the model $y_t = \beta x_t + u_t$ we would observe serial correlation in the residuals because y_{t-1} and x_{t-1} are "missing." But this does not mean that we have a model with serially correlated errors.

By contrast, the approach suggested by Hendry, which is a "top-down" or "general to specific" approach, starts with a very general dynamic model, which is "over-parametrized," that is, has more lags than you would consider necessary. The model is then progressively simplified with a sequence of "simplification tests." The significance levels for the sequence of tests is known unlike the case of the sequence of tests we perform in the "specific to general" approach. The significance level for the jth test is[26]

$$1 - \prod_{i=1}^{j}(1 - \gamma_i)$$

where γ_i is the significance level for the ith test in the sequence. The sequential testing procedures are used to select a "data coherent specialization."

Hendry argues that only after these steps should one test economic theories. "Until the model characterizes the data generation process, it seems rather pointless trying to test hypotheses of interest in economic theory."[27]

12.7   Selection of Regressors

In Section 12.6 we outlined some general approaches to the model selection problem. We now concentrate on a specific issue, the problem of selection of regressors.

In Chapter 4 we considered a multiple regression of an explained variable y on a set of k explanatory variables $x_1, x_2, \ldots, x_k$. It was assumed that the set of variables to be included in the equation is given. In practice this is rarely the case. There is typically a very large number of potential explanatory variables or regressors and one is faced with

---

[26]This result was derived by T. W. Anderson in the paper cited in Section 10.11. This result has been proved for dynamic econometric models by J. D. Sargan (in an unpublished London School of Economics discussion paper).

[27]Hendry, "Predictive Failure," p. 226.

a problem of choosing a subset of these. This is the problem often referred to as the problem of *selection of regressors*.

Suppose that there is a potential set of k regressors from which we have to select a smaller number. In the 1960s a number of stepwise regression methods were suggested.[28] Some of these started with a regression, including all the k variables and successively proceeded to eliminate variables with t-ratios less than a prespecified value (say, 1). This is called a backward selection procedure. Others started with a single variable which had the highest correlation with y and then picked at each stage the variable with the highest partial correlation coefficient (this is called a forward selection procedure). Some procedures combined the elements of the forward and backward selection procedures at each stage (i.e., deleted some variables and added some others).

This sort of mechanical picking of variables by the computer is no longer popular among econometricians. Fortunately, although economists do not have an *exact* idea of all the variables that have to be included in an equation, they do have an idea of what variables are likely to be very important and what variables are doubtful. In this case we can specify a small number of alternative models and then we need to choose one of these alternatives. Since theory cannot give us any guidance at this stage we have to make a choice on statistical grounds.

There are many criteria that have been suggested in the literature. Some of these are listed in Table 12.3. We discuss them briefly. The criteria that we have chosen in Table 12.3 are applicable to regression models only and we have chosen those criteria that depend on some summary measures commonly used like residual sum of squares.

Let RSS denote the residual sum of squares from the jth model with k_j explanatory variables. We define

$$\hat{\sigma}_j^2 = \frac{\text{RSS}_j}{n - k_j}$$

an estimate of σ^2 from the jth model. We denote $\hat{\sigma}_m^2$ as the estimate of σ^2 from a model that includes *all* the k explanatory variables.

Table 12.3 Some criteria for choice among regression models

Criterion	Minimize[a]
Theil's $\bar{R}^2$ (1961)	$\text{RSS}_j/(n - k_j)$
Hocking's S_p (1976)	$\text{RSS}_j/[(n - k_j)(n - k_j - 1)]$
Mallows' C_p (1973)	$\text{RSS}_j + 2k_j\hat{\sigma}_m^2$
Amemiya's PC (1980)	$\text{RSS}_j(n + k_j)/(n - k_j)$
Akaike's AIC (1973, 1977)	$\text{RSS}_j \exp[2(k_j + 1)/n]$

[a]k_j, number of explanatory variables; RSS_j, residual sum of squares for the jth model; $\hat{\sigma}_m^2$, (residual sum of squares)/$(n - k)$ in the model that includes all the k explanatory variables.

---

[28]These methods are not popular at present. However, those interested in a discussion of stepwise procedures can refer to N. Draper and H. Smith, *Applied Regression Analysis*, 2nd ed. (New York: Wiley, 1981), Chap. 6.

We now discuss briefly the criteria listed in Table 12.3.

Theil's $\overline{R}^2$ Criterion

Theil's criterion[29] is based on the assumption that one of the models considered is the correct model. In this case if $\hat{\sigma}_j^2 = \text{RSS}_j/(n - k_j)$ is the estimate of σ^2 from the jth model, then $E(\hat{\sigma}_j^2) = \sigma^2$ for the correct model but is $\geq \sigma^2$ for the misspecified model.[30] Thus, choosing the model with the minimum $\hat{\sigma}^2$ will *on the average* lead us to pick the correct model. Since minimizing $\hat{\sigma}^2$ is the same as maximizing $\overline{R}^2$ [see equation (4.21)], we refer to the rule alternatively as the maximum $\overline{R}^2$ rule.

A major problem with this rule is that a model that has all the explanatory variables of the correct model but also a number of irrelevant variables will also give $E(\hat{\sigma}^2) = \sigma^2$. Thus the rule will not help us pick the correct model in this case. This indeed is confirmed by the results in Schmidt and Ebbeler[31] concerning the power function of the maximum $\overline{R}^2$ criterion. The probability of picking the correct model is considerably below 1 when the alternative model includes a number of irrelevant variables.

Criteria Based on Minimizing the Mean-Squared Error of Prediction

Theil's criterion is based on minimizing the standard error of the regression. The following three criteria are based on minimizing the mean-squared error of prediction:

1. Mallows' C_p criterion.[32]
2. Hocking's S_p criterion.[33]
3. Amemiya's PC criterion.[34]

Suppose that the correct equation involves k variables and the equation we consider involves k_1 $(< k)$ variables. The problem is how to choose the number k_1, as well as the particular set of k_1 variables. In the prediction criteria we are considering

---

[29] H. Theil, *Economic Forecasts and Policy*, 2nd ed. (Amsterdam: North-Holland, 1961).

[30] The proof of this result can be found in several books. See, for instance, G. S. Maddala, *Econometrics* (New York: McGraw-Hill, 1977), pp. 461–462. It is shown there that a model that has all the explanatory variables of the correct model but also a number of irrelevant variables will also give $E(\hat{\sigma}^2) = \sigma^2$.

[31] P. Schmidt, "Calculating the Power of the Minimum Standard Error Choice Criterion," *International Economic Review*, February 1973, pp. 253–255. The numerical errors in Schmidt's paper are corrected in D. H. Ebbeler, "On the Probability of Correct Model Selection Using the Maximum $\overline{R}^2$ Choice Criterion," *International Economic Review*, June 1975, pp. 516–520. There are three types of misspecifications considered in these papers: omitted variables, irrelevant variables, and wrong variables. For the first two cases, Ebbeler shows that some simple analytical results are available.

[32] C. L. Mallows, "Some Comments on C_p," *Technometrics*, November 1973, pp. 661–676. The criterion was first suggested by Mallows in 1964 in an unpublished paper.

[33] R. R. Hocking, "The Analysis and Selection of Variables in Multiple Regression," *Biometrics*, March 1976, pp. 1–49. This has been further discussed in two papers by M. L. Thompson, "Selection of Variables in Multiple Regression, Part 1: A Review and Evaluation," and "Part 2: Chosen Procedures, Computations and Examples," *International Statistical Review*, Vol. 46, 1978, pp. 1–19 and 129–146. Also see U. Hjorth, "Model Selection and Forward Validation," *Scandinavian Journal of Statistics*, Vol. 9, 1982, pp. 1–49.

[34] T. Amemiya, "Selection of Regressors," *International Economic Review*, Vol. 21, 1980, pp. 331–354.

this is done by minimizing the mean-squared error (MSE) of prediction $E(y_f - \hat{y}_f)^2$, where y_f is the future value of y_f and $\hat{y}_f$ is the predicted value. If we denote the future values of the explanatory variables by x_{if}, then $E[y_f - \hat{y}_f)^2 | x_{if}]$ is called the conditional MSE of prediction and $E(y_f - \hat{y}_f)^2$ is called the unconditional MSE of prediction.

To get the unconditional MSE of prediction we have to make some assumptions about x_{if}. Amemiya assumes that the regressors for the prediction period are stochastic and that the values of x_{if} have the same behavior as the variables x_{it} during the sample period. Under this assumption he shows that[35]

$$\text{estimate of } E(y_f - \hat{y}_f)^2 \simeq \frac{2k_1}{n}\sigma^2 + \frac{\text{RSS}_1}{n}$$

where RSS_1 is the residual sum of squares from the model with k_1 regressors.

Now σ^2 has to be estimated. If we use $\hat{\sigma}_m^2 = \text{RSS}/(n - k)$, where RSS is the residual sum of squares from the complete model with k explanatory variables, we get Mallows' C_p criterion. On the other hand, if we use $\hat{\sigma}_1^2 = \text{RSS}_1/(n - k_1)$, then we get Amemiya's PC criterion. Note, however, that $\text{RSS}_1/(n - k_1)$ is an upward-biased estimate of σ^2 because of the fact that it is an estimate from a misspecified regression.[36] On the other hand, $\hat{\sigma}_1^2$ is an unbiased estimate of σ^2 if it is assumed that the model with k_1 variables is the correct model and the model with k variables includes a number of irrelevant variables. This is the "optimistic" assumption that Amemiya makes. However, if we are comparing different models with different sets of variables by the PC criterion, we cannot make the "optimistic" assumption that every one of these is the true model. This is one of the major problems with Amemiya's PC criterion. It is more reasonable to assume that $\hat{\sigma}_m^2$ is the appropriate estimate of σ^2 as assumed in Mallows' C_p criterion.

The important thing to note in the discussion above is that the regressors in the sample period are assumed nonstochastic, whereas they are assumed stochastic in the prediction period. Hocking, by contrast, assumes the regressors to have a multivariate normal distribution and derives the S_p criterion given in Table 12.3 by minimizing the unconditional MSE of prediction. Kinal and Lahiri[37] show that in the stochastic regressor case Amemiya's PC and Mallows' C_p both reduce to Hocking's S_p criterion. Breiman and Freedman[38] give an alternative justification for Hocking's S_p criterion. It is not necessary for us to go through the different ways in which the criteria C_p and S_p have been derived and justified. This discussion can be found in the papers by Thompson cited earlier. The important thing to note is that Amemiya's PC and Mallows' C_p depend on the assumption of nonstochastic regressors, whereas Hocking's S_p depends on the assumption of stochastic regressors. A consequence of this assumption is that (as noted by Kinal and Lahiri) both the C_p and PC criteria require an estimate of the variance σ^2

---

[35]We will not be concerned with the proof here. It can be found in Amemiya, "Selection of Regressors."

[36]This is in fact the basis for the maximum $\overline{R}^2$ rule.

[37]T. Kinal and K. Lahiri, "A Note on 'Selection of Regressors,'" *International Economic Review*, Vol. 25, No. 3, October 1984.

[38]L. Breiman and D. Freedman, "How Many Variables Should Be Entered in a Regression Equation?," *Journal of the American Statistical Association*, March 1983, pp. 131–136.

of the disturbance in the true model, whereas S_p does not. It just requires an estimate of the variance of the disturbance term in the restricted model.

One more important thing to note is that the maximum $\bar{R}^2$ criterion and the predictive criteria C_p, S_p, and PC answer two different questions. In the case of the maximum $\bar{R}^2$ criterion, what we are trying to do is pick the "true" model, assuming that one of the models considered is the "true" one. In the case of the prediction criteria, we are interested in "parsimony" and we would like to omit some of the regressors (even if a model that includes them is the true model) if this improves the MSE of prediction. For the latter problem, the question is whether we need to assume the existence of a true model or not. For the C_p and PC criteria, as we have seen, we do need to think in terms of a "true" model. For the S_p criterion (or in the stochastic regressor case), we do not have to worry about whether one of the models is the true model or not and what regressors there are in the "true" model.

Akaike's Information Criterion

Akaike's information criterion[39] (AIC) is a more general criterion that can be applied to any model that can be estimated by the method of maximum likelihood. It suggests minimizing

$$\frac{-2 \log L}{n} + \frac{2k}{n}$$

where k is the number of parameters in L. For the regression models this criterion implies minimizing [RSS exp($2k/n$)], which is the criterion listed in Table 12.3.

We have included AIC in our list because it is the one that is commonly used (at least in nonlinear models) and like the other criteria listed in Table 12.3, it involves RSS_j and k_j only. Thus it can be computed using the standard regression programs.

12.8   Implied *F*-Ratios for the Various Criteria

We saw earlier (Section 4.10) that maximizing $\bar{R}^2$ implies deletion of variables with an F-ratio <1. We can derive similar conditions for the C_p, S_p, and PC criteria discussed in Section 12.7.

Consider the restricted model with k_1 ($<k$) variables, so that k_2 variables are deleted ($k = k_1 + k_2$). Define λ = RRSS/URSS, where RRSS and URSS are the residual sum of squares from the restricted and unrestricted models, respectively.

Then, as derived in Section 4.8, the F-ratio for testing the hypothesis that the coefficients of the k_2 excluded variables are zero is

$$F = \frac{(\text{RRSS} - \text{URSS})/k_2}{\text{URSS}/(n-k)} = \frac{(\lambda - 1)(n-k)}{k_2} \tag{12.4}$$

---

[39]This criterion is derived in H. Akaike, "Information Theory and an Extension of the Maximum Likelihood Principle," in B. N. Petrov and F. Csaki (eds.), *2nd International Symposium on Information Theory* (Budapest: Akadémiai Kiadó, 1973), and H. Akaike, "On Entropy Maximization Principle," in P. R. Krishniah (ed.), *Applications of Statistics* (Amsterdam: North-Holland, 1977).

If the restricted model is chosen, then for the $\overline{R}^2$ criterion, this means that

$$\frac{\text{RRSS}}{n - k_1} < \frac{\text{URSS}}{n - k} \quad \text{or} \quad \lambda < \frac{n - k_1}{n - k} \tag{12.5}$$

Substituting in equation (12.4) and noting that $k = k_1 + k_2$, we get the condition $F < 1$. For Amemiya's PC criterion we have

$$\lambda < \frac{n - k_1}{n + k_1} \frac{n + k}{n - k} \tag{12.6}$$

Substituting this in equation (12.4) and simplifying, we get

$$F < \frac{2n}{n + k_1} \tag{12.7}$$

For the C_p criterion we have

$$\lambda < 1 + \frac{2k_2}{n - k} \tag{12.8}$$

and thus $F < 2$. For the S_p criterion

$$\lambda < \frac{(n - k_1)(n - k_1 - 1)}{(n - k)(n - k - 1)} \tag{12.9}$$

and thus

$$F < 2 + \frac{k_2 + 1}{n - k - 1} \tag{12.10}$$

For the AIC criterion

$$\lambda < \frac{\exp(k/n)}{\exp(k_1/n)} \tag{12.11}$$

Substituting this in equation (12.4), we do not get any easy expression as in the other cases, but we can tabulate the values for different values of k/n and k_1/n.

For n large relative to k, we have

$$\exp\left(\frac{k}{n}\right) = 1 + \frac{k}{n}$$

and hence

$$\lambda < \frac{n + k}{n + k_1} \tag{12.12}$$

Substituting this in equation (12.4), we get

$$F < \frac{n - k}{n + k_1} \quad \text{which is } < 1 \tag{12.13}$$

The F-values for deletion of the k_2 variables implied by the different criteria are shown in Table 12.4. They stand in the following relation:

$$F(\text{AIC}) < F(\overline{R}^2) < 1 < F(\text{PC}) < F(C_p) < 2 < F(S_p) \qquad (12.14)$$

If n is large relative to k, note that PC, C_p and S_p all imply a cutoff value of $F = 2$.

The choice between the restricted and unrestricted models is based on an F-test for the restrictions. The use of the F-ratios in Table 12.4 implies two things:

1. The significance level that we use for the F-tests, for testing the restrictions, is not the conventional 5% level of significance. In fact, we use a much higher level of significance.
2. The significance level used, in general, decreases with the sample size. This is particularly true for the cases where we use a constant F-ratio like 1 or 2, irrespective of the sample size. It is also true of Amemiya's PC criterion, where the F-ratio is less than 2 for small samples and approaches 2 as $n \to \infty$. However, with Hocking's S_p criterion, the cutoff point of F declines toward 2 as the sample size increases. Thus in this case we cannot say unambiguously that the significance level decreases with sample size.

The common procedure of using a constant level of significance in hypothesis testing irrespective of sample size has been often criticized on grounds that with a sufficiently large sample every null hypothesis can be rejected. The procedure increasingly distorts the interpretation of data against a null hypothesis as the sample size grows. The significance level should, consequently, be a decreasing function of sample size.[40] As we have seen, the criteria for choice of regressors imply a decreasing significance level as the sample size increases. However, some Bayesian arguments have led to more substantial changes in the significance levels with sample size than are implied by the criteria in Table 12.4.

Table 12.4 F-values for different criteria

Criterion	Choose the Restricted Model if the F-Ratio for Testing the Restrictions Gives:
Maximum $\overline{R}^2$	$F < 1$
Mallows' C_p	$F < 2$
Amemiya's PC	$F < \dfrac{2n}{n + k_1}$
Hocking's S_p	$F < 2 + \dfrac{k_2 + 1}{n - k - 1}$
Akaike's AIC (for n large relative to k)	$F < \dfrac{n - k}{n + k_1}$

---

[40]This argument was made in D. V. Lindley, "A Statistical Paradox," *Biometrika*, Vol. 44, 1957, pp. 187–192, and since then in many Bayesian papers on model selection.

We will discuss one such criterion, that of Leamer,[41] but before that we will explain briefly what the Bayesian approach is.

Bayes' Theorem and Posterior Odds for Model Selection

Bayes' theorem is based on the definition of conditional probability. Let E_1 and E_2 be two events. Then by the definition of conditional probability, we have

$$P(E_1|E_2) = \frac{P(E_1E_2)}{P(E_2)} \quad \text{and} \quad P(E_2|E_1) = \frac{P(E_1E_2)}{P(E_1)}$$

Hence

$$P(E_1|E_2) = \frac{P(E_2|E_1)P(E_1)}{P(E_2)}$$

Now substitute H (hypothesis about the model that generated the data) for E_1 and D (observed data) for E_2. Then we have

$$P(H|D) = \frac{P(D|H)P(H)}{P(D)} \tag{12.15}$$

Here $P(D|H)$ is the probability of observing the data given that H is true. This is usually called the *likelihood*. $P(H)$ is our probability that H is true *before* observing the data (usually called the *prior probability*). $P(H|D)$ is the probability that H is true *after* observing the data (usually called the *posterior probability*). $P(D)$ is the unconditional probability of observing the data (whether H is true or not). Often $P(D)$ is difficult to compute. Hence we write the relation above as

$$P(H|D) \propto P(D|H)P(H)$$

That is: Posterior probability varies with (or is proportional to) likelihood times prior probability.

If we have two hypotheses H_1 and H_2, then

$$P(H_1|D) = \frac{P(D|H_1)P(H_1)}{P(D)} \quad \text{and} \quad P(H_2|D) = \frac{P(D|H_2)P(H_2)}{P(D)}$$

Hence

$$\frac{P(H_1|D)}{P(H_2|D)} = \frac{P(D|H_1)}{P(D|H_2)} \frac{P(H_1)}{P(H_2)} \tag{12.16}$$

The left-hand side is called *posterior odds*. The first term on the right-hand side is called the *likelihood ratio*, and the second term on the right-hand side is called the *prior odds*. Thus we have:

Posterior odds equals likelihood ratio times prior odds

---

[41]Leamer, *Specification Searches*, pp. 114–116.

In the problem of choice of regressors, H_1 and H_2 involve some parameters, say β and γ. The likelihood ratio is computed by a weighting procedure, the weights being determined by the prior distributions of these parameter sets. Thus we have

$$\frac{P(H_1|\text{data})}{P(H_2|\text{data})} = \frac{\int L_1 P_1(\beta)\,d\beta}{\int L_2 P_2(\gamma)\,d\gamma}\frac{P(H_1)}{P(H_2)} \tag{12.17}$$

where L_1 and L_2 are the respective likelihoods and P_1 and P_2 are the respective prior distributions for the parameters in models 1 and 2. The first term on the right-hand side is sometimes called the *Bayes factor*.

There have been many suggestions in the literature for P_1 and P_2 and thus for the computation of Bayesian posterior odds.[42] Since our purpose here is to illustrate how the implied F-ratio changes with the sample size according to some Bayesian arguments, we will present one formula suggested by Leamer. He suggests that the posterior probabilities should satisfy the following properties:

1. There must be no arbitrary constants.
2. The posterior probability of a model should be invariant to linear transformations of the data.
3. There should be a degrees of freedom adjustment: of two models that both yield the same residual sum of squares, the one with the fewer explanatory variables should have the higher posterior probability.

Based on these criteria, Leamer suggests prior distributions P_1 and P_2 and computes the posterior odds as prior odds times the Bayes factor given by (in the notation we are using)

$$B = \left(\frac{\text{RRSS}}{\text{URSS}}\right)^{n/2} n^{k_2/2} \tag{12.18}$$

We say that the evidence favors the restricted model if $B < 1$. Using the F-ratio defined in equation (12.14), we get the condition as

$$F < \frac{n-k}{k_2}(n^{k_2/n} - 1) \tag{12.19}$$

Compared with the F-ratios presented in Table 12.4, this criterion produces large changes in the F-ratios as the sample size n changes. The F-ratios Leamer's criterion implies are presented in Table 12.5.

12.9 Cross-Validation

One of the major criticisms of the different criteria for selection of regressors that we discussed in the preceding section is that a model we choose may be the best for the

---

[42]An early survey is in K. M. Gaver and M. S. Geisel, "Discriminating Among Alternative Models: Bayesian and Non-Bayesian Methods," in P. Zarembka (ed.), *Frontiers of Econometrics* (New York: Academic Press, 1974).

Table 12.5 Critical F-values implied by Bayesian posterior odds criterion

	$n - k$	5	10	50	100
$k_2 = 1$	$k = 1$	1.74	2.44	4.01	4.68
	3	1.48	2.18	3.89	4.60
	5	1.29	1.98	3.78	4.53
	10	0.99	1.62	3.53	4.37
	5% point of F	6.60	4.96	4.03	3.94
$k_2 = 3$	$k = 1$	2.42	3.08	4.34	4.90
	3	1.97	2.69	4.20	4.82
	5	1.66	2.40	4.07	4.74
	10	1.20	1.89	3.79	4.56
	5% point of F	5.41	3.71	2.79	2.70
$k_2 = 5$	$k = 1$	3.45	3.95	4.70	5.13
	3	2.67	3.36	4.54	5.05
	5	2.16	2.93	4.40	4.96
	10	1.47	2.23	4.07	4.76
	5% point of F	5.05	3.33	2.40	2.30

Source: E. E. Leamer, *Specification Searches* (New York: Wiley, 1978), p. 116.

period used in estimation but may not be the best when we use it for prediction in future periods. To handle this criticism, it is often suggested that we use only part of the data for the purpose of estimation and save the rest for the purpose of prediction and to check the adequacy of the model chosen. We estimate the different models using the first part and then use the estimated parameters to generate predictions for the second part. The model that minimizes the sum of squared prediction errors is then chosen as the best model.

This procedure of splitting the data into two parts — one for estimation and the other for prediction — is called *cross-validation*. Actually, we have two sets of prediction errors. The prediction errors for the first part (estimation period) are known as *within-sample* prediction errors. The sum of squares of these prediction errors is the usual residual sum of squares. The prediction errors from the second part are known as the *out-of-sample* prediction errors. Different criteria in cross-validation depend on different weights given to the sums of squares of these two sets of prediction errors. A criterion often used is to give equal weights to these two sets of prediction errors.

What the cross-validation procedure does is to impose a penalty for parameter instability. If the parameters are not stable between the estimation period and the prediction period, the sum of squared out-of-sample prediction errors will be large even if the sum of squared within-sample prediction errors is small. Thus the procedure of model selection by cross-validation implies choosing the model that minimizes: the usual residual sum of squares plus a penalty for parameter instability.

Instead of splitting the data into two sets and using one for estimation and the other for prediction, we can follow the procedure of using one observation at a time for prediction (and the remaining observations for estimation). That is, in fact, the idea behind "predicted residuals" discussed earlier in Section 12.4. There the sum of squares of the predicted residuals, PRESS, was suggested as a criterion for model choice. Note that at each stage $(n - 1)$ observations are within-sample (i.e., used for estimation) and the remaining observation is out-of-sample (i.e., used for prediction). PRESS is the sum of squares of out-of-sample prediction errors.

Instead of using PRESS (the sum of squares of predicted residuals) as a criterion for model choice, we can consider the sum of squares of studentized residuals as a criterion of model choice.[43] As discussed in Section 12.4, the studentized residual is just the predicted residual divided by its standard error. The sum of squares of studentized residuals can be denoted by SSSR and the sum of squares of predicted residuals as SSPR. This would be a better terminology, in keeping with the use of the term "residual" for an "estimated error." From the derivations in Section 12.3 we note that both SSPR and SSSR are weighted sums of squares of the least squares residuals $\hat{u}_i$. The $\overline{R}^2$ criterion also involves minimizing a weighted sum of squares of least squares residuals (we minimize $\sum \hat{u}_i^2/\text{d.f.}$). To be a valid criterion of model choice we should be able to show that the expected value of the quantity minimized is less for the true model than for the alternative models. If this is not the case, the criterion does not consistently select the true model. Leamer[44] shows that the $\overline{R}^2$ criterion, and the SSSR criterion, which minimizes the sum of squares of studentized residuals (this is Schmidt's SSPE criterion), satisfy this test and are valid criteria, but that the PRESS criterion and other criteria suggested in cross-validation are not valid by this test. Thus if one is interested in using predicted residuals for model choice, the best procedure appears to be not one of splitting the sample into two parts, but deriving studentized residuals (the SAS regression program gives them) and considering minimization of the sum of squares of studentized residuals (SSSR) as a criterion of model choice (i.e., use Schmidt's SSPE criterion).

12.10   Hausman's Specification Error Test

Hausman's specification error test[45] is a general and widely used test for the hypothesis of no misspecification in the model.

Let H_0 denote the null hypothesis that there is no misspecification and let H_1 denote the alternative hypothesis that there is a misspecification (of a particular type). For instance, if we consider the regression model

$$y = \beta x + u \tag{12.20}$$

in order to use the OLS procedure, we specify that x is independent of u. Thus the null and alternative hypotheses are:

$$H_0 : x \text{ and } u \text{ are independent}$$

$$H_1 : x \text{ and } u \text{ are not independent}$$

[43]This is the criterion proposed in Peter Schmidt, "Choosing Among Alternative Linear Regression Models," *Atlantic Economic Journal*, 1974, pp. 7–13.

[44]E. E. Leamer, "Model Choice and Specification Analysis," in Z. Griliches and M. D. Intrilligator (eds.), *Handbook of Econometrics*, Vol. 1 (Amsterdam: North-Holland, 1983), Chap. 5, pp. 285–330.

[45]J. A. Hausman, "Specification Tests in Econometrics," *Econometrica*, Vol. 46, No. 6, November 1978, pp. 1251–1271.

To implement Hausman's test, we have to construct two estimators $\hat{\beta}_0$ and $\hat{\beta}_1$, which have the following properties:

$\hat{\beta}_0$ is consistent and efficient under H_0 but is not consistent under H_1.
$\hat{\beta}_1$ is consistent under *both* H_0 and H_1 but is not efficient under H_0.

Then we consider the difference $\hat{q} = \hat{\beta}_1 - \hat{\beta}_0$. Hausman first shows that

$$\text{var}(\hat{q}) = V_1 - V_0$$

where $V_1 = \text{var}(\hat{\beta}_1)$ and $V_0 = \text{var}(\hat{\beta}_0)$, both variances being computed under H_0. Let $\hat{V}(\hat{q})$ be a consistent estimate of $\text{var}(\hat{q})$. Then we use

$$m = \frac{\hat{q}^2}{\hat{V}(\hat{q})}$$

as a χ^2-distribution with d.f. 1 to test H_0 against H_1. This is an asymptotic test.

We have considered only a single parameter β. In the general case where β is a vector of k parameters, V_1 and V_0 will be matrices, $\hat{\beta}_1$, $\hat{\beta}_0$, and $\hat{q}$ will all be vectors, and the Hausman test statistic is

$$m = \hat{\mathbf{q}}'[\hat{\mathbf{V}}(\hat{\mathbf{q}})]^{-1}\hat{\mathbf{q}}$$

which has (asymptotically) a χ^2-distribution with d.f. k.

Since a consideration of the k-parameter case involves vectors and matrices, we discuss the single-parameter case. The derivations in the k-parameter case are all similar.

To prove the result $\text{var}(\hat{q}) = V_1 - V_0$, we first have to prove the result that

$$\text{cov}(\hat{\beta}_0, \hat{q}) = 0$$

The proof proceeds as follows. Under H_0, both $\hat{\beta}_0$ and $\hat{\beta}_1$ are consistent estimates for β. Hence we get

$$\text{plim } \hat{q} = \text{plim } \hat{\beta}_1 - \text{plim } \hat{\beta}_0 = \beta - \beta = 0$$

Consider a new estimator for β defined by

$$\hat{d} = \hat{\beta}_0 + \lambda\hat{q}$$

where λ is any constant. Then plim $\hat{d} = \beta$. Thus $\hat{d}$ is a consistent estimator of β for all values of λ.

$$V(\hat{d}) = V_0 + \lambda^2 \text{ var}(\hat{q}) + 2\lambda \text{ cov}(\hat{\beta}_0, \hat{q}) \geq V_0$$

Since $\hat{\beta}_0$ is efficient. Thus

$$\lambda^2 \text{ var}(\hat{q}) + 2\lambda \text{ cov}(\hat{\beta}_0, \hat{q}) \geq 0 \tag{12.21}$$

for all values of λ. We will show that the relationship (12.21) can be satisfied for all values of λ only if $\text{cov}(\hat{\beta}_0, \hat{q}) = 0$.

Suppose that $\text{cov}(\hat{\beta}_0, \hat{q}) > 0$. Then by choosing λ negative and equal to $-\text{cov}(\hat{\beta}_0, \hat{q})/\text{var}(\hat{q})$, we can show that the relationship (12.21) is violated. Thus $\text{cov}(\hat{\beta}_0, \hat{q})$ is not greater than zero.

Similarly, suppose that $\text{cov}(\hat{\beta}_0, \hat{q}) < 0$. Then by choosing λ positive and equal to $-\text{cov}(\hat{\beta}_0, \hat{q})/\text{var}(\hat{q})$, we show that the relationship (12.21) is violated. Thus $\text{cov}(\hat{\beta}_0, \hat{q})$ cannot be greater than or less than zero. Hence we get $\text{cov}(\hat{\beta}_0, \hat{q}) = 0$.

Now since $\hat{\beta}_1 = \hat{\beta}_0 + \hat{q}$ and $\text{cov}(\hat{\beta}_0, \hat{q}) = 0$, we get

$$\text{var}(\hat{\beta}_1) = \text{var}(\hat{\beta}_0) + \text{var}(\hat{q})$$

or

$$\text{var}(\hat{q}) = \text{var}(\hat{\beta}_1) - \text{var}(\hat{\beta}_0) = V_1 - V_0$$

which is the result on which Hausman's test is based.

An Application: Testing for Errors in Variables or Exogeneity

Consider now the model given by equation (12.20). The model can be regarded as an errors in variables model (Chapter 11), where x is correlated with the error term u because it is an error-ridden explanatory variable. In this case our interest is in testing whether there is an error in this variable or not.

Alternatively, equation (12.20) can be regarded as one equation in a simultaneous equations model (Chapter 9) and x is correlated with u because it is an endogenous variable. We are interested in testing whether x is exogenous or endogenous. If x is not correlated with u, we are justified in estimating the equation by OLS.

Under H_1, $\hat{\beta}_0$ is not consistent. To get a consistent estimator for β we have to use the instrumental variable (IV) method. Let us denote the instrumental variable by z. Then the IV estimator is

$$\hat{\beta}_1 = \frac{\sum yz}{\sum xz} = \beta + \frac{\sum uz}{\sum xz} \qquad V_1 = \text{var}(\hat{\beta}_1) = \sigma^2 \frac{\sum z^2}{\left(\sum xz\right)^2}$$

$\hat{\beta}_1$ is consistent under both H_0 and H_1. It is, however, less efficient than $\hat{\beta}_0$, under H_0.

Defining $\hat{q} = \hat{\beta}_1 - \hat{\beta}_0$, we have

$$\text{var}(\hat{q}) = V_1 - V_0 = \sigma^2 \left[\frac{\sum z^2}{\left(\sum xz\right)^2} - \frac{1}{\sum x^2} \right]$$

$$= \frac{\sigma^2}{\sum x^2} \left[\frac{\sum x^2 \sum z^2}{\left(\sum xz\right)^2} - 1 \right] = \frac{\sigma^2}{\sum x^2} \left(\frac{1}{r^2} - 1 \right)$$

$$= V_0 \frac{1 - r^2}{r^2}$$

where r^2 is the squared correlation between x and the instrumental variable z.[46] The test statistic is

$$m = \frac{\hat{q}^2 r^2}{(1 - r^2)\hat{V}_0}$$

which we use as χ^2 with d.f. 1.

Some Illustrative Examples

As an illustration, let us consider the data on the Australian wine industry in Chapter 9 (Table 9.2). Let us consider the equation (all variables in log form)

$$Q_t = \alpha + \beta p_t^w + u_t$$

We are interested in testing the hypothesis that p_t^w is exogenous. The OLS estimator of β is

$$\beta_0 = \frac{1.78037}{0.507434} = 3.5085$$

Using the index of storage costs s as an instrumental variable, we get the IV estimator as

$$\hat{\beta}_1 = \frac{2.75474}{0.500484} = 5.4862$$

$$\hat{q} = \hat{\beta}_1 - \hat{\beta}_0 = 1.9777$$

The squared correlation coefficient between p_t^w and s_t is $r^2 = 0.408$. We also have

$$\hat{\sigma}^2 = 0.09217 \quad \text{and} \quad \hat{V}_0 = \frac{0.09217}{0.507434} = 0.18164$$

The test statistic is

$$m = \frac{(\hat{q}r)^2}{(1 - r^2)\hat{V}_0} = 14.84$$

This is significant at the 1% level (from the χ^2-tables with d.f. 1). Thus we cannot treat p^w as exogenous and we have to consider a simultaneous equations model.

Let us see what happens if we use per capita disposable income y_t as the instrumental variable. In this case we have

$$\hat{\beta}_1 = \frac{2.215}{0.4592} = 4.8236$$

$$r^2 = 0.624$$

$$\hat{q} = 4.8236 - 3.5085 = 1.3151$$

---

[46]Note that both V_1 and V_0 depend on σ^2. But when we get an estimate of var$(\hat{q})$, the estimate of σ^2 we use is the one obtained under H_0.

The test statistic is now

$$m = \frac{(1.3151)^2(0.624)}{0.376(0.18164)} = 15.80$$

Again, this is significant at the 1% level, indicating that we have to treat p^w as endogenous.

As yet another example, consider the demand and supply model for pork considered in Chapter 9 (data in Table 9.1). Let us consider the hypothesis that Q is exogenous in the demand function (normalized with respect to P):

$$P = \alpha + \beta Q + \gamma Y + u$$

The OLS estimate of β is

$$\hat{\beta} = -1.2518 \text{ with SE} = 0.1032$$

The 2SLS estimate of β is

$$\tilde{\beta} = -1.2165$$

Thus

$$\hat{q} = \tilde{\beta} - \hat{\beta} = 0.0353$$

$$\hat{V}_0 = (0.1032)^2 = 0.01065$$

The instrumental variable that is implied by the use of 2SLS is $\hat{Q}$, the predicted value of Q from the reduced form. The squared correlation between Q and $\hat{Q}$ is the R^2 from the reduced-form equation for Q, which is 0.898. Hence the test statistic is

$$m = \frac{(0.0353)^2(0.898)}{(1 - 0.898)(0.01065)} = 1.03$$

which is not significant even at the 25% level (from the χ^2-tables with d.f. 1).

Thus we can treat Q as exogenous and estimate the demand equation by OLS. Note that this was our conclusion in Section 9.3.

An Omitted Variable Interpretation of the Hausman Test

There is an alternative way of implementing the Hausman test. Returning to equation (12.20), let $\hat{x}$ be the predicted value of x from a regression of x on the instrumental variable z, and $\hat{v}$ the estimated residual. That is, $\hat{v} = x - \hat{x}$. Then estimate by OLS the equation

$$y = \beta x + \gamma \hat{x} + \varepsilon$$

or

$$y = \beta x + \gamma \hat{v} + \varepsilon$$

and test the hypothesis $\gamma = 0$. These equations are known as *expanded regressions*. This test is identically the same as the test based on the statistic m derived earlier.

We will not prove this result[47] but we will explicitly state what the OLS estimate $\hat{\gamma}$ will turn out to be. We have

$$\hat{\gamma} = \frac{\hat{\beta}_1 - \hat{\beta}_0}{1 - r^2} = \frac{\hat{q}}{1 - r^2}$$

where r^2 is the squared correlation between x and z. Also,

$$\text{var}(\hat{\gamma}) = \frac{V_0}{r^2(1 - r^2)}$$

Thus

$$\frac{\hat{\gamma}^2}{\text{var}(\hat{\gamma})} = \frac{\hat{q}^2 r^2}{(1 - r^2)V_0} = m$$

the statistic obtained earlier.

This omitted variable interpretation enables us to generalize the test to the case where we have more variables whose exogeneity we are interested in testing.

Suppose that one of the equations in a simultaneous equations model is

$$y_1 = \beta_2 y_2 + \beta_3 y_3 + \alpha_1 z_1 + u_1 \tag{12.22}$$

We want to test the hypothesis that y_2 and y_3 are exogenous (i.e., independent of u_1), the alternative hypothesis being that they are not. The variable z_1 is considered exogenous.

To apply the test, we need to have at least two instrumental variables, say z_2 and z_3. But there could be more in the system. Then what we do is regress y_2 and y_3 on the other exogenous variables in the system and obtain the predicted values $\hat{y}_2$ and $\hat{y}_3$. Now we estimate the *expanded regression equation*

$$y_1 = \beta_2 y_2 + \beta_3 y_3 + \alpha_1 z_1 + \gamma_2 \hat{y}_2 + \gamma_3 \hat{y}_3 + \varepsilon \tag{12.23}$$

by ordinary least squares and test the hypothesis $\gamma_2 = \gamma_3 = 0$ (by the methods described in Chapter 4). This is the Hausman test for exogeneity.

Let us define $\hat{v}_2 = y_2 - \hat{y}_2$ and $\hat{v}_3 = y_3 - \hat{y}_3$. Then, instead of equation (12.23), we can also estimate

$$y_1 = \beta_2 y_2 + \beta_3 y_3 + \alpha_1 z_1 + \gamma_2 \hat{v}_2 + \gamma_3 \hat{v}_3 + \varepsilon \tag{12.24}$$

by OLS and test the hypothesis $\gamma_2 = \gamma_3 = 0$.

This procedure applies *only* if we are testing the exogeneity of all the variables under question and does not apply for testing the exogeneity of a subset of these variables. For instance, in equation (12.22) suppose we assume that y_2 is endogenous and z_1 is exogenous. What we want to do is test the hypothesis that y_3 is exogenous. Now we cannot just estimate equations like (12.23) and (12.24) and just test $\gamma_3 = 0$. Nor does the equivalence between (12.23) and (12.24) apply anymore.[48]

---

[47]For a proof, see Hausman, "Specification Tests," p. 1261.

[48]This is pointed out in Alberto Holly, "A Simple Procedure for Testing Whether a Subset of Endogenous Variables Is Independent of the Disturbance Term in a Structural Equation," discussion paper, University of Lausanne, November 1982.

In this case we have to obtain the 2SLS estimates of β_3 under two assumptions:

1. y_3 *is exogenous.* Call this estimate $\hat{\beta}_3$ with variance V_0.
2. y_3 *is endogenous.* Call this estimate $\tilde{\beta}_3$ with variance V_1.

Then $\hat{q} = \tilde{\beta}_3 - \hat{\beta}_3$ and $\text{var}(\hat{q}) = V_1 - V_0$. We now apply the Hausman test as explained earlier. Note that both V_1 and V_0 depend on $\sigma^2 = \text{var}(u_1)$. However, when we get an estimate of $\text{var}(\hat{q})$ we have to use the estimate of σ^2 under H_0, that is, from the 2SLS estimation treating y_3 as exogenous.

The omitted variable method in this case is somewhat complicated, but consists of the following steps:

1. First we get the reduced-form residuals for the endogenous variables y_2 and y_3 as before. Call these residuals $\hat{v}_2$ and $\hat{v}_3$. However, we do not use these as the omitted variables. We construct linear combinations of these as explained in the next step.
2. Form the covariance matrix of these residuals and get its inverse. Denote this by

$$\begin{pmatrix} C_{22} & C_{23} \\ C_{32} & C_{33} \end{pmatrix}$$

In our simple case we have

$$C_{22} = \frac{\sum \hat{v}_3^2}{\Delta} \qquad C_{33} = \frac{\sum \hat{v}_2^2}{\Delta} \qquad C_{23} = C_{32} = -\frac{\hat{v}_2 \hat{v}_3}{\Delta}$$

where $\Delta = \sum \hat{v}_2^2 \sum \hat{v}_3^2 - (\sum \hat{v}_2 \hat{v}_3)^2$.
3. Define

$$x_2 = C_{22}\hat{v}_2 + C_{23}\hat{v}_3$$
$$x_3 = C_{32}\hat{v}_2 + C_{33}\hat{v}_3$$

These are the missing variables we use.
4. Estimate the following equation by OLS:

$$y_1 = \beta_2 y_2 + \beta_3 y_3 + \alpha_1 z_1 + \gamma_2 x_2 + \gamma_3 x_3 + \varepsilon$$

and test the hypothesis $\gamma_3 = 0$. This is the required test for the hypothesis that y_3 is exogenous.

The test is actually not very complicated. In fact, step 1 has to be used in any 2SLS estimation. Only step 2 involves matrix inversion. Once this is done, step 3 is easy and step 4 is just OLS estimation.

12.11   The Plosser–Schwert–White Differencing Test

The Plosser–Schwert–White (PSW) differencing test[49] is, like the Hausman test, a general test for model misspecification, but is applicable for time-series data only. The test involves estimation of the regression models in levels and in first differences. If the model is correctly specified, the estimators from the differenced and undifferenced models have the same probability limits and hence the results should corroborate one another. On the other hand, if there are specification errors, the differenced regression should lead to different results. The PSW test, like the Hausman test, is based on a comparison from the differenced and undifferenced regressions.

Davidson, Godfrey, and MacKinnon[50] show that, like the Hausman test, the PSW test is equivalent to a much simpler omitted variables test, the omitted variables being the sum of the lagged and one period forward values of the variables.

Thus if the regression equation we are considering is

$$y_t = \beta_1 x_{1t} + \beta_2 x_{2t} + u_t$$

the PSW test involves estimating the expanded regression equation

$$y_t = \beta_1 x_{1t} + \beta_2 x_{2t} + \gamma_1 z_{1t} + \gamma_2 z_{2t} + u_t$$

where

$$z_{1t} = x_{1,t+1} + x_{1,t-1}$$

$$z_{2t} = x_{2,t+1} + x_{2,t-1}$$

and testing the hypothesis $\gamma_1 = \gamma_2 = 0$ by the usual F-test.

If there are lagged dependent variables in the equation, the test needs a minor modification. Suppose that the model is

$$y_t = \beta_1 y_{t-1} + \beta_2 x_t + u_t$$

Now the omitted variables would be defined as

$$z_{1t} = y_t + y_{t-2}$$

and

$$z_{2t} = x_{t+1} + x_{t-1}$$

There is no problem with z_{2t} but z_{1t} would be correlated with the error term u_t because of the presence of y_t in it. The solution would be simply to transfer it to the left-hand side and write the expanded regression equation as

$$(1 - \gamma_1)y_t = \beta_1 y_{t-1} + \beta_2 x_t + \gamma_1 y_{t-2} + \gamma_2 z_{2t} + u_t$$

---

[49]C. I. Plosser, G. W. Schwert, and H. White, "Differencing as a Test of Specification," *International Economic Review*, October 1982, pp. 535–552.

[50]R. Davidson, L. G. Godfrey, and J. G. MacKinnon, "A Simplified Version of the Differencing Test," *International Economic Review*, October 1985, pp. 639–647.

This equation can be written as

$$y_t = \beta_1^* y_{t-1} + \beta_2^* x_t + \gamma_1^* y_{t-2} + \gamma_2^* z_{2t} + u_t^*$$

where all the starred parameters are the corresponding unstarred ones divided by $(1 - \gamma_1)$.

The PSW test now tests the hypothesis $\gamma_1^* = \gamma_2^* = 0$. Thus, in the case where the model involves the lagged dependent variable y_{t-1} as an explanatory variable, the only modification needed is that we should use y_{t-2} as the omitted variable, not $(y_t + y_{t-2})$. For the other explanatory variables, the corresponding omitted variables are defined as before. Note that it is only y_{t-1} that creates a problem, not higher order lags of y_t, like y_{t-2}, y_{t-3}, and so on.

12.12   Tests for Nonnested Hypotheses

Consider the problem of testing two hypotheses:

$$H_0: \quad y = \beta x + u_0 \quad u_0 \sim \text{IN}(0, \sigma_0^2) \tag{12.25}$$

$$H_1: \quad y = \gamma z + u_1 \quad u_1 \sim \text{IN}(0, \sigma_1^2) \tag{12.26}$$

The hypotheses are said to be *nonnested* since the explanatory variables in one of the hypotheses are not a subset of the explanatory variables in the other.

It is a common occurrence in economics that there are many competing economic theories trying to explain the same variable (consumption, investment, etc.), and the explanatory variables in the different theories contain nonoverlapping variables. An extreme example is the paper by Friedman and Meiselman[51] around which there was a considerable amount of controversy in the 1960s. The Keynesian and monetarist theories were formulated in their simplified form as

$$C_t = \alpha_0 + \beta_0 A_t + u_{0t} \quad \text{(Keynesian)}$$

$$C_t = \alpha_1 + \beta_1 M_t + u_{1t} \quad \text{(monetarist)}$$

where C_t = consumption expenditure in constant dollars
$\quad A_t$ = autonomous expenditure in constant dollars
$\quad M_t$ = money supply

The Davidson and MacKinnon Test

There have been several tests that have been suggested for testing such nonnested hypotheses.[52] The first such test is the Cox test. However, we will outline some simple

---

[51] M. Friedman and D. Meiselman, "The Relative Stability of Monetary Velocity and the Investment Multiplier in the U.S. 1897–1958," in *Stabilization Policies* (Commission on Money and Credit) (Englewood Cliffs, NJ: Prentice Hall, 1963).

[52] Two surveys of this extensive literature are: J. G. MacKinnon, "Model Specification Tests Against Non-nested Alternatives" (with discussion), *Econometric Reviews*, Vol. 2, 1983, pp. 85–158, and M. McAleer and M. H. Pesaran, "Statistical Inference in Non-nested Econometric Models," *Applied Mathematics and Computation*, 1986.

alternative and asymptotically equivalent tests suggested by Davidson and MacKinnon[53] that are easy to apply. Their test procedure for testing H_0 against H_1 (H_0 is the maintained hypothesis) is as follows:

1. Estimate equation (12.26) by OLS. Let $\hat{y}_1 = \hat{\gamma}z$ be the predicted value of y.
2. Estimate the regression equation

$$y = \beta x + \alpha \hat{y}_1 + u \tag{12.27}$$

and test the hypothesis $\alpha = 0$.

If the hypothesis is not rejected, then H_0 is not rejected by H_1. If the hypothesis is rejected, then H_0 is rejected by H_1.

A test of H_1 against H_0 would be based on analogous steps.

1. Estimate equation (12.25) by OLS. Let $\hat{y}_0 = \hat{\beta}x$ be the predicted value of y.
2. Estimate the regression equation

$$y = \gamma z + \delta \hat{y}_0 + v \tag{12.28}$$

and test the hypothesis $\delta = 0$.

If the hypothesis is not rejected, then H_1 is not rejected by H_0. If the hypothesis is rejected, then H_1 is rejected by H_0.

The outcome of these two tests can be summarized as follows:

Hypothesis: $\delta = 0$	Hypothesis: $\alpha = 0$	
	Not Rejected	Rejected
Not rejected	Both H_0 and H_1 are acceptable	H_1 is acceptable but H_0 is not
Rejected	H_0 is acceptable but H_1 is not	Neither H_0 nor H_1 is acceptable

The motivation behind the tests suggested by Davidson and MacKinnon is the following. The models given by H_0 and H_1 can be combined into a single model

$$y = (1 - \alpha)\beta x + \alpha(\gamma z) + u \tag{12.29}$$

testing $\alpha = 0$ versus $\alpha = 1$. However, there is no way of estimating β, γ, and α from this model. All we get are estimates of $(1 - \alpha)\beta$ and $\alpha\gamma$. Davidson and MacKinnon show that we can substitute $\hat{y} = \hat{\gamma}z$ for γz in equation (12.29) and then test $\alpha = 0$. They show that under H_0, $\hat{\alpha}$ from equation (12.27) is asymptotically $N(0, 1)$. They call this the J-test

[53]R. Davidson and J. G. MacKinnon, "Several Tests for Model Specification in the Presence of Alternative Hypotheses," *Econometrica*, Vol. 49, 1981, pp. 781–793. The survey paper by MacKinnon contains additional references to the papers by Davidson and MacKinnon.

(because α and β are estimated *jointly*). Note that the J-tests are one degree of freedom tests irrespective of the number of explanatory variables in H_0 and H_1.

The relationship between the J-test and optimum combination of forecasts is as follows. We have two forecasts of y from the two models (12.25) and (12.26). Call these $\hat{y}_0$ and $\hat{y}_1$, respectively. The two forecasts can be combined to produce a forecast with a smaller forecast error.[54] The combination can be written as

$$\hat{y} = (1 - \alpha)\hat{y}_0 + \alpha\hat{y}_1$$

The value of α that gives the minimum forecast error is

$$\alpha = \frac{\lambda_1^2 - \rho\lambda_1\lambda_2}{\lambda_1^2 + \lambda_2^2 - 2\rho\lambda_1\lambda_2}$$

where λ_1^2 and λ_2^2 are, respectively, the variances of the forecast errors $(y - \hat{y}_0)$ and $(y - \hat{y}_1)$ and ρ is the correlation between these forecast errors. Also,

$$\alpha \gtreqless 0 \quad \text{if and only if} \quad \frac{\lambda_1}{\lambda_2} \gtreqless \rho$$

Corresponding to the optimum combination of forecasts, equation (12.29) can also be written as

$$y = (1 - \alpha)\hat{y}_0 + \alpha\hat{y}_1 + v$$

where v is the error term. This can also be written as

$$y - \hat{y}_0 = \alpha(\hat{y}_1 - \hat{y}_0) + v$$

If we estimate this equation and the estimate of α is not significantly different from zero, we can say that H_1 does not add anything to explaining y over H_0. If α is significantly different from zero, H_1 explains y over and above H_0.

We will not pursue the extensions of the J-test here.[55] We will, however, discuss a few of the limitations.[56] One limitation of the test is that sometimes it rejects both H_0 and H_1 or accepts H_0 and H_1. Although this conclusion suggests that we should go back and examine both models, in many cases we would like to have some ranking of the models.

An alternative procedure is to embed the two models given by H_0 and H_1 into a comprehensive model

$$y = \beta x + \gamma z + u \tag{12.30}$$

---

[54]See C. W. J. Granger and P. Newbold, *Forecasting Economic Time Series*, 2nd ed. (New York: Academic Press, 1986), pp. 266–267, on combination of forecasts.

[55]McAleer and Pesaran, "Statistical Inference." G. R. Fisher and M. McAleer, "Alternative Procedures and Associated Tests of Significance for Non-nested Hypotheses," *Journal of Econometrics*, Vol. 16, 1981, pp. 103–119, suggest what is known as the *JA* test. Unlike the *J*-test, which is asymptotic, the *JA* test is a small-sample test (if x and z are fixed in repeated samples).

[56]A good review and discussion of the limitations of nonnested tests is L. G. Godfrey, "On the Use of Misspecification Checks and Tests of Non-nested Hypotheses in Empirical Econometrics," *Economic Journal* (supplement), 1985, pp. 69–81.

and test H_0 by testing $\gamma = 0$, test H_1 by testing $\beta = 0$. When there is more than one variable in x and z, these tests will be F-tests. This is in contrast to the J-test, which is a one degree of freedom test whatever the number of explanatory variables in H_0 and H_1.

The Encompassing Test

At first sight it would appear that there is no relationship between the F-tests and the J-test. This is not so. Mizon and Richard[57] suggest a more general test called the "encompassing test" of which the F-test and J-test are special cases. The encompassing principle is based on the idea that a model builder should analyze whether his model can account for salient features of rival models.[58] The encompassing test is a formulation of this principle. If your model is specified by H_0 and the rival model by H_1, a formal test of H_0 against H_1 is to compare $\hat{\gamma}$ and $\hat{\sigma}_1^2$ obtained under H_1 from equation (12.26), with the probability limits of these parameters under your hypothesis H_0. Comparing $\hat{\gamma}$ with plim $\hat{\gamma}|H_0$ gives the *mean encompassing test*. Comparing $\hat{\sigma}_1^2$ with plim $\hat{\sigma}_1^2|H_0$ gives the *variance encompassing test*. Mizon and Richard show that the F-test is a mean encompassing test and the J-test is a variance encompassing test. This explains why the J-test is a one degree of freedom test no matter how many explanatory variables there are in the models given by H_0 and H_1. The complete encompassing test (CET) suggested by Mizon and Richard is a *joint* test that compares $\hat{\gamma}_1$ and $\hat{\sigma}_1^2$ with their probability limits under H_0. A discussion of this joint test is beyond the scope of this book. Further, there is not much empirical evidence on it. The F-test and J-test, on the other hand, can be very easily implemented.

In summary, to test the nonnested hypothesis H_0 against H_1, we need to apply two tests:

1. The J-test, testing $\alpha = 0$ based on equation (12.27).
2. The F-test, testing $\gamma = 0$ in the comprehensive model (12.30).

As to how these tests perform in small samples, some experimental evidence suggests that the one degree of freedom J-test is better than the F-test at rejecting the false model. However, this is no consolation because it has also been found that the J-test tends to reject the true model too frequently with the estimated small-sample significance levels being so large that it is often difficult to justify asymptotically valid critical values.[59] Yet another shortcoming of the nonnested tests is that if both H_0 and H_1 are false, these tests are inferior to standard diagnostic tests (discussed in earlier sections of this chapter).[60]

---

[57] G. E. Mizon and J. F. Richard, "The Encompassing Principle and Its Application to Testing Non-nested Hypotheses," *Econometrica*, Vol. 54, 1986, pp. 657–678.

[58] J. E. H. Davidson and D. F. Hendry, "Interpreting Econometric Evidence: The Behavior of Consumers' Expenditures in the U.K.," *European Economic Review*, Vol. 16, 1981, pp. 179–198.

[59] Godfrey, "On the Use," p. 76.

[60] Godfrey, "On the Use," p. 79. Godfrey quotes N. R. Erickson's Ph.D. thesis (1982) at the London School of Economics, which provides a numerical example in which F and one degree of freedom tests reject only one of the two competing models, but misspecification tests decisively reject H_0, H_1, and the comprehensive model.

What all this suggests is that in testing nonnested hypotheses, one should use the J-test with higher significance levels and supplement it with the F-test on the comprehensive model and standard diagnostic tests.

A Basic Problem in Testing Nonnested Hypotheses

The specification implied by equations (12.25) and (12.26) does not by itself enable us to make a valid comparison of the two models. In fact, this is the problem with testing nonnested models. Equation (12.25) specifies the conditional distribution of y *given* x. Similarly, equation (12.26) specifies the conditional distribution of y *given* z. How can we compare these two conditional distributions unless the role of z under H_0 and the role of x under H_1 are specified? What we are given are two noncomparable conditional distributions. H_0 does not specify anything about the relationship between y and z. H_1 does not specify anything about the relationship between y and x. Thus to compare the two models given by (12.25) and (12.26), we should be able to derive the conditional distributions of $f(y|x)$ and $g(y|z)$ under *both* H_0 and H_1. To do this we have to supplement equations (12.25) and (12.26) by more equations. This is what is done by Mizon and Richard.

Hypothesis Testing Versus Model Selection as a Research Strategy

We have discussed several examples where the choice between different models is made on the basis of hypothesis tests. There is one major problem with this: the use of common significance levels (1%, 5%) in the hypothesis tests, which is arbitrary. We have discussed this problem in Section 12.8. Hence a better strategy is to use model selection criteria.[61] As noted in Section 12.8, in the problem of selection of regressors, the model selection criteria imply the use of significance levels that are not the same for all sample sizes and are different from the usual 1% and 5% levels.

Summary

1. Diagnostic tests are tests that "diagnose" specific problems with the model we are estimating. The least squares residuals can be used to diagnose the problems of heteroskedasticity, autocorrelation, omission of relevant variables, and ARCH effects in errors (see Section 12.2). Tests for heteroskedasticity and autocorrelation have been discussed in Chapters 5 and 6, respectively. To test for omitted variables, we first estimate the equation by OLS and use $\hat{y}_t^2$ and higher powers of $\hat{y}_t$ as additional variables, reestimate the equation, and test that the coefficients of these added variables are zero. A test based on a regression of $\hat{u}_t$, the estimated residual on $\hat{y}_t^2$ and higher powers of $\hat{y}_t$ is not a valid

[61] This argument has been elaborated recently in C. Granger, M. L. King, and H. White, "Comments on Testing Economic Theories and the Use of Model Selection Criteria," *Journal of Econometrics*, Vol. 67, 1995, pp. 173–188.

test. To test for ARCH effects, we estimate the regression

$$\hat{u}_t^2 = \gamma_0 + \gamma_1 \hat{u}_{t-1}^2 + e_t$$

and test $\gamma_1 = 0$.

2. There are two problems with the least squares residuals. They are heteroskedastic and autocorrelated even if the true errors are independent and have a common variance of σ^2 (see Section 12.3). To solve these problems, some alternative residuals have been suggested (see Section 12.4). Two such residuals, which are uncorrelated and have a common variance, are the BLUS residuals and recursive residuals. The BLUS residuals are more difficult to compute than the recursive residuals; moreover, in tests of heteroskedasticity and autocorrelation, their performance is not as good as that of least squares residuals. Hence we consider only recursive residuals. Two other types of residuals are the predicted residuals and studentized residuals. Both of these are, like the least squares residuals, heteroskedastic and autocorrelated. However, some statisticians have found the predicted residuals useful in choosing between regression models and the studentized residuals in the detection of outliers. The predicted residuals, studentized residuals, and recursive residuals can all be computed using the dummy variable method.

3. The usual approach to outliers based on least squares residuals involves looking at the OLS residuals, deleting the observations with large residuals, and reestimating the equation. During recent years an alternative criterion has been suggested. This is based on a criterion called DFFITS which measures the change in the fitted value $\hat{y}$ of y that results from dropping a particular observation. Further, we do not drop outliers. We merely see that their influence is minimized. This is what is known as bounded influence estimation (Section 12.5). The SAS regression program computes DFFITS.

4. According to Leamer, the process of model building involves several types of specification searches. These can be classified under the headings: hypothesis-testing search, interpretive search, simplification search, proxy variable search, data selection search, and post-data model construction.

5. Hendry argues that most of empirical econometric work starts with very simplified models and that not enough diagnostic tests are applied to check whether something is wrong with the maintained model. His suggested strategy is to start with a very general model and then progressively simplify it by applying some data-based simplification tests. (The arguments for this are discussed in Section 12.6.)

6. A special problem in model selection that we often encounter is that of selection of regressors. Several criteria have been suggested in the literature: the maximum $\overline{R}^2$ criterion and the predictive criteria PC, C_p, and S_p. These criteria are summarized in Section 12.7. There is, however, some difference in these criteria. In the case of the maximum $\overline{R}^2$ criterion what we are trying to do is pick the "true" model assuming that one of the models considered is the "true" one. In the case of prediction criteria, we are interested in parsimony and we would like to omit some of the regressors if this improves the MSE of prediction. For this problem the question is whether or not we need to assume the existence of a true model. For the PC and C_p criteria we need to assume the existence of a true model. For the S_p criterion we do not. For this reason the S_p criterion appears to be the most preferable among these criteria.

7. In Section 12.8 we discuss the critical F-ratios implied by the different criteria for selection of regressors. We show that they stand in the relation

$$F(\overline{R}^2) < 1 < F(\text{PC}) < F(C_p) < 2 < F(S_p)$$

We also present the F-ratios implied by Leamer's posterior odds analysis. This method implies that the critical F-ratios used should be higher for higher sample sizes. For most sample sizes frequently encountered, F-ratios are > 2, which is another argument against $\overline{R}^2$ criterion and the PC and C_p criteria.

8. Cross-validation methods are often used to choose between different models. These methods depend on splitting the data into two parts: one for estimation and the other for prediction. The model that minimizes the sum of squared prediction errors is chosen as the best model. A better procedure than splitting the data into two parts is to leave out one observation at a time for prediction, derive the studentized residuals (the SAS regression program gives these), and use the sum of squares of the studentized residuals as a criterion of model choice.

9. A general test for specification errors that is easy to use is the Hausman test. Let H_0 be the hypothesis of no specification error and H_1 the alternative hypothesis that there is a specification error (of a particular type). We compute two estimators $\hat{\beta}_0$ and $\hat{\beta}_1$ of the parameter β. $\hat{\beta}_0$ is consistent *and* efficient under H_0 but is not consistent under H_1. $\hat{\beta}_1$ is consistent under both H_0 *and* H_1 but is not efficient under H_0. If $d = \hat{\beta}_1 - \hat{\beta}_0$, then $V(d) = V(\hat{\beta}_1) - V(\hat{\beta}_0)$. Hausman's test depends on comparing d with $V(d)$. If we are interested in testing for errors in variables or for exogeneity, Hausman's test reduces to a test of omitted variables.

10. Another general specification test (applicable in time-series models) is the PSW differencing test. In this test we compare the estimators from levels and first difference equations. The idea is that if the model is correctly specified, the estimates we get should not be widely apart. This test can also be viewed as an omitted variable test (Section 12.11).

11. Very often, the comparison of two economic theories implies the testing of two nonnested hypotheses. The earliest test for this is the Cox test, but the alternative (and asymptotically equivalent) J-test is easier to apply. It can also be viewed as an omitted variable test. There are, however, some conceptual problems with nonnested tests. The two hypotheses H_0 and H_1 specify two conditional distributions with different conditioning variables [e.g., $f(y|x)$ and $g(y|z)$] and it does not really make sense to compare them. A proper way is to derive the conditional distributions $f(y|x)$ and $g(y|z)$ under both H_0 and H_1 and compare them, that is, we have to have the same conditioning variables under both hypotheses. This is the idea behind the encompassing test. What it amounts to is supplementing the J-test with an F-test based on a comprehensive model.

Exercises

1. Explain the meaning of each of the following terms:
   (**a**) Least squares residual.
   (**b**) Predicted residual.

(c) Studentized residual.
(d) Recursive residual.
(e) BLUS residual.
(f) DFFITS.
(g) Bounded influence estimation.
(h) ARCH errors.
(i) Post-data model construction.
(j) Overparametrization with data-based simplification.
(k) Posterior odds ratio.
(l) Cross-validation.
(m) Selection of regressors.
(n) Diagnostic checking.
(o) Specification testing.
(p) Hausman's test.
(q) J-test.
(r) Encompassing test.
(s) Differencing test.

2. Examine whether the following statements are true, false, or uncertain. Give a short explanation. If a statement is not true in general but is true under some conditions, state the conditions.

(a) Since the least squares residuals are heteroskedastic and autocorrelated, even when the true errors are independent and homoskedastic, tests for homoskedasticity and serial independence based on least squares residuals are useless.

(b) There is a better chance of detecting outliers with predicted residuals or studentized residuals than with least squares residuals.

(c) In tests of significance we should not use a constant level of significance. The significance level should be a decreasing function of the sample size.

(d) To test for omitted variables, all we have to do is get some proxies for them, regress the least squares residual $\hat{u}_t$ on the proxies, and test whether the coefficients of these proxies are zero.

(e) The procedure of estimating the regression equation

$$\hat{u}_t^2 = \gamma_0 + \gamma_1 \hat{u}_{t-1}^2$$

where $\hat{u}_t$ are the least squares residuals, does not necessarily test for ARCH effect.

(f) The $\overline{R}^2$ criterion of deciding whether to retain or delete certain regressors in an equation implies using a 5% significance level for testing that the coefficients of these regressors are zero.

(g) The criteria for selection of regressors proposed by Amemiya, Hocking, and Mallows imply using a higher significance level for testing the coefficients of regressors than the $\overline{R}^2$ criterion.

(h) The $\overline{R}^2$, C_p, and PC criteria for selection of regressors depend on the assumption that one of the models considered is a "true" model, whereas the S_p criterion does not. Hence given the choice between these criteria, we should use only the S_p criterion.

(i) The maximum $\overline{R}^2$ criterion and the predictive criteria PC, C_p, and S_p for selection of regressors are not really comparable since they answer different questions.

(j) For comparing different models we should always save part of the sample for prediction purposes.

(k) In the model

$$y_1 = \beta_2 y_2 + \beta_3 y_3 + \gamma_1 x_1 + u_1$$

where x_1 is exogenous, to test whether y_2 and y_3 are endogenous, we estimate the equation

$$y_1 = \beta_2 y_2 + \beta_3 y_3 + \gamma_1 x_1 + \alpha_2 \hat{v}_2 + \alpha_3 \hat{v}_3 + w$$

($\hat{v}_2$ and $\hat{v}_3$ are the estimated residuals from the reduced form equations for y_2 and y_3).

(l) In the model in part (k), if x_1 is specified as exogenous and y_2 as endogenous, to test whether y_3 is endogenous, we estimate the equation

$$y_1 = \beta_2 y_2 + \beta_3 y_3 + \gamma_1 x_1 + \alpha_3 \hat{v}_3 + w$$

and test $\alpha_3 = 0$.

3. Comment on the following: In a study on the demand for money, an economist regressed real cash balances on permanent income. To test whether the interest rate has been omitted, she regressed the residual from this regression on the interest rate and found that the coefficient was not significantly different from zero. She therefore concluded that the interest rate does not belong in the demand for money function.

4. Explain how each of the following tests can be considered as a test for the coefficients of some extra variables added to the original equation:
   (a) Test for serial correlation.
   (b) Test for omitted variables.
   (c) Test for errors in variables.
   (d) Test for exogeneity.
   (e) *J*-test.
   (f) PSW differencing test.
In each case explain how you would interpret the results of the test and the actions you would take.

Appendix to Chapter 12

(1) Least Squares Residuals

We have $\hat{y} = X(X'X)^{-1}X'y = Hy$. $H = (h_{ij})$ is known as the *hat matrix*. The least square residuals are $\hat{u} = (I - H)y = (I - H)u$. This gives equation (12.1). $\text{Var}(\hat{u}) = (I - H)\sigma^2$ since $I - H$ is idempotent. Hence $\text{var}(\hat{u}_i) = (1 - h_i)\sigma^2$, which is equation (12.3) and $\text{cov}(\hat{u}_i, \hat{u}_j) = -h_{ij}\sigma^2$. Thus the least squares residuals are heteroskedastic and correlated.

(2) The $\overline{R}^2$ Criterion

The $\overline{R}^2$ criterion or minimum $\hat{\sigma}^2$ criterion for the choice of models is based on the following result. Suppose that:

$\mathbf{y} = \mathbf{X}\boldsymbol{\beta} + \mathbf{u}$ is the true model. $\mathbf{X}$ is $n \times k$.
$\mathbf{y} = \mathbf{Z}\boldsymbol{\delta} + \mathbf{v}$ is the misspecified model. $\mathbf{Z}$ is $n \times r$.

We estimate the misspecified model. Consider the estimate of the residual variance from this model. It is

$$\tilde{\sigma}^2 = \frac{1}{n-r}\mathbf{y}'\mathbf{N}\mathbf{y} \quad \text{where } \mathbf{N} = \mathbf{I} - \mathbf{Z}(\mathbf{Z}'\mathbf{Z})^{-1}\mathbf{Z}'$$

Since $\mathbf{y} = \mathbf{X}\boldsymbol{\beta} + \mathbf{u}$ and $E(\mathbf{u}\mathbf{u}') = \mathbf{I}\sigma^2$, we have $\mathbf{y}'\mathbf{N}\mathbf{y} = (\mathbf{X}\boldsymbol{\beta} + \mathbf{u})'\mathbf{N}(\mathbf{X}\boldsymbol{\beta} + \mathbf{u}) = \boldsymbol{\beta}'\mathbf{X}'\mathbf{N}\mathbf{X}\boldsymbol{\beta} + \mathbf{u}'\mathbf{N}\mathbf{u} + 2\boldsymbol{\beta}'\mathbf{X}'\mathbf{N}\mathbf{u}$. Since $E(\mathbf{u}) = 0$ the last term has expectation zero. Also, $E(\mathbf{u}'\mathbf{N}\mathbf{u}) = (n-r)\sigma^2$ since $\mathbf{N}$ is idempotent of rank $(n-r)$. Hence we get $E(\tilde{\sigma}^2) = \sigma^2 + 1/(n-r)\,\boldsymbol{\beta}'\mathbf{X}'\mathbf{N}\mathbf{X}\boldsymbol{\beta}$. Since the second term in the expression is ≥ 0, we have

$$E(\tilde{\sigma}^2) \geq \sigma^2$$

Thus the estimate of the error variance from the misspecified equation is upward biased. This is the basis of what is known as the "minimum σ^2" or the "maximum $\tilde{R}^2$" rule. The rule says that if we are considering some alternative regression models, we should choose the one with the minimum estimated error variance. The idea behind it is that "on the average," the misspecified model has a larger estimated error variance that the "true" model. Of course, the suggested rule is based on the assumption that one of the models being considered is the "true" model. It should be noted, however, that $E(\tilde{\sigma}^2) = \sigma^2$ even for a misspecified model if $\mathbf{X}'\mathbf{N} = 0$. This will be the case if $\mathbf{Z}$ consists of the variables $\mathbf{X}$ and any number of irrelevant variables. This does not make these models any better than models with a few omitted variables for which $E(\hat{\sigma}) > \sigma^2$.

The preceding discussion shows that there are some drawbacks in choosing between models on the basis of estimated error variance. Hence some alternative criteria in terms of estimated mean-squared error of prediction have been suggested. These criteria, called C_p, PC, S_p, have been discussed in Section 12.7.

13 Introduction to Time-Series Analysis

What is in this Chapter?

This chapter discusses the basic time-series models: autoregressive (AR) and moving average (MA) models, stationary and nonstationary time series, and the Box–Jenkins approach to time-series modeling. Some R^2 measures applicable in evaluating goodness of fit in time-series models are also discussed.

13.1 Introduction

A *time series* is a sequence of numerical data in which each item is associated with a particular instant in time. One can quote numerous examples: monthly unemployment, weekly measures of money supply, M_1 and M_2, daily closing prices of stock indices, and so on. In fact with the current progress in computer technology we have daily series on interest rates, the hourly "telerate" interest rate index, and stock prices by the minute (or even second). A cartoon in the *New Yorker* magazine shows a digital display at a bank:

Time: 11.23
Temperature: 83
Interest rate: 8.62

An analysis of a single sequence of data is called *univariate time-series analysis*. An analysis of several sets of data for the same sequence of time periods is called *multivariate time-series analysis* or, more simply, *multiple time-series analysis* (e.g., an analysis on the basis of monthly data, the relationships among unemployment, price level, money supply, etc., falls under multiple time-series analysis). The purpose of time-series analysis is to study the *dynamics or temporal structure* of the data.

For a long time there has been very little communication between econometricians and time-series analysts. Econometricians have emphasized economic theory and a study of contemporaneous relationships. Lagged variables were introduced but not in any systematic way, and no serious attempts were made to study the temporal structure of the data. Theories were imposed on the data even when the temporal structure of the data was not in conformity with the theories. The time-series analysts, on the other hand, did not believe in economic theories and thought that they were better off allowing the data to determine the model. Since the mid-1970s these two approaches — the time-series approach and the econometric approach — have been converging. Econometricians now use some of the basic elements of time-series analysis in checking the specification of their econometric models, and some economic theories have influenced the direction of time-series work.

13.2 Two Methods of Time-Series Analysis: Frequency Domain and Time Domain

Time-series analysis can be roughly divided into two types of methods: *frequency domain* methods and *time domain* methods. In this chapter we discuss time domain methods only. We shall, however, explain what these two methods are.

In models underlying the frequency domain analysis, the time series X_t is expressed as the sum of independently varying cosine and sine curves with random amplitudes. We thus write X_t as

$$X_t = \mu + \sum_j [Y_j \cos(2\pi f_j t) + Z_j \sin(2\pi f_j t)]$$

where Y's and Z's are uncorrelated random variables with zero expectations and variances $\sigma^2(f_j)$, and the summation is over all frequencies. The frequencies $f_1, f_2, f_3, \ldots$ are equally spaced and separated by a small interval Δf. The purpose of the analysis is to see how the variance of X_t is distributed among oscillations of various frequencies. The technique of analysis is called *spectral analysis*.

Time domain methods are based on direct modeling of the lagged relationships between a series and its past. The methods are similar to the type of analysis discussed in earlier chapters and involve fitting of linear autoregressions and cross-regressions. In any case it would be more difficult for beginning students to understand the spectral methods. Hence this introductory chapter on time series deals with time domain methods only.

13.3 Stationary and Nonstationary Time Series

From a theoretical point of view a time series is a collection of random variables $\{X_t\}$. Such a collection of random variables ordered in time is called a *stochastic process*. The word *stochastic* has a Greek origin and means "pertaining to chance." If it is a continuous variable, it is customary to denote the random variables by $X(t)$, and if t is a discrete variable, it is customary to denote them by X_t. An example of the continuous variable $X(t)$ is the recording of an electrocardiogram. Examples of discrete random variables X_t are the data on unemployment, money supply, closing stock prices, and so on, that we mentioned earlier. We will not go into the theory of stochastic processes here in great detail. We will just outline those elements that are necessary for time-series analysis. Furthermore, we will be considering discrete processes only, and so we shall use the notation X_t or $X(t)$ interchangeably.

The random variables $\{X_t\}$ are, in general, not independent. Furthermore, we have just a sample of size 1 on each of the random variables (e.g., if we say that the unemployment rate at the end of this week is a random variable, we have just one observation on this particular random variable). There is no way of getting another observation, so we have what is called a *single realization*. These two features—dependence and lack of replication—compel us to specify some highly restrictive models for the statistical structure of the stochastic process.

Strict Stationarity

One way of describing a stochastic process is to specify the joint distribution of the variables X_t. This is quite complicated and not usually attempted in practice. Instead, what is usually done is that we define the first and second moments of the variables X_t. These are:

1. The mean $\mu(t) = E(X_t)$.
2. The variance $\sigma^2(t) = \text{var}(X_t)$.
3. The autocovariances $\gamma(t_1, t_2) = \text{cov}(X_{t1}, X_{t2})$.

When $t_1 = t_2 = t$, the autocovariance is just $\sigma^2(t)$. One important class of stochastic processes is that of *stationary* stochastic processes. Corresponding to these we have the concept of stationary time series. A time series is said to be *strictly stationary* if the joint distribution of any set of n observations $X(t_1), X(t_2), \ldots, X(t_n)$ is the same as the joint distribution of $X(t_1 + k), X(t_2 + k), \ldots, X(t_n + k)$ for all n and k.

The definition above of strict stationarity holds for all values of n. Substituting $n = 1$, we get $\mu(t) = \mu$ a constant and $\sigma^2(t) = \sigma^2$ a constant for all t. Furthermore, if we substitute $n = 2$, we get the result that the joint distribution of $X(t_1)$ and $X(t_2)$ is the same as that of $X(t_1 + k)$ and $X(t_2 + k)$. Writing $t_1 + k = t_2$, we see that this is the same as the distribution of $X(t_2)$ and $X(t_2 + k)$. Thus, it just depends on the difference $(t_2 - t_1)$, which is called the *lag*. Hence, we can write the autocovariance function $\gamma(t_1, t_2)$ as $\gamma(k)$ where $k = t_2 - t_1$ the lag. Thus $\gamma(k) = \text{cov}[X(t), X(t + k)]$ is the autocovariance coefficient at lag k. $\gamma(k)$ is called the *autocovariance function* and will be abbreviated as *acvf*. $\gamma(0)$ is, of course, the variance of σ^2.

Since the autocovariance coefficients depend on the units of measurement of $X(t)$, it is convenient to consider the autocorrelations that are free of the units of measurement. Since $\text{var } X(t) = \text{var } X(t + k) = \sigma^2 = \gamma(0)$, we have the autocorrelation coefficient $\rho(k)$ at lag k as

$$\rho(k) = \frac{\gamma(k)}{\gamma(0)}$$

$\rho(k)$ is called the *autocorrelation function* and will be abbreviated as *acf*. A plot of $\rho(k)$ against k is called a *correlogram*.

Weak Stationarity

For a strictly stationary time series the distribution of $X(t)$ is independent of t. Thus it is not just the mean and variance that are constant. All higher order moments are independent of t. So are all higher order moments of the joint distribution of any combinations of the variables $X(t_1), X(t_2), X(t_3), \ldots$ In practice this is a very strong assumption, and it is useful to define stationarity in a less restrictive way. This definition is in terms of first and second moments only.

A time series is said to be *weakly stationary* if its mean is constant and its *acvf* depends only on the lag, that is,

$$E[X(t)] = \mu \quad \text{and} \quad \text{cov}[X(t), X(t+k)] = \gamma(k)$$

No assumptions are made about higher order moments. Alternative terms used for this weakly stationary time series are *wide-sense stationary, covariance stationary*, or *second-order stationary*.

If $X(t_1), X(t_2), \ldots, X(t_n)$ follow a multivariate normal distribution, since the multivariate normal distribution is completely characterized by the first and second moments, the two concepts of strict stationarity and weak stationarity are equivalent. For other distributions this is not so. In Figure 13.1 we show the graph of a stationary time series. It is the graph of X_t where $X_t = 0.7X_{t-1} + \varepsilon_t$ and $\varepsilon_t \sim \text{IN}(5, 1)$. Because of the assumption of normality, this time series is strongly stationary.

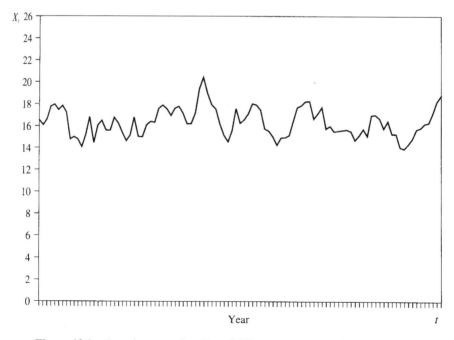

Figure 13.1   A stationary series. $X_t = 0.7X_{t-1} + \varepsilon_t$; $\varepsilon_t \sim \text{IN}(5, 1)$; $X_0 = 16.7$

Properties of Autocorrelation Function

There are two important points to note about the autocorrelation function *acf*. These are the following:

1. The *acf* is an *even* function of the lag k [i.e., $\rho(k) = \rho(-k)$]. This follows from the result

$$\gamma(k) = \text{cov}(X_t, X_{t+k}) = \text{cov}(X_{t-k}, X_t) \quad \text{because of stationarity} = \gamma(-k)$$

2. For a given *acf*, there will be only one normal process. But it is possible to find several nonnormal processes that have the same *acf*. Jenkins and Watts[1] give an example of two different stochastic processes that have the same *acf*.

Nonstationarity

In time-series analysis we do not confine ourselves to the analysis of stationary time series. In fact, most of the time series we encounter are *nonstationary*. A simple nonstationary time-series model is $X_t = \mu_t + e_t$, where the mean μ_t is a function of time and e_t is a weakly stationary series. μ_t, for example, could be a linear function of t (a linear trend) or a quadratic function of t (a parabolic trend). In Figure 13.2 we show the graph of a nonstationary time series. It is clear that apart from a linear trend, holiday season peaks dominate the movements in the series.

13.4 Some Useful Models for Time Series

In this section we discuss several different types of stochastic processes that are useful in modeling time series: (1) a purely random process, (2) a random walk, (3) a moving average (MA) process, (4) an autoregressive (AR) process, (5) an autoregressive moving average (ARMA) process, and (6) an autoregressive integrated moving average (ARIMA) process.

Purely Random Process

This is a discrete process $\{X_t\}$ consisting of a sequence of mutually independent identically distributed random variables. It has a constant mean and a constant variance and the *acvf* is

$$\gamma(k) = \text{cov}(X_t, X_{t+k}) = 0 \quad \text{for } k \neq 0$$

The *acf* is given by

$$\rho(k) = \begin{cases} 1 & \text{for } k = 0 \\ 0 & \text{for } k \neq 0 \end{cases}$$

A purely random process is also called *white noise*.

---

[1]G. M. Jenkins and D. G. Watts, *Spectral Analysis and Its Applications* (San Francisco: Holden-Day, 1968), p. 170.

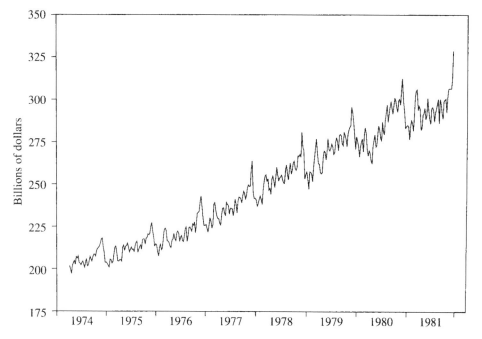

Figure 13.2 Weekly average total transactions deposits component of M_1 for May 15, 1974–January 6, 1982. *Source:* D. A. Pierce, M. R. Grupe, and W. P. Cleveland, "Seasonal Adjustment of the Weekly Monetary Aggregates," *Journal of Business and Economics Statistics*, Vol. 2, 1984, p. 264

Random Walk

This is a process often used to describe the behavior of stock prices (although there are some dissidents who disagree with this random walk theory). Suppose that $\{\varepsilon_t\}$ is a purely random series with mean μ and variance σ^2. Then a process $\{X_t\}$ is said to be a random walk if

$$X_t = X_{t-1} + \varepsilon_t$$

Let us assume that X_0 is equal to zero. Then the process evolves as follows:

$$X_1 = \varepsilon_1$$

$$X_2 = X_1 + \varepsilon_2 = \varepsilon_1 + \varepsilon_2 \quad \text{and so on}$$

We have by successive substitution

$$X_t = \sum_{i=1}^{t} \varepsilon_i$$

Hence $E(X_t) = t\mu$ and $\mathrm{var}(X_t) = t\sigma^2$. Since the mean and variance change with t, the process is nonstationary, but its first difference is stationary. Referring to share prices, this says that the changes in a share price will be a purely random process.

Moving Average Process

Suppose that $\{\varepsilon_t\}$ is a purely random process with mean zero and variance σ^2. Then a process $\{X_t\}$ defined by

$$X_t = \beta_0 \varepsilon_t + \beta_1 \varepsilon_{t-1} + \cdots + \beta_m \varepsilon_{t-m}$$

is called a moving average process of order m and is denoted by MA(m). Since the ε's are unobserved variables, we scale them so that $\beta_0 = 1$. Since $E(\varepsilon_t) = 0$ for all t, we have $E(X_t) = 0$. Also, $\mathrm{var}(X_t) = \left(\sum_{i=0}^{m} \beta_i^2\right)\sigma^2$ since the ε_i are independent with a common variance σ^2. Further, writing out the expressions for X_t and X_{t-k} in terms of the ε's and picking up the common terms (since the ε's are independent), we get

$$\gamma(k) = \mathrm{cov}(X_t, X_{t-k})$$

$$= \begin{cases} \sigma^2 \sum_{i=0}^{m-k} \beta_i \beta_{i+k} & \text{for } k = 0, 1, 2, \ldots, m \\ 0 & \text{for } k > m \end{cases}$$

Also considering $\mathrm{cov}(X_t, X_{t+k})$, we get the same expressions as for $\gamma(k)$.

Hence $\gamma(-k) = \gamma(k)$. The *acf* can be obtained by dividing $\gamma(k)$ by $\mathrm{var}(X_t)$. For the MA process, $\rho(k) = 0$ for $k > m$, that is, they are zero for lags greater than the order of the process. Since $\gamma(k)$ is independent of t, the MA(m) process is weakly stationary. Note that no restrictions on the β_i are needed to prove the stationarity of the MA process.

To facilitate our notation we shall use the *lag operator L*. It is defined by $L^j X_t = X_{t-j}$ for all j. Thus $LX_t = X_{t-1}$, $L^2 X_t = X_{t-2}$, $L^{-1} X_t = X_{t+1}$, and so on.

With this notation the MA(m) process can be written as (since $\beta_0 = 1$)

$$X_t = (1 + \beta_1 L + \beta_2 L^2 + \cdots + \beta_m L^m)\varepsilon_t = \beta(L)\varepsilon_t \quad (\text{say})$$

The polynomial in L has m roots and we can write

$$X_t = (1 - \pi_1 L)(1 - \pi_2 L)\cdots(1 - \pi_m L)\varepsilon_t$$

where $\pi_1, \pi_2, \ldots, \pi_m$ are the roots of the equation

$$Y^m + \beta_1 Y^{m-1} + \cdots + \beta_m = 0$$

After estimating the model we can calculate the residuals from $\varepsilon_t = [\beta(L)]^{-1} x_t$ provided that $[\beta(L)]^{-1}$ converges. This condition is called the *invertibility condition*. The condition for invertibility is that $|\pi_i| < 1$ for all i.[2] This implies that an MA(m) process can be written as an AR(∞) process.

For instance, for the MA(2) process

$$X_t = (1 + \beta_1 L + \beta_2 L^2)\varepsilon_t$$

π_1 and π_2 are roots of the quadratic equation $Y^2 + \beta_1 Y + \beta_2 = 0$.

The condition $|\pi_i| < 1$ gives

$$\left| \frac{-\beta_1 \pm \sqrt{\beta_1^2 - 4\beta_2}}{2} \right| < 1$$

This gives the result that β_1 and β_2 must satisfy

$$\beta_1 + \beta_2 > -1$$
$$\beta_2 - \beta_1 > -1 \qquad\qquad (13.1)$$
$$|\beta_2| < 1$$

[The last condition is derived from the fact that $\beta_2 = \pi_1 \pi_2$, the product of the roots. The first two conditions are derived from the fact that if $\beta_1^2 - 4\beta_2 > 0$, then $(\beta_1^2 - 4\beta_2) < (2 + \beta_1)^2$ or $(\beta_1^2 - 4\beta_2) < (2 - \beta_1)^2$.]

Moving average processes arise in econometrics mostly through trend elimination methods. One procedure often used for trend elimination is that of successive differencing of the time series X_t. If we have

$$X_t = a_0 + a_1 t + a_2 t^2 + \varepsilon_t$$

where ε_t is a purely random process, successive differencing of X_t will eliminate the trend but the resulting series is a moving average process that can show a cycle. Thus the trend-eliminated series can show a cycle even when there was none in the original series. This phenomenon of spurious cycles is known as the *Slutsky effect*.[3]

Autoregressive Process

Suppose again that $\{\varepsilon_t\}$ is a purely random process with mean zero and variance σ^2. Then the process $\{X_t\}$ given by

$$X_t = \alpha_1 X_{t-1} + \alpha_2 X_{t-2} + \cdots + \alpha_r X_{t-r} + \varepsilon_t \qquad\qquad (13.2)$$

---

[2] An alternative statement often found in books on time series is that the roots of the equation $1 + \beta_1 Z + \beta_2 Z^2 + \cdots + \beta_m Z^m = 0$ all lie outside the unit circle.

[3] E. E. Slutsky, "The Summation of Random Causes as a Source of Cyclic Processes," *Econometrica*, Vol. 5, 1937, pp. 105–146.

is called an autoregressive process of order r and is denoted by AR(r). Since the expression is like a multiple regression equation, it is called "regressive." However, it is a regression of X_t on its own past values. Hence it is autoregressive.

In terms of the lag operator L, the AR process (13.2) can be written as

$$X_t = (\alpha_1 L + \alpha_2 L^2 + \cdots + \alpha_r L^r)X_t + \varepsilon_t$$

or

$$(1 - \alpha_1 L - \alpha_2 L^2 - \cdots - \alpha_r L^r)X_t = \varepsilon_t \tag{13.3}$$

or

$$X_t = \frac{1}{1 - \alpha_1 L - \alpha_2 L^2 \cdots \alpha_r L^r}\varepsilon_t$$

$$= \frac{1}{(1 - \pi_1 L)(1 - \pi_2 L)\cdots(1 - \pi_r L)}\varepsilon_t$$

where $\pi_1, \pi_2, \ldots, \pi_r$ are the roots of the equation

$$Y^r - \alpha_1 Y^{r-1} - \alpha_2 Y^{r-2}\ldots\alpha_r = 0$$

The condition that the expansion of equation (13.3) is valid and the variance of X_t is finite is that $|\pi_i| < 1$ for all i.

To find the *acvf*, we could expand (13.2), but the expressions are messy. An alternative procedure is to assume that the process is stationary and see what the $\rho(k)$ are. To do this we multiply equation (13.2) throughout by X_{t-k}, take expectations of all the terms, and divide throughout by var(X), which is assumed finite. This gives us

$$\rho(k) = \alpha_1 \rho(k - 1) + \cdots + \alpha_r \rho(k - r)$$

[substituting $k = 1, 2, \ldots, r$ and noting $\rho(k) = \rho(-k)$ we get equations to determine the r parameters $\alpha_1, \alpha_2, \ldots, \alpha_r$]. These equations are known as the *Yule–Walker equations*.

To illustrate these procedures we will consider an AR(2) process

$$X_t = \alpha_1 X_{t-1} + \alpha_2 X_{t-2} + \varepsilon_t$$

π_1 and π_2 are the roots of the equation

$$Y^2 - \alpha_1 Y - \alpha_2 = 0$$

Thus $|\pi_i| < 1$ implies that

$$\left| \frac{\alpha_1 \pm \sqrt{\alpha_1^2 + 4\alpha_2}}{2} \right| < 1$$

This gives

$$\alpha_1 + \alpha_2 < 1$$

$$\alpha_1 - \alpha_2 > 1 \tag{13.4}$$

$$|\alpha_2| < 1$$

[The conditions are similar to the conditions (13.1) derived for the invertibility of the MA(2) process.]

In the case of the AR(2) process we can also obtain the $\rho(k)$ recursively using the Yule–Walker equations. We know that

$$\rho(0) = 1 \text{ and } \rho(1) = \alpha_1\rho(0) + \alpha_2\rho(-1)$$

$$= \alpha_1\rho(0) + \alpha_2\rho(1) \text{ or } \rho(1) = \frac{\alpha_1}{1 - \alpha_2}$$

Thus

$$\rho(2) = \alpha_1\rho(1) + \alpha_2\rho(0) = \frac{\alpha_1^2}{1 - \alpha_2} + \alpha_2$$

$$\rho(3) = \alpha_1\rho(2) + \alpha_2\rho(1) = \frac{\alpha_1(\alpha_1^2 + \alpha_2)}{1 - \alpha_2} + \alpha_1\alpha_2$$

and so on.

As an example, consider the AR(2) process

$$X_t = 1.0X_{t-1} - 0.5X_{t-2} + \varepsilon_t$$

Here $\alpha_1 = 1.0$ and $\alpha_2 = -0.5$. Note that conditions (13.4) for weak stationarity are satisfied. However, since $\alpha_1^2 + 4\alpha_2 < 0$ the roots are complex and $\rho(k)$ will be a sinusoidal function. A convenient method to derive $\rho(k)$ is to use the recurrence relation (also known as the Yule–Walker relation)

$$\rho(k) = \rho(k - 1) - 0.5\rho(k - 2)$$

noting that $\rho(0) = 1$ and $\rho(1) = \alpha_1/(1 - \alpha_2) = 0.6666$. We then have

$\rho(2) = 0.1666$	$\rho(3) = -0.1666$
$\rho(4) = -0.25$	$\rho(5) = -0.1666$
$\rho(6) = -0.0416$	$\rho(7) = 0.0416$
$\rho(8) = 0.0624$	$\rho(9) = 0.0416$
$\rho(10) = 0.0104$	$\rho(11) = -0.0104$
$\rho(12) = -0.0156$	$\rho(13) = -0.0104$

This method can be used whether the roots are real or complex.

A plot of this correlogram is left as an exercise.

Autoregressive Moving Average Process

We will now discuss models that are combinations of the AR and MA models. These are called autoregressive moving average (ARMA) models. An ARMA(p, q) model is defined as

$$X_t = \alpha_1X_{t-1} + \cdots + \alpha_pX_{t-p} + \varepsilon_t + \beta_1\varepsilon_{t-1} + \cdots + \beta_q\varepsilon_{t-q}$$

where $\{\varepsilon_t\}$ is a purely random process with mean zero and variance σ^2. The motivation for these methods is that they lead to parsimonious representations of higher order AR(p) or MA(q) processes.

Using the lag operator L, we can write this as

$$\Phi(L)X_t = \theta(L)\varepsilon_t$$

where $\Phi(L)$ and $\theta(L)$ are polynomials of orders p and q, respectively, defined as

$$\Phi(L) = 1 - \alpha_1 L - \alpha_2 L^2 - \cdots - \alpha_p L^p$$

$$\theta(L) = 1 + \beta_1 L + \beta_2 L^2 + \cdots + \beta_q L^q$$

For stationarity we require that the roots of $\Phi(L) = 0$ lie outside the unit circle. For invertibility of the MA component, we require that the roots of $\theta(L)$ lie outside the unit circle. For instance, for the ARMA(2, 2) process these conditions are given by equations (13.1) and (13.4). The *acvf* and *acf* of an ARMA model are more complicated than for an AR or MA model.

We will derive the *acf* for the simplest case: the ARMA(1, 1) process

$$X_t = \alpha_1 X_{t-1} + \varepsilon_t + \beta_1 \varepsilon_{t-1}$$

In terms of the lag operator L this can be written as

$$X_t - \alpha_1 X_{t-1} = \varepsilon_t + \beta_1 \varepsilon_{t-1}$$

or

$$(1 - \alpha_1 L)X_t = (1 + \beta_1 L)\varepsilon_t$$

or

$$\begin{aligned}
X_t &= \frac{1 + \beta L}{1 - \alpha L}\varepsilon_t \\
&= (1 + \beta L)(1 + \alpha L + \alpha^2 L^2 + \cdots)\varepsilon_t \\
&= [1 + (\alpha + \beta)L + \alpha(\alpha + \beta)L^2 + \alpha^2(\alpha + \beta)L^3 + \cdots]\varepsilon_t
\end{aligned}$$

Since ε_t is a pure random process with variance σ^2 we get

$$\begin{aligned}
\text{var}(X_t) &= [1 + (\alpha + \beta)^2 + \alpha^2(\alpha + \beta)^2 + \cdots]\sigma^2 \\
&= \left(1 + \frac{(\alpha + \beta)^2}{1 - \alpha^2}\right)\sigma^2 = \frac{1 + \beta^2 + 2\alpha\beta}{1 - \alpha^2}\sigma^2
\end{aligned}$$

Also

$$\begin{aligned}
\text{cov}(X_t, X_{t-1}) &= [(\alpha + \beta) + \alpha(\alpha + \beta)^2 + \alpha^2(\alpha + \beta)^2 + \cdots]\sigma^2 \\
&= \left(\alpha + \beta + \frac{(\alpha + \beta)^2\alpha}{1 - \alpha^2}\right)\sigma^2 \\
&= \frac{(\alpha + \beta)(1 + \alpha\beta)}{1 - \alpha^2}\sigma^2
\end{aligned}$$

Hence

$$\rho(1) = \frac{\text{cov}(X_t, X_{t-1})}{\text{var}(X_t)} = \frac{(\alpha + \beta)(1 + \alpha\beta)}{1 + \beta^2 + 2\alpha\beta}$$

Successive values of $\rho(k)$ can be obtained from the recurrence relation $\rho(k) = \alpha\rho(k-1)$ for $k \geq 2$. For the AR(1) process of $\rho(1) = \alpha$, it can be verified that $\rho(1)$ for the ARMA(1, 1) process is $> \alpha$ or $< \alpha$ depending on whether $\beta > 0$ or < 0, respectively.

Autoregressive Integrated Moving Average Process

In practice, most time series are nonstationary. One procedure that is often used to convert a nonstationary series to a stationary series is successive differencing. Let us define the operator $\Delta = 1 - L$, so that $\Delta X_t = X_t - X_{t-1}$, $\Delta^2 X_t = (X_t - X_{t-1}) - (X_{t-1} - X_{t-2})$, and so on. Suppose that $\Delta^d X_t$ is a stationary series that can be represented by an ARMA(p, q) model. Then we say that X_t can be represented by an autoregressive integrated moving average (ARIMA) model ARIMA(p, d, q). The model is called an *integrated* model because the stationary ARMA model that is fitted to the differenced data has to be summed or "integrated" to provide a model for the nonstationary data. Actually, even if there is no need for a moving average component in modeling X_t, the procedure of differencing X_t will produce a moving average process (the Slutsky effect mentioned in our discussion of the MA process).

13.5 Estimation of AR, MA, and ARMA Models

The estimation of AR models is straightforward. We estimate them by ordinary least squares by minimizing $\sum \varepsilon_t^2$. The only problem is that of the choice of the degree of autoregression. This is discussed in Section 13.7. There is also a loss in the number of observations used as the lag length increases. This is not a problem if we have a long time series.

Estimation of MA Models

We shall illustrate the estimation of MA models with a simple second-order MA process. Consider the MA(2) model

$$X_t = \mu + \varepsilon_t + \beta_1\varepsilon_{t-1} + \beta_2\varepsilon_{t-2}$$

In the case of MA models, we cannot write the error sum of squares $\sum \varepsilon_t^2$ as simply a function of the observed x's and the parameters as in the AR models. What we can do is to write down the covariance matrix of the moving average error and assuming normality, use the maximum likelihood method of estimation.[4] An alternative procedure suggested

---

[4]For this see D. R. Osborne, "Maximum Likelihood Estimation of Moving Average Processes," *Annals of Economic and Social Measurement*, Vol. 5, 1976, pp. 75–87, and J. E. H. Davidson, "Problems with the Estimation of Moving Average Processes," *Journal of Econometrics*, Vol. 19, 1981, pp. 295–310.

by Box and Jenkins[5] is the *grid-search procedure*. In this procedure we compute ε_t by successive substitution for each value of (β_1, β_2) given some initial values, say $\mu = \bar{x}$ and $\varepsilon_0 = \varepsilon_{-1} = 0$. We then have, for the MA(2) model,

$$\varepsilon_1 = x_1 - \mu$$

$$\varepsilon_2 = x_2 - \mu - \beta_1 \varepsilon_1$$

$$\varepsilon_t = x_t - \mu - \beta_1 \varepsilon_{t-1} - \beta_2 \varepsilon_{t-2} \quad \text{for} \quad t \geq 3$$

Thus successive values of ε_t can be generated and $\sum \varepsilon_t^2$ can be computed for each set of values of (β_1, β_2). This grid search is conducted over the admissible range of values for (β_1, β_2) given by equations (13.1) and the set of values (β_1, β_2) that minimizes $\sum \varepsilon_t^2$ is chosen. This grid-search procedure is, of course, not very practicable if we have many parameters in the MA process. However, in practice one usually uses a low-order MA process or a low-order MA component in an ARMA process.

Estimation of ARMA Models

We can now consider the estimation of ARMA models. Again, the problem is with the MA component. Either we have to write down the covariance matrix for the errors in the MA component and use ML methods, or use the grid-search procedure for the MA component. We shall discuss the latter procedure. Consider an ARMA(2, 2) model

$$X_t = \alpha_1 X_{t-1} + \alpha_2 X_{t-2} + \varepsilon_t + \beta_1 \varepsilon_{t-1} + \beta_2 \varepsilon_{t-2}$$

This can be written as

$$(1 - \alpha_1 L - \alpha_2 L^2) X_t = \varepsilon_t + \beta_1 \varepsilon_{t-1} + \beta_2 \varepsilon_{t-2}$$

or

$$X_t = \frac{1}{1 - \alpha_1 L - \alpha_2 L^2} (\varepsilon_t + \beta_1 \varepsilon_{t-1} + \beta_2 \varepsilon_{t-2}) \tag{13.5}$$

Let

$$Z_t = \frac{1}{1 - \alpha_1 L - \alpha_2 L^2} \varepsilon_t$$

Multiplying both sides by $(1 - \alpha_1 L - \alpha_2 L^2)$ we get

$$Z_t - \alpha_1 Z_{t-1} - \alpha_2 Z_{t-2} = \varepsilon_t \tag{13.6}$$

Also, from equation (13.5) we have

$$X_t = Z_t + \beta_1 Z_{t-1} + \beta_2 Z_{t-2}$$

[5]G. E. P. Box and G. M. Jenkins, *Time Series Analysis, Forecasting and Control*, rev. ed. (San Francisco: Holden-Day, 1976), Chap. 7.

or

$$Z_t = X_t - \beta_1 Z_{t-1} - \beta_2 Z_{t-2}$$

The grid-search procedure is as follows. Starting with $Z_0 = Z_{-1} = 0$, we generate successive values of Z_t for different sets of values for (β_1, β_2) in the region given by equations (13.1) as follows:

$$Z_1 = X_1$$

$$Z_2 = X_2 - \beta_1 Z_1$$

$$Z_t = X_t - \beta_1 Z_{t-1} - \beta_2 Z_{t-2} \quad \text{for} \quad t \geq 3$$

We then use the generated Z_t to estimate the parameters (α_1, α_2) in equation (13.6) by ordinary least squares. We choose those values of (β_1, β_2) that minimize $\sum \hat{\varepsilon}_t^2$. The corresponding values $\hat{\alpha}_1$ and $\hat{\alpha}_2$ give the estimates of α_1 and α_2.

For ARIMA models the procedure described above is used after successively differencing the given series until it is stationary. We have discussed the grid-search procedure here. Given the current high-speed computers, it is possible to compute the exact maximum likelihood estimates as well. An algorithm for this is described in Ansley.[6]

Residuals from the ARMA Models

After obtaining estimates of the parameters $(\alpha_1, \alpha_2, \beta_1, \beta_2)$, we get the predicted residuals from equation (13.6). We have

$$\hat{\varepsilon}_t = \hat{Z}_t - \alpha_1 \hat{Z}_{t-1} - \alpha_2 \hat{Z}_{t-2}$$

Note that $\hat{Z}_t$ are obtained from the X's and the final estimates $\hat{\beta}_1$ and $\hat{\beta}_2$ of β_1 and β_2, respectively. These residuals are useful for forecasting from ARMA models. This is discussed in the next section.

An alternative way of obtaining the residuals is to solve the ARMA(2, 2) model by expanding the expressions in terms of the lag operator L. Note that the model $(1 - \alpha_1 L - \alpha_2 L^2)x_t = (1 + \beta_1 L + \beta_2 L^2)\varepsilon_t$ gives

$$\varepsilon_t = (1 + \beta_1 L + \beta_2 L^2)^{-1}(1 - \alpha_1 L - \alpha_2 L^2)x_t$$

Since this is a power series in L, we should write it as

$$(1 + \gamma_1 L + \gamma_2 L^2 + \gamma_3 L^3 + \gamma_4 L^4 + \cdots)x_t$$

We have to find the γ_i. This can be done by noting that $(1 + \beta_1 L + \beta_2 L^2)(1 + \gamma_1 L + \gamma_2 L^2 + \gamma_3 L^3 + \cdots) = (1 - \alpha_1 L - \alpha_2 L^2)$ and equating the coefficients of like powers of L. This gives

$$\text{coefficient of } L = \beta_1 + \gamma_1 = -\alpha_1 \quad \text{or} \quad \gamma_1 = -(\alpha_1 + \beta_1)$$

[6]C. F. Ansley, "An Algorithm for the Exact Likelihood of Mixed Autoregressive Moving Average Process," *Biometrika*, Vol. 66, 1979, pp. 59–65.

$$\text{coefficient of } L^2 = \beta_2 + \beta_1\gamma_1 + \gamma_2 = -\alpha_2 \quad \text{or}$$

$$\gamma_2 = -(\alpha_2 + \beta_2) + \beta_1(\alpha_1 + \beta_1)$$

$$\text{coefficient of } L^3 = \beta_1\gamma_2 + \beta_2\gamma_1 + \gamma_3 = 0 \quad \text{or}$$

$$\gamma_3 = -(\beta_1\gamma_2 + \beta_2\gamma_1)$$

The rest of the γ's can be obtained recursively from the relation

$$\text{coefficient of } L^{j+1} = \gamma_{j+1} = -(\beta_1\gamma_j + \beta_2\gamma_{j-1})$$

Once we get the γ_j, we can write $\varepsilon_t = x_t + \gamma_1 x_{t-1} + \gamma_2 x_{t-2} + \cdots$ and get the estimated residual $\hat{\varepsilon}_t$ by substituting $\hat{\gamma}$ for γ. We shall not provide examples here; they are provided in the exercises at the end of the chapter.

Testing Goodness of Fit

When an AR, MA, or ARMA model has been fitted to a given time series, it is advisable to check that the model does really give an adequate description of the data. There are two criteria often used that reflect the closeness of fit and the number of parameters estimated. One is the *Akaike information criterion* (AIC), and the other is the *Schwartz Bayesian criterion* (SBC). The latter is also called the *Bayesian information criterion* (BIC). If p is the total number of parameters estimated, we have

$$\text{AIC}(p) = n \log \hat{\sigma}_p^2 + 2p$$

$$\text{BIC}(p) = n \log \hat{\sigma}_p^2 + p \log n$$

Here n is the sample size. If RSS is the residual sum of squares, $\sum \hat{\varepsilon}_t^2$, then $\hat{\sigma}_p^2 = \text{RSS}/(n - p)$. If we are considering several ARMA models, we choose the one with the lowest AIC or BIC. (The two criteria can lead to different conclusions.) These goodness of fit criteria are more like the $\bar{R}^2$ or minimum $\hat{\sigma}^2$-type criterion. In addition, we have to check the serial correlation pattern of the residuals — that is, we need to be sure that there is no serial correlation. One can look at the first-order autocorrelation among the residuals. However, as discussed in Chapter 6, one cannot use the Durbin–Watson statistic. With autoregressive models, we have to use Durbin's h-test, or the LM test discussed in Section 6.8.

Box and Pierce[7] suggest looking at not just the first-order autocorrelation but autocorrelations of all orders of the residuals. They suggest calculating $Q = N \sum_{k=1}^{m} r_k^2$, where r_k is the autocorrelation of lag k and N is the number of observations in the series. If the model fitted is appropriate, they argue that Q has an asymptotic χ^2-distribution with $m - p - q$ degrees of freedom, where p and q are, respectively, the orders of the AR and MA components.

---

[7]G. E. P. Box and D. A. Pierce, "Distribution of Residual Autocorrelations in Autoregressive Integrated Moving Average Time Series Models," *Journal of the American Statistical Association*, Vol. 65, 1970, pp. 1509–1526.

Actually, though the Q-statistic is quite widely employed by those using time-series programs (there is no need to list here the hundreds of papers, books, and programs that still use them), it is not appropriate in autoregressive models (or models with lagged dependent variables). The arguments against its use are exactly the same as those against the use of the DW statistic, as discussed in Chapter 6. One can use Durbin's h-test but that tests for only first-order autocorrelation. The Q-statistic is designed to test correlations of higher orders as well. For this purpose it is appropriate to use the LM test as suggested in Section 6.8.

The discussion in the time-series literature does not pay any attention to this aspect of the inappropriateness of the Q-statistic. The Box–Pierce paper appeared in 1970 and Durbin's paper, which showed the inappropriateness of using the DW test with lagged dependent variables (autoregressive models) and suggested an alternative, also appeared in the same year. In spite of the fact that the discussion of the Q-statistic in the time-series literature was all in the 1970s after Durbin's paper appeared, it all concentrated on the "low power" of the Q-statistic. For instance, Chatfield and Prothero[8] fitted four different ARIMA models to the same set of data, but all four models gave a nonsignificant value of Q. Ljung and Box[9] suggest a modification of the Q-statistic for moderate sample sizes. They suggest $Q^* = N(N+2)\sum_{k=1}^{m}(N-k)^{-1}r_k^2$ instead of the Q-statistic. However, even this statistic was found to have low power by Davies and Newbold.[10] This too is inappropriate, just the way Q is, in autoregressive models.

Thus one has to replace the Q-test with some other tests. One alternative that has been suggested is to use Lagrange multiplier (LM) tests.[11] We discussed this earlier in Section 6.8. They are, as shown there, very simple to implement. Godfrey[12] discusses a different type of LM test. This is to check the adequacy of the degree of autoregression in the ARMA model.

Suppose that we estimate an ARMA(p, q) model and ask whether we should be estimating the extended ARMA($p+m, q$) model. As before, α_i represent the parameters in the AR part and β_j represent the parameters in the MA part.

Denote by $\hat{\varepsilon}_t$ the computed residuals from the ARMA(p, q) model. Now consider the extended ARMA($p+m, q$) model and compute

$$\frac{\partial \varepsilon_t}{\partial \alpha_i} = v_{it} \quad \text{and} \quad \frac{\partial \varepsilon_t}{\partial \beta_j} = w_{jt} \qquad \begin{aligned} i &= 1, 2, \ldots, p+m \\ j &= 1, 2, \ldots, q \end{aligned}$$

Let $\hat{v}_{it}$ and $\hat{w}_{jt}$ be the values of v_{it} and w_{jt}, respectively, evaluated at the ML estimates of the restricted ARMA(p, q) model (i.e., setting $\hat{\alpha}_i = 0$ for $i = p+1, \ldots, p+m$). Now estimate a regression of $\hat{\varepsilon}_t$ on the $(p+m+q)$ variables $\hat{v}_{it}$ and $\hat{w}_{jt}$. Let R^2 be

---

[8]C. Chatfield and D. L. Prothero, "Box–Jenkins Seasonal Forecasting: Problems in a Case Study," *Journal of the Royal Statistical Society, Series A*, Vol. 136, 1973, pp. 295–336.

[9]G. M. Ljung and G. E. P. Box, "On a Measure of Lack of Fit in Time Series Models," *Biometrika*, Vol. 65, 1978, pp. 297–303.

[10]N. Davies and P. Newbold, "Some Power Studies of a Portmanteau Test of Time Series Model Specification," *Biometrika*, Vol. 66, 1979, pp. 153–155.

[11]See J. R. M. Hosking, "Lagrange Multiplier Tests of Time Series Models," *Journal of the Royal Statistical Society, Series B*, Vol. 42, 1980, pp. 170–181, for a general discussion.

[12]L. G. Godfrey, "Testing the Adequacy of a Time Series Model," *Biometrika*, Vol. 66, 1979, pp. 67–72.

the coefficient of determination and N the number of observations. The LM statistic is given by

$$LM = NR^2$$

which has (asymptotically) a χ_m^2-distribution.

Godfrey studies the finite sample properties of the LM test in the context of overfitting an AR(1) process by higher order autoregressive models. He finds that the power of the LM test is higher than that of the Q and Q^* tests unless the number of overfitted parameters is large. In the special case where m is large, the LM test and the tests like Q and Q^* coincide. This explains why the Q-statistic or Q^*-statistic is not very useful, because when we are testing the adequacy of the ARMA(p, q) model, the alternative we have in mind is an ARMA($p + m, q$) model with large m.

Godfrey's procedure of using auxiliary regression of $\hat{\varepsilon}_t$ on $\hat{v}_{it}$ and $\hat{w}_{jt}$ is also applicable when the alternative is ARMA($p + k_1, q + k_2$) with $m = \max(k_1, k_2)$, as shown in Poskitt and Tremayne.[13] Despite its limitations discussed here, there are numerous studies that quote the Box–Pierce Q-statistic and argue that if it is not significant (at the 5% level), this is confirmatory evidence that the fitted model is adequate. The available evidence shows that the LM tests are more appropriate, and they can be implemented by some regression routines. However, until they are built into computer programs, they are not likely to be used. Currently, most time-series programs have the Q-statistic built into them despite all the limitations discussed here.

13.6 The Box–Jenkins Approach

The Box–Jenkins approach[14] is one of the most widely used methodologies for the analysis of time-series data. It is popular because of its generality; it can handle any series, stationary or not, with or without seasonal elements, and it has well-documented computer programs. It is perhaps the last factor that contributes most to its popularity. Although Box and Jenkins have been neither the originators nor the most important contributors in the field of ARMA models,[15] they have popularized these models and made them readily accessible to everyone, so much that ARMA models are sometimes referred to as Box–Jenkins models.

The basic steps in the Box–Jenkins methodology are (1) differencing the series so as to achieve stationarity, (2) identification of a tentative model, (3) estimation of the model, (4) diagnostic checking (if the model is found inadequate, we go back to step 2), and (5) using the model for forecasting and control. Schematically, we can describe the steps as in Figure 13.3. We will now discuss these steps in turn.

1. Differencing to achieve stationarity: How do we conclude whether a time series is stationary or not? We can do this by studying the graph of the correlogram of the

---

[13] D. S. Poskitt and A. R. Tremayne, "Testing the Specification of a Fitted ARMA Model," *Biometrika*, Vol. 67, 1980, pp. 359–363.

[14] See Box and Jenkins, *Time Series Analysis*. The first edition of the book appeared in 1970.

[15] These models were discussed earlier in M. H. Quenouille, *The Analysis of Multiple Time Series* (London: Charles Griffin, 1957).

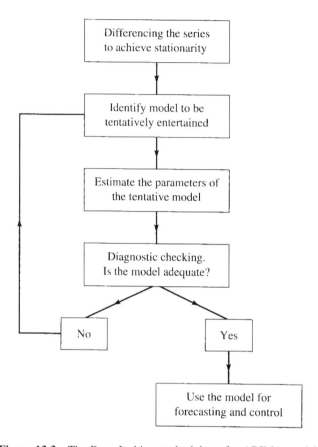

Figure 13.3 The Box–Jenkins methodology for ARIMA models

series. The correlogram of a stationary series drops off as k, the number of lags, becomes large, but this is not usually the case for a nonstationary series. Thus the common procedure is to plot the correlogram of the given series y_t and successive differences Δy, $\Delta^2 y$, and so on, and look at the correlograms at each stage. We keep differencing until the correlogram dampens.

2. Once we have used the differencing procedure to get a stationary time series, we examine the correlogram to decide on the appropriate orders of the AR and MA components. The correlogram of a MA process is zero after a point. That of an AR process declines geometrically. The correlograms of ARMA processes show different patterns (but all dampen after a while). Based on these, one arrives at a tentative ARMA model. This step involves more of a judgmental procedure than the use of any clear-cut rules.

3. The next step is the estimation of the tentative ARMA model identified in step 2. We have discussed in the preceding section the estimation of ARMA models.

4. The next step is diagnostic checking to check the adequacy of the tentative model. We discussed in the preceding section the Q and Q^* statistics commonly used in diagnostic

checking. As argued there, the Q-statistic is inappropriate in autoregressive models and thus we need to replace it with some LM test statistic.

5. The final step is forecasting. We shall now discuss this problem.

Forecasting from Box–Jenkins Models

To fix ideas we shall illustrate forecasting from the ARMA(2, 2) model we have been considering. Suppose that we have estimated the model with n observations. We want to forecast x_{n+k}. This is called a k-period ahead forecast. It is denoted by $\hat{x}_{n,k}$. The first subscript gives the time period when the forecast is made, and the second subscript denotes the time periods ahead for which the forecast is made. Let us start with $k = 1$ so that we need a forecast of x_{n+1} at time period n. We have

$$x_{n+1} = \alpha_1 x_n + \alpha_2 x_{n-1} + \varepsilon_{n+1} + \beta_1 \varepsilon_n + \beta_2 \varepsilon_{n-1}$$

We observe x_n and x_{n-1}. We can replace ε_n and ε_{n-1} by the predicted residuals (obtaining the residuals was described in the preceding section). The only unknown is ε_{n+1}. This we replace by its expected value zero. Hence

$$\hat{x}_{n,1} = \hat{\alpha}_1 x_n + \hat{\alpha}_2 x_{n-1} + \hat{\beta}_1 \hat{\varepsilon}_n + \hat{\beta}_2 \hat{\varepsilon}_{n-1}$$

Now let us go to $k = 2$. We have

$$x_{n+2} = \alpha_1 x_{n+1} + \alpha_2 x_n + \varepsilon_{n+2} + \beta_1 \varepsilon_{n+1} + \beta_2 \varepsilon_n$$

We replace ε_{n+2} and ε_{n+1} by zero, their expected value. x_{n+1} is not known, but we have the forecast $\hat{x}_{n,1}$. Thus we get

$$\hat{x}_{n,2} = \hat{\alpha}_1 \hat{x}_{n,1} + \hat{\alpha}_2 x_n + \hat{\beta}_2 \hat{\varepsilon}_n$$

We continue like this. The procedure is:

1. Write out the expression for x_{n+k}.
2. Replace all future values x_{n+j} ($j > 0$, $j < k$) by their forecasts.
3. Replace all ε_{n+j} ($j > 0$) by zero.
4. Replace all ε_{n-j} ($j \leq 0$) by the predicted residuals.

An alternative procedure is to write x_t in terms of all the lagged x's. For this we use the procedure outlined in the preceding section. We have

$$(1 + \gamma_1 L + \gamma_2 L^2 + \gamma_3 L^3 + \ldots)x_t = \varepsilon_t$$

The γ's are obtained as discussed in the preceding section. Now we have

$$x_{t+1} = -[\gamma_1 x_t + \gamma_2 x_{t-1} + \gamma_3 x_{t-2} + \cdots] + \varepsilon_{i+1}$$

To get $\hat{x}_{t,1}$, we replace ε_{t+1} by zero, its expected value, and the γ's by their estimates. The procedure is the same as earlier except that we do not have to deal with the predicted residuals.

Illustrative Example

As an illustrative example we consider the problem of forecasting hog marketings considered by Leuthold et al.[16] It is an old study, but the example illustrates how the correlogram can be used to arrive at a model that uses higher than first-order differences. The data consist of 275 daily observations. The correlograms for the original data are presented in Figure 13.4. The correlogram does not damp, thus indicating nonstationarity. The peaks at 5, 10, 15, . . . indicate a strong 5-day weekly effect. Figure 13.5 shows the correlogram of first differences. It still shows peaks at 5, 10, 15, and so on, and it does not show any sign of damping. Since the peaks do not damp, it suggests a fifth-order MA component as well. We next try fifth differences, that is $X_t - X_{t-5}$. The correlogram, shown in Figure 13.6, damps. But the initial decline and oscillation suggest the use of an ARMA model rather than a pure AR or MA model. Leuthold et al. finally arrive at the model

$$(1 - \phi L^5)(1 - \alpha_1 L - \alpha_2 L^2)x_t = (1 - \theta L^5)(1 + \beta_1 L + \beta_2 L^2)\varepsilon_t$$

There are three parameters in the MA part. Hence they use the grid-search procedure on the three parameters θ, β_1, and β_2. The estimated parameters were

$$\phi = 0.90 \quad \alpha_1 = 1.44 \quad \alpha_2 = -0.47$$
$$\theta = 0.70 \quad \beta_1 = -1.52 \quad \beta_2 = 0.66$$

The model therefore is

$$(1 - 0.90L^5)(1 - 1.44L + 0.47L^2)x_t = (1 - 0.70L^5)(1 - 1.52L + 0.66L^2)\varepsilon_t$$

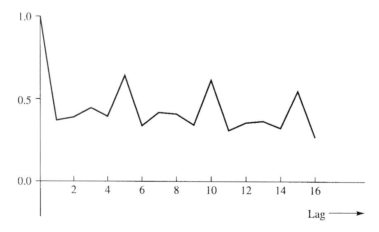

Figure 13.4   Autocorrelation function of levels

[16]R. M. Leuthold, A. M. A. MacCormick, A. Schmitz, and D. G. Watts, "Forecasting Daily Hog Prices and Quantities: A Study of Alternative Forecasting Techniques," *Journal of the American Statistical Association*, March 1970, pp. 90–107.

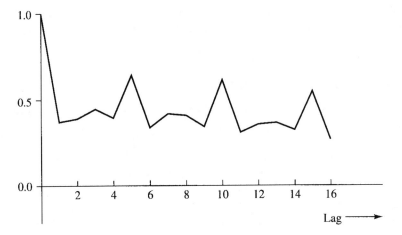

Figure 13.5 Autocorrelation function of first differences

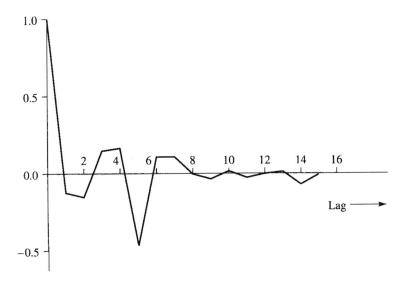

Figure 13.6 Autocorrelation function of fifth differences

This gives

$$x_t = 1.44x_{t-1} - 0.47x_{t-2} + 0.90x_{t-5} - (0.90 \times 1.44)x_{t-6}$$
$$+ (0.90 \times 0.47)x_{t-7} + e_t - 1.52e_{t-1} + 0.66e_{t-2} - 0.70e_{t-5}$$
$$+ (0.70 \times 1.52)e_{t-6} - (0.70 \times 0.66)e_{t-7}$$

This is the equation we use for forecasting purposes, using the methods outlined earlier. Note that β_1 and β_2 satisfy the conditions in (13.1) and α_1 and α_2 satisfy the conditions in (13.4). There were no diagnostic tests and comparison with alternative models. But the example is presented here as an illustration of how first differences were not appropriate but fifth differences were.

Trend Elimination: The Traditional Method

The Box–Jenkins method eliminates trend by differencing the series. A more traditional method adopts the *ratio to moving average method*. An example of this is the Beveridge price index.[17] This is a historically interesting time series of wheat prices in western and central Europe from 1500 to 1869 (370 years). The index is made up from prices in nearly 50 places in various countries (with the mean for 1700–1745 = 100). Beveridge gets a trend-free index by expressing the index for a given year as a percentage of the mean of the 31 years for which it is the center. For instance, for the year 1600, we divide the index for 1600 by the average of the index over the years 1585–1615 and convert this to a percentage. This is the ratio to moving average method. Note that you lose 15 observations at the beginning and 15 observations at the end. The last ones are often critical.

Table 13.2 (available on the Web) gives the Beveridge index and Figure 13.7 gives the correlogram of the trend-free index, which shows that the series is stationary. Calculation

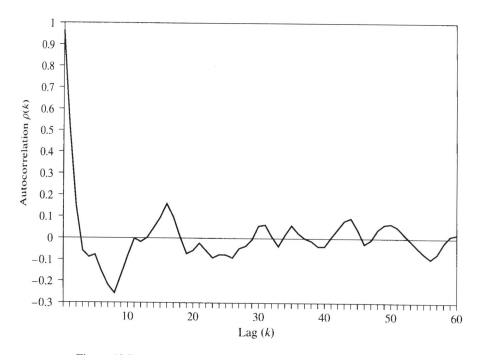

Figure 13.7   Correlogram for the Beveridge trend-free price index

---

[17]W. H. Beveridge, "Weather and Harvest Cycles," *Economic Journal*, Vol. 31, 1921, pp. 429–452.

of the correlogram of the raw index and the first difference of the series is left as an exercise.

A Summary Assessment

The Box–Jenkins models were very popular in the early 1970s because of their better forecasting performance compared to econometric models. The main drawback of econometric models at that time was that inadequate attention was paid to the time-series structure of the underlying data and the specification of the dynamic structure. Once this is done, the forecasting performance of econometric models improves considerably, and the econometric models started to do better than univariate time-series models.[18] Later it was argued that the appropriate comparison should be between econometric models and multivariate time-series models (not univariate time-series models). However, in the early 1970s what was being argued is that even univariate ARIMA models did better in forecasting than econometric models. At least this claim can be put to rest by taking care of the dynamics in the specification of econometric models. As for multivariate time-series models versus econometric models, there is still some controversy.

Quite apart from the forecasting aspect, the Box–Jenkins methodology involves a lot of judgmental decisions and a considerable amount of "data mining." This data mining can be avoided if we can confine our attention to autoregressive processes only. Such processes are easier to estimate and easier to undertake specification testing. We start with a fairly high-order AR process and then simplify it to a parsimonious model by successive "testing down." This procedure has been suggested by Anderson.[19] For ARMA models, on the other hand, moving from the specific to the general is difficult. This is why Box and Jenkins suggest starting with a parsimonious model and building up progressively if the estimated residuals show any systematic pattern (see the earlier discussion on diagnostic checking).

The reason why one may not be able to avoid the MA part in the Box–Jenkins methodology is that the MA part can be produced by the differencing operation undertaken to remove the trend and produce a stationary series. For instance, if the true model is

$$y_t = \alpha + \beta t + \varepsilon_t$$

taking second differences we eliminate the trend but the residual series $\varepsilon_t - 2\varepsilon_{t-1} + \varepsilon_{t-2}$ is a MA(2) process and it is not even invertible.

Seasonality in the Box–Jenkins Modeling

Suppose that we have monthly data. Then observations in any month are often affected by some seasonal tendencies peculiar to that month. A classic example is the upward jump in sales in December because of Christmas shopping. The observation in December

---

[18] An illustration of this comparison is D. L. Prothero and K. F. Wallis, "Modelling Macroeconomic Time-Series" (with discussion), *Journal of the Royal Statistical Society, Series A*, Vol. 139, 1976, pp. 468–500.

[19] See the discussion of Anderson's test in Section 10.11.

1991 is more likely to be highly correlated with observations in December of past years than with observations in other months closer to December 1991.

Just as the Box–Jenkins' method accounts for trends by using first differences, it accounts for seasonality by using the twelfth difference, that is, (January 1991 − January 1990), (February 1991 − February 1990), (March 1991 − March 1990), and so on. If we denote the first difference operator by $\Delta = 1 - L$, the seasonal difference will be denoted by $\Delta_{12} = 1 - L^{12}$. With quarterly data we use the seasonal difference operator $\Delta_4 = 1 - L^4$. Note that $\Delta_{12} \neq \Delta^{12}$ because $1 - L^{12} \neq (1 - L)^{12}$. If the original series is y_t, we get $\Delta y_t = y_t - y_{t-1}$, $\Delta_4 y_t = y_t - y_{t-4}$, $\Delta_{12} y_t = y_t - y_{t-12}$. If we have monthly data and we eliminate both trend and the monthly seasonal, we use both the operators Δ and Δ_{12} — that is, we use both first differences and twelfth differences. Instead of using a first difference, that is, $(1 - L)$, we can sometimes consider a quasi-first difference, that is, $(1 - \alpha L)$ [e.g., $(1 - 0.8L)$ or $(1 - 0.75L)$]. Similarly, for the seasonal, instead of using $(1 - L^{12})$, we might use $(1 - 0.8L^{12})$, and so on.

Chatfield[20] gives an example of some telephone data analyzed by Tomasek[21] using the Box–Jenkins method. Tomasek developed the model

$$(1 - 0.84L)(1 - L^{12})(y_t - 132) = (1 - 0.60L)(1 + 0.37L^{12})\varepsilon_t$$

which when fitted to all the data, explained 99.4% of the total variation about the mean [i.e., $\sum(y_t - \bar{y})^2$]. On the basis of this good fit, Tomasek recommended the use of the Box–Jenkins method for forecasting.

Chatfield argues that if one looks at the data, one finds an unusually regular seasonal pattern which itself explains 97% of the total variation. For this model once the seasonal element is accounted for, nearly any forecasting method gives good results. For instance, an adaptive forecasting equation would be

$$\hat{y}_{t,1} = \lambda y_t + (1 - \lambda)\hat{y}_{t-1,1} \quad 0 < \lambda < 1$$

(i.e., the forecasts are revised on the basis of the most recent forecast errors).

The differencing operation in the Box–Jenkins procedure is also considered one of its main limitations in the treatment of series that exhibit moving seasonal and moving trend. The Box–Jenkins procedure accounts for the trend and seasonal elements through the use of differencing operators and then pays elaborate attention to the ARMA modeling of what is left. This inordinate attention to ARMA modeling obscures some other aspects of the time series that need more attention. It has been found that other procedures that permit adaptive revision of the seasonal elements, trend term and the residual, may give better forecasts than the Box–Jenkins method.

13.7 R^2 Measures in Time-Series Models

First let us consider pure autoregressive models: AR(p). How do we choose the order p? One might think of using R^2 and other criteria discussed in Section 12.7, but most of these criteria were discussed under the assumption of nonstochastic regressors. One

---

[20]C. Chatfield, *The Analysis of Time Series: Theory and Practice* (London: Chapman & Hall, 1975), p. 103.

[21]The reference to Tomasek and the data used can be found in Chatfield's book, p. 103.

procedure that is popular for choosing the order p is Akaike's FPE criterion.[22] This says: Choose the order p by minimizing

$$FPE = \hat{\sigma}_p^2 \left(1 + \frac{1+p}{n}\right)$$

where $\hat{\sigma}_p^2$ is the estimate of $\sigma^2 = \text{var}(\varepsilon_t)$ when the order of the autoregressive process is p, that is, $\hat{\sigma}_p^2 = \text{RSS}/(n - p - 1)$.

Time-series observations normally show a strong trend (upward or downward) and strong seasonal effects. Any model that is able to pick up these effects will have a high R^2. The question is: How good and reliable is this? For instance, Box and Jenkins (1976, Chap. 9) have a data set consisting of 144 monthly observations on the variable y_t, defined as the logarithm of the number of airline passengers carried per month. Regressing y_t on time trend and seasonal dummies gives $R^2 = 0.983$. Is this a good model?

Harvey[23] suggests some measures of *relative* R^2's to judge the usefulness of a model. Note that the criterion on which the usual R^2 is based is the residual sum of squares from the model relative to the residual sum of squares from a naive alternative (that consists of the estimation of the mean only). For instance if $S_{yy} = \sum(y_t - \bar{y})^2$ and RSS is the residual sum of squares from the model,

$$R^2 = 1 - \frac{\text{RSS}}{S_{yy}} \quad \text{(see Chapter 4)}$$

Thus the "norm" R^2 judges a model compared with a naive model, where only the mean is estimated. In time-series models with strong trends and seasonals, this is not a meaningful alternative. The meaningful alternative is a random walk with drift, or with seasonal data, a random walk with drift with seasonal dummies added. Harvey suggests two alternative R^2 measures. One is

$$R_D^2 = 1 - \frac{\text{RSS}}{\sum\limits_{t=2}^{T}(\Delta y_t - \overline{\Delta y_t})^2}$$

The numerator RSS is the residual sum of squares from the model we estimate. The denominator $\sum_{t=2}^{T}(\Delta y_t - \overline{\Delta y_t})^2$ is the residual sum of squares from a random walk with drift, that is, $y_t = y_{t-1} + \beta + \varepsilon_t$, $t = 2, \ldots, T$. For most time-series data this is the "naive alternative." A model for which R_D^2 is negative should be discarded. To adjust for degrees of freedom, we divide the numerator and denominator in R_D^2 by the appropriate degrees of freedom. The denominator d.f. is $(T - 2)$. The numerator d.f. is $(T - k)$, where k is the number of parameters estimated. The R_D^2 adjusted for d.f. can be called $\overline{R}_D^2$.

With seasonal data, Harvey suggests

$$R_S^2 = 1 - \frac{\text{RSS}}{\text{RSS}_0}$$

[22] H. Akaike, "Fitting Autoregressions for Prediction," *Annals of the Institute of Statistical Mathematics*, Vol. 21, No. 2, 1969, pp. 243–247.

[23] A. C. Harvey, "A Unified View of Statistical Forecasting Procedure," *Journal of Forecasting*, Vol. 3, 1984, pp. 245–275.

where RSS is, as before, the residual sum of squares from the model and RSS_0 is the residual sum of squares from the naive model — which in this case is the random walk with drift with seasonal dummies, that is,

$$\Delta y_t = \alpha_1 S_1 + \cdots + \alpha_k S_k + \varepsilon_t$$

where $S_1, S_2, \ldots, S_k$ are the k seasonal dummies. For quarterly data $k = 4$, and for monthly data $k = 12$. For most time-series data this naive model fits well and any alternative model has to do better than this. A model for which $R_S^2 < 0$ should be discarded as useless. Again, we can adjust the numerator and denominator in R_S^2 for degrees of freedom and define the resulting measure as $\overline{R}_S^2$.

As an example, with the airline data mentioned earlier, $R^2 = 0.983$ and RSS $= 0.47232$. But $RSS_0 = 0.19405$ (from the random walk with seasonal dummies). Hence $R_S^2 = 1 - 0.47232/0.19405 = -1.416$. This indicates that the model with $R^2 = 0.983$ is indeed weak even though it has a high R^2.

As yet another example, consider the Nelson and Plosser data on per capita real GNP (PCRGNP) in Table 13.3 (available on the Web). In this case, $\sum(\Delta y_t - \overline{\Delta y_t})^2$ is 1.057 and the R_D^2 for the model $y_t = \alpha + \beta t + \varepsilon_t$ is -3.13. This suggests that the model $y_t = \alpha + \beta t + \varepsilon_t$ with $R^2 = 0.86$ is inadequate.

Let us illustrate the procedure of fitting autoregressions of different order for these data. Figures 13.8 and 13.9 show the correlograms for the logarithm of PCRGNP in levels as well as first differences. The correlograms suggest that the series are nonstationary in the levels form but stationary in the first differences. Also, the fluctuation in the correlogram

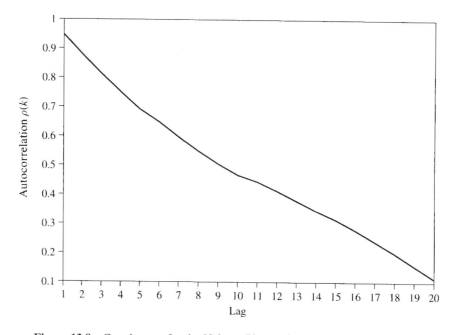

Figure 13.8   Correlogram for the Nelson–Plosser data on real per capita GNP

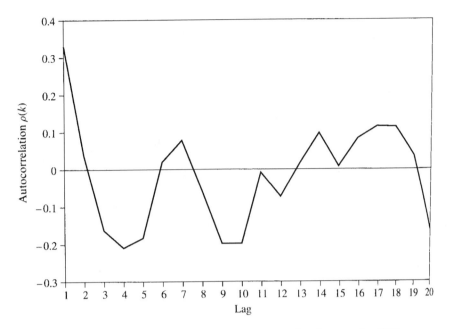

Figure 13.9 Correlogram for first differences of real per capita GNP

Table 13.1 Partial autocorrelations and goodness of fit measures for Δy_t

p	Partial Autocorrelation	R_D^2	$\overline{R}_D^2$	Akaike's FPE
1	0.3315	0.1097	0.0790	0.0041
2	−0.0802	0.1155	0.0523	0.0042
3	−0.1799	0.1466	0.0518	0.0043
4	−0.1101	0.1624	0.0335	0.0045
5	−0.0917	0.1911	0.0294	0.0046
6	0.0952	0.1996	−0.0006	0.0048
7	−0.0001	0.2112	−0.0289	0.0050
8	−0.1810	0.2472	−0.0265	0.0050
9	−0.1891	0.3045	0.0064	0.0049

suggests that AR models are appropriate. We therefore fitted autoregressive models AR(1), AR(2), AR(3), and so on, for Δy_t. The appropriate order of the autoregression can be chosen on the basis of the *partial autocorrelations*. The partial autocorrelations of order 1, 2, 3, and so on, are defined as the last coefficients in the AR(1), AR(2), AR(3), and so on, regressions. It has been proved that each of the partial autocorrelations has SE $= 2/\sqrt{N}$. We can also compute the $\overline{R}_D^2$ for these models as well as the model $y_t = \alpha + \beta t + \varepsilon_t$. Table 13.1 shows the partial autocorrelations, R_D^2, $\overline{R}_D^2$, and Akaike's FPE for Δy_t. The partial autocorrelations, $\overline{R}_D^2$, and FPEs all suggest that the appropriate order of autoregression is 1.

Summary

1. Time series can be classified as stationary and nonstationary. When we refer to stationary time series, we mean covariance stationarity.

2. Some models that are of common use to model stationary series are the autoregressive moving average (ARMA) models. Conditions are given for the stability of the AR models and the invertibility of the MA models. If the MA model satisfies the invertibility condition, we can write it as an infinite autoregression.

3. AR models can be estimated by OLS, but estimation of MA models is somewhat complex. In practice, however, the MA part does not involve too many parameters. A grid-search procedure is described for the estimation of MA models.

4. After the estimation of the ARMA model, one has to apply tests for serial correlation to check that the errors are white noise. Tests for this are described. Also, different ARMA models can be compared using the AIC and BIC criteria. For comparing different AR models, Akaike's FPE criterion can also be used.

5. Another goodness of fit measure is R^2. However, time-series data usually have strong trends and seasonals and the R^2's we get are often very high. It is difficult to judge the usefulness of a model by just looking at the high R^2. Some alternative measures have been discussed, and these should be used.

Exercises

1. Figure 13.1 shows the graph of the stationary series $X_t = 0.7X_{t-1} + \varepsilon_t$ with $\varepsilon_t \sim$ IN(5, 1). To generate the series we need the starting value X_0. We took it as $\mu = E(X_t)$. We find it from the equation $E(X_t) = 0.7E(X_{t-1}) + E(\varepsilon_t)$ or $\mu = 0.7\mu + 5$. This gives $\mu = 5/0.3 \approx 16.67$. Using the same X_0, graph the nonstationary series $X_t = 10 + t + 0.7X_{t-1} + \varepsilon_t$ for $t = 1, 2, \ldots, 100$. This is called a trend-stationary series.

2. Starting with the same initial value X_0, graph the difference stationary series $X_t - X_{t-1} = 10 + \varepsilon_t$.

3. Which of the following AR(2) processes are stable?
   (a) $X_t = 0.9X_{t-1} - 0.2X_{t-2} + \varepsilon_t$.
   (b) $X_t = 0.8X_{t-1} + 0.4X_{t-2} + \varepsilon_t$.
   (c) $X_t = 1.0X_{t-1} - 0.8X_{t-2} + \varepsilon_t$.

4. Which of the following MA(2) processes are invertible?
   (a) $X_t = \varepsilon_t - 0.9\varepsilon_{t-1} + 0.2\varepsilon_{t-2}$.
   (b) $X_t = \varepsilon_t - 1.8\varepsilon_{t-1} + 0.4\varepsilon_{t-2}$.
   (c) $X_t = \varepsilon_t - 0.8\varepsilon_{t-1} + 0.4\varepsilon_{t-2}$.

5. Compute the *acf* for the following AR(2) processes and plot their correlograms:
   (a) $X_t = 1.0X_{t-1} - 0.5X_{t-2} = \varepsilon_t$. (The *acf* is given in the text. Just plot the correlogram.)
   (b) $X_t = 0.9X_{t-1} - 0.2X_{t-2} + \varepsilon_t$.

6. Table 13.2 gives the Beveridge index, and Figure 13.2 gives the correlogram for the trend-free index (with trend eliminated by the ratio to moving average method). Plot the correlograms for the raw index and the first differences of the series.

7. Consider the ARMA model

$$X_t = 1.0X_{t-1} - 0.5X_{t-2} + \varepsilon_t - 0.9\varepsilon_{t-1} + 0.2\varepsilon_{t-2}$$

Express ε_t as a function of X_t and lagged values of X_t by expanding $\varepsilon_t = (1 - 0.9L + 0.2L^2)^{-1}(1 - 1.0L + 0.5L^2)X_t$ in powers of L.

8. For a second-order AR process, show that the (theoretical) partial autocorrelation coefficient of order 2 is given by $(\rho_2 - \rho_1^2)/(1 - \rho_1^2)$.

9. Suppose that the correlogram of a time series consisting of 100 observations has $r_1 = 0.50$, $r_2 = 0.63$, $r_3 = -0.10$, $r_4 = 0.08$, $r_5 = -0.17$, $r_6 = 0.13$, $r_7 = 0.09$, $r_8 = -0.05$, $r_9 = 0.12$, $r_{10} = -0.05$. Suggest an ARMA model that would be appropriate. [*Hint:* The SE of each of the correlations $\sim 1/\sqrt{N} = 0.10$. Values greater than $|2/\sqrt{N}|$ are significant. Thus only the first 2 are significant. Hence a MA(2) process is appropriate.]

10. Table 13.7 gives data on monthly short-term interest rate (MR1) and the long-term interest rate (MR240) for the period February 1950–December 1982. For each of the series estimate a regression on a time trend and seasonal dummies. Compute the R^2. Using the discussion of the different R^2 measures suggested in Section 13.7, check whether these R^2's are good or not.

11. In Exercise 10 compute the *acf* and plot the correlogram to determine whether the data are trend stationary or difference stationary. If they are difference stationary, determine the appropriate order of autoregression for the first differences of the two series using the methods in Table 13.1.

12. The seasonal effect in the two series in Table 13.7 can be taken into account by using seasonal dummies or by seasonal differencing as in the Box–Jenkins approach. Which of these two methods is appropriate for these data sets?

13. Repeat Exercise 10 with the quarterly data on consumption and income in Table 13.4.

14. Repeat Exercise 11 with the data in Table 13.4.

15. Repeat Exercise 12 with the data in Table 13.4.

16. Illustrate the use of the AIC and BIC criteria in the choice between different ARMA models using one of these data sets.

Data Sets

The following data sets are available on the Web.

Table 13.2 Beveridge trend-free wheat price index.

Table 13.3 Nelson and Plosser's data.

Table 13.4 Quarterly data on consumption and income.

Table 13.5 Quarterly data on GNP and money (nominal money supply measured by M_2).

Table 13.6 Real stock price (S&P) and real dividends (S&P) 1871–1985.

Table 13.7 Monthly data on interest rates.

Table 13.8 Acreage and yields on corn, soybeans, and wheat.

14 Vector Autoregressions, Unit Roots, and Cointegration

What is in this Chapter?

This chapter discusses work on time-series analysis starting in the 1980s. First there is a discussion of vector autoregression models, work on which started around 1980 after Sims' paper. Next we talk of the different unit root tests. The Box–Jenkins methods used ad hoc procedures for the analysis of this problem.

Finally, we discuss cointegration, which is a method of analyzing long-run relationships between nonstationary variables. We discuss tests for cointegration and estimation of cointegrating relationships. We also discuss the use of cointegration methodology in testing the rational expectations hypothesis and the market efficiency hypothesis.

14.1 Introduction

In Chapter 13 we discussed time-series analysis as it stood about two decades ago. The main emphasis was on transforming the data to achieve stationarity and then estimating ARMA models. The differencing operation used to achieve a stationarity involves a loss of potential information about long-run movements.

In the present chapter we discuss three major developments during the last two decades, mainly to handle nonstationary time series: vector autoregressions (VARs), unit roots, and cointegration. The Box–Jenkins method of differencing the time series after a visual inspection of the correlogram has been formalized in the tests for unit roots. The VAR model is a very useful starting point in the analysis of the interrelationships between the different time series. The literature on unit roots studies nonstationary time series which are stationary in first differences. The theory of cointegration explains how to study the interrelationships between the long-term trends in the variables, trends that are differenced away in the Box–Jenkins methods. In the following sections we discuss the VAR models, unit roots, and cointegration. Unlike previous chapters, in this chapter we use matrix notation at some places.

14.2   Vector Autoregressions

In previous sections we discussed the analysis of a single time series. When we have several time series, we need to take into account the interdependence between them. One way of doing this is to estimate a simultaneous equations model as discussed in Chapter 9 but with lags in all the variables. Such a model is called a *dynamic simultaneous equations model*. However, this formulation involves two steps: first, we have to classify the variables into two categories, endogenous and exogenous, and second, we have to impose some constraints on the parameters to achieve identification. Sims[1] argues that both these steps involve many arbitrary decisions and suggests as an alternative, the vector autoregression (VAR) approach. This is just a multiple time-series generalization of the AR model.[2] The VAR model is easy to estimate because we can use the OLS method.

Consider two economic time series, y_{1t} and y_{2t}. If we are considering the relationship between money growth and inflation rate, then y_{1t} and y_{2t} are, respectively, the rate of growth of money supply and the GNP deflator. The VAR model with only one lag in each variable (suppressing constants) would be

$$y_{1t} = \alpha_{11}y_{1,t-1} + \alpha_{12}y_{2,t-1} + \varepsilon_{1t}$$
$$y_{2t} = \alpha_{21}y_{1,t-1} + \alpha_{22}y_{2,t-1} + \varepsilon_{2t}$$
(14.1)

We can also add lagged values of some "exogenous" variables z_t, but then we again face the problem of classifying variables as endogenous and exogenous. In practice there would often be more than two endogenous variables and often more than one lag. In this case with k endogenous variables and p lags, we can write the VAR model in matrix notation as

$$\mathbf{y}_t = \mathbf{A}_1\mathbf{y}_{t-1} + \cdots + \mathbf{A}_p\mathbf{y}_{t-p} + \boldsymbol{\varepsilon}_t$$

where $\mathbf{y}_t$ and its lagged values, and $\boldsymbol{\varepsilon}_t$ are $k \times 1$ vectors and $\mathbf{A}_1, \ldots, \mathbf{A}_p$ are $k \times k$ matrices of constants to be estimated.

---

[1]C. A. Sims, "Macroeconomics and Reality," *Econometrica*, Vol. 48, January 1980, pp. 1–48.

[2]The multiple time-series analog of the ARMA model is the VARMA model. But given the complexities in the estimation of MA models discussed earlier, it is clear that estimation of the VARMA model is still more complicated for our purpose. The VARMA model was introduced by G. C. Tsiao and G. E. P. Box, "Modelling Multiple Time Series with Applications," *Journal of the American Statistical Association*, Vol. 76, 1981, pp. 802–816.

To fix ideas, let us go back to the two-equation system (14.1). We can write the system in terms of the lag operator L as

$$\begin{bmatrix} 1 - \alpha_{11}L & -\alpha_{12}L \\ -\alpha_{21}L & 1 - \alpha_{22}L \end{bmatrix} \begin{bmatrix} y_{1t} \\ y_{2t} \end{bmatrix} = \begin{bmatrix} \varepsilon_{1t} \\ \varepsilon_{2t} \end{bmatrix}$$

This gives the solution

$$\begin{bmatrix} y_{1t} \\ y_{2t} \end{bmatrix} = \begin{bmatrix} 1 - \alpha_{11}L & -\alpha_{12}L \\ -\alpha_{21}L & 1 - \alpha_{22}L \end{bmatrix}^{-1} \begin{bmatrix} \varepsilon_{1t} \\ \varepsilon_{2t} \end{bmatrix}$$

$$= \frac{1}{\Delta} \begin{bmatrix} 1 - \alpha_{22}L & \alpha_{12}L \\ \alpha_{21}L & 1 - \alpha_{11}L \end{bmatrix} \begin{bmatrix} \varepsilon_{1t} \\ \varepsilon_{2t} \end{bmatrix} \tag{14.2}$$

where

$$\Delta = (1 - \alpha_{11}L)(1 - \alpha_{22}L) - (\alpha_{12}L)(\alpha_{21}L)$$

$$= 1 - (\alpha_{11} + \alpha_{22})L + (\alpha_{11}\alpha_{22} - \alpha_{12}\alpha_{21})L^2$$

$$= (1 - \lambda_1 L)(1 - \lambda_2 L) \quad \text{say}$$

where λ_1 and λ_2 are the roots of the equation

$$\lambda^2 - (\alpha_{11} + \alpha_{22})\lambda + (\alpha_{11}\alpha_{22} - \alpha_{12}\alpha_{21}) = 0$$

In order that we have a convergent expansion for y_{1t} and y_{2t} in terms of ε_{1t} and ε_{2t} we should have $|\lambda_1| < 1$ and $|\lambda_2| < 1$. Following the results in the appendix to Chapter 7 we note that this is the same condition that the roots of $|\mathbf{A} - \lambda\mathbf{I}| = \mathbf{0}$ are less than one in absolute value, where $\mathbf{A}$ is the matrix of the lag coefficients

$$\begin{bmatrix} \alpha_{11} & \alpha_{12} \\ \alpha_{21} & \alpha_{22} \end{bmatrix}$$

Once the condition for stability is satisfied, we can express y_{1t} (and y_{2t}) as functions of the current and lagged values of ε_{1t} and ε_{2t}. These are known as the *impulse response functions*. They show the current and lagged effects over time of changes in ε_{1t} and ε_{2t} on y_{1t} and y_{2t}. For instance, in the simple model of money (y_{1t}) and prices (y_{2t}), we have, from equation (14.2),

$$y_{1t} = \Delta^{-1}[(1 - \alpha_{22}L)\varepsilon_{1t} + \alpha_{12}L\varepsilon_{2t}]$$

and expanding Δ^{-1} in powers of L and gathering the expressions with the same powers of L, we get

$$y_{1t} = \varepsilon_{1t} + \alpha_{11}\varepsilon_{1,t-1} + (\alpha_{11}^2 + \alpha_{12}\alpha_{21})\varepsilon_{1,t-2} + \cdots$$

$$+ \alpha_{12}\varepsilon_{2,t-1} + \alpha_{12}(\alpha_{11} + \alpha_{22})\varepsilon_{2,t-2} + \cdots$$

with a similar expression for y_{2t}. Thus a price shock in period t has no effect on money until period $(t + 1)$, and vice versa for the effect of a money shock on prices. Of course, these lags are a consequence of the one period lags in the VAR model (14.1).

14.3   Problems with VAR Models in Practice

We have considered only a simple model with two variables and only one lag for each. In practice, since we are not considering any moving average errors, the autoregressions would probably have to have more lags to be useful for prediction. Otherwise, univariate ARMA models would do better. Suppose that we consider say six lags for each variable and we have a small system with four variables. Then each equation would have 24 parameters to be estimated and we thus have 96 parameters to estimate overall. This *overparameterization* is one of the major problems with VAR models. The unrestricted VAR models have not been found very useful for forecasting and other extensions using some restrictions on the parameters of the VAR models have been suggested. One such model that has been found particularly useful in prediction is the Bayesian vector autoregression (BVAR).[3] In BVAR we assign some prior distributions for the coefficients in the vector autoregressions. (See Section 2.5 for prior distributions.) In each equation, the coefficient of the own lagged variable has a prior mean 1, all others have prior means 0, with the variance of the prior decreasing as the lag length increases. For instance, with two variables y_{1t} and y_{2t} and four lags for each, the first equation will be

$$y_{1t} = \alpha_1 y_{1,t-1} + \sum_{j=2}^{4} \alpha_j y_{1,t-j} + \sum_{j=1}^{4} \beta_j y_{2,t-j} + \varepsilon_{1t}$$

The prior for α_1 will have mean 1 and variance λ with $\lambda < 1$. The priors for α_2, α_3, α_4 will have means 0 and variance λ^2, λ^3, λ^4, respectively. The priors for β_1, β_2, β_3, β_4 will have means 0 and variance λ, λ^2, λ^3, λ^4, respectively. Since $\lambda < 1$, as the lag length increases, the variance decreases; that is, we are more and more sure that the coefficient is zero. With the second equation, the priors are similar. The coefficient of $y_{2,t-1}$ will have a prior with mean 1. All other coefficients will have prior 0, with the coefficients of the distant lags having priors more tightly concentrated around zero.

The example of priors above is just meant to illustrate the flavor of the BVAR method. Other priors can be incorporated using the RATS program. The practical experience with the BVAR model has been very good. It has produced better forecasts than many structural simultaneous equation models.[4] It has, however, been criticized as being "a-theoretical econometrics" because it just does not use any economic theory. Sims criticized the traditional simultaneous equations models on the grounds that they relied on ad hoc restrictions on the parameters to achieve identification. However, the BVAR model brings in some restrictions through the back door. The question is: What interpretation can be given to these restrictions?[5] Estimation of the VAR and BVAR models is left as an exercise using some of the data sets listed at the end of Chapter 13.

---

[3]The RATS computer program is the one commonly used for the estimation of VAR and BVAR models.

[4]R. B. Litterman, "Forecasting with Bayesian Vector Autoregression: Five Years of Experience," *Journal of Business and Economic Statistics*, Vol. 4, 1986, pp. 25–38.

[5]There have been other procedures of imposing constraints on the coefficients in the vector autoregressions that give them a structural interpretation. An example is O. J. Blanchard, "A Traditional Interpretation of Macroeconomic Fluctuations," *American Economic Review*, Vol. 79, 1989, pp. 1146–1164.

14.4 Unit Roots

The single topic in the 1980s that attracted the most attention and to which most econometricians have devoted their energies is that of testing for unit roots. The number of papers on this topic runs into the hundreds.[6] We have given a brief introduction to this in Section 6.10, where we discussed the difference between *trend stationary* (TS) and *difference stationary* (DS) time series and the Dickey–Fuller test. We review the problems in greater detail here.

The issue of whether a time series is TS or DS has both economic and statistical implications. If a series is DS, the effect of any shock is permanent. For instance, consider the model

$$y_t = y_{t-1} + \varepsilon_t$$

where ε_t is a zero-mean stationary process. Suppose that in some time period, say, y_T, there is a jump C in ε_T. Then $y_T, y_{T+1}, y_{T+2}, \ldots$ all increase by C. Thus the effect of the shock C is permanent. On the other hand, if we have the model

$$y_t = \alpha y_{t-1} + \varepsilon_t \quad |\alpha| < 1$$

the effect of the shock fades away over time. Starting with y_T, which will jump by C, successive values of y_t will increase by $C\alpha, C\alpha^2, C\alpha^3, \ldots$. Since monetary shocks probably do not have a permanent effect on GNP, if real GNP is DS, fluctuations in real GNP have to be explained by real shocks, not by monetary shocks. Thus the issue of whether in the autoregression, $y_t = \alpha y_{t-1} + \varepsilon_t$, the root α is equal to 1 or < 1, that is, whether there is a unit root or not, is very important for macroeconomists.

On the statistical side, there are two issues. The first is about the trend removal methods used (by regression or by differencing). As pointed out by Nelson and Kang (1981) and as discussed in Section 6.10, spurious autocorrelation results whenever a DS series is de-trended or a TS series is differenced.

The second statistical problem is that the distribution of the least squares estimate of the autoregressive parameter α has a nonstandard distribution (not the usual normal, t, or F) when there is a unit root. This distribution has to be computed numerically on a case-by-case basis, depending on what other variables are included in the regression (constant term, trend, other lags, and so on). This accounts for the proliferation of the unit root tests and the associated tables.

Returning to the economic issue, it does not really make sense to hinge an economic theory on a point estimate of a parameter, on whether or not there is a unit root (i.e., $\alpha = 1$). A model with $\alpha = 0.95$ is really not statistically distinguishable from one with $\alpha = 1$ in a small sample.[7] The relevant question is not whether $\alpha = 1$ or not, but how big the autoregressive parameter is or how long it takes for shocks in GNP

---

[6]See F. X. Diebold and M. Nerlove, "Unit Roots in Economic Time Series: A Selective Survey," in T. Fomby and G. Rhodes (eds.), *Advances in Econometrics*, Vol. 8 (Greenwich, CT: JAI Press, 1990). This "selective" survey lists more than 200 papers in the 1980s.

[7]J. H. Cochrane, "A Critique of the Application of the Unit Root Tests," *Journal of Economic Dynamics and Control*, Vol. 15, No. 2, 1991, pp. 275–284.

to die out.[8] Cochrane argued that GNP does revert toward a "trend" following a shock, but that this reversion occurs over a time horizon characteristic of business cycles — several years at least. Yet another point is that as we noted earlier, the effect of a shock is permanent if $\alpha = 1$ and goes to zero progressively if $\alpha < 1$. However, in many economic problems, what we are concerned with is the present value of future streams of y_t. If the discount factor is β, the present value of the effect of a shock C is $C/(1 - \beta\alpha)$. Without discounting ($\beta = 1$) this is finite if $\alpha < 1$ and infinite with $\alpha = 1$. Thus the unit root makes a difference. But if $\beta < 1$ (i.e., with discounting), the effect is finite for all $\alpha < (1/\beta)$. Thus the existence of a unit root is not important.[9]

14.5   Unit Root Tests

Consider first the model

$$y_t = \alpha y_{t-1} + \varepsilon_t$$

where ε_t is white noise. In the random walk case ($\alpha = 1$) it is well known that the OLS estimation of this equation produces an estimate of α that is biased toward zero. However, the OLS estimate is also biased toward zero when α is less than but near to 1. Evans and Savin (1981, 1984)[10] provide Monte Carlo evidence on the bias and other aspects of the distributions.

To discuss the Dickey–Fuller tests, consider the model

$$y_t = \beta_0 + \beta_1 t + u_t$$

$$u_t = \alpha u_{t-1} + \varepsilon_t$$

where ε_t is a covariance stationary process with zero mean. The reduced form for this model is

$$y_t = \gamma + \delta t + \alpha y_{t-1} + \varepsilon_t \tag{14.3}$$

where $\gamma = \beta_0(1 - \alpha) + \beta_1 \alpha$ and $\delta = \beta_1(1 - \alpha)$. This equation is said to have a unit root if $\alpha = 1$ (in which case $\delta = 0$).

Dickey–Fuller Test

The Dickey–Fuller tests are based on testing the hypothesis $\alpha = 1$ in equation (14.3) under the assumption that ε_t are white noise errors. There are three test statistics

$$K(1) = T(\hat{\alpha} - 1) \quad t(1) = \frac{\hat{\alpha} - 1}{\text{SE}(\hat{\alpha})} \quad F(0, 1)$$

---

[8]J. H. Cochrane, "How Big Is the Random Walk in GNP?," *Journal of Political Economy*, Vol. 96, 1988, pp. 893–920.

[9]See S. R. Blough, "Unit Roots, Stationarity and Persistence in Finite Sample Macroeconometrics," Discussion Paper, Johns Hopkins University, 1990.

[10]G. Evans and N. E. Savin, "Testing for Unit Roots: I," *Econometrica*, Vol. 49, 1981, pp. 753–779, and "Testing for Unit Roots: II," *Econometrica*, Vol. 52, 1984, pp. 1241–1269.

where $\hat{\alpha}$ is the OLS estimate of α from equation (14.3), $\text{SE}(\hat{\alpha})$ is the standard error of $\hat{\alpha}$, and $F(0, 1)$ is the usual F-statistic for testing the joint hypothesis $\delta = 0$ and $\alpha = 1$ in (14.3). These statistics do not have the standard normal, t, and F distributions. The critical values for $K(1)$ and $t(1)$ are tabulated for $\delta = 0$ in Fuller (1976) and the critical values for the $F(0, 1)$ statistic are tabulated in Dickey and Fuller (1981).[11]

The Serial Correlation Problem

Dickey and Fuller, Said and Dickey (1984), Phillips (1987), Phillips and Perron (1988),[12] and others developed modifications of the Dickey–Fuller tests when ε_t is not white noise. These tests, called the "augmented" Dickey–Fuller (ADF) tests, involve estimating the equation

$$y_t = \gamma + \delta t + \alpha y_{t-1} + \sum_{j=1}^{k} \theta_j \Delta y_{t-j} + e_t \qquad (14.4)$$

The purpose in adding the terms Δy_{t-j} is to allow for ARMA error processes. But if the MA parameter is large, the AR approximation would be poor unless k is large.[13]

After estimating this augmented equation, the tests $K(1)$, $t(1)$, and $F(0, 1)$ discussed earlier are used. These test statistics have been shown to have asymptotically the same distribution as the Dickey–Fuller test statistics and hence the same significance tables can be used.

The discussion that follows is based on chapter 4 of G. S. Maddala and I. M. Kim, *Unit Roots, Cointegration and Structural Change* (Cambridge: Cambridge University Press, 1988). We shall make frequent references to this book.

The Dickey–Fuller (DF) and the augmented Dickey–Fuller (ADF) tests are frequently used in testing for unit roots although there are several problems (size distortions and low power) with these tests. With the ADF test there is the problem of selection of lag length. Information criteria like AIC and BIC (see Chapter 12) are used often but they have been found to select a low value of the lag length k. Ng and Perron[14] did a detailed Monte Carlo analysis and found that the general to specific approach is the best choice (starting with a high value of k and progressively going down, see Hendry's approach in Section 12.6).

Phillips and Perron suggest nonparametric alternatives to the ADF test. These tests are the Z_α and Z_t tests (also known as the PP tests). We shall omit the details and refer to section 3.6.3 of Maddala and Kim (1998).

---

[11] W. A. Fuller, *Introduction to Statistical Time Series* (New York: Wiley, 1976), Table 8.5.2. The reference to Dickey and Fuller and excerpts from their tables are shown in Section 6.10.

[12] S. E. Said and D. A. Dickey, "Testing for Unit Roots in ARMA Models of Unknown Order," *Biometrika*, Vol. 71, 1980, pp. 599–607; P. C. B. Phillips, "Time Series Regression with a Unit Root," *Econometrica*, Vol. 55, 1987, pp. 277–302; P. C. B. Phillips and P. Perron, "Testing for a Unit Root in Time Series Regression," *Biometrika*, Vol. 75, 1988, pp. 335–346.

[13] G. W. Schwert, "Tests for Unit Roots: A Monte Carlo Investigation," *Journal of Business and Economic Statistics*, Vol. 7, 1989, pp. 147–159. His conclusion is that the best test is the ADF with a long k.

[14] S. Ng and P. Perron, "Unit Root Tests in ARMA Models With Data-Dependent Methods for the Selection of the Truncation Lag," *Journal of the American Statistical Association*, Vol. 90, 1995, pp. 268–281.

The Low Power of Unit Root Tests

Schwert (1989) first presented Monte Carlo evidence to point out the size distortion problems of the commonly used unit root tests: the ADF and PP tests. Whereas Schwert complained about size distortions, DeJong et al.[15] complained about the low power of unit root tests. They argued that the unit root tests have low power against plausible trend-stationary alternatives. They argue that the PP tests have very low power (generally less than 0.10) against trend-stationary alternatives but the ADF test has power approaching 0.33 and thus is likely to be more useful in practice. They conclude that tests with higher power need to be developed. Section 4.3 in Maddala and Kim (1998) lists several solutions to the problems of size distortions and low power of unit root tests. Here we shall discuss one solution: the DF-GLS test.

The DF-GLS Test

This test suggested by Elliott, Rothenberg, and Stock[16] is as follows: Let y_t be the process we consider. The DF-GLS t-test is performed by testing the hypothesis $a_0 = 0$ in the regression

$$\Delta y_t^d = a_0 y_t^d + a_1 \Delta y_{t-1}^d + \cdots + a_p \Delta y_{t-p}^d + \text{error}$$

where y_t^d is the locally de-trended series y_t. The local de-trending depends on whether we consider a model with drift only or a linear trend. The latter is the most commonly used. In this case we have

$$y_t^d = y_t - \hat{\beta}_0 - \hat{\beta}_1 t$$

where $(\hat{\beta}_0, \hat{\beta}_1)$ are obtained by regressing $\bar{y}$ on $\bar{z}$ where

$$\bar{y} = [y_1, (1 - \bar{\alpha}L)y_2, \ldots, (1 - \bar{\alpha}L)y_T]$$
$$\bar{z} = [z_1, (1 - \bar{\alpha}L)z_2, \ldots, (1 - \bar{\alpha}L)z_T]$$

and $z_t = (1, t)', \bar{\alpha} = 1 + c/T$. $c = -7$ in the model with drift and $c = -13.5$ in the linear trend case. Elliott et al. provide critical values for this DF-GLS test. These are presented in Table 14.1.

What are the Null and Alternative Hypotheses in Unit Root Tests?

The question of whether to de-trend or to difference a time series prior to further analysis depends on whether the time series is trend stationary (TSP) or difference stationary (DSP). If the series is TSP then the data generating process (DGP) for y_t can be written as

$$y_t = \gamma_0 + \gamma_1 t + e_t$$

[15]D. N. DeJong, J. C. Nankervis, N. E. Savin, and C. H. Whiteman, "The Power Problems of Unit Root Tests in Time Series with Autoregressive Errors," *Journal of Econometrics*, Vol. 53, 1992, pp. 323–343.

[16]G. Elliott, T. J. Rothenberg, and J. H. Stock, "Efficient Tests For an Autoregressive Unit Root," *Econometrica*, Vol. 64, 1996, pp. 813–836.

Table 14.1 Critical values for the
DF-GLS test for a model with linear trend
$(c = -13.5)$

Sample Size	Critical Value		
	1%	5%	10%
50	−3.77	−3.19	−2.89
100	−3.58	−3.03	−2.74
200	−3.56	−2.93	−2.64
∞	−3.48	−2.89	−2.57

Source: Elliott et al., Table 1, p. 825.

where t is time and e_t is a stationary ARMA process. If it is DSP then the DGP for y_t can be written as

$$y_t = a_0 + y_{t-1} + u_t$$

where u_t is a stationary ARMA process.

Following Bhargava[17] we can nest these two models in the following model:

$$y_t = \gamma_0 + \gamma_1 t + u_t \quad y_t = \rho u_{t-1} + e_t$$

so that

$$y_t = \gamma_0 + \gamma_1 t + \rho[y_{t-1} - \gamma_0 - \gamma_1(t-1)] + e_t$$

If $\rho = 1$, y_t is difference stationary. If $|\rho| < 1$, then y_t is trend stationary.

This equation can be written as

$$y_t = \beta_0 + \beta_1 t + \rho y_{t-1} + e_t \qquad (14.5)$$

or

$$\Delta y_t = \beta_0 + \beta_1 t + (\rho - 1)y_{t-1} + e_t$$

where $\beta_0 \equiv \gamma_0(1 - \rho) + \gamma_1\rho$ and $\beta_1 \equiv \gamma_1(1 - \rho)$. Note that if $\rho = 1$, then $\beta_1 \equiv 0$.

If we have a quadratic trend, then we have

$$y_t = \gamma_0 + \gamma_1 t + \gamma_2 t^2 + \rho[y_{t-1} - \gamma_0 - \gamma_1(t-1) - \gamma_2(t-1)^2] + e_t$$

which can be written as

$$y_t = \beta_0 + \beta_1 t + \beta_2 t^2 + \rho y_{t-1} + e_t \qquad (14.6)$$

where

$$\beta_0 \equiv \gamma_0(1 - \rho) + (\gamma_1 - \gamma_2)\rho$$

---

[17]A. Bhargava, "On the Theory of Testing for Unit Roots in Observed Time Series," *Review of Economic Studies*, Vol. 53, 1986, pp. 137–160.

$$\beta_1 = \gamma_1(1 - \rho) + 2\gamma_2\rho$$

$$\beta_2 \equiv \gamma_2(1 - \rho)$$

Thus, if $\rho = 1$, then $\beta_2 \equiv 0$

What this says is that in equation (14.5) the null hypothesis is not $H_0 : \rho = 1$ but $H_0 : \rho = 1$, $\beta_1 = 0$. Similarly, in equation (14.6) the null hypothesis is $H_0 : \rho = 1$, $\beta_2 = 0$. The alternative hypothesis in both cases is $H_1 : |\rho| < 1$.

Tests with Stationarity as Null

The null hypothesis considered in the unit root tests is

$$H_0 : y_t \text{ is difference stationary vs. } H_1 : y_t \text{ is (trend) stationary}$$

That is

$$H_0 : y_t \text{ is nonstationary vs. } H_1 : y_t \text{ is stationary}$$

In the classical theory of hypothesis testing, the null hypothesis and the alternative are not on the same footing. The null hypothesis is on a pedestal and is rejected only when there is overwhelming evidence against it. That is why one uses the 5% and 1% levels of significance. If on the other hand, the null and alternative were to be

$$H_0 : y_t \text{ is stationary vs. } H_1 : y_t \text{ is nonstationary}$$

the conclusion would be quite different. In the Bayesian approach, H_0 and H_1 are on the same footing and hence this asymmetry does not arise.[18] Tests for unit roots with the null hypothesis being stationary (no unit root) have also been developed and they often give results contrary to those of the unit root tests with the unit root as null.

There are many tests for unit roots with stationarity as null but the most common ones are the KPSS test due to Kwiatowski et al. and the Leybourne and McCabe test.[19] All the tests for moving average unit roots can be regarded as tests with stationarity as null.

The KPSS test is an analog of the Phillips–Perron test whereas the Leybourne–McCabe test is an analog of the ADF test. They start with the model

$$\Phi(L)y_t = \alpha_t + \beta t + \varepsilon_t$$

$$\alpha_t = \alpha_{t-1} + \eta_t \quad \alpha_0 = \alpha \quad t = 1, 2, \ldots, T$$

where $\varepsilon_t \sim \text{IID}(0, \sigma_\varepsilon^2)$, $\eta_t \sim \text{IID}(0, \sigma_\eta^2)$, ε_t and η_t are independent and $\Phi(L)$ is a pth-order autoregression.

---

[18]D. N. DeJong and C. H. Whiteman, "Reconsidering Trends and Random Walks in Macroeconomic Time Series," *Journal of Monetary Economics*, Vol. 28, 1991, used a Bayesian method and found only two of the Nelson–Plosser series to be of DS type.

[19]D. Kwiatowski, P. C. B. Phillips, P. Schmidt, and Y. Shin, "Testing the Null Hypothesis of Stationarity Against the Alternative of a Unit Root," *Journal of Econometrics*, Vol. 54, 1992, pp. 159–178, and S. J. Leybourne and B. P. M. McCabe, "A Consistent Test for a Unit Root," *Journal of Business and Economic Statistics*, Vol. 12, 1994, pp. 157–166.

The test for stationarity in this model is

$$H_0 : \sigma_\eta^2 = 0 \quad \text{vs.} \quad H_1 : \sigma_\eta^2 > 0$$

Under H_1 the model is an ARIMA model. The Leybourne–McCabe test is carried out as follows:

1. Estimate the ARIMA(p, 1, 1) model by ML

$$\Delta y_t = \beta + \sum_1^p \phi_i \Delta y_{t-i} + u_t - \theta u_{t-1}$$

to get $\hat{\phi}_i$.
2. Construct $y_t^* = y_t - \sum \hat{\phi}_i y_{t-i}$.
3. Regress y_t^* on an intercept and time trend, to get the residual $\hat{\varepsilon}_t$. The test statistic is

$$LM = \hat{\varepsilon}' \mathbf{V} \hat{\varepsilon} / \hat{\sigma}_\varepsilon^2 T^2$$

where $\hat{\sigma}_\varepsilon^2 = \hat{\varepsilon}' \hat{\varepsilon} / T$ and $\mathbf{V}$ is a $T \times T$ matrix with (i, j)th element equal to $\min(i, j)$.

Leybourne and McCabe find that in empirical work their test and the KPSS test give different results. This is confusing from the practical point of view.

Confirmatory Analysis

It has been argued that tests with stationarity as null can be used to confirm the results of the usual unit root tests. The two tests are:

Test 1 (usual test)	Test 2
$H_0 : y_t$ nonstationary (unit root)	$H_0 : y_t$ stationary
$H_1 : y_t$ stationary	$H_1 : y_t$ nonstationary (unit root)

If both tests reject their nulls, then we have no confirmation. But if test 1 rejects the null but test 2 does not (or vice versa) we have confirmation. Burke[20] did a detailed Monte Carlo study to determine the usefulness of confirmatory data analysis. He used the ADF unit root test and KPSS stationarity test. His main conclusions are that:

1. Using 10% significance levels gives better results than using 5% significance levels.
2. Joint rejections are relatively infrequent but joint nonrejections are far more common.
3. Even if confirmation occurs, this may not be correct. Burke found that if the true model is trend stationary, the proportion of confirmations is 50–60% and about half these are correct. When the true model is difference stationary, the proportion of confirmations is 60–65% of which about 82% are correct.

---

[20] S. P. Burke, "Confirmatory Analysis: The Joint Applications of Stationarity and Unit Root Tests," Discussion Paper #20, University of Reading, U.K., 1994.

The overall conclusion is that it is more important to consider better unit root tests than to use confirmatory analysis with defective tests.

Panel Data Unit Root Tests

During recent years panel data unit root tests have become very popular. It is argued that it is one way of obtaining more observations and solving the low power problem of unit root tests. But this is a specious argument. The null and alternative hypotheses are entirely different. The most commonly used tests are the Levin–Lin (LL) tests, followed by the Im–Pesaran–Shin (IPS) test, and the Maddala–Wu (MW) test.[21]

Consider $y_{it} = \rho y_{i,t-1} + e_{it}$, $i = 1, 2, \ldots, N$ for N countries. The test for a unit root, say, for country 1 is based on

$$H_0 : \rho_1 = 1 \quad \text{vs.} \quad H_1 : \rho_1 < 1$$

It is argued that this test has low power. The panel data LL unit root test is based on a test of

$$H_0 : \rho_1 = \rho_2 = \cdots = \rho_N = \rho = 1 \quad \text{vs.} \quad H_1 : \rho_1 = \rho_2 = \cdots = \rho_N = \rho < 1$$

It is argued that this test has higher power. But how can you compare the power of two tests for which both the null and the alternative are different? It does not make any sense.

IPS test the hypothesis

$$H_0 : \rho_i = 1 \text{ vs. } H_1 : \rho_i < 1 \text{ for } i = 1, 2, \ldots, N$$

and suggest a $\bar{t}$-test, and talk of it as a generalization of the LL test. But this is an entirely different test. What you have are N unit root tests. The combined evidence is evaluated on the basis of the $\bar{t}$-statistic.

Suppose each of the unit root tests uses the *same* ADF test with the *same* number of lags. Then the t-statistics from the N countries have the same distribution with, say, mean M and variance σ^2. The mean $\bar{t}$ of these t-statistics will have mean M and variance σ^2/N. You can use the normal approximation to test $\bar{t}$. The quantities M and σ^2 are obtained by simulation.

Note that the problem being solved here is that of combining the evidence from several unit root tests. This problem actually has a long history in statistics. See Section 2.11 where the test suggested by R. A. Fisher in 1932 is discussed. Maddala and Wu suggest the use of the Fisher test for this problem. Their paper compares it with the IPS test and argues that it is more flexible (different unit root tests can be used) than the IPS test. They give arguments why the Fisher test is overall preferable to the IPS test. To use the Fisher

---

[21] A. Levin and C. F. Lin, "Unit Root Tests in Panel Data: Asymptotics and Finite Sample Properties," Discussion Paper #93-23, University of California at San Diego; A. Levin and C. F. Lin, "Unit Root Test in Panel Data: New Results," Discussion Paper #93-56, University of California at San Diego; K. S. Im, M. H. Pesaran, and Y. Shin, "Testing for Unit Roots in Heterogeneous Panels," *Econometrica*, 1998, in press; G. S. Maddala and S. Wu, "A Comparative Study of Panel Data Unit Root Tests and a New Simple Test," paper presented at the Econometric Society Meeting, New Orleans, 1997; *Oxford Bulletin of Economics and Statistics*, Vol. 61, November 1999, pp. 631–652.

test we have to get the P-values P_i for each of the N tests. Then $\lambda = -2\sum_i \log_e P_i$ has a χ^2-distribution with d.f. $2N$.

This is an exact test. The P-values have to be obtained by simulation.

Structural Change and Unit Roots

In all the studies on unit roots, the issue of whether a time series is of the DS or TS type was decided by analyzing the series for the entire time period during which many major events took place. The Nelson–Plosser series, for instance, covered the period 1909–1970, which includes the two world wars and the Depression of the 1930s. If there have been any changes in the trend because of these events, the results obtained by assuming a constant parameter structure during the entire period will be suspect. Many studies done using the traditional multiple regression methods have included dummy variables (see Sections 8.2 and 8.3) to allow for different intercepts (and slopes). Rappoport and Richlin (1989) show that a segmented trend model is a feasible alternative to the DS model.[22]

Perron (1989) argues that standard tests for the unit root hypothesis against the trend-stationary (TS) alternatives cannot reject the unit root hypothesis if the time series has a structural break.[23] Of course, one can also construct examples where, for instance,

$y_1, y_2, \ldots, y_m$ is a random walk with drift

$y_{m+1}, \ldots, y_{m+n}$ is another random walk with a different drift

and the combined series is not the DS type. Perron's study was criticized on the argument that he "peeked at the data" before analysis — that after looking at the graph, he decided that there was a break. But Kim (1990), using Bayesian methods, finds that even allowing for an unknown breakpoint, the standard tests of the unit root hypothesis were biased in favor of accepting the unit root hypothesis if the series had a structural break at some intermediate date.[24]

When using long time series, as many of these studies have done, it is important to take account of structural changes. Parameter constancy tests have frequently been used in traditional regression analysis. But somehow, all the traditional diagnostic tests are ignored when it comes to the issue of the DS versus TS analysis. The main issue with economic time series is how best to model dynamic economic models. The testing for unit roots has received a lot more attention than the estimation aspect.

---

[22]P. Rappoport and L. Reichlin, "Segmented Trends and Non-stationary Time Series," *Economic Journal*, Vol. 99, conference 1989, pp. 168–177.

[23]P. Perron, "The Great Crash, the Oil Price Shock and the Unit Root Hypothesis," *Econometrica*, Vol. 57, 1989, pp. 1361–1401.

[24]In-Moo Kim, "Structural Change and Unit Roots," unpublished Ph.D. dissertation, University of Florida, 1990. Kim studies the Nelson–Plosser and Friedman–Schwartz real per capita GNP series for U.S. (annual) and quarterly OECD data. Another study that argues that many of the U.S. economic time series that were considered to be DS type are not necessarily so and that the evidence on the DS versus TS issue is mixed is G. D. Rudebusch, "Trends and Random Walks in Macroeconomic Time Series: A Re-examination," Federal Reserve Paper 1139, Washington, DC, December 1990.

14.6 Cointegration

An important issue in econometrics is the need to integrate short-run dynamics with long-run equilibria. The traditional approach to the modeling of short-run disequilibria is the partial adjustment model discussed in Section 10.9. An extension of this is the ECM (error correction model), which also incorporates past period's disequilibrium. The analysis of short-run dynamics is often done by first eliminating trends in the variables, usually by differencing. This procedure, however, throws away potential valuable information about long-run relationships about which economic theories have a lot to say. The theory of cointegration developed in Granger (1981) and elaborated in Engle and Granger (1987)[25] addresses this issue of integrating short-run dynamics with long-run equilibria. We discussed this briefly in Section 6.10. We now go through it in greater detail.

We start with a few definitions. A time series y_t is said to be integrated of order 1 or I(1) if Δy_t is a stationary time series. A stationary time series is said to be I(0). A random walk is a special case of an I(1) series, because, if y_t is a random walk, Δy_t is a random series or white noise. White noise is a special case of a stationary series. A time series y_t is said to be integrated of order 2 or I(2) if Δy_t is I(1), and so on. If $y_t \sim$ I(1), and $u_t \sim$ I(0), then their sum $Z_t = y_t + u_t \sim$ I(1).

Suppose that $y_t \sim$ I(1) and $x_t \sim$ I(1). Then y_t and x_t are said to be cointegrated if there exists a β such that $y_t - \beta x_t$ is I(0). This is denoted by saying y_t and x_t are CI(1, 1).[26] What this means is that the regression equation

$$y_t = \beta x_t + u_t$$

makes sense because y_t and x_t do not drift too far apart from each other over time. Thus there is a long-run equilibrium relationship between them. If y_t and x_t are not cointegrated, that is, $y_t - \beta x_t = u_t$ is also I(1), they can drift apart from each other more and more as time goes on. Thus there is no long-run equilibrium relationship between them. In this case the relationship between y_t and x_t that we obtain by regressing y_t on x_t is "spurious" (see Section 6.3).

In the Box–Jenkins method, if the time series is nonstationary (as evidenced by the correlogram not damping), we difference the series to achieve stationarity and then use elaborate ARMA models to fit the stationary series. When we are considering two time series, y_t and x_t say, we do the same thing. This differencing operation eliminates the trend or long-term movement in the series. However, what we may be interested in is explaining the relationship between the trends in y_t and x_t. We can do this by running a regression of y_t on x_t, but this regression will not make sense if a long-run relationship does not exist. By asking the question of whether y_t and x_t are cointegrated, we are asking whether there is any long-run relationship between the trends in y_t and x_t.

The case with seasonal adjustment is similar. Instead of eliminating the seasonal components from y and x and then analyzing the de-seasonalized data, we might also

---

[25]C. W. J. Granger, "Some Properties of Time Series Data and Their Use in Econometric Model Specification," *Journal of Econometrics*, Vol. 16, No. 1, 1981, pp. 121–130; R. F. Engle and C. W. J. Granger, "Cointegration and Error Correction: Representation, Estimation and Testing," *Econometrica*, Vol. 55, No. 2, 1987, pp. 251–276.

[26]More generally, if $y_t \sim$ I(d) and $x_t \sim$ I(d), then y_t and $x_t \sim$ CI(d, b) if $y_t - \beta x_t \sim$ I(d − b) with $b > 0$.

be asking whether there is a relationship between the seasonals in y and x. This is the idea behind "seasonal cointegration."[27] Note that in this case we do not consider first differences or I(1) processes. For instance, with monthly data we consider twelfth differences $y_t - y_{t-12}$. Similarly, for x_t we consider $x_t - x_{t-12}$.

When we talk of common trends, we have to distinguish between what are commonly called *deterministic* and *stochastic* trends. In Section 6.10 we talked about these as the TSP (trend stationary process) and DSP (difference stationary process). De-trending (by running a regression on time) assumes the presence of a deterministic trend, and differencing assumes the presence of a stochastic trend. The concept of cointegration refers to the idea of *common stochastic trends*. But this is not the only kind of common trend. One can also have *common deterministic trends*.[28] The same concept extends to seasonals as well. Seasonal adjustment using dummy variables assumes a *deterministic seasonal*, and seasonal adjustment by differencing as discussed in the Box–Jenkins approach in Section 13.6 assumes a *stochastic seasonal*. The concept of seasonal cointegration applies to stochastic seasonal. In practice, both deterministic and stochastic components could be present in a time series, so that we can write the time series as

$$x_t = T_t + S_t + \mu_t + \eta_t + \varepsilon_t$$

where T_t represents deterministic trends (e.g., a polynomial in t), S_t represents a deterministic seasonal (e.g., seasonal dummy variables), μ_t represents a stochastic trend [e.g., an I(1) process], and η_t represents a stochastic seasonal [e.g., with quarterly data, $(1 - L^4)$ is stationary].

Ignoring the presence of deterministic components leads to some misleading inferences on cointegration. But to simplify our analysis and to concentrate on the issues of cointegration, we shall assume that there are no deterministic elements in the time series we consider.

14.7 The Cointegrating Regression

To fix ideas, we shall consider the simple example considered by Engle and Granger (1987, p. 263). Consider two possibly correlated white noise errors, e_{1t} and e_{2t}. Let x_{1t} and x_{2t} be two series generated by the following model:

$$x_{1t} + \beta x_{2t} = u_{1t} \quad u_{1t} = u_{1,t-1} + e_{1t} \tag{14.7}$$

$$x_{1t} + \alpha x_{2t} = u_{2t} \quad u_{2t} = \rho u_{2,t-1} + e_{2t} \quad |\rho| < 1 \tag{14.8}$$

$$e_{1t} \sim IN(0, \sigma_1^2)$$

$$e_{2t} \sim IN(0, \sigma_2^2)$$

$$\text{cov}(e_{1t}, e_{2t}) = 0$$

---

[27] S. Hylleberg, R. F. Engle, C. W. J. Granger, and S. Yoo, "Seasonal Integration and Co-integration," *Journal of Econometrics*, Vol. 44, 1990, pp. 215–238.

[28] See H. Kang, "Common Deterministic Trends, Common Factors, and Co-integration," in Fomby and Rhodes (eds.), *Advances in Econometrics*, pp. 249–269.

Note that $u_{1t} \sim I(1)$ and $u_{2t} \sim I(0)$. The model is internally consistent only if $\alpha \neq \beta$. The reason for this constraint is that if $\alpha = \beta$, it is impossible to find *any* values for x_{1t} and x_{2t} that simultaneously satisfy both equalities. The parameters α and β are unidentified in the usual sense because there are no exogenous variables, and the errors are correlated. The reduced forms for x_{1t} and x_{2t} are

$$x_{1t} = \frac{\alpha}{\alpha - \beta} u_{1t} - \frac{\beta}{\alpha - \beta} u_{2t}$$

$$x_{2t} = -\frac{1}{\alpha - \beta} u_{1t} + \frac{1}{\alpha - \beta} u_{2t}$$

They are linear combinations of u_{1t} and u_{2t}, and hence, they are both $I(1)$. Note that equation (14.8) describes a linear combination of two $I(1)$ variables that is stationary. Thus, x_{1t} and x_{2t} are cointegrated.

In this case a linear least squares regression of x_{1t} on x_{2t} produces a consistent estimate of α that is actually "superconsistent," that is, it tends to the true value faster than the usual OLS estimator. In the usual case, if $\hat{\beta}$ is the least squares estimator of β, $\sqrt{T}(\hat{\beta} - \beta) \to 0$ whereas in the case here $T(\hat{\beta} - \beta) \to 0$ as $T \to \infty$. This regression of x_{1t} on x_{2t} is called the "cointegrating regression." All other linear combinations of x_{1t} and x_{2t}, other than the cointegrating regression (14.8), will have an infinite variance. There is no simultaneous equations bias in the estimation by OLS of equation (14.8) because the correlation between x_{2t} and u_{2t} is of a lower order in T than the variance of x_{2t} which tends to infinity as $T \to \infty$. This is the case whether we regress x_1 on x_2 to get an estimate of $(-\alpha)$ or we regress x_2 on x_1 to get an estimate of $(-1/\alpha)$. Note that if $\rho = 1$, u_{2t} is also $I(1)$ and then we do not have a cointegrating regression.

Note that equations (14.7) and (14.8) can be written in the autoregressive form

$$\Delta x_{1t} = \beta \delta x_{1.t-1} + \alpha \beta \delta x_{2.t-1} + \eta_{1t}$$
$$\Delta x_{2t} = -\delta x_{1.t-1} - \alpha \delta x_{2.t-1} + \eta_{2t}$$
$$(14.9)$$

where $\delta = (1 - \rho)/(\alpha - \beta)$ and η_{1t} and η_{2t} are linear combinations of the e's. If we define $z_t = x_{1t} + \alpha x_{2t}$, we can write these as

$$\Delta x_{1t} = \beta \delta z_{t-1} + \eta_{1t}$$
$$\Delta x_{2t} = -\delta z_{t-1} + \eta_{2t}$$
$$(14.10)$$

Equations (14.9) give the VAR (vector autoregressions) representation for this simple model.

An error correction model (ECM) is of the form

$$\Delta y_t = \alpha \Delta x_t + \gamma(y - \beta x)_{t-1} + u_t$$

It relates the change in y to the change in x and the past period's disequilibrium. The ECM in this form for the model we have been considering can be derived simply by noting that we have defined $z_t = x_{1t} + \alpha x_{2t}$. Hence, by equation (14.8), we have

$$z_t = \rho z_{t-1} + e_{2t} \quad \text{or}$$

$$\Delta z_t = (\rho - 1)z_{t-1} + e_{2t} \quad \text{or} \tag{14.11}$$

$$\Delta x_{1t} = -\alpha \Delta x_{2t} + (\rho - 1)z_{t-1} + e_{2t}$$

However, note that when estimated by OLS, this equation gives inconsistent estimates of the parameters because of the correlation between x_{2t} and e_{2t}. Note also that all the variables in this equation are I(0).

Equations (14.10) can also be regarded as ECM representations except that in this model Δx_{1t} does not involve Δx_{2t}, and vice versa. When estimated by OLS, equations (14.10) give consistent estimates of the parameters because η_{1t} and η_{2t} are serially uncorrelated. We can get a consistent estimate of β from the estimation of equations (14.10).

One question we might ask at this stage is: How have we managed to identify the parameters α and β in equations (14.7) and (14.8)? The answer is that we have done this by exploiting the information in the specification of the error terms. u_{1t} is a random walk and u_{2t} is I(0). Although by considering a linear combination of the two equations we can generate an equation that looks like each, no linear combination can generate an I(0) error in equation (14.8). Hence α is identified. Similarly, no linear combination can generate a random walk error as in (14.7). Thus β is identified. Equation (14.8) can be estimated by OLS to get a consistent estimate of α. This is free of the simultaneity bias because of the nature of x_{2t}, which is I(1), and u_{2t}, which is I(0). We then construct z_t and get an estimate of β from equation (14.10).

Engle and Granger suggest estimating the cointegrating regression first (note that this is a static regression, that is, a regression with no dynamics or lags) and then estimating the short-run dynamics through variants of the ECM by a two-stage estimation method using the estimated coefficient from the cointegrating regression. As discussed in Section 6.10, others have suggested estimating the long-run parameters and short-run dynamics simultaneously. Banerjee et al.[29] perform a Monte Carlo study based on a model similar to that given by equations (14.7) and (14.8) and find that in small samples, the estimates of α from the static regression (14.8) are biased. They suggest that it is better to estimate the long-run parameter through a dynamic model.

What has been said about the regressions in the I(1) variables can also be said about seasonal data. Our discussion of regressions involving variables with stochastic trends suggests that if y is differenced and x is not, so that y is I(0) and x is I(1), a regression of y on x does not make sense. If both y and x have trends, so that $y \sim$ I(1) and $x \sim$ I(1), a regression of y on x does not make sense unless they are cointegrated, that is, there exists a β such that $y - \beta x \sim$ I(0). This is a case of common stochastic trends. Similar is the case with seasonal data. If y is seasonally adjusted and x is not, a regression of y on x does not make sense. If both y and x have stochastic seasonal elements, a regression of y on x makes sense only if they are seasonally cointegrated, that is, there are common

---

[29]A. Banerjee, J. Dolado, D. F. Hendry, and G. Smith, "Exploring Equilibrium Relationships in Econometrics Through Static Models: Some Monte Carlo Evidence," *Oxford Bulletin of Economics and Statistics*, Vol. 48, 1986, pp. 253–277.

seasonal elements. Also note that if y_t and x_t are both I(1), a regression of the form $\Delta y_t = \beta \Delta x_t + \gamma x_{t-2} + u_t$ does not make sense because Δy_t, Δx_t, and u_t are all I(0) but x_{t-2} is not. It is I(1). Thus all the variables are not on the same level.

14.8   Vector Autoregressions and Cointegration

There is a simple relationship between vector autoregressions and cointegration. In the two-variable case we have considered, if the characteristic roots of the matrix of coefficients[30] in the VAR model are both equal to unity, the series are both I(1) but *not* cointegrated; if precisely one of the roots is unity, the series are cointegrated. If neither of the roots is unity, the series are stationary, so they are neither integrated nor cointegrated. In the example we have considered the VAR model given by equation (14.9) can be written as

$$x_{1t} = (1 + \beta\delta)x_{1,t-1} + \alpha\beta\delta x_{2,t-1} + \eta_{1t}$$

$$x_{2t} = -\delta x_{1,t-1} + (1 - \alpha\delta)x_{2,t-1} + \eta_{2t}$$

The matrix of coefficients is

$$\mathbf{A} = \begin{bmatrix} 1 + \beta\delta & \alpha\beta\delta \\ -\delta & 1 - \alpha\delta \end{bmatrix}$$

The characteristic roots are 1 and $1 - \alpha\delta + \beta\delta$. Thus the series are cointegrated. Note that if $\rho = 1$, then $\delta = 0$ and we have two unit roots. In this case x_1 and x_2 are *not* cointegrated. If we consider the matrix of coefficients in the equations (14.9), we have to talk of zero roots rather than unit roots since the matrix of coefficients is $\mathbf{A} - \mathbf{I}$. Note that $\mathbf{A} - \mathbf{I}$ is a singular matrix. It can be written as

$$\mathbf{A} - \mathbf{I} = \begin{bmatrix} -\beta \\ 1 \end{bmatrix} [-\delta - \alpha\delta] \qquad (14.12)$$

   How do we find the cointegrating relationship from the VAR model? The procedure is as follows. Find the characteristic roots. Then corresponding to each root, find the characteristic vector. This is obtained by solving the equations $(\mathbf{A} - \lambda\mathbf{I})\mathbf{C} = 0$. For instance, corresponding to the root $\lambda = 1$, we have

$$\beta\delta C_1 + \alpha\beta\delta C_2 = 0$$

$$-\delta C_1 + \alpha\delta C_2 = 0$$

This gives $C_1 = -\alpha, C_2 = 1$. Similarly, for the other root $(1 - \lambda\delta - \beta\delta)$ we get the characteristic vector as $C_1 = -\beta, C_2 = 1$. Consider the matrix with these vectors as columns. This is

$$\mathbf{R} = \begin{bmatrix} -\alpha & -\beta \\ 1 & 1 \end{bmatrix}$$

---

[30] See appendix to Chapter 7 for a discussion of characteristic roots.

Now invert this matrix. We have

$$\mathbf{R}^{-1} = \frac{1}{\beta - \alpha} \begin{bmatrix} 1 & \beta \\ -1 & -\alpha \end{bmatrix}$$

Then the rows in this matrix give the required linear combinations

$x_1 + \beta x_2$ is nonstationary (corresponding to the unit root)

$- x_1 - \alpha x_2$ is stationary

In this example, we started out with a VAR model with one unit root. In practice, we have to test for the unit roots. We do this as follows. Let the root closest to 1 be denoted by $\hat{\gamma}$. Then we consider $n(\hat{\gamma} - 1)$ and refer to the tables for $n(\hat{\rho} - 1)$ or $n(\hat{\rho}_\mu - 1)$ in Fuller (1976, p. 371), depending on whether μ is known or estimated. n is the sample size. As an example, consider the VAR model with $y_t =$ income and $C_t =$ consumption, based on 53 observations (1898–1950), which produced the following results:[31]

$$\begin{bmatrix} \Delta y_t \\ \Delta C_t \end{bmatrix} = \begin{bmatrix} 34.16 \\ 31.50 \end{bmatrix} + \begin{bmatrix} 0.055 & -0.110 \\ 0.291 & -0.371 \end{bmatrix} \begin{bmatrix} y_{t-1} \\ c_{t-1} \end{bmatrix}$$

The matrix $\mathbf{A} - \mathbf{I}$ has characteristic roots -0.0424 and -0.2740. The roots of $\mathbf{A}$ are obtained by adding 1 to each. They are 0.9576 and 0.7260. To test whether the root 0.9576 is significantly different from 1, consider $53(0.9576 - 1) = -2.20$. This is not less than the tabulated 5% value in Fuller (1976, p. 371), which is -13.29. Thus this root is not significantly different from 1. We next compute the matrix $\mathbf{R}$ of characteristic vectors and $\mathbf{R}^{-1}$. (These computations are left as an exercise.) The two rows of $\mathbf{R}^{-1}$ give the result that $(C_t - 2.99 y_t)$ is (approximately) a unit root process and $(C_t - 0.88 y_t)$ is (approximately) stationary. The latter result says that 0.88 is the long-run marginal propensity to consume.

In the two-variable case, the cointegration coefficient, if it exists, is uniquely determined. Also, in this case, the matrix $(\mathbf{A} - \mathbf{I})$ for the VAR model has rank 1. As we saw in equation (14.12), it can be expressed as $\mathbf{CB}'$, where $\mathbf{C}$ and $\mathbf{B}$ are row vectors and $\mathbf{B}'$ gives the cointegrating vector. In the case of more than two variables, there can be more than one cointegrating regression and these need not be uniquely determined. For instance, suppose that there are n variables. Suppose there are $(n - r)$ unit roots and r cointegrating vectors. In this case the matrix $\mathbf{A} - \mathbf{I}$ will be of rank $r < n$. As before, we can then write

$$\mathbf{A} - \mathbf{I} = \mathbf{CB}'$$

where $\mathbf{C}$ and $\mathbf{B}$ are $n \times r$ matrices. The rows of $\mathbf{B}'$ are the r distinct cointegrating vectors. However, they may not all have meaningful economic interpretation and we have to choose the linear combinations that make economic sense. In the case where there are $(n - 1)$ unit roots, so that $r = 1$, the cointegrating vector, if it exists, will be unique. The

---

[31]This example is from D. A. Dickey, "Testing for Unit Roots in Vector Processes and Its Relation to Cointegration," in Fomby and Rhodes (eds.), *Advances in Econometrics*, pp. 87–105.

determination of the cointegrating vectors (and their number) for a general VAR model with n variables and k lags is described by Johansen.[32]

The steps in the Johansen procedure are:

1. Regress Δx_t on $\Delta x_{t-1}, \ldots, \Delta x_{t-k+1}$ and get the residuals. Call these R_{0t}. Regress x_{t-1} on these same variables. Call the residuals R_{1t}.
2. Define $\begin{bmatrix} \mathbf{S}_{00} & \mathbf{S}_{01} \\ \mathbf{S}_{10} & \mathbf{S}_{11} \end{bmatrix}$ as the matrix of sums of squares and sums of products of R_{0t} and R_{1t}. Each of $\mathbf{S}_{00}, \mathbf{S}_{01}$ and $\mathbf{S}_{11}$ are of order $p \times p$ where p is the number of elements in x_t.
3. Find the characteristic roots of the determinantal equation $|\mathbf{S}_{11}^{-1} \mathbf{S}_{10} \mathbf{S}_{00}^{-1} \mathbf{S}_{01} - \lambda \mathbf{I}| = 0$.

See the appendix to Chapter 7 for the definition of characteristic roots. If there are r cointegrating vectors, then $(p - r)$ characteristic roots (eigenvalues as they are called) are zero. Johansen suggests two tests for this: the trace test and the maximum eigenvalue test. The CATS program computes these statistics. (CATS stands for "cointegration analysis of time series.") Details can be found in the papers quoted in footnote 31 and in Maddala and Kim (1998), Chap. 6.

The Johansen procedure is very popular because there is a well-documented computer program: CATS. But several problems with the procedure have been noted, which empirical researchers should note:

1. The estimates are very sensitive to departures from the normality assumption made on the errors.
2. If the variables are not I(1), there is a possibility of finding spurious cointegration.
3. The procedure is also very sensitive to the misspecification of the lag length k of the VAR model we start with.
4. Several Monte Carlo studies show that though showing less bias than other estimators, the estimators from the Johansen procedure exhibit large variation, and there is a high probability of outliers.

For more details on these problems and a comparison with other methods, see chapters 5 and 6 of Maddala and Kim (1998).

The Johansen method is a system method. It also determines the *number* of cointegrating vectors. Since linear combinations of cointegrating vectors are also cointegrated, there is the problem of economic interpretation. So one has to bring in some restrictions from economic theory to interpret the cointegrating vectors.

The alternatives to this system method are single-equation methods where you are interested in estimating only a single cointegrating vector.

Consider for simplicity a two-variable equation $y_{1t} = \beta y_{2t} + u_t$. y_{1t} and y_{2t} are I(1). u_t is I(0).

---

[32]S. Johansen, "Statistical Analysis of Cointegration Vectors," *Journal of Economic Dynamics and Control*, Vol. 12, 1988, pp. 231–254, and S. G. Hall, "Maximum Likelihood Estimation of Cointegration Vectors: An Example of the Johansen Procedure," *Oxford Bulletin of Economics and Statistics*, Vol. 51, No. 2, 1989, pp. 213–218, and D. A. Dickey, D. W. Jansen, and D. L. Thornton, "A Primer on Cointegration with an Application to Money and Income," *Federal Reserve Bank of St. Louis*, March–April 1991, pp. 58–78.

There are two problems associated with this model. Endogeneity of the regressor y_{2t} (that is y_{2t} and u_t are correlated) and serial correlation in u_t. All estimation methods depend on how these two problems are solved. (In the Johansen procedure they are solved by considering the VAR model with lags.)

There are two types of single-equation methods: the FM-OLS (fully modified OLS) method of Phillips and Hansen is in the spirit of the Phillips–Perron unit root test, in the sense that it starts with the OLS estimator and applies corrections to it to take care of the endogeneity and serial correlation problems. The other methods depend on adding leads and lags of y_{1t} and y_{2t} to the equation. These are in the spirit of the ADF test in that they modify the estimating equation. In these methods the selection of the lag length is crucial. The lag length is often chosen by using information criteria like AIC and BIC. But these are not recommended. It is best to start with a long lag and test down (the "general to specific" modeling strategy).

To simplify the exposition, we have discussed the VAR model with only one lag. Suppose instead that we have a general VAR model with k lags:

$$\mathbf{x}_t = \mathbf{A}_1 \mathbf{x}_{t-1} + \mathbf{A}_2 \mathbf{x}_{t-2} + \cdots + \mathbf{A}_k \mathbf{x}_{t-k} + \boldsymbol{\varepsilon}_t \tag{14.13}$$

This can be written as

$$\Delta \mathbf{x}_t = \mathbf{B}_1 \Delta \mathbf{x}_{t-1} + \mathbf{B}_2 \Delta \mathbf{x}_{t-2} + \cdots + \mathbf{B}_{k-1} \Delta \mathbf{x}_{t-k+1} + \mathbf{B}_k \mathbf{x}_{t-k} + \boldsymbol{\varepsilon}_t \tag{14.14}$$

where $\mathbf{B}_i = -\mathbf{I} + \mathbf{A}_1 + \mathbf{A}_2 + \cdots + \mathbf{A}_i$, $i = 1, 2, \ldots k$. If $\mathbf{x}_t$ is I(1), then $\Delta \mathbf{x}_t$ is I(0). If some linear combinations of $\mathbf{x}_t$ are stationary, that is, there are some cointegrating relationships among the variables in $\mathbf{x}_t$, then the matrix $\mathbf{B}_k$ should not be of full rank, where $\mathbf{B}_k = -\mathbf{I} + \mathbf{A}_1 + \mathbf{A}_2 + \cdots + \mathbf{A}_k$.

If some of the variables in a VAR model are cointegrated, this implies some restrictions on the parameters of the VAR model. In Section 14.3 we pointed out that predictions from the unrestricted VAR models were not good, and hence some restrictions on the parameters were imposed in the Bayesian VAR (BVAR) approach. The cointegration theory gives a theoretical basis for imposing some restrictions on the VAR model. It has been found that predictions from the VAR model improved with restrictions imposed by cointegration theory.[33] However, many of the comparisons made have been with unrestricted VAR rather than BVAR. What we need to do is compare the predictions from VAR models that use cointegration restrictions with those generated by BVAR. Note that as we described in Section 14.3, the Bayesian VAR approach, by assuming a prior coefficient of unity on the own lagged terms, implicitly assumes that all the variables in the VAR model are unit root processes.

Suppose we consider a set of three variables, all of which are unit root processes. Suppose also that there are two cointegrating relationships among them. Then since any linear combination of cointegrated relationships is also cointegrated, it becomes very difficult to give any economic interpretation to the cointegrated relations. Each of them is a long-run equilibrium relationship, and all linear combinations are equilibrium

---

[33]R. F. Engle and B. S. Yoo, "Forecasting and Testing in Cointegrating Systems," *Journal of Econometrics*, Vol. 35, 1987, pp. 143–159.

relationships. There is, thus, an identification problem, and unless we have some extraneous information, we cannot identify the long-run equilibrium relationship. This has been the experience with the estimation of some long-run demand for money functions. For instance, Johansen and Juselius[34] estimate the demand for money functions for Denmark and Finland using quarterly data. For the Danish data the sample was 1974–1 to 1987–3 (55 observations). For the Finnish data the sample was 1958–1 to 1984–3 (67 observations). For the Danish data, there was only one cointegrated relationship, and this simplified the interpretation of the cointegrating vector as a long-run demand for money function. But for the Finnish data there were three cointegrating vectors, and this caused problems of interpretation.

This is not surprising because "cointegration" is a purely statistical concept based on properties of the time series considered. It is "a-theoretical econometrics." Cointegrated relationships need not have any economic meaning. But even if they do not, they can be used to improve predictions from the VAR models.

One important contribution of cointegration tests is to the modeling of VAR systems, whether they should be in levels or first differences or both with some restrictions. For this purpose the cointegration relationships need not have any economic interpretation. The cointegrated relations are of value only in determining the restrictions of the VAR system. (It is all part of a-theoretical econometrics anyway.)

If a set of unit root variables satisfies a cointegration relation, simple first differencing of *all* the variables can lead to econometric problems.[35] In the general VAR system with n variables, if all the variables are nonstationary, using an unrestricted VAR in levels is appropriate. If the variables are all I(1) but no cointegration relation exists, then application of an unrestricted VAR in first differences is appropriate. If there are r cointegrating relationships, then we need to model the system as a VAR in the r stationary combinations and $(n - r)$ differences of the original variables.

In any case, when our interest is in forecasting, the existence of some cointegrating relationships, even if they do not have any economic interpretation, should help us to improve the forecasts from the VAR models. The multiplicity of cointegrating vectors (and the resulting identification problems mentioned earlier) need not worry us. Cointegration relationships that do not make any economic sense need not be discarded. In fact, this is the most important use of cointegration tests and cointegrating relationships.

14.9 Cointegration and Error Correction Models

If x_t and y_t are cointegrated, there is a long-run relationship between them. Furthermore, the short-run dynamics can be described by the error correction model (ECM). This is known as the *Granger representation theorem*.

If $x_t \sim$ I(1), $y_t \sim$ I(1), and $z_t = y_t - \beta x_t$ is I(0), then x and y are said to be cointegrated. The Granger representation theorem says that in this case x_t and y_t may be considered to

[34]S. Johansen and K. Juselius, "Maximum Likelihood Estimation and Inference on Cointegration with Applications to the Demand for Money," *Oxford Bulletin of Economics and Statistics*, Vol. 52, 1990, pp. 169–210.

[35]See P. C. B. Phillips, "Optimal Inference in Cointegrated Systems," *Econometrica*, Vol. 59, 1991, pp. 283–306.

be generated by ECMs of the form

$$\Delta x_t = \rho_1 z_{t-1} + \text{lagged}(\Delta x_t, \Delta y_t) + \varepsilon_{1t}$$

$$\Delta y_t = \rho_2 z_{t-1} + \text{lagged}(\Delta x_t, \Delta y_t) + \varepsilon_{2t}$$

where at least one of ρ_1 and ρ_2 is nonzero and ε_{1t} and ε_{2t} are white noise errors.

Granger and Lee[36] suggest a further generalization of the concept of cointegration. Define $w_t = \sum_{j-0}^{t} z_{t-j}$ that is, w_t is an accumulated sum of z_t or $\Delta w_t = z_t$. Since $z_t \sim I(0)$, w_t will be I(1). Then x_t and y_t are said to be *multicointegrated* if x_t and w_t are cointegrated. In this case y_t and w_t will also be cointegrated. It follows that $u_t = w_t - \alpha x_t \sim I(0)$, where α is the cointegration constant. If x_t and y_t are multicointegrated, Granger and Lee show that they have the following (generalized) ECM representation:

$$\Delta x_t = \rho_1 z_{t-1} + \delta_1 u_{t-1} + \text{lagged}(\Delta x_t, \Delta y_t) + \varepsilon_{1t}$$

$$\Delta y_t = \rho_2 z_{t-1} + \delta_2 u_{t-1} + \text{lagged}(\Delta x_t, \Delta y_t) + \varepsilon_{2t}$$

Examples of this are: x_t = sales, y_t = production, $z_t = y_t - x_t$ = inventory change, and w_t = inventory. Sales, production, and inventory are all I(1) and possibly cointegrated; z_t, the inventory change, is I(0).

14.10   Tests for Cointegration

An important ingredient in the analysis of cointegrated systems is tests for cointegration. Consider, first, the case of two variables, x and y. We first apply unit root tests to check that x and y are both I(1). We next regress y on x (or x on y) and consider $\hat{u} = y - \hat{\beta}x$. We then apply unit root tests on $\hat{u}$.

If x and y are cointegrated, $u = y - \beta x$ is I(0). On the other hand, if they are not cointegrated, u will be I(1). Since unit root tests will be applied to u, the null hypothesis (as we discussed in Section 14.5) is that there is a unit root. Thus the null hypothesis and the alternative in cointegration tests are

$$H_0 : u \text{ has a unit root or } x \text{ and } y \text{ are } not \text{ cointegrated}$$

$$H_1 : x \text{ and } y \text{ are cointegrated}$$

The additional problem here is that u is not observed. Hence we use the estimated residual $\hat{u}$ from the cointegrating regression. Engle and Granger (1987) suggest several cointegration tests but suggest that using the ADF test to test for unit roots in $\hat{u}_t$ is best.

An alternative procedure is to use the VAR model, compute the characteristic roots of the matrix $\mathbf{A}$ of the coefficients of the VAR model [or the roots of the matrix $\mathbf{B}_k$ in equation (14.14) in the case of a general AR model] and apply the tests described earlier; that is, consider $n(\hat{\lambda} - 1)$ and use the tables in Fuller (1976, p. 371).

---

[36]G. W. J. Granger and Tae-Hwy Lee, "Multicointegration," in Fomby and Rhodes (eds.), *Advances in Econometrics*, pp. 71–84.

The case with more than two variables is more complicated. If there is only one unit root, the procedures we described earlier based on the VAR model can be used. If there is more than one unit root, the Johansen procedure (referred to earlier) has to be used.

Of particular importance since the significance levels used are the conventional 1% and 5% levels is the meaning of the null and alternative hypotheses in cointegration tests. In the unit root tests, the null hypothesis is that there is a unit root. That is, we maintain that the time series are difference stationary. This null hypothesis is maintained unless there is overwhelming evidence to reject it. In the case of cointegration tests, the null hypothesis is that there is *no* cointegration. That is, we maintain that there are no long-run relationships. This null hypothesis is maintained unless there is overwhelming evidence to reject it. The way the null hypothesis and the alternatives are formulated and the significance levels commonly used for these tests suggest that the dice are loaded in favor of unit roots and no cointegration.

We can reverse the null and alternative hypotheses for the cointegration test if we reverse the null and alternative hypotheses for the unit root tests. That is, we adopt the null hypothesis and alternative in unit root tests as

$$H_0 : x_t \text{ is stationary}$$

$$H_1 : x_t \text{ is a unit root process}$$

with similar hypotheses for y_t. Then for the cointegration test we have

$$H_0 : x_t \text{ and } y_t \text{ are cointegrated}$$

$$H_1 : x_t \text{ and } y_t \text{ are } not \text{ cointegrated}$$

We mentioned in Section 14.5 some unit root tests that use the null hypothesis of stationarity.

14.11   Cointegration and Testing of the REH and MEH

During recent years, cointegration theory has been used for testing the rational expectations hypothesis (REH) and the market efficiency hypothesis (MEH). In Section 10.14 we described some tests for the rationality of y_t^e, where y_t^e is the expectation of y_t (obtained from survey data or other sources). The tests described there are, however, not valid if y_t and/or y_t^e are I(1). For the validity of REH, $y_t - y_t^e$ has to be I(0) or else y_t and y_t^e will be drifting further apart over time, in which case the rationality of y_t^e is violated. However, it is not sufficient that the forecast error $y_t - y_t^e$ be I(0). The forecast error has to be free of serial correlation or be white noise. Hence for the rationality of expectations we require the following three conditions:

1. y_t and y_t^e must be cointegrated.
2. The cointegrating factor must be 1.
3. The difference $(y_t - y_t^e)$ must be a white noise process.

Since the cointegrating factor is specified to be 1, we use what is known as the restricted cointegration test. That is, we first test, using unit root tests, whether y_t and y_t^e are both I(1).

We next consider $\mu_t = y_t - y_t^e$ and apply unit root tests to μ_t. If the null hypothesis of a unit root (a null hypothesis of *no* cointegration) is rejected, y_t and y_t^e are cointegrated with a cointegrated factor of 1. We next test by using the Q-statistic described in Section 13.5 for the presence of serial correlation in μ_t.[37]

As with the regression tests of the REH, the regression tests of the MEH are also not valid if the variables under consideration have unit roots. In this case, the cointegration tests should be applied. The exact form of the MEH differs, depending on the markets being considered. For instance, in the case of the gold and silver markets, it should not be possible to forecast one price from the other. Thus gold and silver prices should not be cointegrated. In the case of foreign exchange rates, if the currency markets are efficient, spot exchange rates should embody all relevant information, and it should not be possible to forecast one spot exchange rate as a function of another. That is, the spot exchange rates across currencies should *not* be cointegrated. The same should be the case with forward rates. On the other hand, the future spot rate and the forward rate should be cointegrated because the forward rate is a predictor of the future spot rate.[38] The test of the last hypothesis in the regression context starts by estimating the equation

$$S_{t+1} = \alpha + \beta F_t + \varepsilon_t$$

The MEH states that $\alpha = 0$ and $\beta = 1$. However, if both S_{t+1} and F_t are I(1) series, the error ε_t is not a stationary white noise process unless the two variables are cointegrated with $\alpha = 0$ and $\beta = 1$. Some economists try to avoid the nonstationary problem by considering the following equation:

$$S_{t+1} - S_t = \alpha + \beta(F_t - S_t) + \varepsilon_t$$

Then they test whether or not $\alpha = 0$ and $\beta = 1$. However, the model is useful only if $(F_t - S_t)$ is nonstationary. For simplicity, assume that both variables are pure random walk processes. Then the left-hand side of the equation is stationary because $(S_{t+1} - S_t)$ is a white noise process. But there is no guarantee that the variable on the right-hand side, $(F_t - S_t)$, is stationary. Note that $(F_t - S_t)$ can be decomposed into $(F_t - F_{t-1}) + (F_{t-1} - S_t)$. While the first component is stationary, the second will have the same property only if the MEH holds.[39] One can think of regressing the first difference of S_{t+1} on the first difference of F_t. But this model is misspecified and gives inconsistent estimates of the parameters because the correct model to be used, if the two variables are cointegrated, is the error correction model

$$S_{t+1} - S_t = \alpha + \beta(F_t - F_{t-1}) + \gamma(F_{t-1} - S_t) + \varepsilon_t$$

---

[37] Examples of such restricted cointegration tests of the REH appear in R. W. Hafer and S. E. Hein, "Comparing Futures and Survey Forecasts of Near Term Treasury Bill Rates," *Federal Reserve Bank of St. Louis Review*, May–June 1989, pp. 33–42, and Peter C. Liu and G. S. Maddala, "Using Survey Data to Test Market Efficiency in the Foreign Exchange Markets," *Empirical Economics*, Vol. 17, 1992, pp. 303–314.

[38] Craig Hakkio and Mark Rush, "Market Efficiency and Cointegration: An Application to the Sterling and Deutsche Mark Exchange Markets," *Journal of International Money and Finance*, March 1989, pp. 75–88.

[39] Thus, if $F_t - S_t$ is stationary, there is no point in further testing the MEH. If $F_t - S_t$ is nonstationary, we have a regression of a stationary variable on a nonstationary variable. Hence plim $\hat{\beta} = 0$ and the MEH is rejected.

The regression in first differences omits the last term, thus causing an omitted variable bias. Thus if the exchange rate is nonstationary, most of the models on testing the MEH are inappropriate. If S_{t+1} and F_t are both I(1), the proper procedure is to use the restricted cointegration test using $(S_{t+1} - F_t)$.

14.12   A Summary Assessment of Cointegration

Cointegration tests have been used for a wide variety of problems, such as testing the permanent income hypothesis, testing rationality of expectations, testing market efficiency in different markets, and testing purchasing power parity. There are, however, many problems with the use of these tests and their interpretation. In a way, in the case of both unit roots and cointegration, there is too much emphasis on testing and too little on estimation.

We discussed earlier the way the null and alternative hypotheses for the unit root tests and cointegration tests are formulated, and we have also discussed the arbitrariness in the universal use of the 5% and 1% significance levels. Conclusions may be reversed if the null and alternative are reversed. For instance, when the test is conducted with the null hypothesis as a unit root, the null hypothesis is not usually rejected if the conventional significance levels are used, and if the null hypothesis is that the time series is stationary (with the alternative that it has a unit root), again the null hypothesis is not rejected when the conventional significance levels are used. The same is the case with cointegration tests when the null hypothesis is of no cointegration, or of cointegration. There is also the problem of the power of these tests, as discussed in Section 14.4.

Another important issue is that of bivariate versus multivariate cointegrating regressions. The issue is similar to simple versus multiple regression. For instance, y and x_1 may not be cointegrated, but y, x_1, and x_2 may be cointegrated. If y, x_1, and x_2 are all I(1) and there exists a linear combination of these that is I(0), so that $y = \beta_1 x_1 + \beta_2 x_2 + \varepsilon$, where ε is I(0), then (y, x_1, x_2) are cointegrated. But when we consider

$$y = \beta x_1 + \mu$$

since $\mu = \beta_2 x_2 + \varepsilon$ is I(1), we will find y and x_1 not to be cointegrated. This is the usual omitted variable problem. In this case it is wrong to make inferences just because the hypothesis of no cointegration has not been rejected. For instance, if y and x refer to prices in two related markets, it is tempting, if the hypothesis of no cointegration is not rejected, to conclude immediately that the two markets are efficient. This is indeed incorrect.

The analogy with the omitted variable case in regression analysis cannot be pushed too far. In the case of the simple versus multiple regression that we have, if x_1 and x_2 are uncorrelated, the coefficient of x_1 will be the same in both the regressions (with and without x_2). In the case of cointegration, this condition is not sufficient. When will the bivariate and multivariate tests of cointegration give the same results? The answer is: when there is only one unit root process driving all the variables. Suppose that we are considering four series on exchange rates. Then if the matrix in the VAR representation (discussed earlier) has only one unit root, the bivariate and multivariate tests will give the same results.

Another issue that arises in estimating the cointegrating regressions is the choice of the dependent variable. In the two-variable case, whether we regress y on x or x on y (and take the reciprocal of the regression coefficient) does not make any difference asymptotically, but it does in small samples. The issue is the same in the case of more than two variables. However, this problem does not arise if one is using the maximum likelihood (ML) method, as in the Johansen procedure. The problem is similar to that of 2SLS versus LIML discussed in Chapter 9. The 2SLS estimates, which depend on the regression method are not, in general, invariant to the normalization adopted, whereas the LIML estimates, which depend on the ML method, are invariant.

While estimating cointegrating regressions, many of the problems that we often discuss in the case of the usual regression and simultaneous equations models (e.g., omitted variables, parameter instability due to structural change, outliers, multicollinearity, heteroskedasticity, etc.) are often ignored, and attention is concentrated on testing for cointegration, as if that were the ultimate objective of all analysis. Even if one is doing an analysis with I(1) variables, many of these problems should not be ignored, and they do affect tests for cointegration as well.

One final issue is that of the long-run equilibrium economic relationships that the cointegrating regressions are supposed to capture. The earlier literature on partial adjustment models (discussed in Sections 10.10 and 10.11) was concerned with the estimation of long-run equilibrium relationships as well as the time lags involved in achieving equilibrium. In discussions of cointegration, the long-run relationships are estimated through static regressions and not much is said regarding the time lags required to achieve the equilibrium unless an ECM is also estimated. As argued earlier, a procedure of estimating both the long-run parameters and short-run dynamics jointly would be a better one and would also be in the spirit of the earlier discussions on the estimation of dynamic models. Also, given that the evidence in favor of unit root processes in most economic time series has been found to be fragile, preoccupation with cointegration as the sole vehicle for studying dynamic economic relationships is unwarranted. Estimation of standard ECM and VAR models with attendant diagnostics might lead to less fragile inference. The ECM's can be used to merge short-run and long-run forecasts in a consistent fashion.

Summary

1. Unrestricted VAR models suffer from the problem of overparametrization. The Bayesian version (BVAR) has been found to give better results and has a good forecasting record.

2. There have been many tests suggested for unit roots. In most of these tests, the null hypothesis is that there is a unit root, and it is rejected only when there is strong evidence against it. Using these tests, most economic time series have been found to have unit roots. However, some tests have been devised that use stationarity as the null and unit root as the alternative hypotheses. Using these tests, most economic time series have been found not to have a unit root. Some other limitations of unit root tests have also been discussed. The evidence of unit roots in economic time series appears to be fragile.

3. The theory of cointegration tries to study the interrelationships between long-run movements in economic time series. Most economic theories are about long-run behavior,

and thus much important information relevant for testing these theories is lost if the time series is de-trended or differenced, as in the Box–Jenkins approach, before any analysis is done.

4. Cointegration implies the existence of an error correction model (ECM). It also implies some restrictions on the VAR model.

5. Tests for cointegration specify the null hypothesis as no cointegration. This is because the unit root tests have the null hypothesis of unit root. Some problems with this have been discussed.

6. Cointegration theory has been used to test the rational expectations hypothesis (REH) and the market efficiency hypothesis (MEH). The former rests on rejecting the hypothesis of no cointegration and the latter on acceptance of this hypothesis. The results of these tests are sensitive to whether we consider bivariate or multivariate relationships. For instance, x and y may not be cointegrated, but x, y, and z may be cointegrated.

Exercises

1. Explain whether the following statements are true (T), false (F), or uncertain (U). If a statement is not true in general but is true under some conditions, state the conditions.
    (a) An unrestricted VAR model gives bad forecasts because of the large number of lagged variables in each equation.
    (b) The overparametrization problem in the VAR model can be solved by using Almon or Koyck lags for the lagged coefficients.
    (c) The Bayesian VAR (BVAR) model introduces very unnatural restrictions on the parameters in the model. Hence it cannot be expected to give good forecasts.
    (d) Unit root tests are all biased toward acceptance of the unit root null hypothesis.
    (e) It is better to have the null hypothesis of stationarity with the alternative as a unit root rather than the other way around.
    (f) The Dickey–Fuller tests are not very useful for testing unit roots. One should use the Phillips tests.
    (g) The Box–Jenkins method of visual inspection of the correlogram in levels and first differences gives the same results as the Dickey–Fuller unit root tests.
    (h) If x_t and y_t both have unit roots, the coefficient of x_{t-1} in the equation for x_t and the coefficient of y_{t-1} in the equation for y_t will both be close to 1 when we estimate a VAR model for these two variables.
    (i) Unit root tests all have low power because the alternative is not well specified.
    (j) Unit root tests applied to macroeconomic time series have low power because of changes in the structure of the economy.
    (k) When considering simultaneous equations models in I(1) variables, we do not have to worry about simultaneity bias. We can estimate the equations by OLS and get consistent estimates of the parameters.
    (l) If x_t and y_t are both I(1) variables, since estimates of the regression coefficient are superconsistent, it really does not matter whether we regress x_t on y_t or y_t on x_t.
    (m) Cointegration implies Granger causality.

(n) Suppose that we have the following pth-order representation of a vector $\mathbf{x}_t$ of random variables:

$$\mathbf{x}_t = \mathbf{A}_1\mathbf{x}_{t-1} + \mathbf{A}_2\mathbf{x}_{t-2} + \cdots + \mathbf{A}_p\mathbf{x}_{t-p} + \boldsymbol{\varepsilon}_t$$

The rank of $\mathbf{A}_p$ gives the number of cointegrating relationships.

(o) The representation in part (n) can be written as

$$\Delta\mathbf{x}_t = \mathbf{B}_1\Delta\mathbf{x}_{t-1} + \cdots + \mathbf{B}_{p-1}\Delta\mathbf{x}_{t-p-1} + \mathbf{B}_p\mathbf{x}_{t-p} + \boldsymbol{\varepsilon}_t$$

The rank of $\mathbf{B}_p$ gives the number of cointegrating relationships.

2. Explain how to construct hypotheses to test the following economic theories by cointegration tests:
   (a) Market efficiency hypothesis.
   (b) Purchasing power parity theory.
   (c) Rational expectations hypothesis.

3. Consider the following hypotheses:

$$H_0 : \alpha = 1 \text{ in } y_t = \mu + \alpha y_{t-1} + u_t \quad (\mu \neq 0)$$

$$H_1 : |\alpha| < 1 \text{ in } Z_t = \mu + \alpha Z_{t-1} + u_t \quad \text{where} \quad Z = y_t - \beta_1\beta_2 t$$

Show that the OLS estimator $\hat{\alpha}$ of α in $y_t = \mu + \alpha y_{t-1} + u_t$ tends to 1 under H_1.

Exercises 4 to 10 are similar except that they use different data sets. Students should select the data set and the appropriate question.

4. Using the data in Table 13.4, estimate a VAR model for C_t and Y_t with one lag and two lags.
   (a) Is the model with two lags better than the model with one lag? Use the AIC and BIC criteria (see Section 13.5). Also check for residual autocorrelations.
   (b) Since the data are quarterly, regress the data on seasonal dummies, and compute the residuals. Repeat the analysis with these residuals (assuming that they are the observations).

5. Consider the VAR models with one and two lags in Exercise 4.
   (a) Estimate the characteristic roots and vectors for the relevant matrices discussed in Section 14.8. Apply tests for unit roots and tests for cointegration.
   (b) If there is a cointegrating regression, estimate it from the characteristic vectors and also from the static regression as suggested by Granger and Engle.
   (c) Are the results different for the VAR models with one and two lags? Are they different from those from the static regressions? What do you conclude from these results?
   (d) Repeat parts (a) to (c) with the seasonally adjusted data (residuals from the regression on seasonal dummies).

6. Repeat Exercises 4 and 5 using the data in Table 13.5.

7. Repeat Exercises 4 and 5 using the data in Table 13.7. This time, when adjusting for seasonality, you have to regress the original series on a constant and 11 monthly dummies.

8. For the data in Table 4.10:
- **(a)** Estimate a regression of HS on y and RR.
- **(b)** Estimate a VAR model with one lag. Compute the characteristic roots. Test for cointegration and estimate the cointegrating vectors, if any.
- **(c)** What sense can you make of the multiple regression estimated in part (a)?
- **(d)** Repeat the analysis with residuals from a regression of the raw data on quarterly dummies.

9. In the data set in Table 13.8, examine which of the time series are trend stationary and which are difference stationary. Also investigate whether there are any cointegrating relationships among the series.

10. Consider the data in Table 13.7. Take yearly data for each month (e.g., Mar 52, Mar 53, Mar 54, ..., Mar 82; similarly, Nov 52, Nov 53, ..., Nov 82). We thus have 12 annual time series.
- **(a)** For each of these series, apply unit root tests.
- **(b)** For each of these series, compute a VAR model with one lag. Apply unit root tests and check for any cointegrating regressions.
- **(c)** Compare the results of this analysis with those in Exercise 7.

Table 14.2 Critical values for unit root tests

Sample Size	K-Test 1%	K-Test 5%	t-Test 1%	t-Test 5%	F-Test[a] 1%	F-Test[a] 5%
AR(1)						
25	−11.9	−7.3	−2.66	−1.95		
50	−12.9	−7.7	−2.62	−1.95		
100	−13.3	−7.9	−2.60	−1.95		
250	−13.6	−8.0	−2.58	−1.95		
500	−13.7	−8.0	−2.58	−1.95		
∞	−13.8	−8.1	−2.58	−1.95		
AR(1) with constant						
25	−17.2	−12.5	−3.75	−3.00		
50	−18.9	−13.3	−3.58	−2.93		
100	−19.8	−13.7	−3.51	−2.89		
250	−20.3	−14.0	−3.46	−2.88		
500	−20.5	−14.0	−3.44	−2.87		
∞	−20.7	−14.1	−3.43	−2.86		
AR(1) with constant and trend						
25	−22.5	−17.9	−4.38	−3.60	7.24	10.61
50	−25.7	−19.8	−4.15	−3.50	6.73	9.31
100	−27.4	−20.7	−4.04	−3.45	6.49	8.73
250	−28.4	−21.3	−3.99	−3.43	6.34	8.43
500	−28.9	−21.5	−3.98	−3.42	6.30	8.34
∞	−29.5	−21.8	−3.96	−3.41	6.25	8.27

[a]$K = T(\hat{\rho} - 1)$, $t = (\hat{\rho} - 1)/\text{SE}(\hat{\rho})$ and F-test is for $\gamma = 0$ and $\rho = 1$ in $y_t = \alpha + \gamma t + \rho y_{t-1} + u_t$. *Source:* W. A. Fuller, *Introduction to Statistical Time Series* (New York: Wiley, 1976), p. 371 for the K-test and p. 373 for the t-test; D. A. Dickey and W. A. Fuller, "Likelihood Ratio Statistics for Autoregressive Time Series with a Unit Root," *Econometrica*, Vol. 49, No. 4, 1981, p. 1063 for the F-test.

15 Panel Data Analysis

What is in this Chapter?

This chapter discusses analysis of panel data. This is a situation where there are observations on individual cross-section units over a period of time. The chapter discusses several models for the analysis of panel data. These are:

1. Fixed effects models.
2. Random effects models.
3. Seemingly unrelated regression model.
4. Random coefficient model.

Next some specification tests in the context of these models are discussed.

In addition, the chapter considers some issues arising from dynamic models and the question of whether or not to pool. A panel data set on energy demand in the U.S. over 20 years for 49 states is provided in Appendix B. This data set can be used to experiment with the methods discussed in the chapter.

15.1 Introduction

The term "panel data" refers to data sets where we have data on the same individual over several periods of time. The main advantage with having panel data as compared to a single cross-section or series of cross-sections with nonoverlapping cross-section units is that it allows us to test and relax the assumptions that are implicit in cross-sectional analysis.

One of the early uses of panel data in economics was in the context of estimation of production functions. The model used is now referred to as the "fixed effects" model and is given by

$$y_{it} = \alpha_i + \beta' x_{it} + u_{it} \qquad \begin{matrix} i = 1, 2, \ldots, N \\ t = 1, 2, \ldots, T \end{matrix} \qquad (15.1)$$

where y_{it} is the output and x_{it} is the vector of inputs for the ith farm in the tth period. α_i captures farm specific inputs (e.g., managerial skills) assumed to be constant over time. This model is also referred to as the "least squares with dummy variables" (LSDV) model. The α_i are estimated as coefficients of dummy variables. We have discussed such dummy variable regressions earlier in Sections 8.2 and 8.3.

15.2   The LSDV or Fixed Effects Model

For simplicity let us consider only one explanatory variable so that the model is

$$y_{it} = \alpha_i + \beta x_{it} + u_{it}$$

We also assume $u_{it} \sim \text{IN}(0, \sigma^2)$.

Define $\bar{x}_i = \dfrac{1}{T} \sum_t x_{it}$, $\bar{y}_i = \dfrac{1}{T} \sum_t y_{it}$. These are group means.

$$W_{xxi} = \sum_t (x_{it} - \bar{x}_i)^2$$

$$W_{xyi} = \sum_t (x_{it} - \bar{x}_i)(y_{it} - \bar{y}_i)$$

$$W_{yyi} = \sum_t (y_{it} - \bar{y}_i)^2$$

These are *within-group* sums of squares and sums of products. Also let $W_{xx} = \sum_i W_{xxi}$ with W_{xy} and W_{yy} defined similarly.

The estimates of the parameters α_i and β are obtained by minimizing $Q = \sum_{i,t}(y_{it} - \hat{\alpha}_i - \hat{\beta}x_{it})^2$ with respect to α_i and β. We get

$$\frac{\partial Q}{\partial x_i} = 0 \Rightarrow \sum_t (y_{it} - \hat{\alpha}_i - \hat{\beta}x_{it}) = 0$$

$$\text{or} \quad \hat{\alpha}_i = \bar{y}_i - \hat{\beta}\bar{x}_i$$

$$\frac{\partial Q}{\partial \beta} = 0 \Rightarrow \sum_{i,t} x_{it}(y_{it} - \hat{\alpha}_i - \hat{\beta}x_{it}) = 0$$

Substituting the expression for $\hat{\alpha}_i$ in the second equation and simplifying we get

$$\hat{\beta} = W_{xy}/W_{xx}$$

The residual sum of squares is $W_{yy} - W_{xy}^2/W_{xx}$. In the case of several explanatory variables, W_{xx} is a matrix and $\hat{\beta}$ and W_{xy} are vectors.

We get

$$\hat{\alpha}_i = \bar{y}_i - \hat{\beta}'\bar{x}_i$$

$$\hat{\beta} = W_{xx}^{-1} W_{xy}$$

This is known as the within-group estimate of β and is often denoted $\hat{\beta}_w$ or $\hat{\beta}_{LSDV}$. Res SS $= W_{yy} - W_{yx}(W_{xx})^{-1}(W_{xy})$. If we define $\bar{x}$ and $\bar{y}$ as deviations from the overall mean (rather than group means) we have $T_{xx} = \sum_{i,t}(x_{it} - \bar{x}_i)^2$ with T_{xy} and T_{yy} defined suitably. If we consider the hypothesis $\alpha_1 = \alpha_2 = \cdots = \alpha_N = \alpha$ then the model is

$$y_{it} = \alpha + \beta x_{it} + u_{it}$$

and in this case $\hat{\alpha} = \bar{y} - \hat{\beta}\bar{x}$ and $\hat{\beta} = T_{xy}/T_{xx}$.

15.3 The Random Effects Model

In the random effects model, the α_i are treated as random variables rather than fixed constants. The α_i are assumed to be independent of the errors u_{it} and also mutually independent. This model is also known as the *variance components* model. It became popular in econometrics following the paper by Balestra and Nerlove[1] on the demand for natural gas.

We shall assume that

$$\alpha_i \sim \text{IID}(0, \sigma_\alpha^2)$$

$$u_{it} \sim \text{IID}(0, \sigma_u^2)$$

and that α_i and u_{it} are independent. (IID stands for independent and identically distributed.)

For the sake of simplicity we shall use only one explanatory variable. The model is the same as equation (15.1) except that α_i are random variables.

Since α_i are random, the errors now are $v_{it} = \alpha_i + u_{it}$ and the presence of α_i produces a correlation among the errors of the same cross-section unit though the errors from the different cross-section units are independent. Thus we have

$$\text{cov}(v_{it}, v_{is}) = \sigma_u^2 + \sigma_\alpha^2 \quad \text{for } t = s$$

$$= \sigma_\alpha^2 \quad \text{for } t \neq s$$

$$\text{cov}(v_{it}, v_{js}) = 0 \quad \text{for all } t, s \text{ if } i \neq j$$

Since the errors are correlated, we have to use generalized least squares (GLS) to get efficient estimates. However, after algebraic simplification the GLS estimator can be

---

[1]P. Balestra and M. Nerlove, "Pooling Cross-Section and Time-Series Data in the Estimation of a Dynamic Model: The Demand for Natural Gas," *Econometrica*, Vol. 34, 1966, pp. 585–612.

written in the simple form[2]

$$\hat{\beta}_{\text{GLS}} = \frac{W_{xy} + \theta B_{xy}}{W_{xx} + \theta B_{xx}} \quad \theta = \frac{\sigma_u^2}{\sigma_u^2 + T\sigma_\alpha^2} \tag{15.2}$$

where W refers to within-group and B refers to between-group data.

$$B_{xx} = T_{xx} - W_{xx}$$

$$B_{xy} = T_{xy} - W_{xy}$$

$$B_{yy} = T_{yy} - W_{yy}$$

where T refers to total (and W refers to within) sums of squares and sums of products defined earlier.

Note that $\hat{\beta}_{\text{OLS}} = T_{xy}/T_{xx}$ and $\hat{\beta}_{\text{LSDV}} = W_{xy}/W_{xx}$. Thus the OLS and LSDV estimators are special cases of the GLS estimator with $\theta = 1$ and $\theta = 0$, respectively.

The arguments in favor of the random effects model are that the LSDV method often results in a loss in a large number of degrees of freedom (if N the number of cross-section units is large) and it also eliminates a large portion of the total variation if B_{xx}, B_{xy}, and B_{yy} are large relative to W_{xx}, W_{xy}, and W_{yy}, respectively. Another argument is that α_i are a total of several factors specific to the cross-section units, and thus α_i represent "specific ignorance" and can be treated as random variables by much the same argument that u_{it} representing "general ignorance" are treated as random variables.

There are two more arguments for the use of the fixed effects models. The first, common in the analysis of variance literature, is that if we want to make inferences about only this set of cross-section units then we should treat α_i as fixed. On the other hand, if we want to make inferences about the population from which these cross-section data came, we should treat α_i as random. In most of the applied econometric work, the latter is the case.

The second argument is as follows: very often we have also some time-invariant explanatory variables. For instance, in earnings equations, years of schooling, family background, etc., are explanatory variables, so that the equation looks like

$$y_{it} = \gamma z_i + \beta x_{it} + \alpha_i + u_{it}$$

If we use the fixed effects model, there is no way we can estimate the parameter γ because α_i captures the effect of z_i. In this case we have to use the random effects model.

There are two things to note about the GLS estimator (15.2). First, if T is large or σ_α^2 is large relative to σ_u^2, θ will be very close to zero, and the GLS estimator is very close to the LSDV estimator. Second, in actual practice θ is not known and must be estimated based on preliminary estimates of σ_u^2 and σ_α^2. Several methods have been suggested in

---

[2]See G. S. Maddala, "The Use of Variance Components Models in Pooling Cross-Section and Time-series Data," *Econometrica*, Vol. 39, 1971, pp. 341–358.

the literature.[3] One of these is the procedure suggested by Nerlove.[4] In this procedure we first estimate the equation by the LSDV method to get estimates of the α_i and σ_u^2. The variance of the $\hat{\alpha}_i$ is taken as an estimate of σ_α^2. The estimates of σ_α^2 and σ_u^2 obtained from this method are biased and not consistent but Nerlove found in his Monte Carlo study that the GLS estimator so obtained outperforms (in terms of mean-squared error) the estimators from the other methods.

Fuller and Battese[5] show that the GLS estimator (15.2) is the same as the OLS estimator from the transformed data

$$y_{it} - \lambda \bar{y}_i \quad \text{and} \quad x_{it} - \lambda \bar{x}_i \quad \text{where } \lambda = 1 - \sqrt{\theta}$$

Nerlove's two-step procedure has been widely used in several empirical studies besides the study by Balestra and Nerlove. However, unlike the Balestra–Nerlove study, these studies found the GLS estimator close to the LSDV estimator. For instance, the results from Houthakker, Verleger, and Shechan[6] were as follows (figures in parentheses are standard errors):

Method	Coefficient of		
	Price	Income	Lagged Consumption
OLS	0.023 (0.012)	0.0031 (0.0039)	0.9894 (0.0037)
LSDV	−0.081 (0.013)	0.341 (0.018)	0.6595 (0.0171)
VC	−0.075 (0.013)	0.303 (0.017)	0.6957 (0.0164)

Note that there is very little difference between the estimates obtained by the LSDV and VC methods. Also, the price and income elasticities are much higher when these methods are used than when the OLS method is used.

The computation of OLS, LSDV, and VC estimates from the data in Table 15.1 (available on the Web) is left as an exercise.

The extension of the above procedures to the case of several explanatory variables is straightforward. W_{xx} and B_{xx} will be matrices and W_{xy} and B_{xy} will be vectors. Equation (15.2) will be

$$\hat{\beta}_{\text{GLS}} = (W_{xx} + \theta B_{xx})^{-1}(W_{xy} + \theta B_{xy})$$

Also, it is easy to extend this model to the case where in addition to cross-section dummies we have time dummies as well and both sets of dummies are treated as random.[7]

---

[3]These are discussed in G. S. Maddala and T. D. Mount, "A Comparative Study of Alternative Estimators for Variance Components Models," *Journal of the American Statistical Association*, Vol. 68, 1973, pp. 324–328.

[4]M. Nerlove, "Further Evidence on the Estimation of Dynamic Economic Relations From a Time-Series of Cross-Sections," *Econometrica*, Vol. 39, 1971, pp. 359–382.

[5]W. A. Fuller and G. E. Battese, "Transformations for Linear Models With Nested Error Structure," *Journal of the American Statistical Association*, Vol. 68, 1973, pp. 626–652.

[6]H. S. Houthakker, P. K. Verleger, Jr., and D. P. Shechan, "Dynamic Demand Analysis for Gasoline and Residential Electricity Demand," *American Journal of Agricultural Economics*, May 1974, pp. 412–418.

[7]See Maddala, "Use of Variance Components." Also, T. D. Wallace and A. Hussain, "The Use of Error-Components Models in Combining Cross-Section and Time Series Data," *Econometrica*, Vol. 37, 1969, pp. 55–72.

15.4　Fixed Effects Versus Random Effects

We have given, in the previous section, some arguments for using the random effects models. Mundlak,[8] however, argued that this dichotomy between fixed effects and random effects models disappears if we make the assumption that α_i depend on the mean values of x_{it}, an assumption he regards as reasonable in many problems. In this case we have

$$\alpha_i = \pi'\bar{x}_i + w_i \tag{15.3}$$

Substituting this in equation (15.1) gives

$$y_{it} = \pi'\bar{x}_i + \beta'x_{it} + w_i + u_{it}$$

Using the Fuller and Battese argument we note that the estimate from the random effects model is obtained by using the OLS in the following equation:

$$\begin{aligned}
y_{it} - \lambda\bar{y}_i &= \pi'(\bar{x}_i - \lambda\bar{x}_i) + \beta'(x_{it} - \lambda\bar{x}_i) + v_{it} \\
&= \beta'(x_{it} - \bar{x}_i) + \delta'\bar{x}_i + v_{it}
\end{aligned} \tag{15.4}$$

where $\delta = (\pi + \beta)(1 - \lambda)$.

Since $\bar{x}_i$ is orthogonal to $(x_{it} - \bar{x}_i)$ and since $\text{cov}[(x_{it} - \bar{x}_i)(y_{it} - \bar{y}_i)] = W_{xy}$ we get the result $\hat{\beta} = W_{xx}^{-1}W_{xy}$, the LSDV estimator. Thus in this case the random effects model gives us the same estimator as the fixed effects. We have given here an easy proof of Mundlak's result. Note that this argument also goes through if instead of equation (15.3) we have

$$\alpha_i = \pi'\bar{x}_i + \gamma'z_i + w_i$$

where z_i are some time-invariant variables. In this case equation (15.4) can be written as

$$y_{it} - \lambda\bar{y}_i = \beta'(x_{it} - \bar{x}_i) + \delta'\bar{x}_i + (1 - \lambda)\gamma'z_i + v_{it}$$

and since $\sum_t(x_{it} - \bar{x}_i)z_i = 0$ we get the estimator of β as $W_{xx}^{-1}W_{xy}$.

Hausman Test

The Hausman test described in Section 12.10 is usually applied to tests for fixed versus random effects models. Actually, the test is not a test for this hypothesis. The Mundlak argument says that α_i are correlated with x_{it} but in a particular way. We can test the hypothesis

$$H_0 : \alpha_i \text{ are } not \text{ correlated with } x_{it}$$

$$H_1 : \alpha_i \text{ are correlated with } x_{it}$$

Under H_0, the GLS estimator is consistent and efficient. On the other hand, the within-group estimator $\hat{\beta}_w$ is consistent whether the null hypothesis is valid or not since all

---

[8]Y. Mundlak, "On the Pooling of Time-Series and Cross-Section Data," *Econometrica*, Vol. 46, 1978, pp. 69–85.

time-invariant effects are subtracted out. Thus we can construct $q = \hat{\beta}_w - \hat{\beta}_{GLS}$. Also $V(q) = V(\hat{\beta}_w) - V(\hat{\beta}_{GLS})$. Hence we use $m = \hat{q}'[\hat{V}(\hat{q})]^{-1}\hat{q}$ as a χ^2-statistic with d.f. k where k is the dimensionality of β.

Breusch and Pagan Test

Yet another specification test is to test $\sigma_\alpha^2 = 0$. This is the case where the individual components do not exist and we can use the OLS method. A test of this hypothesis is given in Breusch and Pagan.[9]

If we denote the residuals from the least squares regression by $\hat{u}_{it}$ and define

$$S_1 = \sum_{i=1}^{N} \left(\sum_{t=1}^{T} \hat{u}_{it} \right)^2$$

$$S_2 = \sum_{i=1}^{N} \sum_{t=1}^{T} \hat{u}_{it}^2$$

and

$$\lambda = \frac{NT}{2(T-1)} \left(\frac{S_1}{S_2} - 1 \right)^2$$

then λ has a χ^2-distribution with d.f. 1.

15.5 The SUR Model

Zellner[10] suggested an alternative method to analyze panel data, the seemingly unrelated regression (SUR) estimation. In this model a GLS method is applied to exploit the correlations in the errors across cross-section units. The random effects model results in a particular type of correlation among the errors. It is an equicorrelated model. In the SUR model the errors are independent over time but correlated across cross-section units:

$$\text{cov}(u_{it}, u_{js}) = \sigma_{ij} \quad \text{if } t = s$$
$$= 0 \quad \text{if } t \neq s$$

This type of correlation would arise if there are omitted variables that are common to all equations.

The estimation of the SUR model proceeds as follows. We first estimate each of the N equations (for the cross-section units) by OLS. We get the residuals $\bar{u}_{it}$. Then we compute $\hat{\sigma}_{ij} = 1/(T-k) \sum \hat{u}_{it}\hat{u}_{jt}$ where k is the number of regressors. After we get the estimates $\hat{\sigma}_{ij}$ we use GLS on all the N equations jointly.

[9]T. Breusch and A. R. Pagan, "The Lagrange Multiplier Test and Its Application to Model Specification in Econometrics," *Review of Economic Studies*, Vol. 47, 1980, pp. 239–253.

[10]A. Zellner, "An Efficient Method of Estimating Seemingly Unrelated Regressions and Tests for Aggregation Bias," *Journal of the American Statistical Association*, June 1962, pp. 348–368.

If we have large N and small T this method is not feasible. Also, the method is appropriate only if the errors are generated by a true multivariate distribution. When the correlations are due to common omitted variables it is not clear whether the GLS method is superior to OLS.[11] The argument is similar to the one mentioned in Section 6.9. See "autocorrelation caused by omitted variables."

15.6 Dynamic Panel Data Models

We shall discuss briefly the extensions of the variance components models in Section 15.3 to dynamic models. When it comes to dynamic panel data models, we have to distinguish between two kinds of panel data models:

1. The serial correlation model

$$y_{it} = \beta x_{it} + \alpha_i + w_{it}$$

$$w_{it} = \rho w_{i,t-1} + u_{it} \quad |\rho| < 1 \tag{15.5}$$

2. The state dependence model

$$y_{it} = \beta x_{i,t-1} + \gamma y_{i,t-1} + \alpha_i + u_{it} \tag{15.6}$$

In both cases $\alpha_i \sim \text{IN}(0, \sigma_\alpha^2)$ and $u_i \sim \text{IN}(0, \sigma_u^2)$ and α_i and u_{it} are independent.

Also, when we consider the ML method of estimation, we have to consider the conditional likelihood function (conditional on the initial value of y_{i0}) and the unconditional likelihood function. In the latter case we assume that the process has been going on for a long time and hence we assume that y_{i0} is an observation from the equilibrium distribution of y_{i0}.

The ML estimation is very tedious to be discussed here. Two references where this can be found are the papers by Maddala and Nerlove.[12] We shall consider some simplified estimators which may not be as efficient as the ML estimators but are much easier to compute.

In all the variance components models, there is the problem of getting estimates of σ_α^2 and σ_u^2. As described in Section 15.3, these are obtained from the LSDV model. They are not consistent but the GLS method based on these estimates performs better than the GLS method based on other estimates. Nerlove (1998) argues against using a method suggested by Greene and Judge et al. in their texts in econometrics and that is built into several computer programs because it gives negative estimates of the variance components and leads to unnecessary rejection of the model as invalid.

---

[11] See P. Rao, "Specification Bias in Seemingly Unrelated Regressions," in W. Sellekaerts (ed.), *Essays in Honor of Tinbergen*, Vol. 2 (New York: International Arts and Science Press, 1974), pp. 101–113.

[12] G. S. Maddala, "Recent Developments in the Econometrics of Panel Data Analysis," *Transportation Research*, Vol. 21A, 1987, pp. 303–326, Section 5 "Estimation of Dynamic Models," and M. Nerlove, "Properties of Alternative Estimators of Dynamic Panel Data Models," in C. Hsiao, K. Lahiri, L. F. Lee, and M. H. Pesaran (eds.), *Analysis of Panels and Limited Dependent Variable Models Essays in Honor of G. S. Maddala* (Cambridge: Cambridge University Press, 1998).

Once the estimates of the variance components have been obtained, we can use the Fuller–Battese transformation discussed in Section 15.3 and use OLS. This is the method of estimation for the model in equation (15.6).

For the model (15.5) we can first estimate the model by the LSDV method and get $\hat{w}_{it}$. Now regress $\hat{w}_{it}$ and $\hat{w}_{i,t-1}$ to get $\hat{\rho}$. Next estimate the transformed equation

$$y_{it}^* = \beta' x_{it}^* + \alpha_i^* + u_{it}$$

where

$$y_{it}^* = y_{it} - \hat{\rho} y_{i,t-1}$$
$$x_{it}^* = x_{it} - \hat{\rho} x_{i,t-1}$$
$$\alpha_i^* = \alpha_i(1 - \rho)$$

Again we estimate this equation by LSDV, get estimates $\hat{\alpha}_i^*$, and take the variance of these as $\hat{\sigma}_\alpha^{*2}$. Using $\hat{\sigma}_u^2$ and this estimate of $\hat{\sigma}_\alpha^{*2}$ we use the Fuller–Battese transformation and the OLS.

Essentially we have described some feasible GLS procedures.

Of course, in the model (15.6), since the errors are not independent, we have a problem of lagged dependent variable and correlated errors. Thus, OLS estimators of the parameters are inconsistent. One can use $x_{i,t-1}$ as instrumental variables (IV) and estimate the equation by IV methods instead of OLS to get consistent estimates.

15.7 The Random Coefficient Model

Consider the model

$$y_{it} = \alpha_i + \beta_i x_{it} + u_{it} \quad i = 1, 2, \ldots, N$$
$$t = 1, 2, \ldots, T$$

In the variance components model α_i are treated as random and $\beta_i = \beta$ for all i; i.e., the intercepts are random and the slope coefficients are all equal.

In the random coefficient model,[13] the β_i are also treated as random. For simplicity let us drop α_i. We consider the model

$$y_{it} = \beta_i x_{it} + u_{it}$$
$$\beta_i = \beta + v_i \quad \text{where } v_i \sim \text{IN}(0, \delta^2) \quad u_{it} \sim \text{IN}(0, \sigma_i^2)$$

We then have the model

$$y_{it} = \beta x_{it} + (u_{it} + v_i x_{it}) = \beta x_{it} + w_{it}$$

---

[13]P. A. V. B. Swamy, "Efficient Inference in a Random Coefficient Model," *Econometrica*, Vol. 38, 1970, pp. 311–323. The random coefficient model was first discussed in C. R. Rao, "The Theory of Least Squares When the Parameters are Stochastic," *Biometrika*, Vol. 52, 1965, pp. 447–458. Swamy generalized this to panel data.

We have

$$\text{cov}(w_{it}, w_{is}) = \sigma_i^2 + \delta^2 x_{it}^2 \quad \text{if } t = s$$

$$= \delta^2 x_{it} x_{is} \quad \text{if } t \neq s$$

$$\text{cov}(w_{it}, w_{js}) = 0 \quad \text{if } i \neq j$$

This is a heteroskedastic model and we have to use GLS.

It can be shown that $\hat{\beta}_{\text{GLS}}$ is a weighted average of the OLS estimators $\hat{\beta}_i$ from the individual cross-section equations

$$\hat{\beta}_{\text{GLS}} = \sum_{i=1}^{N} w_i \hat{\beta}_i \tag{15.7}$$

where

$$w_i = \frac{1/(\delta^2 + v_i)}{\sum_{i=1}^{N} [1/(\delta^2 + v_i)]} \tag{15.8}$$

where $v_i = \sigma_i^2 / \sum_{t=1}^{T} x_{it}^2$ is the variance of $\hat{\beta}_i$. If δ^2 is large compared with v_i, then the weights in equation (15.8) are almost equal and the weighted average would be close to a simple average of the $\hat{\beta}_i$.

In practice the GLS estimator cannot be computed because the parameters δ^2 and σ_i^2 in equation (15.8) are not known. To obtain these we estimate separate equations for the N cross-section units and get the residuals $\hat{u}_{it}$. Then

$$\hat{\sigma}_i^2 = \frac{1}{T} \sum_t \hat{u}_{it}^2 \quad \text{and} \quad \delta^2 = \text{var}(\hat{\beta}_i)$$

Swamy suggests an unbiased estimator for δ^2 but this can be negative.

The generalization of this to the case of several explanatory variables is obvious. δ^2 will be a matrix which we can denote by Δ. $\hat{\beta}_i$ are vectors and v_i are matrices. $v_i = (x_i' x_i)^{-1} \sigma_i^2$ and w_i are also matrices.

$$\hat{\beta}_{\text{GLS}} = \sum w_i \hat{\beta}_i$$

$$\text{where } w_i = (\Delta + v_i)^{-1} \left[\sum_{i=1}^{N} (\Delta + v_i)^{-1} \right]^{-1}$$

Alternative procedures for the estimation of σ_i^2 and Δ that have been suggested in the literature are reviewed in Table 1 of Maddala et al.[14] We have given above one procedure for the estimation of σ_i^2 and δ^2 to be used in the GLS estimation.

---

[14]G. S. Maddala, H. Li, R. P. Trost, and F. Joutz, "Estimation of Short-Run and Long-Run Elasticities of Energy Demand From Panel Data Using Shrinkage Estimators," *Journal of Business and Economic Statistics*, Vol. 15, 1997, pp. 90–100.

Summary

1. This chapter first discusses the fixed effects and random effects models and the issues related to the choice between these models. Hausman's specification error test is discussed and it is explained what *exactly* it tests. There are some misconceptions about the test among empirical researchers. Next the seemingly unrelated regression (SUR) model is described.

2. The chapter then discusses dynamic models. The exact maximum likelihood methods for these models are complicated and hence references are given. Some simplified procedures are discussed.

3. Finally the chapter discusses the random coefficient model and describes the GLS estimator as a weighted average of the OLS estimators for the individual cross-section units.

All these models can be estimated using the data in Table 15.1 on the Web. This is left as an exercise. Hence no exercises have been added to this chapter.

Panel data analysis is now very popular, particularly because of the assembly of several cross-country data sets. The most popular of these data sets is the Penn–World tables by Summers and Heston which have been used in many studies on economic growth. These data are publicly available from the NBER Website at ftp://pwt.econ.upenn.edu/

An amusing example of such cross-country regressions is that of Wall,[15] who used the data from 95 noncommunist nonOPEC countries from the Penn–World tables and estimated the following regressions:

$$g = 103.9 - 43.0 D_c + 80.3 D_b$$
$$\underset{(15.1)}{} \quad \underset{(14.4)}{} \quad \underset{(39.9)}{}$$

where g = growth rate of real per capita income between 1960 and 1990, D_c and D_b are dummies indicating cricket and baseball countries.

The conclusions are:

1. For emerging countries without a history of cricket or baseball, baseball instruction and subsidies should be an immediate priority. United States and Japan can provide those subsidies.
2. Countries playing cricket should abolish cricket and switch to baseball.

---

[15]H. J. Wall, "Cricket vs. Baseball as an Engine of Economic Growth," *Royal Economic Society Newsletter*, July 2–3, 1995.

16 Large-Sample Theory

What is in this Chapter?

This chapter discusses two methods of estimation that have desirable properties in large samples. The method of maximum likelihood (ML) and the method of generalized moments (GMM). It also discusses the asymptotic tests of significance based on the ML method of estimation: likelihood ratio (LR) test, Wald (W) test, and Rao's score test, also known as the Lagrangian multiplier (LM) test. We illustrate these with reference to the linear regression model but they are all of general applicability. Two important references on asymptotic theory are:

1. C. R. Rao, *Linear Statistical Inference and Its Applications*, 2nd ed., Section 2.C "Limit Theorems," pp. 108–130 and Chap. 5 "Criteria of Estimation in Large Samples" (Wiley, 1973).
2. T. Amemiya, *Advanced Econometrics*, Chap. 3 "Large Sample Theory," pp. 80–104 (Harvard University Press, 1985).

Our discussion will be more elementary. Proofs will be omitted. They can be found in the above books.

Earlier in Chapter 2 (Section 2.6) we discussed asymptotic properties of estimators. In this chapter we discuss methods of estimation and tests of significance.

We start with the ML method of estimation (see also appendix to Chapter 3).

16.1 The Maximum Likelihood Method

Consider a sample $y_1, y_2, \ldots, y_n$ from the density $f(y, \theta) > 0$. The joint distribution of the observation is $f(y_1, y_2, \ldots, y_n, \theta)$. $\int \int \ldots \int f(y_1, y_2, \ldots, y_n, \theta) \, dy_1 \, dy_2 \ldots dy_n = 1$. We shall write this compactly as $\int f(\mathbf{y}, \theta) \, d\mathbf{y} = 1$. $f(\mathbf{y}, \theta)$ regarded as a function of θ given $y_1, y_2, \ldots, y_n$ is called the likelihood function denoted by $L(\theta|\mathbf{y})$ or compactly as

$L(\theta)$. We therefore have $\int L\,d\mathbf{y} = 1$. Differentiate both sides with θ. We get

$$\int \frac{\partial L}{\partial \theta}\,d\mathbf{y} = 0 \quad \text{or} \quad \int \left(\frac{1}{L}\frac{\partial L}{\partial \theta}\right) L\,d\mathbf{y} = 0 \quad \text{or} \quad \int \left(\frac{\partial \log L}{\partial \theta}\right) L\,d\mathbf{y} = 0$$

But, for any function $g(\mathbf{y})$, $\int g(\mathbf{y}) f(\mathbf{y}, \theta)\,d\mathbf{y}$ is just $E[g(\mathbf{y})]$. Hence we have $E[\partial \log L/\partial \theta] = 0$. The quantity $\partial \log L/\partial \theta$ is denoted by $S(\theta)$ and is called "score." The ML estimate of θ is obtained by solving the equation $\partial \log L/\partial \theta = 0$ or $S(\theta) = 0$. This is called the *likelihood equation*. Take

$$\int \left(\frac{\partial \log L}{\partial \theta}\right) L\,d\mathbf{y} = 0$$

and differentiate both sides again with θ. We get

$$\int \left[\frac{\partial^2 \log L}{\partial \theta^2} L + \frac{\partial \log L}{\partial \theta}\frac{\partial L}{\partial \theta}\right] d\mathbf{y} = 0$$

Write the second part of this as $(\partial \log L/\partial \theta)(\partial \log L/\partial \theta)L$. This says

$$E\left[\frac{\partial^2 \log L}{\partial \theta^2} + \left(\frac{\partial \log L}{\partial \theta}\right)^2\right] = 0$$

or

$$E\left[-\frac{\partial^2 \log L}{\partial \theta^2}\right] = E[S(\theta)]^2 = V[S(\theta)]$$

since $E[S(\theta)] = 0$. The quantity $E[-\partial^2 \log L/\partial \theta^2]$ is denoted by $I(\theta)$. It has been proved that under general conditions the variance of $\hat{\theta}_{mL}$ is equal to $1/I(\theta)$ (for a proof see Rao, 1973 and Amemiya, 1985 cited earlier).

In the case of several parameters the $I(\theta)$ is a matrix and the covariance matrix of the ML estimators is $[I(\boldsymbol{\theta})]^{-1}$ where $I(\boldsymbol{\theta})$ is the expected value of the matrix of second derivatives of $\log L$ with a minus sign. $I(\boldsymbol{\theta})$ is also known as the *information matrix*.

16.2   Methods of Solving the Likelihood Equations

The likelihood equations $S(\theta) = 0$ are usually nonlinear and have to be solved using the methods described in Chapter 10, in particular, the Newton–Raphson method. However, there are two other methods available. The method of scoring and the Brendt et al. method. The method of scoring works as follows.

If θ_0 is the trial value of θ, then expanding $(\partial \log L/\partial \theta)$ and retaining only the first power of $\delta\theta = \theta - \theta_0$ we get

$$\frac{\partial \log L}{\partial \theta} = \frac{\partial \log L}{\partial \theta_0} + \delta\theta \frac{\partial^2 \log L}{\partial \theta_0^2}$$

At the maximum, $\partial \log L / \partial \theta = 0$. This gives $\delta\theta$. In large samples, we can substitute $-I(\theta_0)$ for $\partial^2 \log L / \partial \theta_0^2$. Hence we get, using the definition of $S(\theta)$, $\delta\theta = [I(\theta_0)]^{-1} S(\theta_0)$.

This gives the next estimate θ as $\theta_1 = \theta_0 + \delta(\theta)$. The difference between the Newton–Raphson method and the method of scoring is that the former depends on the *observed* second derivatives and the latter depends on *expected* values of the second derivatives. There seems to be some evidence that the method of scoring, where feasible, is to be preferred.

In the appendix to Chapter 3 we illustrate the scoring method with respect to the regression model

$$y_i = \frac{1}{x_i - \beta} + u_i$$

Both the Newton–Raphson and the scoring methods depend on the second derivatives of the likelihood function.

The method by Berndt et al.[1] uses only the first derivatives. The rationale is as follows. Since

$$L = \prod_{i=1}^{T} f(Y_i, \theta)$$

$$\log L = \sum_{i=1}^{T} \log f(Y_i, \theta)$$

$$\frac{\partial \log L}{\partial \theta} = \sum_{i=1}^{T} \frac{\partial \log f(Y_i, \theta)}{\partial \theta}$$

$$\frac{\partial^2 \log L}{\partial \theta^2} = \sum_{i=1}^{T} \frac{\partial^2 \log f(Y_i, \theta)}{\partial \theta^2}$$

As we showed earlier

$$E\left[\frac{\partial \log f(Y_i, \theta)}{\partial \theta}\right] = 0$$

and

$$E\left[-\frac{\partial^2 \log f(Y_i, \theta)}{\partial \theta^2}\right] = E\left[\frac{\partial \log f(Y_i, \theta)}{\partial \theta}\right]^2$$

The BHHH algorithm replaces

$$\frac{-\partial^2 \log f(Y_i, \theta)}{\partial \theta^2} \quad \text{by} \quad \left(\frac{\partial \log f(Y_i, \theta)}{\partial \theta}\right)^2$$

Hence we get the following algorithms:

---

[1] E. R. Berndt, B. H. Hall, R. E. Hall, and J. A. Hausman, "Estimation and Inference in Non-Linear Structural Models," *Annals of Economic and Social Measurement*, 1974, pp. 653–665.

Newton–Raphson

$$\theta_1 = \theta_0 + \left[\frac{-\partial^2 \log L}{\partial \theta_0^2}\right]^{-1} S(\theta_0)$$

Scoring Method

$$\theta_1 = \theta_0 + [I(\theta_0)]^{-1} S(\theta_0)$$

BHHH

$$\theta_1 = \theta_0 + \left[\sum_{i=1}^{T} \left(\frac{\partial \log f(Y_i, \theta)}{\partial \theta_0}\right)^2\right]^{-1} S(\theta_0)$$

In vector notation this is

$$\theta_1 = \theta_0 + \left[\sum_{i=1}^{T} \frac{\partial \log f(Y_i, \boldsymbol{\theta})}{\partial \boldsymbol{\theta}} \frac{\partial \log f(Y_i, \boldsymbol{\theta})}{\partial \boldsymbol{\theta}'}\right]^{-1}_{\theta=\theta_0} S(\theta_0)$$

16.3   The Cramer–Rao Lower Bound

Let T be an unbiased estimator of θ. Then $V(T) \geq 1/I(\theta)$. This is known as the Cramer–Rao lower bound for the variance of T. The quantity $1/I(\theta)$ is called the "information limit to the variance of T."

The proof runs roughly as follows.

$$E(T) = \theta$$

Hence

$$\int T L(\mathbf{y}) \, d\mathbf{y} = \theta$$

Differentiating both sides with respect to θ we get

$$\int T \frac{\partial L}{\partial \theta} \, d\mathbf{y} = 1 \quad \text{or} \quad \int T \frac{\partial \log L}{\partial \theta} L \, d\mathbf{y} = 1$$

Since $E[\partial \log L/\partial \theta] = 0$ we have $\text{cov}(T, \partial \log L/\partial \theta) = 1$. Now $\text{cov}^2(T, \partial \log L/\partial \theta) \leq V(T)V(\partial \log L/\partial \theta)$, but $\text{var}(\partial \log L/\partial \theta) = I(\theta)$. Hence we get $1 \leq V(T)I(\theta)$ or $V(T) \geq 1/I(\theta)$.

This result also holds good if T is a consistent estimator of θ (see Rao, 1973). The ML estimator attains the Cramer–Rao lower bound.

16.4   Large-Sample Tests Based on ML

There are three tests based on the ML method: the likelihood ratio (LR) test, the Wald (W) test, and Rao's score test, also known as the Lagrangian multiplier (LM) test. The LR test is the most commonly discussed test and was suggested by Neyman and Pearson in 1928.

The Wald test was suggested by Abraham Wald in 1943. The score test was suggested by C. R. Rao in 1948. Aitchisan and Silvey suggested the same test under the name "the Lagrangian multiplier" test in a series of papers in 1958–1960. The score test is commonly referred to as the LM test in the econometric literature (except in the book by Amemiya who refers to it as the score test and does not use the terminology LM test at all).

We shall denote

$$\hat{\theta}_{\text{ML}} \text{ or } \hat{\theta} \text{ as the unrestricted MLE}$$

$$\tilde{\theta} \text{ as the restricted MLE}$$

The LR test uses both $\hat{\theta}$ and $\tilde{\theta}$. The W test uses $\hat{\theta}$ only. The score test uses $\tilde{\theta}$ only.

In many problems computing the restricted MLE is easier because it is a simpler model. That is why the score test (LM test) is very popular in econometrics. The intuitive idea of the score test is as follows.

Earlier we derived the result that $E[S(\theta)] = \mathbf{0}$, $\text{var}[S(\theta)] = I(\theta)$, and $S(\hat{\theta}) = \mathbf{0}$ if $\hat{\theta}$ is MLE. If the null hypothesis is that θ is subject to some restrictions, then $S(\tilde{\theta}) \approx \mathbf{0}$ for the restricted MLE $\tilde{\theta}$. Also, $I(\theta) \approx I(\tilde{\theta})$. Hence the score test statistic is given by

$$T_s : S(\tilde{\theta})'[I(\tilde{\theta})]^{-1}S(\tilde{\theta}) \sim \chi_r^2$$

where r is the number of restrictions. There are several forms of the score test depending on how $I(\tilde{\theta})$ is estimated. T_s is significantly different from zero if $\tilde{\theta}$ is significantly different from $\hat{\theta}$, or the null hypothesis is not true.

The likelihood ratio test considers the ratio

$$\lambda = \frac{\max L(\theta) \text{ under the restriction (or } H_0)}{\max L(\theta) \text{ without the restriction}}$$

λ will necessarily be less than 1 since the restricted maximum will be less than the unrestricted maximum. If the restrictions are not valid, λ will be significantly less than 1. If they are valid, λ will be close to 1. The LR test consists of using $-2\log\lambda$ as a χ^2-distribution with d.f. k where k is the number of restrictions imposed by H_0.

The Wald test uses the covariance matrix $[I(\hat{\theta})]^{-1}$ of the unrestricted ML estimates to construct tests of the null hypothesis.

More discussion of the relationship between the LR, W, and score (LM) tests can be found in the appendix to Chapter 3.

16.5 GIVE and GMM

Consider the linear regression model

$$\mathbf{y} = \mathbf{X}\boldsymbol{\beta} + \mathbf{u} \quad E(\mathbf{u}\mathbf{u}') = \mathbf{I}\sigma^2$$

$$E(\mathbf{X}'\mathbf{u}) = \mathbf{0} \text{ (this is known as an orthogonality condition)}$$

$$V(\mathbf{X}'\mathbf{u}) = (\mathbf{X}'\mathbf{X})\sigma^2$$

The OLS estimators are obtained by minimizing $\mathbf{u}'\mathbf{u}$ or $(\mathbf{y} - \mathbf{X}\boldsymbol{\beta})'(\mathbf{y} - \mathbf{X}\boldsymbol{\beta})$.

The generalized method of moments (GMM) estimation method minimizes $\mathbf{u'XWX'u}$, where $\mathbf{W}$ is a "weighting matrix." Minimizing $(\mathbf{y} - \mathbf{X}\beta)'\mathbf{XWX'}(\mathbf{y} - \mathbf{X}\beta)$ we get

$$\mathbf{X'XWX'X}\hat{\beta} = \mathbf{X'XWX'y}$$

If $(\mathbf{X'X})$ is nonsingular and $\mathbf{W}$ is nonsingular, we get $\hat{\beta} = (\mathbf{X'X})^{-1}\mathbf{X'y}$, which is OLS. Thus, the weighting matrix does not matter. We shall see later that it does matter in some cases.

Consider the case where $E(\mathbf{X'u}) \neq \mathbf{0}$. Let $\mathbf{Z}$ be the set of instruments. $\mathbf{Z}$ is of the same dimension as $\mathbf{X}$. Write the orthogonality conditions as

$$E(\mathbf{Z'u}) = \mathbf{0} \quad V(\mathbf{Z'u}) = (\mathbf{Z'Z})\sigma^2$$

The usual IV estimator is obtained by setting

$$\mathbf{Z'u} = \mathbf{0} \quad \text{or} \quad \mathbf{Z'}(\mathbf{y} - \mathbf{X}\beta) = \mathbf{0} \quad \text{or} \quad \hat{\beta}_{\text{IV}} = (\mathbf{Z'X})^{-1}\mathbf{Z'y}$$

Sargan (*Econometrica*, 1958, "Estimation of Economic Relationship with Instrumental Variables") proposed minimizing

$$(\mathbf{y} - \mathbf{X}\beta)'\mathbf{Z}(\mathbf{Z'Z})^{-1}\mathbf{Z'}(\mathbf{y} - \mathbf{X}\beta)$$

This is known as the generalized instrumental variable estimator (GIVE). If $E(\mathbf{uu'}) = \Omega$, then the GIVE estimator minimizes

$$(\mathbf{y} - \mathbf{X}\beta)'\mathbf{Z}(\mathbf{Z'}\Omega\mathbf{Z})^{-1}\mathbf{Z'}(\mathbf{y} - \mathbf{X}\beta)$$

Note that the GMM minimizes

$$\mathbf{u'ZWZ'u} \quad \text{or} \quad (\mathbf{y} - \mathbf{X}\beta)'\mathbf{ZWZ'}(\mathbf{y} - \mathbf{X}\beta)$$

$$\Rightarrow \quad (\mathbf{X'Z})\mathbf{W}(\mathbf{Z'X})\hat{\beta} = (\mathbf{X'Z})\mathbf{WZ'y}$$

If $(\mathbf{X'Z})$ is nonsingular and so is $\mathbf{W}$, we have

$$\hat{\beta}_{\text{GMM}} = (\mathbf{X'ZWZ'X})^{-1}(\mathbf{X'ZWZ'y})$$

Hansen (*Econometrica*, 1982) shows that the optimal choice of $\mathbf{W}$ is $(\mathbf{Z'Z})^{-1}/\sigma^2 = [V(\mathbf{Z'u})]^{-1}$. It is $(\mathbf{Z'}\Omega\mathbf{Z})^{-1}$ if $E(\mathbf{uu'}) = \Omega$.

Thus the GMM in this case is

$$\hat{\beta} = [\mathbf{X'Z}(\mathbf{Z'}\Omega\mathbf{Z})^{-1}\mathbf{Z'X}]^{-1}[\mathbf{X'Z}(\mathbf{Z'}\Omega\mathbf{Z})^{-1}\mathbf{Z'y}]$$

The covariance matrix of $\hat{\beta}_{\text{GMM}}$ is

$$[\mathbf{X'Z}(\mathbf{Z'}\Omega\mathbf{Z})^{-1}\mathbf{Z'X}]^{-1}$$

The GMM method has been used often in the estimation of nonlinear rational expectations models and cases where $\Omega = E(\mathbf{uu'})$ has a very general specification.

The above discussion is an introduction to GMM and GIVE in the context of linear regression models.

There are two good survey papers on GMM in G. S. Maddala, C. R. Rao, and H. D. Vinod (eds.), *Handbook of Statistics*, Vol. 11 (Amsterdam: Elsevier Science, 1993). These are: (i) A. Hall, "Some Aspects of GMM Estimation," pp. 393–417; and (ii) M. Ogaki, "GMM: Econometric Applications," pp. 455–488. There is also a computer program and user's guide. See M. Ogaki, "GMM: A User's Guide," RCER Working Paper #348, University of Rochester, 1993. W. H. Greene, *Econometric Analysis*, 3rd ed. (Prentice Hall, 1997) has a more detailed discussion of GMM in Section 11.5.

Summary

1. This chapter gives a brief introduction to large-sample theory. We first discuss the maximum likelihood (ML) method, methods of solving the likelihood equations, the Cramer–Rao lower bound, and large-sample tests of significance based on the ML method. These are the likelihood ratio (LR) test, the Wald (W) test, and Rao's score test [also known as the Lagrangian multiplier (LM) test].

2. Finally, we describe the generalized instrumental variable estimation (GIVE) method and the generalized method of moments (GMM) method in relation to linear regression models.

References are provided for further study.

17 Small-Sample Inference: Resampling Methods

What is in this Chapter?

In the previous chapter we discussed methods of estimation (ML, GMM) and tests of significance (LR, W, LM) that produce estimators and test statistics with desirable large-sample properties. In small samples we would like to know the relative performance of two estimators or test statistics that have the same asymptotic distribution and we would also like to know how reliable the asymptotic inference is. There are some finite sample results that can be obtained by Edgeworth expansions but these are beyond our scope and are very complicated.

In this chapter we discuss resampling alternatives — methods based on drawing repeated samples. Two methods we discuss are: Monte Carlo methods and bootstrap methods.

17.1 Introduction

The LR, W, and LM tests that we have discussed before have asymptotic normal or χ^2 distributions. In practice, however, we do not know how these tests perform in small samples. Many of these tests exhibit substantial size distortions, i.e., you many be testing at the 5% level using the asymptotic normal or χ^2 distributions, but the actual significance level could be 25%. Also there may be two estimators that have the same asymptotic normal distribution but in small samples their performance can be different.

To examine these problems, we shall discuss two resampling methods, or methods that depend on drawing repeated samples:

1. Monte Carlo methods.
2. Bootstrap methods.

They solve different aspects of small-sample inference. Method 1 is used to choose between, say, two estimators or two test statistics. Method 2 is used to get the small-sample distribution of the chosen estimator or test statistic.

17.2   Monte Carlo Methods[1]

In Monte Carlo methods you choose a model, consider a sample size N, fix the parameters at certain values, and draw repeated samples from the distribution of the error term. This generates the data of size N from which the parameter estimates are calculated. Repeat this M times. Then the distribution of the M parameter estimates gives the sampling distribution of the parameter estimates for samples of size N. We can then compare this sampling distribution with the asymptotic distribution. Or we can get the sampling distributions of two estimators and compare them.

Consider, for instance, the regression model

$$y_t = \beta x_t + u_t \quad u_t \sim \text{IN}(0, \sigma^2)$$

where x_t are given values. This is not a case where one would do a Monte Carlo study but it is considered here to illustrate the procedure.

Let us consider $\beta = 4.0$, $\sigma^2 = 1.0$ and a sample size 50. We draw random numbers from the $N(0, 1)$ distribution. Many computer packages (SAS, SHAZAM and others referred to in Appendix C) have random number generators. Call these $(u_1, u_2, \ldots, u_{50})$. Using these, the given x_t and $\beta = 4.0$, we generate the sample values of y: $(y_1, y_2, \ldots, y_{50})$. We can now use these sample values to get an estimate $\hat{\beta}$ of β. We repeat this M times ($M = 1000$, say). Then the distribution of $\hat{\beta}_j$ $(j = 1, 2, \ldots, 1000)$ gives the distribution of the least squares estimator $\hat{\beta}$. We will find $\bar{\beta} = \frac{1}{1000} \sum_1^{1000} \hat{\beta}_j$ would be very close to 4.0 in this case.

This is a very simple example to illustrate the procedure. In this case we know the small-sample distribution of $\hat{\beta}$ so we do not need the Monte Carlo study. But, consider the model

$$y_t = \beta x_t + u_t \quad u_t = \rho u_t - 1 + e_t \quad e_t \sim \text{IN}(0, \sigma^2) \tag{17.1}$$

and we use the Cochrane–Orcutt two-step estimator described in Chapter 6 (Section 6.4). First we get the OLS estimate $\hat{\beta}$ and the least squares residuals $\hat{u}_t$. We then regress $\hat{u}_t$ on $\hat{u}_{t-1}$ to get $\hat{\rho}$. We use this to transform the data and get the GLS estimate β^* of β.

---

[1]Our exposition is concise, more details can be found in D. F. Hendry, "Monte Carlo Experimentation in Economics," Chap. 16 in Z. Griliches and M. D. Intrilligator (eds.), *Handbook of Econometrics*, Vol. 2 (Amsterdam: North-Holland, 1984), and Section 3.6 of D. F. Hendry, *Dynamic Econometrics* (Oxford: Oxford University Press, 1995).

We do not know the small-sample distribution of β^*. The asymptotic distribution of β^* is normal with mean 0 and variance $(\mathbf{x}'\mathbf{\Sigma}^{-1}\mathbf{x})^{-1}$ where $\mathbf{x}' = (x_1, x_2, \ldots, x_N)$ and $\mathbf{\Sigma}$ is the covariance matrix of the errors u_t.

The Monte Carlo experiment runs as follows. Suppose we consider a sample of size 50 and we are given $(x_1, x_2, \ldots, x_{50})$ which remain the same in all replications. We fix the value of the parameters (β, ρ, σ^2). We draw a random sample $(e_1, e_2, \ldots, e_{50})$ from the $N(0, \sigma^2)$ distribution. To generate u_t, we need the starting value u_0. It is customary to take u_0 as a sample value from the equilibrium distribution of u_t which is $N(0, \sigma^2/(1 - \rho^2))$. Using the $\hat{u}_t$, we now generate y_t. Now we have a sample of size 50: $(y_t, x_t), t = 1, 2, \ldots, 50$. We use the Cochrane–Orcutt procedure to get the GLS estimate $\hat{\beta}_{\text{GLS}}$. We repeat this, say, 1000 times. We then get 1000 values of $\hat{\beta}_{\text{GLS}}$ and this gives the small-sample distribution of $\hat{\beta}_{\text{GLS}}$.

More Efficient Monte Carlo Methods

The procedure described can be improved upon. Hendry discusses two methods: the method of antithetic variables and the method of covariances. We shall not go into the details here.[2] The method of antithetic variates reuses the drawn random samples of the errors, e.g. if $(e_1, e_2, \ldots, e_{50})$ is a random sample of errors, so is $(-e_1, -e_2, \ldots, -e_{50})$.

Response Surfaces

The Monte Carlo results we described are for one set of parameter values (θ) and one sample size N. For instance, we get the bias (B say) for the GLS estimator for parameter value θ, sample size N. We may have results from several other Monte Carlo experiments for different values of θ and N. An easy way of summarizing these results is to compute a *response surface*.[3] This is a regression of the form

$$B_j = \alpha + \beta_1\theta_j + \beta_2 N_j + u_j \quad j = 1, 2, \ldots, K$$

where K is the number of different values of θ and N for which we conducted Monte Carlo experiments. From the estimated regression equation, we can get predictions of the bias (B) in the GLS estimator for several values of θ and N for which we have not conducted a Monte Carlo study. The response surface method is a convenient and useful way of summarizing the results of several Monte Carlo experiments.[4] The Monte Carlo method we described can be used

---

[2]See Hendry (1984) and Hendry (1995, Sections 3.6.2 and 3.6.3).

[3]More details on the response surface methodology can be found in Hendry (1984), cited earlier.

[4]This method has been used by MacKinnon to summarize the results from several Monte Carlo experiments to get critical values for cointegration tests. See J. G. MacKinnon, "Critical Values for Cointegration Tests," in R. F. Engle and C. W. J. Granger (eds.), *Long Run Economic Relationships* (Oxford: Oxford University Press, 1991), pp. 267–276.

to compare the small-sample performance of different estimators or test statistics. We compute the different estimators and test statistics with each of the samples generated.

17.3 Resampling Methods: Jackknife and Bootstrap

In the previous section we described the Monte Carlo method where repeated samples are drawn from the assumed error distributions. There are several other methods where samples are drawn *from the given sample*. Two such methods are the jackknife introduced by Quenouille[5] and the bootstrap introduced by Efron.[6] In these methods the information in the sample is "recycled" to get the sampling distributions of the statistics of interest. The jackknife deletes a number of observations at each cycle of computation and the bootstrap does random sampling of the sample observations at each cycle of computation. The simplest "delete-one" jackknife runs as follows: Let $\hat{\theta}$ be the estimator from $y_1, y_2, \ldots, y_n$ the set of observations. The steps for jackknife estimation are:

1. Compute $\hat{\theta}_i$ by deleting y_i from the set of observations.
2. Compute $p_i = n\hat{\theta} - (n-1)\hat{\theta}_i$.
3. The jackknife estimator of θ is $\theta^* = \sum P_i / n$.
4. The jackknife variance estimator is $V^* = \sum(p_i - \theta^*)^2 / n(n-1)$.

The jackknife is not commonly used in econometrics and hence we shall not pursue it in more detail. More advanced jackknife methods are discussed in Wu.[7]

The bootstrap method is another resampling method for the same purpose as the jackknife: to reduce bias and provide more reliable standard errors. The bootstrap method works as follows: Let $(y_1, y_2, \ldots, y_n)$ be the given sample. Draw a sample of size n from this sample *with replacement*. Call this $B_j = (y_1^*, y_2^*, \ldots, y_n^*)$. This is the bootstrap sample. Each y_i^* is a random pick from $(y_1, y_2, \ldots, y_n)$. We do this for $j = 1, 2, \ldots, m$ and compute $\hat{\theta}_j$ from each of the bootstrap samples β_j. The distribution of $\hat{\theta}_j$ is the bootstrap distribution of the estimator θ. The bootstrap estimates of the bias and variance of θ are derived from this bootstrap distribution.

Note that resampling does not add any new information to the original sample. The advantage of methods like the bootstrap must be the result of the way the sample information is processed. In the case of the normal distribution all the information about the sample mean is summarized in the sample mean and sample variance. Thus, other ways of processing the sample information do not yield better results in this case. It is in cases where there is no readily available finite sample distribution of the statistics that the bootstrap is useful.

---

[5]M. Quenouille, "Notes on Bias in Estimation," *Biometrika*, Vol. 43, 1956, pp. 353–360.
[6]B. Efron, "Bootstrap Methods: Another Look at the Jackknife," *Annals of Statistics*, Vol. 7, 1979, pp. 1–26.
[7]C. F. J. Wu, "Jackknife, Bootstrap and Other Re-sampling Methods in Regression Analysis," *Annals of Statistics*, Vol. 14, 1986, pp. 1261–1295.

The bootstrap distribution can often be skewed. In this case, it is not sufficient to look at the bootstrap variance. Several early applications in econometrics used the bootstrap method to get the variance of the sample statistics. Even if the asymptotic and bootstrap standard errors are the same in any given example, the confidence intervals can be different if the bootstrap distribution is skewed. For the autoregressive model $y_t = y_{t-1} + e_t$ based on Wolfer's sumspot numbers for 1770–1889, Efron and Tibshirani[8] got $\hat{\rho} = 0.815$ with asymptotic standard error 0.053. The bootstrap standard error based on 1000 bootstrap samples was 0.055, agreeing nicely with the asymptotic result. But the bootstrap distribution was skewed to the left. Thus, the confidence intervals are different.

Some Illustrative Examples

Example 1: Computing SE's of LR Parameter Estimates

A problem that occurs often is the computation of standard errors of nonlinear functions of parameter estimates in econometric applications. Consider the dynamic model (all variables in logs) estimated by OLS

$$y_t = \hat{\alpha} y_{t-1} + \hat{\beta}_1 x_t + \hat{\beta}_2 x_{t-1} + \hat{u}_t$$

The estimate of the long-run elasticity is $\hat{\theta} = (\hat{\beta}_1 + \hat{\beta}_2)/(1 - \hat{\alpha})$. The problem is to get the SE of θ. There are several methods available. We discussed the Fieller method in Section 3.10 and the Taylor series expansion method in Section 6.9 (under the heading "Wald test"). Li and Maddala[9] found in a Monte Carlo study that the bootstrap method gives better estimates than Fieller's method as well as Taylor series expansions.

For the bootstrap, we resample $\hat{u}_t$, get different estimates of $(\hat{\alpha}_1, \hat{\beta}_1, \hat{\beta}_2)$ and hence $\hat{\theta}$, and the bootstrap distribution of $\hat{\theta}$. If this bootstrap distribution is skewed, then as argued earlier, looking at the standard error is not sufficient, but one can construct confidence intervals for θ from the bootstrap distribution.

Example 2: Testing for Serial Correlation in Models with Lagged Dependent Variables

In Section 6.8 we discussed an LM test for higher order serial correlation. The tests described are large-sample tests. Their behavior in small samples is not known. Some Monte Carlo studies found that the use of the asymptotic χ^2-distribution leads to misleading inferences. The bootstrap method can be used to get more accurate small-sample inference in these cases.[10]

---

[8] B. Efron and R. Tibshirani, "Bootstrap Methods for Standard Errors, Confidence Intervals and Other Measures of Statistician Accuracy," *Statistical Science*, Vol. 1, 1986, pp. 54–77.

[9] H. Li and G. S. Maddala, "A Comparative Study of Alternative Methods for Obtaining Standard Errors of LR Parameter Estimates in Econometrics Models," paper presented at the Far Eastern Meeting of the Econometric Society, Hong Kong, 1997.

[10] These results have been reported to me by H. Li.

Example 3: Forecast Intervals when Forecast Period Exogenous Variables are Stochastic

Very often in forecasting, in regression models, the explanatory variables are not known with certainty. They are themselves forecast. In this case, the distribution of the forecast error is not normal. The bootstrap method can be used to construct prediction intervals.[11]

These are a few examples where the statistics under consideration have unknown asymptotic distribution or known asymptotic distribution which produces misleading inferences in small samples. In all these cases the bootstrap method has been shown to help.

Other Issues Relating to Bootstrap

In the subsequent sections we discuss several issues relating to the bootstrap:

1. Bootstrap confidence intervals (Section 17.4).
2. Hypothesis testing with the bootstrap (Section 17.5).
3. Bootstrapping residuals versus bootstrapping data (Section 17.6).
4. NonIID errors and nonstationary models (Section 17.7).
5. Miscellaneous other applications (Section 17.8).

The following papers are surveys on bootstrap methods in econometrics where these problems are discussed:

1. J. L. Horowitz, "Bootstrap Methods in Econometrics: Theory and Performance," in D. M. Kreps and K. F. Wallis (eds.), *Advances in Economics and Econometrics: Theory and Applications*, Vol. III (Cambridge: Cambridge University Press, 1997).
2. J. Jeong and G. S. Maddala, "A Perspective on Application of Bootstrap Methods in Econometrics," in G. S. Maddala, C. R. Rao, and H. D. Vinod (eds.), *Handbook of Statistics*, Vol. 11 (Amsterdam: Elsevier Science, 1993), pp. 573–610.
3. H. Li and G. S. Maddala, "Bootstrapping Time Series Models" (with discussion), *Econometric Reviews*, Vol. 15, 1996, pp. 115–195.
4. H. Li and G. S. Maddala, "Bootstrapping Cointegrating Regressions," *Journal of Econometrics*, Vol. 80, 1997, pp. 297–318.
5. G. S. Maddala and H. Li, "Bootstrap Based Tests in Financial Models," in G. S. Maddala and C. R. Rao (eds.), *Handbook of Statistics*, Vol. 14 (Amsterdam: Elsevier Science, 1996), pp. 463–488.
6. G. S. Maddala and I. M. Kim, *Unit Roots, Cointegration and Structural Change* (Cambridge: Cambridge University Press, 1998), Chap. 10 "Small Sample Inference: Bootstrap Methods."

---

[11]See B. D. McCulloch, "Consistent Forecast Intervals When the Forecast-period Exogenous Variables are Stochastic," *Journal of Forecasting*, Vol. 15, 1996, pp. 293–304.

17.4 Bootstrap Confidence Intervals

The bootstrap distribution can be used to get confidence intervals for θ. This method of constructing confidence intervals is known as the *percentile method*. However, it has been found that the coverage probabilities of these confidence intervals are not correct. That is a 95% confidence interval is not a 95% interval. To correct for these biases Efron suggested two modifications of the simple bootstrap, called the "bias corrected" and "accelerated bias corrected" intervals. Since these are not often used in econometrics, we shall not discuss them here. Details can be found in B. Efron and R. Tibshirani, *An Introduction to the Bootstrap* (London: Chapman & Hall, 1993).

Another alternative to the percentile method is the *percentile-t* or *bootstrap-t* method, which Hall[12] shows gives an improvement over the method of constructing confidence intervals based on asymptotic distributions. This is the percentile method based on the *t*-statistic $t = \sqrt{n}(\hat{\theta} - \theta)/s$ where s is a consistent estimator of the standard error of $\sqrt{n}(\hat{\theta} - \theta)$. This procedure is often known as *studentization*.

The bootstrap-*t* is often used in econometrics. It has one major problem — it produces bad results if the estimate of the variance is poor.

17.5 Hypothesis Testing with the Bootstrap

Two important issues concerning hypothesis testing using bootstrap methods are:

1. What test statistic to bootstrap.
2. How to generate bootstrap samples.

Suppose we want to test the hypothesis $H_0 : \theta = \theta_0$ vs. $H_1 : \theta \neq \theta_0$. Given an estimator $\hat{\theta}$ of θ the usual test procedure would be based on $T = \hat{\theta} - \theta_0$, and the significance levels and *P*-values are obtained from the distribution of T under H_0. A direct application of the bootstrap procedure would suggest using the bootstrap distribution of $T^* = \hat{\theta}^* - \theta_0$, where $\hat{\theta}^*$ is the value of $\hat{\theta}$ from the bootstrap sample. However, Hall (1992, Section 3.12) discusses the bad behavior of the power of this test arguing that T^* does not approximate the null distribution when the sample comes from a distribution with parameter θ away from θ_0. Hall and Wilson[13] therefore consider the distribution of $(\hat{\theta}^* - \hat{\theta})$. They propose two guidelines for hypothesis testing. First, use the bootstrap distribution of $(\hat{\theta}^* - \hat{\theta})$ but not $(\hat{\theta}^* - \theta_0)$. Second, use a properly studentized statistic: $(\hat{\theta}^* - \hat{\theta})/\hat{\sigma}^*$ where $\hat{\sigma}^*$ is the estimate of $\hat{\sigma}$ from the bootstrap sample.

---

[12]P. Hall, "Theoretical Comparison of Bootstrap Confidence Intervals," *Annals of Statistics*, Vol. 16, 1988, pp. 927–953, and P. Hall, *The Bootstrap and Edgeworth Expansion* (New York: Springer-Verlag, 1992).

[13]P. Hall and S. R. Wilson, "Two Guidelines for Bootstrap Hypothesis Testing," *Biometrics*, Vol. 47, 1997, pp. 757–762.

Next there is the question of how to generate the bootstrap sample. We shall discuss this with reference to the regression model

$$y = \beta x + \varepsilon \quad \varepsilon \sim \text{IID}(0, \sigma^2)$$

Let $\hat{\beta}$ and $\hat{\sigma}$ be the OLS estimators of β and σ, respectively and $\hat{\varepsilon}$ the OLS residual. Let $\hat{\varepsilon}^*$ be the bootstrap residuals obtained by resampling of $\hat{\varepsilon}$. Then we can consider the following sampling schemes for the generation of bootstrap samples:

$$S_1 : y^* = \hat{\beta}x + \varepsilon^*$$
$$S_2 : y^* = \beta_0 x + \varepsilon^*$$

where β_0 is the value of β specified by H_0.

$$S_3 : y^* = \beta_0 x + \varepsilon_0^*$$

where ε_0^* is the bootstrap sample from $\varepsilon_0 = y - \beta_0 x$.

In both S_1 and S_2 we use resampling based on OLS residuals. S_3 is based on resampling of restricted residuals. The corresponding test statistics are

$$T_1 : (\hat{\beta}^* - \hat{\beta})/\hat{\sigma}^*$$
$$T_2 : (\hat{\beta}^* - \beta_0)/\hat{\sigma}^*$$

Hall and Wilson consider S_1 and T_1. But T_2 is valid for sampling schemes S_2 and S_3. In fact using T_2 under S_3 is the best choice.[14]

17.6 Bootstrapping Residuals Versus Bootstrapping the Data

The preceding discussion was all based on bootstrapping the residuals. An alternative method is to bootstrap the data, e.g. in the regression model

$$y_i = \beta x_i + u_i$$

the methods we talked about referred to bootstrapping the residuals $\hat{u}_i$. But for the regression model with stochastic regressors, we bootstrap the pairs (y_i, x_i) and not the residuals $\hat{u}_i$. This is called the *direct method* of generation of bootstrap samples. Even for the regression model with fixed regressors, the direct method of sampling (y_i, x_i) is useful in the case of heteroskedastic errors because it gives a correct estimate of the covariance matrix of $\hat{\beta}$. See Jeong and Maddala (1993, pp. 577–578).

In dynamic models the residual based method uses more information than the direct method and hence should be the preferred choice, e.g. suppose the model is

$$y_t = \alpha_1 y_{t-1} + \beta_1 x_t + \beta_2 x_{t-1} + u_t$$

---

[14]See H. Li and G. S. Maddala, "Bootstrapping Time Series Models," *Econometric Reviews*, Vol. 15, 1996, pp 115–195.

but the errors u_t are AR(1): $u_t = \rho u_{t-1} + e_t$, where e_t are IID$(0, \sigma^2)$. The direct method resamples $(y_t, y_{t-1}, x_t, x_{t-1})$. In the residual based method we resample $\hat{e}_t$ after estimating $(\alpha_1, \beta_1, \beta_2, \rho)$. The residual method uses more information than the direct method. This is also the case with cointegrating regressions. See Maddala and Kim (1998, Section 10.6) and Li and Maddala (1996).

17.7 NonIID Errors and Nonstationary Models

Heteroskedasticity and Autocorrelation

Most of the bootstrap applications are based on IID errors which is an unrealistic assumption in econometric work. In the previous section we discussed the case of nonIID errors: the problems of heteroskedasticity and autocorrelation. In the case of heteroskedasticity, we said that bootstrapping the data, instead of bootstrapping the residuals, is the preferred choice. On the other hand, in the case of autocorrelation in the errors, with a known structure (e.g. AR(1), AR(2), etc.) the method of bootstrapping the residuals from the estimated autoregressions is the preferred choice.

Unit Root Tests Based on the Bootstrap

In the case of nonstationary models, we consider bootstrap based unit root tests and cointegration tests. For unit root tests, the use of the sampling scheme S_1 and test statistic T_1 (discussed in Section 17.5) is not valid. It is test statistic T_2 with sampling schemes S_2 or S_3 that are valid. For more details see Li and Maddala (1996) and Maddala and Kim (1998).

Cointegration Tests

This discussion is based on Maddala and Kim (1998, Section 10.6).

Consider the case $y_t = \beta x_t + u_t$ where y_t and x_t are both I(1). A test for no cointegration is a test for unit root in u_t. The previous discussion on valid test statistics and sampling schemes is applicable here.

Another issue is on tests of hypotheses regarding the cointegrating parameter β, if there is cointegration. Note that the direct method of resampling (y_t, x_t) cannot be used in the case of cointegrating regressions because the I(1) property of the variables is not preserved under random resampling.

Suppose there is no endogeneity problem (that is x_t and u_t are not correlated) and there is no serial correlation problem (that is u_t are serially independent.) The OLS estimator $\hat{\beta}$ of β is nuisance parameter free and one can apply the bootstrap procedure. Even then it is better to use the bootstrap-t method rather than to bootstrap $\hat{\beta}$ itself for constructing the confidence intervals or using tests of significance. The bootstrap procedure runs as follows:

1. Get $\hat{u}_t$ by estimating the equation by OLS. Also get the residuals $\hat{v}_t = \Delta x_t$.
2. After centering these residuals, bootstrap the pairs $(\hat{u}_t, \hat{v}_t)$.
3. Construct x_t^* using the recursive method and y_t^* using $\hat{\beta}$, u_t^* and x_t^*.

In case there are endogeneity and serial correlation problems, using the OLS estimation method and bootstrapping the OLS residuals is not valid. We have to use the FM-OLS or Johansen methods (see Chapter 14) and bootstrap the residuals from these estimation methods. We shall not pursue the details here. They can be found in Li and Maddala (1997) and Maddala and Kim (1998, Section 10.6).

17.8   Miscellaneous Other Applications

Bootstrap methods have been widely used in financial applications. For a review, see Maddala and Li (1996). Apart from the standard use to get standard errors, confidence intervals and tests of significance, there is one application in finance that is novel: use of bootstrap methods for model selection based on trading rules. The procedure is as follows: First get a measure of profits generated by a trading rule using the actual data. Next estimate the postulated model and bootstrap the residuals to generate bootstrap samples. Generate trading rule profits for each of the bootstrap samples. Compare this bootstrap distribution of the trading rule profits with the profits from the actual data. Do this for each of the models considered. The basic idea is to compare the time-series properties of the generated series from the given model with the time-series properties of the given data. Measures like R^2 and other goodness of fit measures do not capture the time-series properties as the trading rule profits do. Examples of this method and the relevant references can be found in Maddala and Li (1996).

In the financial literature the use of the percentile method is very common. Maddala and Li (1996) point out that the percentile-t is preferable and should be used more often.

Summary

1. In this chapter we discuss two resampling methods for small-sample inference: Monte Carlo methods and bootstrap methods. The Monte Carlo methods help in the choice between different estimators and test statistics. The bootstrap methods help in making small-sample inference on the chosen estimator and test statistic.

2. We discussed two bootstrap data generation methods: the residual based method and the direct method of bootstrapping the data. We discussed different methods of constructing confidence intervals: the percentile method and the percentile-t method, and argued that the latter method is the preferred choice. We also discussed bootstrap based tests in regression models, in unit root models, and cointegrated regression models.

3. Finally, we discussed a method of choosing between different models based on bootstrapping trading rule probits.

There are many instances where defective bootstrap methods have been used. See Maddala and Li (1996). This raises the question: Is a defective bootstrap method still better than asymptotic inference? There are several examples in the literature where this is not so. One example is in the unit root literature (bootstrap based on S_1 and T_1 defined in Section 17.5). However, when no asymptotic inference is available, it is better to use a bootstrap method. Also, when a correct bootstrap method is complicated, and not feasible, a theoretically imperfect bootstrap method might still improve asymptotic inference, as discussed in Li and Maddala (1997). Thus, unless proven otherwise, some bootstrap may be better than no bootstrap.

Appendices

The appendices consist of statistical tables, description of data sets on the Web, and discussion of computer programs.

Appendix A: Data Sets

Many of the macroeconomic time series are available in the Economic Report of the President, Citibase, and so on. Foreign exchange data are available from the IMF. There are large data sets available from the longitudinal survey conducted by the Center for Human Resources at the Ohio State University, Columbus, OH.

The Website related to this book contains some original data sets made available to the author. These are in Tables 4.7, 4.12, and 15.1. The others are from published sources.

There is no paucity of data that can be obtained from several sources: each of these data sets might have been collected with a specific purpose in mind.

Table A.1 Ordinates of the normal density function

$$\phi(x) = \frac{1}{\sqrt{2\pi}} e^{-x^2/2}$$

x	0.00	0.01	0.02	0.03	0.04	0.05	0.06	0.07	0.08	0.09
0.0	0.3989	0.3989	0.3989	0.3988	0.3986	0.3984	0.3982	0.3980	0.3977	0.3973
0.1	0.3970	0.3965	0.3961	0.3956	0.3951	0.3945	0.3939	0.3932	0.3925	0.3918
0.2	0.3910	0.3902	0.3894	0.3885	0.3876	0.3867	0.3857	0.3847	0.3836	0.3825
0.3	0.3814	0.3802	0.3790	0.3778	0.3765	0.3752	0.3739	0.3725	0.3712	0.3697
0.4	0.3683	0.3668	0.3653	0.3637	0.3621	0.3605	0.3589	0.3572	0.3555	0.3538
0.5	0.3521	0.3503	0.3485	0.3467	0.3448	0.3429	0.3410	0.3391	0.3372	0.3352
0.6	0.3332	0.3312	0.3292	0.3271	0.3251	0.3230	0.3209	0.3187	0.3166	0.3144
0.7	0.3123	0.3101	0.3079	0.3056	0.3034	0.3011	0.2989	0.2966	0.2943	0.2920
0.8	0.2897	0.2874	0.2850	0.2827	0.2803	0.2780	0.2756	0.2732	0.2709	0.2685
0.9	0.2661	0.2637	0.2613	0.2589	0.2565	0.2541	0.2516	0.2492	0.2468	0.2444
1.0	0.2420	0.2396	0.2371	0.2347	0.2323	0.2299	0.2275	0.2251	0.2227	0.2203
1.1	0.2179	0.2155	0.2131	0.2107	0.2083	0.2059	0.2036	0.2012	0.1989	0.1965
1.2	0.1942	0.1919	0.1895	0.1872	0.1849	0.1826	0.1804	0.1781	0.1758	0.1736
1.3	0.1714	0.1691	0.1669	0.1647	0.1626	0.1604	0.1582	0.1561	0.1539	0.1518
1.4	0.1497	0.1476	0.1456	0.1435	0.1415	0.1394	0.1374	0.1354	0.1334	0.1315
1.5	0.1295	0.1276	0.1257	0.1238	0.1219	0.1200	0.1182	0.1163	0.1145	0.1127
1.6	0.1109	0.1092	0.1074	0.1057	0.1040	0.1023	0.1006	0.0989	0.0973	0.0957
1.7	0.0940	0.0925	0.0909	0.0893	0.0878	0.0863	0.0848	0.0833	0.0818	0.0804
1.8	0.0790	0.0775	0.0761	0.0748	0.0734	0.0721	0.0707	0.0694	0.0681	0.0669
1.9	0.0656	0.0644	0.0632	0.0620	0.0608	0.0596	0.0584	0.0573	0.0562	0.0551
2.0	0.0540	0.0529	0.0519	0.0508	0.0498	0.0488	0.0478	0.0468	0.0459	0.0449
2.1	0.0440	0.0431	0.0422	0.0413	0.0404	0.0396	0.0387	0.0379	0.0371	0.0363
2.2	0.0355	0.0347	0.0339	0.0332	0.0325	0.0317	0.0310	0.0303	0.0297	0.0290
2.3	0.0283	0.0277	0.0270	0.0264	0.0258	0.0252	0.0246	0.0241	0.0235	0.0229
2.4	0.0224	0.0219	0.0213	0.0208	0.0203	0.0198	0.0194	0.0189	0.0184	0.0180
2.5	0.0175	0.0171	0.0167	0.0163	0.0158	0.0154	0.0151	0.0147	0.0143	0.0139
2.6	0.0136	0.0132	0.0129	0.0126	0.0122	0.0119	0.0116	0.0113	0.0110	0.0107
2.7	0.0104	0.0101	0.0099	0.0096	0.0093	0.0091	0.0088	0.0086	0.0084	0.0081
2.8	0.0079	0.0077	0.0075	0.0073	0.0071	0.0069	0.0067	0.0065	0.0063	0.0061
2.9	0.0060	0.0058	0.0056	0.0055	0.0053	0.0051	0.0050	0.0048	0.0047	0.0046
3.0	0.0044	0.0043	0.0042	0.0040	0.0039	0.0038	0.0037	0.0036	0.0035	0.0034
3.1	0.0033	0.0032	0.0031	0.0030	0.0029	0.0028	0.0027	0.0026	0.0025	0.0025
3.2	0.0024	0.0023	0.0022	0.0022	0.0021	0.0020	0.0020	0.0019	0.0018	0.0018
3.3	0.0017	0.0017	0.0016	0.0016	0.0015	0.0015	0.0014	0.0014	0.0013	0.0013
3.4	0.0012	0.0012	0.0012	0.0011	0.0011	0.0010	0.0010	0.0010	0.0009	0.0009
3.5	0.0009	0.0008	0.0008	0.0008	0.0008	0.0007	0.0007	0.0007	0.0007	0.0006
3.6	0.0006	0.0006	0.0006	0.0005	0.0005	0.0005	0.0005	0.0005	0.0005	0.0004
3.7	0.0004	0.0004	0.0004	0.0004	0.0004	0.0004	0.0003	0.0003	0.0003	0.0003
3.8	0.0003	0.0003	0.0003	0.0003	0.0003	0.0002	0.0002	0.0002	0.0002	0.0002
3.9	0.0002	0.0002	0.0002	0.0002	0.0002	0.0002	0.0002	0.0002	0.0001	0.0001

Table A.2 Cumulative normal distribution

$$\Phi(x) = \int_{-\infty}^{x} \frac{1}{\sqrt{2\pi}} e^{-t^2/2} dt$$

x	0.00	0.01	0.02	0.03	0.04	0.05	0.06	0.07	0.08	0.09
0.0	0.5000	0.5040	0.5080	0.5120	0.5160	0.5199	0.5239	0.5279	0.5319	0.5359
0.1	0.5398	0.5438	0.5478	0.5517	0.5557	0.5596	0.5636	0.5675	0.5714	0.5753
0.2	0.5793	0.5832	0.5871	0.5910	0.5948	0.5987	0.6026	0.6064	0.6103	0.6141
0.3	0.6179	0.6217	0.6255	0.6293	0.6331	0.6368	0.6406	0.6443	0.6480	0.6517
0.4	0.6554	0.6591	0.6628	0.6664	0.6700	0.6736	0.6772	0.6808	0.6844	0.6879
0.5	0.6915	0.6950	0.6985	0.7019	0.7054	0.7088	0.7123	0.7157	0.7190	0.7224
0.6	0.7257	0.7291	0.7324	0.7357	0.7389	0.7422	0.7454	0.7486	0.7517	0.7549
0.7	0.7580	0.7611	0.7642	0.7673	0.7704	0.7734	0.7764	0.7794	0.7823	0.7852
0.8	0.7881	0.7910	0.7939	0.7967	0.7995	0.8023	0.8051	0.8078	0.8106	0.8133
0.9	0.8159	0.8186	0.8212	0.8238	0.8264	0.8289	0.8315	0.8340	0.8365	0.8389
1.0	0.8413	0.8438	0.8461	0.8485	0.8508	0.8531	0.8554	0.8577	0.8599	0.8621
1.1	0.8643	0.8665	0.8686	0.8708	0.8729	0.8749	0.8770	0.8790	0.8810	0.8830
1.2	0.8849	0.8869	0.8888	0.8907	0.8925	0.8944	0.8962	0.8980	0.8997	0.9015
1.3	0.9032	0.9049	0.9066	0.9082	0.9099	0.9115	0.9131	0.9147	0.9162	0.9177
1.4	0.9192	0.9207	0.9222	0.9236	0.9251	0.9265	0.9279	0.9292	0.9306	0.9319
1.5	0.9332	0.9345	0.9357	0.9370	0.9382	0.9394	0.9406	0.9418	0.9429	0.9441
1.6	0.9452	0.9463	0.9474	0.9484	0.9495	0.9505	0.9515	0.9525	0.9535	0.9545
1.7	0.9554	0.9564	0.9573	0.9582	0.9591	0.9599	0.9608	0.9616	0.9625	0.9633
1.8	0.9641	0.9649	0.9656	0.9664	0.9671	0.9678	0.9686	0.9693	0.9699	0.9706
1.9	0.9713	0.9719	0.9726	0.9732	0.9738	0.9744	0.9750	0.9756	0.9761	0.9767
2.0	0.9772	0.9778	0.9783	0.9788	0.9793	0.9798	0.9803	0.9808	0.9812	0.9817
2.1	0.9821	0.9826	0.9830	0.9834	0.9838	0.9842	0.9846	0.9850	0.9854	0.9857
2.2	0.9861	0.9864	0.9868	0.9871	0.9875	0.9878	0.9881	0.9884	0.9887	0.9890
2.3	0.9893	0.9896	0.9898	0.9901	0.9904	0.9906	0.9909	0.9911	0.9913	0.9916
2.4	0.9918	0.9920	0.9922	0.9925	0.9927	0.9929	0.9931	0.9932	0.9934	0.9936
2.5	0.9938	0.9940	0.9941	0.9943	0.9945	0.9946	0.9948	0.9949	0.9951	0.9952
2.6	0.9953	0.9955	0.9956	0.9957	0.9959	0.9960	0.9961	0.9962	0.9963	0.9964
2.7	0.9965	0.9966	0.9967	0.9968	0.9969	0.9970	0.9971	0.9972	0.9973	0.9974
2.8	0.9974	0.9975	0.9976	0.9977	0.9977	0.9978	0.9979	0.9979	0.9980	0.9981
2.9	0.9981	0.9982	0.9982	0.9983	0.9984	0.9984	0.9985	0.9985	0.9986	0.9986
3.0	0.9987	0.9987	0.9987	0.9988	0.9988	0.9989	0.9989	0.9989	0.9990	0.9990
3.1	0.9990	0.9991	0.9991	0.9991	0.9992	0.9992	0.9992	0.9992	0.9993	0.9993
3.2	0.9993	0.9993	0.9994	0.9994	0.9994	0.9994	0.9994	0.9995	0.9995	0.9995
3.3	0.9995	0.9995	0.9995	0.9996	0.9996	0.9996	0.9996	0.9996	0.9996	0.9997
3.4	0.9997	0.9997	0.9997	0.9997	0.9997	0.9997	0.9997	0.9997	0.9997	0.9998

x	1.282	1.645	1.960	2.326	2.576	3.090	3.291	3.891	4.417
$\Phi(x)$	0.90	0.95	0.975	0.99	0.995	0.999	0.9995	0.99995	0.999995
$2[1 - \Phi(x)]$	0.20	0.10	0.05	0.02	0.01	0.002	0.001	0.0001	0.00001

Source: Reprinted from A. M. Mood, F. A. Graybill, and D. C. Boes, *Introduction to the Theory of Statistics,* 3rd ed. (New York: McGraw-Hill, 1973), by permission of the publishers.

Table A.3 Cumulative χ^2-distribution

$$F(u) = \int_0^u \frac{x^{(n-2)/2} e^{-x/2} dx}{2^{n/2}\Gamma(n/2)}$$

n \ F	0.005	0.010	0.025	0.050	0.100	0.250	0.500	0.750	0.900	0.950	0.975	0.990	0.995
1	0.0^4393	0.0^3157	0.0^3982	0.0^2393	0.0158	0.102	0.455	1.32	2.71	3.84	5.02	6.63	7.88
2	0.0100	0.0201	0.0506	0.103	0.211	0.575	1.39	2.77	4.61	5.99	7.38	9.21	10.6
3	0.0717	0.115	0.216	0.352	0.584	1.21	2.37	4.11	6.25	7.81	9.35	11.3	12.8
4	0.207	0.297	0.484	0.711	1.06	1.92	3.36	5.39	7.78	9.49	11.1	13.3	14.9
5	0.412	0.554	0.831	1.15	1.61	2.67	4.35	6.63	9.24	11.1	12.8	15.1	16.7
6	0.676	0.872	1.24	1.64	2.20	3.45	5.35	7.84	10.6	12.6	14.4	16.8	18.5
7	0.989	1.24	1.69	2.17	2.83	4.25	6.35	9.04	12.0	14.1	16.0	18.5	20.3
8	1.34	1.65	2.18	2.73	3.49	5.07	7.34	10.2	13.4	15.5	17.5	20.1	22.0
9	1.73	2.09	2.70	3.33	4.17	5.90	8.34	11.4	14.7	16.9	19.0	21.7	23.6
10	2.16	2.56	3.25	3.94	4.87	6.74	9.34	12.5	16.0	18.3	20.5	23.2	25.2
11	2.60	3.05	3.82	4.57	5.58	7.58	10.3	13.7	17.3	19.7	21.9	24.7	26.8
12	3.07	3.57	4.40	5.23	6.30	8.44	11.3	14.8	18.5	21.0	23.3	26.2	28.3
13	3.57	4.11	5.01	5.89	7.04	9.30	12.3	16.0	19.8	22.4	24.7	27.7	29.8
14	4.07	4.66	5.63	6.57	7.79	10.2	13.3	17.1	21.1	23.7	26.1	29.1	31.3
15	4.60	5.23	6.26	7.26	8.55	11.0	14.3	18.2	22.3	25.0	27.5	30.6	32.8
16	5.14	5.81	6.91	7.96	9.31	11.9	15.3	19.4	23.5	26.3	28.8	32.0	34.3
17	5.70	6.41	7.56	8.67	10.1	12.8	16.3	20.5	24.8	27.6	30.2	33.4	35.7
18	6.26	7.01	8.23	9.39	10.9	13.7	17.3	21.6	26.0	28.9	31.5	34.8	37.2
19	6.84	7.63	8.91	10.1	11.7	14.6	18.3	22.7	27.2	30.1	32.9	36.2	38.6
20	7.43	8.26	9.59	10.9	12.4	15.5	19.3	23.8	28.4	31.4	34.2	37.6	40.0
21	8.03	8.90	10.3	11.6	13.2	16.3	20.3	24.9	29.6	32.7	35.5	38.9	41.4
22	8.64	9.54	11.0	12.3	14.0	17.2	21.3	26.0	30.8	33.9	36.8	40.3	42.8
23	9.26	10.2	11.7	13.1	14.8	18.1	22.3	27.1	32.0	35.2	38.1	41.6	44.2
24	9.89	10.9	12.4	13.8	15.7	19.0	23.3	28.2	33.2	36.4	39.4	43.0	45.6
25	10.5	11.5	13.1	14.6	16.5	19.9	24.3	29.3	34.4	37.7	40.6	44.3	46.9
26	11.2	12.2	13.8	15.4	17.3	20.8	25.3	30.4	35.6	38.9	41.9	45.6	48.3
27	11.8	12.9	14.6	16.2	18.1	21.7	26.3	31.5	36.7	40.1	43.2	47.0	49.6
28	12.5	13.6	15.3	16.9	18.9	22.7	27.3	32.6	37.9	41.3	44.5	48.3	51.0
29	13.1	14.3	16.0	17.7	19.8	23.6	28.3	33.7	39.1	42.6	45.7	49.6	52.3
30	13.8	15.0	16.8	18.5	20.6	24.5	29.3	34.8	40.3	43.8	47.0	50.9	53.7

Source: Abridged from "Tables of Percentage Points of the Incomplete Beta Function and of the Chi-Square Distribution," *Biometrika*, Vol. 32, 1941. It is published here with the kind permission of its author, Catherine M. Thompson, and the editor of *Biometrika*.

Table A.4   Cumulative student's t-distribution

$$F(t) = \int_{-\infty}^{t} \frac{\Gamma\left(\dfrac{n+1}{2}\right)}{\Gamma(n/2)\sqrt{\pi n}\left(1 + \dfrac{x^2}{n}\right)^{(n+1)/2}}\,dx$$

n \ F	0.75	0.90	0.95	0.975	0.99	0.995	0.9995
1	1.000	3.078	6.314	12.706	31.821	63.657	636.619
2	0.816	1.886	2.920	4.303	6.965	9.925	31.598
3	0.765	1.638	2.353	3.182	4.541	5.841	12.941
4	0.741	1.533	2.132	2.776	3.747	4.604	8.610
5	0.727	1.476	2.015	2.571	3.365	4.032	6.859
6	0.718	1.440	1.943	2.447	3.143	3.707	5.959
7	0.711	1.415	1.895	2.365	2.998	3.499	5.405
8	0.706	1.397	1.860	2.306	2.896	3.355	5.041
9	0.703	1.383	1.833	2.262	2.821	3.250	4.781
10	0.700	1.372	1.812	2.228	2.764	3.169	4.587
11	0.697	1.363	1.796	2.201	2.718	3.106	4.437
12	0.695	1.356	1.782	2.179	2.681	3.055	4.318
13	0.694	1.350	1.771	2.160	2.650	3.012	4.221
14	0.692	1.345	1.761	2.145	2.624	2.977	4.140
15	0.691	1.341	1.753	2.131	2.602	2.947	4.073
16	0.690	1.337	1.746	2.120	2.583	2.921	4.015
17	0.689	1.333	1.740	2.110	2.567	2.898	3.965
18	0.688	1.330	1.734	2.101	2.552	2.878	3.922
19	0.688	1.328	1.729	2.093	2.539	2.861	3.883
20	0.687	1.325	1.725	2.086	2.528	2.845	3.850
21	0.686	1.323	1.721	2.080	2.518	2.831	3.819
22	0.686	1.321	1.717	2.074	2.508	2.819	3.792
23	0.685	1.319	1.714	2.069	2.500	2.807	3.767
24	0.685	1.318	1.711	2.064	2.492	2.797	3.745
25	0.684	1.316	1.708	2.060	2.485	2.787	3.725
26	0.684	1.315	1.706	2.056	2.479	2.779	3.707
27	0.684	1.314	1.703	2.052	2.473	2.771	3.690
28	0.683	1.313	1.701	2.048	2.467	2.763	3.674
29	0.683	1.311	1.699	2.045	2.462	2.756	3.659
30	0.683	1.310	1.697	2.042	2.457	2.750	3.646
40	0.681	1.303	1.684	2.021	2.423	2.704	3.551
60	0.679	1.296	1.671	2.000	2.390	2.660	3.460
120	0.677	1.289	1.658	1.980	2.358	2.617	3.373
∞	0.674	1.282	1.645	1.960	2.326	2.576	3.291

Source: Abridged from R. A. Fisher and Frank Yates, *Statistical Tables* (Edinburgh and London: Oliver & Boyd, 1938). It is published here with the kind permission of the authors and their publishers.

Table A.5   Critical values for the Durbin–Watson test: 5% significance level[a]

n	$k = 3$ L	U	$k = 6$ L	U	$k = 9$ L	U	$k = 12$ L	U	$k = 15$ L	U	$k = 21$ L	U
10	0.70	1.64	0.24	2.82								
15	0.95	1.54	0.56	2.22	0.25	2.98						
20	1.10	1.54	0.79	1.99	0.50	2.52	0.26	3.06	0.10	3.54		
25	1.21	1.55	0.95	1.89	0.70	2.28	0.47	2.70	0.27	3.12	0.04	3.79
30	1.28	1.57	1.07	1.83	0.85	2.14	0.64	2.48	0.45	2.82	0.16	3.47
35	1.34	1.58	1.16	1.80	0.97	2.05	0.78	2.33	0.60	2.62	0.30	3.19
40	1.39	1.60	1.23	1.79	1.06	2.00	0.90	2.23	0.73	2.47	0.43	2.97
45	1.43	1.62	1.29	1.78	1.14	1.96	0.99	2.16	0.84	2.37	0.55	2.81
50	1.46	1.63	1.34	1.77	1.20	1.93	1.06	2.10	0.93	2.29	0.66	2.68
55	1.49	1.64	1.37	1.77	1.25	1.91	1.13	2.06	1.00	2.23	0.75	2.57
60	1.51	1.65	1.41	1.77	1.30	1.89	1.19	2.03	1.07	2.18	0.84	2.49
65	1.54	1.66	1.44	1.77	1.34	1.88	1.23	2.01	1.12	2.14	0.91	2.42
70	1.55	1.67	1.46	1.77	1.37	1.87	1.27	1.99	1.17	2.11	0.97	2.36
75	1.57	1.68	1.49	1.77	1.40	1.87	1.31	1.97	1.22	2.08	1.03	2.32
80	1.59	1.69	1.51	1.77	1.43	1.86	1.34	1.96	1.25	2.06	1.08	2.28
85	1.60	1.70	1.53	1.77	1.45	1.86	1.34	1.96	1.25	2.06	1.08	2.24
90	1.61	1.70	1.54	1.78	1.47	1.85	1.40	1.94	1.32	2.03	1.16	2.21
95	1.62	1.71	1.56	1.78	1.49	1.85	1.42	1.93	1.35	2.01	1.20	2.19
100	1.63	1.72	1.57	1.78	1.51	1.85	1.44	1.92	1.37	2.00	1.23	2.16
150	1.71	1.76	1.67	1.80	1.62	1.85	1.58	1.90	1.54	1.94	1.44	2.04
200	1.75	1.79	1.72	1.82	1.69	1.85	1.65	1.89	1.62	1.92	1.55	1.99

[a]k is the number of explanatory variables + 1 (constant term).

Source: This table is adapted from N. E. Savin and K. J. White, "The Durbin–Watson Test for Serial Correlation with Extreme Sample Sizes or Many Parameters," *Econometrica*, Vol. 45, 1977, pp. 1989–1996. We have given the table only for some sample sizes and number of variables. For intermediate sample sizes or number of variables, interpolation can be used. Given the limitations of the DW test, we find detailed tables unnecessary.

Table A.6 F-distribution, upper 5% points $(F_{0.95})^a$

Degrees of Freedom for Numerator

	1	2	3	4	5	6	7	8	9	10	12	15	20	24	30	40	60	120	∞
1	161	200	216	225	230	234	237	239	241	242	244	246	248	249	250	251	252	253	254
2	18.5	19.0	19.2	19.2	19.3	19.3	19.4	19.4	19.4	19.4	19.4	19.4	19.4	19.5	19.5	19.5	19.5	19.5	19.5
3	10.1	9.55	9.28	9.12	9.01	8.94	8.89	8.85	8.81	8.79	8.74	8.70	8.66	8.64	8.62	8.59	8.57	8.55	8.53
4	7.71	6.94	6.59	6.39	6.26	6.16	6.09	6.04	6.00	5.96	5.91	5.86	5.80	5.77	5.75	5.72	5.69	5.66	5.63
5	6.61	5.79	5.41	5.19	5.05	4.95	4.88	4.82	4.77	4.74	4.68	4.62	4.56	4.53	4.50	4.46	4.43	4.40	4.37
6	5.99	5.14	4.76	4.53	4.39	4.28	4.21	4.15	4.10	4.06	4.00	3.94	3.87	3.84	3.81	3.77	3.74	3.70	3.67
7	5.59	4.74	4.35	4.12	3.97	3.87	3.79	3.73	3.68	3.64	3.57	3.51	3.44	3.41	3.38	3.34	3.30	3.27	3.23
8	5.32	4.46	4.07	3.84	3.69	3.58	3.50	3.44	3.39	3.35	3.28	3.22	3.15	3.12	3.08	3.04	3.01	2.97	2.93
9	5.12	4.26	3.86	3.63	3.48	3.37	3.29	3.23	3.18	3.14	3.07	3.01	2.94	2.90	2.86	2.83	2.79	2.75	2.71
10	4.96	4.10	3.71	3.48	3.33	3.22	3.14	3.07	3.02	2.98	2.91	2.85	2.77	2.74	2.70	2.66	2.62	2.58	2.54
11	4.84	3.98	3.59	3.36	3.20	3.09	3.01	2.95	2.90	2.85	2.79	2.72	2.65	2.61	2.57	2.53	2.49	2.45	2.40
12	4.75	3.89	3.49	3.26	3.11	3.00	2.91	2.85	2.80	2.75	2.69	2.62	2.54	2.51	2.47	2.43	2.38	2.34	2.30
13	4.67	3.81	3.41	3.18	3.03	2.92	2.83	2.77	2.71	2.67	2.60	2.53	2.46	2.42	2.38	2.34	2.30	2.25	2.21
14	4.60	3.74	3.34	3.11	2.96	2.85	2.76	2.70	2.65	2.60	2.53	2.46	2.39	2.35	2.31	2.27	2.22	2.18	2.13
15	4.54	3.68	3.29	3.06	2.90	2.79	2.71	2.64	2.59	2.54	2.48	2.40	2.33	2.29	2.25	2.20	2.16	2.11	2.07
16	4.49	3.63	3.24	3.01	2.85	2.74	2.66	2.59	2.54	2.49	2.42	2.35	2.28	2.24	2.19	2.15	2.11	2.06	2.01
17	4.45	3.59	3.20	2.96	2.81	2.70	2.61	2.55	2.49	2.45	2.38	2.31	2.23	2.19	2.15	2.10	2.06	2.01	1.96
18	4.41	3.55	3.16	2.93	2.77	2.66	2.58	2.51	2.46	2.41	2.34	2.27	2.19	2.15	2.11	2.06	2.02	1.97	1.92
19	4.38	3.52	3.13	2.90	2.74	2.63	2.54	2.48	2.42	2.38	2.31	2.23	2.16	2.11	2.07	2.03	1.98	1.93	1.88
20	4.35	3.49	3.10	2.87	2.71	2.60	2.51	2.45	2.39	2.35	2.28	2.20	2.12	2.08	2.04	1.99	1.95	1.90	1.84
21	4.32	3.47	3.07	2.84	2.68	2.57	2.49	2.42	2.37	2.32	2.25	2.18	2.10	2.05	2.01	1.96	1.92	1.87	1.81
22	4.30	3.44	3.05	2.82	2.66	2.55	2.46	2.40	2.34	2.30	2.23	2.15	2.07	2.03	1.98	1.94	1.89	1.84	1.78
23	4.28	3.42	3.03	2.80	2.64	2.53	2.44	2.37	2.32	2.27	2.20	2.13	2.05	2.01	1.96	1.91	1.86	1.81	1.76
24	4.26	3.40	3.01	2.78	2.62	2.51	2.42	2.36	2.30	2.25	2.18	2.11	2.03	1.98	1.94	1.89	1.84	1.79	1.73
25	4.24	3.39	2.99	2.76	2.60	2.49	2.40	2.34	2.28	2.24	2.16	2.09	2.01	1.96	1.92	1.87	1.82	1.77	1.71
30	4.17	3.32	2.92	2.69	2.53	2.42	2.33	2.27	2.21	2.16	2.09	2.01	1.93	1.89	1.84	1.79	1.74	1.68	1.62
40	4.08	3.23	2.84	2.61	2.45	2.34	2.25	2.18	2.12	2.08	2.00	1.92	1.84	1.79	1.74	1.69	1.64	1.58	1.51
60	4.00	3.15	2.76	2.53	2.37	2.25	2.17	2.10	2.04	1.99	1.92	1.84	1.75	1.70	1.65	1.59	1.53	1.47	1.39
120	3.92	3.07	2.68	2.45	2.29	2.18	2.09	2.02	1.96	1.91	1.83	1.75	1.66	1.61	1.55	1.50	1.43	1.35	1.25
∞	3.84	3.00	2.60	2.37	2.21	2.10	2.01	1.94	1.88	1.83	1.75	1.67	1.57	1.52	1.46	1.39	1.32	1.22	1.00

^{a}Interpolation should be performed using reciprocals of the degrees of freedom.

Source: Reproduced from M. Merrington and C. M. Thompson, "Tables of Percentage Points of the Inverted Beta (F) Distribution," *Biometrika*, Vol. 33, 1943, p. 73, with the permission of the Biometrika Trustees.

Table A.7 *F*-distribution, upper 1% points $(F_{0.99})^a$

Degrees of Freedom for Numerator

	1	2	3	4	5	6	7	8	9	10	12	15	20	24	30	40	60	120	∞
1	4052	5000	5403	5625	5764	5859	5928	5982	6023	6056	6106	6157	6209	6235	6261	6287	6313	6339	6366
2	98.5	99.0	99.2	99.3	99.3	99.3	99.4	99.4	99.4	99.4	99.4	99.4	99.5	99.5	99.5	99.5	99.5	99.5	99.5
3	34.1	30.8	29.5	28.7	28.2	27.9	27.7	27.5	27.3	27.2	27.1	26.9	26.7	26.6	26.5	26.4	26.3	26.2	26.1
4	21.2	18.0	16.7	16.0	15.5	15.2	15.0	14.8	14.7	14.5	14.4	14.2	14.0	13.9	13.8	13.7	13.7	13.6	13.5
5	16.3	13.3	12.1	11.4	11.0	10.7	10.5	10.3	10.2	10.1	9.89	9.72	9.55	9.47	9.38	9.29	9.20	9.11	9.02
6	13.7	10.9	9.78	9.15	8.75	8.47	8.26	8.10	7.98	7.87	7.72	7.56	7.40	7.31	7.23	7.14	7.06	6.97	6.88
7	12.2	9.55	8.45	7.85	7.46	7.19	6.99	6.84	6.72	6.62	6.47	6.31	6.16	6.07	5.99	5.91	5.82	5.74	5.65
8	11.3	8.65	7.59	7.01	6.63	6.37	6.18	6.03	5.91	5.81	5.67	5.52	5.36	5.28	5.20	5.12	5.03	4.95	4.86
9	10.6	8.02	6.99	6.42	6.06	5.80	5.61	5.47	5.35	5.26	5.11	4.96	4.81	4.73	4.65	4.57	4.48	4.40	4.31
10	10.0	7.56	6.55	5.99	5.64	5.39	5.20	5.06	4.94	4.85	4.71	4.56	4.41	4.33	4.25	4.17	4.08	4.00	3.91
11	9.65	7.21	6.22	5.67	5.32	5.07	4.89	4.74	4.63	4.54	4.40	4.25	4.10	4.02	3.94	3.86	3.78	3.69	3.60
12	9.33	6.93	5.95	5.41	5.06	4.82	4.64	4.50	4.39	4.30	4.16	4.01	3.86	3.78	3.70	3.62	3.54	3.45	3.36
13	9.07	6.70	5.74	5.21	4.86	4.62	4.44	4.30	4.19	4.10	3.96	3.82	3.66	3.59	3.51	3.43	3.34	3.25	3.17
14	8.86	6.51	5.56	5.04	4.70	4.46	4.28	4.14	4.03	3.94	3.80	3.66	3.51	3.43	3.35	3.27	3.18	3.09	3.00
15	8.68	6.36	5.42	4.89	4.56	4.32	4.14	4.00	3.89	3.80	3.67	3.52	3.37	3.29	3.21	3.13	3.05	2.96	2.87
16	8.53	6.23	5.29	4.77	4.44	4.20	4.03	3.89	3.78	3.69	3.55	3.41	3.26	3.18	3.10	3.02	2.93	2.84	2.75
17	8.40	6.11	5.19	4.67	4.34	4.10	3.93	3.79	3.68	3.59	3.46	3.31	3.16	3.08	3.00	2.92	2.83	2.75	2.65
18	8.29	6.01	5.09	4.58	4.25	4.01	3.84	3.71	3.60	3.51	3.37	3.23	3.08	3.00	2.92	2.84	2.75	2.66	2.57
19	8.19	5.93	5.01	4.50	4.17	3.94	3.77	3.63	3.52	3.43	3.30	3.15	3.00	2.92	2.84	2.76	2.67	2.58	2.49
20	8.10	5.85	4.94	4.43	4.10	3.87	3.70	3.56	3.46	3.37	3.23	3.09	2.94	2.86	2.78	2.69	2.61	2.52	2.42
21	8.02	5.78	4.87	4.37	4.04	3.81	3.64	3.51	3.40	3.31	3.17	3.03	2.88	2.80	2.72	2.64	2.55	2.46	2.36
22	7.95	5.72	4.82	4.31	3.99	3.76	3.59	3.45	3.35	3.26	3.12	2.98	2.83	2.75	2.67	2.58	2.50	2.40	2.31
23	7.88	5.66	4.76	4.26	3.94	3.71	3.54	3.41	3.30	3.21	3.07	2.93	2.78	2.70	2.62	2.54	2.45	2.35	2.26
24	7.82	5.61	4.72	4.22	3.90	3.67	3.50	3.36	3.26	3.17	3.03	2.89	2.74	2.66	2.58	2.49	2.40	2.31	2.21
25	7.77	5.57	4.68	4.18	3.86	3.63	3.46	3.32	3.22	3.13	2.99	2.85	2.70	2.62	2.53	2.45	2.36	2.27	2.17
30	7.56	5.39	4.51	4.02	3.70	3.47	3.30	3.17	3.07	2.98	2.84	2.70	2.55	2.47	2.39	2.30	2.21	2.11	2.01
40	7.31	5.18	4.31	3.83	3.51	3.29	3.12	2.99	2.89	2.80	2.66	2.52	2.37	2.29	2.20	2.11	2.02	1.94	1.80
60	7.08	4.98	4.13	3.65	3.34	3.12	2.95	2.82	2.72	2.63	2.50	2.35	2.20	2.12	2.03	1.94	1.84	1.73	1.60
120	6.85	4.79	3.95	3.48	3.17	2.96	2.79	2.66	2.56	2.47	2.34	2.19	2.03	1.95	1.86	1.76	1.66	1.53	1.38
∞	6.63	4.61	3.78	3.32	3.02	2.80	2.64	2.51	2.41	2.32	2.18	2.04	1.88	1.79	1.70	1.59	1.47	1.32	1.00

^{a}Interpolation should be performed using reciprocals of the degrees of freedom.

Source: Reproduced from M. Merrington and C. M. Thompson, "Tables of Percentage Points of the Inverted Beta (*F*) Distribution," *Biometrika*, Vol. 33, 1943, p. 73, with the permission of the Biometrika Trustees.

Appendix B: Data Sets on the Web

Several of the data sets in the book are available on the Web. Some of these short data sets are printed in the book. Others on the Web are not in the book. Here is a listing of the data sets.

Data sets in the book and also on the Web

These are: Tables 3.11, 4.7–4.11, 5.5, 7.2, 8.2, 9.1, 9.3.

Data sets available on the Web only

Table 4.12	Auction prices of apartments in Moscow (data provided by Yasushi Toda).
Table 8.7	Data set on bride–groom characteristics and dowry (ICR, SAT-VLS data) south central rural India (data provided by A. B. Deolalikar).
Tables 13.2 to 13.8	Time-series data (these are listed at the end of Chapter 13).
Table 15.1	Panel data set on demand for electricity and natural gas in the U.S. (based on Maddala et al., *Journal of Business and Economic Statistics*, January 1997).

Appendix C: Computer Programs

There are now many computer programs that do everything discussed in this book. The commonly used programs are:

1. SHAZAM (latest version 8.0) by Ken White.
2. MICROFIT (latest version 4.0).
3. RATS.
4. SAS.
5. MICRO-TSP.
6. CATS in RATS for cointegration analysis.

MICROFIT 4.0 also has cointegration analysis. LIMDEP used to be the program used for limited dependent variable models, but for the simple models (logit, probit, and tobit) discussed in this book, the other programs are more accurate.

One thing to note is that different programs can give different answers for the same problem. For instance, in the logit or probit models, one can get different results with SAS vs. LIMDEP. In such cases it is better to take the SAS results. LIMDEP is designed to be used for very complicated limited dependent variable models.

For most purposes for the problems discussed in this book the first two programs SHAZAM and MICROFIT are enough.

Lovell and Selover[1] compare the results from SHAZAM, MICROFIT, RATS, and MICRO-TSP, and discuss the merits and drawbacks of each of these programs and discuss the differences in the results obtained.

---

[1] M. C. Lovell and D. Selover, "Econometric Software Accidents," *Economic Journal*, Vol. 104, 1994, pp. 713–725.

Index